Harvard English Studies 20

AMERICAN BABEL

American Babel

Literatures of the United States from Abnaki to Zuni

EDITED BY Marc Shell

HARVARD UNIVERSITY PRESS

Cambridge, Massachusetts, and London, England

2002

Library of Congress Cataloging-in-Publication Data

American Babel : literatures of the United States from Abnaki to Zuni /
edited by Marc Shell
  p. cm — (Harvard English studies ; 20)
ISBN 0-674-00644-5 (cloth : alk. paper) — ISBN 0-674-00661-5 (pbk. : alk. paper)
  1. United States—Literatures—History and criticism. 2. American literature—
Minotity authors—History and criticism. 3. Minorities in literature.
I. Shell, Marc. II. Series.

PN849.U5 A48 2002
809'.8973—dc21   2002023123

Preface

American Babel is the last volume in the series *Harvard English Studies* (1970-2002). Many of the previous books in this series focused mainly on the anglophone tradition in the United States. Their editors were always aware, however, that American anglophone literature is often influenced by and defines itself in terms of literatures written in the United States in languages other than English. Those literatures allow special access to issues of ethnic, linguistic, and national identity as well as to myriad problems of multilingualism, metaphorization, and translation.

My colleagues and I first discussed publishing *American Babel* at a three-day seminar on "The Non-English Literatures of the United States," which met in Mexico at an annual meeting of the American Comparative Literature Association (1997). Almost all scholars present at that seminar contributed an essay to the present collection. Other contributors participated in programs offered at Harvard by its Department of Comparative Literature, Department of English and American Language and Literature, Program in American Civilization, and the Longfellow Institute for the Study of the Non-English Languages and Literatures of the United States.

Werner Sollors and I founded the Longfellow Institute in 1994. The Institute was designed to pull together past efforts to study the non-English writings in what is now the United States and to reexamine the English-language tradition in the context of American multilingualism. Named after Henry Wadsworth Longfellow — the polyglot nineteenth-century poet who, in his translations and academic work, helped to develop literary study across linguistic boundaries — the Institute has set itself the task of identifying, and bringing back as the subject of study, the multitude of historically important and aesthetically outstanding American texts that were written in languages other than English. Publishing activity so far includes *The Multilingual Anthology of American Literature: A Reader of Original Texts with English Translations* (2000).

Most of the essays in *American Babel* focus on particular linguistic tradition in what is now the United States: Arabic, French, German, Spanish, Yiddish, Zuni, and so on. A few essays concern the same tradition: there are three contributions about American Welsh, for example, and three about American Chinese. Taken together, the essays suggest the general thematic, historical, and theoretical issues that inform the study of American literatures and that often ground the study of diasporic languages and literatures in a wider international and global context.

I should like to thank Susan Lisa Meld Shell, who presented a paper at the seminar in Mexico that could not be included in the present collection. The copyeditor and designer at Harvard University Press did outstanding work on this often-difficult manuscript from many hands. Lindsay Waters's encouragement and advice has been decisive all along. Last — a placement that means to convey emphasis — I am grateful to Yota Batsaki, whose essay is a crucial contribution to *American Babel* and whose work as editorial associate was indispensable to the project as whole.

Contents

PART I. INTRODUCTION

1. Babel in America   3
   MARC SHELL

2. The Name of America   34
   ALEXANDER DEL MAR

PART II. RESISTANCE AND ASSIMILATION

3. "And in a Christian Language They Sold Me":   41
   Messages Concealed in a Slave's Arabic-Language
   Autobiographical Narrative
   ALA ALRYYES

4. Unfaithful Translation: Bilingual Versions as   55
   Greek-American Strategies of Concealment
   YOTA BATSAKI

5. Disturbing the Language Peace: German-Jewish   74
   Women Poets in *Aufbau*, 1933–1993
   ELISABETH LENCKOS

6. *Mordecai and Haman:* The Drama of Welsh   93
   America
   ESTHER WHITFIELD

7. Ferdinand Kürnberger's *Der Amerika-Müde* (1855):   117
   German-Language Literature about the United
   States, and German-American Writing
   WERNER SOLLORS

PART III. AUTHORITATIVE AND
         NONAUTHORITATIVE LANGUAGES

8. "Neither the King's English nor the Rebbetzin's   133
   Yiddish": Yinglish Literature in the United States
   JAMES LOEFFLER

9. Homing Pidgins: Another Version of Pastoral 163
in Hawai'i
SUSANNAH YOUNG-AH GOTTLIEB

10. Irish Gaelic Literature in the United States 188
KENNETH NILSEN

11. Alfred Mercier's Polyglot Plantation Novel 219
of Louisiana
LAWRENCE ROSENWALD

12. Written in Sound: Translating the Multiple 238
Voices of the Zuni Storyteller
DENNIS TEDLOCK

PART IV. LOSS AND GAIN

13. Contrapuntal Languages: The Games They 263
Play in Spanish
DORIS SOMMER

14. America, Everybody's Other World 283
ALICIA BORINSKY

15. The Gothic and the American-Exotic: Baron 297
Ludwig von Reizenstein's *Die Geheimnisse von
New-Orleans*
STEVEN ROWAN

16. Grave Matters: Poetry and the Preservation 307
of the Welsh Language in the United States
MELINDA GRAY

17. Beyond the National Tradition: Thuong Vuong- 322
Riddick's *Two Shores/Deux Rives*
DAN DUFFY

PART V. NATIONALISM AND INTERNATIONALISM

18. The Welsh Atlantic: Mapping the Contexts   343
    of Welsh-American Literature
    DANIEL WILLIAMS

19. Carved on the Walls: The Archaeology and   369
    Canonization of the Angel Island Chinese Poems
    TE-HSING SHAN

20. Immigration Blues: The Portrayal of Chinatown   386
    Life in Chinese-Language Literature in America
    XIAO-HUANG YIN

21. "China" in the American Diaspora   404
    QIAN SUOQIAO

22. Haitian Literature in the United States,   431
    1948–1986
    JEAN JONASSAINT

23. Translingualism and the American Literary   450
    Imagination
    STEVEN G. KELLMAN

24. What Is *Aufklärung* (in Pennsylvania)?   465
    PETER FENVES

PART VI. AFTERWORD

25. "Prized His Mouth Open": Mark Twain's *The*   491
    Jumping Frog of Calaveras County: in English, then
    in French, then clawed back into a civilized language
    once more by patient, unremunerated toil
    MARC SHELL

Illustrations

3.1. Manuscript fragment from the "Autobiography of Omar Ibn Said." Permission Derrick Beard. Photograph by Marc Shell and Ala Alryyes. p. 43

4.1. "A Future American." From Henry Pratt Fairchild, *Greek Immigration to the United States* (New Haven: Yale University Press, 1911), frontispiece. p. 58

8.1. Yiddish text in Hebrew script by James Loeffler, translating a passage from Philip Roth's story "Epstein" (1958). p. 147

8.2. Yiddish text in Hebrew script by James Loeffler: another passage from "Epstein." p. 149

15.1. "Encampment on 6th June [1852]." Lithograph by H. Lawrence, 86 John St., New York City. Copy in the Thomas Jefferson Library, University of Missouri-St. Louis. Reproduced in Randolph B. Marcy and George B. McClellan, *Exploration of the Red River of Louisiana, in the Year 1852, With Reports on the Natural History of the Country, and Numerous Illustrations*, Executive Document, House of Representatives, 33rd Congress, 1st Session (Washington: A. O. P. Nicholson, Public Printer, 1854), plate 3. p. 302

15.2. "Head of Ke-Che-Ah-Que-Ho-Ho, or the main branch of the Red River." Lithograph by H. Lawrence. Reproduced in Marcy and McClellan, *Exploration of the Red River*, plate 10. p. 303

20.1. Chinese text with English words interspersed. From Zhou Li, *Manhadun de Zhongguo Nuren* (Beijing: Beijing Chubanshe, 1992), p. 322. p. 389

25.1. W. Fr. Bowen, "A Complete Word." From Appendix to Mark Twain, *A Tramp Abroad*, first edition (Hartford, Conn.: American Publishing Co., 1879). p. 495

25.2. F. W. Strothman, "My Re-Translation from the French." From Mark Twain, *The Jumping Frog of Calaveras County: in English, then in French, then clawed back into a civilized language once more by patient,* *unremunerated toil.* Illustrations by F. W. Strothman (New York: Harper and Bros., 1903), 56/57. Collection Selechonek.   p. 503

25.3. F. W. Strothman, "Turn one summerset, or maybe a couple." *Jumping Frog* 24/5.   p. 505

25.4. F. W. Strothman, detail from 25.2 above.   p. 506

25.5. F. W. Strothman, "It might be a canary, maybe, but it ain't — it's only just a frog." *Jumping Frog* 46/37.   p. 509

25.6. Joseph Goodhue Chandler, *Daniel Webster at Bunker Hill.* Undated. Courtesy Hood Museum of Art, Dartmouth College, Hanover, N.H.; purchased through the Julia L. Whittier Fund.   p. 512

25.7. F. W. Strothman, "Dan'l Webster." *Jumping Frog* 30/31.   p. 513

Part I

INTRODUCTION

CHAPTER ONE

Babel in America

■ **MARC SHELL**

What really is the language of the United States?

The common American response to this question is to dismiss it as outlandishly naïve and lacking cultural or political significance. After all, isn't the United States, though a land of immigrants, fundamentally English-speaking? Didn't founder John Jay insist in the *Federalist Papers* "that Providence has been pleased to give this one connected country, to one united people . . . speaking the same language"?[1] And isn't America's linguistic union one of the great historical feats of social language-engineering?[2]

The familiar rhetoric of inevitable linguistic union ranges from the humorous to the imperialistically oppressive. ("Melting pot, yes. Tower of Babel, no!")[3] And the one-language idea still informs most studies of the politics of language in America and histories of the anglicization of America.[4] But this rhetoric serves to obscure or explain away the facts that the revolutionary colonies were markedly polyglot, that neither the Constitution of the United States nor other official documents name an official language, and that there has been a crucial dialogue, nowadays generally submerged but nevertheless ready to surface, about whether the United States should have an official language — or several official languages — and, if so, which one.[5]

What, besides the predilection to confuse America with the world before Babel, impels Americans to accept the fiction of original American monolingualism for the reality of American multilingualism? Is there a link between the impressive bilingualism of America's former population in its many languages and its current population's high rate of illiteracy in even one language?

3

MANY LANGUAGES

Inside and outside the often changing borders of the American colonies between 1750 and 1850, if ever there were a polyglot place on the globe — other than Babel's spire — this was it. Here four continents — North America, Africa, Europe, and Asia — met one another. As early as 1789, visiting Frenchmen reported on the multiplicity of languages in America.[6]

Between the mid-eighteenth and the mid-nineteenth century, native English speakers were not as numerous as has been generally assumed. First, non-English European settlers made up one quarter of the total white population: two-fifths of Pennsylvania's population alone spoke German.[7] Second, the Amerindians — called "Aborigines" by George Washington — spoke numerous languages.[8] Third, the blacks, mostly slaves who numbered more than one-fifth of the total population, had their own African languages.[9] (Had a slave the courage to speak his native language, however, punishment was sometimes severe; there are reports of blacks having their tongues cut out.)

Outside the colonies, in addition to the various Amerindian languages, French and Spanish were common. Thomas Jefferson even suggested that Americans should travel to Canada in order to acquire a knowledge of French, and he emphasized that Spanish was an important influence in the New World. This internationalist pose was partly Jefferson's short-term strategy during a border-changing, expansionist period.[10] After the Louisiana Purchase (1803) — under President Jefferson — francophones were Americanized. A later example is the Treaty of Guadalupe Hidalgo (1848). By this treaty Mexico ceded almost half its territory to the United States, and language rights were supposed to devolve to the newly Americanized Spanish-speaking population.[11] (It is worth comparing here the language rights guaranteed to francophone Catholics by the British North America Act of 1867, which was for a century or more Canada's constitutive document.)

ONE LANGUAGE

The polyglot situation in the newly constituted United States had its problems. How could people of one language get along with others of a different one? Thomas Paine wrote, "if there is a country in the world where concord, according to common calculation, would be least expected, it is America. Made up, as it is, of people . . . speaking different languages."[12]

Concern for commercial and political concord, as well as an Enlightenment search for affinity among languages or for a universal language — abetted by American missionaries' and presidents' research into Amerindian languages — led to discussion, itself still little researched, about the need or desire to have only one language in America. This research into the diversity of languages was thus generally to foster linguistic homogeneity rather than to encourage linguistic heterogeneity.[13]

The chief question was, of course, *which* language should predominate in America. The factors that militated for English are well known. The commercially dominant plurality were English speakers schooled in the rhetoric of the British Empire, and many believed in the manifest destiny of their own tongue. Not a few figured that English would soon become something like what Latin had been among Catholics or European intellectuals: a universal language.[14] In a letter to Noah Webster, Benjamin Franklin noted that one day English would outflank French as the universal secular language.[15]

But other factors militated against English. Some American republicans argued that independence from England — and from British imperialism — required independence from English. This notion, with its shades of English anti-Normanism, led to discussion of several strategies.[16] Some of these may seem bizarre, but the outlandishly successful social language-engineering projects in the twentieth century — the miraculous Israeli renaissance of Hebrew, say, and the imperialist Russification of the Soviet colonies — suggest that very few of the proposals in the American case were preposterous, and all speak eloquently of their designers' hopes and fears.[17]

First was the idea of starting a new language — something like Esperanto or Boontling (a unique language experiment in a California town).[18] As the contemporary *The Quarterly Review* commented, "Nor have [Americans] been wanting projects among them for getting rid of the English language . . . by substituting a new language of their own."[19] Second was the idea of the renaissance of an ancient language. Both Hebrew and Greek were proposed as alternatives to English on the model of the famously tolerant and much discussed ancient "Hebrew commonwealth."[20] As the Marquis de Chastellux reported in the 1780s, "the Americans have carried [their anti-British aversion] so far, as seriously to propose introducing a new language; and some persons were desirous, for the convenience of the public, that the *Hebrew* should be substituted for the English. The proposal was, that it should be taught in the schools, and made use of in all public acts." Concerning ancient Greek, Charles Astor Bristed wrote in 1855: "it is still on record that a legislator seriously proposed that the young republic should complete its independence by adopting a different language from that of the mother-country, 'the Greek for instance,' which proposition was summarily extinguished by a suggestion of a fellow representative [Roger Sherman of Connecticut, delegate to the Continental Congress and a member of the committee that drafted the Declaration of Independence] that 'it would be more convenient for us to keep the language as it was, and *make the English speak Greek.'*" Third were the modern languages. Among these was French, of which the etymologist Herbert Croft wrote in 1797 (in his *A Letter from Germany to the Princess Royal of England,* published in Hamburg) that "during the American revolution, the idea was started of revenging themselves on England, by rejecting its language and adopting that of France."[21] And there was German, whose experience in the United States belies the widespread belief in America that there were no serious attempts to make the country or its states officially bilingual.[22]

OFFICIAL GERMAN

A brief history of the controversies surrounding German as a proposed official American language might begin with Benjamin Franklin, ace newspaper publisher, book seller, and editor of *The New England Courant.* He opened his own printing shop in 1724, at age eighteen, and operated the *Pennsylvania Gazette* as proprietor at age twenty-three. In the early 1730s, Franklin taught himself French, German, Italian, Spanish, and Latin. And he seems to have believed enough in multilingualism to publish in 1732 the first German-language newspaper in North America, the *Philadelphische Zeitung.*[23]

However, Franklin's German newspaper failed, and "a better qualified

German printer" cornered the German book market. The failure may have been critical for the subsequent linguistic history of Pennsylvania if not the entire continent. Forever thereafter, Franklin's writings about American "foreign"-language speakers took a sharply xenophobic turn. In 1750, for example, he complained that Pennsylvania "will in a few Years become a German colony: Instead of their Learning our Language, we must learn their's, or live as in a foreign Country."[24] In "Observations Concerning the Increase of Mankind" (1751), he grumbled likewise about "Palatine Boors" who "swarm into our Settlements and . . . establish their Language"; he asked, "Why should *Pennsylvania*, founded by the *English*, become a Colony of Aliens, who will shortly be so numerous as to Germanize us instead of our Anglifying them, and will never adopt our Language or Customs any more than they can acquire our Complexion?"[25] Even in 1784, in the face of the considerable distrust of Englishmen that one would expect in the revolutionary period, Franklin complained about "Foreigners of all Nations and Languages, who by their Numbers may drown and stifle the English," and argued in favor of a continuing/increased immigration of Englishmen, so that English would "become in the course of two centuries the most extensive Language in the World, the Spanish only excepted."[26]

It is unclear how much influence Franklin had, or how many shared his views. But whether thanks to English speakers' fear of another language's parity with English, or to non-English speakers' desire for such equality, stories, with at least a germ of truth, began to circulate about how one or another language, usually German, "almost" became official. A Congressional committee recommended that "the laws be translated, and printed in the German language.'"[27] And, writing in German, Frank Löhrer reported about attempts at German language parity in Pennsylvania: "in the vote on this question, whether the dominant speech in the Assembly, in the courts, and in the records of Pennsylvania should be the German language — the votes were tied."[28]

The German language remained a strong, unofficial presence in the United States throughout the nineteenth century.[29] Many argued that anglophone Americans should learn German and endorsed the view of Benjamin Rush, who proposed that there should be a German-language college.[30] Indeed, bilingual schools were not unusual. But eventually, as a result of the hostilities of World War I and fears of a third column, anti-German and isolationist sentiment was strengthened. In 1916, it became illegal even to teach many foreign languages in American Schools![31] President Theodore Roosevelt, in his still influential 1917 appeal entitled "The Children of the Crucible," said that "we must . . . have but one language. That must be the language of the Declaration of Independence."[32]

The problem was partly that of "language loyalty."[33] Roosevelt, characterizing all Americans as willing immigrants, did not consider that blacks and Amerindians were, one way or another, conquered peoples. Nor did he mention the French, whose territory was forcibly bought, nor the Dutch and Germans, who had been settlers before the signing of the Declaration of Independence.[34] More tellingly, Roosevelt did not consider the Spanish speakers, for whom the Treaty of Guadalupe Hidalgo might have involved official language rights, or the bilingual constitution of New Mexico (1912), which actually partly provided those rights. (During debates in 1878 about whether the Mexican territories should become states, Mexican-Americans had been called simply "foreigners."[35]) When the state constitution of New Mexico was finally ratified in 1912, however, Mexican-Americans were promised official language rights on a two-decade "trial basis."[36] About these matters Roosevelt remained as silent as are most Americans — both anglophone and Spanish-speaking — today.

President Roosevelt's wartime ideology — that the United States must have only one language just as it has one flag, and that this language must be English — has remained the effective unofficial view of America's political officials ever since. But, of course, there is more to the unofficial culture of English as the one official American language than merely the wartime xenophobia of World War I.

NON-ENGLISH LANGUAGES AND DIALECT

Since 1750, people had argued about whether there should be only one official language and which language that should be: English or one of the "foreign," that is, non-English languages, whether ancient or modern. That issue was sometimes expressed in the form of literary debates about whether the American language itself was essentially a "foreign" — that is, non-English — language. This turn in the discussion helps to explain the still widespread phenomenon in America of treating the politics of language mainly in terms of changes, called politically symptomatic, to the English language. It also serves to divert attention from the question of an official or national language.

To begin with, the view that the American language ought to become something essentially other than the English language seemed to involve notions about fundamental lexis, syntax, and even truth.[37] Early on, William Thornton wrote in *Cadmus* that American English should become a language of new political truth: "You have corrected the dangerous doctrines of European powers, correct now the language you have imported ... The AMERICAN LANGUAGE will thus be as distinct as the government, free from all the follies of unphilosophical fashion, and resting upon truth as its only regulator."[38] But James Herron saw, in the polyglot heritage of the new republic, the possibility of creating a new language. Thus he wrote in *American Grammar* that "we express our own free thoughts in a *language* our own, adopted from the tongues of the many nations, of our forefathers ... Consequently, LANGUAGE in the UNITED STATES is *Polyglot* — national with our people — not borrowed from any one distinct tongue." In the same vein, Noah Webster claimed that the United States "will produce, in a course of time, a language in North America, as different from the future language of England, as the modern Dutch, Danish and Swedish are from German, or from one another."[39]

Webster was wrong about this. And just why the language did not develop as he envisioned it is an interesting question of sociolinguistics. Yet the thought of some non-English American language emerging from a polyglot population was no more exotic than that of the United States or one of its states — say, Pennsylvania (German) or New Mexico (Spanish) — becoming officially bilingual. Moreover, the Americanist assimilationist vision of the natural metamorphosis of one language into another language — that is, the hypothesis of an American English language that would be both foreign and familiar to English — made it easier to drop the idea that English would necessarily predominate instead of some new language.

In the ensuing years, Webster and his followers came to realize that the English language would predominate, and even argued outright that it should. (The revisionist Webster now said that "our language is the *English* and it is desirable that the language of the United States and Great Britain should continue to be the same").[40] And so, the argument that the declared political separation from the English people meant also a linguistic separation from the English language gave way to the consideration of practical language issues — "fonetic" spellings and the like.[41] The debate about official language was thus displaced onto questions of dialect and race. Dialect as such became both a popular subject and medium for anglophone fiction writers in America — Irving, Poe, Melville, Twain, and many others.

Comparing the language issue in an unofficially biracial United States to that of an officially bilingual Québec may be helpful here for understanding the distinctive American linkage between dialect and race. Whereas in Québec the subject of dialect *supplemented* without supplanting that of language, in the unofficially unilingual and (until recently) officially biracial United States, an often exclusive focus on dialect serves to mask the disappearance of actual languages.[42] Whereas some present-day Québécois call themselves the *nègres* of Canada, refuse to "speak white" (that is, English, *Franglais,* or *joual* — a quasi-dialect sometimes loosely translated as "French jive talk" or "French gumbo"), and try in various ways to return to pure French, the once legally defined group of American blacks had lost its various original mother tongues and adopted the "master's" language along with his religion.[43] (The brutal Philomelan history has yet to be told, owing to a continuing failure on both sides — white and black — to acknowledge fully as their inheritance the effective conditions of American race slavery. The failure is abetted and masked by diversions into such interesting and otherwise important topical areas as Africanisms in American English, Gullah as an essentially African language rather than an essentially English one, syntactic similarities between Creole and African-American, and African-American bi-dialectism.[44])

In Twain's unsettling and bi-dialectic *Pudd'nhead Wilson,* for example, the nurse-mother-slave Roxana looks white and is legally black (that is, she has one-sixteenth black ancestry), but she is treated as black because she speaks black. Similarly, Roxana's changeling "Tom Driscoll" (né *Valet de Chambres,* in the "malappropriated" French of Mississippi planters) looks white and is legally black (that is, he has one-thirty-second black ancestry), but he is treated as white because he talks white. Finally, Roxana's master's changeling *"Valet de Chambres"* (né Tom Driscoll), looks white and is legally white (he has fully white ancestry), but even after everyone learns he is really white, he is treated as black and thinks of himself as black because he talks black.[45] (America's often prosperous elocution schools and best-selling elocution manuals offered to rid clients of just such foreign, regional, and black accents.)[46] Spanish *limpieza de sangre* (blood purity), adapted to the needs of the distinctively American institution of race slavery, thus infected America's peculiarly unspoken rhetoric of language purity.[47]

LANGUAGE AND RACE

The rhetoric about language often resembles that for race.[48] The linguistic and natural historians' terms for genus and species are thus often the same, and, as Charles Darwin put it, "the proofs that [different languages and distinct species] have been developed through a gradual process, are curiously the same."[49] Despite various intelligent formulations, nineteenth-century ideologues of linguistic historiography (Grimm), in their dialectics of universal-particular and terminus-origin, differ little from those of species historiography (Darwin) or racial historiography (Gobineau).[50] The common sentiment remains that "language is by itself the nearest approach to a perfect test of national extraction."[51]

How language mediates the politics of race or nationhood in North America depends on whether the state is essentially unilingual or multilingual. In the United States, for example, citizens generally have political rights (including that of free speech) as individuals rather than as members of one or another particular linguistic or racial group. Thus every American has the right to go to school or to argue in court, but there is no constitutionally or officially *guaranteed* right in the United States to attend school or to plead in court in the language of one's choice, if one's choice is *not* English. Perhaps, officially, even if one's choice *is* English, American courts do sometimes grant permission to plead in a non-English language, especially where there are many people who speak Spanish, but when differences appear between the meaning of the law as written in English and its meaning in translation, the courts make their disposition according to the original wording in English.

In contrast, the Canadian province of Québec often heeds the group rights of Canada's two constitutive nations (variously called English-speakers and French-speakers, or Protestants and Catholics, or British stock and French stock), generally subordinating the rights of these two official groups *both* to the individual rights of any particular citizen *and* to the group rights, if any, of linguistic, religious, and racial groups other than the official two. In this respect, Québec differs from the United States, which generally heeds the equal rights of individuals as members of one ideally unilingual nation, generally subordinating to these rights the status of citizens as members of particular linguistic groups. (Under some circumstances the United States does grant to certain people, as members of groups, an anomalous treatment under the law. The fact that Spanish-language speakers, all grouped as Hispanics, are covered by various affirmative action rulings tends to lessen the difference in American ideology between race and language; the term *Hispanic* seems to indicate now a racial group, now a linguistic one.)

Official bilingualism in Québec has included the constitutive right of members of the two originary national groups, Protestants and Catholics, to attend schools in their respective religions (there are no purely secular schools of the American sort).[52] On the basis of this right, guaranteed by the British North America Act (1867), Protestant and Catholic leaders argued successfully that schoolchildren had the derivative right to attend school in their respective language, Protestants being generally English-speaking and Catholics French-speaking.[53] Further, they asserted the religious and linguistic group rights of persons who are British "blood stock," or *britannique de souche,* and those who are French Canadian "blood stock," or *québécois de souche.*

What happens to immigrants to Québec who are neither French-speaking nor English-speaking, neither English nor French?[54] The answer tempers unrealistic enthusiasms for the Canadian cultural mosaic. In the United States, diverse immigrants all become American citizens by virtue of the civic ritual of naturalization (they are reborn or regenerated fictively as American: *e pluribus unum*); in Québec, all immigrants become members of one official group or the other. Official *nationhood* in Québec thus has a bi- or multilateral meaning.

In the 1980s, for example, immigrants to Québec from non-English-speaking countries (called allophones), and even those from some English-speaking countries (anglophones), were classified, for educational and taxation purposes, as French (francophone). This meant that a person with Greek-speaking, Greek Orthodox parents was francophone. Likewise, a monolingual English-speaking person from Singapore who was not *britannique de souche* was classified as francophone. By a similar fiction, Jews in Québec were generally classified as English Protestants (and so attended Protestant schools) even when they were, like the Morocco-born Sephardim, native French- or Arabic-speakers.[55] The fact that the Jews of Montréal, whether Ashkenazim or Sephardim, constituted something like one nation as a *group* (with one sacred written language) and spoke various native languages besides French or English as *individuals,* tended discomfortingly to challenge the thesis, dear to European linguistic nationalists, that a common spoken language is the main distinguishing characteristic of nationhood.

THE VEIL OF CULTURAL DIVERSITY

Out of anxiety about cultural dependence on the English "mother tongue" and a sense of competition with English writers, anglophone American writers and literary critics have fabricated the idea of American as a primary — even independent — language and literature.[56] This is in contrast to the Canadian experience, which involves the dependence both of the English language and of the French language on their respective "mother countries" — a dependence fostered and abetted by the competition within Québec itself between English and French. That is why there is no Canadian "national literature" in the American sense of the term.

Anglophone Americans' various fictive idealizations of an independent American language buttressed the spectacular development in the United States of a distinctly monoglottal national literature and culture. Yet neither in literature nor in American politics generally was the question of official language discussed successfully. Although American writers in French and German did produce a plethora of books in their respective languages, which can be found in America's parish churches and great public and private libraries, their work is little studied by scholars in the institutionalized academic discipline called "American language and civilization." In many American universities, professors of literature still say that nonanglophone American literature — in German, say, or Chinese — belongs properly neither to departments of foreign languages nor to departments of English and American language and literature. For decades, such literature had no institutional home.

The American academy's passing over most nonanglophone American languages and literatures is, of course, partly explicable by the fact that it is easier to talk about other peoples' cultures in English than to learn their languages. But the main explanation is that literary America, despite its horror of race slavery and its ideal of race blindness, has always liked to emphasize racial difference instead of language difference. This preference arises from the traditional American pretense that culture is not largely linguistic or, rather, that culture ought to be English.[57] Monoglot Tereus fears the nightingale's song.

Even as the American university claims to foster a tolerant heterogeneity of cultures, then, it perseveres in the traditional American homogenization of the world as English. At Hampshire College in Amherst, for example, one third of the curriculum in 1994 was devoted to courses in "cultural diversity," but there was not a single foreign language course. Yet Hispanic literature written in English or read only in English translation is still Anglo — the name Hispanics sometimes give to "white" anglophones. Obliviousness of this fact serves to obscure an ineradicable tension, crucial to understanding American ideology, between the argument that speakers of other languages should yield to English and the argument that they really cannot yield because, as Herder suggested, culture *is* (essentially) language. This is the tension informing thoughtful American writers in a tradition extending from Roger Williams's *Key into the Language of America* (1643) to Benjamin Whorf's *Language, Thought, and Reality* (1956), in which a "standard average European" language is compared with the language of the Hopi.[58] (Much relevant anthropological, linguistic, and missionary investigation similarly concerns aspects of the languages of Amerindian tribes and thus often seems, like Whorf's book itself, to transform American silence about Amerindian genocide into something like a ventriloquist's whisper of America. From Abnaki to Zuni.)[59]

It may be useful here to compare academic literary criticism in the United States and Québec. Few American literary critics work on the vast multilingual literature of the United States. Most simply raise up English-language works written by members of America's various ethnic and racial groups — often in the name of multicultural diversity — even as they dismiss American literary works written in languages other than English. Thus they encourage reading English-language literature by Americans of Chinese ethnicity but ignore Chinese-language American literature.[60]

When scholars in the field of American studies, so called, do read non-anglophone American writings in the original language, they still generally exhibit distinctly monolingual methodological tendencies; they treat American literature in German as a discrete, non-American entity, for example, or they provide a five-hundred-year Spanish-language history of an unrealistically remote literature of New Mexico, or they depict American Yiddish as a language basically disconnected from American English.[61] (Not surprisingly, non-American students of American literature have often been better at this sort of work: European, Canadian, and Chinese scholars have made important contributions.)[62]

Tellingly, the American brand of comparative literature has been domesticated in such a way that, despite its multilingualism and its historical origin (at the beginning of the nineteenth century) in problems of linguistic and national difference, it generally avoids studying the linguistically multifaceted American literary experience, and sometimes even conceals that experience. The problem here is not so much that Americanized comparative literature has become a political rest home for professional refugees and discards from linguistically unilingual literature departments (although, of course, in some cases it has). The problem is rather that professors project uncritically the linguistically homogenized domestic agenda of the United States onto the screens of faraway literary theories and national differentiations.

Among scholars in Québec, in contrast, the emphasis is bifocal almost to the point of myopia. The traditional literary history of Québec's various languages and literatures also faces a fascination with diglossia (as in *Kamouraska*); a scholarly respect for *joual* together with the old distrust of it; and renewed interest in the problem of translating French texts that contain English words into English and translating English texts that contain French words into French (as in *Volkswagen Blues*).[63] Québecois intellectuals are greatly concerned with the role of so-called *transfuge* writers, and there is a still growing movement to increase the number of French anthologies of English writers, and interest in publishing bilingual journals.[64]

It would be tempting here to look outside the American academy to such popular American counterparts to these critical Québecois tendencies as the contemporary bilingual novel of the American Southwest and the multilingual — Spanish, English, and Haitian French — rap or hip-hop of Miami.[65] But American popular culture has always been *just* beginning to comprehend its own multilingual elements. And American cultural criticism, in its inability or unwillingness to recognize America's centuries-long negotiations with such issues (or in its buoyant service to the national anglophone identity of the American literary tradition), still turns a blind eye to America's past — and to its future.

CONCLUSION

What the United States evidences nowadays is both a continual rise in the number of non-English speakers and a unilingual policy without overt official sanction.[66] Any social or intellectual movement toward official bilingualism — legally mandated bilingualism in court, say, with equally weighted versions of the law — would have little positive means of expression in current culture. (The reverse does have a negative impact, however, as when the self-styled "Japanese-American" former senator S. I. Hayakawa, in a legal tradition dating back to 1923, introduced a bill to make English the one and only official language of the country.)[67] Moreover, legislative bills with doublespeak misnomers like Bilingual Education Act — bills that turn out to mean something like "help for the linguistically disabled" — divert public attention from official language as much as does talk about quirkily regional literary traditions.[68] And, for many Americans caught up in problems of civil warring and an almost official biracialism, the example of an always apparently dividing, officially bilingual Canada looms as a warning against any experiments in bilingualism. Thus Edward

A. Steiner wrote in 1916 that "a cleavage in the language (of the United States) now would mean to us a cleavage of the nation in its most vulnerable if not in its most essential part."[69] So it is that a country once polyglot, with thousands of bilingual schools, has become unilingual, if barely literate, in the twenty-first century.[70]

More startling than American lack of intellectual concern with official bilingualism is the lack of political interest in the problems and opportunities of the reality of multilingualism. Were it not that official bilingualism affirming the rights of two dominant linguistic groups over all other linguistic groups often means political problems greater than those of unofficial monolingualism, America's long-standing attempts to decentralize political power by "balancing" one power against another would seem almost to make official bilingualism palatable. (Such bilingualism would mean that the Spanish version of the Constitution would have equal "weight" with the English version; translation would thus partly replace interpretation of the English words of the document's authors.) Recent controversies about language in the workplace would seem to goad America to consider the legal issue, as when commercial corporations seek to outlaw the use of Asian languages or Spanish in the lunchroom.[71] Also, there are disagreements about the appropriate language for private or public signs, as when anglophones want to outlaw unilingual non-English signs in California.[72] In this case the court upheld the right to have unilingual non-English signs, but it is significant that the court made its ruling not on the basis of any argument about official (or unofficial) language but only on First Amendment rights — free speech. Thus America's generally laudable concern with free speech served, as usual, to distract Americans from the issue of official language and even to veil it. It is the apparent contrast between the rights of individuals (American free speech) and the rights of groups (American race rights, Canadian language rights) that sheds light on why the free-speech arena is not the politically realistic place to stage effectively an American debate about official languages and multilingualism.

It might seem easier nowadays to raise the issue of constitutional bilingualism, thanks to contemporary discussions of American statehood for Puerto Rico and of a North American union for Canada, the United States, and Mexico. Puerto Rico's argumentation about whether to "elevate" English to the status of official language has again made many terms of the language debate quasi-official. In 1993, "Governor Pedro Rosselló [of Puerto Rico] signed into law a bill that [gave] English equal status with Spanish as the official language of this American territory. 'Now we have two hymns, two flags, two languages,' Mr. Rosselló, a statehood advocate, declared to hundreds of cheering supporters at a signing ceremony . . . He dismissed as 'a rhetorical storm' the arguments of critics who had sought to safeguard Spanish's 21-month-old status as the island's sole official language."[73] To an unofficially unilingual American populace, still uncertain even whether the term *Hispanic* refers to a linguistic or a racial grouping, official Spanish/English bilingualism in Washington, D.C., still means only "a rhetorical storm" — and babble in education, law, and the workplace. It is useful to rephrase the question of Spanish/English bilingualism with the crucible metaphor that has informed discussion of ethnicity since before Israel Zangwill's *The Melting-Pot* (1908) and Theodore Roosevelt's "Children of the Crucible" (1917). In these perhaps too familiar terms, the main question is not how long the Spanish language can resist melting in the anglophone pot of America. Nor is the question whether Spanish will "break the [linguistic] melting pot" in the sense that Webster meant when he surveyed the linguistic diversity of the United States in the late eighteenth century and predicted that all the American languages — English, German, French, and so on — would eventually melt together to become a distinctly nonanglophone language.[74] Rather, the main question would be whether the Spanish language will become, in the United States, *another* linguistic melting pot, just as the English language has already become a second official linguistic pot in Puerto Rico. As such, the Spanish language in the United States would become not just the language of a "nation within a nation" — which is what Martin Delany called American blacks in 1852, and Clermont-Tonnerre called French Jews in 1789 — but a twin language alongside English, whether as an officially unofficial language, which is what English is in the present, or, more fractious toward the ideology of one melting pot, as an official language, which is what the English language itself would also be likely to become in such circumstances.[75]

Similarly, it might appear simpler these days to raise issues of official multilingualism thanks to contemporary American hopes for — or fears of — such North American economic and political unions as NAFTA joining together the United States, Mexico, and Canada. This union, should it ever amount to more than "free trade," would seem to project and fulfill Americans' dream of a single manifest destiny north and south, Mexicans' vision of again crossing the Rio Grande legally, and francophone Canadians' traditional conviction that they would have been better off with anglophone Americans than with anglophone Canadians. In the first years, moreover, such a union might well weaken federal governments and simultaneously strengthen local cultures (hence languages), much as the contemporary political unification of multilingual Europe seems to be doing. But the problems and opportunities for this North American future are properly accessible to debate only in a language that still shows the specific "nationalizing" resistance that was, for centuries, part of America's unifying motive.

Thus the story of America's social language-engineering needs to be understood and perhaps wisely redirected. It is a remarkable, and some would say heroic, story of immigration, forced, illegal, and voluntary; of treaties, purchases, and constitutions by which Spanish, French, German, and Amerindian languages, among many others, were subsumed; of a once new and powerfully nationalist literary movement that still informs devotedly monolingual American university departments. Most Americans, however, cannot yet tell the story, or they do not want to tell the real story, not so much because the languages are forgotten (though they are), but mainly because forgetting language difference — and hence, more critically, partly suppressing the category of "language" itself — is still the urgent component of unofficially anglophone America's understanding of itself. America's otherwise laudable concerns with free speech, dialect, bilingual education, ethnicity, and cultural diversity serve effectively to mask substantive language issues. Comprehending the full magnitude of multilingualism in the United States — and defining the problem of the language rights of "people" both within it and without it — probably requires a radical revision of the political history of languages in North America. "Babel in America" is an introductory essay in that direction.

Notes

1. John Jay writes "that Providence has been pleased to give this one connected country, to one united people; a people descended from the same ancestors, speaking the same language, professing the same religion," in Alexander Hamilton, James Madison, and John Jay, *The Federalist Papers: A Collection of Essays Written in Support of the Constitution of the United States,* ed. Roy P. Fairfield (Garden City, N.Y.: Anchor Books, 1966), p. 6.

2. I use the terms *America* and *United States* as near synonyms; at the same time I examine the international and intranational political significance of how the rhetoric of the term *American* — indicating here the English language as spoken in the United States — takes the part for the whole (i.e. the "United States of America" for an ideal "union of the Americas North, Central, and South") or the one for the many (i.e. anglophone unilingualism for plurilingualism).

3. Saul Bellow is (perhaps wrongly) reported to have said this about the goals of U.S. English, a group bent on making English the one and only official language of the United States. Bellow has said that he is not a member of U.S. English (quoted in S. I. Hayakawa, *One Nation — Indivisible? The English Language Amendment,* excerpted as "The Case for Official English" in *Language Loyalties: A Source Book on the Official Language Controversy,* ed. James Crawford [Chicago: University of Chicago Press, 1992], p. 100). Compare Arthur M. Schlesinger's complaint: "The national ideal had once been *e pluribus unum.* Are we now to belittle *unum* and glorify *pluribus?* Will the center hold? or will the melting pot yield to the Tower of Babel?" (quoted in Werner Sollors, "E Pluribus Unum; or, Matthew Arnold Meets George Orwell in the Multiculturalism Debate," Working Paper no. 53, for the John F. Kennedy Institut für Nordamerikastudien at Freie Universität Berlin [1992]:22).

4. Silence about official language in America characterizes analyses from the left and right sides of the political spectrum. Both sides assume the hegemony of English as a fact of life and define the politics of language in the United States mainly in terms of the characteristics of a specifically American English. Among such analysts are Michael P. Kramer, *Imagining Language in America: From the Revolution to the Civil War* (Princeton: Princeton University Press, 1992), and David Simpson, *The Politics of American English 1776–1850* (New York: Methuen, 1986); they fail to consider fully the significance of America's polyglot past and its unofficially official monoglot present.

5. See Shirley Brice Heath, "English in Our Language Heritage," in *Language in the USA,* ed. Charles A. Ferguson and Heath (Cambridge: Cambridge Univer-

sity Press, 1981), pp. 6–20. Yet it is worth recalling that: (1) various treaties with the Indians and the Spanish seem to have meant to guarantee some sort of official language parity with the English; (2) the Constitution was translated into other languages; (3) in our own century there have been movements to make English the one official language. For translation of the Constitution into French, see Benjamin Franklin, letter to Robert R. Livingston, 22 July 1783, *Franklin: Writings*, ed. J. A. Leo Lemay (New York: Viking, 1987), p. 1071.

6. See Richard W. Bailey, *Images of English: A Cultural History of the Language* (Ann Arbor: University of Michigan Press, 1991), p. 102.

7. See *The Federalist Papers*, pp. 287–88 n4. The linguistic "stock" of some of the white people of 1790 has been studied with some care; see American Council of Learned Societies, *Report of Committee on Linguistic and National Stocks in the Population of the United States*, in *The Annual Report of the American Historical Association*, 3 vols. (Washington, D.C., 1932), vol. 1, pp. 103–441. Compare Jack Citrin, "Language Politics and American Identity," *The Public Interest* 99 (Spring 1990):96–109. See also Frank Ried Diffenderffer, *The German Immigration into Pennsylvania through the Port of Philadelphia, 1770–1775* (Lancaster, Pa.: Published by the author, 1900), pp. 102–6.

8. George Washington, letter to the Marquis de Lafayette, 10 Jan. 1788, *The Writings of George Washington from the Original Manuscript Sources, 1745–1799*, ed. John C. Fitzpatrick, 39 vols. (Washington, D.C., U.S. Govt. Print. Off., 1931–1944), vol. 29, p. 374. The numbers of the Amerindians are not known, because the official census reports for the various tribes were ludicrously and inaccurately low.

9. For black population figures, see Lisa A. Bull, "The Negro," in *The Ethnic Contribution to the American Revolution*, ed. Frederick Harling and Martin Kaufman (Westfield, Mass.: Westfield Bicentennial Committee, 1976), pp. 67–74. The study of how slaves lost their various tribal languages (hence also a comparative history of those languages) has yet to be fully undertaken; but see Daniel C. Littlefield, *Rice and Slaves: Ethnicity and the Slave Trade in Colonial South Carolina* (Baton Rouge: Louisiana State University Press, 1981), and Guion Griffis Johnson, *A Social History of the Sea Islands, with Special Reference to St. Helena Island, South Carolina* (1930; rpt. New York: Negro Universities Press, 1960), pp. 77–78.

10. See R. Merritt Cox, "Thomas Jefferson and Spanish: 'To Every Inhabitant Who Means to Look beyond the Limits of His Farm,'" *Romance Notes* 14 (Autumn 1972):116–21. Merritt focuses more on Spain than the local areas.

11. By 1878 in New Mexico and Arizona — after the large influx of English speak-

ers during the gold rush — Spanish language rights, if ever they existed, were rescinded. See Rodolfo Acuña, *Occupied America: The Chicano's Struggle toward Liberation* (San Francisco: Canfield Press, 1972), p. 104.

12. Paine quoted in Hayakawa, "The Case for Official English," p. 95.

13. The European settlers, including Thomas Jefferson, researched languages of the Amerindians. See Alexander F. Chamberlain, "Thomas Jefferson's Ethnological Opinions and Activities," *American Anthropologist* 9 (July–Sept. 1907):499–509. The compilers of Indian vocabularies were generally either military men or missionaries: for example, David Zeisberger, a Moravian missionary, who wrote a book about Delaware Indian (and English) "spellings." George Washington sent this to Lafayette, as well as a *Vocabulary of the Shawanese and Delaware Languages* by Richard Butler. In a letter to Lafayette of January 10, 1788, Washington wrote: "To know the affinity of tongues seems to be one step towards promoting the affinity of nations. Would to god, the harmony of nations was an object that lay nearest to the hearts of Sovereigns; and that the incentives to peace (of which commerce and facility of understanding each other are not the most inconsiderable) might be daily encreased! Should the present or any other efforts of mine to procure information respecting the different dialects of the Aborigines in America, serve to reflect a ray of light on the obscure subject of language in general, I shall be highly gratified. For I love to indulge the contemplation of human nature in a progressive state of improvement and melioration; and if the idea would not be considered visionary and chimerical, I could fondly hope, that the present plan of the great Potentate of the North might, in some measure, lay the foundation for *that assimilation of language, which, producing assimilation of manners and interests, should one day remove many of the causes of hostility from amongst mankind.*" (*Writings of George Washington*, p. 374; emphasis added).

14. Thomas Paine brings up a religious aspect of the problem of unilingualism: "But how was Jesus Christ to make anything known to all nations? He could speak but one language, which was Hebrew, and there are in the world several hundred languages. Scarcely any two nations speak the same language, or understand each other; and as to translations, every man who knows anything of languages knows that it is impossible to translate from one language into another, not only without losing a great part of the original, but frequently mistaking the sense"; Paine, *The Age of Reason*, in *The Life and Works of Thomas Paine*, ed. William M. Van der Weyde, 10 vols. (New Rochelle, N.Y.: Thomas Paine National Historical Association, 1925), vol. 8, p. 42. St. Paul, that great traveler, might say that in the New Dispensation there will be no longer Hebrew or Greek; but language differences are not transcended — except in silence, or, in the "old" elevation, as uniquely sacred Hebrew (among

the Jews) and, in the "new" elevation, as Roman imperial Latin or Christian Church Latin.

15. Franklin, noting that the universal language of the eighteenth century was French, wrote that "our English bids fair to obtain the second Place" and expressed the conviction that one day it would be English that would be first (Franklin, letter to Noah Webster, 26 Dec. 1789, *Franklin: Writings*, p. 1175).

16. The English colonists' rebellious discussions of ridding the United States of the English language and concomitant English political institutions were themselves variations of English nationalist demands, common since Anglo-Norman times, that the English language be purged of its "foreign" elements, chiefly Norman, and that pure English become, as Edmund Spenser put it, "the kingdom of our own language." Quoted in Richard Helgerson, *Forms of Nationhood: The Elizabethan Writing of England* (Chicago: University of Chicago Press, 1992), p. 25. Hugh MacDougall points out that John Hare had argued for freedom from French, saying that English usages and constitutive laws of Norman origin should be "'devested of their French rages [rags]. . . be restored into the [original] English or Latine tongue.' All French words should be purged from the language and replaced with words and terms 'from the old Saxon and the learned tongues.'" Hugh A. MacDougall, *Racial Myth in English History: Trojans, Teutons, and Anglo-Saxons* (Montréal: Harvest House, 1992), p. 61.

17. Historically, the political underdog generally conflates oppression by a conquering *people* with oppression by that people's *language*. Likewise the conqueror often argues that no language is inherently — that is, lexically or syntactically — oppressive. Stalin led a murderous experiment in social language-engineering and argued implicitly that a new Russian unilingualism would help destroy economic inequalities. See Joseph Stalin, *Marxism and Linguistics*, trans. Margaret Schlauch (New York: International Publishers, 1951).

18. Boontling was spoken from 1880 to 1920 in the area near Boonville (in northern California); it was not intelligible to outsiders. See Charles C. Adams, *Boontling: An American Lingo* (Austin: University of Texas Press, 1971).

19. Quoted in Dennis E. Baron, *Grammar and Good Taste: Reforming the American Language* (New Haven: Yale University Press, 1982), p. 12.

20. On ideas about the commonwealth in England and Amsterdam in the seventeenth century, see Marc Shell, "Marranos (Pigs), or from Coexistence to Toleration," *Critical Inquiry* 17 (Winter 1991):306–35.

21. See Baron, *Grammar*, pp. 12–13.

22. See Bailey, *Images of English*, p. 104: "Despite persistent folklore promulgated

by subsequent writers, there were no serious attempts to adopt some language other than English for the new nation."

23. See Franklin, "The German Language in Pennsylvania," in *Language Loyalties*, p. 18n9. See also Oswald Seidensticker, *The First Century of German Printing in America, 1728–1830; Preceded by a Notice of the Literary Work of F. D. Pastorius* (Philadelphia: German Pionierverein of Philadelphia, 1893).

24. Franklin's letter to James Parker, 20 Mar. 1750, is quoted in Robert A. Feer, "Official Use of the German Language in Pennsylvania," *Pennsylvania Magazine of History and Biography* 76 (Oct. 1952):401.

25. See Franklin's diatribe against the Germans in a letter to Peter Collinson, 9 May 1753, *The Papers of Benjamin Franklin*, ed. Leonard W. Labaree et al., 29 vols. (New Haven: Yale University Press 1959–), vol. 4, pp. 479–86 (quoted in Feer, "Official Use," p. 401). In the same tradition as Franklin, William Smith wrote in 1755 that "I know nothing that will hinder them, either from soon being able to give us Law and Language, or else, by joining with the *French*, to eject all the *English* Inhabitants" (quoted in ibid., p. 402).

26. Franklin's letter to William Strahan, 19 Aug. 1784, in *Franklin: Writings*, p. 1102. Franklin offers the Irish of Pennsylvania as an example of how a minority group can dominate the government.

27. Feer, "Official Use," p. 399. The committee recommendation followed an incident in the Third Congress of the United States whereby "'a petition of a number of Germans, residing in the State of Virginia' was presented to the House of Representatives . . . 'praying that a certain proportion of the laws of the United States may be printed in the German language'" (ibid., p. 398).

28. Löhrer writes that "half of them (in the Assembly) were for the introduction of the German language, and this was certainly of great importance when one considers that here it was a question of making a German state where English had previously been the official language. Then the speaker of the Assembly, a Muhlenberger, through his vote, gave the decision in favor of the English language" (quoted in Feer, "Official Use," p. 395). What was "involved was a request, made by a group of Virginia Germans, to have certain laws issued in German *as well as* in English. The proposal was rejected by [only] one vote"; David Crystal, *Cambridge Encyclopedia of Language* (Cambridge: Cambridge University Press, 1987), p. 365. See also Heath and Frederick Mandabach, "Language Status Decisions and the Law in the United States," in *Progress in Language Planning*, ed. Juan Cobarrubias and Joshua A. Fishman (The Hague: Mouton Publishers, 1983), pp. 87–105.

29. Joseph Ehrenfried argued in 1834 that "the prevalence of the German language in many parts of the United States should form a powerful inducement

of men in every situation of life to become, at least partially acquainted with it" (quoted by Heath, "English in Our Language Heritage," p. 11).

30. Rush was a member of the Continental Congress and signer of the Declaration of Independence. See Benjamin Rush, *The Letters of Benjamin Rush*, ed. L. H. Butterfield, 2 vols. (Princeton: Princeton University Press, 1951), vol. 1, pp. 356–66. See also Rush, *Information to Europeans Who are Disposed to Migrate to the United States* (Philadelphia: Carey, Stewart, 1790).

31. See Edward Sagarin and Robert J. Kelly, "Polylingualism in the United States of America: A Multitude of Tongues amid a Monolingual Majority," in *Language Policy and National Unity*, ed. William R. Beer and James E. Jacob (Totowa, N.J.: Rowman and Allenheld, 1985), pp. 20–44. One might also consider here the conflict between the Germanic (Hegelian) philosophers of Missouri (as well as Ohio and Chicago) and the New England transcendentalists. See Carl Wittke, *German-Americans and the World War with Special Emphasis on Ohio's German-Language Press* (Columbus: Ohio State Archeological and Historical Society, 1936). See also Carolyn Toth, *German-English Bilingual Schools in America: The Cincinnati Tradition in Historical Context* (New York: P. Lang, 1990).

32. Roosevelt continued, "The greatness of this nation depends on the swift assimilation of the aliens she welcomes to her shores" (Theodore Roosevelt, "The Children of the Crucible," excerpted as "One Flag, One Language," in *Language Loyalties*, p. 85).

33. See Joshua A. Fishman, *Language Loyalty in the United States: The Maintenance and Perpetuation of Non-English Mother Tongues by American Ethnic and Religious Groups* (The Hague: Mouton, 1966).

34. On the long-term use of "Dutch" elsewhere than in Pennsylvania, see Philip E. Webber, *Pella Dutch: The Portrait of a Language and Its Use in One of Iowa's Ethnic Communities* (Ames: Iowa State University Press, 1988) and various linguistic histories of New York, once called "New Amsterdam."

35. Thus we read in the Congressional record: "*Mr. Tinnin:* 'We have here in the Capital now tons and tons of documents published in Spanish for the benefit of foreigners.' *Mr. Rolfe:* 'Do you call the native population of this State foreigners?'" (Quoted in *Language Loyalties*, p. 53.)

36. See U.S. Commission on Civil Rights, *The Excluded Student: Educational Practices Affecting Mexican Americans in the Southwest*, excerpted as "Language Rights and New Mexico Statehood," in *Language Loyalties*, p. 62. On the bilingualism of the older New Mexico constitutions, see Dorothy Cline, *New Mexico's 1910 Constitution: A Nineteenth-Century Product* (Santa Fe: The Lightning Tree, 1985). The bilingual provision was renewed in 1931 and 1943, but was apparently omitted in 1949.

37. Larzer Ziff writes that Americans at the time of the revolution had "inherited a medium shaped by centuries of monarchal government . . . [which had] encoded in its diction, syntax, and especially its literary conventions the values of hierarchal society" (quoted in David Bromwich, "When Books Are to Blame," review of *Writing in the New Nation: Prose, Print, and Politics in the Early United States* by Larzer Ziff, *Times Literary Supplement*, 22 May 1992, p. 13).

38. Quoted in Geoffrey Nunberg, "The Official English Movement: Reimagining America," in *Language Loyalties*, p. 485.

39. Herron is quoted in Baron, *Grammar*, p. 14. Webster is quoted in Bailey, *Images of English*, p. 104. Webster also said that in the Federal Procession there was "a scroll, containing the principles of a [new] *Federal* language" (Webster, *The New York Packet*, 5, 1788).

40. Noah Webster, *Dissertations on the English Language: With Notes, Historical and Critical*, excerpted as "Declaration of Linguistic Independence," in *Language Loyalties*, p. 35 n33. The two languages — English and American — should be the same, Webster wrote, "except so far as local circumstances, laws and institutions shall require a few particularities in each country" (ibid.).

41. Webster's ideas for his *"Federal* English" — to which Adams, Franklin, Jefferson, and Madison contributed their notions — were not so revolutionary as the "fonetic" pronunciation-spellings used by some writers in France in the eighteenth century. William Thornton's proposed phonetic alphabet was sometimes discussed; see also Charles Jared Ingersoll, *Remarks on the Review of Inchinquin's Letters* (Boston, 1815), pp. 138–39; cited in Baron, *Grammar*, p. 12.

42. "As soon as I began to write," Gérald Godin had written in *Parti pris* in 1965, "I realized that I was a barbarian, i.e., a foreigner, according to the etymological meaning of the term. My mother tongue was not French but *franglais*. I had to learn French almost as a foreign language"; quoted in Lise Gauvin, "From Octave Crémazie to Victor-Lévy Beaulieu: Language, Literature, and Ideology," trans. Emma Henderson, *Yale French Studies* 65 (1983):38–39. Gaston Miron discussed in 1973 the linguistic schizophrenia and alienation that informed the diseased cultural life of Québec, including the "debilitating effects" of bilingual signs on the "purity" of the "French language," and called for a new "linguistic decolonization" in "Décoloniser la langue: Interview/ témoignage with Gaston Miron," *Maintenant* 125 (Apr. 1973):12. Jacques Godbout had claimed similarly in 1975 that the "ideology" of *joual* was an "infantile disease of nationalism" (quoted in Gauvin, "From Crémazie to Victor-Lévy Beaulieu," p. 43).

43. See Pierre Vallières, *Nègres blancs d'Amérique: Autobiographie précoce d'un "terroriste" québécois* (Paris, 1969); Kathy Mezei, "Speaking White: Literary Translation as a Vehicle of Assimilation in Québec," *Canadian Literature* 117

(Summer 1988):11–23; and Michèle Lalonde, "Speak White," *Change* 30–31 (Mar. 1977):100–104. Malcolm X compares some American blacks' intention not to assimilate (to the white racial majority of the United States) to some French Canadians' intention not to assimilate (to the linguistic majority of Canada). See Malcolm X and Alex Haley, *The Autobiography of Malcolm X* (New York: Grove Press, 1965), p. 277.

44. On distinct Africanisms in African-American language, see *Africanisms in Afro-American Language Varieties,* ed. Salikoko S. Mufwene and Nancy Condon (Athens: University of Georgia Press, 1993), which concerns the influence of African languages on English. Compare Joseph E. Holloway and Winifred K. Vass, *The African Heritage of American English* (Bloomington: Indiana University Press, 1993). On Gullah as a "language" or "dialect," see Charles W. Joyner, *Down by the Riverside: A South Carolina Slave Community* (Urbana: University of Illinois Press, 1984), and on some of its social implications, see my *Money, Language, and Thought: Literary and Philosophical Economies from the Medieval to the Modern Era* (Berkeley: University of California Press, 1982), chap. 1. On the views that "black English" is a type of Creole, see *Verb Phrase Patterns in Black English and Creole,* ed. Walter F. Edwards and Donald Winford (Detroit: Wayne State University Press, 1991). On its syntax, see Edgar W. Schneider, *Morphologische und syntaktische Variablen im amerikanischen Early Black English* (Tuscaloosa: University of Alabama Press, 1989). See also Hanni U. Taylor, *Standard English, Black English, and Bidialectalism: A Controversy* (New York: P. Lang, 1991).

45. Compare David R. Sewell, *Mark Twain's Languages: Discourse, Dialogue, and Linguistic Variety* (Berkeley: University of California Press, 1987) and Shelley Fisher Fishkin, *Was Huck Black? Mark Twain and African-American Voices* (New York: Oxford University Press, 1993). In his Uncle Remus stories, Joel Chandler Harris blended "black" and "white" into a society of dialect-speaking humanoid "brethren" (as in Brer Rabbit and Brer B'ar).

46. A few examples of early general manuals may be helpful here. Noah Webster's *Grammatical Institute of the English language (Pt. 3),* 3d ed. (Philadelphia, 1787) already included in its subtitle "rules in elocution and directions for expressing the principal passions of the mind." John Walker's *Elements of Elocution* includes "copper-plates explaining the nature of accent" (Boston: D. Mallory, 1810). John Frost's *The American Speaker* (Philadelphia: F. W. Greenough and Thomas Cowperthwait, 1839) likewise announces its stress "on pronunciation, pauses, inflections, accent, and emphasis" and its goal "to improve the pupil in . . . recitation." See also William Russell, *The American Elocutionist; Comprising "Lessons in Enunciation," "Exercises in Elocution," and "Rudiments of Gesture"* (Boston: Jenks, Palmer, 1844). Closer to Twain's period, see Alexander Melville Bell, *Elocutionary Manual: The Principles of Elocution,* 4th ed. (Sa-

lem, Mass.: J. P. Burbank, 1878), with its focus on, as its subtitle has it, "the principles of elocution, with exercises and notations for pronunciation, intonation, emphasis, gesture and emotional expression," and Loomis J. Campbell, *The New Franklin Fourth Reader* (New York: Taintor Bros., 1884).

47. See Marc Shell, "From Coexistence to Toleration; or Marranos (Pigs) in Spain," in *Children of the Earth: Literature, Politics, and Nationhood* (New York: Oxford University Press, 1993), pp. 22–40.

48. Even the term *Aryan*, once applied only to language families, as in Thomas Young's article in *The Quarterly Review* (1813), came to be applied also to biological groupings. Language thus became a test for race.

49. Charles Darwin, *The Descent of Man, and Selection in Relation to Sex* (1871; Princeton: Princeton University Press, 1981), p. 59.

50. Max Müller, recanting some of his earlier views, wrote in 1888 that "to me an ethnologist who speaks of an Aryan race, Aryan blood, Aryan eyes and hair, is as great a sinner as a linguist who speaks of a *dolichocephalic* dictionary or a *brachycephalic* grammar. It is worse than a Babylonian confusion of tongues — it is downright theft. We [linguists] have made our own terminology for the classification of languages; let ethnologists make their own for the classification of skulls, and hair, and blood"; Max Müller, *Biographies of Words and the Home of the Aryans* (London: Longmans, Green, 1888), pp. 120–21.

Indeed, many natural historians have hypothesized a human "monogenesis" — one genetic origin of all presently living human beings, sketching a family tree that illustrates a supposed divergence of humankind from a single DNA stock. Many historical linguists likewise hypothesize a single original source or locale for all human languages, some claiming to "have reconstructed the ancestor of all living languages." See Vitaly Shevoroshkin, "The Mother Tongue: How Linguists Have Reconstructed the Ancestor of All Living Languages," *The Sciences* 30 (May/June 1990):20–28; this was, of course, the pre-Babel, Ur language that seventeenth-century theorists called Adamic, the "language" that modern linguists sometimes call Nostratic. See David S. Katz, *Philo-Semitism and the Readmission of the Jews to England, 1603–1655* (Oxford: Clarendon Press, 1982), esp. chap. 2. Belief in the historical existence of this unitarian language is "a kind of religion" that "emphasize[s] the unity of humankind and the need of brotherhood" (Juha Janhunen, quoted in Robert Wright, "Quest for the Mother Tongue," *Atlantic Monthly*, April 1991, p. 48). On the racialist rhetoric of German romantic linguistics in the eighteenth and nineteenth centuries, see also Martin Bernal, *The Fabrication of Ancient Greece, 1785–1985*, vol. 1 of *Black Athena: The Afroasiatic Roots of Classical Civilization* (New Brunswick: Rutgers University Press, 1987), pp. 224–72. On Gobineau, see Shell, *Children of the Earth*, pp. 178–79, 276n15.

51. William Stubbs, *The Constitutional History of England in Its Origin and Development*, 3 vols. (1870; Oxford: Clarendon, 1891), vol. 1, p. 7.

52. For relevant details about the language issue in Québec, see Shell, *Children of the Earth*, esp. chap. 3, and "La Publicité bilingue au Québec: Une Langue fourchue," *Journal canadien de recherche sémiotique* 5-2 (1977):55–76. The Québec government's Parent Act of 1964 introduced a few supposedly non-confessional (or secular) schools. Various governments since then have tried to secularize the entire school system.

53. In this same vein, Martin Luther wrote in 1518, "I thank God that I am able to hear and find my God in the German language. Whom neither I nor you could ever find in Latin or Greek or Hebrew"; quoted in Arno Borst, *Der Turmbau von Babel: Geschichte der Meinungen über Ursprung und vielfalt der Sprachen und Völker*, 4 vols. in 6 (Stuttgart: A. Hiersemann, 1957–63), vol. 3, p. 1006.

54. On the routing of Montréal's "ethnic minorities" into French language schools, see Conseil de la langue française, *Vivre la diversité en français: Le Défi de l'école français à clientèle pluriethnique de l'île de Montréal* (Québec: Le Conseil, 1987). For an analysis of "immigrant anglicisation" and the *commission des écoles catholiques de Montréal* in the 1980s (as seen from the viewpoint of the Italian community), see Donat J. Taddeo and Raymond C. Taras, *Le Débat linguistique au Québec* (Montréal: Presses de l'Université de Montréal, 1987). On Montréal's efforts at the *tri*lingual education of "Néo-Canadiens," see Michael D. Behiels, "*The Commission des écoles catholiques de Montréal* and the Neo-Canadian Question: 1947–63," *Canadian Ethnic Studies* 13-2 (1986):38–64.

55. In previous decades, some members of the Jewish community had favored the assimilationist tendencies of this arrangement.

56. See Walt Whitman, *An American Primer*, ed. Horace Traubel (Boston: Small, Maynard, 1904).

57. See Johann Gottfried Herder's suggestion that the essential "constituent" in national *culture* is language: "Jede Nation spricht also, nach dem sie denkt, und denkt, nach dem sie spricht." Johann Gottfried Herder, *Über die neüre Deutsche Litteratur: Fragmente erste Sammlung* (1768), *Sämmtliche Werke*, ed. Bernhard Suphan, 33 vols. (Berlin: Weidmann, 1877–1913), vol. 2, p. 18. See also Herder, pt. 1 of *Ideen zur Philosophie der Geschichte der Menschheit* (1784), *Sämmtliche Werke*, vol. 13, pp. 354–66.

58. Whorf was a student of Edward Sapir's, author of the influential *Language* (New York: Harcourt, Brace, 1921). See also Frans Boas, *Handbook of American Indian Languages* (Washington, D.C.: U.S. Govt. Print. Off., 1911) and *Race, Language, and Culture* (New York: Macmillan, 1940).

59.   See especially Jonathan Edwards, *Observations on the Language of the Muhhekaneew Indians; in which the Extent of that Language in North-America is Shewn; its Genius is Grammatically Traced; some of its Peculiarities, and Some Instances of Analogy between that and the Hebrew are Pointed Out* (New Haven: Josiah Meigs, 1788). For many works written in the Amerindian languages themselves, see Robert Kruse, *The Henry Rowe Schoolcraft Collection: A Catalogue of Books in Native American Languages in the Library of the Boston Athenaeum* (Boston: Boston Athenaeum, 1991). Being encouraged by economic or political circumstances — and sometimes being compelled by law — to speak a language other than one's own, at least in the public sphere, is part of the experience of most nonanglophone immigrants. Some critics of this ambiguously involuntary anglicization call it cultural or linguistic genocide. However, a better analogy would be forced conversion.

60.   Werner Sollors, *Beyond Ethnicity: Consent and Descent in American Culture* (New York: Oxford University Press, 1986) has barely a word to say about linguistic difference and official language, but see *Ethnicity and Language*, ed. Winston A. Van Horne (Milwaukee: University of Wisconsin System, Institute on Race and Ethnicity, 1987).

61.   See Robert Elmer Ward, *A Bio-Bibliography of German-American Writers, 1670–1970* (White Plains, N.Y.: Kraus International Publications, 1985); Brent Orlyn Peterson, *Popular Narratives and Ethnic Identity: Literature and Community in Die Abendschule* (Ithaca: Cornell University Press 1991); and Stephen Clausing, *English Influence on American German and American Icelandic* (New York: P. Lang, 1986).
      On literature in Spanish, see several essays in *Pasó por aquí: Critical Essays on the New Mexican Literary Tradition, 1542–1988*, ed. Erlinda Gonzales-Berry (Albuquerque: University of New Mexico Press, 1989). As Heinz Kloss argues, in *American Bilingual Tradition* (Rowley, Mass.: Newbury House, 1977), p. 126, "the entire life of New Mexico is colored by the coexistence of these two language groups," that is, Spanish and English. It would be worth considering also the role of the unofficial languages, that is, the native American languages, in a quasi-bilingual New Mexico.
      On the possible effects of Yiddish on English, Henry James writes: "the accent of the very ultimate future, in the States, may be destined to become the most beautiful on the globe . . . ; but whatever we shall know it for, certainly, we shall not know it for English — in any sense for which there is existing literary measure"; see Henry James, *The American Scene* (1907; New York: C. Scribner's Sons, 1946), p. 139. See also Cynthia Ozick, "Envy; or, Yiddish in America," *The Pagan Rabbi and Other Stories* (New York: Knopf, 1971), pp. 39–100.

62.   For American German, see Sigrid Bauschinger, *Die Posaune der Reform: Deut-*

sche Literatur im Neuengland des 19. Jahrhunderts (Bern: Francke, 1989). For American "Dutch", see Kurt Rein, *Religiöse Minderheiten als Sprachgemein-schaftsmodelle: Deutsch Sprachinseln täufer ischen Ursprungs in den Vereinigten Staaten von Amerika* (Wiesbaden: Steiner, 1977). For American Spanish, see Antonio Blanco S., *La lengua española en la historia de California: Contribución a su estudio* (Madrid: Cultura Hispánica, 1971); Yves-Charles Grandjeat et al, *Écritures hispaniques aux États-Unis: Mémoires et mutations* (Aix-en-Provence: Université de Provence, 1990); *European Perspectives on Hispanic Literature of the United States,* ed. Geneviève Fabre (Houston: Arte Publico Press, 1988); and parts of *Spanish in the United States: Sociolinguistic Aspects,* ed. Jon Amastae and Lucía Elías-Olivares (New York: Cambridge University Press, 1982). For American Chinese: Mimi Chan and Helen Kwok, *A Study of Lexical Borrowing from Chinese into English with Special Reference to Hong Kong* (Hong Kong: Centre of Asian Studies, University of Hong Kong, 1985). For North America as a whole: Gilles Bibeau, *L'Éducation bilingue en Amérique du Nord* (Montréal: Guerin, 1982), and Fernand Baldensperger, *Note sur les moyens d'action intellectuelle de la France à l'étranger* (Paris, 1917).

63. On Anne Hébert's *Kamouraska* (Paris: Editions du Seuil, 1970), see, among others, Ben-Z. Shek, "Diglossia and Ideology: Socio-Cultural Aspects of 'Translation' in Québec," *Études sur le texte et ses transformations: Traductions et Cultures* 1-1 (1988):85–91.

On French/English issues, see Jacques Poulin, *Volkswagen Blues* (Montréal: Quebec/Amerique, 1984), p. 85; trans. Sheila Fischman, under the title *Volkswagen Blues* (Toronto: McClelland and Stewart, 1988). The Volkswagen in this novel has the Heideggerian inscription "Die Sprache ist das Haus des Seins." Compare Mezei, "Speaking White."

64. On *transfuge* writers, see Pierre Monette, "Mon français mais Montréal," in *L'Avenir du français au Québec,* ed. Jacques Folch-Ribas (Montréal, 1987), p. 115. Monette points out that "la plupart des écrivains majeurs sont des transfuges" (ibid.). On anthology, see Paul Morisset, "La Face cachée de la culture québécoise," in *Le Québec en textes: Anthologie 1940–1986,* ed. Gérard Boismenu, Laurent Mailhot, and Jacques Rouillard (Montréal: Boreal, 1986), pp. 531–38. On bilingual journals, see *Vice Versa, Montréal Now,* and *Ellipse.*

65. See Cormac McCarthy's novel *All the Pretty Horses* (New York: Knopf, 1992), one part of *The Border Trilogy.* Set in Texas and Mexico, this book includes a good deal of Spanish. On Miami's current multilingualism generally, see *Miami Now! Immigration, Ethnicity, and Social Change,* ed. Guillermo Grenier and Alex Stepick (Gainesville: University of Florida Press, 1992).

66. In the 1980s, the total number of United States residents age five and over who spoke a language other than English at home rose by 14% to 31,845,000 in 1990. The number of people who speak Spanish and French — the two

most frequently spoken non-English languages — rose by 50.1% to 17,339,000 and by 8.3% to 1,703,000 respectively. The figure for French speakers includes French Canadians in New Hampshire and Maine, but it does not include Haitian Creole speakers, whose number rose by 65.4% to 188,000, or Louisiana Cajun speakers. It is not only the rate of immigration (50.1%) that explains the high number of Spanish speakers. Some immigrant groups have higher rates of immigration: Chinese up 97.7% to 1,249,000; Tagalog (Philippines) up 88.6% to 843,000; Koreans up 127.2% to 626,000; and Vietnamese up 149.5% to 507,000. It is also the case that Spanish has a certain staying power deriving, on the one hand, from the feeling in some parts of the country — principally in such border states as New Mexico and California, with 33.5% and 31.5% non-English speakers — that enough people already speak Spanish to make the language "self-sustaining," and, on the other hand, from the belief that Spanish speakers have a historical "right" to the land. A similar belief may help account for the rise in the number of French speakers and of Navaho speakers (up 20.6% to 149,000).

67. Hayakawa had proposed the constitutional amendment that would have made English the official language of the United States. See Jon Stewart, "Saving America from Foreign Tongues," *Seattle Post-Intelligencer* 31 May 1981, p. B2. For a discussion of this amendment, see Hayakawa, *One Nation — Indivisible?* The twentieth-century legal movement to make "American" the official language of the United States dates from about 1923, when Congressman Washington J. McCormick introduced a bill to Congress to this effect. Though the bill died in committee, it was later adopted by Illinois. See Washington J. McCormick, "'American' as the Official Language of the United States," in *Language Loyalties*, pp. 40–41. The 1986 debate about California's English Language Amendment is exemplary. During the debate, Richard D. Lamm argued that "we should be color-blind but linguistically cohesive" (Richard D. Lamm, "English Comes First," *New York Times*, 1 July 1986, p. 23); compare Lamm and Gary Imhoff, *The Immigration Time Bomb: The Fragmenting of America* (New York: Truman Talley Books, 1985); on the other side, the American Civil Liberties Union stated that it did not "believe that the ability to be protected by the State Constitution should be dependent upon proficiency in English" (quoted in Marcia Chambers, "California Braces for Change with English as Official Language," *New York Times*, 26 Nov. 1986, p. 20).

68. On bilingual education see, among others, Alfred Bruce Gaarder, *Bilingual Schooling and the Survival of Spanish in the United States* (Rowley, Mass.: Newbury House, 1977); Joshua A. Fishman et al., *Bilingualism in the Barrio: The Measurement and Description of Language Dominance in Bilinguals* (Bloomington: University of Indiana Press, 1971); *The New Bilingualism: An American Dilemma*, ed. Martin Ridge (New Brunswick: Rutgers University Press, 1981); and perhaps Nathan Glazer, *Towards a Bilingual Democracy?* (Chicago: Institute for Political

Philosophy and Policy Analysis, Loyola University of Chicago, 1982). See too Fishman, "Bilingualism and Separatism," *The Annals of the American Academy of Political and Social Science* 487 (Sept. 1986):169–80.

69. Quoted in Heath, "English in Our Language Heritage," p. 8.

70. This is the regular condition, we say, of "developing" nations. See *Language Problems of Developing Nations,* ed. Fishman, Charles A. Ferguson, and Jyotirindra Das Gupta (New York: Wiley, 1968).

71. *Gutiérrez v. Municipal Court* (838 F.2d 1031, 9th Cir. 1988) outlawed English-only rules in the workplace. Concerning various other English-only rulings, see Edward M. Chen, "Language Rights in the Private Sector," in *Language Loyalties,* pp. 269–77. For various cases relating to the Spanish language, see Bill Piatt, *Language on the Job: Balancing Business Needs and Employee Rights* (Albuquerque: University of New Mexico Press, 1993) and *Only English? Law and Language Policy in the United States* (Albuquerque: University of New Mexico Press, 1990).

72. In 1988, the city of Pomona enacted an ordinance providing that if local businesses "displayed signs featuring 'foreign alphabetical characters,' they must 'devote at least one-half of the sign area to advertising copy in English alphabetical characters'" (Crawford, introduction to *Asian American Business Group v. City of Pomona,* in *Language Loyalties,* pp. 284–85). See also *Bilingualism in the Southwest,* ed. Paul R. Turner (Tucson: University of Arizona Press, 1973) and "Indian Language Renewal," in *Human Organization* 47 (Winter 1988):283–329. Law cases include discrimination in the workplace against those who speak a non-English language, those who speak English dialects, and those who speak English with a foreign accent.

73. "Puerto Rico Elevates English," *New York Times,* 29 Jan. 1993, p. A6.

74. Compare Thomas Weyr, *Hispanic U.S.A.: Breaking the Melting Pot* (New York: Harper and Row, 1988).

75. Martin Robison Delany, *The Condition, Elevation, Emigration, and Destiny of the Colored People of the United States* (1852; New York: Arno Press, 1968), p. 12. Compare Comte Stanislas de Clermont-Tonnerre, *Opinion relativement aux persecutions qui menacent les juifs d'Alsace* (Versailles, 1789).

CHAPTER TWO

The Name of America

■ ALEXANDER DEL MAR

Alexander Del Mar is a remarkable writer. There is stuff in him. He is the sort of
man you need in America. He knows what he is about. He is the sort of man to put
things right in your country, or in any country.

—John Stuart Mill, at Avignon; interview published
in *Philadelphia Press*, August 16, 1874

That the American Continent derived its name from the Florentine merchant and geographer, Emerigo Vespucci, and that thereby an injustice was
done to Columbus, is an impression which still retains a firm hold on the
popular mind; yet many proofs have been offered that before Columbus
landed, the name America was found scattered over the Southern Continent from the Caribbean Sea to the Pacific Ocean and from the Maracaibo
Gulf and the Amaracapana coast, near the Orinoco's outlet, to the moun-
tainous regions of Cax-Amaraca around Bogotá and over the heights of the
Andes as far to the south as Peru.

Ex-President Harrison added his influence to the popular impression
with the remark that the continent should have been named for Columbus;

---

* Alexander Del Mar (c. 1837–1920), a multilingual American statesman and scholar born in
Algeria, knew most of the tens of works about the toponymy of the Western hemisphere that
had been published in Central, South, and North America between 1860 and 1910. These
works, written in Portuguese, Spanish, German, Dutch, Arabic, French, English, and at least
two native languages, contest in various ways the much freighted belief that America got its
name from the explorer Amerigo Vespucci. Del Mar too claims that the name came from elsewhere, and modern linguistic and navigational evidence partly supports his conclusions.

Alexander Del Mar's heretofore unpublished work, "The Name of America" (1911),
is here transcribed, unaltered, by Marc Shell from the typescript at the New York Public
Library.

thereby implying that it was in fact named for Vespucci. The only evidence to sustain this assumption is the letter of a Florentine bishop, in which he writes rather boastfully "and well may our new world be named America, since its discovery was due to our eminent countryman, Amerigo Vespucci," etc.

On the other hand the proofs that the country bore a title much nearer to "America" than "Emerigo," may be summarized in the following citations:

Girolemo Benzoni, a Milanese, in his "Historia delle Mondo Nuovo," published at Venice in 1565, says (p. 7 of trans.): "The Governor shortly after left Cumana with all his company, and coasting westward, went to *Amaracapanna;* this was a town of about forty houses, and four hundred Spaniards resided there constantly, who annually elected a captain."

Humboldt, in his "Relations Historiques," a narrative of personal observations, chiefly in South America, from 1799 to 1804, writes, Vol. l, p. 324, that "the first settlement of the Spaniards on the mainland was at Amaracapanna." The coast between the Capes Paria and de la Vela, appears under the names of Amaracapana and Maracapana in Codazzio's map of Venezuela, showing the voyages of Columbus and others.

Hererra, in his *History of the West Indies,* narrates the voyage of Ojeda (1499), whom Amerigo Vespucci accompanied as a merchant, and says: "Finally he arrived at a port, where they saw a village on the shore, called Maracaibo by the natives, which had twenty-six large houses of bell shape, built on pillars or supports, with swinging bridges leading from one to another; and as this looked like Venice in appearance, he gave it that name," which was subsequently adopted by the Republic of Venezuela. This sentence affords a presumption that at the time Vespucci made his first landing in the Western Continent, the port he stopped at was called Amaracai-bo or America-land.

Sir Walter Raleigh reached the same region (1595) and wrote of it as "the Bewtiful valley of Amerioca-pana." Sir Walter also, writing in 1596, describes one of the younger brothers of Atahualpa, the Inca of Peru (whom the Spaniards under Pizarro had slain), as taking thousands of the soldiers and nobles of Peru, and with these "vanquishing all that tract and valley of America situated between the Rivers Orinoco and Amazon."

Besides this, the name given to the whole country between the "Coast of Amaraca," which stretched from the Orinoco River to Maracai-bo bay, and thence to the whole country between Maracai-bo bay and the Pacific, was called Amaraca, while the whole country now known as Bogotá and stretching down to Peru was called Cax-Amaraca. Along the heights of the Andes in this region the name again appears in the Capital City, which was also called Cax-Amaraca, in one of its near-by towns, called Pult-Amaraca, and in the three other local names strewn to the southward along the Andes, of And-Amaraca and Catamaraca. Down near the mouth of the River Cumana was Amaraca-pana, previously mentioned, while out in the Caribbean Sea, off the Coast of Amaraca-pana, was the large island of Tamaraque, a Spanish mode of spelling the same word; it was also a name given to one of the gods, or one of the names given to the Great Spirit of the natives.

To these citations may be added the probability that had there been any intention to name the continent after Vespucci, his surname would have been used, so that the result would have been something like Vespugia, instead of Emeriga. In short there seems to be little room to doubt that the world has been misled through the complimentary notice of the Florentine bishop.

There seems to be a law for the evolution of continental names from names of a divinity or names of small localities, which through use by the persons first coming into contact with a continental area beginning at that point, spreads gradually over the whole. Thus Europa originally designated only a small village in Thessaly, but as it lay to the west of the Bosphorus and the Hellespont, it must have been spoken of by Asiatic neighbors in a manner to facilitate its more extended application. "Asia" indicated originally a very small part of what is now called Asia Minor. Africa meant originally only that small part of the continent around Carthage, that with which the Romans came in contact. It was much less extended than Libya. Egypt was the name by which the Greeks knew a small seaport town near the mouth of the Nile. It bears no resemblance to the name "Black Country," by which the ancient Egyptians designated their own land. The name China spread from a petty mountain region on the borders of India, because it was there that the Europeans first came into any considerable contact with the empire, and it was by Europeans that the name came to be obtruded on an empire which knew itself only as The Middle Kingdom. This shows that it is more commonly from the spread of local names, indigenous to a small region, that large regions are named, than from the given names of individuals. I have much respect for Vespucci, but more for the belief that America is a native name.

Part II

RESISTANCE AND ASSIMILATION

"And in a Christian Language They Sold Me": Messages Concealed in a Slave's Arabic-Language Autobiographical Narrative

▪ ALA ALRYYES

Omar Ibn Said begins his *Life* with a surprising demurral: "I cannot write my life, I have forgotten much of my language as well as the language of the Maghreb."[1] His apology seems to make the usual rhetorical claim that the author is not up to the task, a *de rigueur* flourish that accompanies many a literary preface. His knowledge of Arabic, however, sets Omar apart from other early African American writers of slave narratives, in that he had "the language" — had been literate — *before* being captured, and wrote in a language that most of his enslavers could not read. Unlike Olaudah Equiano, author in 1789 of the first slave narrative by an African, or even Frederick Douglass, it was not in captivity that Omar learned the language in which he wrote his autobiography.

Although other slave writings in Arabic survive, such as letters by Abd al-Rahman Jallo, who, after forty years of slavery, was freed and returned to Africa, Omar's manuscript is of singular importance, for it is the only extant autobiography by a slave in Arabic. The text is in two parts: first, a chapter from the Koran, *Surat al-Mulk,* followed by Omar's narrative proper, which opens with an apology in advance for his performance, addressed to a "Sheikh Hunter" — presumably the man who asked Omar to write the narrative. Omar — rhetorically, it seems, judging from the quality of his text — protests that he has forgotten his language as well as Arabic, though he had been writing in Arabic well before 1831, the date of the autobiography.

The narrative relates Omar's life in Africa, where he was born in the region which lies between the Senegal and Gambia rivers in West Africa: "My name is Omar Ibn Said; my birthplace is *Fut Tur*, between the two rivers." Omar describes his scholarly education, which lasted for twenty-five years under three sheiks, and the grisly circumstances of his capture in 1807: "Then there came to our country a big army. It killed many people. It took me and walked me to the big sea, and sold me into the hands of a Christian man."[2] The text is silent on the horrors of the notorious Middle Passage; the author only mentions that it lasted a month and a half.

Landing in Charleston, Omar is sold to his first American owner. Although he is laconic when he describes the course of his life under slavery, Omar's poignant awareness of his linguistic alienation and subjection marks this stage: "In a Christian language," he writes, "they sold me." The "evil" Johnson, his first owner, puts him to work in the fields even though Omar is a "small man who cannot do hard work."

Omar escapes, hiding for about a month in what he describes as "houses." It is not clear just what he means by "houses." Were they churches or homes of sympathetic Southerners? They may refer to public places; Omar relates that he was turned in by a young man on horseback who came into the "house." Eventually captured by a chase party, Omar is made to walk to Fayetteville, North Carolina, and imprisoned in the Cumberland County jail for "sixteen days and nights." The runaway is eventually sold to Jim Owen, the brother of a former governor of North Carolina, but before that, "a man called Mitchell" tries to buy him and asks him if he wants to "walk to a place called Charleston." The question is outrageous; and Omar's horror, and his enduring memory of his first owner's cruelty, is reflected in his unequivocal refusal: seven "no's."

Omar concludes his *Autobiography* with an encomium to his owner: "I continue in the hands of Jim Owen, who does not beat me, nor calls me bad names . . . During the last twenty years I have not seen any harm at the hands of Jim Owen." From this account, as well as other contemporary reports, it appears that the Owens were kind masters. Yet Omar was never freed; and any statements regarding his masters must remain under this shadow.

Omar Ibn Said's manuscript consists of twenty-three pages of quarto

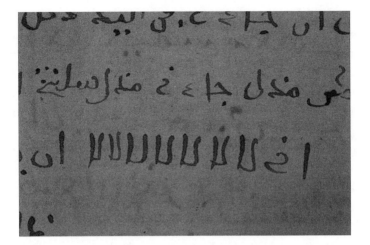

3.1. Manuscript fragment from the "Autobiography of Omar Ibn Said," a slave narrative written in Arabic.

paper, of which pages six to thirteen are blank. It includes a title page, probably a later addition, written in English in a different hand, identifying the author as "Omar ben Saeed, called Morro, a Fullah slave, in Fayetteville, N.C., owned by Governor Owen." The narrative, according to the inscription, was "Written by himself in 1831 & sent to Old Paul, or Lahmen Kebby, in New York, in 1836, Presented to Theodore Dwight by Paul in 1836, Translated by Hon. (Alexander) Cotheal, Esq., 1848." Theodore Dwight (1796–1866), a Free-Soiler who had graduated from Yale in 1814, opposed the spread of slavery, as he argued in his book *The Kansas Wars*, published in 1859. "Dwight," remarked J. Franklin Jameson, who wrote the introduction to the first published translation of Omar's manuscript in 1925, "was deeply interested in West Africa, and made special efforts to obtain information from or respecting Mohammedan slaves in the United States."[3] Jameson noted that the translation he presented had been done by the Rev. Isaac Bird (1793–1835), "who had been for a dozen years (1823–1835) a missionary in Syria," and had been revised "through the kindness of Dr. F. M. Moussa, secretary of the Egyptian Legation in Washington."[4]

Old Paul was the slave name of Lahmen Kebby, or Lamen Kebe, a former slave who was freed in 1835, after forty years of bondage. He was also a Muslim who hailed from Omar's province. He impressed Dwight, a founder of the American Ethnological Society, with his pedagogical experience as a former schoolmaster in Africa. "Paul was a schoolmaster in Footah, after pursuing a long course of preparatory studies," wrote Dwight in 1864. "Schools were generally established through the country, provision being made by law for educating children of all classes, the poor being taught gratuitously."[5]

Because the central text that Paul's culture studied and taught, the Koran, is written in Arabic, not in native languages, the pedagogical system in which Kebe taught was, already in the eighteenth century, remarkably attuned to the subtleties of bilingualism. Dwight observed that "Lamen Kebe [Paul] has a high opinion of a certain process practised in some of the institutions of his native land, which he calls doubling . . . [in which] the meaning of the Arabic word is explained as well as translated. He inquires with some interest, whether the doubling or explaining [bilingual] system is properly cultivated in the United States."[6] Allan Austin, in a detailed though uneven study of the lives of several African Muslims, notes: "[Dwight] also found Kebe to be an exemplary teacher and published some of his advice in the *American Annals of Education and Instruction,* making Kebe the only African quoted at length in a contemporary American professional journal."[7]

Kebe managed to have himself sent back to Africa as an agent of the American Colonization Society. Founded in 1817, the ACS dedicated itself to solving both the slavery problem and the "problem" of the incompatibility of the races by encouraging free blacks to emigrate to, and colonize, what is today Liberia.[8] According to Ralph Gurley, the secretary of the ACS, Kebe corresponded in Arabic with his countryman, Omar. Unfortunately these letters are currently unavailable. However, in addition to this autobiography, a number of his scattered writings in Arabic survive. In a particularly moving two-page fragment intimating his desire to go home, Omar wrote in 1819, "I want to be seen in a place called Africa in a place called Kaba in Bewir."[9]

The journey of Omar Ibn Said's manuscript underscores the point that he was in fact fairly famous. Several evangelists and members of the ACS had met him and wrote about him. Their accounts debated his conversion to Christianity; some outlandishly saw in him an Arabian prince rescued by his kind owner from a fate apparently fit only for blacks. Omar's reference to "Sheikh Hunter," who had presumably asked him to write his story, remains obscure. It seems significant that Omar was asked to pen his narrative in 1831, for this was the year of the fiery rebellion of Nat Turner — in the words of William Styron, "the only effective, sustained revolt in the annals of American Negro slavery" — which shook Virginia and the slave-owning South in general.[10] It was the quiet before the storm that unnerved slave owners: "It will thus appear, that whilst every thing upon the surface of society wore a calm and peaceful aspect; whilst not one note of preparation was heard to warn the devoted inhabitants of woe and death," marveled magistrate T. R. Gray, who recorded Turner's confession, "a gloomy fanatic was revolting in the recesses of his own dark, bewildered and overwrought mind schemes of indiscriminate massacre to the whites."[11]

As terror swept the South, were slave owners looking for a "good" slave narrative to counter the effects of Turner's dangerous example? The results of Turner's rebellion were striking. Scores of blacks were murdered by vengeful vigilantes; official and unofficial steps were taken to "bar black preachers and to forbid public funerals without a white man present to officiate." More telling reactions included "laws against teaching slaves to read and write," as well as increased attention to the religion of slaves and "encouragement of oral instruction of slaves in the Christian faith."[12] It is difficult to believe that, in this charged atmosphere, Sheikh Hunter's request was unrelated to the repercussions of the rebellion. I would like to offer some speculations as to how Omar's narrative may have been related directly to the events of August 1831.

It is possible that Omar's good masters wanted to dissuade some of the more hard-line masters from further acts of cruelty. An autobiography by a "good" slave might prove that not all (literate) slaves were contemplating murder, that Turner's was an isolated example. Another possibility, not unrelated to this one, emphasizes the Kebe connection. Recall that the Arabic manuscript was sent to Kebe a year before he emigrated to Liberia, supported by the African Colonization Society. It is conceivable that the ACS wanted to capitalize on the Turner aftermath to support its policy of encouraging former slaves to emigrate. The ACS received some support in the Upper South; were its members collecting information from plantations with sympathetic owners? As mentioned above, the Rev. Ralph Gurley, a prominent member of the ACS, met and interviewed Omar in 1837, six years after he wrote his narrative. Earlier connections are likely. It is possible that "Sheikh Hunter" was a member of the ACS, who had heard of Omar through Kebe and traveled to North Carolina to meet him. Others spoke of Omar emigrating to Africa much earlier. Omar's two-page manuscript of 1819 mentioned above was sent by a John Louis Taylor to Francis Scott Key, of "Star-Spangled Banner" fame, accompanied by a letter in which Taylor informed Key that Omar might not mind being sent back to Africa.[13]

Only on the surface, however, does Omar's autobiography appear to be a "safe" pro-slavery story, praising his owner for his good life in America. I will argue, to the contrary, that the *Life* is replete with concealed utterances that not only hide his views from potentially dangerous readers, but also test the readers, sifting them into those who can interpret the utterances and are therefore within Omar's closed circle — his community — and those who cannot decipher them, and are outside it.

Before beginning his own narrative, Omar interpolates a chapter from the Koran, choosing *Surat al-Mulk* as a kind of prologue. This choice seems deliberate and highly significant in the context of a slave narrative. The first two *ayas,* or verses, in the *Sura* read: "Blessed be He in whose hand is the *mulk* and who has power over all things. He created death and life that He might put you to the proof and find out which of you had the best work; He is the most Mighty, the Forgiving One." The noun *al-mulk* comes from the tripartite Arabic root *malaka,* meaning both "to own" and "to have dominion."[14] The title of the *Sura* is, therefore, the perfect allusion to slavery: absolute power through ownership. The verb and the noun conflate persons and things. The *Sura* contends that it is God who is the owner of all and everything; through his choice of this Koranic chapter, Omar seems to refute the right of his owners over him, since only God has the *mulk,* the power and the ownership.

There is a striking similarity between Omar's counter-argument from divine possession and the language employed in David Walker's well-known *Appeal in Four Articles; Together with a Preamble, to the Coloured Citizens of the World*. Walker, suggestively modeling his appeal on the American Constitution, analyzes slavery and concludes that modern American and European bondage is far crueler than that of the Greeks and the Romans. Jeremiah-like, he asks for divine punishment "in behalf of the oppressed." Walker, in his preamble, refutes the right to hold slaves because "All persons who are acquainted with history, and particularly the Bible . . . who are willing to admit that God made man to serve Him *alone,* and that man should have no other Lord or Lords but Himself — that God Almighty is the *sole proprietor* or *master* of the WHOLE human family. . . ."[15] This argument against slavery is essentially the same as the one presented by Omar — though esoterically — by citing the aforementioned *Sura.*

Walker published his *Appeal* in 1829; its power and popularity made him a hated man in the South. When a number of people in Virginia sought to bar black ministers from preaching to their own people, it was partly because, as slaveholders feared, some would use the *Appeal* as their text. Clearly, the work was very popular; and although one visitor criticized Omar's "broken English," it is likely that Omar would have been familiar with parts of Walker's text. Indeed, as Omar's *Life* dates from 1831, he may have been a recipient and, possibly, an imitator of Walker's argument. The reverse interpretation is equally possible. For what if a particularly Muslim argument against slavery, which finds its expression in *Surat al-Mulk,* had spread orally and was incorporated by Walker in his *Appeal?* It is noteworthy that Walker interpolates several verses from the Bible into his tract and draws the reader's attention to the appropriate chapter and verse. However, when he mentions that "God Almighty is the *sole proprietor,*" Walker does not refer to the Bible. Was this, then, an argument which Walker had coined on his own, or a borrowing from *Surat al-Mulk?* In either case, Walker would probably have approved of Nat Turner's rebellion, but he did not live to see it. He died suddenly in June 1830, possibly poisoned by his southern enemies.

In the penultimate page of his *Life,* Omar explicitly condemns the injury done to him: "I reside in our country here because of the great harm," he writes. Throughout the autobiography, however, Omar's views are most often expressed esoterically, that is, they are intended for a group of readers "within a circle."[16] In introducing the 1925 translation, Jameson writes, "The earlier pages of the manuscript are occupied with quotations from the Koran which Omar remembered, and these might be omitted as not auto-biographical . . . but it has been thought best to print the whole."[17] I disagree. In my view, the *Sura* was placed there for a concealed purpose, and bears a possible connection to Walker's anti-slavery argument. Jameson's view is predicated on the assumption that the writer is free to deliver his message directly. Such freedom is denied the slave, for revolt, even in the eyes of the most benign of masters, is an unpardonable offense.

How does Omar openly address his enslavers? There are in his narrative two moments of his encounter with "the other's" language which seem to me to function as polar opposites. The first occurs when he describes the earliest moments of his capture. "In a Christian language," he writes, "they sold me." At that moment perhaps the entire crime is encapsulated in the foreignness of that incomprehensible language that turns a man into chattel in America. Later, however, Omar addresses his audience: not only the Sheikh Hunter who asked him to compose the narrative, but indeed the "people of America, all of you." This is a moment of reaching out. Between these two instances, however, Omar's language is rich in hidden meanings, with nuances that seem to separate him from the white community of his owners, to guard his identity even as a slave.

In the *Odyssey*, Homer deploys what the text itself refers to as *ainoi* (plural of *ainos*, which translates as "riddling utterance"), and *semata* (plural of *sêma*, one of whose meanings is "sign," related to our word "semiotics" for example). Each of these utterances constitutes a narrative code, whose true message requires an act of interpretation which, in turn, as Gregory Nagy argues, requires the decoder to possess certain moral, intellectual, and emotional ties to the utterer or encoder of the message.[18] The Homeric narrative sifts the characters within Odysseus's household (Telemachus, Penelope, her suitors, as well as the maids and servants) into two groups: those who can read Odysseus's "language" — his *ainoi* and *semata* — and therefore may join the new community he will establish, and those who cannot, and are excluded.[19]

Omar's concealed utterances, like Odysseus's riddles, not only allow him to let out steam, as it were, but they also enable him to be the master of language, to establish a home in that language that his enslavers cannot enter. In Nagy's terms, therefore, Omar seems to be setting himself apart from those not bound to him by moral, intellectual, or emotional ties. These double utterances — like his use of *Surat al-Mulk* — more than enable Omar to conceal his deeper message; they permit him to reconstruct a community that is not circumscribed by slavery. Similarly, other forms of slaves' literary production, for example, Negro spirituals, "became an almost secretive code for the slave's critique of the plantation system, and his search for freedom in this world."[20]

Omar uses *Surat al-Mulk* not only to argue against slavery, but also to cast a symbolic role for himself in that resistance. Prominent in the *Sura* is a verse that describes the suffering and torture in hell (in Arabic, *juhanam*) of those who did not accept the message of the prophet Muhammad:

> When they are flung into its flames, they shall hear it roaring and seething, as though bursting with rage. And every time a multitude is thrown therein, its keepers will say to them: "Did no one come to warn you?" "Yes," they will reply, "he did come, but we rejected him (as a liar) and said: 'God has revealed nothing: you are in grave error.'" And they will say: "If only we had listened and understood, we should not now be among the heirs of the Fire."

Who is the "one come to warn you" — in the original Arabic the word is *natheer*, "he who warns"? On the surface, it is Muhammad, bringing the message of Islam to the *kuffar*, the infidels who denied him. Islam, however, like Christianity, is a proselytizing religion. It is the duty of Muslims to call others to Islam, to warn them of the consequences of not believing. Hence, in the hidden meaning, Omar Ibn Said was the messenger in his time, suffered for the message, and was denied. And those who should confess their errors and be judged are not only the unbelievers among Muhammad's tribe of *Quraish* in Mecca — for whom the original *Sura* is intended — but also Omar's unbelieving owners.

That Omar did not choose this particular *Sura* at random, but, as I have argued, to fit the context of his life, is supported by evidence from his other writings. Although Omar used *Surat al-Mulk* more than once — for example, earlier in the 1819 letter sent to Francis Scott Key — he wrote other Koranic *Suras*. Remarkably, his last known writing, in 1857, is *Surat al-Nasr*, the Victory: "When God's help and Victory come, and you see people embrace God's faith in multitudes, give glory to your Lord and seek His pardon. He is ever disposed to mercy."[21] This *Sura* can be interpreted as an invocation to God: a wish for victory, for liberation from slavery, which calls into question Omar's supposed contentment in the hands of the Owens.

It is telling that this *Sura* was given to Muhammad on the occasion of the prophet's victory over his own tribe and his triumphant, and merciful, entry into Mecca in 630 AD. Muhammad's victory and return to Mecca, his native city, from which he had escaped eight years earlier under cover of night to flee death, was vital to the survival and spread of Islam. Again, Omar analogically links himself with Muhammad, setting his own hoped-for vindication in parallel with Muhammad's actual victory.

Omar's education in an Islamic *madrasa*, or religious school, would have comprised not only Koranic exegesis, but also the memorization of large tracts of the Koran, if not the whole text. Omar says that he "sought knowledge" under the direction of various Sheiks for twenty-five years. Therefore, it is not unlikely, even after twenty-four years in America, for him to remember much of the Koran in the original words, which he had undoubtedly recited many times. Most of *Surat al-Mulk*, which Omar interpolates in his *Life*, is perfect in its reproduction of the Arabic Koranic text. I have relied on it as a sort of Rosetta stone to resolve certain problems inherent in reading Omar's idiosyncratic orthography. Yet, as I remark in my translation of Omar's *Life*, there are some errors in Omar's *Sura*. This is proof, I think, that Omar was writing from memory and not copying. Such a view is supported by contemporary witnesses' observation that Omar owned a copy of an English Koran, not an Arabic one.[22]

To sum up, Omar's deliberate choice of the two *Suras* above — *al-Mulk* and *al-Nasr* — and the fact that he remembered them, can best be understood as occasional: Omar cites from memory the *Suras* that fit the context of the story of his own life. To my mind, the Koranic fragments that Omar often inscribed into his writings have the same double significance. Just as he analogically figures his experiences to stand for Muhammad's suffering or victory, Omar reenacts the occasionality of the delivery of the Koran itself to Muhammad. For, as Muslims believe, the Koran was not delivered to the prophet in one installment. Nor was it, like the New Testament, a compilation of various accounts of Muhammad's life and words. Instead, as the example of *Surat al-Nasr* demonstrates, the *Suras* that Muhammad received from God addressed the specific contexts and occasions of their delivery.

Resistance to slavery did not, of course, always mean rejection of the master's religion. It could also frequently mean, as is vividly manifested in the case of Nat Turner, interpreting the master's religion in a way he did not like. Omar's use of the Koranic *Sura* in an occasional context raises fundamental issues regarding his resistance to slavery, and changes the terms in which the matter of his conversion should be cast. Did Omar, as some of his contemporaries claimed, convert to Christianity, or did he, as others suspected, remain a Muslim? In addition to *Surat al-Mulk* in his *Life* and *Surat al-Nasr* later, other evidence supports the belief that Omar did not abandon the "bloodstained Koran" to worship "at the feet of the Prince of Peace."[23]

Omar's persistence in his Islamic beliefs is revealed in a subtle phrasing. After he has praised his masters because "They are good men for whatever they eat, I eat; and whatever they wear they give me to wear," he continues:

> Before I came to the Christian country, my religion *was* [emphasis added] the religion of Muhammad, the prophet of Allah, may Allah bless him and grant him peace. I used to walk to the mosque [*masjid*] before dawn, and to wash my face, head, hands, feet. I used to hold the noon prayers, the afternoon prayers, the sunset prayers, the night prayers. I used to give alms [*zakat*] every year in gold, silver, harvest, cattle, sheep, goats, rice, wheat and barley — all I used to give in alms. I used to join the *Jihad* every year against the infidels [*Kuffar*]. I used to walk to Mecca and Medinah as did those who were able.

The message of the passage is ambiguous, in that Omar does not use the Arabic past construction (*kana*) to render the past state of his religion, (the underscored "was"), matching the time of the adverb "before." The literal translation into English would thus read: "Before . . . my religion is the religion of Muhammad." So either this is a grammatical error, or an indication that indeed his religion was, and is, that of Muhammad.

Furthermore, it may seem on the surface that Omar is merely relating what he used to practice back in Africa, before converting to Christianity. It is more probable, however, that he is enumerating some of the tenets and duties, or *arkan* and *furod*, respectively, by way of instruction in Islam, rather than describing what he had done. It is unlikely that he "used to walk to Mecca and Medinah," or that he gave alms in all of nine different products, some of which, like rice and wheat, were not available in West Africa. Maybe he performed the pilgrimage once; he probably gave alms of money and livestock. However, the language he uses echoes that of an instructional book. I think Omar is mixing a description of his particular deeds, such as praying five times a day, with catechizing, such as "one should go to Mecca and Medinah if able." It is courageous for a slave to catechize his native religion when he is supposed to be extolling his conversion.

Omar did not convert in the sense that Gurley (and probably the Owens) believed. He retained the faith that he brought with him from Africa. Yet, as Genovese acutely observes: "From the moment the Africans lost the social basis of their religious community life, their religion itself had to disintegrate as a coherent system of belief. From the moment they arrived in America and began to toil as slaves, they could not help absorbing the religion of the master class."[24] Omar may, I believe, have escaped losing his religion because his faith in Islam allowed him some leeway in dealing with Christian efforts to convert him. A Muslim believes that Christians and Jews are people of the book, that Moses and Jesus were precursors of Muhammad. Omar, in fact, copied out various Christian pieces, such as the Lord's Prayer — which he includes in his *Life* and interjects on other occasions — and the 23rd Psalm, "The Lord is my Shepherd." Neither of these pieces, however, contradicts Islamic beliefs. Omar never, for example, alludes to the godhead of Jesus or to his crucifixion, which Islam rejects.

Abducted in the waning days of the Atlantic slave trade, Omar — whose English remained elementary — may have held aloof from "homegrown" African American slaves, or he may have been snubbed by a Creole black population now thoroughly in control of the New World's language and customs. In reading his Arabic Bible and going to church, Omar may have sought out spiritual Christians to make up for a slave's inevitable loss of community, as Genovese asserts. Yet it is also likely that his religion did not disintegrate because he used it as a means of resistance. That Omar narrates his tale of slavery gives the reader a rare glimpse of a slave's agency, an account largely missing from the historical record. That Omar wrote in Arabic complicates the view that all literate slaves in the United States owed their literacy to their masters. It also inserts Arabic into the linguistic map of America, making it an "American" language. Ironically, Arabic comes to join the European languages in the United States precisely from the area where it had, more than eleven centuries earlier, entered Western Europe: Africa.[25] That the last Arabic-speaking Muslim enclave in Europe, Granada in Spain, fell in 1492 — to the same Ferdinand and Isabella who sponsored Columbus — further reminds us that Arabic has always been connected to America.

Notes

1. All translations are from *"O, People of America": Autobiography of Omar Ibn Said, an Arabic-Speaking Slave,* trans. and ed. Ala A. Alryyes (forthcoming from Johns Hopkins University Press).

2. Omar dated the narrative in 1831, and wrote that he had "been residing in the Christian country for twenty-four years."

3. J. Franklin Jameson, ed., "Autobiography of Omar ibn Said, Slave in North Carolina, 1831," *American Historical Review* 30-4 (July 1925):788.

4. Ibid., p. 789.

5. Ibid., p. 788.

6. Theodore Dwight, "Remarks on the Sareeulehs, an African Nation, Accompanied by a Vocabulary of Their Language," *American Annals of Education and Instruction* 5 (1835):451–56.

7. Allan D. Austin, *African Muslims in Antebellum America: Transatlantic Stories and Spiritual Struggles* (New York: Routledge, 1997), p. 116.

8. In 1822 the ACS established Monrovia (later Liberia, with Monrovia as its capital) on the west coast of Africa. Over the next forty years the Society set-

tled some 12,000 African Americans in that country. Although the Society existed until 1912, after 1860 it functioned primarily as the "caretaker" of the settlement in Liberia.

9. Quoted in Austin, *African Muslims*, p. 137.

10. Denmark Vesey's abortive revolt in 1822 was better organized, but it was betrayed, and he and his recruits were captured before they had even started.

11. T. R. Gray, "The Confessions of Nat Turner" (Richmond, 1832).

12. Eugene D. Genovese, *Roll, Jordan, Roll: The World the Slaves Made* (New York: Vintage, 1972), pp. 186–94.

13. Austin, *African Muslims*, p. 131.

14. All Arabic words derive from a tripartite root, usually the third-person singular past tense of the related verb.

15. David Walker, *Appeal in Four Articles; Together with a Preamble, to the Coloured Citizens of the World*, in *The Norton Anthology of African American Literature*, ed. Henry Louis Gates, Jr. and Nellie Y. McKay (New York: Norton, 1997), p. 181.

16. It is possible that, since the "great harm" had taken place 24 years earlier, Omar may have felt safe to condemn it explicitly.

17. Jameson, "Autobiography of Omar," p. 791.

18. Gregory Nagy, *Pindar's Homer: The Lyric Possession of an Epic Past* (Baltimore: Johns Hopkins University Press, 1990), p. 148.

19. Consider what Charles Taylor calls "language in a broad sense, covering not only the words we speak, but also other modes of expression whereby we define ourselves," in *Multiculturalism: Examining the Politics of Recognition* (Princeton: Princeton University Press, 1994), p. 32.

20. Melvin Dixon, "Singing Swords: The Literary Legacy of Slavery," in *The Slave's Narrative*, ed. Charles Davis and Henry Louis Gates (Oxford: Oxford University Press, 1985), p. 298.

21. Omar's last writing, in 1857, is preserved at the University of North Carolina at Chapel Hill.

22. It is worth noting that Omar's version of *Surat al-Nasr* (not the translation I have provided) intercalates an extraneous addition, a verse promising victory to Muslims. That it is the *Sura* is beyond doubt, however.

23. For example, Ralph Gurley declared that Omar "had completely converted to Christianity," whereas the Rev. Mathew B. Grier, "the minister of the church Omar last attended . . . expressed some doubt about the absoluteness of his conversion to Christianity." See Austin, *African Muslims*, pp. 131–32.

24. Genovese, *Roll, Jordan, Roll*, p. 184.

25. 711 A.D. is the date of the beginning of the Muslim conquest of Andalusia.

CHAPTER FOUR

Unfaithful Translation: Bilingual Versions as Greek-American Strategies of Concealment

■ YOTA BATSAKI

The first decades of the twentieth century were a particularly turbulent period in modern Greek history, marked by a succession of wars culminating in the migration of ethnic Greeks from Asia Minor "back" to mainland Greece. This period also roughly coincides with the beginning and consolidation of Greek immigration to America, which began comparatively late, in the 1890s, and reached its peak in the early 1920s. Greek immigration, which formed part of the new wave of immigration characterized by a high proportion of emigrants from southern and eastern Europe, displays some striking characteristics. In the first two decades of the century, over 90 percent of the emigrants were men between the ages of fourteen and forty-four. Their motives were predominantly economic, and initially they envisaged only a temporary stay. The absence of Greek women and relatively low rates of intermarriage meant that many of these men often lived in groups in bachelor establishments, working in the railways, factories, or steel mills.[1] The proportion of their earnings that they sent back to the home country was one of the highest among ethnic groups in the United States. In short, the goals of Greek immigration at the beginning of the twentieth century were temporary and old-country oriented.

Two forms of publication in the Greek language proliferated at that time. Newspapers appeared in New York and Chicago, where the Greeks tended to settle. Ἀτλαντίς [*Atlantis*], one of the oldest and most influential, began publication as a four-page weekly in 1894 and became a daily in 1905. It remained the major Greek paper until the advent of Ἐθνικός Κήρυκας [*The National Herald*], in 1915.[2] These early New York newspapers were followed by a number of publications that catered to the interests of the early immigrants by privileging news from the old country over American issues.[3] Theodore Saloutos, in his seminal study of the Greeks in the United States, sums up the relationship between the early press and its readership: "The absorption of the overwhelming majority of Greek Americans with the politics of the old country, their comparative short residence in the country, and the failure of most of them to become citizens meant that American problems had less appeal than Greek problems. Consequently, the Greek language press sought to capitalize on the partisan Old World preferences of its readers."[4]

Literary production in the form of poems and short stories was first published in the newspapers. These, along with fantastic stories of thieves and lovelorn maidens, oriental tales, fictional accounts of Byzantium and anecdotes from the Greek War of Independence, seem to make up the main reading material of the Greek newcomers in the United States.[5] This, at least, is the complaint of Serapheim Canoutas, who, in a book published in 1919, admonishes the immigrant to turn to the study of profitable books, whether in Greek or English: «ὄχι ἀνάγνωση Μπερτόλδου, Χαλιμάς, Παπουτσωμένου Γάτου, Ἱστορίας τῶν Ληστῶν καί τόσων ἄλλων χυδαίων ἀναγνωσμάτων, τά ὁποῖα εὑρίσκει τις ἔν ἀφθονία εἴς τά δωμάτια τῶν Ἑλλήνων μεταναστῶν» ["No more reading of Bertold, the Arabian Nights, Puss in Boots, Tales of the Brigands and so many other vulgar readings one finds strewn all over the rooms of the Greek immigrants"].[6]

Canoutas proceeds to improve both the rooms and the readings through his involvement in the second genre flourishing in the period, that of immigrant guidebooks or manuals. These can be found in a variety of forms, as didactic tales in verse, autobiographical accounts interspersed with general advice, legal guides also offering tips on hygiene, economy, and learning English, even pseudo-historical accounts of the Greeks in the United States going back all the way to Columbus as a Greek nobleman.[7] In fact, my reference to these varied works as belonging to a single genre is largely based on their common and often self-proclaimed instructive purpose, rather than on any stylistic resemblance.[8] This didactic impulse links such manuals to the early newspapers: common guidebook headings include "Business Counsel, Rules of Conduct, Naturalization Laws," while the papers often provide articles on hygiene, business, and the advantages of American citizenship. Λοξίας [*Loxias*],[9] for example, a newspaper published in Chicago from 1908, features on its front page a column entitled "Good Advise" (sic), while Θεσσαλονίκη [Saloniki], also from Chicago, has a section on "Character" offering advice on education and social behavior. Moreover, like the newspapers, these guides sometimes appear in bilingual format.

This emphasis on instruction and self-representation should be regarded as both a contribution and a response to the contemporary debate over "the immigrant problem" and the issue of Americanization. This debate focused mainly on the phenomenon of the "new wave," and was generally framed as a concern over the "quality" of the new immigration. A number of contemporary sociological and ethnographic accounts employ a discourse of race to discuss assimilation as the process of creation of the composite "American type," to which the various incoming races would inevitably contribute. The respective desirability of these races is then assessed by means of statistic tables comparing crime and mendicancy rates, attitudes to intermarriage, literacy levels, and linguistic competence (in English), among other categories.[10]

The photograph below, captioned "A Future American," appears on the frontispiece to Henry Pratt Fairchild's *Greek Immigration to the United States.*[11] The book is an accompaniment to Fairchild's more general works on immigration, such as his 1913 *Immigration: A World Movement and Its American Significance,* and approaches the Greek movement as a particular case study. The author, as both sociologist and anthropologist, undertakes fieldwork back in the old country in order to observe and assess the qualities and drawbacks of its emigrants and "future Americans."

Fairchild's project can be considered in the context of nineteenth-century travels to Greece and the Orient. Like the Romantic travelers to Greece, and despite the scientific claims of his observation, Fairchild cannot help constantly comparing the modern Greeks (and their language) to the ancients. And, like the Romantics' judgment of modern Greeks, his too is ambivalent; on the one hand he finds that they fall short of their illustrious "ancestors," while on the other hand he appears to detect in them mythic attributes surviving through the centuries, notably Odyssean cun-

4.1. "A Future American," photo used as frontispiece to Henry Pratt Fairchild, *Greek Immigration to the United States* (1911).

ning, an aptitude for commerce, and an impulse towards travel.[12] He is, however, suspicious of the Greek immigrants' avowedly mercenary motives for expatriation.

> It is almost impossible to get even an intelligent Greek to comprehend your meaning if you ask him what was the immediate cause of the new emigration. These people are not fitted by mental equipment or training for analytical reasoning; they habitually look only at the surface of things. About all the answer you can hope to get is something as follows: "Why, our country is poor and America is rich. They go there because they can get more money." (p. 74)

The Greeks' self-seeking motives for immigration to the United States were worrying, insofar as they might constitute a separate interest group, always contemplating nostalgically a return to the home country, and undermining the project of a common American citizenship. The Greeks' resistance to the lofty project of Americanization could be detected in their insistent desire for repatriation and in their impressive dedication to sending money back home. Concomitantly, the most frequent charges leveled against the Greeks, as obstacles to their proper Americanization, were their unwillingness to learn the American language (insisting, for example, that their wives and children speak Greek) and their neglect of naturalization and the vote. This attitude could be interpreted as reluctance to participate in the two most important American institutions.

The link between the American idiom and the American republic, as products of a new environment that can provide a basis for the establishment of a national identity, is emphatically drawn in Mencken's well-known essay on the American language.[13] The project of constructing a "national character" is envisaged as an evolutionary linguistic process unfolding in anthropomorphic terms. Narrow-minded conservatism is personified in the figure of the schoolma'am, rendered ludicrous in her attempt to impose a normative spelling and pronunciation:

> New words and idioms swarm around her in such numbers that she is overwhelmed, and her function as an arbiter of speech withers away. In this great free Republic the verdict of life and death upon a neologism is

not brought in by schoolma'ams . . . but by a jury resembling a *posse comitatus*, on which even schoolboys sit. In brief, the American language is molded by a purely democratic process, and, as on the political level, this process is grounded upon the doctrine that any American is as good as any other.[14]

As good as any other, in other words, so long as he contributes to the democratic process of fashioning the national character through, among other things, the national (if not official) language.[15] The gendered polarity on which Mencken's scheme hinges is striking. The schoolma'am is contrasted to the schoolboy, the citizen is envisaged in terms of Tacitus's belligerent yet tight-knit *posse comitatus*, while at the very end of the essay the General American idiom is contrasted to effeminate Oxford English and described in terms of the stereotype of the American: practical, efficient, vigorous:

> "General American is much clearer and more logical than any of the other dialects, either English or American. It shows a clear if somewhat metallic pronunciation, gives all necessary consonants their true values, keeps to simple and narrow speech tunes, and is vigorous and masculine."[16]

The Greek newspapers and manuals engaged in this general debate about the relationship of language and citizenship in two crucial ways, which reflected both their commitment to the process of successful adaptation and their concern about the pressure on incoming groups to define themselves and to function along ethnic lines. The newspapers and manuals operated didactically on the level of the individual reader, whom they were directly addressing, but also with self-representation and self-justification in mind with regard to the wider American audience. The editor of *Saloniki*, for example, justified the newspaper's choice of the purist (*kathareuousa*) over the popular (demotic) linguistic register as a concern with ethnic definition in the eyes of outside observers.[17] He argued that

> Many professors and American students of the Greek language read Greek newspapers in order to retain or achieve familiarity with the language. If they discover Greek newspapers written in this dialect, which is not only coarse, but is also full of Slavic words, they will be sure to

think that the Greeks are a spurious race, as some people have dared to contend.[18]

The possibility of wooing a wider American audience (those students of the classics who wished to improve their ancient Greek by reading modern Greek publications), necessitated the careful concealment of a skeleton in the closet; the coarse modern "dialect" which undermined the linguistic continuity of the Greek language (and race) from antiquity to the present.

During the war period strategies of self-representation took on increasing importance. For the editor of *Saloniki*, the implicit strategy for recognition of the Greek and of Greekness by an American audience consisted in addressing that audience in a shared language that it could understand. The guidebook suggests a different approach; one important achievement of C. S. Calodikes's bilingual Ἡ Χρυσή Βίβλος/ *The Golden Book* is its recasting of the problem of translation as successful movement *between* Greek and American.

First published in 1917, the book is a compilation in bilingual form, with the American text on the left-hand side and the Greek on the right-hand side. Far from being a one-way manual of instruction of the Greek, in Greek, this work aspires to a bipolar translation for both groups, Greeks and Americans. From the very beginning, however, the bilingual pledge is compromised. The book's somewhat blasphemous title, Χρυσή Βίβλος, is rendered into English as the more acceptable "The Golden Book."[19] Moreover, the book's programmatic statement of translation appears solely in Greek, and this places the whole enterprise under a different light — a point to which we will return. I quote the entire prologue, followed by my own translation from the Greek:

Πρόλογος

Σκοπός τῆς παρούσης ἐκδόσεώς μας εἶναι ἡ ἀποκρυστάλλωσις ἑνός πόθου, τόν ὁποῖον πρό πολλοῦ ἐτρέφομεν εἰς τά στήθη μας. Ἡ δημοσίευσις τουτέστιν παντός ἐκλεκτοῦ ὕμνου, ὅστις ἐγράφη διά τήν Ἑλλάδα μας ὑπό τῶν μεγαλητέρων σοφῶν καί ποιητῶν τοῦ κόσμου διά μέσου τῶν αἰώνων. Οὕτως ὥστε τόσον ἡμεῖς, ὅσον καί οἱ Ἀμερικανοί, νά ἴδωμεν ὡς ἐν κατόπτρω τό μεγαλεῖον τῆς φυλῆς μας.[20]

Πάντα τά ἀναγνώσματα φιλολογικά, ἱστορικά, ποιητικά, πολιτικά,

πατριωτικά εἶναι ἐκ παραλλήλου γεγραμμένα Ἀγγλιστί καί
Ἑλληνιστί, μετά πιστοτάτης μεταφράσεως, οὕτως ὥστε ἐάν τις ἤθελεν
ἀναγνώσει αὐτά εἰς τήν Ἑλληνικήν θά ὠφελεῖτο εἰς τήν γλῶσσαν του,
ἐάν δέ ἤθελε παραβάλη αὐτά πρός τό ἀντίστοιχον ἀγγλικόν κείμενον θά
ὠφελεῖτο καί εἰς τήν Ἀγγλικήν. Τελείαν δέ καί συντομωτάτην ἐπίλυσιν
τῆς προφορᾶς τῆς Ἀγγλικῆς θέλει εὕρη ὁ ἀναγνώστης εἰς τό τέλος τοῦ
βιβλίου.

Οὐδέποτε μέχρι σήμερον ἐξεδόθη βιβλίον μέ τόσον ὑψηλόν σκοπόν
καί μέ τόσην χρησιμότητα.

Διά τοῦτο οὐδείς Ἕλλην φιλοπρόοδος καί θέλων νά αἰσθανθῆ
ὑπερηφάνειαν ἀναγιγνώσκων τό μεγαλεῖον τῆς πατρίδος του, οὐδεμία
Ἑλληνική οἰκογένεια χάριν τῆς ἀναπτύξεως καί ἐξοικειώσεως τῶν
τέκνων τῆς πρός τό ἐθνικόν μεγαλεῖον δέν πρέπει νά μείνη χωρίς νά
ἀποκτήση τήν ὄνομα καί πρᾶγμα Χρυσήν Βίβλον, ἥτις θέλει χρησι-
μεύση ὡς μοναδικόν ἐγκόλπιον διά πάντα Ἕλληνα τῆς Ἀμερικῆς,
θέλοντα νά ἐμπερικλείση ἐν ἑαυτῶ τό Ἑλληνικό πνεῦμα μετά τοῦ Ἀμερι-
κανικοῦ.

[Prologue

The aim of our current publication is the fulfillment of a long-
harbored wish. Namely, the compilation of every choice hymn written
about our Greece by the greatest sages and poets of the world throughout the centuries, in order that both we and the Americans may behold,
as in a mirror, the greatness of our race.

All the excerpts, philological, historical, poetic, political, patriotic are
presented in parallel both in English and in Greek, in most faithful translation, so that were someone to read them in Greek, he would reap the
benefits in his own language, and were he to compare them to the relevant English text, he would benefit in English too.[21] The reader will also
find a full and most concise key to English pronunciation at the end of
the book.

Never until now has a book of such high aspiration and usefulness
been published.

Therefore, no Greek who is a lover of progress and wishes to feel
proud reading about the glory of his motherland, no Greek family, for

the sake of the introduction of its offspring to the glory of their nation, should remain without this literally Golden Bible, which aims to serve as a unique guide to every Greek in America, wishing to encompass within him the Greek spirit as well as the American.]

The reader is confronted with a medley of texts that address issues of both Greek and American nationality and citizenship. In a reference to its wartime context, the book begins with President Woodrow Wilson's address to Congress on the occasion of America's entering the war, and also features Theodore Roosevelt's speech on "True Americanism." Next to the Greek and American national anthems are two poems by Byron, the Romantic poet whose works fueled the early nineteenth-century philhellenic movement in Europe: "The Isles of Greece" and "Maid of Athens."[22] There are other philhellenic extracts, "Greece, the Mother of Europe" and "The Hellenic Ideals," as well as some practical pieces of advice on how to succeed in business by Carnegie and Rothschild. There is an excerpt on how the Greeks won the Trojan War by means of the ruse of the Wooden Horse. The book concludes with a translation of Shelley's drama *The Cyclops* and a short, untranslated guide to English pronunciation. As the final expression of the book's ideological stance, this guide-within-the-guide highlights the work's implicit faith in the possibility of bilingualism; learning English is easier than you think, provided you are equipped with a well-thought-out strategy.

How does this bilingual project comment on issues of translation? The choice of bilingual versions facing each other seems to subordinate the relationship between originality and faithful reproduction (the thorniest of issues in theories of translation) to a scheme of equivalence. The arrangement on the page does not depend on the language of the original, but on the arbitrary decision of juxtaposition, which consistently places the English text on the left and the Greek on the right. The theoretical question of the possibility of linguistic approximation or correspondence between languages is accorded pragmatic treatment, since Calodikes usually translates — not unsuccessfully — almost word for word.

Bearing in mind the date of the first edition, one can also interpret this voluntary, two-way translation, along with its pledge to accuracy, as a gesture of good will. By flaunting a linguistic transparency that defuses the threat of a separate ethnic interest in the midst of the nation, wartime translation serves as proof of good citizenship. The press equivalent would be the statement attached to front-page editorials in the paper *Loxias:* "True translation filed with the Postmaster at Chicago, Ill. [. . .] as required by the Act of Oct. 6th 1917." This notice was included on the front pages of foreign-language newspapers in compliance with Section 19 of the Act, which specified that:

> until the end of the war it shall be unlawful for any person, firm, corporation, or association, to print, publish, or circulate [. . .] in any foreign language, any news item, editorial or other printed matter, respecting the Government of the United States, or of any nation engaged in the present war, its policies, international relations, the state or conduct of the war, or any matter relating thereto: *Provided,* That this section shall not apply to any print, newspaper or publication where the publisher or distributor thereof, on or before offering the same for mailing, or in any manner distributing it to the public, has filed with the postmaster at the place of publication, in the form of an affidavit, a true and complete translation of the entire article [. . .] and has caused to be printed, in plain type in the English language, at the head of each such item [. . .] the words "True translation filed with the postmaster . . ." (Sixty-fifth Congress, Sess. I, Chs. 106–107).

To translate from the ethnic to the national group is to show that you have nothing to hide. Yet.

I have referred to equivalence as the fundamental assumption behind Calodikes's bilingual project of translation. The strategy followed to achieve this on the discursive level, as opposed to the visual, is at least twofold. First, the problematic issue of continuity from ancient to modern Greek is dexterously ignored, through a straightforward and unproblematic translation of references to both modern and ancient Greece as just "Hellas." In this way, the book can appropriate praise of ancient Greece into the general and vague category of the Hellenic. Difference is translated into linguistic identity.

The second strategy hinges on a comparison that seeks to remind Americans, proud of their republican principles, of the roots of democracy that make the Greek an integral part of the American. The first volume is dedicated

> To President Wilson
> The New Pericles
> of the United States.

The dedication establishes a relation of metaphoric reincarnation and repetition. (This discursive strategy had already been used to advantage by the Greeks and their European supporters during the nineteenth-century Greek War of Independence).[23] Similarly, Polenis's Ἐγκόλπιον Μεταναστου [Immigrant's Manual] features a photograph of President Roosevelt with the caption: Ο ΜΕΓΑΣ ΠΡΟΕΔΡΟΣ ΤΩΝ ΗΠΑ, ΑΥΤΟΣ Ο ΝΕΩΤΕΡΟΣ ΠΕΡΙΚΛΗΣ [The Great President of the United States, that Modern Pericles]. According to the metaphorical scheme, the splendor of ancient Greek democracy (embodied in historical figures such as Pericles) lives again in its modern progeny (the American presidents and the American republic). Wilson or Roosevelt stand to the United States as Pericles does to ancient Athens. The American republic is equated with ancient Greek democracy and, combined with the first strategic equation, both are equivalent to modern Greece.

This scheme is by no means potentially beneficial only to the Greek side; equivalence can also be construed as a relationship of mutual debt and obligation, as in the "Address by Prof. Solomon H. Clark of the University of Chicago, Before the Greek Liberal League, on Sunday, Oct. 21, 1917," featured on the front page of *Loxias* of Oct. 25, 1917. In this speech, printed in English (in which it was delivered), "the first gift of the Greek race to humanity: [t]he love of liberty!" is pompously celebrated in order to convince the "Greeks, who have for centuries been shedding their life blood for democracy and liberty" to "stand behind Uncle Sam" by investing in Liberty Loans. The same paper informs its audience in capital letters that the "Greek Government Issued a Proclamation, Authorizing Greek Subjects, Residing in the U.S., to Enlist at Once in the American Army" (*Loxias*, Jan. 31, 1918). The newspaper's Greek-language editorials denounce the cowardice and hypocrisy of those who exploit their immigrant status to evade service, and urge readers to enlist in the army of either country (the armies, too, appear to be equivalent). The article concludes with a challenge, in bold English characters: "Up to you!"

Nevertheless, Calodikes's structure of equivalence is revealed to be ultimately misleading. The Greek element is *in excess*, if only because there is more of untranslated Greek text than there is of translation. Having began to understand what might be at stake in faithful translation, we may be able to identify potential sites of conflict by detecting the points where translation glosses over problematic issues of ethnic and national identity. In another excerpt quoted by Calodikes, "Greece, the Mother of Europe, in Balkan War is Fighting for Great Idea," Garret P. Serviss urges the West to help Greece, the cradle of civilization, in its war against Turkey and Bulgaria, and exhorts his readers: "We cannot excuse ourselves by saying that the Greeks of to-day are *degenerate* and are not the true descendants of the men of Marathon, and of the contemporaries of Pericles, Socrates, Plato and Aristotle. It is true that there has been an intermixture of other blood in Greece [. . .] but the old blood, the old names, the old spirit are not extinguished."[24] The Greek text translates "degenerate" accurately, as ἐκπεφυλισμένοι; the statement quoted denies, after all, that any serious adulteration has taken place. Moreover, the translation uses a tripartite paragraph structure to render a unified portion of English text, as if wishing to transform a chance remark into a rigorous argument. But when Byron, in the poem "The Isles of Greece," laments the loss of the ancient world, his philhellenic claim to "Hellas" undermines the term's potential as a marker of nationality/citizenship. When, as a citizen of an ideal "Hellas," Byron asks "And where art thou, my country . . . And must thy lyre, so long divine, / *Degenerate* into hands like mine?,"[25] the Greek text speaks of a broken or tuneless lyre (να χαλάσῃ), not a degenerate one.

This way of leaving items untranslated or translated differently than a faithful translation would warrant is a significant undercurrent running through the compilation. My previous comments on the project of self-representation presupposed a bilingual audience, and Calodikes's Prologue would seem to bear this out — joined by the figure of the Postmaster General, haunting the front page and demanding faithful translations. Although Calodikes's Prologue is in Greek, it claims that the book is addressed to both Greeks and Americans. In fact, the reviews from the Greek-American press quoted at the beginning of the second edition advertise it as "the best gift that the Greek of America can offer to his friends." ("Beware of Greeks bearing gifts" was the moral of the Wooden Horse incident at Troy.) This, however, downplays the fact that only the Greek part of the audience enjoys potential access to both versions. The same problem arises with the newspaper claim of a "true translation filed with the Postmaster." The wording here as well as in the Act itself suggests that it is the editor of the foreign paper who is responsible for providing the Postmaster with translations. How can Americans judge the translation's accuracy, since it is highly unlikely that they speak modern Greek — or ancient Greek for that matter? The issue is passed over in silence by Calodikes, who claims to have proceeded «μετά πιστοτάτης μεταφράσεως» ["in most faithful translation"].

In fact, the guidebook's pedagogic strictures to the individual immigrant reader hint that bilingual equality or equivalence might not be quite such a good strategy for success. One extract, for instance, about business, contains a hint for success that undermines the book's ostensibly bilingual politics or pretense of "faithful translation." The aspiring businessman is told by Andrew Carnegie to concentrate his endeavors on one enterprise, as "I have never yet met the man who fully understood two different kinds of business; you cannot find him any sooner than you can find a man who thinks in two languages equally, and does not invariably think in one."[26] The implication is that one can speak a second language, but ought not to speak it too fluently; at any rate, one can think, or scheme, successfully only in one, presumably the mother tongue.

Calodikes exploits this one-sided linguistic privilege of his audience in order to convey a secret ethnic message in an untranslated two-page article entitled: Η ΙΣΧΤΣ ΕΝ ΤΗ ΕΝΩΣΕΙ. ΤΑ ΖΑΧΑΡΟ-ΠΛΑΣΤΕΙΑ ΚΑΙ ΤΑ ΑΝΘΟΠΩΛΕΙΑ ΜΑΣ [Power in Unity: Our Pastry Stores and Flower Shops].[27] Despite the urge to Americanize in order to join the national civic community, the "we" here signals the linguistic boundary that delimits the ethnic group and simultaneously creates a persuasion of shared interest. The "we" speaks into existence the ethnic group that it aims to summon and mobilize under the auspices of a language incomprehensible to the wider national community: «ὑπό ἕνα ἀρχηγόν καί μίαν ἀρχήν, διά νά ἀποτελέσωμεν μίαν τεραστίαν δύναμιν συμπαγῆ καί ἀκαταγώνιστον, ἵνα δυνηθῶμεν ἀποτελεσματικῶς ν'ἀντεπεξέλθωμεν ἐναντίον τοῦ ἀνά τάς διαφόρους ἐνταῦθα ἐθνικότητας ὑφιστάμενον πρός ἐπικράτησιν συναγωνισμοῦ» ["under one leader and one rule, to form a great, solid and unconquerable force in order to successfully counteract the competition for dominance practiced by the various ethnicities here present"].[28]

Imagery of warfare surfaces on the level of economic competition, as models of citizenship and community give way to the play of ethnic interests. But in this strange linguistic scheme there is no common enemy, and no mention of the "American": «Παρά τό πλευρόν τοῦ Γερμανοῦ, τοῦ Ἄγγλου, τοῦ Γάλλου, Ἰταλοῦ καί Εβραίου συναγωνίζεται καί ὁ Ἕλλην ἐμπορικῶς» ["By the side of the German, the Englishman, the Frenchman, the Italian and the Jew the Greek also competes in business"]. The composite American character is dissolved into a series of competing ethnicities. And competition demands ethnic solidarity and a common policy if, in this Darwinian environment, the species is to survive: the Greek of America who, Calodikes warns, is «εὐπρόσβλητος εἰς τά βέλη τοῦ ἀτέγκτου καί παμφάγου συνεταιρισμοῦ, τόν ὁποῖον τόσον συστηματικῶς εφαρμόζουν οἱ ξένοι» ["vulnerable to the darts of the merciless and omnivorous partnerships, systematically practiced by the foreigners"].[29] The word xenos and its derivative, xenitia ("exile," "living abroad") has a long history in the Greek literary tradition and is often used to denote a "foreigner." Here, it is manipulated to express a Greek community and to legitimize it in the midst of xenitia.

The possibility of wartime ethnic subversion is the obvious reason behind the Act of 1917 and its imperative of translation. The compilation appears to give playful expression to this subversive potential in its references to the Trojan War, won, Calodikes reminds us, through Odysseus's ruse of the Wooden Horse. Could the ethnic language serve as a similar ruse? The book ends with the drama The Cyclops, translated from Euripides's ancient Greek by Shelley and retranslated from the English into modern Greek by Calodikes. The play describes one of the adventures of

Odysseus, primordial figure of the Greek traveler, migrant, and cunning entrepreneur. The account is cut short, but the story is well known: Odysseus and his companions, on a brief visit to the isle of the Cyclops to replenish their supplies, sneak into Polyphemus's cave, plunder his goods, and steal out again, strapped under the bellies of his flock. Later they evade the blinded Polyphemus's attempt at revenge through a linguistic sleight of hand. While the ship is sailing away, Polyphemus taunts Odysseus to tell him his name, but the cunning Greek shouts in reply: "I am Nobody." When his companions return and offer to help him, Polyphemus asks them to punish his enemy, but he is unable to reveal the enemy's identity. To their questions he can only reply: "Nobody blinded me."

I have argued that, while Calodikes's bilingual scheme seeks to valorize the Greek contribution to the American picture, it also manipulates the ruse of unfaithful translation to convey its linguistic-ethnic message: keep (or use) your language cunningly in order to survive. If language can play the role of the Trojan horse, every Greek-speaking Greek-American willing to band together with his ethnic-linguistic kind is a potential Odysseus. But then, how can we account for the fact that the ruse is there for all to behold, in the Greek text that occupies all of the two pages that should have been bilingual? Is it by being all-too-conspicuous, like the enormous wooden horse left outside the walls of Troy, that it can best serve its purpose?

At any rate, the possibility of unfaithful translation appears to have been conceivable only briefly. In the second edition of 1923, Calodikes's article on ethnic business solidarity gives way to the text of the Declaration of Independence, the Constitution, and its Amendments. Even more graphically, the drama of Odysseus and the Cyclops is supplanted by the staged drama of naturalization, providing the questions and answers to the ritual of the court where the judge interrogates the immigrant and prospective citizen on the history and the institutions of the United States. The evasiveness of the foreign-language text and the exploitation of the ethnic's advantage over a monolingual American audience, undertaken through the scheme of bilingual translation, yields to the ritual of naturalization. And that is a ritual to be undergone in English only.

Notes

1. Life in these establishments, or *bekiarika*, is described in the short stories of Elias Tzanetes (a.k.a. Phil Nax). His humorous vignettes first appeared in Greek-American newspapers and magazines in the 1920s and 1930s, and were later published as a collection entitled Ἡ Αὐτοῦ Μεγαλειότης ὁ Μετανάστης [His Royal Highness the Immigrant] (New York: Anatolia Press, 1946). Theano Papazoglou-Margare, in two volumes of stories, Ἕνα Δάκρυ γιά τόν Μπάρμπα Τζίμη [A Tear for Uncle Jimmy] (Athens: Diphros, 1958) and Χρονικό τοῦ Χόλστεντ Στρήτ [Chronicle of Holstead Street] (Athens: Ekd. Oikos Phexe, 1962), also portrays vividly the experience of Greek immigrants before and during the two World wars.

2. Ἐθνικός Κήρυκας [*The National Herald*], New York: Enossis Publishing, 1915–.

3. For an overview of the Greek press in the beginning of the century see also: Charles Jaret, "The Greek, Italian, and Jewish American Ethnic Press: A Comparative Analysis," *Journal of Ethnic Studies* 7-2 (1940):45–65; Theodore Giannakoulis, "The Greek Press in America," *Athene* 2-8 (1941):16–32; Victor Papacosma, "The Greek Press in America," *Journal of the Hellenic Diaspora*, 5-4 (1980):45–61; and Robert F. Park, *The Immigrant Press and Its Control* (New York: Harper & Brothers, 1922).

4. Theodore Saloutos, *The Greeks in the United States* (Cambridge: Cambridge University Press, 1964), p. 183.

5. Demetra Vaka Brown's *The Unveiled Ladies of Stamboul* (Boston: Houghton Mifflin, 1923) appeared in English; Corinne Canoutas's Greek-language Τό Τέλος Ἑνός Ππρίγκηπος [The Last Ottoman Prince] (New York: Kosmos, 1917), a tale of incest, politics, and murder in Istanbul, was published in Greek. See the interesting pamphlet "The Greek Immigrant and His Reading," by Alison B. Alessios (Chicago: American Library Association, 1926; series: Library Work With the Foreign Born), for the way that it represents the Greek immigrant from an American perspective, and for the suggested bibliography in the modern Greek language to be acquired by librarians for the Greeks in their communities. The pamphlet's headings include: "Reading Tastes," "Racial Background," "Americanization."

6. Serapheim Canoutas, Σύμβουλος καί Πρακτικός Δικηγόρος [Adviser for Greeks in America] (New York: Kosmos, 1919], p. 30. Translations from the Greek, unless otherwise indicated, are my own.

7. See Christopher Canoutas, *Christopher Columbus a Greek Nobleman* (New York: St. Mark's, 1943).

8. A selective list of guidebooks, widely understood, includes: John Booras, Αἴ Ἐθνικαί Θερμοπύλαι [The National Thermopylae] (New York?: n. pub., 1911?); Serapheim Canoutas, Ἑλληνοαμερικανικός Ὁδηγός [Greek-American Business Directory] (New York: S. G. Canoutas, 1910) and Σύμβουλος καί Πρακτικός Δικηγόρος [Adviser for Greeks in America]; C. S. Calodikes, Χρυσή Βίβλος [The Golden Book or the Greek and American Spirit] (New York: n. pub., 1917; 2nd ed. with changes, New York: n. pub., 1923); Babes Malaphoures, Ἕλληνες τῆς Ἀμερικῆς, 1528–1948 [Greeks in America: 1528–1948] (New York: I. Goldmann, 1948); Babes Marketos, Ἡ Ἑλλάς στό Σταυροδρόμι [Greece at the Crossroads] (New York: Ekd. Ethnikou Kyrekos, 1942); Emmanouel Polenis, Ἐγκόλπιον Μετανάστου [Immigrant's Manual] (Athens: n. pub., 1945); and the anonymous Τό Κλειδί τοῦ Ἕλληνος στήν Ἀμερική [A Key for the Greek in America: The Greek as Citizen as Soldier as Sailor of the United States; includes the Declaration of Independence and the Constitution in English and Greek] (New York: Vivliop. Ethnikou Kyrekos, 1917).

9. The newspaper *Loxias* was published in Chicago by D. S. Eutaxias, 1908–.

10. A list of contemporary works on the Greek immigration includes: Grace Abbot, "A Study of the Greeks in Chicago," *The American Journal of Sociology* (Nov. 1909); Thomas Burgess, *Greeks in America: An Account of Their Coming, Progress, Customs, Living, and Aspirations: With a Historical Introduction and the Stories of Some Famous Greek-Americans* (Boston: Sherman French, 1913); Christopher Canoutas, *Hellenism in America or the History of Greeks in America* (Boston: S. G. Canoutas, 1918); Park, *The Immigrant Press and Its Control;* Henry Pratt Fairchild, *Immigration: A World Movement and Its American Significance* (New York: Macmillan, 1913), and *Greek Immigration to the United States* (New Haven: Yale University Press, 1911); Thomas Lacey, *A Study of Social Heredity as Illustrated in the Greek People* (New York: F. S. Lacey, 1916); Theodore Saloutos, *The Greeks in the United States* (Cambridge, Mass.: Harvard University Press, 1964); Franklin B. Sanborn, *Michael Anagnos, Memoir* (Boston: Wright & Potter, 1907); and J. P. Xenides, *The Greeks in America* (New York: G. H. Doran, 1922).

11. Fairchild, *Greek Immigration to the United States.*

12. This kind of comparison of moderns to ancients is a common *topos* in accounts of the early Greek immigrant. See, for example, the report written by William I. Cole, professor of applied sociology, for the Massachusetts Bureau of Immigration, "Immigrant Races in Massachusetts: The Greeks" ([Boston], c. 1919), Widener Library, Harvard University. Like Alessios in "The Greek Immigrant and His Reading," Cole comments on the Greeks' business abilities and argues that "they join hands with the ancient Greeks in the possession of certain mental and moral characteristics whatever may be their kinship with them in blood."

13. H. L. Mencken, "The American Language," in *Literary History of the United States*, eds. Robert E. Spiller, Willard Thorp, et al., 4th ed. (New York: Macmillan, 1974).

14. Ibid., p. 665.

15. For an account of how the question of the official language of the United States elided its earlier multilingual context and was displaced instead onto, among other things, the difference between English and American English, see Marc Shell, "Babel in America," in this volume.

16. Mencken, "The American Language," p. 675.

17. Bilingualism was a predicament familiar to the Greek immigrant even before leaving home. Many Greeks spoke Turkish or Albanian; moreover, during much of the twentieth century the "language question" in Greece revolved around the competition for dominance between the purist and the popular register, and mirrored closely the debate over national definition and the proper nature of "Greekness." Καθαρεύουσα, (from καθαρός, "clean," "pure," "unadulterated"), an artificial language based on ancient Greek forms, was espoused by the proponents of continuity as a link with the classical past. The demoticists, on the other hand, defended the popular linguistic register, arguing that it would best serve the purposes of national definition, since it expressed the "soul of the people" through popular art forms such as the folksong. *Kathareuousa* persisted until the 1970s, and the demotic did not become the official language until the Education Act of 1976.

18. Editorial of Feb. 26, 1916, quoted (in translation) in Jaret, "The Greek, Italian, and Jewish American Ethnic Press," p. 60. One such notable contender was Jacob Philipp Fallmerayer. In a lecture on the origin of the modern Greeks to the Bavarian Academy of Sciences in 1835, he argued that all ancient Greek traces had been erased by the Slavic invasions of the Greek mainland during the Byzantine period. For an account of the process by means of which Fallmerayer achieved "Satanic" proportions in modern Greek culture as an embodiment of anti-Hellenism, see Stathis Gourgouris, *Dream Nation: Enlightenment, Colonization and the Institution of Modern Greece* (Stanford: Stanford University Press, 1996), pp. 141–50.

19. "The Golden Bible"; the old meaning of *he biblos*, "book," has been taken over by the neuter form *to biblio(n)*.

20. The function of the possessive pronoun μας — and, by implication, the attribution of greatness — is tellingly ambiguous. It may refer solely to the Greek race, or to Greek and American respectively commanding mutual respect; but it also seems to perform, on the grammatical level, a fusion of the two.

21. In this case, "benefiting" conveys the idea of self-improvement not merely by grasping the meaning of the text at hand, but also by improving one's linguis-

tic skills in the language in which it is written. The guidebook thus provides both important information and language instruction, in whatever language (English or Greek) the reader happens to be less fluent.

22. Lord Byron, the most famous of philhellenes, died in Greece during the siege of Messolonghi. Philhellenism, a literary phenomenon that evolved into a political attitude, played an interesting role in the politics of early nineteenth-century Europe. Greek propaganda in Europe during the War of Independence stressed the continuity between ancient Greeks and their modern counterparts in order to secure political and financial support. Concomitantly, the European philhellenes' support for the Greek cause was also a reaction against conservative regimes at home. See William St. Clair, *That Greece Might Still Be Free* (London: Oxford University Press, 1972), esp. ch. 2.

23. On philhellenism as a discourse of repetition and reincarnation in this earlier context, and with reference to French painting of the Greek War, see Nina Athanassoglou Kallmyer, *French Images of the Greek War of Independence* (New Haven: Yale University Press, 1989), esp. ch. 3.

24. Calodikes, *The Golden Book*, p. 50, my emphasis.

25. Ibid., p. 68, my emphasis.

26. Ibid., p. 84.

27. Articles in the Greek press urging cooperation and even partnership among Greek businessmen are not uncommon at this time. See, for example, the articles in *Loxias* on "Greek Candy-Makers," March 7, 1918, p. 1, and on "The Coffee Houses," March 14, 1918, p. 1; also, Saloutos on the establishment of the American Association of Greek Restaurant Keepers, incorporated on Dec. 1, 1919, pp. 268–269.

28. Calodikes, *The Golden Book*, p. 122.

29. Ibid., p. 123.

CHAPTER FIVE

Disturbing the Language Peace: German-Jewish Women Poets in *Aufbau*, 1933–1993

■ **ELISABETH LENCKOS**

The women of German-Jewish origin who published in the German-language New York magazine *Aufbau* [*Reconstruction*] between 1933 and 1993, considered themselves artistic agitators and educators whose poetry tested the tenets of cultural diversity and tolerance that supposedly governed American society. To write in a minority language was a symbolic act of protest against the paradox of a social ideology that advocated the idea of "the melting pot," yet inflicted a strict monolingual dictate upon its immigrants. Since the majority of these women were mothers who witnessed the rigorous American indoctrination of their offspring, their work is permeated with a passionate resistance against the politics of forced cultural assimilation. A prominent *Aufbau* contributor, Mascha Kaléko (1912–1975) compared the ostracism that she experienced as a Jew in Germany to the hostility that her son encountered in the United States in her poem "Interview mit mir selbst — Anno Neunzehnhunderfünfundvierzig" ["Interview with Myself — In the Year 1945"]:

> ... Das war einmal. In einem andern Leben,
> Doch unterdessen, wie die Zeit verrinnt,
> Hat sich auch biographisch was ergeben:
> Nun hab ich selbst ein Emigrantenkind.
>
> Das lernt das Wörtchen "alien" buchstabieren
> Und spricht zur Mutter: "Don't speak German, dear."
> Muss knapp acht Jahre alt Diskussionen führen,

Dass er "alright" ist, wenn auch nicht von hier.
Grad wie das Flüchtlingskind beim Rektor May!
Wenn ich mir dies Dacapo so betrachte . . .[1]

[. . . Once upon a time. In another life,
But in the meantime, how time flies,
There's been a change in my biography:
I now have an immigrant child.

The word "alien" he learns to spell
And tells his mother: "Don't speak German, dear."
Eight years of age, he has to lead discussions

To state that he's "alright," even if not from here.
Just as the fugitive child had once to Principal May!
When I look at this repetition . . .[I rage]

Kaléko's outrage at the societal demand for justification of her son's presence in the United States in 1945 resembles the great distress expressed by Rahel Varnhagen, the famous German Jewish writer and leader of literary Berlin between 1790 and 1806: "How dreadful it is to always be forced to legitimize oneself! That is why it is so disgusting to be a Jewish woman!"[2] The similarity of their reactions bears testimony to the politics of exclusion aimed at Jews in the Western world in the past two hundred years. While Varnhagen suffered from Prussian legislation that denied her the rights of a citizen, Kaléko had to endure the culturally and racially motivated resistance of American society against the integration of newcomers.

The shared experiences of various forms of discrimination resulted in a strong common bond and a cultural tradition uniting German-Jewish women across countries and generations in a characteristic stance of opposition. The very fact that German Jews considered their political and social exclusion in the United States not as a transitory episode, but as an affirmation of the permanency of their exile, strengthened their ability to exist and even prosper in the position of the outsider and to impose on themselves the challenging task of social agitator. Women in particular renewed their "social contract" with enthusiasm because of their heightened awareness of the importance of personal cultivation *(Bildung)*, whose tenets Jewish women writers had propagated in Germany since the Enlightenment and which they now sought to integrate into the politics of the North American educational system. The poetry of German-Jewish women thus occupies a place of extraordinary importance in the exile literature of the United States because of the special role which Jewish women intellectuals had taken up when they resided in Germany and which they subsequently transferred to the New World: that of the "disturber of the civil peace."[3]

While in Germany, Jewish women poets and thinkers had since the eighteenth century contested conservative assumptions about political and cultural unity. Upon their arrival in the United States, they continued their tradition of opposition, but changed the object of their attack because they felt threatened not by the actuality of the American legal and political system but by its ideology of cultural harmony and ethnic unity. Although the majority of these poets mastered English, they persisted in their use of German as the idiom of their poetry because it tested the American claim that all kinds of diversity, including that of language, were welcome in the New World. The poets thus acted as disturbers of "the linguistic peace" and continued their work of agitation until the very end of their lives. Their motivation, however, sprang not only from their ingrained tendency towards political controversy, but also from a deeply felt affinity with the German language and culture. The particularly passionate and problematic nature of this connection had been described by the nineteenth-century German-Jewish poet Ludwig Börne: "[Because . . . I am] at once a German and a Jew, and . . . was not born in a fatherland, I long more hotly for a fatherland . . . because for me, for whom the foreign land began outside the closed doors [of my birthplace] . . . the great fatherland stretches as far as its language."[4] His declaration indicates the place of privilege that the German language held in the minds and achievements of Jewish citizens living in German territories prior to the advent of National Socialism, and provides a further explanation as to why the majority of German Jewish poets who came to the United States after 1933 continued to write in the medium of their modern cultural experience. They stood in the tradition not only of Börne, but also of the great Heinrich Heine, who had declared the "German word . . . the most sacred good and a fatherland for those who are de-

nied a fatherland."[5] Even after expatriation, German-Jewish women insisted on using their *Muttersprache* (mother tongue) and on grounding their
identity in the consciousness of being the guardians of an exalted, yet embattled cause. Margarete Kollisch explained that "The German language is
the home that never sent me into exile"; Anna Krommer said that "I write
in German because it is my mother tongue"; and Vera Lachmann explained simply: "I compose in German, because I have no alternative."[6]

Their constancy to the language included their loyalty to the literature
and culture of their former homeland. Even after 1933, German Jews pains-
takingly distinguished between their cultural background and the contemporary situation in Germany. The poetry of German Jews therefore remained permeated with a sense of defiance that attested to their refusal to
be deprived of their artistic heritage after having been displaced from their
rightful place in the homeland.[7] Hilde Marx (1911–1986) expressed this
sentiment in one of her early political poems, "Das freie Wort" ["Free
Speech"]:

> Schwer war der Abschied von geliebten Orten
> und Menschen. Und der Weg war voll Gefahr.
> Doch meine Heimat blieb in meinen Worten
> und meine Worte blieben frei und wahr.[8]
>
> [The farewell from beloved places
> And friends was hard. Dangers lurked on the way.
> But my home remained in my words,
> And my words remained free and true.]

Writing in German meant fighting the Nazi enemy, whose goal had been
both the actual annihilation of the Jewish population and the symbolic era-
sure of its immense contribution to German art and culture. Although German-Jewish poets could not prevent the slaughter, they kept the traces of
their sufferings and their accomplishments alive in their verse. Thus *Aufbau*
poet Ilse Blumenthal-Weiss described her poems as *Mahnmale* ["Monu-
ments of Admonishment"], and the theme of *remembering* features prominently in the poetry of her peers.[9]

The role of agitators and educators in a minority language placed high demands on these poets. Many of them experienced a "language trauma" because societal pressure urged them to compose poetry in the English language.[10] They fell victim to a profound disorientation which temporarily tested their ability as poets, because they found it strenuous and even impossible to describe their experiences under Nazi rule in a language other than German. Rose Ausländer, who published frequently for *Aufbau*, at first called German "the language of murderers" and attempted to write exclusively in English between 1948 and 1956, but eventually felt compelled to return to German in order to come to terms with her past as a victim of National Socialism.[11] Another result was that many poems by *Aufbau* contributors such as Maria Berl-Lee, Anna Krommer, Erika Guetermann, and Ilse Blumenthal-Weiss, although written in German, seemed to be grappling with syntactic fragmentation. The broken style of their verse alludes to each poet's inner struggle with the threat of losing the intrinsic qualities of her poetry, which were intimately connected with her use of the idiomatic properties of her native language.

The preoccupation with the possibility of creative inertia reflected more than the poet's sense of displacement, however. It also reflected her realization that in the perception of the greater American society, the German-Jewish poet remained a nonentity, since society proved unwilling to propagate languages other than English in the United States. Monolinguistic social attitudes thus forced German-Jewish poets into "niche-writing" and prompted them to concentrate on their immediate surroundings. Consequently, they depicted their neighborhoods as quasi-Utopias, half-idealized places that resisted social and technological change, yet gradually transformed themselves into sites of greater ideological freedom and higher moral principles than were being enjoyed by the rest of American society:

> Aber was mich mehr besticht
> Als der Technik stolze Zeichen,
> Sind die Strassen, gestrig, schlicht,
> Die noch keinem Fortschritt weichen.
>
> Wo das alte Brauchtum währt,
> Mitgebracht aus anderen Breiten,

Edle Fracht, die zollfrei fährt.
Sie versöhnt die Zeit den Zeiten.[12]

[But I am enchanted
Less by technology's proud signifiers,
Than by modest streets of yesterday transplanted,
They remain progress deniers.

Where old customs are prevailing,
Preserved from other areas,
Noble freight without tax entailing,
Time is reconciled with eras.]

Gertrude Urzidil's (1898–1977) "Zwischen Hudson und East River" ["Between the Hudson and the East River"] translates immigrant neighborhoods into symbolic scenes of philosophical reconciliation. She asserts that they unite future and past because they are assailed by the changing times, yet combat change ardently. The controversial view of the immigrant communities as signifying loci, where social transformation and ethnic assimilation are ideally transcended, can be found in many poems by German-Jewish immigrants.[13] It is the result of the understanding that the ethical obligation of German-Jewish culture and literature consisted in the protection and preservation of an identity founded not on a firm and unadulterated knowledge of place, but on a fragile sense of affinity in shared hybrid customs and rhetorical traditions. German-Jewish neighborhoods were depicted now as staunchly old-fashioned (in terms of modern technology), now as radically progressive (in terms of democratic principles), in order to suggest that they represented the perfect synthesis of the conflicting forces that drive society; utopias where the immigrant could live in political liberty yet remain magically untouched by machine progress.

German-Jewish women poets who had immigrated to the United States continued to consider the state of exile and the quest for home as the defining experiences of their existence. Anna Krommer (1924–), whose poetry is almost parsimonious in its use of language, summarized this plight in poems that continue to amaze with their strikingly concise lyricism. Although she concentrated on three allegorically vague locations (the street, the garden, and the cemetery), she described these sites in an evocative style which greatly moves the reader with the gentle intimation of the suffering they conceal.

"JÜDISCHER FRIEDHOF" (SLOWAKEI, 1977)

Stufenweise
führen Erinnerungen
ins Trüblicht von Gestern.
Für immer
geschlossen die Pforte
wo der Friedhof verwaist.
Über Gräber
streichen Himmelszeichen,
schweifen Heimatwinde,
setzt die Verlassenheit
die grosse Ruhe.[14]

["JEWISH CEMETERY" (SLOVAKIA, 1977)

Step by step
Memories lead
Into the dull light of yesterday.
Forever
Closed the gate
Where the cemetery is orphaned.
Above graves
Heavenly signs pass,
Homebound winds roam,
Desolation places
Great quiet.]

"FRIEDHOF"

Geheimnisvoller
Garten der Toten —
Zinnoberblumen

magisch verpflanzt;
kreisendes Licht
Gräber betastend.
Marmorsteine. Urnen.
Schwarzer Kater
auf Schleichwegen.
Flieder. Goldregen.
Vergissmeinnicht . . .[15]

["CEMETERY"

Prodigiously mysterious
Garden of the Dead —
Vermilion flowers
Magically transplanted;
Circling light
Touching graves.
Marble stones. Urns.
Black tomcat
On secret paths.
Lilac. Laburnum.
Forget-me-not . . .]

Krommer's elliptical style greatly differs from the often verbose and lengthy poems of many of her fellow immigrant poets. Krommer's work, continuing well after many of her fellow poets had either ceased writing or died, constitutes the moment when German Jewish poetry abandons its historic specificity in favor of philosophical transcendence and transfigures, in the American tradition of Emily Dickinson, the meaning of the trope of exile from the ethnic to the universal, from the realistic to the mythical, and from the personal to the lyrical. This shift is evident in the titles of the two cemetery poems, one of which makes reference to the Holocaust, while the other merely names a location. The contrast between the two sites is striking; the Jewish cemetery is a desert of desolation that bears no sign of life, whereas the unknown cemetery is a virtual garden of light and animation. The graves in the Jewish cemetery lack any human or heavenly reference; the graves in the other cemetery, by contrast, are lovingly tended by human hands and by nature. The heartrending implication is clear: Jewish grave sites are consigned to oblivion, whereas gardens of the dead hold intense communication with the living.

The linguistic "coincidence" of the flower's name in German and English ("Vergissmeinnicht," "Forget-me-not . . .") establishes a symbolic correspondence between the two languages which in reality ruled the life and creativity of the German-Jewish woman poet in the United States. It also proposes a resolution both to the conflict of linguistic predominance and to the poetic fight against social indifference. Krommer's implicit reference to a third and universal idiom, the floral emblem, attests to her aspiration to transcend linguistic barriers and to establish a more accessible system of signs for a broader audience. The fact that her poems are particularly amenable to English translation corroborates the assumption that Krommer's poetry is meant to act as *metaphor* in the most elemental sense; an enigmatic symbol which is unraveled when decoded and translated within the context of idiomatic signification. The hint of mystery and obscurity inherent in Krommer's poetic language transports her poetry from its confinement in an ethnic and linguistic niche to transcendence of the forces which stand in the way of the long journey to healing the rift between the two languages. A line from one of her poems, "The Refuge of Silence," represents a fitting self-analysis of her poetry, whose fragmentary images threaten to dissolve into the vagueness of allusions and require the participation of the reader.[16] The reason for this elusiveness is that Krommer's poems are designed as epitaphs, concise and spare inscriptions on the bare slates over the tombs of the forgotten dead. Krommer's poems bring them back to memory and challenge us to resurrect the ghosts of those who lie buried beneath our oblivion. Like her peers Urzidil and Blumenthal-Weiss, Krommer is "a disturber of the peace" and points to the decades-long conspiracy of silence about the Holocaust and its devastating effects upon victims and survivors. Her poetry asks us to continue and bring to fruition her quest for recognition.

Krommer's poetry also demonstrates that eventually the role of agitator has extended from that of social critic of current circumstances to that of poet on a universal scale. Between 1933 and 1993, *Aufbau* poets rewrote the annals of Jewish persecution and redefined both the German and the American attitudes toward the Holocaust, especially in the first two decades after the Second World War, when it was not yet a commonly discussed subject. The momentous work of correcting and revising the modern history of the German Jewry was another important reason for German-Jewish immigrant poets in the United States to continue writing in their native tongue. A great part of their poetry remained in dialogue with their former homeland, reminding its citizens of the Jewish claim to German language and culture. As a very select group of survivors of a historical epoch, German-Jewish poets documented this chapter for posterity, but also started on a new chapter: that of the (German) Jews in North America. They commented on many important events that influenced immigrant existence, including urban conditions, politics, crime, the landing on the moon, and expressed the various human emotions that touched the alien resident — among them, the initial feeling of alienation upon arriving in the New World and the never-relenting sense of estrangement that they experienced, even late in life, as ethnic minorities. The sum of their motivations is described by Ilse Blumenthal-Weiss (1899–1987) in her poem "Anweisungen" ["Advice"]:

> Ohne Erfahrung sein
> Und Wort und Gebärde
> Den Wolken anvertrauen
> Und dem verschwiegenen Meer.
>
> Keine Antwort geben
> Auf Vergangenheitsfragen
> Nur im Schweigen den Schmerz überstehn
> Und die Untiefe Schuld.
>
> Dem Auftrag Vergessen
> Keine Folge leisten.
> Das ragende Mahnmal
> Hält die Erinnerung wach . . .
>
> [To be without experience
> Without word and gesture

To trust the clouds
And the silent sea.

To give no answer
To questions about the past.
To survive pain solely in silence
And the fathomless guilt.

To fail to obey
The order to forget.
The towering monument
Keeps memory awake.]

Her work describes deep conflicts: between an individual's ardent wish to regain innocence and the absolute refusal to forget the personal contamination inflicted by the Holocaust; between the longing for peace and coming to terms with suffering, and the ethical duty to fight universal oblivion. The plea for silence reflects the great burden that the poet feels in having to pollute the beauty and purity of her language with the Nazi rhetoric of atrocity and violence. For Blumenthal-Weiss, language, which can cast a magic spell, can also turn into a curse that pronounces and propounds the poet's sense of separation:

Aber die Sehnsucht führt keine Sprache heim.
Nur im Blick der Schlafenden
Und im Zifferblatt der Träume
Flüstert noch ein Amenhauch.

Denn die Worte haben den Weg verloren . . .[17]

[Longing finds no home in language.
Only in the gaze of the sleepers
And in the face of dreams
Whispers the breath of an amen.

For the words have lost the way . . .]

The startling ambiguity of the first line, "Aber die Sehnsucht führt keine Sprache heim," depicts the confusion of the exiled poet who is unable to feel at home in her language, yet doubts that her new home offers a solution in another language. "Abendweihe" ["Evensong"] thus represents a resounding renunciation of the quest for finding reconciliation in one's native language. As Blumenthal-Weiss rejects the exiled poet's punishing claim to cultural independence and individual self-sufficiency, she takes recourse in a signifying silence; the name of God that must not be spoken and yet lights her way ("Nur der unaussprechliche Name / Leuchtet über mir": "Only the unspeakable name / Shines above me"). Her plea resembles Krommer's exploration of an allusive form of communication to compensate for the obfuscation of linguistic sense-making. Similarly, Kaléko critically re-examines her former inability to find a voice in her new country of residence because the language of her childhood is different from that of her new compatriots:

> Auch ich ward fremd und muss oft danke sagen,
> Das macht: Ich hab hier Murmeln nie gespielt,
> Geheimstes dieser Sprache nie erfühlt
> In Worten, wie sie Träumer wagen.
> Doch Dank der Welle, die mich hergetragen,
> Und Dank dem Wind, der mich an Land gespült.
>
> Sagst du auch stars, sind's doch die gleichen Sterne,
> Und moon der Mond, den du als Kind gekannt,
> Und Gott hält seinen Himmel ausgespannt,
> Als folgte er uns auch in die fernste Ferne.
>   — Im Traume nur schreckt mich die Mordskaserne,
> Und ich ruh aus von meinem Vaterland. . .[18]
>
> [I am foreign and have to say more thanks than I care to,
> I mean: I never played marbles here,
> Never felt the most secret sense of this language — mere
> Words — the way dreamers dare to.
> But I thank the wave that brought me near,
> Thanks to the wind that took me to this land so dear.
>
> Even if you say "star," it is the same star
> And "moon" the moon that you knew as a child.

And God keeps his suspended heavens mild,
As if he followed us into the distance far.
— Only in dreams I am terrified by the murderer's band,
And I take refuge from my fatherland . . .]

For Kaléko, the commonality of experience began to relieve the passionate dependence on the German language in the thinking of German-Jewish immigrants. Similarly, Rose Ausländer's (1901–1988) poem "Wiederkäuer" ["Ruminators"] reflects a disenchanted but sophisticated understanding of the ideological function of language, which results in a new and critical exploration of rhetorical manipulation:

Im übersättigten
Hungerjahrhundert
kaue ich die Legende
Frieden
und ich werde nicht satt.

Kann nicht verdauen
die Kriege sie liegen
mir wie Steine im Magen
Grabsteine

Der Frieden
liegt mir am Herzen
ich kaue, kaue
das wiederholte Wort
und werde nicht
satt.[19]

[In the overfed
Famine century
I ruminate the legend
Peace
My hunger I can't satiate.

I cannot digest
The Wars, they lie

In my stomach like stones
Gravestones

Peace
Is in my heart
I ruminate, ruminate
The repeated word
My hunger I can't
Satiate.]

Ausländer's poetry plays with the commonplaces and confusions of language, the comparisons and metaphors that supposedly capture the deepest human emotions and concerns in words, yet fail to convey essential truths. The images of repetition and regurgitation refer to the feckless abuse of political rhetoric, which deprives language of its magical capacity to create a meaningful likeness and instead perverts it into inane metonymy. "Ruminators" attests to the ideological and spiritual distance that Ausländer has put between herself and her "mother tongue"; language is no longer seen as a friend in one's solitude, but rather as a deadly enemy that must be vanquished.

But the attack on the reverence for one's language also results in an embracing of linguistic and cultural diversity. This moment is celebrated in Gertrude Urzidil's poem "Zinshaus tief in Queens" ["Tenement House in the Middle of Queens"]:

Auf der Insel, die sich Walt Whitmans rühmt,
sind wir eines Hauses hundertachtzigste Partei.
Man grüsst einander, wie es sich ziehmt,
nur selten geht jemand vorbei.

Es ist besser, wenn man mit anderen wohnt,
als die Welt zu messen nach seinem Gartenbeet.
Von den hundertachtzig Arten Lärm bleibt niemand verschont.
Aber man fühlt sich nicht als Mitte, um die sich alles dreht.

Keines der Kinder heir ist ohne Gespielen,
sepiafarbig, gelb, schwarz und weiss.

. . . . .

Wenn man da ihre Rufe durchs Fenster hört,
Zu jeder Jahreszeit und immer beschwingt,
Glaube keiner, der gute graue Barde fühle sich gestört,
Denn er ists ja, der den Kindern von den Grashalmen singt.[20]

[On the island that boasts Walt Whitman,
We are in a house the hundred-and-eightieth apartment.
Here it is the custom to greet your fellow man,
Rarely, someone passes by without a comment.

It is better to live with others in communities,
Than to measure the world by one's hearth,
No one can avoid the hundred-and-eighty cacophonies.
They remind you, you're not the center of the earth.

No child here is without a pal,
Sepia, yellow, black and white

. . . . .

Through the windows one hears them calling
In any season, in voices always bright,
Don't think the good gray bard finds this appalling,
For he sings to the children of the Leaves of Grass.]

Urzidil presents the tenement house as the realization of Whitman's ideal of vast and massive urban individuality. Her reference to the variety of skin colors demonstrates that she no longer single-mindedly celebrates the German-Jewish immigrant neighborhoods, but instead promotes ethnic mobility and linguistic variety. Whereas her depiction of the sense of companionship resounding with the "hundred-and-eighty cacophonies" reflects her idealistic beliefs, the apartment building is a more open and universal place than Urzidil had imagined fourteen years earlier, in her poem "Between the Hudson and the East River." By 1963, her dream of German-Jewish cultural isolation and linguistic contraction has given way to a vision of international expansion and idiomatic freedom. Like Krommer, Kaléko, and Blumenthal-Weiss, she searches for alternative modes of communication and finds these in music and the verbal art forms most closely connected with music: song and poetry. Urzidil's poem, filled with the sounds of neighborly greetings, the manifold noises of children at play, and the cheerful voices of adults at the task of caring for their progeny, brings together the personal and societal, the high and the low, the immigrant and the indigenous aspects of American culture in an allegorical chant in the great tradition of Longfellow and Whitman.

Urzidil's poem describes the change of heart and mind in German-Jewish poets, as they gradually learned to appreciate the importance of ethnic and linguistic versatility and to regard their ability to move between various idioms and cultural identities as the principal source of their creative individuality and capacity for personal tolerance and sympathy. Many of the *Aufbau* women began to write poems in a similar vein, empathizing with members of American society who shared their background of persecution and ostracism, including Mascha Kaléko's "Einer Negerin im Harlem Express" ["To an African American Woman on the Harlem Express"], Hilde Marx's "Dunkle Schwester" ["Dark Sister"], and Mimi Grossberg's "A Southern Ballad."[21] In her poem, Kaléko tried to communicate with others in the silent language of glances:

> Dunkles Mädchen eines fremden Stammes,
> Tief im Dschungel dieser fremden Stadt,
> Deiner Augen schwarz verhangne Trauer
> Sagt mir, was Dein Herz gelitten hat.
>
> Immer möchte ich dich leise fragen:
> Weisst du, dass wir heimlich Schwestern sind?
> Du des Kongos dunkelbraune Tochter,
> Ich, Europas blasses Judenkind.[22]
>
> [Dark girl of a foreign tribe,
> Deep in the jungle of this foreign city,
> Your eyes, veiled in black pain, tell me
> That your heart's suffering I must pity.
>
> I want to ask you quietly,
> Do you know we are secretly sisters?

> You, the dark-brown daughter of the Congo,
> I, Europe's Jewish pale child.]

However, the expression of affinity through suffering ultimately represents a plea for understanding the speaker's own plight. Kaléko's poem represents one of her last, moving bequests to readers of exile poetry, who retain as the final image of the poet her silent despair that hopes for nothing more than a short, mute exchange of misery with a stranger.[23] But we are also left with the impression of a fighter; a poet who, like her fellows Krommer, Urzidil, and Blumenthal-Weiss, documents life on the margins of society with unrelenting honesty and self-deprecating accuracy.

Although their poetry reflects these women's profound sense of alienation, it must be recognized for the sublimely contending aesthetic effort that it certainly was; a continuous rebellion against a lasting destiny of persecution and exile that was designed to obliterate their persistent creativity. But neither banishment nor discrimination could silence these German-Jewish women poets; each poem defies the powers that persecuted, oppressed, or ignored them. They had scarce opportunity to publish their work in media other than *Aufbau* and were largely unnoticed by the English-speaking public, yet in contrast to the majority of writers who tended to idealize life in the United States, they remained completely honest and uncorrupted in their depictions of the contemporary American situation as they found it. Their verse still attests to the temerity of its creators, who defied linguistic assimilation and stayed true to their role as disturbers of the public life. Through their poems we come to realize that aesthetic work can in fact enter into the debate on ethics and ethnicity, as a restorer of lost memory of past wrongdoing and suffering. Even if this poetry is written in a language other than English, it deserves our attention, as it teaches us the necessity of writing in an *idiom of one's own*, as if it were in *a room of one's own*. It is up to us to enter the accomplishments of these poets into the record of American literary history.

Notes

1. *Aufbau*, 19 Sept. 1966. All of the translations in this article are my own and form part of an ongoing project, a bilingual anthology of German-Jewish women's poetry written and published in the United States between 1933 and 1993. Thus far it includes poems by Rose Ausländer, Maria Berl-Lee, Ilse Blumenthal-Weiss, Anita Daniel, Mimi Grossberg, Erika Guetermann, Mascha Kaléko, Margarete Kollisch, Anna Krommer, Vera Lachmann, Helga Nathorff, and Gertrude Urzidil.

2. Rahel von Varnhagen, *Briefwechsel: Rahel und ihre Freunde*, ed. Friedhelm Kemp, 3 vols., 2nd ed. (Munich: Winkler Verlag, 1979), vol. 3, p. 54.

3. I take this term from the title of the book by Marcel Reich-Ranicki, *Über Ruhestörer: Juden in der deutschen Literatur* (Munich: Deutscher Taschenbuchverlag, 1993), who describes the cultural position of Jewish poets and intellectuals in Germany. The argument of my article is indebted to his excellent analysis.

4. Ludwig Börne, *Sämtliche Schriften*, ed. Inge and Peter Rippman, 3 vols. (Düsseldorf: Joseph Melzer Verlag, 1964), vol. 3, p. 511.

5. Quoted from Reich-Ranicki, *Über Ruhestöre*, pp. 86–88.

6. All quotes taken from Lisa Kahn, ed., *Reisegepäck Sprache: Deutschschreibende Schriftstellerinnen in den USA 1938–1978* (Munich: Wilhelm Fink Verlag, 1979), pp. 75, 80, 84.

7. On this point, see in more detail: Gert Niers, *Frauen schreiben im Exil: Zum Werk der nach Amerika emigrierten Lyrikerinnen Margarete Kollisch, Ilse Blumenthal-Weiss und Vera Lachmann* (Frankfurt: Peter Lang, 1988).

8. "Das freie Wort" ["Free Speech"], *Aufbau*, 20 Nov. 1942.

9. See Kaléko's "Jom Kippur" ["Yom Kippur"], "Enkel Hiobs" [Job's Progeny"], "Nachtgedanken" ["Night Thoughts"]; Blumenthal-Weiss's "Heimkehr aus dem Konzentrationslager" ["Return from the Concentration Camp"], "Displaced Persons," "Unbewältigte Vergangenheit" ["We're Yet to Come to Terms with the Past"], "Gebet" ["Prayer"], "Anweisungen" ["Advice"]; Hilde Marx's "Nie Wieder" ["Never Again"], "Seelenfeier" ["All Souls"], "Ewiger Frühling" ["Eternal Spring"], "Gedanken in Dachau" [Thoughts in Dachau"]; Gertrude Urzidil's "Worte des Andenkens" [Words of Remembrance"], "Jüdisches Schicksal" ["Jewish Fate"]; Anna Krommer's "Jüdischer Friedhof" ["Jewish Cemetery"]; Erika Guetermann's "An der Klagemauer des Tempels" [At the Temple's Wailing Wall"]; Rose Ausländer's "Wiederkäuer" ["Ruminators"];

Maria Berl-Lee's "Der Mohn" ["Poppies"]; Margarete Voss's "Suchanzeige" ["Missing"].

10. On language trauma, see for example the statements made by immigrants and cited in Claudia Schoppmann, *Im Fluchtgepäck die Sprache: Deutschsprachige Schriftstellerinnen im Exil* (Frankfurt: Fischer, 1995), pp. 11–37.

11. Helmut Braun, Afterword, in Rose Ausländer, *The Forbidden Tree: Englische Gedichte* (Frankfurt: Fischer, 1995), pp. 261–63.

12. *Aufbau*, 12 Dec. 1947.

13. See, for example, Erika Guetermann, "Frühling an der Battery" ["Spring at the Battery"]; Gertrude Urzidil, "Zinhaus tief in Queens" ["Apartment House Deep in Queens"]; Hilde Marx, "Meinem Nachbarn im Roominghouse" ["To My Rooming-House Neighbor"]; Mascha Kaléko, "New York, Ende Dezember" ["New York at the End of December"].

14. *Aufbau*, 1 Dec. 1978.

15. *Aufbau*, 16 Feb. 1990.

16. From her poem "Refugium" ["Refuge"], *Aufbau*, 28 Sept. 1978.

17. "Abendweihe" ["Evensong"], *Aufbau*, 22 Sept. 1961.

18. "Immigranten-Frühling" ["Immigrant Spring"], *Aufbau*, 26 April 1940.

19. *Aufbau*, 1 Feb. 1974.

20. *Aufbau*, 20 Sept. 1963.

21. On this point, see also Christine Backhaus-Lautenschläger, *Und standen ihre Frau: Das Schicksal deutscher Emmigrantinnen in den USA nach 1933* (Pfaffen-weiler: Centaurus, 1991), pp. 207–18.

22. Mascha Kaléko, *In meinen Träumen läutet es Sturm; Gedichte und Epigramme aus dem Nachlass*, ed. Gisela Zoch-Westphal (Munich: Deutscher Taschenbuch-verlag, 1977), p. 48.

23. The poem was published posthumously, see n22.

CHAPTER SIX

Mordecai and Haman:
The Drama of Welsh America

▓ ESTHER WHITFIELD

Henry M. Edwards wrote *The Sacred Drama of Mordecai and Haman*, about the savior and the arch-enemy of the Jews exiled in Persia, five years after his emigration from Wales to the United States.[1] The challenges of creating a new homeland touched his life, his work, and the philosophy which he developed over the years for himself and for his compatriots. After leaving Blackwood, Monmouthshire, he and his family stayed briefly in Carbondale, Pennsylvania, and then laid down new roots in neighboring Scranton in 1864. This town especially became home to migrants from all over Europe seeking a better life in the rapidly expanding America of the second half of the nineteenth century, ready as they were to try their luck in the area's many coal mines and, as time went on, in the social apparatus growing up around these. Edwards remembered being drawn toward his own American dream, which he described for readers of *The Druid* (newspaper) in 1909: "Following the impulse stirring within me, conviction came that America was the land of the greatest Opportunity (a big O, please)."[2]

Among the different national communities which clustered in Scranton, the Welsh was one of the more economically successful, and also one of the more colorful inside and outside the workplace. Many Welshmen arrived as skilled miners and thus were more valued than their fellow Europeans; this appreciation bred among them an entrepreneurial spirit, so that by the end of the century they had built up a well-oiled infrastructure of banks, services and newspapers for an affluent second generation.[3] Henry M. Edwards had carved out a comfortable niche in this society, becoming one of its most active and distinguished members. Soon after his arrival he em-

93

barked upon what was to be a lifelong interest in journalism, which served him well as he sought a medium for his formulations of an emerging Welsh-American identity. In addition to commenting on local affairs, Edwards developed expertise in legal matters, and in 1892 he was nominated by the local Republican faction for a place on the bench of Lackawanna County, where he served unopposed until 1923. He had by that time become a legendary figure in local politics, and one of the longest-serving judges in the country.

While the Judge undoubtedly made his mark on the legal and administrative institutions of Scranton during their formative years, he had a second public face which was known and loved just as well around the city. To many, Judge Edwards was the unofficial guardian of a very precious patrimony, the "Welshness" of his compatriots. He was a figurehead for the Welsh community, "the 'éminence grise' behind most Welsh cultural activity in Scranton in the late nineteenth and early twentieth centuries," as William D. Jones describes him, and, moreover, a deep and careful thinker on the identity and integration of the Welsh in the United States.[4] The Judge's personal views on education and ambition mirrored and indeed directed the course of the Welsh community in Scranton. Welsh language and culture ought to be known and respected, yes, but as much for being an asset in the enterprise of becoming American as for their bonds with the old country. The first installments of the Judge's memoirs in the newspaper *The Druid* in 1909 read like a manual for getting ahead, respectably, in the United States, peppered as they are with tributes to learning, opportunity, and success.

The Welsh community underpinned its economic success with an intricate network of religious and cultural institutions, many transplanted directly from Wales. At the root of the community were its churches — the Congregationalist, the Baptist, and the Calvinistic Methodist — and these created an institutional framework within which the Welsh could preserve the language and traditions of their home country. For they, like other immigrant communities in Scranton and elsewhere, were afraid of losing their heritage in their new context, and clung to it with remarkable tenacity. In the 1860s and 1870s, the decades which Judge Edwards remembered as the most passionately Welsh in Scranton's history, the city hummed with the sounds of Bible school classes, singing groups, and the hundreds-strong choirs which brought international acclaim to the Welsh of America. Debates, literary meetings, and concerts were scheduled regularly and were enlivened by the inspired participation of much of the community, speaking and singing in the language of Wales. The Judge records in *The Druid* that during that period Scranton was known as "the Welsh Athens of America."[5] At the same time, to thousands of incoming Welshmen, it was "another Wales."[6]

THE EISTEDDFOD

Nowhere was the interaction of Welsh and American cultures staged more dramatically than in the Eisteddfod, a Welsh celebration whose origins are uncertain, although the word is derived from the verb *eistedd*, meaning "to sit," and the practice already had something of a history when Lord Rhys of Deheubarth hosted a gathering of bards and minstrels at Cardigan Castle, in west Wales, on Christmas Day of 1176.[7] It was at an Eisteddfod held in aid of the Welsh Baptist Church of Providence, Pennsylvania, that *The Sacred Drama of Mordecai and Haman* came before the public on 17 March 1869, just as the festival was beginning to gain ground in the United States. The Eisteddfod had been in steady decline throughout the seventeenth and eighteenth centuries, but in the late 1800s a large-scale revival began. This was set under way, interestingly, by a society based outside Wales, the London Gwyneddygion. In 1792, Iolo Morgannwg introduced the Gorsedd of the Bards, a deeply ceremonial assembly of poets and bards whose rituals were integrated into Eisteddfod pageantry in 1858, and argued successfully for a freer metric code for the long poem than the one that had been in force since the sixteenth century.[8] In 1861, in response to a number of factors — among them the internal debate over literary standards, the crippling blow dealt to the Welsh language by the government's "Blue Books" report on Welsh education, and, as E. G. Hartmann has suggested, the increasing national consciousness brought about by intense emigration — a National Eisteddfod was established.[9] From 1880 on, it was organized by a national association. The event is held annually in different Welsh towns to this day, and continues to be the foremost celebration of Welsh culture.

Efforts to transport the Eisteddfod to the United States were boosted by its full revival at home by the time Welshmen began to cross the Atlantic in unprecedentedly large numbers. This eased its passage to the status of tradition, to the misty realms of nostalgia which it in fact reached rather prematurely. Beginning in the 1860s, the Eisteddfod made appearances all over the United States, and it soon became the sine qua non of every self-respecting Welsh community. The Scranton area, already "the Welsh Athens of America" and home to a number of bards when Edwards arrived there, was the natural venue for many Eisteddfodau, but the festival also took root in New York, Ohio, and Colorado. The Denver Eisteddfod of 1897 prompted Edwards's reflection that "With the Westward stride of emigration and civilization the Welshman went along . . . Wherever he went, he was, as a general rule, on the side of industry, honesty, morality and religion; and, if he was in any place in sufficient numbers, he held an Eisteddfod. Hence, I have found many an excellent Eisteddfod held in the Western States."[10]

Among the most important of the Eisteddfodau, both for Edwards and in a broader American context, were two: one held in Hyde Park, Scranton, in 1875, and the other at the Chicago World's Fair in 1893. The Hyde Park Eisteddfod was heralded as the country's first "National Eisteddfod" — "national" for the first time referring to the United States and not to Wales. It was at this gathering that Governor Hartanft of Pennsylvania addressed his predominantly Welsh-origin audience with words which must have been music to their ears, even amidst the accomplished performances they had heard that day: "Welshmen have shown that while they adhere to the traditions and customs of their native land, they are not insensible to the claims of their adopted country, and in the hour of peril their blood and their lives have been freely given in her service."[11]

The Chicago World's Fair Eisteddfod, staged for four days during the Columbian Exposition, brought 40,000 Welshmen from far and wide, many directly from Wales despite the Welsh National Eisteddfod's having refused an invitation to move its event to the United States for that year. The Gorsedd ceremony was performed for the first time outside Wales and was presided over by Archdruid Hwfa Môn of the Welsh Gorsedd, who, in the words of Judge Edwards, imbued the event with a peculiar magic, for "he seemed to belong to an ancient order of things."[12] The Eisteddfod counted among its guests from Wales several adjudicators, a cluster of choirs, and an enthusiastic audience, although just as significant in terms of the festival's fate in the United States were the numbers of Americans, new and long-established, who made their way to the Welsh pavilion to see for themselves the culture which they were to influence irrevocably.[13]

While the Victorian Eisteddfod in Wales retained enough of its literary heritage to steer a course towards a far more aesthetically rigorous twentieth-century version, in the United States the choral cavalcade triumphed. In Edwards's heyday, the musical numbers were applauded the most enthusiastically, but the Chairing of the Bard and the principal poetic competitions were still in force. As the decades wore on, however, and as Wales became an increasingly distant memory for her children and grandchildren, the Eisteddfod became a musical affair, crystallizing in the 1920s into the hearty hymn-singing gathering known as the Cymanfa Ganu.[14] This trend was already in full swing when *The Druid* began publishing Edwards's reminiscences. The differences between the Eisteddfod as it had been practiced in Wales and the form which developed in the United States were of great interest to him in his de facto capacity as an authority on Welsh-American culture, for they encapsulated the changes which the Welsh population was undergoing as it acclimatized to American society.

The Welsh language underwent a rapid decline in the United States after the mid-nineteenth century. This was accompanied — and largely caused — by a concerted Welsh endeavor to prosper and integrate. These were precisely the goals which H. M. Edwards signaled, and most certainly encouraged, in his discussion of the Eisteddfod in America. He noted the entrepreneurial popularization of the festival: "The masses of Welsh people in Wales and the United States have taken the Eisteddfod into their own hands; whereas, a century and less ago, the Eisteddfod was held mainly for the benefit of scholars, antiquarians and the Welsh literati generally."[15] To his mind this was a means of flaunting and, indeed, selling the Welsh culture. The purpose of the 1902 Scranton Eisteddfod, with which he was closely associated, was "to exhibit to the people, particularly the English-speaking people, an ideal Eisteddfod" and, more firmly, "to Americanize the old institution."[16] The paradox of this endeavor, as William D. Jones has shown, was that the more the festivals and traditions were opened to the community as a whole, the weaker the Welsh content became. English being the lingua franca of Scranton's many ethnic groups, and success as an American being the common dream, the cultural heritage of Wales eventually transformed far beyond its original shape, giving way to a distinctly American brand of Welshness.

The decline of the Welsh character of the Eisteddfod certainly caused the Judge some sadness, but this was primarily intellectual, for while he maintained that "it would be a calamity to allow the iconoclastic tendencies of the twentieth century to destroy the Eisteddfodic tradition of the fathers and to obliterate the historic identity of the institution," he more than anyone was at pains to expose the festival to the country at large. Nor was the gradual dilution of the Welsh language a cause of unequivocal regret to him, despite his being one of its most eloquent speakers and the most vocal champion of its arts. Making the quite accurate predictions, in 1909, that "it is safe to say that fifteen years hence there will be very little Welsh spoken" in Scranton, and that "the all-conquering Anglo-Saxon tongue will prevail universally," he concluded that "this will be as it should be." He was convinced that the richness of the Welsh language was self-perpetuating, "the glory of a language and a people that have existed for so many centuries will continue to live in poetry and song for centuries yet to come, although sung in another tongue."[17] The fact remains, though, that adaptation was a priority for Edwards, and linguistic and cultural patrimony were not to be preserved for their own, nostalgia-driven sake.

The educator, the entrepreneur, and the public man in Edwards were destined to triumph over the sentimentalist; it was ultimately far more important to him that Welsh culture should play a determining role in the United States than that it should be preserved intact. Thus it was not only with Judge Edwards's blessing, but with his active encouragement, that the Eisteddfod was to come into twentieth-century America in a hugely compromised and eventually barely recognizable form. For the Judge there was no tension between Welsh and American loyalties; rather, the Welsh of America were to place their birthright in the service of their American aspirations. Remembering the Welsh of Utica, New York, whose descendants, "well-dressed, and bearing the marks of prosperity and culture, constitute a high type of American citizenship," Edwards commended their ability to "preserve the Welsh language and to foster the Welsh spirit, without impairing in any way their obligations to their adopted country."[18] With similar negotiating skills, Edwards lived as both a passionate participant in Welsh cultural affairs, and as a wealthy, successful, and much-admired Pennsylvanian judge who coined — and, indeed, incarnated — the term "Welsh-American."

THE STORY OF MORDECAI AND HAMAN

"Mordecai and Haman" was set as the subject for the Dramatic Poem, in free verse, at the 1869 Providence Eisteddfod. This was very much a subject of its time, for drama in nineteenth-century Wales was firmly under the rein of the Church.[19] This particular story, from the Book of Esther, has had considerable currency in Welsh literature: in the year of Edwards's emigration, Glan Alun, a popular preacher and playwright, published a drama entitled *Esther,* and in the following decades a number of smaller works appeared on this same subject, including an operetta by James Davies and J. J. Williams and a play by the journalist and author Beriah Gwynfe Evans.[20] The twentieth century has seen the highly acclaimed screenplay *Esther* (1965) by Saunders Lewis, the foremost Welsh playwright of his time and a founding member of Plaid Cymru, the Welsh National Party. Saunders Lewis's *Esther* is a strong political allegory of the struggle for the Welsh language, and Edwards's play, too, has some bearing upon the particular sociopolitical situation of the Welsh in America. At the same time, however, its style, its subject, and the circumstances of its writing give it a place in a long-established tradition.

Jean Racine claimed to have found inspiration for his *Esther* (1689) in "the great truths of the Scriptures, and the sublime manner in which they are pronounced."[21] He set out to make his characters noble, their sentiments pure, and their language in keeping with the deep tragedy in which the story is steeped. Edwards's play has no classical pretensions, but it does aspire to a certain grandeur of style and expression. It has five acts and is written in free verse, the rhyme structure and syllable count varying between scenes but not within them, except at two moments of high tension: in the second act, when Mordecai prays (2:2, 91–114), and throughout the fourth act, when Haman is seized by anger. The most "sublime" characters of *Mordecai and Haman* are raised to celestial heights by elegant figures of speech worthy of the most tragic heroes and heroines. Queen Vashti's beauty is such that "Near her the stars above / Blush and conceal their faces"(1:1, 61–72); and Queen Esther is "Like a sweet moon guiding the heavenly stars"(2:2, 69–70). Evil is of a comparable order; endowed with superhuman magnitude, it too draws its images from nature and the elements. As Bigthan and Theresh plot to kill the king, like Shakespeare's Macbeth they associate murder with a huge bird whose shadow eclipses the world:[22]

> Mae'r nos yn lledu ei hesgyll duon dros
> Ein daear; dwfn ddystawrwydd fel y bedd
> Sydd yn teyrnasu. (3:1, 1–3)
>
> [Night is spreading her blackened wings over
> Our earth; silence, deep as the darkest grave
> Reigns over us.]

Line by line this play picks up echoes of earlier tragedies, and in so doing it works its way into a tradition greater than that within which it was ostensibly written, namely that of the Welsh Eisteddfod. Edwards pays homage not only to his historical sources but to his literary masters, to the great poets and playwrights of his past, to Shakespeare and Racine as well as to the long line of Welsh bards — with whom, upon winning an Eisteddfod Chair, he gained an almost filial relationship. In taking from all of these in order to appeal to the Eisteddfod, Edwards seeks to open his audience's ears to worlds beyond their specifically Welsh-American one, and to forge links between his contemporaries and peoples of earlier times and places.

Despite such gestures toward the past, Edwards makes his own mark, and that of his generation, on the story of Mordecai and Haman. He does so principally in terms of the plot. In it Mordecai, a Jew in exile in Persia, encourages his niece Esther to marry the country's King Ahasuerus after Queen Vashti has been banished for disobedience, and Esther does win the throne. One day Mordecai overhears two of the king's servants, Bigthan and Theresh, plotting to kill their master, and he speaks out to prevent this treason. Haman, the king's right-hand man who bears a grudge against Mordecai, then seeks and obtains royal approval for his plan to exterminate all the Jews in Persia. Mordecai persuades Esther to beg for her husband's mercy, at great peril to herself, for this means both appearing unsolicited before the king and revealing to him that she is Jewish. The bravery of both Mordecai and Esther is finally rewarded: Ahasuerus remembers Mordecai's loyalty and bestows upon him all Haman's political power. Haman, meanwhile, is condemned to the fate which he had planned for the Jew he hated, and goes to the gallows.

Edwards declares, in his Foreword, that his sources are primarily "the Canonical account," namely the Bible's Book of Esther and the chronicles of the Roman-Jewish historian Flavius Josephus, whose work includes "a number of interesting facts not recorded in the Book of Esther, but which are of the same importance, to the historian and the poet, as they would be had they been chronicled by the pen of the inspired scribe." Edwards claims to be faithful to his sources, and attributes any deviation to narrative necessity: "I draw on my imagination," he insists, "no further than to fill in a gap here and there in the cohesion of events." As is perhaps to be expected from such a profession of innocence, this "filling in" takes on considerable importance in *The Sacred Drama of Mordecai and Haman.*

Three moments stand out as the fruits of Edwards's imagination. The most substantial of these is Hegai's performance in the second act. Hegai is mentioned almost in passing in the Bible, as "keeper of the women," and not at all in the chronicles of Josephus.[23] In contrast, readers of Edwards's dramatic poem are treated to joke after bawdy joke, thirty lines of comic relief to dissipate the gravity of Mordecai's prayers and Esther's promises in the preceding scene. Hegai takes it upon himself not only to guard but also to verbally dissect each of the prospective brides who have sought to replace the disgraced Queen Vashti in the king's affections. The keeper is merciless, and until the arrival of Esther no candidate escapes the malice of his tongue:

Mae hon yn cael ei chyfrif yn ei chartre'
Fel seren wen y nos, neu haul y bore
Os gwir yw hyn, na foed i seren wenu
A pheidied haul y nefoedd a thywynu. (2:2, 8–12)

[This maiden is considered in her hometown
The whitest star of night, or the morning sun.
If this be true, let no star be seen smiling
Let the sun there in the heavens cease to shine.]

Of another unfortunate lady, he recalls that:

a'i thrwyn yn esgyn rhwng ei gruddiau,
fel yr ymddyrcha un o byramidiau
Yr Aipht i'r nen o ganol y gwastadedd? (2:2, 19–21)

[from between her cheeks
her nose arose, as pyramids in Egypt
Rise to heaven from the middle of the plain.]

It is striking that this rather vulgar and ungenerous character should have recourse to the figurative language of the nobler characters, and that his demeaning portrayals should draw from a similar store of images, namely the heavens, the sun, and the stars. The blatantly disrespectful use of this otherwise solemn language introduces a note of irony, subtly undermining the play's lofty pretensions. At the same time, the entire scene represents a "filling-in" of the story, and with his jokes Hegai undoubtedly sows the seeds of a break with the past. Admittedly, it is with the strictly historical sources — with the Bible and the writings of Josephus — that Hegai makes the cleanest break; the figure of the comic gatekeeper has a number of theatrical precursors, not least among them the drunken "porter of hell-gate" who guards the ramparts of *Macbeth*'s Dunsinane.[24]

A second supplement to the historical sources is the far more prominent, almost symbolic, role of Queen Vashti in *Mordecai a Haman*. The first two scenes of Edwards's play set King Ahasuerus and his queen in direct opposition to one another, in what is a perfectly overt confrontation between the two sexes. *Mordecai a Haman* opens with a rowdy banquet at which the king and his noblemen drink to good wine, food, and military glory and decide, eventually, that to complete their happiness they are in need of a beautiful woman. Thereupon the king sends for Vashti, and the scene gives way to another banquet, a mirror image of the first but attended, this time, by the queen and her ladies in waiting. Their express intention here, unlike in the Bible and the histories of Josephus where the queen wants to celebrate her husband's territorial conquests, is to rival the men's revelry:

> Mae'r brenin gyda'i luoedd tywysogion
> Yn chwareu uwch eu gwin mewn llonder calon
> Eu henaid sydd yn amlwg ar eu gwefus
> A'u nefoedd gant mewn asbri rhydd a nwyfus
> Os ydynt hwy yn sugno eu hyfrydwch
> O gwpan aur, dan lewyrchiadau harddwch
> Paham nad allwn ninau hefyd ymddifyru
> A chwerthin ar y gwin pan fo yn gwenu?   (1:2, 5–12)

> [The king is ever with his hosts of princes,
> Playing, drinking wine, to their hearts' content;
> Their souls upon their lips displayed quite clearly,
> They find a heaven in this lively mischief.
> If they can thus imbibe so great a pleasure
> From a golden cup, in the glare of beauty,
> Then why cannot we, too, seek entertainment
> And laughter in the wine which smiles upon us?]

When she is summoned, Queen Vashti will not agree to appear before the king; and for this she is banished. In Josephus's account, the queen bases her refusal on a Persian law which prohibits royal wives from being seen by strangers; the Bible gives no reason for this disobedience. In *Mordecai and Haman*, however, although Vashti cites the country's law, she acts expressly in the name of women. She weighs her love for her husband and her duty to the crown against the honor of her sex, for which, she claims, she is willing to die. It is in a spirit of struggle and self-sacrifice that she faces her fate, knowing that she will be banished for choosing to take this path:

Pa beth a wnaf? Mae'm calon yn anwylo
Y brenin, ac nis gallaf wrthod iddo
Ufudd-dod ym mhob peth sydd yn rhesymol —
Mae ufuddhau i reswm yn naturiol;
Ond er mor gryfed ydyw cariad calon
Ac er mor barod wyf i'w holl orch'mynion
I dalu y warogaeth angenrheidiol
Mi fyddaf dros fy rhyw yn ddewr a gwrol;
Am hyny, at y brenin dos, Harbona,
A dywed nad yw uchel gyfraith Persia,
Yn caniatau i wraig y brenin ddangos
Ei hun o flaen dyeithriaid f'ont yn aros
Yn y brenhindy; gwell f'ai genyf farw
Nas dwyn fy hun i'r fath ddirmygawl sylw.   (1:2, 5–12)

[What will I do? For in my heart I cherish
The king, and it is not right to refuse him
Obedience in all reasonable matters —
It is most natural to obey reason;
But however strong the love within my heart,
However ready I may be to render
The homage due to each command he utters,
I will now, for my sex, be brave and fearless
For this reason, go to the king, Harbona,
And tell him that the highest law of Persia
Does not permit the king's wife to exhibit
Herself before strangers, though they be the guests
Of the king's palace; I would prefer to die
Than bring myself before such scornful audience.]

It is significant that Queen Vashti should underpin her challenge to the king, and to the demands made upon her solely because she is a beautiful woman, with the word *gwrol.* I have translated this as "fearless," as this had been its principal use for some time prior to the publication of *Mordecai a Haman,* but like the Latin *virtus, virtutis,* it is a word whose direct root is in the noun for "man," in this case the Welsh *gwr.*[25] Even in its more general usage, *gwrol* retains heavily masculine connotations; it describes, for example, warriors in the national anthem which was written just a decade be-fore Edwards's emigration.[26] Indeed, throughout this play the word betrays an underlying sexual tension. In the first scene the king, anticipating the appetite which will make him seek out Vashti, talks of wine as a fortifier of men, as the charm which makes them "gwrol": "Ei ddirgel-dreiddiol rin / A wna y gwan yn wrol" [Its deep and piercing charm / Makes the weak man fearless] (1:1, 49). The same word is used later by another woman and man who, in terms of the plot, are in direct opposition to each other. Esther vows to be *gwrol* in her bid for the throne; she tells Hegai she is "yn ofnus, eto'n wrol" [fearful, but yet brave] (2:2, 39). Haman, over whom Esther finally triumphs, attributes his former rise to power to this same fearless-ness: "Ond enill wneuthym I drwy ddal yn wrol" [But I won with fearless perseverance] (4:1, 24). In a strange twist to the story, then, Vashti shows her allegiance to women by being "manly," and it is by taking a similar stance that Esther is able to save her people.

One of the more dramatic departures from the story as it had previously been told is in the ending of *Mordecai a Haman*. Both the Book of Esther and the chronicles of Josephus recount in detail the celebrations which fol-lowed Haman's defeat and gave rise to the Jewish festival of Purim. The Book of Esther closes with an account of the Jews' revenge on Haman's family, and an exhortation that the suffering and salvation of this people be remembered: "And that those days should be remembered, and ob-served throughout all generations, and all families, and all states too, and all cities: so that the days of Purim shall not cease amongst the Jews, and that there shall be no end to their commemoration amongst their off-spring" (Esther IX, v. 28).[27] Josephus, too, insists upon the lasting legacy of this story to the Jewish people: "Mordecai also wrote to those Jews that lived in the kingdom of Artaxerxes [Ahasuerus] to observe those days, and celebrate them as festivals, and to deliver them down to posterity, that this festival might continue for all time to come, and that it might never be bur-ied in oblivion, for since they were about to be destroyed on these days by Haman, they would do a right thing, upon escaping the danger in them, and on them inflicting punishments on their enemies, to observe those days, and give thanks to God on them; for which cause the Jews still keep the aforementioned days, and call them days of Phurim [or Purim]."[28]

Mordecai and Haman, in contrast, brings the story to a rather abrupt end, making no mention of either Purim or the central importance of Esther's story to the history of the Jewish people. No sooner has Haman been disclosed as a traitor and condemned to death than the king closes the play with a political honor for Mordecai, and a royal blessing upon his name. He addresses these words to Queen Esther:

> Y cyfan fydd, yn un
> A'th gais, a Mordecai dy gâr a gaiff
> Ddyrchafiad yn y llys; efe a fydd
> Yn ail yn y Llywodraeth; trwy y wlad
> Ei glod a genir tra bo tonau'r môr
> Yn arllwys ei cyfrinion ar y traeth. (5:6, 71–76)

> [All of this shall be
> As you ask, and Mordecai your kinsman
> Will be advanced in court; soon he will be
> Second in my Government; through the land
> His praises will be sung, for as long as
> The waves pour out their secrets on the shore]

In ending thus Edwards effectively strips Mordecai and Haman's story of its Jewishness. Not only is the story's place in posterity secondary to the more immediate prospect of Mordecai's promotion in court; in heaping all honor on Mordecai and on Mordecai alone, the playwright manages to sidestep the omnipotence of God (to which Mordecai, at least, attributes the outcome of this episode), and omits the fact that the "praises" of the closing lines will be sung by Mordecai's descendants, the Jews. The tremendous symbolic significance of this story to Judaism, articulated as clearly in the Bible as in the histories of Flavius Josephus, is silenced, simply set aside, in *Mordecai and Haman.*

A STORY OF TRANSLATION

Edwards's imaginative "filling in of gaps" in his sources — or, in the case of Purim, his omission — modernizes the story of Mordecai and Haman for his American Eisteddfod-goer. Hegai, the comic character, was certain to cut a popular figure amongst the large, loud, and increasingly less sophisticated crowds that were beginning to dictate the course of the Eisteddfod in the United States. In a similar vein, the curiously male voice assumed by Vashti, and later by Esther, might well have curried favor with the Welsh women of Scranton, who were securing for themselves an ever more active position in their community and in the Eisteddfod. The *Scranton Republican* reported that most of the participants in the 1875 Eisteddfod were women.[29] In 1905, moreover, the town witnessed a strange reenactment of the opening scenes of *Mordecai a Haman* when, in angry response to an all-male banquet hosted by the Cymmrodorion Society, a "Daughters of Gwalia" committee was formed to prepare a rival feast.[30]

The play's abrupt ending, too, demonstrates a certain sensitivity to the religious climate of Edwards's Scranton. By underplaying the importance which the Old Testament gives to this account of Jewish salvation, and by explicitly omitting to mention Purim, Edwards would have rendered his work especially palatable to the Baptist, Congregationalist, and Calvinist Methodist churches whose worship was firmly grounded in the New Testament. The churches, as the mainstay of Welsh cultural life in Scranton, had unofficial representatives on the adjudicating committee of every Eisteddfod, and congregations whose numbers were depended upon to fill the performance halls; it was certainly in each competitor's interest to bear this in mind when presenting a piece for the Eisteddfod.

Mordecai and Haman's subtle deviations from previous versions of the story shape the play, and not only this current English rendition of it, as a translation in a very broad sense: Edwards rewrites an old story in a new language and a new context, making certain changes to facilitate the understanding of his particular audience but retaining as he sees fit the wealth of his sources. The drama of Mordecai and Haman had passed from age to age, through geographical translocations and linguistic transmutations, before it reached this playwright in his Welsh enclave of nineteenth-century Scranton, and Edwards himself might have read from sources in a number of languages, amongst them Latin, Greek, Hebrew, English, and Welsh. The Mordecai and Haman story itself, from its earliest form, embodies similar processes of migration and resettlement as the Jews sought to make a new home in Persia. It is, then, not only a story which has undergone innumerable translations, but one spawned from the act of translation. Written against a background of intense expatriation and readjustment, and amidst very real threats to the survival of the Welsh language, *Mordecai and Haman* owes much of its creative force to its negotiation between the past and the present, between the weight of tradition and the impulse towards self-definition.

It is a singular achievement of Edwards's work that the processes of translation through which the Mordecai and Haman story has been kept alive should be brought together, in all their irreducibility, by one word: *cenedl.* Each time I came across this word in my own efforts to translate the drama, it brought me to a standstill. The word lends itself to any number of meanings, the lowest common denominator of these being merely some sense of grouping, of belonging to an entity greater than oneself. In *Mordecai and Haman,* in this story in which the notion of collective identity plays so great a part, *cenedl* serves as an all-embracing but resolutely nonspecific term; insofar as identities are formed and reformed through translations, then *cenedl* acts as a force which orders signification but, perhaps for this reason, resists being translated itself. The University of Wales Dictionary offers an eclectic and almost impossibly broad range of English approximations for the word: "nation; tribe, clan, kindred; generation; *bibl.* gentile; Norsemen; sort, species, kind, sex; gender; voice of a verb." The Dictionary provides a longer description in Welsh:

> (a) Cymdeithas o bobl yn byw fel rheol dan yr un llywodraeth mewn gwlad arbennig ac a gysylltir ynghyd yn aml gan undod hanes a thraddodiad ac iaith, nasiwn; *Cyfr.* llwyth, gwelygordd, tylwyth neu deulu hyd at y nawfed ach; cenhedlaeth; *Beibl.* (yn y ff. *Cenhedloedd*) pobl heb fod yn Iddewon; gwyr Llychlyn; rhywogaeth, rhyw, math; (b) *Gram.* Rhyw enw neu rhagenw neu ansoddair; ystad (am ferf).

> [(a) A community of people living as a rule under the same government in a particular country and which is bound together often by a unity of history and tradition and language, nation; *Law.* tribe, stock, kindred or family up to the ninth remove; generation; *Bible* (in the plural

Cenhedloedd) people who are not Jews; men of Scandinavia; species, sex, kind; (b) *Gram.* Gender of a noun or pronoun or adjective; state (i.e. voice) of a verb.][31]

Cenedl is derived from the Greek [genethli], which has a similar, if somewhat less evolved, definition as "a family in the widest sense."[32] The Welsh word has, quite fittingly, come into being through a process of translation and supplementation. The breadth of meaning to which the Welsh word has opened out is demonstrated by the usage of the plural form, "cenedloedd," to denote "Gentiles," whereas throughout *Mordecai a Haman,* and very often in the Welsh Bible, it refers to Jews. This lack of discrimination between one group and its opposite reveals at its starkest the mockery which *cenedl* makes of specificity of meaning. In this connection it is imperative to note that for each of the Dictionary's English suggestions, with the exception of the grammatical terms, there is at least one possible alternative to *cenedl.* This word simply does not enter into relationships of equivalence with other words. Rather, it gathers into its vast orbit specific meanings which have in common a deeper, more general sense of belonging to a group. It is in this sense that the word is evoked each time it is uttered in *Mordecai a Haman,* and this is what gives a peculiar depth to the work.

The first instance of *cenedl* is in Mordecai's prayer for Esther's quest to become queen, and he uses the word again at the end of the play:

> Ein cenedl sydd yn gruddfan
> A'r estron yn ei fri;
> O Dduw! ein hunig amcan
> Yw codi'th enw di.   (2:1, 17)

> [Our [*cenedl*] is lamenting
> The foreigner is proud;
> O God! Our one ambition
> Is to exalt your name!]

> Fy nghares hoff — beth yw dy fywyd di
> Neu'm heiddo inau, i'w gymharu â
> Chadwraeth cenedl gyfan.   (5:2, 12–14)

> [My dearest kinswoman — what is your life?
> What are all our possessions, compared to
> Salvation of a [*cenedl*]]

In both scenes Mordecai is in the company of his niece, and his use of *cenedl* reiterates their family bond, such that "kin" and "generation" are appropriate translations. When Mordecai's words are addressed to God, "race" and "faith" also come to mind, as what Eve Sedgwick, in her discussion of Esther's "closeting" of her Jewishness, calls "ethnic/cultural/religious" terms.[33] Mordecai's opposition of his *cenedl* to the "foreigner" suggests, too, a political translation, such as "nation." "People" does cover these meanings to some extent, although it lacks the emotive force of *cenedl*.

Haman, Mordecai's adversary, speaks twice of *cenedl* when he is trying to turn the king against the Jews:

> O, ardderchocaf frenin! Yn dy deyrnas
> Mae cenedl sydd yn warthrudd i dy urddas. (4:2, 1–2)

> [Oh, most illustrious sovereign! In your kingdom
> There is a race which disgraces your honor]

> Nyni — y Persiaid, alwant yn estroniaid
> Oherwydd fod eu cenedl hwy'n *Hebreaid!* (4:2, 11–12)

> [And we, the Persians, they have named foreigners
> Because their [*cenedl*] is of the *Hebrew* people.]

Haman's wife, Zeres, utters *cenedl* in the same murderous tones:

> Boed Mordecai rhwng nef a llawr yn warth
> genedl, ac yn brawf fod urddas un
> O weis y brenin yn teilyngu parch. (5:4, 34-36)

> [Let Mordecai, between earth and heaven,
> Pour shame upon his [*cenedl*], prove that the honor
> Of a royal servant commands respect.

In all three instances, the term invokes the Jews as enemies; here, they are a community to be destroyed. "Nation," in this context, seems too empowering a translation. Race might be more appropriate as its charge is less narrowly political, and although it spans less semantic ground, it does wield much of the symbolic force of *cenedl*. Anthony Appiah, in his essay "The Uncompleted Argument: Du Bois and the Illusion of Race," proposes that W. E. B. Du Bois raised "race" to extraordinary heights by defining it as "a vast family of human beings, generally of common blood and language, always of common history, traditions and impulse"; he was, however doomed by the abstract singular's having broken up into a plurality of "races," each claiming its own quite specific grounds for difference.[34] This dual function, as both mode of signification and meaning, or as both connotation and denotation, is the downfall of "race," for as Appiah concludes, "The truth is that there are no races: there is nothing in the world that can do all we ask 'race' to do for us."[35] For this very reason, the attempt to delimit a meaning for *cenedl* is bound to be frustrated, for its power lies in its presiding over meanings.

An unnamed Jew, one of the small chorus who joins Mordecai in pleading for God's mercy following the king's order that the Jews be destroyed, uses *cenedl* in the plural *cenedloedd*:

UN O'R IDDEWON: A wnaethost furiau in' o donau'r môr; —
YR AIL: A foddaist ynddo y gelynol lu; —
YTRYDYDD: A droaist yr Iorddonen yn ei hol; —
Y PEDWERYDD: A leddaist y cenedloedd yn dy lid. (5:1, 16–19)

[ONE OF THE JEWS: You who made walls from the waves of the sea; —
THE SECOND JEW: And drowned in it our hosts of enemies; —
THE THIRD: And sent the River Jordan in their wake; —
THE FOURTH: And slaughtered [*cenedloedd*] in your wrath.]

Here, the translation "Gentiles" presents itself as the most likely, as it is the Jews' enemies who have been slaughtered. Strictly speaking, though, the term for "Gentiles" is a proper noun, *Y Genedloedd*, and here both capitalization and the definite article are omitted. The plural form in these strongly implies number, an implication which is not brought out particularly well in the translation "Gentiles"; "generations" gives a better sense of both the magnitude and the legacy of God's parting of the Red Sea. A compromise between these two terms would perhaps be "scores of gentiles."

Finally, Queen Esther implores her husband to save the Jews and to recognize their loyalty and monetary donations to the Persian crown. The Jews, she argues, have proved themselves capable of immense gratitude and support for a foreign authority even while retaining their difference from the rest of the population. *Cenedl* could here be translated as "people," as Esther is referring to the Jews as a social rather than religious or political group; nevertheless, this translation sacrifices much of the passion and fear which the queen's appeal carries:

> Nid oes — ni fu — ni ddaw, un genedl fwy
> Deyrngarol i'th Lywodraeth di na hon;
> Yn llanw'th goffrau mae ei threthi hi,
> Ac ychwanega at adnoddau'th wlad.   (5:6, 21–24)

> [There is — was not — will not be a [*cenedl*]
> More loyal to your government than this;
> It is their taxes which fill up your coffers
> Augmenting the resources of this land.]

Cenedl's momentous appearance — the one which bridges the distance between the work and its reader, between the ancient and the modern, and, indeed, between the Jews, the Welsh, and the Americans — is in the playwright's Foreword. As he shifts his gaze toward faraway Persia, these are Edwards's parting words to his readers:

> Os yn annheilwng o gefnogaeth, eheded yr adgof o hono i fro annghof; ond os cyfrifir ef, gan fy nghydgenedl, yn deilwng o goffawdwriaeth yn eu plith, bydd hyny yn ddigonol gydnabyddiaeth i'r AwDUR.

> [If it [this play] is unworthy of praise, then let the memory of it fly swiftly to the realms of oblivion, but if it should be esteemed by my [*cydgenedl*], worthy of record among them, then this will be acknowledgment enough for THE AUTHOR.]

The prefix "cyd" corresponds to the English "co-," or "fellow" and here binds the author more closely to what might be his nation, his race, his kin, or his generation. In Edwards's case these possible English translations suggest a number of distinct groups, among them the playwright's immediate family, the Welsh left behind in their country, and the American nation as a whole. As *Mordecai a Haman* was first presented at the Providence Eisteddfod, here it is most certainly an appeal to the nascent community of Welsh-Americans, to the men and women of Edwards's generation — in a loose sense, his kin — who with him cherished the language and traditions of Wales. The translations "countrymen" and "compatriots" retain a degree of ambiguity, but a plainly inadequate on. It cannot be unequivocally clear to whom Edwards is addressing his Foreword and his dramatic poem; nor, I think, would such clarity be at all in keeping with this work, for through the resolutely imprecise word *cenedl* it opens the bonds of community to indefinite breadths.

Mordecai a Haman [Mordecai and Haman] mimics the performance of *cenedl*. The work not only puts into play certain meanings to which the word has lent itself, but, more fundamentally, it reproduces the processes which lead to the construction of meaning and the formation of identities. By not naming directly the *cenedl* of his Foreword, and at the same time echoing there the most highly charged word of the whole play, Edwards conjures up a whole series of human ties — family ties, linguistic ties, national, racial, and religious ties. He invokes these very much as relations in themselves, unfettered by the restraints of a specific context, although it is only in lending themselves to such contexts that these relations can take on immediate significance. People — and, most particularly, displaced peoples — draw from this pool of relations in attempting to stabilize themselves as a community. *Cenedl*, as a word which balances many versions of belonging, is central to the experience of a people in formation, to individuals as they appeal to the ties that bind them together.

Edwards tests the strength of old ties in new surroundings by supplementing the Mordecai and Haman story with telltale traits of his own time and place. He introduces a comic gatekeeper, two "manly" queens, and an abrupt ending without Purim for the Welsh who were, when *Mordecai and Haman* first appeared, in the process of establishing themselves and shaping new lives in America. This audience was, however, inventing the Welsh-American in the company of thousands of other immigrants with a similar project — the Irish-Americans, the German-Americans, and the Polish-Americans, to name but a few of Edwards's fellow citizens — and *cenedl*, as a guiding and all-encompassing project, is what the new Americans being born to Scranton shared. In this work, Edwards offers his own *cyd-genedl* a degree of self-recognition by giving them a place in a number of old traditions, historical and literary, and also in a new America. Where better to herald this gift than at the Eisteddfod, the forum for celebration and anticipation, for a proud glance at the past and a strategic one toward the future? And what better medium for doing so than the endlessly translated and translocated story of Mordecai and Haman?

Notes

1. Henry M. Edwards, *Drama Gysegredig Mordecai a Haman* (Scranton: The Republican Press, 1869). All citations are from my own unpublished translation.

2. *The Druid* (Scranton, Pennsylvania), 7 Oct. 1909, p. 1.

3. William D. Jones, *Wales in America: Scranton and the Welsh, 1860–1920* (Cardiff: University of Wales Press, 1993) gives a thorough account and analysis of this period in Welsh-American history, to which I am greatly indebted for much of the factual detail of this introduction.

4. Jones, *Wales in America*, p. 87.

5. "Eisteddfodic Reminiscences," *The Druid*, 7 Oct. 1909.

6. *The Druid*, 21 Oct. 1909.

7. See Hywel Teifi Edwards, *The Eisteddfod* (Cardiff: University of Wales Press, 1990) for a short history of the Welsh Eisteddfod.

8. An account of Iolo Morgannwg's Gorsedd is given in Geraint Bowen, *Golwg ar Orsedd y Beirdd* (Cardiff: University of Wales Press, 1992); and, more briefly, in Meic Stephens, *The Oxford Companion to the Literature of Wales* (Oxford: Oxford University Press, 1986).

9. The "Blue Books," which were completed in 1847, blamed poor standards in schools and pupils' inability to speak English on the Welsh language and religious Nonconformity. On national consciousness of emigrants, see Edward

G. Hartmann, "The Eisteddfod, the Gorsedd, and the Gymanfa Ganu," ch. 7 of *Americans from Wales* (Boston: Christopher Publishing, 1967), pp. 139–155.

10. *The Druid,* 2 Dec. 1909.

11. Recorded in *The Druid,* 21 Oct. 1909.

12. *The Druid,* 11 Nov. 1909.

13. Hywel Teifi Edwards has devoted a book to the Chicago Eisteddfod and its implications for Welsh and American culture, *Eisteddfod Ffair y Byd: Chicago 1893* (Llandysul: Gwasg Gomer, 1990). See also Jones, *Wales in America,* ch. 4.

14. E. G. Hartmann chronicles this development in *Americans from Wales.*

15. *The Druid,* 17 Feb. 1910.

16. Ibid.

17. "Eisteddfodic Reminiscences," *The Druid,* 21 Oct. 1909.

18. *The Druid,* 27 Jan. 1910.

19. O. LLew Owain discusses this period in *Hanes y Ddrama yng Nghymru 1850– 1943* [A History of Drama in Wales 1850–1943]. (Liverpool: Gwasg y Brython, for Council of the National Eisteddfod, 1948).

20. Mentioned in an appendix to O. Llew Owain, *Hanes y Ddrama.*

21. In the preface to *Esther,* Racine writes of "les grandes vérités de l'Écriture, et la manière sublime dont elles y sont énoncées"; it is these qualities of the biblical story which persuade him to present his play, written for private performance by the young ladies of Saint-Cyr convent, before a public audience. Jean Racine, *Théatre Complet,* Vol. 2 (Paris: Garnier-Flammarion, 1965), p. 258.

22. Macbeth's words as he goes to kill Banquo are: "Light thickens, and the crow / Makes wing to the rooky wood; / Good things of day begin to droop and drowse, / While night's black agents to their preys do rouse." *Macbeth,* Act 3 Scene 3, 50–53.

23. Biblical references throughout this introduction are to the Welsh Holy Bible, *Y Beibl Cyssegr-Lan,* as first translated into Welsh in 1588 by Bishop William Morgan. This translation was in circulation in Wales and the United States throughout the nineteenth century, and it is still the most readily available. For the writings of Josephus, I have consulted *The Complete Works of Flavius Josephus,* trans. William Whiston (Chicago: Thompson & Thompson, 1901).

24. *Macbeth* Act 2 Scene 3, 1–42.

25. The University of Wales Dictionary, *Geiriadur Prifysgol Cymru* (Cardiff: University of Wales Press, 1965–), cites such usages of *gwrol* from as early as the thirteenth century.

26. The opening lines of the anthem, composed in 1856 by Evan and James James, are as follows: "Mae hen wlad fy nhadau yn annwyl i mi / Gwlad

beirdd a chantorion, enwogion o fri / Ei *gwrol* rhyfelwyr, gwladgarwyr tra mâd / Tros ryddid gollasant eu gwaed." An approximate translation would be: "The land of my fathers is dear to me / Land of bards, singers and scores of illustrious people / Her fearless warriors, her great patriots / For freedom they shed their blood."

27. My translation from the *Beibl Cyssegr-Lan:* "Ac y bydde y dyddiau hynny i'w cofio, ac i'w cynnal drwy bob cenhedlaeth, a phob teulu, pob talaith hefyd, a phob dinas: sef na phalle y dyddiau Pwrim hynny o fysc yr Iddewon, ac na ddarfydde eu coffadwriaeth hwynt o blith eu hâd."

28. *The Complete Works of Flavius Josephus,* book XI, ch. 6, p. 13.

29. Scranton *Weekly Republican,* 22 Sept. 1875; cited in Jones, *Wales in America,* p. 102.

30. Recounted by Jones, *Wales in America,* pp. 116–117.

31. *Geiriadur Prifysgol Cymru,* 461.

32. *The Oxford Classical Dictionary* (Oxford: Clarendon, 1949).

33. Eve Sedgwick, *Epistemology of the Closet* (Berkeley: University of California Press, 1990), p. 75.

34. W. E. B Du Bois, "The Conservation of Races" in *W. E. B. Du Bois Speaks: Speeches and Addresses 1890–1919,* ed. Philip S. Foner (1897; New York, 1970), pp. 75–76. Quoted in Anthony Appiah, "The Uncompleted Argument: Du Bois and the Illusion of Race," in *"Race," Writing and Difference,* ed. Henry Louis Gates (Chicago: University of Chicago Press, 1986), pp. 21–37, 23.

35. Appiah, "Uncompleted Argument," p. 35.

CHAPTER SEVEN

Ferdinand Kürnberger's *Der Amerika-Müde* (1855): German-Language Literature about the United States, and German-American Writing

■ WERNER SOLLORS

Dr. Moorfeld, the idealistic protagonist of Ferdinand Kürnberger's novel *Der Amerika-Müde: Amerikanisches Kulturbild* (1855) [The Man Who Was Weary of America: An American Cultural Portrait], is a keen observer of damning details on the American scene. When he enters the house of Staunton, his New York host, he notices numerous features of the interior, from statues and the absence of a library to wallpapers, curtains, and furniture. The fabric covering the couch "glittered in a powerful orange color pattern that struck the eye vividly enough, but the pattern represented nothing less than a — forest fire. Moorfeld reacted with more than a smile to the invitation — untempered by aesthetic considerations — that he be seated on fiery flames."[1]

Satirical descriptions characterize many German-language books about America; for example, the weary narrator of Max Frisch's *Montauk* (1976) notes that a "jauchefarbener Spannteppich" (manure-colored wall-to-wall carpet) brightens up his Long Island motel room. Kürnberger's detail of the flaming sofa is the first burst of the hero's somewhat excessive America-fatigue, his weariness of the aesthetically impossible, politically disappointing, religiously hypocritical, economically ruthless, and generally ridiculous hell that is the New World. The Bible — tellingly, the only book in the Staunton household — is ostentatiously displayed on a round table in front of the "forest-fiery sofa." And a little later, Staunton invites Moorfeld to "burn himself, i.e., he offered him the couch to sit on."[2] Fittingly, the American *Urwald* (forest primeval) that Moorfeld searches for turns out to be literally a burned-over district, and at the end, he barely escapes an anti-German riot in New York that culminates in an apocalyptic conflagration of the German-American neighborhood of *Kleindeutschland*. All the while that new immigrants arrive chanting praises of free America, "Vivat das freie Amerika" (the novel's ironic last line), the reader and Moorfeld know better: going back to Europe represents an Exodus from the "pillar of cloud" of burning *Kleindeutschland*. The fiery ending marks the sinister recurrence of the pillar of fire (*lichterlohe Feuersäule*) that Moorfeld observed over a frame house (*sogenanntes Framehaus*) during the comic Sunday spectacle of the mock-chivalric firemen's competition at the beginning of the novel.

Along with elaborate fire symbolism, countless details make America look hellish: its terrible cuisine (women don't care to cook) and the boorishness of mixing champagne and brandy in the same glass; the disgusting spittoons in a government office building and the complete absence of hygiene on the steamboat where one "equality-towel" serves all; the repetitive, square, checkerboard-like grid in the layout of Philadelphia; and the ridiculous origin of the song "Yankee Doodle." Bad taste rules American arts (from the shrill colors of lithographs to what passes as sculpture), and scandalous financial speculations permeate all areas of life. Children act as if they had complete superiority over their parents, and the educational system is a travesty. Black slavery and inhuman treatment of Indians (there is a scene in which an Indian maiden is cannibalized) round off the picture of a world in which God's commandments are simply meaningless. In *Der Amerika-Müde*, the New World is worse than the Old in every way; even the windows open only halfway in America.

The thin plot serves as an excuse to include not only narratorial observations, but also lengthy discussions and letters in which Kürnberger's heterogeneous cultural bits proliferate. Though the novel targeted America, and its Austrian author (1821–1879) had a remarkable flair for scathing descriptiveness, it has not been translated into English. It still holds interest for readers on the political left as well as the right. Some might be intrigued by the 1848 revolutionary backdrop of some of Kürnberger's assessments and by his general anticapitalist and occasional explicitly socialist pronouncements, whereas others might find the novel's anti-Americanism congenial on the basis of the spiritual and aesthetic superiority of internally homogeneous European nation states over the vulgar decadence of the heterogeneous United States.

It is telling that Max Weber drew on and partly adopted Kürnberger's satirical portrait of Benjamin Franklin when he launched his own critique in *The Protestant Ethic and the Spirit of Capitalism* (1904–05), so much better known than *Der Amerika-Müde*.[3] In the novel Kürnberger lets his fictional schoolmaster, Mr. Mockingbird, introduce Franklin's "Advice to a Young Tradesman" with the comment: "The conversion of human existence into shillings and pounds only deserves our pardon because of the invention of the lightning rod. Without it, this would be the doctrine . . . make tallow out of cattle and money out of men."[4] Weber cites this passage in his discussion of Franklin. Contemporary readers might be impressed by Kürnberger's Marxian and quite systemic critique of the spiderlike quality of capitalism that makes deception and humbug normative.[5] They would perhaps also be surprised by Kürnberger's observation of the state penitentiary in Pennsylvania that anticipates Michel Foucault's famous critique of the panopticon: "To be sure, it's a miracle of human intelligence. One single guard has five hundred cells under surveillance! That character sits like a spider in its sack: from him the whole terrible building fans out; no cell window looks into another one, and yet he can look into all of them!"[6] After speaking with some miserable prisoners who relive the horrors of their lives in their lonely cells, Moorfeld concludes that while European censors merely murder thoughts, American prisons surrender prisoners to their own thoughts, making their haunting fantasies the breeding ground of insanity. To this thought he responds with "Cut, censors, cut" and "May the abyss devour the Pennsylvanian system."

On the cultural plane, Kürnberger's America does not even merit such dismissive comparisons. It is clear that, within the code of the book, the United States simply has no culture, no *Kultur*, and it is this very richly developed aspect of the novel that would seem to account for its conservative Eurocentric appeal. Moorfeld's first aesthetic pleasure (*Kunstgenuß*) right after his arrival in America is representative: in a café where he stops to have ice cream, a black band is playing: "A strangely cut-up rhythm, the beat of which was somewhat obscure and, moreover, handled rather independently by each artist! But how did our listener feel when the melody suddenly, without any mediation, jumped from sharp to flat?"[7] Moorfeld knows no better than to tear the violin out of the hand of the first violinist and to show the band how to play the figure correctly. Yet after a polite response, it turns out that when the band plays again, the same "barbarism" recurs at the same point in the piece as before. Neither Moorfeld nor his author has much of an ear for polyrhythms or blue notes, except as mistakes and flaws that need to be corrected. The other side of the coin is American treatment of European genius: here Kürnberger takes a poetic license to link the death of Mozart's librettist Lorenzo Da Ponte (he died in America in 1838) to the mob riot in New York, in the novel's final section. Beauty and America are simply incompatible in innumerable ways.

For Kürnberger, the United States is not the kind of integrated country that could develop culture or beauty. At best, the Americans are an incomplete people (*ein unfertiges Volk*); at worst, they are hopeless barbarians who will never acquire a sense of art or of other higher ideals. Moorfeld's friend (and later antagonist) Benthal specifically deplores ethnic heterogeneity in the newly expanded union and doubts that the Puritan in Boston and the Frenchman in New Orleans, the palm country of Florida and the icy stretches of Maine and Vermont, could have anything in common. When, as in the case of Texas, a new star joins the Stars and Stripes, what looks like an increase in national power merely accelerates the prospect of its ultimate demise (*Beförderung des Zerfalls*); and Kürnberger anticipates not only a Civil War between North and South, but also one between Atlantic and Pacific America. Even where ethnic mixing leads to fusion rather than to disunity and conflict, the result is horrifying rather than stimulating, as Moorfeld's letter to Benthal from Harrisburg deplores in its dismissal of Pennsylvania Dutch. He mocks such untranslatable sentences as a carpenter's statement, "Wenn Sie ein *loghouse* bauen wollen und dasselbe inwendig *geplastert* und von außen *geclapboardet* wird, so kostet es siebenhundert Dollars." And Kürnberger includes a long and rather funny German-American dialogue of a couple, the first at six months and the second at six years after their wedding. Moorfeld comments: "Can one imagine a poet in this tongue? Yet a nationality which is unable to produce poets is like a tree that does not bloom. It is dead. That is the case with the Pennsylvania Dutch."[8] This mixed language is *Kauderwelch* and simply an abomination in the context of the cultural purism of *Der Amerika-Müde*. Such dismissals of German America have not been uncommon in German literature about the United States, well into the twentieth century. If German America was too un-German for Kürnberger, however, it was too provincially German and un-American for writers like Wolfgang Koeppen, whose *Amerikafahrt* (1959) described the German section of New York as a "German nightmare" and a *Kitschmuseum*.

Kürnberger may be an unusual source for his observations of the New World: he never came to America, and all his descriptive details were either secondhand (he even cites some of the literature about America) or simply made up. His novel was a specific response to Heinrich Heine's term "europamüde" (weary of Europe) that had been popularized by Ernst Willkomm's novel *Die Europa-Müden* (1838). Kürnberger based his novel on idealized accounts of the poet Nikolaus Lenau's brief and disappointing stay in America in 1832–33; and he shares with Lenau the motif of the impoverished natural scene of the New World. This was a theme that eighteenth-century European intellectuals from de Pauw to Buffon had circulated, and that Jefferson attempted to counter in his *Notes on the State of Virginia* (1787).

Columbus reported in a 1493 letter to Luis de Santangel that the (European) nightingale and other birds of a thousand kind were singing when he landed on Hispaniola. Many later observers of America were hesitant to project such European sounds onto the New World; and to say that America was a continent without nightingales became a cultural statement. For Lenau, this was a serious and symbolic shortcoming. Was not the absence of the beloved European singing bird symptomatic of the general depravity of the New World, where aesthetics has been sacrificed to economics? Just a few days after landing in America, Lenau lamented in a famous letter: "The nightingale is right not to visit these scoundrels. I see a deep and serious significance in the fact that America has no nightingale. It seems like a poetic curse. It would take the voice of Niagara to preach to these villains that there are higher gods than those coined in the mint."[9] The land of the dollar was simply not a home for nightingales; and Kürnberger's choice to give the Franklinesque teacher the name "Mockingbird" is, of course, a sarcastic comment on this fact. The only time the word "nightingale" appears in the novel is in a French song, in which the line *Nous entendrons le rossignol chanter* (we shall hear the nightingale sing) strikes Moorfeld as ironic as he walks through the American forest. With characteristic excess the novelist represents the American *Urwald* as an eerily silent forest without *any* birds, butterflies, or animal sounds, in which European trees exist only "pseudonymously," so that even the celebrated fall season seems more vulgar and less appealing in the northeastern American woods than in the European forest.

Kürnberger may have been an extreme representative of the Americophobic pole of German writing about America. (Ironically, though not very convincingly, Kürnberger begins and ends his book on the opposite note of Americophilia.) Writers who actually went to America were likely to be more ambivalent than Kürnberger. It is telling, for example, that in his novel *Nach Amerika* [Toward America, 1855] Friedrich Gerstäcker apparently chose to poke fun at Lenau's no-nightingale topos: upon landing in New Orleans, "the full, mourning tone of a nightingale could be heard clear as a bell — a bird brought across the Atlantic by emigrants."[10] Perhaps even more complex was the negotiation of German literature and American themes for those who decided to stay in the United States or who were American-born of German ancestry. (Nearly seven million Germans emigrated to the United States between 1820 and 1970, and over twenty-five million Americans claim German descent.) At least 25,000 titles were published in German in the United States, and there were many texts in English and other languages. These works are now collecting dust on the shelves of archives, awaiting new readers.

The German-American tradition begins with the intriguing manuscript by Francis Daniel Pastorius, called *Bee Hive* (1696).[11] It is a collection of excerpts, parental advice to his children, and autobiographical observations, often cast in the language of bee-keeping. Like the nightingale, the bee has associations with Europeans in American literature; as Washington Irving put it in *A Tour on the Prairies* (1835), Indians consider bees "the harbinger of the white man." Pastorius's manuscript contains several thousand "honey combs" filled with numerous subjects. Pastorius wrote this work in several languages, moving back from one to another with ease. The title page of his manuscript is suggestive of the *Bee Hive*'s multilingual project, as it offers the author's name and title in Greek, Latin, English, German, Dutch, Italian, and French, followed by an opening poem:

> In these seven Languages I this Book do own,
> Friend, if thou find it, Send the same to Germantown;
> Thy recompense shall be half a Crown . . .[12]

If he should fail to keep the promise for lack of money,

> A Cup of Drink may do: Or else, alas! thou must
> Trust unto me a while. As I to others Trust,
> To which I have no lust: But must per Force, poor Dust.

At this point, he switches into German:

> Freund, Was du findest, wiedergieb,
> Sonst hält man Dich vor einen Dieb . . .

This leads him to the golden rule — in German and Latin:

> Zu thun, wie man Gethan will seÿn
> Quod Tibi vis fieri, hoc facias Alÿs.

Pastorius uses the focus on the bee not only to mine the ancients and the moderns for bee wisdom, but also to develop something like an aesthetic of the small form: "Do not scorn small things. Small things have their own particular grace."

As a pioneer, Pastorius may at least be known by name. But this is not the case for many other authors of German-American poems, autobiographies, and countless essays — many never-before-translated, and virtually all of them little known in Germany and the United States. The period during which Kürnberger published was particularly fruitful in generating German-American novels, several of which followed the urban "mysteries" format in the wake of Eugène Sue's *Mystères de Paris* (1842ff). One of the first was the anonymous *Geheimnisse von Philadelphia* (1850), of which only the beginning chapters have survived, including lively interracial scenes in a black-German bar, and a remarkable account of some Philadelphia upstarts' efforts to create the illusion that they spend endless hours shopping in expensive and fashionable stores, so as to appear to be richer than they are. Correspondingly, the shop owners arrange to have many coaches wait outside of shops, to suggest that they are more popular than they are. "If business gets 'sluggish' [*flau*], that is, if more carriages stand in front of other shops than this one, the business manager dispatches his errand-boy to those places where carriage drivers gather and orders . . . six, eight, or ten carriages, to drive up from various sides and wait for a half hour or even a full hour in front of the shop" (unpublished; trans. Elliott Shore). This author's critique of Philadelphia's capitalist world of illusions surrounding conspicuous consumption is marked by far more ironic amusement than contempt.

Emil Klauprecht's *Cincinnati, oder Geheimnisse des Westens* (1854–55) departs from Kürnberger in his enjoyment of mixed languages and of melting-pot encounters. Klauprecht enriches a sensationalist plot with such interesting words as "Neuigkeits*item*" (news item) or "Quadronenball" (quadroon ball) and such sentences as "Ich stelle die Moh'schen" (I make the motion) — all suggesting a considerable extent of linguistic interaction in Cincinnati. Klauprecht also sets a scene in the Hotel Dumas for "free colored," a substantial four-story building with a ten-window facade, a delicate cast-iron balcony, and a two-pillared foyer opening to Cincinnati's McAllister Street. Inside, the walls are decorated with portraits of Toussaint L'Ouverture and (a Germanized) *Friedrich* Douglass, and scenes of the freeing of the slaves in the West Indies, of Cinqué's rebellion on the *Amistad*, and illustrations from *Othello*.

Ludwig von Reizenstein's *Die Geheimnisse von New-Orleans* may well be the most lurid of the German-American "mysteries" — indeed, its publication in book form was suppressed at the end of its long serialization in the *Louisiana Staats-Zeitung* in 1854 and 1855.[13] In addition to an interracial love comedy plot, the novel also contains a remarkably candid chapter entitled "Lesbische Liebe." The narrator frames the amorous dialogue between the German-Creole woman Orleana (who lives on New Orleans's Toulouse Street and has just been harassed by a drunken German immigrant) and Claudine de Lesuire, who has just left her husband. "An authority from ancient Greece tells us that women once lived on the island of Lesbos who did not allow themselves to be touched by any man, since a whim of nature had given them the gift of being happy among themselves."[14] The love dialogue between Orleana and Claudine is fairly extensive, interrupted only by the narrator's explanation that their relationship — even though it is like that of flower cups that will not accept male pollen — may be of a kind as widespread in New Orleans as in Lesbos, Meran, or the emigrant Reizenstein's native southern Germany. There is no reference to bees here.

"Do you really love me, Claudine?"
"Oh, how the fresh warmth of your proud shoulders drives me wild!"
"How your breasts make my blood boil!"
"Orleana, Orleana, how excitingly loose your clothes are!"
"Claudine, Claudine, how tightly you are corseted!"
"Orleana, Orleana, how easily your clothes fall away!"
"Claudine, Claudine, how difficult it is for me to get these things off from you!"
"Orleana, how pure and white your shoulders are!"
"Claudine, where did you get the scars on yours?"
"Orleana, Orleana — Albert did that."
"And you really love me, Claudine?"[15]

And so on. This chapter is certainly unlike anything in English-language American fiction; and the binational location may also have made Reizenstein bolder than most German writers of the 1850s.

One of the most distinguished novels of manners in the German-American tradition is a nearly completely forgotten and as yet untranslated book by Reinhold Solger, *Anton in Amerika* (1862), which purports to be a sequel to Gustav Freytag's *Soll und Haben* (1855), the anti-Semitism of which Solger fortunately chose not to follow. The novel takes place partly in New York, followed by travels to the West and return to New York at the end. It also takes the readers into many different social worlds, among them a party at the fashionable house of a bankrupt New York businessman, Mr. Dawson, whose creditors, surprisingly, enjoy his hospitality as they prefer to keep him in business than to lose all of their investments.[16] The predators, who pounce like a starved ship's crew upon the cocktail hors-d'œuvres served by white-gloved black servants, have to be imagined in a setting where lewdness seems to govern aesthetic taste in sculptures (which the narrator observes from an amused, ironic distance). The Dawsons' salon contains startling statues of naked women — but displayed with an excuse, or better, with some authority, to make them seem part of ordinary everyday life: "There was an Iphigenia, who was just about to be sacrificed at Aulis. People who indulge in such a superstition and do not shrink back from such an atrocity just to get a little wind would of course also not hesitate to undress the poor victim." The sculptures of a Greek slave girl and of a modern white slave woman are justified by other motives, transparent to the narrator who sustains his ironic voice in the most detailed descriptions. (One expects a flaming sofa.) *Anton in Amerika* is a good example of a Balzacian eye in New York. This is also true for Caspar Stürenberg's *Klein-Deutschland: Bilder aus dem New Yorker Alltagsleben* (1885), in which a tenement building is the central subject and setting, its multilingual tenants giving it the combined qualities "of Noah's ark and the tower of Babel" (p. 3) as refuge and multilingual residence of the poor.

Kürnberger's dismissal of American nature, and especially of the American forest, had a complex thematic parallel. German-born Konrad Nies was one of the first writers to draw attention in 1904 to the environmental problem of deforestation in one of his most remarkable poems, "Die Rache der Wälder" [The Revenge of the Forest Primeval], for which he was awarded first prize at a German-American Baltimore festival.[17] The balladesque poem gives (a German romantic) voice to the American forests that the white man had cut down:

> With rapacious destruction and wanton crime
> They brutally plundered our wealth,
> And they squandered a trust of immortal time
> With cunning, connivance, and ruthless stealth.
>
> But ere we submit to their boundless desire,
> Felled victims and subjects in thrall,
> Avenge us, o storm! hear us o fire!
> Save us, ye earth and ye waters withal!

While the form of the poem recalls the German ballad tradition, its theme anticipates the rise of "green" literature.

Mixed languages that Kürnberger had feared as gobbledygook *(Kauder-welch)* were not only used by prose writers like Klauprecht, but have also inspired poets as possible poetic languages — exactly in the way that Kürnberger thought deplorable or impossible in his dismissal of Pennsylvania Dutch. This is the case in German-American plays such as the anonymous *Die Emigranten* (1882), in which an amusing duet is performed by a brother and a sister who associate German and American meanings with the sound of *Schoppen* [drink]/shoppin'. A master of "Germerican" as a comic poetic idiom is Kurt Stein (K.M.S.). In numerous poems code-switching was medium and subject, such as "Die schönste Lengevitch" or "Gemixte Pickles." A stanza from "Das Picnic [Etwas nach Johnnie Go-thee sei Erlkönig]" (reprinted 1953) is representative of K.M.S.'s idiom:

> "O Papa, O Papa! Hörst du denn nicht?
> Da is e Bumblebee wo mich sticht!"
> "Keep shtill, mei Sohn, und mach hurryop,
> Ich kauf auch a bottle mit rotem Pop."[18]

Stein's code-switching send-ups of "Faust," "Die neue Lorelei," or "Lohengrin" are impressive (and hilarious) responses to obsolete demands for linguistic purity, and to the worship of *Kultur* that was so characteristic of Dr. Moorfeld.

German-American literature does not exist in the kind of cultural isolation for which *Der Amerika-Müde* yearned, but implies in the very hyphenation of its adjective that it is part of an *interaction*. It is this double perspective that may have endowed some works with a unique ability to record manners ironically, while others achieve a prophetic quality in foreshadowing thematic concerns (same-sex love or green politics) and linguistic aspects (code-switching or bilingual puns) of the transnational period that has all but replaced the nationalist era in which "German America" may have had something unnatural, oxymoronic, or merely comic about it, as it had for Kürnberger. Perhaps the tree of German America did bloom after all.

Notes

1. Ferdinand Kürnberger, *Der Amerikamüde: Amerikanisches Kulturbild* (repr. Frankfurt: Insel Taschenbuch, 1986), p. 37.

2. Kürnberger, *Der Amerika-Müde,* p. 29.

3. Winfried Fluck, "The Man Who Became Weary of America: Ferdinand Kürnberger's novel *Der Amerika-Müde* (1855)," in *German? American? Literature?,* ed. Winfried Fluck and Werner Sollors (New York: Peter Lang, 2002).

4. Kürnberger, *Der Amerika-Müde,* p. 33.

5. Rüdiger Steinlein, "Ferdinand Kürnberger's 'Der Amerika-Müde': Ein 'amerikanisches Kulturbild' als Entwurf einer negativen Utopie," in *Amerika in der deutschen Literatur: Neue Welt — Amerika — USA,* ed. Sigrid Bauschinger, Horst Denkler, and Wilfried Malsch (Stuttgart: Reclam, 1975), pp. 154–77. See also Harold Jantz, "Amerika im deutschen Dichten und Denken," in *Deutsche Philologie im Aufriss,* ed. Wolfgang Stammler, 2nd ed. (Berlin: Erich Schmidt-Verlag, 1962), pp. 310–71.

6. Kürnberger, *Der Amerika-Müde,* p. 326.

7. Ibid., p. 20.

8. Ibid., p. 343.

9. Lenau's letter is quoted in Ritchie Robertson, "German Idealists and American Rowdies: Ferdinand Kürnberger's Novel *Der Amerika-Müde,*" in *Gender and Politics in Austrian Fiction,* ed. Ritchie Robertson and Edward Timms (Edinburgh: Edinburgh University Press, 1996), pp. 22–23.

10. Manfred Durzak, "Nach Amerika: Gerstäckers Widerlegung der Lenau-Legende," in *Amerika in der deutschen Literatur,* ed. Bauschinger et al., p. 146.

11. Pastorius, *Bee Hive,* introduced by Alfred Brophy, in *The Multilingual Anthology of American Literature: A Reader of Original Texts with English Translations,* ed. Marc Shell and Werner Sollors (New York: New York University Press, 2000).

12. Pastorius, *Bee Hive,* p. 20. All the quotes are from the same page.

13. Ludwig von Reizenstein, *Die Geheimnisse von New-Orleans,* trans. and introduced by Steven Rowan, in *The Multilingual Anthology of American Literature,* ed. Shell and Sollors, pp. 185–209.

14. Reizenstein, *Die Geheimnisse von New-Orleans,* p. 199.

15. Ibid., p. 303.

16. Reinhold Solger, *Anton in Amerika,* 2 vols. (New York: E. Steiger, 1872), vol. 1, p. 43.

17. Konrad Nies, "Die Rache der Wälder," introduced by Regine Wieder and trans. by Christoph Lohmann, in *The Multilingual Anthology of American Literature*, ed. Shell and Sollors, pp. 377–83.

18. K. M. S., *Die Allerschönste Lengevitch: Die Schönste Lengevitch mit Gemixte Pickles und Limberger Lyrics zusammen downgeboilt, und plenty geseasont mit Additions von Neugehatchter Nonsense* (New York: Crown, 1953), p. 36.

Part III

AUTHORITATIVE AND NONAUTHORITATIVE LANGUAGES

"Neither the King's English nor the Rebbetzin's Yiddish": Yinglish Literature in the United States

▪ JAMES LOEFFLER

They . . . had it in their heads to be Jews in a way no one had ever dared to be a Jew in our three-thousand-year history: speaking and thinking American English, *only* American English, with all the apostasy that was bound to beget.

— Philip Roth, *Operation Shylock*

A dozen rivers can't wash away the Yiddish accent.

— Primo Levi, *Se non ora, quando?*

Du, honey chile,
it's a farginigen to have dir mit mir afn range.
We'll take a look on the nissim fun mudder's nature.
Heh heh, mudder's nature:
beymer, blumen, and vumen.
Side bayn side we'll take a shmek,
a shmek tabok.
I'm gonna take you places honey,
I'm gonna take you to Oy Vegas.
I'll also take to you the mountains, to the Boulders.
Boulders, shmoulders, abi gezunt, honey chile,
honey kneydl, honey lekekh, honey knish you are.
I'll take you to the hills dortn,
and in hills we're going to kill — we're going to derhag a mountain lion.

You don't know what it is a mountain lion? A mountain lion is an alter cougar!!

[You, honey child,
It's a pleasure to have you with me on the range.
We'll take a look on the miracles of Mother nature.
Heh, heh, Mother nature:
Trees, flowers, and women
Side by side we'll take a sniff,
a sniff of tobacco.
I'm gonna take you places honey.
I'm gonna take you to Las Vegas.
I'll also take you to the mountains, to the Boulders,
Boulders, shmoulders, as long as you're healthy, honey child,
honey matzoh ball, honey cake, honey knish you are.
I'll take you to the hills there,
and in the hills we're going to kill — we're going to murder a mountain lion.
You don't know what a mountain lion is? A mountain lion is an old fart!![1]]

In the fall of 1947, Mickey Katz and his Kosher Jammers released a 78 rpm Victor recording entitled "Haim Afen Range" — the text just quoted.[2] In New York alone, 10,000 copies were sold within the first three days of its release. Total sales shot upwards of the 200,000 record mark.[3] Musically, this brilliant piece of parody is clearly recognizable as "Home on the Range," the classic nineteenth-century American folk ballad. But the lyrics are a curious linguistic melange — not quite Yiddish and not quite English — that has come to be known as Yinglish.

Mickey Katz was an entertainer and comedian, and in his mind his lyrics were merely "English-Yiddish parodies of the top hits of the day," not necessarily examples of a new literature or language.[4] But even as he joined other performers in using Yinglish deliberately for comic effect, he was sensitive to the powerful and tricky audience responses.[5] Interviewed in 1953, Katz reported that "Straight Yiddish is offensive to some people, and a combination of Yiddish and English makes for a happy result."[6] He understood that Yinglish rests at the boundary between English and Yiddish, dialect and language. As a result, linguists have been engaged in the study of and debate over Yinglish for the past several decades.[7] Yet in the academic discipline that could benefit most from the serious study of Yinglish, Jewish-American literature, scholars have been slow to grasp its linguistic presence and cultural implications.[8]

Jewish-American literature has been consistently read as a monolingual and culturally ambiguous category of ethnic literature rather than a linguistically marked — if not circumscribed — literary corpus. Such a neglect of the obvious is all the more startling given the strong case that scholars of Yiddish and Hebrew literature have made for multilingualism in general, and bilingualism and diglossia in particular, as deeply felt characteristics of Jewish literature throughout its history. Citing the Yiddish literary critic Baal Makhshoves, Hana Wirth-Nesher explains Jewish literature's bilingualism to be "not only the literal presence of two languages, but also the echoes of another language and culture detected in the prose of the one language of which the text is composed."[9] This line of reasoning has led many critics to note places in Jewish-American literature where "The Yiddish may just glow through the English" or "Yiddish is the absent source language," creating both literal and psychological effects of translation.[10] Yet a true understanding of the interactions between Yiddish and English in Jewish-American literature necessitates a closer examination of the points where the bilingual framework breaks down and the presence of a third language, Yinglish, is revealed.

ROOTS OF THE CONTROVERSY / A CONTROVERSY OF ROOTS

Any reference to a Yiddish-derived dialect of English or a new Jewish language must first reckon with the confused and dramatic relationship between Yiddish and German. Through nearly one thousand years of Central and East European Jewish experience, Yiddish was the definitive Jewish language. The debates about dialect, purity, authenticity, and Jewishness that marked its linguistic history are characteristic of all Jewish languages.[11]

Sometime around the ninth century, Jews from northern France and northern Italy migrated to the German Rhine valley, joining a small community of German Jews.[12] The newcomers spoke varieties of Romance languages mixed with Hebrew and Aramaic — Judeo-French and Judeo-Italian — while the established group spoke a strain of medieval High German crossed with Hebrew and Aramaic. The double fusion of these linguistic elements produced the earliest Yiddish, sometime before the thirteenth century. Throughout the following centuries, Yiddish grew side by side with modern German, but the two languages evolved in different directions. Yiddish acquired a large minority of Slavic elements and new Hebrew-Aramaicisms, and lost much of its original Romance component. Thus by the time modern German developed in the sixteenth century, Yiddish had already established itself for a few hundred years as its own language.[13]

Despite this complex yet distinct history, Yiddish was consistently misunderstood and derided throughout the centuries as little more than a dialect or Jewish corruption of German.[14] Many scholars have noted the role of names in assigning negative value to Yiddish, including the common term *zhargon* [jargon], the misnomer *jüdish-deutsch* [Judeo-German], and even the confusing words *jüdisch* [German for "Jewish"] and *yidish* [literally translatable as "Jewish"].[15] Sociolinguist Joshua Fishman reports some of the terms commonly applied to Yiddish and other Jewish languages: "'ugly,' 'rasping,' 'corrupted,' 'crippled,' 'bastardized' . . . 'mishmash,' 'grammarless,' 'undisciplined' . . . 'dwarfed,' 'hunchbacked,' and 'hoarse.'"[16] Cultural historian Sander Gilman has documented Christian Europe's stereotypes of Jewish languages: "[There is an] extensive and venerable Western tradition which labels the language of the Jew as corrupt and corrupting, as the sign of the inherent difference of the Jew. This tradition sees the Jew as inherently unable to have command of any 'Western,' that is, cultural language."[17]

The Jewish Enlightenment [*Haskala*] writers praised Hebrew as elegant, classical, and spiritually uplifting. Yiddish became linked in their minds to the perceived backwardness and decrepitude of Hasidism and of traditional Jewish life. The pioneering leader of the German Jewish Enlightenment, Moses Mendelssohn, himself a native Yiddish speaker, went so far as to remark: "I am afraid this jargon has contributed not a little to the immorality of the common man. Depending on the situation pure German or pure Hebrew should be spoken. But no mixing of the languages!"[18] The same exaltation of Hebrew as a noble and pure language and denigration of Yiddish as a diasporic relic occurred with the birth of Zionism and its efforts to revive spoken Hebrew as the Jewish national language.[19]

A MIXED MARRIAGE: YIDDISH AND ENGLISH IN THE UNITED STATES

Mid-nineteenth-century England was the first point of contact between the Yiddish and English languages, owing to the arrival of East European Jews.[20] But the explosion of linguistic interaction did not occur until the masses of Eastern European Jews began to pour into the United States in the final decades of the nineteenth century.[21] The first Yiddish book published in the United States, an 1877 collection of poetry, already contained several English loanwords, including "Yenkee," "missus," "fotsen" [fortune], and "beyzamen" [basement], as well as neologisms such as "dzshentleyt un dzshentlevumens" [gentlemen and gentlewomen], and "Yenkizirkayt" [Americanization, literally Yankification].[22] Within a short time the grammar, pronunciation, and vocabulary of American English began to reflect the influence of Yiddish. Hundreds of Yiddish words entered the press, literature, and slang of great immigration centers, including words such as "kibitz," "chutzpah," "kosher," "maven," "mensch," and so on. At the same time, words such as "faker," "customer," "peddler," "college boy," "payde" [paid], "yunyon" [union], "vindeh" [window], "tickets," "paintner" [painter], and "bluffer" either replaced Yiddish equivalents or filled vocabulary gaps in standard American Yiddish of the late nineteenth and early twentieth centuries.[23]

This great interlinguistic exchange was bound to lead to various syntheses, and eventually to the prospect (at least in theory) of a third, mixed language. Word coinings such as "holdupnik," "boychik," "allrightnik," and "trouble makher" resulted from linguistic hybridization of English and Yiddish, foreshadowing later, more complex permutations. While it is natural to assume that these new Yinglish words reflect to some degree an ordinary refashioning of language toward the needs of the moment, the standardization and canonization of Yinglish developments in American culture owed much to the output of journalists and writers.

If ever there was a progressive advocate of language change for immigrant American Jews, that figure was Abraham Cahan (1860–1951). Legendary founder and editor of *Der Forverts* [*The Jewish Daily Forward*], Cahan played a fundamental role in determining the direction of Jewish literature and culture in the United States from the 1880s well into the 1940s. Unlike his colleagues in the English-language press, who continued to refer to Yiddish as "jargon" or "the queer lingo that passes for Hebrew in the East Side," Cahan did not resist or lament new developments in Jewish languages.[24] Instead, he viewed them as necessary for both the evolution of Yiddish and the improvement of Jewish immigrants' vital knowledge of English. He welcomed many English words as replacements for Yiddish ones in the pages of the newspaper, and even went so far as to append a glossary of English (and Yinglish) words to the second volume of his mammoth five-part memoir, *Bleter fun mayn lebn* (1926).[25] His journalism strongly promoted and standardized the borrowing of English words and expressions in Yiddish.[26]

Cahan's firm and prescriptive opinions on language dovetailed naturally with the guiding philosophy of his own literary ambitions, the doctrine of social realism. Along with his fellow writer-journalists of the late nineteenth century, Jacob Riis, Stephen Crane, and Hutchins Hapgood, Cahan sought to document the rapidly emerging world of urban New York. But he went a step further than his peers, for he embraced the challenge of representing immigrant Jewish speech as accurately as possible.[27] Cahan's writing continually exposes the blurred boundaries between accent, dialect, and language in vernacular speech. Central to his array of strategies for dealing with Yiddish and English is a basic opposition between the two. In his first English work, the short novel *Yekl: A Tale of the New York Ghetto* (1896), Cahan reverses the expected narrative flow, stating that the characters are speaking in Yiddish.[28] Yiddish dialogue is thus carried out in standard literary English, while the immigrants' poor English is expressed through broken English passages full of Yiddishisms.[29] For the (English-speaking) reader, this convention makes the text appear strangely foreign, almost as if it were translated from another language. Hana Wirth-Nesher has described this effect in later Jewish-American literature, but her comments apply equally well to Cahan's work: "The odd result is that English, the language in which the text is written, can itself be experienced as alien by the reader as well as the characters, as a type of self-distancing or reverse interference."[30] To further complicate matters, loanwords — whether English or Yiddish — are preserved through italicization, as Cahan explains in a footnote, "English words incorporated in the Yiddish of the characters of this narrative are given in italics."[31] Despite all of his careful system of linguistic rules, the two languages begin to blur the first time he employs this technique: "I knew a *feller*, so he was a *preticly* friend of John Shullivan's . . . Like here, in New York, where the Jews are a *lot* of *greenhornsh* and can not speak a word of English? Over there every Jew speaks English like a stream."[32] How are we to evaluate the word *green-hornsh?* Cahan's italics indicate the word to be non-Yiddish, but it is clearly not the standard English form of the word "greenhorns," which also appears italicized in the same dialogue (to indicate its borrowing from English), nor the common Yiddish word, *grine*.[33] We must conclude that Cahan is inconsistent in his own linguistic strategies, especially with regard to the complicated use of italics.[34]

At moments, though, a third language seems to peek more blatantly through the tangle of vernacular speech. Talking of his recently arrived wife who has retained her Old World ways, the protagonist, Jake, reflects, "'Never min . . . she will *oyshgreen** herself and I shall get used to her.'"[35] Here Cahan feels compelled to insert an asterisk to explain that this is "a verb coined from the Yiddish *oys*, out, and the English *green*, and signifying to cease being green."[36] Yinglish rears its head at last. Slightly later this verb appears again, this time without comment: "'She is still *green*,' Jake apologized for her, in Yiddish. *'Never min'*, she will soon *oysgreen* herself,' Mamie remarked."[37] In the latter example the verb has lost a consonant, "h," thereby shifting closer to Yiddish grammar and completing the process of standardization common to Yinglish constructions.

Though Cahan could shift easily from Yiddish to English, embracing Yinglish as heard on the streets of the Lower East Side, he still refrained from changing the language of the narration itself. Determining the dividing line between these snatches of misspoken or heavily accented English and Yiddish (or Yinglish) remains quite difficult, but language, dialect, and accent operate only within the less problematic realm of dialogue sequences. To cross the languages within the narration itself would wreak havoc on the sober opposition between Yiddish and English upon which Cahan's work ultimately rests. Or perhaps it would simply produce a strange and ironic effect in the style of much dialect humor. This is precisely the tack that the next generation of Jewish writers took in the 1920s and 1930s, especially with the whole genre of dialect humor which mocked immigrant accents and improper English pronunciation.

Milt Gross (1895–1953) was one of the most successful American newspaper cartoonists of the 1920s and 1930s.[38] Essentially imitating the poor speech of his immigrant parents, Yiddish-speaking residents of the Bronx, Gross published several parodies of immigrant life and of classics of Western literature, usually written entirely in a dialect style.[39] *Famous fimmales witt odder ewents from heestory* (1928) is just one such work, a collection of comic retellings of famous tales from the Bible, the ancient world, and other periods of history. Here is the beginning of chapter four, "Iv" [Eve]:

> So de foist human bing wot it axeested was entitled "Heddem."
> So Heddem leeved heppily in a plaze wot it was de Godden from Iddin. So in de Godden from Iddin was extrimmingly gudgeous, wot it was dere all kinds from fency fruits . . .[40]

> [So the first human being that existed was called 'Adam.'
> So Adam lived happily in a place known as the Garden of Eden. So in the Garden of Eden it was extremely gorgeous since there were all kinds of fancy fruits there . . .]

Judging from Gross's careful avoidance of Yiddish phrases or distinctive Yiddish words, this dialect style is apparently meant to convey a generic European immigrant speech as much as a Jewish one. Here nondistinctive accented English stands in for Jewish ethnicity for comic effect. Even in this de-ethnicized form, however, Yiddish linguistic elements shine through. The phrase "wot it was de Godden from Iddin" is a near-literal translation of the Yiddish syntactical construction of the same phrase, *vos es iz geven dem ganeydn.* Other passages in the book reflect the presence of Yinglish even more dramatically, as in the following comment by an animal upon seeing a human being for the first time, "Noo, frick, where is by you de tail, ha??" [Well, freak, where is your tail, ha??][41] In this case an actual Yiddish word, *nu,* is employed. In addition, the Yiddish prepositional construction *bay aykh* [with you/for you] is used here, expanding the meaning of a similar English language preposition, "by," and creating a Yinglish structure.

Gross's writing raises several questions about the changing interactions among English, Yiddish, and Yinglish. The scrupulous avoidance of Yiddish words, even in the ethnicized versions of biblical stories, is an obvious act of linguistic assimilation. But this tactic is compromised by various occurrences of Yiddish and Yinglish and the overall nature of the text. This 123-page book is written entirely in a language that everywhere implies Yiddish or Yinglish but only rarely marks itself as such explicitly. And yet by the yardstick of standard English, the book is quite understandable. Nu, what gives?

A bit of history helps to put the issue in perspective. The 1920s witnessed the severe curtailment of immigration by restrictive legislation, along with a marked increase in the cultural and linguistic assimilation of immigrant Jews and their American-born children. Jewish-Americans of that time joined other European-American ethnic groups in proclaiming their national loyalty and Americanness. Language was a common testing ground. As a result, all immigrants were lumped together in a general category of inferior or exotic English speakers. Gross's work clearly takes that stance. Ethnic language (or ethnicity itself) was intrinsically comic, clearly outdated but recognizable, and, most of all, a corruption of English.[42] There is only one language in the United States — English — and those who speak it with an accent are therefore immigrants.

Appropriately, predictions of the decline of Yiddish and its replacement by a new Jewish language also date from the 1920s.[43] Most caustic in their attitudes were the Yiddishists, ideological advocates of Yiddish and secular Jewish culture who quickly denounced the emergence of Yinglish as a corrupt dialect and a threat to pure Yiddish: "When one thinks of Yiddish in America, one must not forget that we have here two brands of Yiddish. One brand is the wild-growing Yiddish-English jargon, the potato-chicken-kitchen language; the other brand is the cultivated language of Yiddish culture all over the world."[44]

The Yiddishist fear of a new language ironically recalls earlier descriptions of Yiddish and other Jewish languages. Yinglish is startlingly portrayed in terms of the baser biological functions: "wild-growing" (read: sexually promiscuous), "Yiddish-English jargon" (read: impure and degenerate), and "potato-chicken-kitchen language" (read: suitable only for food). The great Yiddish novelist Isaac Bashevis Singer echoed this tone in a 1943 essay on the writing of Yiddish literature in America: "Words, like people, sometimes endure a severe disorientation when they emigrate, and often they remain forever helpless and not quite themselves. This is precisely what happened to Yiddish in America . . . What they did to Yiddish here had — from a linguistic point of view — a negative effect. They vulgarized the language, mixing in hundreds of English and anglicized words and expressions, and creating a gibberish which no self-respecting Yiddish writer could use in good conscience."[45] The demonization of Yinglish also signifies a shift from regarding it as a mere unremarkable dialect to a recognition of the idea of a third language, the linguistic offspring of Yiddish and English.

NAMING NAMES: FROM HYPHEN TO COMPOUND

As might be expected for any language related to Yiddish, the issue of naming posed a serious challenge to the very idea of a new language. Would the transformations of Yiddish lead to a new Jewish language? The answer still depended first and foremost on how Yiddish itself would be described.[46] Thus an academic Germanist speculated in 1928 on what he perceived to be the relationship of Yiddish (or Judeo-German) to the new language: "Judeo-German in America is inevitably doomed . . . There is no reasonable doubt that American Yiddish will within a very few years lose its identity, at least as Judeo-German, will turn into Judeo-English, expire quietly, and finally become as delightfully musty and passé a subject for doctor's theses as Anglo-Saxon is today."[47]

The more dominant name for the new Jewish language would emerge not from academia, however, but from a central branch of contemporary Jewish-American culture: the Borscht Belt. This Jewish-American cultural industry built around the "hybridization of language," musical style, and comedy began to bloom in New York and elsewhere during the 1920s and 1930s thanks to the national radio, recording, and theater industries.[48] It is to them that we owe the name "Yinglish." In a 1951 *Commentary* review of two Borscht Belt musicals, the authors describe a "language neither the King's English nor the *Rebbetzin's* Yiddish but a crossbreed that we might call 'Yinglish.'"[49] From these origins the term moved quickly into popular usage, joining the general growing awareness of hybrid languages in the postwar period.[50]

Despite much brilliant Yiddish linguistic scholarship and literary publications in the half century before 1950, Yiddish languished in an uncertain state in the mid-twentieth century. A shockingly high number of Americans (including Jews) continued to view Yiddish as a dialect, not a language. Comedians and other entertainers often equated the Yiddish language with Yiddish-accented English.[51] No one could deny that Yiddish was on the decline. Some eighty percent of the world's Yiddish speakers were murdered during the Holocaust. The generation of immigrants' children, who themselves viewed Yiddish as "a badge of shame . . . the indelible indicator of lowly immigrant status or of immigrant parentage . . . the 'jargon' of the ignorant," had now produced a new generation of American Jews.[52] These second- and third-generation Americans were culturally secure enough to perceive Yiddish itself — not just Milt Gross's Yiddish accent — with greater ease and humor: "Yiddish was bagels and lox and ribald ditties for those who more regularly savored steak and Gershwin tunes. Yiddish was to be enjoyed in the manner of a spectator sport. Corrupted though they were, Yiddish and its hand-maiden, Yinglish, were a very fine vaudeville team. The second generation learned to laugh at Yiddish rather than merely to shudder at the mere sound of it."[53]

"THE RAPE OF YIDDISH"

Following the Borscht Belt hijinks and popular culture parodies of the preceding decades, the 1950s ushered in a new era in Jewish-American literature. A whole host of young, "technically advanced, more inner-directed and self-conscious" Jewish authors such as Saul Bellow, Bernard Malamud, and Philip Roth began to make their mark on the American literary scene.[54] One might have assumed that with the decline of Yiddish and the rise of Yinglish, this new wave of Jewish literature would have marked a turning point for Yinglish in Jewish-American culture. After all, historically, the appearance of a new Jewish language in writing marked a turning point for its social acceptance. Yiddish gained much ammunition against the critics who labeled it a dialect once the flowering of modern Yiddish literature began in the late nineteenth century, with the works of Sholem Abramovitsh (Mendele Mokher Sforim), Sholem Rabinovitsh (Sholom Aleichem), and I. L. Peretz. Similarly, the unprecedented degree of self-consciousness conferred on Yinglish by Jewish-American literature of the 1950s might have been assumed to improve its recognition and status. Yiddish and Yinglish did play a significant role in these authors' work, and the quick rise to fame in the world of American letters that these writers shared certainly also helped matters.[55]

Yet the reaction of critics was mixed and largely antagonistic on this score. Witness the case of Philip Roth's short story, "Epstein."[56] In 1958 Roth published this story in *The Paris Review*. This brief tale describes a middle-aged Jewish businessman named Lou Epstein who, dissatisfied and depressed by the 1950s suburban material success he has achieved for himself and his family, initiates a disastrous affair with a neighbor. Included in Roth's 1959 debut collection of fiction, *Goodbye, Columbus,* "Epstein" drew immediate, widespread attention.[57] Roth himself later recalled the most common question prompted by the story, "Why all the *schmutz?*"[58] His response, "The story is the *schmutz,*" was deliberately ironic, for it evokes one of the principal subjects of criticism: language. Put briefly, Roth was accused of everything — from Jewish self-hatred to "the rape of Yiddish" — for creating Jewish characters that speak "a language of their own": "This is the unique patois whose lineage obviously descends from Yiddish with all the inversions, omissions, and tune inflections which that language has in contrast to the usual pattern of spoken English."[59]

Continuing his attack, the reviewer charged Roth with linguistic anti-Semitism, arguing that he had done his characters a disservice since "nobody thinks with an accent."[60] Essayist Marie Syrkin was another ferocious critic of Roth's language, lambasting him with the charge that, "An emancipated Jew does not invariably refer to gentile girls as *shikses;* his vocabulary and imagination are more flexible."[61]

These critiques are all the more striking given that in the context of his peer group of Jewish-American authors, Roth stands out the least for his language:

> Roth's prose is not dominated by the overt Yiddishisms of Malamud and Richler or the cerebral aggression of Bellow's Jewish intellectuals. While Yiddish, the language of the immigrants, and the brilliant intellectual aggressiveness of the new generation of Jewish professionals play a significant part in his work, the linguistic quickness and agility of urban life is its primary quality, mirroring the nimbleness with which his characters move through the dynamic American suburb and cityscape. Writing in a new, supple, vivid American English, Roth stakes out a new area for Jewish writing. He defines the shape of Jewish literature — that is, writing which charts the fateful experiences of the Jews — in a non-Jewish language accessible to all Americans.[62]

What, then, is the exact nature of Yiddish and Yinglish in Roth's writing?[63] Many of these critics rightly acknowledge Jewish languages as an influence and a presence, but by positing that the language of Roth's characters is everyday vernacular speech, they avoid subjecting it to any necessary vigorous analysis. For these critics, questions of Yinglish are questions of dialect, not linguistics.[64] To be fair, much of this disregard stems from the relatively small number of truly explicit Yiddish and Yinglish words in the story (as distinguished from the underlying syntactical and grammatical constructions). Not including the name "Epstein," there are exactly twenty-four words (including repetitions) of identifiable Yiddish or Hebrew origin throughout the story's total of roughly 8,400 words. While this low percentage might at first seem to confirm the non-Jewish nature of Roth's "new, supple, vivid American English," his array of contradictory uses and strategies only serves to heighten further the symbolic potency of language in his work.

Continuing a long-standing strategy, Roth employs italics for certain words in "Epstein." Presumably intended to identify and distinguish among Yiddish, Hebrew, and Yiddish-origin words, the inconsistent application of italics instead raises confusing, if subtle, questions. It comes as little surprise that the word "rabbi," which entered modern English from old English as a Hebrew loanword sometime in the Middle Ages, is not italicized, while the word *oysgamitched* (exhausted or worn out), spoken by Epstein in describing his own failed efforts to impregnate his wife Goldie, is underscored. The questions come from the more ambiguous middle ground. What about the Yiddish words *oy* (oh!) and *shah* (quiet)?[65] Certainly they are interjections and hence retain the illusion of universality. Yet can it really be argued that these words are less clearly Jewish or more common to standard English than the word *mensch,* which appears italicized toward the story's end?

A different kind of linguistic question comes up in the opening paragraph of the story, as Roth lays the scene of a house late at night: "The only light burning was downstairs in the dining room where the *shabus* candles flickered in their tall golden holders and Herbie's *jahrzeit* candle trembled in its glass."[66] The linguistic contrast of these two non-English words is quite striking and peculiar. The Yiddish/Hebrew word *shabus* (Sabbath) is given in a normal romanization, while *jahrzeit* is the archaic Germanic spelling of the Yiddish word for death anniversary. This mix typifies confusion about how to present and incorporate Jewish words in the English language.[67] On the one hand, writing (and especially literature) act to standardize and validate linguistic practice, even when it is replete with errors. At the same time, though, it is possible to view these inconsistencies as part of the mixed-bag heritage of Yinglish. The dividing line between literature-driven change — intentional or not — and natural linguistic evolution remains quite elusive.[68]

Other linguistic patterns in the story also deserve comment. At various times, for instance, the characters use expressions which are obviously intended to appear to many readers as Jewish or Yiddish. Many of these phrases do have Yiddish echoes, such as the description of the widow Ida Kaufman's response to Epstein's question, "suddenly she raised her arms in front of her, and shrugged her shoulders as though to say, 'Who knows, Epstein, who knows?'"[69] This phrase is a direct translation of the Yiddish *ver veyst?* into English. Again, when Goldie wishes good health to her nephew, she declares, "you should live and be well," a fairly direct translation of the Yiddish expression *zol lebn un zayn gezunt.*

At other times, though, a clear Yiddish analogue cannot always be found. The logical implication is that if what sounds Yiddish does not come from Yiddish, it therefore is in fact Yinglish. Here translations may be of assistance. The following dialogue exchange between Epstein and his wife is here presented in the original, in romanized Yiddish, and in Yiddish (my translation). Note that Roth himself does not italicize any words, suggesting that the entire passage is in English. Yet according to the critical and popular consensus, the flavor of the characters' speech is undeniably Yiddish or Yiddish-derived:

Goldie looked at him, mystified, while Epstein searched for words appropriate to his posture.
    At last: "You had a nice bath."
    "Nice, shmise, it was a bath," his wife mumbled.[70]

[Goldy hot im gegebn a kuk, mystifirt, vayl epshteyn hot durkhgetsukht far verter ongemostn tsu dos haltn zikh.
    Endlikh: "Du host zikh gut gebodn?"
    "Ikh hob zikh gebodn?" ir froy hot gemurmult.]

גאָלדי האָט אים געגעבן אַ קוק, מיסטיפֿירט,
ווייל עפּשטיין האָט דורכגעצוכט פֿאַר
ווערטער אָנגעמאָסטן צו דאָס האַלטן זיך.
ענדליך: "דו האָסט זיך גוט געבאָדן?"
"איך האָב זיך גוט געבאָדן?", זײַנע פֿרוי
האָט געמורמולט.

Attempting to put the passage into Yiddish exposes much of the Yinglish nature of Roth's language. As the translation exercise demonstrates, this dialogue centers on Goldie's wordplay. She uses the Yiddish construction "shm-" for the "deprecating formula which states a word and then repeats the root with the addition of the particle SHM- as in VAYB, SHMAYB (wife, shmife) or KLIGER-SHIMIGER (smart one — shmart one)."[71] Linguist Lillian Mermin Feinsilver points out that this construction clearly expanded its scope during the 1950s to include all kinds of verbal situations, including Roth's application.

Roth's use is problematic, though, for there is no clear corresponding adjective for "nice" in Yiddish. Nor is there a verbal construction corresponding to "to take / to have a bath." These difficulties determine that the closest possible translation of "You had a nice bath?" will emerge roughly as "You have bathed well?" The appropriate response can only be achieved through an ironic repetition, such as "I have bathed well?" Yet though some of the ironic emphasis and verbal jousting has been preserved in the Yiddish translation, Roth's original Yiddish-derived construction itself has vanished. This paradox of translation is further evidence for Roth's writing as a form of Yinglish.[72]

The issue of translatedness triggers the question of whether Roth's passage has an English translatability factor as well. Can the language be proven to be non-English or not standard English through translation? Were we to attempt to translate "Nice, *shmise,* it was a bath" into standard English, the result might be something like "Nice — yeah right — it was a bath," or "Nice — really nice — it was a bath." Such a translation does not prove that Yinglish is a language distinct from English, especially if we apply the test of comprehensibility. But it can be argued, as Philip Roth himself suggests, that certain linguistic and cultural meanings will be lost on the non-Jewish reader. An interviewer recalls her conversation with Roth: "Roth suggested that a gentile reader might have a different 'range of tolerance' for his work and made the comparison between the way he would be likely to read Flannery O'Connor and the way a Southerner might. He and the reader more familiar with the southern dialect might, he speculated, both be in the same range of interpretation, but there would be a certain patina to O'Connor's work that he would miss."[73]

Let us take a final glance at "Epstein" to address the issue of codeswitching as a specifically new linguistic strategy employed by Roth. To linguists conversational codeswitching is what occurs when a speaker uses different languages or linguistic registers — types of speech — in a single conversation.[74] Interrogating her husband, Goldie engages in an episode of codeswitching between English and Yiddish/Yinglish:

"What is *that?*"

"What?"

"That!"

He could not look into the eyes of her face, so concentrated instead on the purple eyes of her droopy breasts.

"A sand rash, I think."

"*Vus far* sand!"

"A rash then."

["Vos is dos?"

"Vos?"

"Dos."

Er hot nisht gekent kukn afn di oygn fun ir ponem un onshtot hot er zikh kontsontrirt af di purplne oygn fun ire arophengendike brist.

"An oyshit fun zamd, meyn ikh."

"Vos far a zamd?"

"Nu, an oyshit."

‫"װאָס איז דאָס?"‬

‫"װאָס?"‬

‫"דאָס."‬

‫ער האָט נישט געקענט קוקן אויף די אויגן‬
‫פֿון איר פּנים און אָנשטאָט האָט ער זיך‬
‫קאָנצאָנטרירט אויף די פּורפּולנע אויגן‬
‫פֿון אירע אַראָפּהענגעדיקע בריסט.‬

‫"אַן אוישיט פֿון זאַמד, מיין איך."‬

‫"װאָס פֿאַר אַ זאַמד!"‬

‫"נו, אַן אוישיט."‬

As the Yiddish translation immediately reveals, Goldie's expression is not standard Yiddish, deleting as it obviously does the crucial article "a" and using the English noun instead of the Yiddish one. While the meaning is basically the same, the sense of codeswitching — built into Yinglish, or resulting from a Yiddish/Yinglish-English shift — is completely lost in any Yiddish translation. So too is the incongruity of the implicating, urgent expression juxtaposed with the banal word "sand." Putting the entire sentence in English would also destroy the codeswitch or hybrid tension. "What sort of sand?" does not convey the "what for a-" and the "what for / for what (why)" implications contained in the original passage. Roth must have sensed all of these nuances, for he opted for italics in this instance.

To summarize, Roth's writing in "Epstein" reflects two contradictory linguistic impulses. One is to casually adopt certain modes of Yinglish, marking certain words as domesticated and others as foreign through italics, and embracing translated syntactical and lexical forms. Whether deliberate or not, these moves clearly suggest a Yinglish aesthetic. At the same time, Roth's strategy of codeswitching reveals a highly selective and thus powerfully symbolic deployment of Yiddish and Yinglish at key emotional cadences of the plot.

TOWARD A NEW YIDDISH?

These two impulses are actually the result of twin — though contradictory — trends in Jewish-American culture. Beginning in the 1960s, a steady stream of works emerged that seized upon the unique cultural resonance of Yiddish or Yinglish, highlighting these linguistic elements as either intrinsically comic or emotionally expressive. Chief among these works was Leo Rosten's landmark work *The Joys of Yiddish* (1968).[75] Moving forward (or backward) from Hyman Kaplan's dialect, Rosten now seized translatability (or the absence thereof) as a phenomenon to be marketed in its own right. Properly speaking, works such as Rosten's (and the sequels) constituted neither actual dictionaries nor conventional prose literature but popular lexicons — word books filled with humor and anecdotes — that treated Yiddish and Yinglish as crude word pools out of which to pluck decontextualized vocabulary items.[76]

Simultaneously, a second school of thought began to appear which argued for Yinglish or Jewish-English as a new language for American Jews.

This ideology was based on the popular and academic assumption that American Jews had already unconsciously begun to use such a language.[77] In a 1970 lecture on American-Israeli relations, Cynthia Ozick outlined the case for a new Jewish language corresponding to Yinglish. Given the fact that "of all Jews alive today, 45 percent live in America, and perhaps 50 percent have English for their mother-tongue," the Jews of the United States can learn to speak a new language known as New Yiddish:

> Like old Yiddish, New Yiddish will be the language of a culture which is centrally Jewish in its concerns and thereby liturgical in nature. . . . Already English merits every condition of New Yiddish, with the vital exception of having a mature literature. But even now for Jews the English vernacular is on its way toward becoming Jewish; already there are traces (in the form of novels) of a Jewish liturgical literature written in English. As for essays, there are dozens, and several actually contain, as in old Yiddish, numerous Hebrew words essential to their intent. . . . When Jews poured Jewish ideas into the vessel of German they invented Yiddish. As we more and more pour not merely the Jewish sensibility, but the Jewish vision, into the vessel of English, we achieve the profoundest invention of all: a language for our need, our possibility, our overwhelming *idea.* [78]

Despite its broad and prophetic idealism, the most obvious fault with Ozick's conception of the new Jewish language is that it remains hopelessly vague.[79] In truth, this same weakness undermines the entire field of Yinglish studies. Yinglish literature needs to be uncovered and decoded before it can be interpreted. More often than not, critics are frustrated by a perplexing inability to keep the subject — a new Jewish language — in focus long enough to certify its existence. Instead, the theoretical pendulum swings wildly between Ozick's New Yiddish, so subtle and unconscious as to be barely visible, and the other extreme of Leo Rosten's Yinglish, so ubiquitous and familiar as to be inconceivable as a language distinct from English.

Perhaps the solution lies in a compromise between Ozick's sweeping cultural program and Rosten's ahistorical lexicography. The appearance or even the mere concept of a new Jewish language always owes its origins as much to a specific set of cultural conditions as to language's "natural" evolution. In other words, the development of Yinglish — or any language — results from broad cultural identities and social forces combined with discrete linguistic variation and philological change. The works of Abraham Cahan, Milt Gross, and Philip Roth amply confirm that just as Jewish-American literature cannot be truly understood without attention to Yinglish, so too does Yinglish require consideration of the constantly changing mishmash of American language.[80]

Notes

Many thanks to Marc Shell and Werner Sollors for their literary comments, and to Marion Aptroot, Sarah Bunin Benor, and Jeremy Dauber for their advice on questions of translation and linguistic theory.

1. This last sentence is a virtually untranslatable pun on the Yiddish phrase *alter kaker* and the expected English "old cougar."

2. Myron Katz, *Papa, Play for Me: The Hilarious, Heartwarming Autobiography of Comedian and Bandleader Mickey Katz* (New York: Simon and Schuster, 1977), p. 123.

3. Ronald L. Smith, *Comedy On Record: The Complete Critical Discography* (New York: Garland, 1988), p. 345.

4. Katz, *Papa*, p. 128.

5. Katz was part of a long tradition of mixed-language Jewish comic songs, both in the earlier American style of Benny Bell and the Barton Brothers and in the older European Yiddish folksong mode.

6. Herbert Gans, "The Yinglish Music of Mickey Katz," *American Quarterly* 5-3 (Fall 1953):216. In his autobiography, Katz describes how a Los Angeles radio station refused to play his records because they were deemed "ethnic records" on account of the use of Yiddish, even though another record with a "[Jewish] accent" was not considered problematic. Katz, *Papa*, p. 128.

7. The most specific definition of Yinglish comes from linguist Sol Steinmetz: any "form of Yiddish- and Hebrew-influenced English used by Jews, regardless of the extent of its hybridization." Sol Steinmetz, "Jewish English in the United States," *American Speech* 56-1 (Spring 1981):14. Linguists work with the assumption that, technically speaking, it is impossible to differentiate a lan-

guage from a dialect. Yiddish linguist Max Weinreich popularized the expression, "A language is a dialect with an army and navy." Max Weinreich, *"Der yivo un di problemen fun undzer tsayt," YIVO Bleter* 25-1 (Jan.–Feb. 1945):13. The oft-quoted expression actually came from an anonymous student of Weinreich's. For more on the distinction between language and dialect, see William O'Grady, Michael Dobrovolsky, and Mark Aronoff, *Contemporary Linguistics* (New York: St. Martin's Press, 1993), p. 576, and R. A. Hudson, *Sociolinguistics,* 1st ed. (Cambridge: Cambridge University Press, 1980), pp. 30–48, and Walt Wolfram and Natalie Schilling-Estes, *American English: Dialects and Variation* (Malden: Blackwell, 1998), esp. pp. 1–22, 165–69, and 307–10.

8. This essay builds on the groundbreaking work of several scholars. See in particular Hana Wirth-Nesher, "Between Mother Tongue and Native Language: Multilingualism in Henry Roth's *Call It Sleep," Prooftexts* 10 (1990):297–312; Wirth-Nesher, *City Codes: Reading the Modern Urban Novel* (Cambridge: Cambridge University Press, 1995); Wirth-Nesher, ed., *What Is Jewish Literature?* (Philadelphia: Jewish Publication Society of America, 1994); Murray Baumgarten, *City Scriptures: Modern Jewish Writing* (Cambridge, Mass.: Harvard University Press, 1982), pp. 157–60, Werner Sollors, "'A World Somewhere, Somewhere Else.' Language, Nostalgic Mournfulness, and Urban Immigrant Family Romance in *Call It Sleep,"* in *New Essays on Call It Sleep,* ed. Hana Wirth-Nesher (Cambridge: Cambridge University Press, 1996), pp. 127–88.

9. Wirth-Nesher, "Between Mother Tongue," p. 298. See also Shmuel Niger, *Bilingualism in the History of Jewish Literature,* trans. Joshua A. Fogel (Lanham: University Press of America, 1990).

10. Sollors, "'A World Somewhere,'" p. 134; Wirth-Nesher, "Between Mother Tongue," p. 302. Murray Baumgarten is even more emphatic. "If these works are written in English, it is a language with Yiddish lurking behind every Anglo-Saxon character . . . Yiddish, as language and culture, [works] to make its presence felt in the character, situation, and narrative voice of the story, as it does in the vocabulary, syntax, and morphology of the western language in which it is written." Baumgarten, *City Scriptures,* pp. 10, 155. See also Irving Howe, *World of Our Fathers* (New York: Harcourt Brace Jovanovich, 1976), p. 588, and Horst Immel, *Literarische Gestaltungsvarianten des Einwanderungsromans in der amerikanischen und anglokanadischen Literatur: Grove, Cahan, Rölvaag, Henry Roth* (Frankfurt: Peter Lang, 1987), pp. 335–50.

11. There is no current consensus of what constitutes a Jewish language, but it is generally understood by linguists and laymen alike to be any language spoken by Jews but not by the other groups in the society around them, often with syntactical and grammatical differences which have developed over time or stem from its origins as a contact language. Furthermore, Jewish

languages are often defined as languages spoken and understood only by Jews, and/or languages derived from the writing of another language in Hebrew characters or with Hebrew and Aramaic added into the standard vernacular language. See Sol Steinmetz, *Yiddish and English: A Century of Yiddish in America* (Tuskaloosa: University of Alabama Press, 1986), p. 10, and Joshua A. Fishman, "The Sociology of Jewish Languages from the Perspective of the General Sociology of Language: A Preliminary Formulation," *International Journal of the Sociology of Language* 30 (1981):5–16.

12. For the most definitive history of the Yiddish language, see Max Weinreich, *History of the Yiddish Language* (Chicago: University of Chicago Press, 1980). For a sampling of recent scholarship, which includes different perspectives, see also Dovid L. Katz, ed., *Origins of the Yiddish Language* (Oxford: Pergamon Press, 1987); David Goldberg, ed., *The Field of Yiddish*, vol. V (Evanston: Northwestern University Press and YIVO Institute for Jewish Research, 1993), and Paul Wexler, "Focus Article," *International Journal of the Sociology of Language* 91 (1991):11–127.

13. Joshua A. Fishman, "Yiddish in America," in Fishman, *Yiddish: Turning to Life* (Amsterdam: John Benjamins Publishing, 1991), p. 155n1.

14. On the ideological debates surrounding the historical relationship between Yiddish and German, see Christopher Hutton, "Normativism and the Notion of Authenticity in Yiddish Linguistics," pp. 11–57 in Goldberg, *Field of Yiddish*.

15. On the history of various names of Yiddish, see Weinreich, *History*, pp. 315–27. On the ideological uses of names, see Jerold C. Frakes, "Critical Ideology in Old Yiddish Studies: The Names of Old Yiddish," *Yiddish* 6-1 (1985):5–14.

16. Joshua A. Fishman, "Post-exilic Jewish Languages and Pidgins/Creoles: Two Mutually Clarifying Perspectives," in Fishman, *Yiddish*, pp. 19–22. The idea of Yiddish as a grammarless, amorphous language lacking a true structure has persisted even into the present. Here, for instance, is the advice of a 1968 popular guide to Yiddish and the use of Yiddish expressions in English: "Yiddish is, perhaps, the ideal pidgin-language because it naturally assumes the syntax of the host language. In spicing your English vocabulary with Yiddish, the general rule is: don't think about grammar, use Yiddish words just as you would English words ... Yiddish and English verbs are perfectly interchangeable." Martin Marcus. *Yiddish for Yankees, or, Funny, You Don't Look Gentile* (Philadelphia: J. B. Lippincott, 1968), p. 46.

17. Sander Gilman, "To Quote Primo Levi: 'Redest keyn yiddisch bist nit keyn jid'" [If you don't speak Yiddish, you're not a Jew], *Prooftexts* 9-2 (1989):139–60. See also Sander Gilman, *Jewish Self-Hatred: Anti-Semitism and the Hidden Language of the Jews* (Baltimore: Johns Hopkins University Press, 1986), esp. pp. 68–86, 139–48, and Steven E. Ascheim, *Brothers and Strangers: The East Eu-*

ropean Jew in German and German Jewish Consciousness, 1800–1923 (Madison: University of Wisconsin Press, 1982), pp. 6–12.

18. Moses Mendelssohn, quoted in Gabriele von Glasenapp, "German versus *Jargon:* Language and Jewish Identity in German Ghetto Writing," in *Ghetto Writing: Traditional and Eastern Jewry in German-Jewish Literature from Heine to Hilsenrath,* ed. Anne Fuchs and Florian Krobb (Columbia: Camden House, 1999), p. 55. Others went even farther in their contempt for Yiddish. Witness the vicious comments of the nineteenth-century German-Jewish historian Heinrich Graetz: "The language of the [Polish] Jews in particular suffered . . . degenerating into a ridiculous jargon, a mixture of German, Polish, and Talmudical elements, an unpleasant stammering, rendered still more repulsive by forced attempts at wit. This corrupt speech, despising all forms, could be understood only by Jews, natives of the country. Together with their language the Polish Jews lost that which constitutes a man, and were thus exposed to the scorn and contempt of non-Jewish society." Graetz, *History of the Jews,* vol. 4, trans. and ed. Bella Lowy (Philadelphia: Jewish Publication Society of America, 1894, p. 641. See also Glaesnapp, pp. 54–65, and Graetz, vol. 4, pp. 640–41; vol. 5, pp. 291–92, 300–01, 328–33.

19. See Benjamin Harshav, *Language in Time of Revolution* (Berkeley: University of California Press, 1993), esp. pp. 139–40, 153–66, 183–94, and Naomi Seidman, *A Marriage Made in Heaven: The Sexual Politics of Hebrew and Yiddish* (Berkeley: University of California Press, 1997), esp. pp. 114–31.

20. For a fascinating example of mid-nineteenth-century Yinglish in Britain, see David L. Gold, "Five Assorted Documents of Yiddish Interest (from 1853, 1871, 1928, and 1936)," *Jewish Language Review* 6 (1986), pp. 150–63.

21. One exception is the Anglo-Jewish author Israel Zangwill, whose works documented Yiddish language and culture among London's East End Jews. Zangwill's most famous novel (1892), *Children of the Ghetto: A Study of Peculiar People* (London: White Lion Publishers, 1972), was the first instance of the appearance of a glossary in an English-language literary work.

22. Yaakov Tsvi Sobel, *Yisroel der alte/Israel ha-zaken,* quoted in Kalman Marmor, *Der onhoyb fun der yiddisher literature in amerike, 1870–1890* [The Birth of Yiddish Literature in America, 1870–1890] (New York: IKUF, 1944), pp. 13–19. See also Marmor, "Tsvey Yubileyen: Dos ersht yidish bikhl in amerike un di ershte tsaytung in yidish in shikage, vos zaynen aroys in yor 1877" [Two Anniversaries: The First Yiddish Book Published in America and the First Yiddish Newspaper Published in Chicago in the Year 1877], *Pinkes* (New York: YIVO Institute, 1928), vol. 1, pp. 38–52, and Moyshe Shtarkman, "Tsu der geshikhte fun yidish in amerike" [Toward the History of the Yiddish Language in America], *YIVO Bleter* 2 (1939), pp. 181–90.

23. George Wolfe, "Notes on American Yiddish," *The American Mercury* 29-116 (1933):474. The word "paintner" is a special instance of a partial loan. Linguist Lillian Mermin Feinsilver explains, "Yiddish is prone to the partial loan: an English word is taken and added to in some way. With nouns, it may add an extra letter, as in PEYNTNER [sic] from 'painter.' This term has been subject to so much reminiscing, from *Commentary* magazine to Alan Sherman's parodying folk song, 'When the Paintners Come Marching In.'" Lillian Mermin Feinsilver, *The Taste of Yiddish* (South Brunswick: Thomas Yosseloff, 1970), pp. 375–76.

24. Jacob Riis, *How the Other Half Lives* (New York: Dover, 1971), p. 43.

25. Abraham Cahan, *Bleter fun mayn lebn* (New York: Forward Association, 1926), vol. 2, pp. 445–58. Cahan gave the glossary the title, *Verter-bukh far nit amerikanishe lezer* [Lexicon for Non-American Readers]. Its contents were defined as "words and expressions which have become a part of the Yiddish language in America (and England) and which are unknown in the language of our old country."

26. Joshua Fishman writes, "Abe Cahan, long time editor of the *Forverts* was one of the major avowed champions of the 'potato-Yiddish' in the daily press." Fishman, "Yiddish in America," p. 158. Cahan suffered many charges of self-hatred and anti-Semitism for his honest depictions of Lower East Side ghetto life. Sanford Pinsker, *The Comedy that 'Hoits'* (Columbia: University of Missouri, 1975), p. 5. For more on Cahan's prescriptive vision of the Yiddish press, see Jeremy Dauber, "Worthy Editor: Theorizing the Advice Column of the Jewish Daily Forward," B.A. thesis, Harvard University, 1995. The central role of popular culture in linguistic change should not be overlooked. For a discussion of language and the immigrant theater and popular song industries, see Mario Maffi, *Gateway to the Promised Land* (New York: New York University Press, 1994), pp. 133–34.

27. For an interesting discussion of Cahan's work in the context of his Jewish-American peers, see Sally Ann Drucker, "Yiddish, Yidgin, and Yezierska: Dialect in Jewish-American Writing," *Yiddish* 6-4 (1987):99–113. While Drucker's analysis suffers from an unquestioning emphasis on dialect as opposed to Yinglish, her attention to the variation in the use and representation of Yiddish and Yinglish is helpful.

28. The starting point for all investigations into Cahan's writing is Jules Chametzsky, *From the Ghetto: The Fiction of of Abraham Cahan* (Amherst: University of Massachusetts Press, 1977). Aviva Taubenfeld has recently achieved a breakthrough in Cahan scholarship by comparing Cahan's English version of *Yekl* with his virtually unknown Yiddish version (published in serial form in a newspaper at roughly the same time). She takes a very different methodological and theoretical approach from mine, concentrating on a side-by-side com-

parison of the two texts. The result is a fascinating interpretation of Cahan as a dual-language immigrant writer simultaneously playing with and trying to escape the dilemma of bilinguality. Taubenfeld, "Only an 'L': Linguistic Borders and the Immigrant Author in Abraham Cahan's *Yekl* and *Yankel der Yankee*," in *Multilingual America: Transnationalism, Ethnicity, and the Languages of American Literature,* ed. Werner Sollors (New York: New York University Press, 1998), pp. 144–165. Other important recent work includes Matthew Jacobson, "The Quintessence of the Jew: Polemics of Nationalism and Peoplehood in Turn-of-the-Century Yiddish Fiction," in *Multilingual America,* pp. 103–11, and Sanford Marovitz, *Abraham Cahan* (New York: Twayne Publishers, 1996).

29. Henry Roth later used this literary technique to great effect in his masterpiece *Call It Sleep* (New York: Noonday Press, 1991). For an analysis of Roth's approach, see Sollors, "'A World Somewhere,'" pp. 129–37, and Wirth-Nesher, "Between Mother Tongue," pp. 298–311.

30. Wirth-Nesher, "Between Mother Tongue," p. 302.

31. Abraham Cahan, *Yekl and the Imported Bridegroom and Other Stories of the New York Ghetto* (New York: Dover Publications, 1970), p. 2.

32. Cahan, *Yekl and . . . Stories,* p. 2.

33. Ibid., p. 5.

34. Italics often drop out unexpectedly throughout the story. Cahan, *Yekl and . . . Stories,* p. 47.

35. Ibid., p. 45.

36. Ibid.

37. Ibid., p. 49.

38. Bill Blackbeard, "Milt Gross," *Dictionary of Literary Biography. Vol. 11: American Humorists, 1800–1950* (Detroit: Gale, 1982), pp. 160–65.

39. For a theoretical overview of dialect in literature, see Sumner Ives, "A Theory of Literary Dialect," in *A Various Language: Perspectives on American Dialects,* ed. Juanita V. Williamson and Virginia M. Burke (New York: Holt, 1971), pp. 146–77. For two linguists' perspectives on dialect in Gross's work, see Robert Menner, "Popular Phonetics," *American Speech* 4 (1929):410–16, and Lawrence M. Davis, "Literary Dialect in Milt Gross' *Nize Baby*," in *Studies in Linguistics in Honor of Raven I. McDavid, Jr.,* ed. Lawrence M. Davis (Tuscaloosa: University of Alabama Press, 1972), pp. 41–47.

40. Milt Gross, *Famous fimmales witt odder ewents from heestory* (Garden City: Doubleday, Doran, 1928), p. 18.

41. Ibid., p. 15.

42. The most famous example of this genre of immigrant speech parody is Leo Rosten's 1937 work, *The Education of H*Y*M*A*N K*A*P*L*A*N* (New York: Harcourt Brace, 1937), which follows the same rules as Gross's work, steadfastly avoiding Yiddish and emphasizing malapropisms, mispronunciations, and errors based on homophones. While Rosten's works sold extremely well, they still elicited standard criticisms as distorted exaggerations of Jewish speech (which they were): "[Rosten's book] is an offensive gimmick revolving around dialogue, although 80 per cent of the American Jewish community has been born in this country, and even of the other 20 per cent, not too many speak Hyman Kaplan's dialect." Judd L. Teller, "The House-Broken Jew," *Midstream* 5-4 (Autumn 1959):94.

43. In fact, there is a long tradition of prophesying the impending death of Yiddish. As early as 1862, a Russian-Jewish Hebrew journalist told Czarist authorities that Yiddish was dying. Yiddish literature scholar Leo Wiener expressed the same pessimism at the turn of the century, even as immigration climbed towards its peak. Steinmetz, *Yiddish*, p. 22.

44. Chaim Zhitlowsky, quoted in Wolfe, "Notes," p. 478. Other references to Yinglish of the time include "the barbaric language" and "the language of the streets" and "pidgin Yiddish" and "dialect" (ibid). Perhaps most extreme is the slightly later reference to a "rape of Yiddish." S. J. Goldsmith, "The Rape of Yiddish," *Congress Bi-Weekly*, June 24, 1963, pp. 21–22; Nahma Sandrow, *Vagabond Stars: A World History of the Yiddish Theatre* (New York: Harper and Row, 1977), p. 294.

45. Isaac Bashevis Singer, "Problems of Yiddish Prose," *Svive* 2 (March-April 1943), trans. Robert H. Wolf and reprinted in *Prooftexts* 9-1 (Jan. 1989):8–9.

46. Many American English speakers refer to Yiddish by the term "Jewish," a direct, though confusing, translation of its name. "Some Old Masters," *New Era* 6-4 (March/April 1905):448.

47. H. B. Wells, "Notes on Yiddish," *American Speech* 4-1 (Oct. 1928):65–66. Compare the Germanist's remark to Yiddishist Irving Howe's comments on Saul Bellow's Yinglish: "Bellow's style draws heavily from the Yiddish, not so much in borrowed diction as in underlying intonation and rhythm . . . so that what we get . . . [is] a vibrant linguistic and cultural transmutation. Precisely at the moment when Yiddish is dying off as an independent language, it has experienced an astonishing, and not always happy, migration into American culture. In two or three decades students of American literature may have to study Yiddish for reasons no worse than those for which students of English literature study Anglo-Saxon." Irving Howe, "Odysseus, Flat on His Back," *The New Republic*, Sept. 19, 1964, pp. 21–26, reprinted in *Critical Essays on Saul Bellow*, ed. Stanley Trachtenberg (Boston: G. K. Hall, 1979), p. 34.

48. William Schack and Sarah Schack, "And Now — Yinglish on Broadway," *Commentary*, Dec. 1951, p. 587.

49. Schack and Schack, "And Now," p. 586. A few years earlier, Yiddish literary critic A. A. Roback offered the following definition: "Yidgin-English: Yiddish-English dialect (*colloquialism*)." A. A. Roback, *Dictionary of International Slurs (Ethnopaulisms)* (Cambridge: Sci-Art Publishers, 1944), p. 72. For an even earlier reference to "Yidgin English," defined as "a purely imaginary language logically related to neither of its parents," see Alter Brody, "Yiddish in American Fiction," *American Mercury* 7 (1926):205. See also Alter Brody, "Yiddish: Our Literary Dominion," *The Nation* 124 (April 20, 1927):435–36.

50. These languages included Spanglish (1954), Franglais (1959), and even Finnglish (1944). Only later in the 1960s and 1970s did large-scale academic research on Yinglish begin. See, for instance, Feinsilver, *The Taste of Yiddish;* Eugene Green, *Yiddish and English in Detroit: A Survey and Analysis of Reciprocal Influences in Bilinguals' Pronunciation, Grammar, and Vocabulary* (Ann Arbor: University of Michigan Press, 1961); and George Jochnowitz, "Bilingualism and Dialect Mixture among Lubavitcher Hasidic Children," *American Speech* 43 (1968):182–200. The name "Jewish English" emerged during the early 1970s and remains the current academic term, though others have been proposed. See Fishman, "The Sociology of Jewish Languages," *International Journal of the Sociology of Language* 30 (1981):5–16; Steinmetz, *Yiddish,* pp. 76–102; David L. Gold, "Jewish English," in *Readings in the Sociology of Jewish Languages,* ed. Joshua A. Fishman (Leiden: E. J. Brill, 1985), pp. 280–298; Gold, "An Introduction to Jewish English," *Jewish Language Review* 6 (1986):94–120; Gold, "On Jewish English in the United States," *Jewish Language Review* 6 (1986):121–36.

51. Much of the ambiguity concerning the difference between Yiddish and the Yiddish accent stems from the long tradition of American dialect humor. Jewish dialect humor actually preceded Yiddish-language humor in America, beginning in the 1880s and continuing straight through to the 1950s. A 1950 survey found that over one-third of the Jewish jokes of the time involved dialect. Milton L. Baron, "A Content Analysis of Intergroup Humor," *American Sociological Review* 15 (1950):90, quoted in Stanley Brandes, "Jewish-American Dialect Jokes and Jewish-American Identity," *Jewish Social Studies* (Summer–Fall 1983):235. For an earlier discussion of Jewish dialect, see C. K. Thomas, "Jewish Dialect and New York Dialect," *American Speech* 7-5 (June 1932):321–26. Nevertheless, the contextualization of Yiddish — its selective use in popular culture — explains much of its comic associations. See Sig Altman, *The Comic Image of the Jew: Explorations of a Pop Culture Phenomenon* (Rutherford, 1971), pp. 60, 84–86, Goldsmith, "The Rape," pp. 21–22, Wells, "Notes on Yiddish," p. 58, and Gans, "Yinglish Music," pp. 216–17.

52. Fishman, "Yiddish in America," p. 126.

53. Ibid., p. 127.

54. Marc Shechner, "The Conversion of the Jews," in Marc Shechner, *The Conversion of the Jews and Other Essays* (New York: St. Martin's Press, 1990), p. 3.

55. On Yiddish in these authors' work, see in particular Howe, "Odysseus," pp. 21–26, and Baumgarten, *City Scriptures*, especially pp. 10; 155–60. A less rigorous lexicon of Yinglish in these authors' work can be found in Gene Bluestein, *Anglish-Yinglish: Yinglish in American Life and Literature*, 2nd ed. (Lincoln: University of Nebraska Press, 1998).

56. Roth was born in New Jersey in 1933. There is no indication from his autobiography, *The Facts* (London: Jonathan Cape, 1989), that he spoke Yiddish or had extensive contact with the language while growing up. See also Ruth Wisse, "Language as Fate: Reflections on Jewish Literature in America," in *Literary Strategies: Jewish Texts and Contexts*, ed. Ezra Mendelsohn (New York: Oxford University Press, 1996).

57. Philip Roth, "Epstein," *The Paris Review* 19 (1958):13–36; Philip Roth, *Goodbye, Columbus* (Boston: Houghton Mifflin, 1959). This work won the National Book Award for Fiction in 1960.

58. Quoted in Pinsker, *Comedy*, p. 24. See also Philip Roth, *Reading Myself and Others* (New York: Farrar, Straus and Giroux, 1975), p. 153, and Theodore Solotaroff, "Philip Roth: A Personal View," in *The Red Hot Vacuum* (New York: Atheneum Books, 1970), p. 312.

59. Goldsmith, "The Rape," pp. 21–22; Alvin Lukashok, "Dialect and Dialogue," *Jewish Frontier* 26 (Nov. 1959):19.

60. Lukashok, "Dialect," p. 19.

61. Marie Syrkin, "The Fun of Self-Abuse," *The State of the Jews* (Washington: New Republic Books, 1980), p. 333. For more on the Jewish communal response to Roth's early work, see Alan Cooper, *Philip Roth and the Jews* (Albany: SUNY Press, 1996), esp. pp. 24–50.

62. Murray Baumgarten and Barbara Gottfried, *Understanding Philip Roth* (Columbia: University of South Carolina Press, 1990), pp. 17–18.

63. For a different reading of Yinglish in Philip Roth, see Bluestein, *Anglish-Yiddish*, pp. 129–47.

64. Critic Murray Baumgarten has explored this problem: "To multiply examples [of Jewish interlinguistics] by listing passages in which Yiddish words and phrases are the pivots of meaning in works written in the modern Western languages is insufficient evidence . . . What we need to focus on is the effect of combination, when lexical borrowing is reinforced by character as well as syntax and narrative voicing; the full situation functions to evoke the panoply of the values of Yiddish culture." Baumgarten, *City Scriptures*, p. 29. Baumgarten's point is well taken, but we might also add that the historical context is equally significant in determining the literary and linguistic effect.

65. Roth, "Epstein," pp. 22, 27, 30–31.

66. Ibid., p. 14.

67. Sol Steinmetz elaborates on this point: "The problem of rendering Jewish-English words in Roman script is complicated by the two discrete pronunciation systems inherited from Hebrew and Yiddish. Though both of these languages use the Hebrew alphabet and spell the words common to both identically, they pronounce these words differently . . . in actual practice many writers will use the more prestigious Hebrew spelling even though they pronounce the word as if it were spelled [in accordance with the Yiddish pronunciation]." Steinmetz, "Jewish English," p. 13.

68. For a discussion of language standardization and writing, see Steinmetz, *Yiddish*, p. 107.

69. Ibid., p. 20.

70. Ibid., p. 21.

71. Feinsilver, *Taste of Yiddish*, p. 45.

72. In the 1959 version of "Epstein," published in *Goodbye, Columbus* and otherwise identical to the original, the sentence is: "Nice, shmice, it was a bath." Assuming it was Roth and not a copy editor responsible for the change, we can surmise that Roth changed the spelling of "shmice" because of Yinglish concerns. Changing the "s" to a "c" corresponds further to the Yinglish formula according to which the two words should appear as identical as possible. Why else would Roth change the spelling from a romanization closer to Yiddish "-ise" to the more Anglicized sound "-ice"? For more on the "shm-" construction, see Lilian Mermin Feinsilver, "On Yiddish Shm-," *American Speech* 36-4 (Dec. 1961):302–03, Leo Spitzer, "Confusion Schmooshun," *Journal of English and Germanic Philology* 51 (1952):226–27, and Leo Rosten, *The Joys of Yinglish* (New York: McGraw Hill, 1989), pp. 4–5.

73. Judith Paterson Jones and Guinevera A. Nance, *Philip Roth* (New York: Frederick Ungar Publishing, 1981), p. 6. Only one of the authors, Jones, conducted the interview and summarized Roth's remarks in the introduction to the volume.

74. Hudson, *Sociolinguistics*, pp. 56–58.

75. Leo Rosten, *The Joys of Yiddish* (New York: McGraw-Hill, 1968).

76. See Leo Rosten, *Hooray for Yiddish* (New York: Simon and Schuster, 1982), Rosten, *The Joys of Yinglish;* Paul Hoffman and Matt Freedom, *Dictionary Shmictionary!: A Yiddish and Yinglish Dictionary* (New York: Quill, 1983); Jackie Mason, *How to Talk Jewish* (New York: St. Martin's Press, 1992); Mollie Katz, *Jewish as a Second Language* (New York: Workman's Publications, 1991); Marcus, *Yiddish for Yankees,* and Dana C. Berkman, *Goyim My Way: A Gentile's Guide to Yiddish* (New York: South Brunswick, A. S. Barnes, 1966).

77. For examples of the academic promotion of American Jewish linguistic distinctiveness that date from this period, see Lawrence M. Davis, "The Phonology of Yiddish-American Speech," Ph.D. diss., University of Chicago, 1967; his "The Stressed Vowels of Yiddish-American English," *Publication of the American Dialect Society* 48 (Tuscaloosa: University of Alabama Press, 1967); J. R. Rayfield, *The Languages of a Bilingual Community* (The Hague: Mouton, 1970); and David S. Disenhouse, "Phonological Manifestations of Ethnic Identification: The Jewish Community of New York City," Ph.D. diss., New York University, 1974.

78. Cynthia Ozick, "America: Toward Yavneh," in Wirth-Nesher, *What Is Jewish Literature?*, pp. 29–34.

79. Nevertheless the phenomenon lives on. See, for instance, Chaim M. Weiser, *Frumspeak: The First Dictionary of Yeshivish* (Northvale: J. Aronson, 1995); Hoffman and Freedom, *Dictionary Shmictionary*; Sidney J. Jacobs, *The Jewish Word Book* (Middle Village, N.Y.: J. David, 1982); Richard Lederer, *Adventures of a Verbiore* (New York: Pocket Books, 1994), pp. 88–91, and Benjamin Bleich, *The Complete Idiot's Guide to Learning Yiddish* (Indianapolis: Alpha Books 2000). Ruth Wisse takes Ozick to task for an "almost complete lack of supportive evidence" while Murray Baumgarten questions Ozick's realism given the dramatic success and obvious potential of modern Hebrew. Ruth Wisse, "American Jewish Writing, Act II," *Commentary* 61–6 (June 1976):41 and Baumgarten, *City Scriptures*, p. 134. See also Wisse, "Language as Fate," p. 132.

80. Recent academic treatments of Yinglish have tended to approach the subject from a sociolinguistic perspective. See Sarah Benor, "Yavnish: A Linguistic Analysis of Columbia's Orthodox Jewish Community," *Iggrot ha-Ari* [Columbia University Student Journal of Jewish Scholarship] 1-2 (Spring 1998):8–50; Benor, "Loan Words in the English of Modern Orthodox Jews: Yiddish or Hebrew?" in *Proceedings of the 25th Annual Meeting of the Berkeley Linguistics Society, 1999, Parasession on Loan Word Phenomena* (Berkeley: Berkeley Linguistics Society, 2000), pp. 287–98; Gold, "Jewish English"; Barbara Ullmann, "Jewish English as an Ethnic Speech Marker: A Lexical Study of an Upstate New York Community," Ph.D. diss., SUNY at Binghamton, 2001, and Sam Weiss, "Book Review: *Frumspeak: The First Dictionary of Yeshivish*, by Chaim M. Weiser," *International Journal of the Sociology of Language* 138 (1999):181–87. For two original literary approaches, see Marc Shell, "Hyphens; between Deitsch and American," in *Multilingual America*, ed. Sollors, pp. 258–71, and Lawrence Rosenwald, "American Anglophone Literature and Multilingual America," in ibid.

CHAPTER NINE

Homing Pidgins: Another Version of Pastoral in Hawai'i

■ **SUSANNAH YOUNG-AH GOTTLIEB**

"FOR DA BIRDS"

Fodor's famous 1969 guide to Hawai'i, with its foreword by James Michener, includes a section on intellectual climate called "Beware of Ideas." The writers offer these helpful guidelines to tourists who may want some sense of life in Hawai'i before planning a trip: "So far there have been no Hawaiian intellectuals. There may never be. . . . A massive immovable literalmindedness characterizes those who are educated in the Islands, especially those of Oriental background. Irony, metaphor, poetry, and other flights of fancy are almost incomprehensible to local college students, to the great despair of their teachers. . . . The virtues of Hawaii are the virtues of love and not syntax."[1]

The authors provide scant clues as to the reasons for the development of the amorous virtues at the expense of virtues of the intellect, except to describe local women as "free," "uninhibited," "generous," "ardent," and even "shameless," and to insist that the local population is largely incompetent in standard English.[2] In a section on language entitled "Island Speech Is Different: Hawaiian Salt and Pidgin Pepper," the authors describe Hawai'i pidgin as the unofficial language of the islands: "It is heard everywhere: on ranches, in warehouses, on beaches, and in the hallowed halls (though not in the classrooms) of the University of Hawaii."[3] To illustrate in what manner pidgin poses an obstacle to the development of a more intellectual climate, the authors offer a story about a professor who "once gave a dramatic reading of Shelley's 'Ode to a Skylark' [sic]" at the University of Hawai'i and asserted that such a masterpiece could not have been written in pidgin. He later overheard a student say, "Who da hell wanna write da kine ode for da birds?"[4]

In a different kind of ornitho-tribute, Joseph P. Balaz, a local writer who sometimes writes in pidgin, was invited to read his poetry at a Colloquium on Pidgin and Creole Languages at the University of Hawai'i at Manoa in Honolulu in August 1986. As a preface to his talk, Balaz offered this tale of avifauna:

DA HISTORY OF PIGEON
(in phonic association to pidgin)

Like different kind words, da world was full of different kind birds: yellow birds, blue birds, red birds, love birds — and den came da pigeon.

Da history of the word pigeon is li'dis — Wen da French-speaking Normans wen conquer England in da year ten-six-six, dey wen bring along wit dem da word pigeon, for da type of bird it was. Da resident Anglo-Saxons used da word dove, or D-U-F-E, as dey used to spell 'um to mean da same bird. It just so happened dat terms in Norman-French wen blend wit Old English sentence structure, to form what we know as Middle English. In da process, da French word became da one dat referred to da pigeon as food. Today in England, if you look for dem, you can find recipes for pigeon pie.

Food for taught, eh — Even back den, da word pigeon wen blend with pigeon for get some moa pigeon. So now days get pigeon by da zoo — get pigeon on da beach — get pigeon in town — get pigeon in coups — and no madda wat anybody try do, dey cannot get rid of pigeon — I guess wit such a wide blue sky, everything deserves to fly.[5]

In his play on the homophones *pidgin* and *pigeon,* Balaz ingeniously interweaves many of the characteristics of the development of a pidgin into his history of pigeon: among them, borrowing and relexification at a point of linguistic contact, and ubiquity — the seeming impossibility of elimination. This account also raises but does not resolve the question of the status of English after the Norman conquest. Despite major modifications of its syntax and a lexicon that absorbed words from everywhere, the emergent English never ceased to be considered a language. Although Hawai'i pidgin has undergone similar transformations, it is not understood as a further evolution in the development of an ever-changing language but, rather, as a corruption of a somehow "pure" language.

Regardless of the difficulty in defining what constitutes a language (rather than a dialect or a corrupted version of a language), there is an almost unanimous insistence that anything called a pidgin is impoverished: not the native language of its speakers, it is generally understood as a contact vernacular, used for limited purposes and arising primarily in situations involving two or more languages other than the standard one used by the dominant culture.[6] Some other characterizations that are fairly uncontroversial among linguists indicate that "a pidgin represents a language which has been stripped of everything but the bare essentials necessary for communication. There are few, if any, stylistic options. The emphasis is on the referential or communicative rather than the expressive function of language."[7] If a pidgin is only a rudimentary medium of communication — one divested of style and stylistic options — how could there be a literature in Hawai'i pidgin? This question may not be a central one for linguistic research into the nature of pidgins and creoles, but it points toward the difficulty of finding a sure criterion by which to distinguish pidgins from creoles and creoles from "standard" languages. If literature emphasizes something other than the referential function of language, pidgin would seem incapable of sustaining a literary tradition. And yet the developing body of literature written in Hawai'i pidgin clearly confounds this contention. Linguists resolve the contradiction by categorizing Hawaiian Pidgin English as a creole, not a true pidgin.[8] But the pidgin writers of Hawai'i nevertheless choose to refer to their language as Hawai'i pidgin or simply pidgin, and their choice suggests that certain linguistic categories and systems of classification do not fully accommodate this language.[9] The question whether a language is suitable for the generation of a literary tradition is rarely a matter of concern for linguists. There is good reason, however, to think that the question of language in general cannot be divorced from the question of something like literary potential; that is, the ability of a communicative mode not only to function in a nonreferential manner, but also to harbor self-referential and self-consciously figural artifacts. In this essay, which moves toward the reading of some stories written in Hawai'i pidgin, I do not seek to respond to the question "what constitutes a language?" Rather, I hope to indicate the questionability of denying the status of language to a language — indeed, one with a significant literary tradition.

In Darrell Lum's story "Beer Can Hat," the narrator tells us that people say of his friend Bobo, "he talk crooked."[10] This statement assumes that the structure of the pidgin sentence "he talk crooked" is straight, and it mirrors the attitude of many speakers of standard English toward Hawai'i pidgin, namely, that its speakers talk crooked and need to be corrected. It seems possible, and at certain moments even necessary, to translate crooked into straight speech, which means in this story, however, to translate garbled language into pidgin. If we take for granted, as the narrator of the story clearly does, that pidgin is a language with a full range of expressive possibilities and is not a crooked, deficient, or defective mode of speaking, then pidgin is straight as it is and does not require correction. Yet even among those who make pidgins the subject of scientific inquiry, they are not only thought to be imperfect versions of one or more languages, but defective versions of language itself. Suzanne Romaine indicates that even a "true pidgin" is not truly a language: "a pidgin always arises from a situation involving a target language and two or more substrate languages, where the socially superior target language is sufficiently inaccessible to the substrate speakers that there is little motivation to improve performance and where a defective version of language can be functionally adequate."[11]

Social stratification determines that one language is the target of speech — a target that the speakers of a pidgin always miss. Instead of being a further development of this or any other language, a pidgin falls short of even the category "language." As a "defective version of language," a pidgin does not descend along a straight line of a language tree and therefore cannot be easily integrated into a system of classification.[12] Pidgins so thoroughly disrupt the idea of straight linguistic lineage that they cannot be presented according to the image of a tree at all. Instead of branching out from and into other languages, pidgins fall out of the language tree altogether, where they remain at the bottom of the linguistic landscape, always below the "true" languages. Without invoking any specific figure, Romaine's presentation of the situation in which a pidgin originates suggests the image of a pyramid: "substrate speakers" looking up to, and aiming for, a superior "target language" but unable — because "unmotivated" — ever to reach it.

"THE SHIT PYRAMID"

On sugar plantations, under English-speaking foremen, Hawai'i pidgin emerged.[13] It developed into a common tongue as plantation overseers gave instructions in a condensed, minimal form of English to newly arrived workers, most of whom came from Asia. Although whites were only about 5 percent of the population at the turn of the century, they held most of the skilled and supervisory positions.[14] And this is hardly surprising: "In 1904, the Hawaiian Sugar Planters' Association passed a resolution that restricted skilled positions to 'American citizens, or those eligible for citizenship.' Asian immigrants were excluded, for they were not 'white' and therefore ineligible to become naturalized citizens according to federal law."[15] During the same period, English was made the official language of the Hawaiian government and the medium of instruction in the public schools. As the children of immigrants from China, Japan, Korea, the Philippines, Portugal, Spain, and Puerto Rico entered these schools — to quote Elizabeth Carr — "the English language, so recently established as the medium of instruction, suffered a kind of 'linguistic swamping.'"[16]

This diversification of the population of Hawai'i and the consequent "swamping" of the linguistic landscape was not an accidental or haphazard process. On the contrary, it was part of a conscious attempt by plantation owners, managers, and stewards to prevent their workers from organizing with one another and thus creating effective unions. George H. Fairfield, manager of the Makee Sugar Company, stated the strategy with particular clarity: "Keep a variety of laborers, that is different nationalities, and thus prevent any concerted action in case of strikes, for there are few, if any, cases of Japs, Chinese, and Portuguese entering into a strike as a unit."[17] The more diversified the population, it was thought, the less likely an effective mass strike for at least one obvious reason: the absence of an interethnic language. Although the first unions were indeed organized as "blood unions" according to ethnic membership, pidgin facilitated communication among laborers of different ethnicities.[18] Less a language of labor than of resistance to the manner in which labor had hitherto been organized, pidgin served as an indispensable link among people whom the Hawaiian Sugar Planters' Association wanted to keep apart.[19] In February of 1920, a united Filipino-Japanese strike brought plantation operations to a stop with calls of "Pau Hana" and "no go work," and on April 23, the Japanese Federation of Labor became an interracial union: the Hawai'i Laborers' Association.

Despite the promise of these early gestures toward interethnic labor cooperation, it took over twenty-five years before notions of class began to replace in widespread fashion the attachments of ethnic cohesion that continued to separate labor, and even longer before sugar workers began to win a respectable share of the industry's wealth. In a massive campaign conducted between 1944 and 1958 on behalf of longshoremen and pineapple and sugar workers, the International Longshoremen's and Warehousemen's Union still needed to spell out, as one of its basic organizing principles, that "ethnic or racial distinctions served only the employers' interests."[20] This principle was responsive to the specific working and living conditions of the sugar plantations, which were organized into a pyramid according to ethnicity so as to keep labor divided. The pyramidal structure was both monetary — workers from different ethnic groups received wages according to different pay scales — and spatially sanctioned in the layout of the plantation.[21] Thus, the overseer's mansion was at the top of the hill, followed by a tiered housing system in which descending levels of the pyramid housed different ethnic groups. The descent down the pyramid was matched by a decline in the quality of the housing: "It was a company town with identical company houses and outhouses, and it was set up like a pyramid. At the tip was Mr. Nelson, then the Portuguese, Spanish, and Nisei *lunas* in their nicer-looking homes, then the identical wooden frame houses of Japanese Camp, then the more run-down Filipino Camp."[22]

In this descriptive early passage from Milton Murayama's revolutionary novel, *All I Asking for Is My Body*, the mention of outhouses anticipates a pivotal revelation near its end. Kiyo, the novel's young narrator, wakes up from a dream — that he could have a happy life on the plantation if only he could marry and enclose himself and his bride in a four-walled paradise of sexual fulfillment. But the world of the plantation cannot be shut out: the realities of poverty and mounting debt deny people the privilege of controlling their bodies and cause all such dreams to vanish. Living on Pig Pen Avenue, Kiyo thinks it better to copulate with a pig: in this way he would not be tempted to dream of a better life. Thus degraded, he sees the plantation as if for the first time:

> It rained so continually a damp smell of the outhouse hung over Pig Pen Avenue. The camp, I realized then, was planned and built around its sewage system. The half dozen rows of underground concrete ditches, two feet wide and three feet deep, ran from the higher slope of camp into the concrete irrigation ditch on the lower perimeter of the camp. . . . Shit too was organized according to the plantation pyramid. Mr. Nelson was top shit on the highest slope, then there were the Portuguese, Spanish, and *nisei lunas* with their indoor toilets which flushed into the same ditches, then Japanese Camp, and Filipino Camp. . . . Shit was the glue which held a group together.[23]

The workers who live at the lowest perimeter of the pyramid are exposed to the sights and smells of the sewage that collects in the ditch at the plantation's base. In Japanese Camp, Kiyo's home is the house nearest to both the pigpens and the ditch. Lacking anything like an elegant veranda or well-appointed parlor where he might invite guests — and unable to enter the women's baths — Kiyo must scheme to meet a woman in the only truly public space of the camp, the outhouse.[24] Kiyo chooses Michie, his young neighbor, but when he addresses her in the outhouse, Michie responds not in the pidgin of their peer group, but in the language of the *haole*.[25] Affronted by her pretensions to standard English, he says: "'You think you haole, eh? Maybe you think you shit ice cream, eh?'"[26] In his irritation, Kiyo has a point: language may be mobile in ways that housing and plumbing are not, but the thought that speaking like a white person could confer on Michie of Pig Pen Avenue the advantages of living at the top of the pyramid is as plausible as the idea of shitting ice cream. But only under the impossible conditions of shit's conversion to ice cream would Michie be liberated from her position amidst the camp's waste: "freedom was freedom from other people's shit."[27]

In the meticulously planned and rigid enterprise of the plantation — "Everything was over-organized" — there could be very little social mobility.[28] The excessive organization of the plantation is remarkably well matched in the minute organization of linguistic systems that, seeking to place pidgin somewhere within the complex of world languages, consign it to its detritus: under the name "Hawaiian Creole," pidgin is listed in Merritt Ruhlen's *Guide to the World's Languages,* for example, as "Classification: Miscellaneous."[29] In each case pidgin and its speakers are relegated to the lowest level of a functioning hierarchy, to be disposed of, hidden, or deposited in its sewers. Thus pidgin-speaking workers can be replaced in a single missive ("Our order for *40 Japs* . . . is now *void.* 25 Chinese . . . will fill our back orders for labor to date"),[30] and pidgin dismissed as a language, for the structures that these workers and this language inhabit were organized on the basis of their disposability.

Pidgin should be considered a language, not a "defective version of language" or a dialect. To consider it a defect is to favor a simple representation of a simple people who do not understand how to use even a simplified version of English grammar. To consider it a dialect is to convert shit into ice cream. Not a defect, to be sure, pidgin is turned into a dessert: something to be enjoyed in leisure hours but unnecessary to the workings of a civilized society. There is no better evidence of this than the words of Elizabeth Carr, who argues for an understanding of Hawai'i pidgin as a dialect: "Some look upon it with despair, it is true, but others regard it fondly as something as typical of the Islands as flower leis and pineapples. This attitude has grown with the realization that the dialect no longer brands a youngster — he can learn a standard or near standard form of English for use in the classroom and during working hours, yet can revert to [pidgin] during casual hours at the beach, on the playing field, in the bus, during coffee breaks, and at home."[31]

"HONOLULU — PARADISE"

In Carr's meditation we see remnants of an old story that continues to assert itself even in scholarly discussion. When Hawai'i pidgin is placed among the flowers and fruits of the land, it is interpreted according to a colonialist image: Hawai'i as pastoral paradise, Hawai'i the last refuge from the city and hence from civilization. As Stephen Sumida points out in his superb study, *And the View from the Shore,* "in Western annals for half a millennium, interesting confusions and blurred relationships have occurred between the pastoral as literary mode (the *concept* of a simpler and truer life) and the pastoral as literal fact (the supposed *reality* of an earthly paradise come true)."[32] Such simplistic confusions of fact and myth create a certain kind of Hawai'i pastoral in which "the writer — that is, the civilized man or woman — believes that the primitives he or she encounters take their own primitive myths literally. In Hawai'i's simple pastoral, the identification of fact with myth is unquestioned: Hawai'i *is* paradise; the native Hawaiians *believe* that Captain Cook *is* their god Lono."[33]

The old story that native Hawaiians viewed Captain Cook as a god may be true or false, but there is no doubt that the European imagination immediately seized upon Hawai'i as a version of pastoral. Seen as a garden shielded from civilization by a vast ocean, it could be figured as an Arcadia, a rural remnant of a golden age. In this way, the original features of pastoral stamped the image of this supposed paradise. So powerful is this image that it has become nearly impossible for a Hawai'i writer to avoid. The image of Hawai'i-as-paradise defines the literary space against which the pidgin writer creates his or her stories. There is perhaps no better proof of the power of this image than the advertising slogan that graces the shirt of Rosa K., the hero of Darrell Lum's "Primo Doesn't Take Back Bottles Anymore": "Honolulu — Paradise."[34] The slogan works even though everyone knows Honolulu is a large city. And no "is" is needed to complete the slogan, because everyone knows that Honolulu is part of Hawai'i, and Hawai'i *is* paradise.

Images of Hawai'i as paradise plant Lum's story firmly in the tradition of pastoral, and the provenance of pidgin in the plantation sends it in the direction of the proletarian pastoral. This latter term is an invention of William Empson, whose investigations into the pastoral tradition sacrifice systematicity for insight into the device by which *some* — but not all — versions of the genre are generated.[35] The pastoral, for Empson, involves a certain "mechanism" or "trick": complexity is simplified, difference made into sameness, or the many are shown to be one. In traditional pastorals, the complex reality of an urban civilization is simplified by making "simple people" — the diminutive characters of the pasture — represent larger figures of the city, as they speak the universal truths of nature: "The essential trick of the old pastoral, which was felt to imply a beautiful relation between rich and poor, was to make simple people express strong feelings (felt as the most universal subject, something fundamentally true about everybody) in learned and fashionable language (so that you wrote about the best subject in the best way)."[36] Less traditional and more "realistic" versions of pastoral make its subjects into critics of the civilization in which they are unable and unwilling to participate: "The realistic sort of pastoral . . . gives a natural expression for a sense of social injustice. So far as the person described is outside society because too poor for its benefits he is independent, as the artist claims to be, and can be a critic of society; so far as he is forced by this into crime he is the judge of the society that judges him."[37] Pastoral can thus serve a critical function — to reveal the ideological mechanisms by which the complexities of social reality are simplified and present them as little more than pastoral tricks: "This is the source of irony."[38] Yet in self-proclaimed proletarian literature Empson discovers — to his own surprise, it seems — something like a traditional pastoral: the lower orders are ennobled as they act heroically and speak universal truths, again "in a learned and fashionable language."

Pastoral accomplishes its defining trick by equating the lower and higher orders of society. It does not so much invert the social pyramid as raze it to the ground — a ground newly freed of its sewers. For who would need sewers if people egested ice cream? This is, for Empson, the great danger of pastoral: a sticky-sweet feeling of oneness captures hold of the reader, who all along remains secure in the knowledge that real social differences are still intact. *Some Versions of Pastoral* can thus be read as an extended investigation into the phenomenon of "slumming." The literary category "pastoral" corresponds to a certain version of tourism. Tourists are attracted to pastoral settings for reasons other than climatic: feeling an underlying sameness with those whom they encounter, they nevertheless know themselves to be different — and superior. Tourism has replaced sugar as Hawai'i's primary industry, and *Fodor's* explains why — no exposed sewers and many colorful people: "Few places on earth can offer a comparable combination of equable climate . . . dazzling flowers and flowering trees plus 20th-century American plumbing and a local population which is at once colorful, exotic and sincerely friendly to the *malihini* or stranger."[39]

The tourist whom *Fodor's* addresses — generally a speaker of standard

English — may be a *malihini*, but is definitely not a stranger. On the contrary, Fodor's tourists need never feel strange, for they carry their own world with them: experiences that can be immediately translated into familiar ones constitute the norm, and every untranslatable experience becomes so much "local color" or "local custom," including the local language. Similarly, when a literary work features pidgin only in the mouths of its characters and does not dignify it as a thoroughgoing medium of literary expression, readers may roam through the text as tourists through paradise. Taking for granted the superior status of their language — for it *is*, after all, a language — they can enjoy the charm of the "customs" of the "natives." A literature written entirely in pidgin, by contrast, offers something different: readers must recognize themselves as strangers to a world that goes on without them.

RECYCLING, ORNAMENT, ART

The writer who insists on pidgin as a language suitable for literature, and not merely as an instrument of local color placed within disavowing quotation marks, doubly develops the critical function of pastoral: exposing the limits of sentimental or idealized visions of Hawai'i as an island paradise, and making the reader aware, as well, of the choice of language — a choice that is not simply a matter of consciousness, but of a complex historical, material, and social configuration. First a language in which orders were issued to workers, then a language of interethnic union organization, it became also a language of domesticity and social life. As single immigrant workers married Hawaiians, or as immigrants from diverse ethnic groups married each other and set up homes, or even as immigrants from within the same ethnic group began to have children, plantation pidgin served as the language of the household. When the children went to school, the language widened to become the language of their peer group and became intimately tied to a local, interethnic identity. With the mechanization of agriculture, the plantation system disappeared but its language survived: it established a home for itself in the islands' complex — and constantly changing — spaces. The process by which this language creates a home for its speakers and writers deserves the title "homing pidgin."

The peculiar development of pidgin makes it particularly well suited to perform, almost as if on its own, the critical function of pastoral: as a local language, it runs counter to pastoral's gestures toward universality. Everywhere it is used, pidgin points away from the primary globalizing structures of the contemporary world, namely, the corporation and the school. Pidgin has not been accepted as a language of scholarship, and the nonliterary character of pidgin, in a very literal sense, is the final thematic punctuation mark of "Primo Doesn't Take Back Bottles Anymore" — a story whose events take place under the shadow of "new management."[40] This story by Darrell Lum, written alternately in English and pidgin, describes a primitive business interaction and how its main character came to be dependent on a way of life that becomes, in the space of five pages, obsolete. As Sumida describes him, "Rosario Kamahele is not the antihero he would appear to be but is again actually a character out of the pastoral, this time an 'unemployed laborer' as swain."[41] Kicked out of school, sent to a boys' home, told by a judge to join the army or get a job, Rosa K. decides to join the union: "he almost became a carpenter's apprentice when he and half the crew got laid off. That was when he started collecting bottles."[42] Recycling bottles is not just a means of getting money, but also a way of tending the island and keeping it free of debris. Rosa the recycler participates, however tenuously, in the island's economy. When recycling comes to an end, Rosa becomes as useless as the things he once collected. He survives, but in the manner that most things survive: only as memories or ironic images and slogans, like those that cover his "silken aloha shirt with hula girls and Diamond Head and 'Honolulu — Paradise' written all over it."[43]

Rosa's chief achievement before he began to collect and redeem bottles is one that he recalls again and again: at one time he was the "bull of the school and ruler of the second floor lavatory," and he supported himself and his brother by stealing from *haoles*.[44] By beating up the white boys, Rosa kept them aware of his existence and the existence of people like him, and he managed at the same time to locate himself at the top of a miniature social pyramid. Rosa thus enacted a pastoral inversion of the plantation system — the bathroom moving to the pinnacle — for he treated his white classmates as the white overseers treated those like Kiyo in *All I Asking for Is My Body*. Just as the plantation system made huge profits from the labor of its workers while leaving them the means of subsistence, Rosa's system generated a profit by intimidating those beneath him while leaving them in a position to provide him with an income: instead of stealing all the money of the *haoles,* he always left them bus fare so that they could return and begin the cycle again.

Once Primo doesn't take back bottles anymore, Rosa is displaced from his second occupation — recycling — and deprived of his only source of income. Bearing along with his case of empties a gift of *opihi* that he picked among the rocks, Rosa expects to find his friend Harry at the brewery, ready to exchange his bottles for money. Instead, he finds the "Receiving Bottle Empties" sign painted over and Harry gone, dismissed from his job. In his agitation, Rosa grabs a brush and writes "F-O-C-K" on the sign. The wet letters momentarily appear in the monochromatic field: "The paint was the same color as the sign but the work was visible as the sun glistened off the dripping letters."[45] Lum does not underline the word *work,* but it is as emphatic — and surprising — as the word *fock.* Rosa creates "a work" at the very moment he loses his job. But the work is even shorter-lasting than the job: superimposed on the newly blanked-out sign, his pidgin self-expression disappears into homogenization. This is a literalization of the nonliterary character of Rosa's language. The story thus concludes with the image of a pidgin writer — one whose work disappears almost as soon as it is written. Like the bottles he collects, the letters Rosa writes cannot be redeemed: they fade out of circulation.

In "Beer Can Hat," Lum moves us into the world that has already been changed by the end of recycling. What can you do with beer cans that cannot be recycled? For Junior, whose pidgin narrative forms the story, the answer is clear: you make hats. Something that can no longer be recycled can still be redeemed as a purely ornamental, rather ridiculous, though still treasured object: in this case, decoration for a knitted hat. Junior presents this hat with its four flattened beer cans as a gift to his friend Bobo. The cans appear as ironic echoes of an often-repeated phrase through which Bobo's life is defined: "no can." Even Junior says, "Bobo no can understand dat good."[46] But Bobo *can* do certain things remarkably well; he demonstrates a kind of knowledge that is absolutely practical, tied to a specific place and a singular ability to deal with people. Lum portrays a child who knows more than he appears to know, and what he knows is how to trick others. Whereas the writer of traditional pastoral makes complex problems simple by projecting them onto simple characters in the countryside, Bobo survives in the city by making himself appear as a simpleton and thereby masking the complexity of his transactions. Although he "stay lolo in da head. Mental, you know," he is smart enough to exploit his own image.[47] As Junior explains: "Bobo he smart fo' time em good, him. He take long time get change fo' quartah at red light, bumbye da light change green and da guy tell, 'Ay, ass okay, keep 'em,' and step da gas. Bobo . . . he time 'em real good."[48] Bobo demonstrates a remarkable sense of timing, but it serves him in only one place. Junior is saving up for "one college edja-kay-shen," but Bobo, who used to spend his days wheeling carts around the supermarket until the manager told him "no can," now pushes a cart around the parking lot, waiting for school to let out so that he and his friend can sell their papers together.[49]

Only Bobo is going nowhere. Even though his father "give Bobo lickin's and shave his head," he is not allowed to move out of his abusive home, because "da social worker say no can." Upset for Bobo and his "bolo head," Junior asks his mother to make his friend a beer can hat, which he gift-wraps "like one real present."[50] Bobo is delighted by his gift, and he fusses excitedly over its placement on his head. But when some "mokes" grab it from Bobo, yelling "Whoo, whoo, Kojak, man," and toss it to be crushed by oncoming traffic, he is inconsolable: "He go by da wall and scrunch up really small into one ball, you know, and only cry. He cry so hard he begin to hit his head on da wall."[51] Bobo's hat may not have protected him from his father, but at least it hid the sign of his humiliation, and the moment he sees it crumpled up, he too crumples up. Its fragility mirrors the futility of all efforts to help Bobo lead a life not entirely defined by "no can." Bobo is able to exploit — but cannot change — his appearance as a simpleton; he can only make himself appear as others already see him: someone who spends his time in supermarket aisles, parking lots, and at intersections; someone, that is, with nowhere to go.

In another of Lum's stories, "Paint," the author takes us under an urban freeway, a place in which the image of going nowhere is cemented. For Coco, the scrawny child graffiti artist who spraypaints on the wall of the underpass, this neglected space provides an opportunity for self-expression. He can make himself — or at least his name — appear big: "'Coco '84' is what I write. I no write um plain, I make um nice, you know. Fat lettahs. Outline um. Wit sparkles. . . . Someting big you know, so dat I stay big, too."[52] Coco does not paint on conventional surfaces, but his work is recognizable as art; his story, in turn, can be interpreted as a naive pastoral in which a small boy acts out the struggles of the great artist to gain recognition and autonomy. But in his artistic efforts, Coco is concerned with nothing so much as the complicated trick by which something small is made to seem larger than it is. He knows that he enlarges his name because he is small, and he therefore cannot *simply* function as a diminutive figure of a universal type, but instead achieves a certain independence from any interpretation that characterizes him as the representative of something greater than himself. Coco comprehends the mechanisms through which he might be depicted as an artist in miniature; which is to say, he reads those who would presume to read him.

As an artist, Coco has to work against the damage and deterioration that routinely threaten his art. Anarchic youth show up from time to time, scrawling things like "Rockerz Rule" on his wall. Community road workers appear regularly to whitewash the wall, covering everything by a large expanse of white. And, of course, the natural forces of sun, wind, and rain contribute to the disappearance of his work. Coco can accept these natural and civic forces of decay, but he soon finds himself confronted with a different kind of enemy: the hippie lady. Far from seeing Coco as an artist in miniature, she fails to see him as an artist at all. A woman who has no appreciation of his artistry, who spraypaints slogans such as REVOLUTION FOR THE 80's over his graffiti, and whose own writing displays no artistic ambitions, the hippie lady forces the unnatural disappearance of his creations. Coco doesn't have enough paint, and specifically, he doesn't have enough paint to paint over her indifferently scrawled letters: "I went check my colors and I figahed would be too hard fo cover da words. . . . I thought I could do Coco '84 mo big but still couldn't cover da lady's words. Would use up all my paint."[53] Here we see the basic material limitation on Coco's expressiveness. The hippie lady explains her proletarian slogans as demands for "money and food and power," but she does not include a plea for paint.

The hippie lady — that's his name for her, she doesn't sign her work —

has no eye for, or interest in, art: no eye for the big name. She scrawls her slogans "not nice wit fat lettahs or sparkles but jes anykine way" right over Coco's creations. By writing on the wall, she wants to direct people away from the wall. No longer a place for self-expression — no longer a space on which the big name is revealed and becomes legible — the wall becomes an instrument for political propaganda. The conflict between Coco and the hippie lady is not, however, simply one between artist and agitprop. Despite his mother's dismissal of the writers of such slogans as Communist, un-American "good fo nuttings," it is not the hippie lady's politics, but her indifferent destruction of his art that enrages Coco. Without revealing his identity, he tries to tell her that she should not write on Coco's wall. She counters that the wall has been liberated for everyone, and no one can claim ownership, not even Coco, for he is just another big name; if the boy fights for Coco, he is simply allowing himself to be oppressed. Such reasoning reveals the hippie lady's own inability to interpret the situation before her, even as she denounces the global structure of domination. Her inability to recognize either Coco or his art is expressed in her slogan WORLD WITHOUT IMPERIALISM, which could mean to say, or could be read as saying, no more big names, including Coco's.[54] Lum's story reveals the conditions in which the writer of pidgin works, as he elaborates the terms of his criticism from the perspective of an anti-imperialist program — or slogan.

The hippie lady's signs, which are written in standard English speech, even though she herself speaks pidgin, overrun the particularity they are meant to protect and liberate. Lum stages a pastoral conflict and a conflict between two versions of pastoral: the hippie lady articulates universal thoughts "in a learned and fashionable language" — "world without imperialism" — whereas Coco expresses particular feelings in an altogether particular, localized, and dated language: "Coco '84." The former language in a literal sense suppresses the latter, even as it calls for an end to oppression. The hippie lady's slogans suppress her own language, and thereby demonstrate that she does not recognize the trick of pastoral: those *haoles* who stop to read her "work" can engage in a feeling of solidarity with its writer, for they all appear to share at least a common language. By contrast, Coco does not engage in the fantasy that a "learned language" is the "best way" to express himself. He writes: LADY — HATE YOU.[55] Standard-English speak-

ers who read this response to the hippie lady's slogan "world without imperialism" would doubtless understand it as an ungrammatical formulation
for "I hate you," whereas pidgin speakers could find something else entirely: "the lady hates you," namely, those who read this message. Thus
does Coco recognize and incorporate the trick of pastoral into his works.

And Coco *does* work, unlike the hippie lady, who does not — who is
anti-imperialist with no apparent proletarian credentials. It is the kind of
work that concludes "Primo Doesn't Take Back Bottles Anymore": work
that issues into a work, more exactly, a graffito or a painting. Coco wants
to establish his work, make it permanent. By painting on the wall, he
claims an ugly, empty space from the urban no man's land and transforms
it into a space of art. Similarly, the pidgin in which the story is narrated —
deemed a nonlanguage, native to none, and consigned to the linguist's
wasteland — is transformed into a language of literary value simply by using it as the language it is. Only when pidgin is recognized as a language in
its own right are the interpretive possibilities of Lum's story disclosed. Re-
trieved from the unclaimed land of "classification: miscellaneous," pidgin
is, of course, a medium suitable for creative expression, and Lum's work in
pidgin is refigured in Coco's work on his wall. When Coco paints "Lady —
Hate You," his pidgin sentence may lack inflection, but this omission —
cleared by a dash — should not be understood as a mark of inarticulateness; it is, rather, an opening onto a beautifully devious ambiguity.

In the end, Coco's rage finds expression in paint, and he furiously creates a face right over the hippie lady's words: "Was one mean and sad face
. . . Da paint went run out when I was fixing up da cheek. Went drip. I
couldn't finish um."[56] Unable to complete his painting, Coco crosses the
street to assess his work. But before he can gain sufficient perspective, road
workers come to whitewash the wall. One of them says, "Eh, try look dis
face. . . . Not bad yeah? Look almost like somebody crying wit dis red drip
ovah here. You know who went do this one? Pretty good artist. Too bad
gotta cover um up."[57] It is only at the moment of its passing that Coco's art
is fully recognized; his lack of paint and the very act of destruction paradoxically complete his creation: the accidental drips consummate the image of sadness he wished to create. The artwork seems to come to life and
shed red tears — for the wall, for itself, for Coco, or perhaps for nothing.

Like his artwork, Coco sheds tears for reasons that likewise escape him. He is, moreover, as incomplete as the image of himself he tries to paint: his life is just beginning when his face is painted over. The story as a whole is also like the artwork, for it comes to an end without being finished. The three dots with which it closes mirror the tears of paint: "I jes went turn around. I started for cry. I donno how come . . ."[58]

These tears — the final ellipsis in which the actions of the writer and the painter coincide — are a mark of incompleteness. They are free of paradox and pathos, however, for they do not result from a series of accidents that leave the story unfinished, and they do not lament the transitory nature of things. Lum's three dots are a critical version of tears — tears that are not watery, not red, and not even sad. Like the dash through which Coco articulates the words *lady* and *hate,* the ellipsis could be understood as an indication of something missing; but from a different perspective, it is a disclosure of possibilities, and only such a disclosure allows a language, like Coco's artwork, to come alive. Coco wants his art to be permanent; but no one, including Coco, would feel its power if it were not vulnerable to forces of destruction. Exposure of his artwork to these forces animates it, and so, too, with pidgin — as with all languages. The dynamism of languages — their openness to change, chance, erosion, and even whitewashing — gives them life. As Lum portrays the fragility of a hat, the waning of a practice, the disappearance of a word, or the obliteration of an artwork, transient things gain a certain fluency. Appearing in the medium of Hawai'i pidgin, they show that transience, too, can be eloquent.

Notes

1. William Davenport et al., *Fodor's Hawaii 1969* (New York: David McKay, 1969), p. 46.

2. Davenport, *Fodor's*, p. 45.

3. Ibid., p. 72.

4. Ibid.

5. Quoted in Suzanne Romaine, *Pidgin and Creole Languages* (New York: Longman, 1988), pp. 112–13. According to one of the less plausible etymologies for *pidgin*, the word indeed derives from the English word *pigeon*, and it arose when speakers of standard English scornfully dismissed the utterances of those they colonized as "the speech of pigeons." At least six other, better-documented etymologies have been offered for this term, and this multiplicity of etymologies is characteristic of pidgin languages, which develop in such a complicated fashion that the words of these languages can rarely be derived from single roots. Most etymologies of *pidgin* link it with terms for trade. According to the *OED* (which also connects *pigeon* to *pidgin* as an alternate spelling), it is a "Chinese corruption" of the English word *business*. More accurate versions of the same etymology refer to Cantonese rather Chinese. Another conjecture along similar lines presents *pidgin* as a Cantonese pronunciation of the Portuguese *ocupação* ("business"). Other linguists derive it from two Chinese characters, *peí-ts'ín*, which mean "paying money." It has also been suggested that the word comes from the Hebrew *pidjon*, which means "exchange" or "trade," especially in the sense of "redemption." Taking *beachee* as the original term, other linguists have proposed that it is a South Seas pronunciation of the English *beach*. Yet another theory disputes the general tendency to find in *pidgin* a term for business or trade and proposes that it comes from *pidian*, the word for "people" in Yayo, a South American Indian language spoken in an area colonized by Britain. See the informative discussion of Ian Hancock, "On the Origin of the Term 'Pidgin,'" in *Readings in Creole Studies*, ed. I. Hancock (Ghent: E. Story-Scientia, 1979), pp. 81–89.

6. Because pidgins and creoles are most commonly understood as solutions to discontinuities in social and linguistic traditions, and since the social pressures to develop cross-linguistic communication differ from case to case, it is extremely difficult to establish an unambiguous and coherent definition of these languages. After noting that there is no agreement among linguists, David DeCamp writes: "Some definitions are based on function, the role these languages play in the community: e.g., a pidgin is an auxiliary trade language. Some are based on historical origins and development: e.g., a pidgin may be

spontaneously generated; a creole is a language that has evolved from a pidgin. Some definitions include formal characteristics: restricted vocabulary; absence of gender, true tenses, inflectional morphology, or relative clauses, etc. Some linguists combine these different kinds of criteria and include additional restrictions in their definition" (D. DeCamp, "The Development of Pidgin and Creole Studies," in *Pidgin and Creole Linguistics,* ed. Albert Valdman [Bloomington: Indiana University Press, 1977], pp. 3–4). It should be noted that attempts to define pidgin generally take place within the context of languages that take their own status for granted.

7.   Romaine, *Pidgin and Creole Languages*, p. 24.

8.   According to many linguists, the main difference between a pidgin and a creole lies in the feature known as "vitality" — whether the language has a viable community of native speakers: "Pidgins are . . . short lived. Rarely does a pidgin survive for a century. . . . The only way in which a pidgin may escape extinction is by evolving into a creole; i.e., the syntax and vocabulary are extended and it becomes the language of a community" (D. DeCamp, "Pidgin and Creole Languages," in *Pidginization and Creolization of Languages,* ed. Dell Hymes [Cambridge: Cambridge University Press, 1971], p. 16). Unlike pidgin, a creole is defined as the native language of the majority of its speakers. Some linguists speak of a linguistic "life-cycle": a spontaneous generation of a pidgin which then evolves into a creole; see, in particular, two works by R. A. Hall: "The Life-Cycle of Pidgin Languages," in *Lingua* 11 (1962):151–56 and *Pidgin and Creole Languages* (Ithaca: Cornell University Press, 1966), esp. pp. 126–30. Other linguists stress the discontinuity between creoles and the pidgins from which they develop: creoles have a large number of shared semantic features that cannot be traced to their pidgin ancestors. Derek Bickerton, who has championed this view, attributes the newly created semantic features to innate universals of language; see D. Bickerton, *Roots of Language* (Ann Arbor: Karoma, 1981).

9.   The use of *Hawai'i* avoids some of the ambiguities of the term *Hawaiian,* which could refer to the geographical location of Hawai'i, to the people of native Hawaiian (that is, Polynesian) ethnic descent, or to the Hawaiian language.

10.   Darrel H. Y. Lum, "Beer Can Hat," in *The Best of Bamboo Ridge: The Hawaii Writers' Quarterly,* ed. Eric Chock and Darrell H. Y. Lum (Honolulu: Bamboo Ridge Press, 1986), p. 175. As a written form, literary pidgin — of which Lum's stories are an outstanding example — reproduces some of the complications of the early period of the language's development as an oral form: because pidgin does not have its own orthography, pidgin writers must develop their own written forms and make decisions at points of language contact.

For example, necessary to the spelling of Hawaiian words is the *'okina* or glottal stop, which appears as a single inverted comma. When words with this sound are anglicized, the *'okina* is generally dropped.

11. Romaine, *Pidgin and Creole Languages,* p. 24.

12. Although there is a dispute between linguists who map languages in terms of trees and those who prefer the model of the wave, neither model easily accommodates pidgin. On these two models, see Merrit Ruhlen, *A Guide to the World's Languages* (Stanford: Stanford University Press, 1991), vol. 1, pp. 256–57.

13. There are many theories about the origin and development of pidgin. One theory holds that pidgin is a much reduced form of English (with borrowings from Portuguese and Cantonese) — a case of simplification and imitation. Another theory contends that it is an outgrowth of nautical jargon used for communication among sailors of different nationalities; see John Reinecke, *Language and Dialect in Hawaii: A Sociolinguistic History to 1935* (Honolulu: University of Hawaii Press, 1969), pp. 23–38. (As an interesting aside, after 1859, about 50% of American seamen on whaling ships were of African descent; as yet, no attempt has been made to assess the significance of this fact for the development and spread of pidgins; see Romaine, *Pidgin and Creole Languages,* p. 85.) According to other linguists, all European-based pidgins and creoles are relexified versions of a fifteenth-century Portuguese pidgin first used along the African coast and later carried to India and East Asia. This pidgin is itself related to Sabir, the medieval Mediterranean lingua franca, believed to be the language of the Crusaders and a common trading language: see Ian Hancock's discussion of *Lorica of Gildas the Briton* in "Recovering Pidgin Genesis: Approaches and Problems," in *Pidgin and Creole Linguistics,* ed. Valdman, pp. 287–91; see also Loreto Todd, *Pidgins and Creoles* (London: Routledge, 1974), pp. 34–42; and Keith Whinnom, "The Origin of 'European-Based' Pidgins and Creoles," *Orbis* 14 (1965):509–27. It is also possible that Hawai'i pidgin is a relexified pidgin Hawaiian; see D. Bickerton, *Roots of Language,* p. 7.

14. See Andrew Lind, *Hawaii's People,* 3rd ed. (Honolulu: University of Hawaii Press, 1967), p. 32. See also Ronald Takaki, *Pau Hana: Plantation Life and Labor in Hawaii, 1835–1920* (Honolulu: University of Hawaii Press, 1983), pp. 76–77.

15. Ronald Takaki, *A Different Mirror: A History of Multicultural America* (New York: Little, Brown, 1993), p. 253. Takaki is here referring to the Nationality Act of 1870, according to which only "free whites" and "African aliens" were allowed to apply for naturalization. In the section of *China Men* entitled "The Laws," Maxine Hong Kingston juxtaposes the adoption of the 14th Amendment to the U.S. Constitution in 1868 (which said that naturalized Americans

have the same rights as native-born citizens) with the Nationality Act of 1870: "Debating the Nationality Act, Congressmen declared that America would be a nation of 'Nordic fiber'" (Maxine Hong Kingston, *China Men* [New York: Knopf, 1980], p. 153). On the Hawaiian Sugar Planters' Association, see n19 below.

16. Elizabeth Ball Carr, *Da Kine Talk: From Pidgin to Standard English in Hawaii* (Honolulu: University of Hawaii Press, 1972), p. 5. Carr's work has been called the "first descriptive book on Hawaiian Island English."

17. Quoted in Takaki, *Pau Hana*, p. 24. Between 1876 and 1905, Hawai'i "imported" 46,000 Chinese men as laborers; 17,500 Portuguese men (along with their families); 6,000 Puerto Ricans; and 8,000 Koreans. The largest group "imported" to the islands' plantations before 1900 came from Japan — 61,000 workers. (A summary of the demographic information can be found in Carr, *Da Kine Talk*, pp. 5–6.) The strength of the Japanese community was cause for concern among politicians and plantation owners in Hawai'i. According to a "Confidential Brief" circulated in House and Senate committees and submitted as testimony in 1921, only the diversification of Hawaii's population would allow its American citizens to overcome the political and economic dangers posed by the presence of "a large alien race": "Hawaii believes that her political and industrial salvation lies in securing labor from some other source than Japan, provided this labor is inherently able to work in her fields and neutralize the effect of the large alien race that now predominates in the Territory." Appendix 4, John Reinecke, *Feigned Necessity: Hawaii's Attempt to Obtain Chinese Contract Labor, 1921–23* (San Francisco: Chinese Materials Center, Inc., 1979), p. 555. Between 1907 and 1931, more than 120,000 workers from the Philippines were imported along with a much smaller number of Spaniards. Talk of importation here is not metaphorical. Orders for workers were no different than for any other commodity. One plantation manager writes: "Our order for *40 Japs* — given you in our letter of the 6th inst., is now *void.* 25 Chinese . . . will fill our back orders for labor to date" (quoted in Takaki, *Pau Hana*, p. 25).

18. On the development of pidgin as an interethnic and working-class language, see Takaki, *Pau Hana*, esp. pp. 118–19: "Speaking Hawaiian English or pidgin, the immigrants and their children were no longer only Korean, Japanese, Chinese, Filipino, Puerto Rican, or Portuguese. On the plantations, pidgin English began to give its users a working class identity as well as a Hawaiian or 'local' identity, which transcended their particular ethnic identity" (p. 119). For additional sources on the complex history of union activity in Hawai'i, see the authoritative studies of Lawrence H. Fuchs, *Hawaii Pono: A Social History* (New York: Harcourt, Brace & World, 1961); Michi Kodama-Nishimoto,

Warren S. Nishimoto, and Cynthia A. Oshira, *Hanahana: An Oral History Anthology of Hawaii's Working People* (Honolulu: Ethnic Studies History Project, University of Hawaii at Manoa, 1984); Dennis M. Ogawa, *Kodomo no tame ni — For the Sake of the Children: The Japanese American Experience in Hawaii* (Honolulu: University of Hawaii Press, 1978); John E. Reinecke, *The Filipino Piecemeal Sugar Strike of 1924–1925* (Honolulu: University of Hawai'i Press, 1996); Ronald Takaki, *Strangers from a Different Shore: A History of Asian Americans* (Harmondsworth: Penguin, 1989). Takashi Tsutsumi, one of the leaders of the Hawaii Labor Association, has left an account of the history of labor and unionization on the islands; see his *History of Hawaii Laborers' Movement*, trans. Umetaro Okumura (Honolulu: Hawaiian Sugar Planters' Association, 1922; microfilm, 1951?).

19. Designed initially as an agricultural research and management information center, the Hawaiian Sugar Planters' Association quickly became the primary mechanism for wage regulation: "the association organized a central labor bureau to coordinate all employment of Asian laborers and to force them to be paid wage rates set by the HSPA.... The Board of Trustees passed a resolution that fixed the maximum rates or wages for all laborers . . . and developed a centralized interisland system of information to monitor movements of laborers trying to bargain for higher wages. When the HSPA learned that sixty Filipino laborers at the Olaa Sugar Company had refused to work under the terms of the labor agreement and left the plantation, it immediately instructed all managers to offer them only the same terms" (Takaki, *Pau Hana*, pp. 83–84).

20. Edward Beechert, *Working in Hawaii: A Labor History* (Honolulu: University of Hawaii Press, 1985), p. 329.

21. See Takaki, *Pau Hana*, esp. pp. 155–56: "In their demand for higher wages, the strikers called for equal pay for equal work; they wanted to end the racially discriminatory wage system" (p. 155). For a discussion of wage disparities among different ethnic groups, see Fuchs, *Hawaii Pono*, esp. pp. 52–67.

22. Milton Murayama, *All I Asking for Is My Body* (Honolulu: University of Hawaii Press, 1988), p. 28.

23. Ibid., p. 96.

24. About the outhouses, Kiyo explains, "you could hear all the farts and everything going on in the other toilets. . . . You were so close in fact you could touch the other guy's ass" (ibid., p. 29).

25. *Haole* is a pidgin term originating in the Hawaiian word for foreigner but later restricted to people of European ancestry, with the exception of plantation workers of Portuguese, Spanish, and Puerto Rican descent.

26. Murayama, *All I Asking for Is My Body*, 63. On the ambivalent attitudes toward standard English in Hawai'i, see John Reinecke "'Pidgin English' in Hawaii: A Local Study in the Sociology of Language," in *Kodomo no tame ni*, ed. D. Ogawa, pp. 209–17.

27. Murayama, *All I Asking for Is My Body*, p. 96.

28. Ibid.

29. Ruhlen, *A Guide to the World's Languages*, vol. 1, p. 377. Of the 21 language groupings covering over 5,000 languages whose lineages Ruhlen seeks to determine, four groupings "cannot be placed in the worldwide classification" (p. 290), and only the invented languages Esperanto and Interlingua are more intractable than pidgins and creoles.

30. See n17 above.

31. Carr, *Da Kine Talk*, 44.

32. Stephen Sumida, *And the View from the Shore: Literary Traditions of Hawai'i* (Seattle: University of Washington Press, 1991), p. 4.

33. Ibid., p. 6.

34. Lum, "Primo Doesn't Take Back Bottles Anymore," in *The Best of Bamboo Ridge*, p. 184.

35. See William Empson, *Some Versions of Pastoral* (New York: New Directions, 1974).

36. Ibid., p. 11.

37. Ibid., p. 16.

38. Ibid.

39. Davenport, *Fodor's*, p. 37.

40. Lum, "Primo Doesn't Take Back Bottles Anymore," p. 188.

41. Sumida, *And the View from the Shore*, p. 104.

42. Lum, "Primo," p. 186.

43. Ibid., p. 184.

44. Ibid., p. 186.

45. Ibid., p. 188.

46. Lum, "Beer Can Hat," in *The Best of Bamboo Ridge*, p. 178.

47. Ibid., p. 175.

48. Ibid.

49. Ibid.

50. Ibid., p. 176.

51. Ibid., p. 178.

52. Lum, "Paint," in *The Best of Bamboo Ridge*, p. 189.

53. Ibid., p. 191.

54. Ibid.

55. Ibid.

56. Ibid., p. 193.

57. Ibid., p. 194.

58. Ibid.

CHAPTER TEN

Irish Gaelic Literature in the United States

■ **KENNETH NILSEN**

In recent United States censuses nearly forty million people claim Irish ancestry. How is it then that so little of the Irish language, Irish Gaelic, is to be found in this country? Why is it that despite a long history of a thriving Irish-American press, Irish Gaelic is limited to one column in one or two Irish-American newspapers? Why do only one or two Irish-American radio programs regularly include *spoken* Irish as part of their broadcasts? Why is it that in nineteenth-century America the Germans, Scandinavians, Jews, Polish, French, and Welsh had a thriving publishing industry in their own languages, but not the Irish?

The answers to these questions must be sought, of course, in Irish history and in the history of the Irish language. The earliest form of Irish is found in inscriptions on some three hundred stones dating from ca. 300–600 A.D. They are written in a script known as Ogham, which consists of series of notches and dots up and down the side of a stone. This early form of Irish is called Goidelic and was the language spoken throughout Ireland at the time of St. Patrick's mission (432 A.D.). St. Patrick brought with him to Ireland Christian learning and knowledge of spoken and written Latin. Within a few decades of Patrick's death, it is believed the Latin alphabet was being employed in the writing of Irish, some time in the period 550–600. This means that Irish is the oldest written vernacular of Western Europe, with an unbroken tradition to the present day. During the period of the Dark Ages, literature in Irish was actually flourishing and continued to prosper for many centuries.

In spite of the Norman invasion of Ireland in 1169, Irish Gaelic culture managed to survive until the seventeenth century. During the sixteenth and seventeenth centuries the English government put increasing pressure on Ireland. Henry VIII's break with the Roman Catholic Church meant that the official state religion of the kingdom was different from that professed by the majority of the Irish population. In the course of the seventeenth century, Ireland was dealt three devastating defeats, which completely destroyed the old native Gaelic system and its schools of law and poetry; at the same time the upper echelon of Gaelic society disappeared because of exile or reduction in status. The introduction of the Penal Laws in the 1690s totally disenfranchised the Catholic population. Catholics were not allowed to have schools; they were barred from public office, the armed services, and from most of the professions. The Catholic clergy was banned. The Irish language had no official status. Thus just at the time when most other languages of Europe, including even Scottish Gaelic and Welsh, were beginning to take advantage of the printing press, Irish works rarely found their way into publication. Indeed, only a handful of Irish books were published in the seventeenth and eighteenth centuries and most of these were religious in nature, some written by Protestants in hopes of converting the native Irish, and others published by Irish Catholic religious orders in exile in France and Belgium to counter the effects of the Reformation.

Because of England's policies of cultural genocide, Irish learning in the eighteenth century was carried on precariously in the so-called hedge schools, mere hovels set up by the side of the road. The hedge school masters were in many cases Gaelic poets who also kept up the manuscript tradition. Since so few books were printed in Irish, if one wanted a copy of an Irish text one had to have a scribe make a handwritten copy of it, just as had been done in medieval times. Breandán Ó Conchúir's study of Irish scribes in County Cork from 1700 to 1850 reveals that 1,400 manuscripts written by Cork scribes in that period are known to exist today. The scribes tended to be antiquaries, and the majority of them were copyists rather than creative writers.

During the last few decades of the eighteenth century, as the Penal Laws were gradually relaxed, a Catholic middle class emerged which saw clearly that a knowledge of the English language opened the door to economic success. Gradually the English language spread throughout the eastern and more prosperous half of Ireland. By the year 1800 it is estimated that half the population spoke English. The half that spoke Irish were the poorest and least educated in the country. The Irish language came to be regarded as a badge of poverty and ignorance. But it is interesting to note that although Irish became nearly dissociated from formal education, it did in fact maintain a vigorous oral tradition, which included one of the richest stores of folktales in Western Europe, and a thriving tradition of folk poetry.

In the nineteenth century various factors contributed to the further decline of Irish. These included the introduction of the National School system by Britain in 1831, which did not recognize the existence of the Irish language; the negative attitude toward Gaelic of many Irish leaders such as Daniel O'Connell; the devastating potato famine, which struck hardest in those areas where Irish was spoken; and the resulting emigration, which drained off a large proportion of the population of the Irish-speaking districts. Even the campaign by Protestant organizations to teach Irish speakers to read the Bible in Irish had an overall negative affect on the language, because the campaign was denounced by many Irish priests and Irish speakers came to assume that any book printed in Irish was Protestant propaganda! By the end of the nineteenth century, the Irish language was spoken only in a few isolated pockets, mostly on the remote west coast.

From the late eighteenth century, even as the language was declining, there arose various organizations and individuals who concerned themselves with the Irish language. The earlier of these were mainly antiquarian in nature, but by the end of the nineteenth century, in 1893, the Gaelic League was established in Dublin with the purpose of promoting the spread of Irish. Although it should be noted that there were some important predecessors of the Gaelic League, including many in the United States, it was the rise of the League which ignited the spark that led to the establishment of Irish classes throughout Ireland and the development of a modern literature in Irish. Within a few years of its foundation, the organization had printed more books in Irish than had been published in the previous three centuries. It was the Gaelic League that was responsible for the comparatively prominent role the Irish language has had in Ireland since the signing of the treaty with Britain in 1921. Irish is taught in virtually all the schools of the Republic of Ireland, and perhaps as many as 10 percent of those who go through the Irish educational system have a fair knowledge of the language. The number of speakers in the Irish-speaking districts has, however, continued to decline, and it is estimated that there are only between 20,000 and 30,000 people in these districts who speak Irish as their daily language.

Given the low status the language had for centuries in Ireland, it is hardly surprising to find that in America its very existence was frequently ignored even by historians of the American Irish. This was especially true twenty or thirty years ago of Irish-American scholars like William Shannon, whose book *The American Irish* devotes less than one paragraph to the question of language. In his book *The Immigrant Church: New York's Irish and German Catholics, 1815–1865,* Jay P. Dolan devotes extensive coverage to the question of the German language vis-à-vis the Church, but dismisses the Irish language by saying that it had died out in the eighteenth century. Only recently have historians of Irish America such as Kerby Miller and David N. Doyle treated the question of the Irish language in the United States as a subject deserving serious research.

There are only occasional references to Irish in colonial America. One of the earliest and most shocking is that of Goody Glover, an Irishwoman living in Boston in the 1680s who was accused of being a witch. At her trial "the court could have no answers from her, but in the Irish; which was her native language, although she understood English very well." The court obtained the services of an interpreter so part of the trial was actually conducted in Irish. But the poor unfortunate Irish-speaking woman was found guilty and was hanged as a witch in Boston in 1688.[1]

David Doyle's research in colonial American newspapers has yielded some interesting references to the Irish in America, such as advertisements for runaway indentured Irish servants. A small number of these advertisements specifically mention that the servants were Irish speakers, such as this one in the *Virginia Gazette,* May 16, 1771.

RUN away from the subscriber, in *Bedford* County on *Great Falling River,* an *Irish* Servant Man named MICHAEL KELLY, about five Feet five Inches high, with short black Hair, wears a cut brown Wig, a blue Broadcloth Coat, spotted Flannel Jacket, and a Pair of old patched Breeches.

Also an *Irish* Servant Woman named MARGARET KELLY, Wife to the said *Michael.* She wore a blue Calimanco Gown and Petticoat. They both speak *Irish,* but neither of them are known to speak *English.* I will give FIVE POUNDS Reward on their being delivered to me, and FIFTY SHILLINGS if they are secured in any Jail in this Colony, upon Information of the same given to WILLIAM HAYTH.[2]

In the early United States of America we find several references to the Irish language, including that it was in use among a considerable number of George Washington's troops. Speaking in the House of Commons on April 2, 1784, about the loss of the American colonies, Luke Gardiner (Lord Mountjoy) said, "America was lost through the Irish emigrants . . . I have been assured on the best authority that the Irish language was commonly spoken in the American ranks." He obtained this information from an army officer who had fought in Pennsylvania.[3] Certainly a number of poems were composed in Ireland in Irish in favor of the American cause. Hopes ran high in Ireland at this time, while Britain was occupied in the colonies, that the Irish Volunteers would be able to obtain freedom for Ireland. Two of these poems, by the Clare poet Thomas Meehan, were edited by Professor Fred Norris Robinson, the pioneer of Celtic Studies at Harvard.

In the early days of the Republic, states that had concentrations of Irish speakers included Maryland, Pennsylvania, and New York and to a lesser extent Massachusetts. Some references to the Catholic Church include mention of the Irish language. For instance, the first Catholic pastor in New York in the 1780s just after the Revolution was Charles Whelan, who was said to be more fluent in Gaelic and French than English. A Father Philip Lariscy who was in Boston and Salem from 1818–1820 was noted for his Gaelic sermons. Lariscy then traveled on to New York and New Jersey, where he was much in demand for hearing confessions in Gaelic. He finally went to Philadelphia, where he died in 1824 at a young age. In Philadelphia he made the acquaintance of Matthew O'Conway, a brilliant Irish-speaking native of Galway who spoke several languages. After compiling a dictionary of Spanish, O'Conway set to work on a dictionary of the Irish language, which by the time of his death in 1842 filled an entire trunk. This work has never been published, but it has been preserved and has been housed in the National Library of Ireland since 1977.

During the first few decades of the nineteenth century, poor Irish laborers were streaming into the United States and obtaining employment doing difficult, physically demanding jobs like digging the Erie canal. Many of these were Irish speakers, but most Irish speakers were illiterate in their own language. Many of these newcomers could not speak English. Among them there were undoubtedly individuals who had retained their attachment to Gaelic culture. One such Irish immigrant who came with his family to the United States in 1826 was Patrick Condon of Ballymacoda, County Cork. He could not speak English, but he was a Gaelic poet and a fine scribe, hardly culturally deprived. He settled on a farm, Deerfield, near Utica, N.Y., and spent the next eight years working to pay off the farm. When he had his bills all paid, he turned to his pen and started writing letters and poems home to Ireland. When they arrived they caused amazement and were widely circulated and copied. The Condon letters are apparently the most impressive collection of Irish-language immigrant material discovered.[4] In all, it consists of some eleven letters and about 24 poems, including a tour de force of 68 quatrains. They give us a picture of the cares and concerns of a nineteenth-century Irish immigrant living in rural America. His first letter, written to Bartholomew Chapel in 1834, tells us about his new home: "I have a fine farm free forever, no one can ask me for rent. Our family can eat their fill of bread and meat butter and milk any day we want all year and so I think it is better here than to stay in Ireland without land, food or clothing. It is a pity that the foolish Irish stay in Ireland. Look at the English and Germans. They come here in droves every year . . . they buy land and live like lords" (p. 27).[5] He goes on to explain why he has chosen this area:

> There is no land in the Barony as good as my land. I paid ten dollars an acre for it. . . . I could have gotten land that would be just as good for a dollar an acre or even less than a dollar, but there would be no priest or Mass nearby. Over here there are no priests, except in the towns and any of the Catholics who come here . . . like to be near a Mass and that makes the land expensive . . .

I am 260 miles northwest of New York, within three miles of a town called Utica in New York State. We have Mass there any day in the year we want. . . .

I would have written to you long ago, but when I took possession of this farm, I only had a small bit of money, but I received credit to cover the rest and I agreed to pay so much every year for seven years, and if I didn't pay it I would have lost the land and the money. For fear that I would not be able to do that I did not want to write boasting about something I did not have. It is all paid up now and I can write of what is true. (p. 27–28)

He concludes the letter with this request: "Write to me soon in the Irish language, and put on the envelope these words in English: Patrick Condon, Utica, County Oneida, State New York" (p. 29).

Condon's poetry is strictly within the Gaelic tradition. What is interesting about it, of course, is that it was composed in Utica, New York. Ireland figures prominently in his verses, many of which are of the *Aisling* or "vision" genre. In *Aisling* poems the scene is set: the poet sees a beautiful maiden who is in distress and he inquires what has caused her sorrow. She replies that her lands have been usurped by foreigners and predicts that her spouse will return from overseas to rid her country of the alien churls. Condon has an interesting twist on this theme in several of his poems. In the first of these, "Iargnó Éireann" [Ireland's Tribulation], the beautiful maiden approaches him, takes his hand and asks:

> "A sháirfhir mhúirnigh, tabhair dam scéala
> Fáth do chúise let dhútha thréigean
> Is crádh liom cúthail tu i gcúige chaothach
> Do chéile is do shleacht bhog óg."

> [My dear good man, explain to me
> Why you have deserted your native land.
> It troubles me to find you, your wife
> And family in a foreign region.]

He tells her what made him leave Ireland:

> [Fair-tressed flower, I'll tell you
> The reason exactly without a lie

(It was) the trickery of crooked neighbors,
And the torture of evil English-speaking boors
Who squeezed the harness beyond endurance
On the pure-blooded Gaels of my ancestral Ireland.] (p. 31–32)

Probably one of his most interesting compositions is one in which he describes some of the difficulties and some of the good points of life in the United States. Parts of it may be compared to the poem "A' Choille Ghruamach" [The Gloomy Forest] written by the bard John MacLean shortly after he emigrated from Scotland to Nova Scotia in 1819. Condon's poem, entitled "Aiste na n-Iarthar" [An Account of the Western Regions] was sent to his old friend Michael Gleason in December 1834:

A shoilbh-fhir léigheanta, shéimh, dheagheóluis,
Tabharfad tásc fém láimh gan gó dhuit
Ar an ndútha ghránna ina ráinig damhsa
Teacht go hársa, fálta, feóidhte . . .

[Dear gentle learned well-educated man
I'll write you a description without a lie
About the ugly land in which I have arrived
Decrepit, old and worn out.
There are no smooth fair fields here,
Just forests and trees and big plains,
Bare grey moss-covered boulders
Hills and valleys and misty regions.
Loud roars and threatening screeches
From panthers, wolves, bears and lions
Wild animals howling for battle
And poisonous snakes wriggling with venom.
The skies colliding, threatening and booming
The air on fire and the ground quaking
Fireballs are thrown in showers on the roads
And indeed they terrify me.

Three seasons are fair enough
The other season is piercing, freezing
With ice and cold constantly stabbing them

It is pitiful how people shake at Shrovetide.
Frost and snow high above their knees
From Christmas to mid-March
Their ears, feet, hands and limbs are numb
With pain.

The summer is hot, scalding, fiery, sunny, painful, sore,
Neither young nor old wear anything but shirt, belt, trousers and shoes.

The people of this land are an ill-tempered lot
Deceitful, murderous, criminal, shameless, accursed
And devious in mind and manners.]

He continues this diatribe against the new land and its inhabitants for six more stanzas but then, apparently having exhausted all their faults, he says:

[As bad as their customs and manners are,
They pay on time and in cash those who are working for them
And they give them their fill of food and drink.

When you get up in the morning from your bed
You'll get a glass of fine whiskey
Bread, butter and tasty peas
A chunk of cheese and a bone of beef.

After eating your meal in a hurry
Off to work they trot you
At break time you'll have a party
Like a wedding, christening or marriage.
There will be mugs being filled with beer
White plates full of delicacies
Fat roasted geese and ganders
And other fowl I won't bother to mention.

They will give you twenty-one minutes to eat
They would not wait any longer for you.
They'll be shouting and calling you
Driving you back to work by force.

Then they have you again back at your job
Your grog is not measured, just drink it
But if you are drunk or late in the afternoon
The boss will give you your walking papers.

As much as I praise their fairness and banquets
Their liquor and drinks and their slabs of meat
I would prefer to have, poor fare though it be,
Potatoes and salt in Ireland.

As you read my lay, be at ease
Smile gently as you used to,
Drink my health at the pub counter
And send overseas a greeting or two to me.

I send over to Ireland a hundred and one greetings
To relatives and friends,
And though I'll never see any of you again
I'll never let you out of my thoughts.] (p. 40–45)

The poem does not end here, but goes on for forty more stanzas, most of which deal with stories from the Bible. Withal, in many of his letters Condon advises his neighbors to come to America. In one which he wrote to James Fitzgerald in 1837, he says:

When you receive this letter I think there is nothing better you could do than sell your place and come, you, your wife and family. The pay for laborers and craftsmen is much better now in America than it was when I came out. Last year a workman could earn twenty dollars a month as well as food and drink. . . .

Give my greeting to my brother, Thomas Condon and tell him not to think of coming here. The work here is too hard for him and if he comes he will regret it. As for me, I have a large family. There are twelve of us now, myself, my wife and ten children, thanks be to God who gave them to us. Seven of them are female, the three that I brought with me from Ireland and four more since I came to America. You know that it is a great cost to keep them in food, clothing and school, for there it not the least respect here for a man or woman without learning, especially young people. Therefore I have no money to send him but if I ever have I will not forget him. I hope to God that it will not be long before I can send him some help.

Your eternally faithful poor friend,
Patrick Condon (p. 71–72)

Condon had his share of hardship in this country, and one of his finest pieces is an elegy entitled "Ó'm Chroí mo Scread" [My Heart Cries Out], which he composed in 1840 on the death of his wife. This poem has been included in a number of Irish poetry anthologies and has recently been translated by Thomas Kinsella.

Condon continued to correspond with old friends in Ireland. In a letter written on the 27th of May 1848 to Thomas O'Brien, after inquiring about the state of the crops in Ireland, Condon lists the price of foodstuffs in New York: "a bushel of oats, a half dollar; a hundred weight of yellow flour, 2 dollars; a hundredweight of beef is three and a half dollars" (p. 79). In another letter to Thomas O'Brien, he laments as follows:

O, poor slaves of Ireland, it is a pity that you are not here where you would get the value of your health. And you, poor girls who have no possessions but your health, alas it is the pity of my heart that you are not here. Look, you couldn't distinguish a rich man's wife or daughter from a poor man's wife or daughter any day that they go out, as far as it concerns attractive showy clothing, and silk and ribbons waving in the wind. Gold earrings in their ears and so on. If I told you that my own children have rings of gold in their ears I think you would laugh, but it is no great wonder here, it's just the style of the country — "If you go to Rome, be a Roman with them." (p. 86)

At this time we also find a few references to the Great Famine. Condon clearly heard about it and mentions it several times, but it seems that he did not quite grasp the enormity of the tragedy. His clearest pronouncement on the event is a poem he composed in 1849. Though he begins with a stanza which explicitly mentions the Famine, the rest of the poem, much like his earlier poetry is a conventional attack on English Protestant rule in Ireland. The first verse goes like this:

A Chláir Luirc m'osna 's dortadh déar mo dhearc
An tásc do chloisim ortsa i gcéin thar lear
Ár is gorta ag coscairt Gaedhal ar fad
Is cáin gan sosadh ag lomadh an méid do mhair.

[Oh Plain of Lorc (that is, Ireland), my sigh and shedding of tears
The news I hear about you from afar overseas
Destruction and famine completely ravaging the Gaels
And tax without end skinning those who remain alive.]

As late as 1852, Condon was still trying to convince neighbors to leave Ireland. In a letter to Thomas Stack he describes the difference between working conditions in the two countries and castigates Irish farmers for their treatment of their workers. Speaking of farm laborers in Ireland, he says that they might have only a bit of a potato and a drop of sour milk to drink. He goes on to say: "If it happened that there was any food better than that, the poor laborer would be far from getting a taste of it: the master would take it all for himself but not at the same table as the workingman; he wouldn't sit with him because of stinginess and contempt for him." Condon contrasts this behavior with that of Americans:

Look at the farmers of this country, they have food and drink every day of the year as good as any gentleman. They, their wives and families have no reluctance to eat at the same table with the workingmen: they all share the same table and the same food. They're not like Sean of the herring who greedily chomps his meal in a separate room. And another impression of people like Sean, it isn't surprising that they are as they are, shy, irritated, oppressed by the foreigners, for it is clear that they themselves would tie the knot just as tight and even tighter if it were in their power to do so. (p. 97)

This comment apparently reminded Condon of an old enemy of his back in Ireland who had just died, and dipping his pen in the venom of satire he composed a mock elegy. A short excerpt will be sufficient to give an idea of the piece:

He was a troublesome snarler, a contrary hunch-backed sulker
A useless dwarf, an evil-minded, murderous fat-bellied frog

And just like him were all those who were nursed on the same breast
as he. (p. 98)

It seems fitting that the last poem we have by Condon, written in 1856, is
an *Aisling* poem. It concludes stereotypically with the prediction by the
spéir-bhean (the beautiful woman representing Ireland) that the Irish will
rise up and slaughter the foreigner.

Condon is an important figure in Irish literature in the United States,
just by virtue of being the only pre-Famine writer in Irish that we had in
this country. He was that exceptional individual, both literate and creative,
who was able put down on paper his thoughts about this country in his native language. The majority of his Irish-speaking countrymen who emigrated here lacked this ability and thus left behind no records in their native language.

After the Famine, the influx of Irish to the United States increased by
huge numbers. Many of these immigrants were Irish speakers. Likewise
many of the exiles from the 1848 Uprising were Irish speakers. Men such
as John O'Mahony and Michael Doheny, well known for their political
activities, also cultivated their interest in the Irish language and literature during their long sojourn in New York City. It was in Brooklyn that
O'Mahony penned his admirable translation into English of Geoffrey
Keating's *Forus Feasa ar Éirinn* [History of Ireland], using manuscripts that
Irish immigrants lent him. One of the most important of these was a copy
written in 1753, now kept at Boston College (Gaelic MS 5). Michael
Doheny frequently supplied the *Irish-American*, a weekly New York newspaper, with the text and his own metrical translations of Irish poems he
had found in manuscripts.

The *Irish-American* deserves special mention here. Founded in 1849, at
first its Gaelic content consisted of only the occasional word or phrase in
an English song or story. On June 21, 1851, however, it printed in its "Poet's
Corner," without any fanfare or particular notice, a three-stanza Irish poem
in praise of one James O'Dwyer, the owner of a pub on Duane Street in
Manhattan. This is probably the first original composition in Irish to be
published in the United States. Below is the corrupt text exactly as it appeared in print.

TO THE EDITOR OF THE IRISH AMERICAN
June 7th, 1851

Gach Oighfhear calma lan mheanamnach flior vouda
Ma mbein leis sealad a chathamh le plensur;
Go Duane street tagach go tapa 'sa steach don Daisy,
Mar a bhfuil ceol da spreaga mar chautain na bhfioreaula.

Ata an sud gan bhladareacht measareacht fioramdachd,
Ata aun brandy flo farsin agus fionu da thaosga;
Gin gan easba mar mheasaim agus beoir le huiliomh,
Aig aun Leemhan mear calma, do mhathaimh agus do chru na gaoidilimh.

A se Seamus an farare geauamnach lau eagneach,
D'fhior flauil chathaseach chlar banaba ba mhor eiliomh;

O'Dasir mar mheata a mam catha chum namhaiddo fhleasga
Le hard ghnionh aigionta da dtreasgairt da mbrugh 'sda leirsgrios.

[Each brave full-spirited well-met young fellow
Who wishes to spend a while in pleasure
To Duane street let him come quickly and into the Daisy
Where music is played like the singing of birds.

There he will find
Without boasting moderation and true companionship
Brandy in plenty and wine being poured
No lack of gin, I believe and beer for the asking
From that swift brave Lion of the noble blood of the Gael.
James is the cheerful, mindful guardian
Of the true blood of the Plain of Banba of great fame

O'Dwyer never cowardly at the break of battle in blasting the enemy
With a high noble deed, defeating them, crushing them and destroying
    them.]

Six years later, in 1857, the paper ordered the first set of Gaelic type to
be struck in America and on July 25, 1857, commenced its Gaelic Department, which was to be a regular feature, with occasional lapses, for the
next half century. The problem of the Gaelic type was a major one. There

was a general feeling that Irish had to be printed using Gaelic font, and yet such type was extremely scarce. Most newspapers were unwilling to go to the expense of procuring a set of Irish type. Therefore this undertaking by the *Irish American* was a major commitment. At the time no newspaper, even in Ireland, had a Gaelic column. The *Irish American's* Irish-language column included poems and tales taken from manuscripts, some of which had never before appeared in print; songs reprinted from the handful of contemporary Gaelic books published in Ireland, such as the translations of Moore's Melodies done by Archbishop MacHale of Tuam; the occasional letter; and, rarely, original compositions in Irish. Its first Gaelic editor was apparently John O'Mahony, assisted by Michael Doheny, both of whom later played an important role in the establishment of the Fenians in America. In the first one hundred weeks of the column, only three poems were created expressly for the Gaelic section. The column was also the first to publish several poems by Patrick Condon, from a manuscript provided by the poet's son, who had moved to Brooklyn after his father's death in 1856.

The importance of the Gaelic column cannot be overstated, yet it has received little credit from Irish scholars. A year after it started, the Dublin *Nation* announced that it too would begin a Gaelic column. The *Irish-American* Gaelic column continued as long as the paper did, until 1915, although there were several significant gaps. But by 1915 it had published 1,500 columns, some of which are extremely interesting, especially in the 1880s and 1890s. It is thus one of the major sources for writing in Irish in this country, and yet its columns have been virtually neglected until now.

The first five original poems of the Gaelic column were sent in by two Irishmen living in Canada (we may also note here that the first one of these appeared on Oct. 10, 1857, and the fifth on March 21, 1863). The first four were by Fr. Thomas O'Boyle, a native of Donegal who wrote under the pen name of Éire go Bráth from Gloucester, Canada West, in what is today the Province of Ontario. John O'Daly of Dublin regarded him as one of the greatest Irish scholars of the time. O'Boyle's poems are written in a strange pseudo-archaic Irish orthography (even the Gaelic editor of the *Irish-Ameri-*

can noted this: "The orthography of the poem is peculiar and antiquated"), which may have resulted from reading too much Old Irish or from the theories of Colonel Vallancey, an eighteenth-century antiquarian. The first poem we have by O'Boyle is "Idh Breasail, no Beg-Arand" a somewhat "Celtic mist" type of poem about the Land of Youth to the West of Ireland. His other compositions ("Aoileann na Trágha," "Duthchas inda n-Gaedhal" or the Land of the Gael, and "A Ghaedhlig mhín, mhilis") are in praise of a beautiful woman, in praise of Ireland, and in praise of the Irish language. His poems were reprinted in later years in the *Irish-American*, and we learn that Fr. O'Boyle apparently met with an early death. It is truly a pity, for he could well have developed into an interesting poet, and he would surely have been an important figure in the incipient Gaelic movement that was developing in North America.

The other man who contributed a composition of his own was William Russell of Buckingham, Canada East, a place that is about thirty miles north of Ottawa. His poem "Maidin Lae Phádraig" [The Morning of Saint Patrick's Day] was published on March 23, 1863, and is a battle cry for the Irish to rise up and throw off England's oppressive yoke of servitude: "Now for Ireland, o children of the warriors / Attack your enemy fiercely / And redden the shafts of your blades and spears / With the blood of every deceitful pillager." As far back as 1854 Russell had sent in from Ottawa an English poem set to a Gaelic tune which the *Irish-American* published on June 10 of that year. In 1869 Russell came to New York at the invitation of the newspaper and became its Gaelic editor until 1871. During this time he continued the tradition of supplying poetry and songs from manuscripts, and only two of his original pieces appeared in those two years. Both of these deal with the theme of exile and the hope for freedom for Ireland. After his stint with the *Irish-American*, Russell moved to Pennsylvania, where he took part in the Irish language movement in the 1880s.

After Russell's departure from the paper, the Gaelic column disappeared for several years. From 1872 to 1876 only three pieces of Gaelic appeared, one of which is a fine elegy composed in the United States by Dermot Kissane upon the death of his brother Fr. William Kissane (*Irish-American* August 15, 1874). It begins in translation:

[As I traveled about in mist alone, at the edge of a field far from Ireland,
I heard, I saw, I was surprised to perceive a troubled maiden lamenting
  alone.

I was troubled by the maiden's sorrow and approached her with pity for
  her wailing
And asked the fine woman the cause of her sorrow and the reason for her
  tears.

The maiden answered us in sorrowful words
"Have you not heard the pitiful tale?
In Knockraw dead is the good-humored priest
Father Kissane beloved by all.

. . . . .

I started at hearing that news, floods of tears came to my eyes
If what you tell me is true, my stay in this world will not be long

It was not long till there arrived under black seal
A letter from across the sea, saying that it was no lie
All that the maiden had said as she tearfully cried
That Death had called for him and he had to depart.]

Two weeks after Kissane's poem had been published, the paper printed
a verse composition copied from the County Galway *Tuam Advertiser* in
praise of the revival of Irish, composed by the Religieuses of the Mercy
Convent, Tuam. This piece is a response to a well-known pathetic poem in
English lamenting the passing of the Irish language by a Father Mullen, entitled "O, 'tis Fading." It shows a degree of involvement in secular matters
that we would hardly expect from a convent of nuns in 1874. But their
interest becomes less surprising when we recall that John MacHale was
the Archbishop of Tuam in the western province of Connacht, which was
still largely Irish-speaking. MacHale was a native Irish speaker, and one of
the few important supporters of the teaching of Irish in the schools. When
all the rest of Ireland had fallen to the English-only National School system, MacHale held out against it. In Tuam in his local training college, St.
Jarlath's, the Irish language was taught for decades. The local weekly paper, the *Tuam News,* started an Irish column in 1873 which continued well

into the twentieth century. So just as the *Irish-American*'s Gaelic column was disappearing, periodicals in Ireland started to publish in Irish. In addition to the *Tuam News*, two weekly magazines, the *Shamrock* and the *Irishman*, had occasional articles in Irish during the 1870s.

At this time another Irish-American paper, the *Irish World*, was established in New York, with Patrick Ford as editor. In the early 1870s the paper received a large number of letters expressing an interest in the Irish language. Michael Logan was one of those who called for the establishment of classes in this country. Logan had arrived in Brooklyn from the Tuam district of Galway in 1871. He had attended St. Jarlath's College in Tuam and arrived fresh, with the gospel of Gaelic still intact. He established an Irish class in Brooklyn in 1872. Soon after that the Philo-Celtic Society was formed in Boston. It started out when one Irishman saw a Gaelic sign in the shop of another. He wrote a poem in Gaelic to the shopkeeper, a poetic correspondence developed, and from that the society was founded. The poets were Michael O'Sullivan and Michael C. O'Shea, both of whom worked for decades afterwards in the Irish-language movement. Shortly after the founding of the Boston society, Michael Logan established a Philo-Celtic Society in Brooklyn. This activity was apparently noted in Ireland, and at the end of 1876 the Society for the Preservation of the Irish Language was founded in Dublin. It published a book of Irish lessons, and soon their influence reverberated across the Atlantic to the United States. In 1877 the *Irish-American* recommenced its Gaelic column, which remained a regular feature until the paper ceased publication in 1915, and in 1878 Gaelic societies were formed all over New York, New Jersey, and Massachusetts.

The new, revitalized *Irish-American* Gaelic column continued to feature ancient poetry and songs, but the paper also started a special sub-category of the column which it called "Written Irish." By this it meant current topics of everyday interest, which had virtually never received treatment in Irish in print before. The first installment of "Written Irish" opened with these words: "From a number of communications in the Irish language, which we have received since resuming our Gaelic publications, we select the following as specimens of what can be done with the Irish as a medium of written correspondence. The letters will serve also as a study of ordinary colloquial language for those who are desirous to learn" (*Irish-American*, Sept. 29, 1877). The first two letters chosen to be published were from Michael O'Sullivan and P. J. O'Daly of Boston. O'Sullivan's letter gives an idea of the excitement that was felt by some Irish speakers at the reawakening of interest in the language. Below is the translation of the letter which the paper published alongside the original in Irish:

Dear Sir, — I was much rejoiced to see in your patriotic paper of the past week the fine Irish song "There is not in the wide world a valley so sweet," translated from the English by that holy prelate, John, Archbishop of Tuam, and the letter from the learned John Fleming, of Rathcormack.

Now, as the people of Dublin and of Ireland generally are exerting themselves to re-enliven the Irish, it is incumbent upon the Irishmen of Boston and New York to unite with you to circulate your paper throughout this country.

Our tongue has been denounced too long by the unmerciful Saxon spoiler; and it is time now we should use our utmost endeavors to elevate it to its pristine eminence.

Surely we are not so charmed by the Saxon tongue that we should forget our own melifluous [sic] language for its sake and the thousands of Irishmen in this country, so successful and comfortable who could associate and resolve to help each other to bring the Irish tongue to life again.

Have we not the same opportunities in this fine broad land that the other European peoples have, to learn our tongue and to read and write the ancient history of Ireland? How beautifully the poet O'Lionain moulds the Irish tongue in these words:

"Nor did Homer of the smooth flowing verse,
Nor gleeful, witty Ovid e'er rehearse
Their thoughts and themes in richer language sing,
Than the Irish tongue that flows like living spring."

Most respectfully,
Michael O'Sullivan,
Number 121 West Second street,
South Boston, Mass.

Unfortunately, one of the main tasks of this column was to criticize the Irish of other writers. This was a real problem, because even though writers may have been excellent Irish speakers, they would have had very little opportunity to develop into adept writers of the language. Furthermore, some of the writers were only learners of Irish and their Irish at times was truly atrocious. The most critical of all the writers was Thomas O'Neill Russell, a student of the language whose own Irish never attained grammatical correctness. Nevertheless, this column was extremely important because it gave people an opportunity to practice writing Irish. Soon some fairly weighty matters were being handled in letters to the paper in Irish, including literary criticism and the 1880 U.S. Presidential election! Some excellent Irish scholars emerged in these years. One was David O'Keeffe of New York, who had been involved in Irish language activity as far back as the 1850s, when he was copying Irish manuscripts in New York; another was Daniel Magnier, a manuscript specialist who published extracts from Irish manuscripts in the *Irish-American* over the course of the 1880s. By 1881 the *Irish-American* had published 450 Gaelic columns since 1857.

In 1881 Michael Logan established a monthly bilingual periodical in Brooklyn called *An Gaodhal* (*The Gael*), which provided an additional outlet for writers of Irish to publish their work. At the time no such periodical existed in Ireland. The appearance of *An Gaodhal* in 1881 almost certainly spurred the Irish at home in Dublin to produce their own bilingual periodical *Irisleabhar na Gaedhilge* (*The Gaelic Journal*) in 1882.[6] While much of *An Gaodhal*'s material is sentimental or overly romantic, one finds some very interesting material in its pages, such as letters in Irish from immigrants describing life in Alabama, Louisiana, and San Francisco. Poetry, of course, is the main vehicle of creative writing.

One frequent contributor to *An Gaodhal* was Patrick O'Byrne, a native of Donegal who settled in New York ca. 1880. His work appeared in many of the Irish-American publications of the time such as the *Irish-American* and *Irish World* of New York and the *Irish Echo,* a bilingual Boston periodical which was published between 1886 and 1894. An elegy he wrote for Ulysses S. Grant was printed in the *New York Herald* on August 10, 1885. His poems covered the language revival movement, politics, nature, history, love, and humor.[7] His poetry, along with that of Douglas Hyde, heralded the tentative beginning of a new era in Irish poetry. One of his poems, "In Aondacht tá Buaidh" [In Unity There Is Victory], published in the *Irish-American* on January 19, 1884, shows a commendable tolerance and understanding of the faction problem:[8]

[O people of Ireland, remember the phrase:-
"In unity there victory; in division misfortune;"
Without unity among people or any nation
There is no way they can get their freedom.

It is because of division among our people, alas,
That the hideous English first came to our country;
They have left division among us ever since,
It is division that is now tightening the noose.

Though brave, upright men have often striven
To break asunder forever the chains of our island,
Though they have shed their life's blood on field and plain,
The battle was always lost due to division

And today the same black hatred as in former times
Is poisoning every heart
And keeping apart the people who should be
United and steadfast against might.

It is the one island that raised us all
It is the one sun that lights our sky,
It is the one land we have as a country, -
To that country we should be true.

If William fought James in days of yore
What do we care which of them was right?
They've both been lying in the ground for long
"Let their fight die with them" — that's my motto.

Should we be criticizing each other for ever
If all Irish do not bend their knee

In the same church at the same altar of God
Or at any other altar, if they wish?

If this is your religion, o foolish people
Freedom is a long way off from the children of the Gael
If hatred for one another is your praise to God
I am a Pagan till I go to the grave.

"Damn the Pope!" "The Pope forever!"
Are these the prayers we should pray?
It would be far better for us to say:
"Here's to Ireland's freedom forever!"

Province or county, let them no longer
Keep people apart
Religion — don't let it be an obstacle
But let the spirit of peace be forever in our hearts.]

One of his finest poems, "Ádhbhar ár m-Bróin" [The Cause of Our Sor-
row] (*Irish-American*, Feb. 12, 1887, p. 3), was written shortly after Fr. Edward McGlynn had been suspended from his duties at St. Stephen's Parish
by the Archbishop of New York, M. A. Corrigan. McGlynn was dismissed
for his outspoken political views, which included support of Henry George
and his socialist policies. The case received a fair amount of coverage in the
Irish-American, and the editors gave their full support to the Archbishop's
decision. Pádraic's poem expresses powerfully the love and reverence the
common people had for McGlynn and their feeling of helplessness in the
conflict. McGlynn is not mentioned by name in the poem and it is certain,
given the editorial stance of the paper, that the piece would not have been
printed had it been written in English.

ÁDHBHAR ÁR M-BRÓIN

A Shagairt a rúin! — A fhíor-shómpla gach maitheas, —
Is cráidhte, croidhe-bhriste do phobal go léir, —
A shómpla gach súbhailce líonas an Flaitheas, —
A shagairt na sagart a d-talamh na saor!

A athair, a chara na n-íosal 'sna n-daidhbhir! —
A shóláis ár m-buaidhirt! — a sholuis ár slighe! —
A shagairt nár chrom 'riamh ag cosaibh na saidhbhir —
Ní féidir nach bh-feicfimíd thusa a choidhch'!

Nach bh-feicfimíd thusa, a shagairt ba ghloine;
Nach bh-feicfimid thusa, a phrionsa na g-cléir! —
Nach g-cluinfimid feasda an gúth sin ba bhinne;
Nach lasfaidh do chaoin-smig a coidhche ár spéir!

Acht, deir siad go raibh tú ceann-dána, easúmhal; —
Gur chán tú na focla nár chóir duit a rádh;
Ghur shiúbhal tú an bealach nár cheart duitse shiúbhal;
Gur theagaisg tú dlíghthe gan ciall a's gan fáth!

Chum tighearnaibh, — go cinnte, — ní raibh tú ro-úmhal;
Is fíor é nár chrom tú do BHODACH no RIGH;
'Gus nár shiúbhal tú an bealach ba mhian leo thú siúbhal,
Óir bhí spioraid na fearamh fearamhleachd' beó in do chroidhe.

Is cinnte gur labhair tú na focla so linne: —
"Tá ceirt ag gach duine a m-bothán no cró, —
Óir níor chruthaigh an Cruthaightheóir talamh na cruinne
Chum mórdhachd' a's glóire aoin bhodaigh no dó."

Acht an tuata lochduigheas thúsa gan smuaineamh
Tar liomsa a n-diú agus seas ins an tígh;
'Na bh-fuil baintreabhach bhocht in a seómra ag caoineadh,
'Gus a dílleachdaidhe beaga, gan deoch a's gan díth!

A's fiafraigh do'n mhnaoi so cad fáth bh-fuil sí caoineadh?
'Gus fiafraigh do'n phaisde annsin ag a glúin
Cad fáth bh-fuil a dheóra ag tuitim gan staonadh?
Cad fáth bh-fuil a osnadh ag briseadh a shuain?

A's deirfidh siad leat: — "Níl aon phighín in ár sparán,
Do chaill sinn an cára a líon é do ghnáth!
Le seachtmhain, tá'n bórd sin lom, folamh, gan arán
Óir díbriúghadh ár sagart; sin ádhbhar ár g-crádh!"

A athair! má bhris tú aon dlighe de na dlíghthibh
A gheall tú do choimhéad gan briseadh go bráth,
Ní tusa tá ciontach, — amach as ár g-croidhthibh
Admhóchaidh do phobal gur b'iadsan an fáth.

Is linne an t-ualach a bhrónaigh do bheatha,
Is tusa an mairtír a thuit in ár g-cúis,
Ba tusa ár d-treóraidhe, 's ag deireadh an chatha
Bhí d'obair-se deunta, ba linne an duais.

A shagairt, ní iongantach do phobal bheith gruama,
'Nuair chídheann siad thusa i mórdachd do ghrádh
Ag iomchar ár n-ualaigh go foighideach, go stúama,
S gan é in ar g-cúmhacht aon fhocal de rádh!

Acht, athair, tá fágtha ag daoinibh gach tíre,
Aon chúirt 'na bh-fuil breitheamh a g-cómhnuidhe 'na shuidhe,
Aon chúirt 'na bh-fuil paidir 'na n-íosal níos fíre
'Ná paidir an bhodaigh, 'ná paidir an rígh.

Do'n chúirt sin, a shagairt, éirigheann ár n-guidhthe,
Go dílis, go dúthrachtach, oidhche 'gus lá,
Go bh-filleidh sé chugainn fíor-shagart ár g-croidhtheadh,
'S go mairfidh sé linne mar threóruidhe go bráth!

[THE CAUSE OF OUR SORROW

Oh dear priest — true example of all goodness, —
All your people are tormented and broken-hearted
Oh model of each virtue that fills Paradise, —
Oh priest of priests in the land of the free!

O father, o friend of the lowly and dejected!
O solace of our sorrow — o light of our way
O priest who never bowed at the feet of the rich —
It is not possible that we shall not see you again!

That we shall not see you, o priest most pure;
That we shall not see you, o prince of the clergy!

That we shall not hear that sweetest of voices;
That your fair countenance will never light up our sky!

For they say that you are stubborn and disobedient;
That you spoke words you should not have said;
That you walked the path you should not have walked;
That you taught laws without sense or reason!

To lords, — indeed, — you were not humble;
It is true that you did not bow down to CHURL or KING;
And that you did not walk the path they wanted you to walk
Because the spirit of manhood was alive in your heart.

It is certain that you spoke these words to us: —
"Everyone has a right to some hut or shack, —
For the Creator did not create this world
For the majesty and glory of one or two churls.

But let the ignoramus who condemns you without thinking
Come with me today and stand in the house
Where there is a poor widow in her room crying,
And her little orphans, without food or drink!

And ask this woman why she is crying?
And then ask the child at her knee
Why his tears are falling without stop?
Why does his sigh disturb his sleep?

And they will tell you: — "There is not a penny in our purse,
We have lost the friend who filled it regularly!
For a week that table has been empty without bread,
Because our priest was banished; that is the cause of our torment!"

O father! if you broke any of the rules
Which you promised to keep unbroken forever,
It's not you who are guilty — out of our hearts
Your people will admit that they are the cause.

Ours is the burden that saddened your life,
You are the martyr who fell in our cause,

You were our leader and at the end of the battle
Your work was done, the prize was ours.

O priest, it is no wonder your people are gloomy,
When they see you, in the magnificence of your love,
Carrying our burden patiently, sedately,
And we powerless to say a word.

But, father, there is left to the people of every country
One court where a judge is always presiding
One court where the plea of the lowly is more trustworthy
Than the plea of a churl or a king.

To that court, o priest, our prayers go up,
Faithfully and earnestly night and day,
May he return to us, our dearly beloved priest,
And may he remain with us as a leader forever!]

Other poems by Padraic show a modern outlook or world view that was rare in Gaelic poetry at this time. A good example is his poem on the Irish Gael and Scottish Gael, in which he says they should overcome their religious differences and unite for their common good.

Pádraic was responsible also for the Irish text of a musical that was staged in New York in 1884. The music was by the Corkman Paul MacSwiney and *An Bard agus an Fó* [The Bard and the Knight] was almost certainly the first Irish-language musical ever produced anywhere in the world. After the turn of the century, Irish-language plays, including some written in this country, were performed in New York right up to the late 1960s. Two early examples are *Ar Son Cháit, a Chéad Ghrádh* [For Kate His First Love], written by Andrew O'Boyle, a native of Sligo who was active in the New York language movement in the first decade of this century, and *Seaghan Ruadh* [Red John], performed in New York in 1906 and written by B. O'Keeney, a native of Donegal who was also a major figure in New York Irish-language circles at the time.

In the 1880s Irish-language columns were appearing in a number of Irish-American newspapers such as the *Chicago Citizen* and the San Francisco *Monitor*. As mentioned above, a bilingual magazine called the *Irish*

Echo ran for several years in Boston. In all of these the material consisted mainly of traditional poetry and prose tales taken from manuscripts or copied from the columns of papers in Ireland, but some new genres did begin to appear. One of these was a wide range of folklore material, especially songs, collected by people like J. J. Lyons and Fr. D. Murphy from the oral recitation of Irish speakers all over the Philadelphia area. Original prose appeared as well in the form of sermons, addresses delivered at meetings, and, after the turn of the century, some pieces which might be considered precursor short stories. Noteworthy in the realm of prose is a series of twelve articles written by Féilim Ua Tuathail (Phelim O'Toole) between December 28, 1889, and April 19, 1890, which appeared in the *Irish-American*. Ua Tuathail, writing from an undisclosed rural location in the American Midwest, discusses the question of the Irish language in the United States with a maturity of style and a command of language seldom seen in Irish prose writing at that time. Some of his comments may have been too pointed, because after the appearance of his April 19 article he disappeared from the Irish-language press and was apparently never heard from again.

Perhaps the most unusual collection of Irish narrative material composed just after the turn of the century is that of the Limerick man, John Cahill, who wrote verse accounts in Irish of his exploits with the U.S. Cavalry fighting the Indians in the "Wild West." The poems seem to have been based partly on Fenian ballads and partly on Wild West dime novels.[9] Cahill seems to have learned some Irish in his late teens or early twenties in Ireland and continued studying it in the United States. He sent copies of his poems to a number of people, including Douglas Hyde in Ireland and Michael McDonnell in New York. The Douglas Hyde copies are preserved at University College of Galway, and the McDonnell copies were obtained for Harvard by Fred Norris Robinson and are now in Houghton Library. The poems included are "An chéad Uair a' mBráighdeanas Ag na th-Indiachaibh Ans' na Sléibhte Carraigeacha" [My First Time in Captivity among the Indians in the Rocky Mountains, 178 stanzas] and "Cionnas do bhuadhaig Tomás Ua Gráda Bean-Phrionsa Indiach mar Mhnaoi-céile" [How Thomas O'Grady Won an Indian Princess as a Wife, 173 stanzas).

There is something artificial in Cahill's language, and for all his study of Irish it is clear that he never developed a natural feeling for it.

Well into this century Irish remained the language of a fair number of newly arrived immigrants. Though many of these were unlettered, some of them were far more adept at composing Irish poetry than John Cahill. One such folk poet was John Russell of West Kerry, who worked in Alaska, Washington State, and the mines of Butte, Montana. Several of his compositions have been collected orally in Ireland. His poem "The Mine Song" tells us some of the hardships he faced:

> [West to America I went
> Hunting early in my life
> Searching for gold under the ground
> And by the side of the mountain.
> Though I have walked every street and city
> From Boston to Carroll Street
> I have seen no place like the home
> That I left in the morning at the dawn of day.][10]

James Moriarty, another Kerryman who spent years in San Francisco and Butte, Montana, published a number of his poems in the *Gaelic American* in the first decade of this century. In one poem he speaks of his disillusionment with life in America:

> [It is a pity that I ever came to this country
> And that I left Ireland behind
> As I think with sorrow on the old days
> When I had merriment and sport.
>
> I received a letter from a friend to go quickly overseas
> That there was gold to be had
> And I would never see a hard or poor day.
>
> I took with me a satchel in which I would put the gold
> I tied a cord around it
> I boarded a ship foolishly
> With my satchel on my back I prayed to God

> To deliver me unharmed to the land
> Where I would be a gentleman all my life.
>
> Ah, but when I landed in that country
> And moved quickly about the city
> I saw no gold on the street corners
> I was a poor displaced wretch
>
> It's better to be in sweet Ireland
> Listening to the music of the birds
> Than to be looking for work from a cheapskate
> Who thinks you are a donkey to be struck with a whip.][11]

Since so many Irish speakers were illiterate in their own language, especially before the general introduction of Irish-language instruction into Irish schools, it is not surprising that written acounts of their experiences in this country are rare. One excellent book-length memoir, *Rotha Mór an tSaoil* [The Great Wheel of Life] by Michael MacGowan, which has been translated into English with the title *The Hard Road to Klondike,* consists of MacGowan's reminiscences of life in this country and in the Klondike during the Gold Rush of the 1890s. His story was delivered orally and recorded on Ediphone by Seán Ó hEochaidh of the Irish Folklore Commission in the 1940s.

In recent years accounts of immigrant experiences in America can be found in the works of Kerry natives Maidhc Dainín Ó Sé, who lived in Chicago in the 1950s, and Muiris Ó Bric, who lives in suburban New York. What is noticeably absent is a major work from the native Irish speakers who are so numerous in the Boston area. Though no counterpart to Isaac Bashevis Singer has yet appeared in their midst, it is still possible that one of these Boston-based Irish speakers will produce a work of significance to illustrate the life of contemporary Irish speakers in the United States.

Notes

1. P. MacAonghusa, "An Ghaeilge i Meiriceá" in *Go Meiriceá Siar*, ed. Stiofán Ó hAnnracháin ([Dublin]: An Clóchomhar Tta a d'fhoilsigh do Chumann Merriman, 1979), pp. 14–15.

2. For references, see David N. Doyle, *Ireland, Irishmen and Revolutionary America, 1760–1820* (Dublin: Mercier Press for The Cultural Relations Committee of Ireland, 1981), p. 249.

3. MacAonghusa, "An Ghaeilge i Meiriceá," p. 15.

4. Before going on to discuss Condon's work, it is important to note what is extant of the original material. Only three pieces survive written in Condon's own hand. The first of these, Maynooth manuscript C.93, is a letter written to Cáit Graidhin of Callan, County Kilkenny, on June 22, 1823, several years before Condon left Ireland. The second piece, written in 1825, is part two of Royal Irish Academy manuscript 23 B 14 and consists of songs. The third piece is a letter written by Condon on March 30, 1852. This occurs in manuscript G.6 in the County Cork Archives and is the only piece written by him in America that has survived.

   A photostat copy of an Irish manuscript, which contains twenty-two of Condon's poetic compositions, is housed in the New York Public Library Rare Book Division. The copy is bound and on the flyleaf is the following note: "Gift of Miss S. Carty, 211 Berkeley Place, Brooklyn, N.Y. Dec. 1930." This seems to be a copy of Condon's own manuscript, but unfortunately the NYPL has no record of how they acquired the photostat nor do they have any idea of what happened to the original.

   The most important source for our knowledge about the poet is the book *Pádraig Phiarais Cúndún,* edited by Risteard Ó Foghludha (Richard Foley) and published in Ireland (Baile Átha Cliath: Oifig Díolta Foillseacháin Rialtais, 1932). Ó Foghludha's edition is the most complete collection of Condon's work. Ó Foghludha himself was a native of the Ballymacoda district. He was one of the indefatigable workers of the early days of the Gaelic League. He had an excellent knowledge of Irish poetry and manuscripts and in the course of his lifetime published nearly twenty editions of the works of various eighteenth- and nineteenth-century Munster poets. Ó Foghludha was in a particularly good position to know about Condon, for his father had known the poet's brothers and Ó Foghludha seems to have gathered a fair amount of oral lore about Condon in the district. In his book on Condon, Ó Foghludha published some thirty-six pieces by the author. Twenty-two of the poems also occur in the New York photostat, but of the eleven American letters

Ó Foghludha gives, only one has come down to us today and that is the one which is in the County Cork Archives. It is most unfortunate that Ó Foghludha did not tell the source for his material. He dedicates the book to his uncle, Eamonn Rua Ó Foghludha who, he says "did the most in his time to preserve the written work of Patrick Condon and furthermore who encouraged me, by his own good example and by bestowing Gaelic manuscripts, to do my best for the language of Ireland." Ó Foghludha not only knew of the existence of the New York manuscript but even knew the line at which it ended. But he gives us no indication of how he knew about it. In spite of the uncertainty, we can be confident that the material he presents is really the work of Condon.

5.   All page references in text are to *Pádraig Phiarais Cúndún*. All translations are my own unless otherwise noted.

6.   The Irish language movement in Dublin was well aware of developments in the United States, as can be seen in these comments from the 1882 Report of the Society for the Preservation of the Irish Language: "The little organ which Brooklyn sends forth, *An Gaodhal*, welcome to our sight as the first daisy which February bears, deserves our commendation as being an effort to meet the need, however imperfectly. We at home will not, I trust, prove untrue to the demand now made upon us" (p. 54); "That our deliberations are being watched with interest across the Atlantic is evident from a letter which I have just received from that enthusiastic philo-celt, Mr. T. O'Neill Russell of Chicago, in which he hopes 'that the Congress will seriously consider the matter of establishing an Irish weekly paper in Dublin . . .'" (p. 55).

7.   See Breandán Ó Conaire "Pádraig Ó Beirn — Fear a D'fhill," in Ó hAnnracháin, *Go Meiriceá Siar*, p. 113.

8.   A poem by Jeremiah O'Donovan Rossa entitled "Éire Trasna 'n t-Sáile" [Ireland across the Sea], with similar sentiments, was published in the *Irish-American* in February 1880.

9.   A prose account, with somewhat similar content, was published in the *Irish-American* on March 15, 1884, with the title "Mícheál Ó Mathghamhnuigh 's na h-Indiachuighe: Cionnus do shaor an Ghaedhilig a bheatha féin agus beatha mórán daoineadh eile" (Michael O'Mahony and the Indians: How Irish Saved His Life and the Lives of Many Others). The piece was contributed by Thomas O'Neill Russell, who wrote it from the recitation of Michael O'Mahony of Galena, Illinois.

10.   "Amhrán na Mianach" (The Mine Song) in Seán Ó Dubhda, *Duanaire Duibhneach* (Baile Átha Cliath: Oifig an tSoláthair, 1933), p. 130.

11.   Ó Dubhda, *Duanaire Duibhneach*, pp. 127–29.

CHAPTER ELEVEN

Alfred Mercier's Polyglot Plantation Novel of Louisiana

■ **LAWRENCE ROSENWALD**

Alfred Mercier's *L'Habitation Saint-Ybars* (The Saint-Ybars Plantation), which takes place in Louisiana in mid-nineteenth century, is a scrupulous dramatization of the relations between Louisiana Standard French and Louisiana French Creole, and thus of interest to students of language, translation, and southern history.[1] But neither author nor novel is widely known, so I should begin by situating them. Mercier was born in Louisiana in 1816.[2] In 1830 he was sent to France for his education, and from then until the end of the Civil War he lived more in Europe than in Louisiana; during the war itself he was practicing medicine in Paris. He returned to Louisiana after the war and spent most of the rest of his life there, until his death in 1894. By training and profession he was a doctor; but by temperament and by long labor in diverse genres he was a man of letters, probably the leading man of letters in francophone Louisiana. He was also the guiding spirit of the Athénée Louisianais, a society founded after the Civil War for the embattled support of francophone Louisiana culture.

L'Habitation Saint-Ybars is often singled out as Mercier's best work, for its loving and careful description of scenes Mercier knew from his childhood. It describes some twenty years in the life of a Louisiana plantation, from 1851 till an unspecified year in the 1870s, and is told chiefly from the viewpoint of Antony Pélasge, a Parisian-born, French-trained, revolutionary Huguenot intellectual. Pélasge has been on the Paris barricades in 1848, has been wounded and imprisoned and deported, and has escaped from an Algerian prison. Now, at the age of twenty-three, seeking a refuge from the political turmoil of Europe, he arrives in Louisiana and finds employ-

219

ment as a tutor. His employer is the passionate and uncontrolled plantation owner, Saint-Ybars; Antony's charges are his employer's two children, a daughter, Chant d'Oisel (Birdsong), and a son, Démon (Demon).

The novel centers on Pélasge. It tells the story of his successes in tutoring, and depicts his affection for his two students; it recounts his participation in the family's furious quarrels and his friendship with Vieumaite, Saint-Ybars' Jekyll-and-Hyde father (the two sides of his face are sharply different, and the plantation slaves call them "sunside" and "shadeside").[3] In addition to particular people, particular places in the plantation—a certain grove and a magnificent tree called "the Old Sachem" — become part of his world. In time he falls in love with Chant d'Oisel, who eventually marries him on her deathbed. Pélasge's grief at Démon's suicide, occasioned by racial prejudice, is followed by his growing isolation and his return to a life of political activity in Europe. We sense other stories in the background, but they matter less; the chapter on the Civil War takes only three pages, one page fewer than the chapter recounting the departure of the Russian music tutor, Mlle Nogolka.

What makes the novel matter, though, is that it is a bilingual novel, perhaps the only systematically bilingual novel in American literature. Most novels that depict a bilingual or multilingual population represent languages other than the narrative language indirectly and selectively — by devices such as "he said in language X," by literal "translation" of language X idioms, by the direct "quotation" of particularly emphatic language X phrases, by narrative characterization of the non-narrative language or languages being spoken. Mercier uses none of these strategies. Instead, he does something very simple and very rare: he makes his characters speak the languages he judges they would have used.[4] When he judges that his characters would have spoken Louisiana standard French (LSF), they speak it. When he judges they would have spoken Louisiana French Creole (LFC), they speak that. This is an easy strategy to describe, to understand, and to defend. But it is very rare; it is hard to think of another American novel of that period that makes use of it in portraying a bilingual or multilingual community.

This is not to say that Mercier's strategy makes *L'Habitation Saint-Ybars* a great novel of languages, on the order of Henry Roth's *Call It Sleep*. For one thing, Mercier seems not to have much of an interest in dialect and idio-lect, or in the range of registers within particular languages. For another, though he has a passion for *recording* multiple languages, he seems to have only a secondary interest in *thematizing* them. His novel does not dwell on how we use language to win power, to fashion an identity, or to bridge the gap between ourselves and others. He seems sometimes to be more of a sociolinguist than a novelist. We can, because of his meticulous precision, find patterns in the uses of language he depicts; we do not, however, feel that he has organized his novel around the patterns we find.

But Mercier's painstaking sociolinguistic exactness is worth our atten-tion. It seems evident that American literature ought to represent the American multilingual scene. But as we read through the classic American novels in search of such representation, what we find is in large part de-ceit and evasion. We may well turn to the work of sociolinguists to as-sure us of what we already know, namely, that we live in an almost chaoti-cally complex multilingual world, and that the languages people speak matter to their individual identities and political communities. A novel like Mercier's, an extended experiment in letting characters actually speak the languages they must speak or choose to speak, affords us a rare opportu-nity for an analysis of the results.

LSF is superior to LFC. (I should add here that Mercier had written a thoughtful, pioneering essay about LFC, describing its forms and defend-ing its grammar as possessing "all the parts of speech necessary for the ex-pression of [the speaker's] thought";[5] its having the lower place in his hier-archy does not reflect any belief on his part that it is something less than a language. But its place is still the lower one.)

French Creole occupies a lower rung partly because it is, for whites, as-sociated with childhood. At the beginning of the novel, much is made of Démon's preference for the conversation of Mamrie, the black nurse and cook, over that of his parents; he is always running off to her kitchen to hear her stories, and he consistently speaks to her in LFC (and calls her *vou* rather than *to*). After the war, when he returns from Europe, he speaks to her in LSF, and uses *tu*.

And Mamrie approves: "To blié parlé créol; mo oua ça; tapé parlé gran bo langage de France; épi asteur, effronté to tutéié to Mamrie. Mo palé grondé toi pou ça; an contraire, ça fé moin plésir to tutéié moin, to acé gran pou ça" (p. 246).[6] ("You've forgotten how to speak creole. I can see that — you speak the big, beautiful language of France. And now, you insolent thing, you say *tu* to your Mamrie. I won't scold you for that; just the opposite. It pleases me that you say *tu* to me. You're big enough for that.") This exchange implies a whole structure of decorum. It is appropriate for Démon in his boyhood to speak LFC with Mamrie and to treat her with the respect implied by *vou;* it is equally appropriate for Démon in his manhood to speak to her in LSF, and to treat her with the intimacy and mastery implied by *tu.* Part of the pathos of Chant d'Oisel's bilingual deathbed scene, in which she speaks LFC to Mamrie and LSF to everyone else, is precisely that she dies before making her own linguistic *rite de passage.*

Knowing this sociolinguistic fact can help us read one of the tensest, most dramatic scenes of the novel. Démon quarrels with his father, whereupon his father attacks him, striking him several times in the face. Mamrie rushes to Démon's aid, tells his father to let him go, and then, when he continues his attack, throws an axe at his head. Later, Demon's father resolves to punish Mamrie; he orders Jim, a slave, to whip her. But before the whipping starts, Démon comes up to Jim and tells him, "si tu as le malheur de donner un seul coup de fouet à Mamrie, tu es mort" ("If you are so unlucky as to give Mamrie even a single lash, you are dead," p. 187). Démon is still a boy; but at this crucial moment, in need of the adult authority he has so far been at odds with, he adopts the linguistic strategies of a man. Like his own father, he now addresses a slave in LSF, and chooses *tu* rather than *vous.* And it works; Jim refuses to do the whipping, and in the end no whipping is done by anyone.

Another feature that makes LSF superior to LFC is that the former is associated with reason, the latter with storytelling. During the war, Pélasge and Chant d'Oisel undertake the education of Blanchette, the illegitimate daughter of the slave Titia and an unnamed white planter's son. In the course of their teaching, says Mercier, "they always spoke to her in the language of reason, and carefully avoided filling her head with tales and legends" (p. 216). That is clearly a good thing to do, and it follows that "the language of reason" is better than "tales and legends."

But there is a strong association in the novel between "tales and legends" and LFC. When Démon runs off to talk with Mamrie in her kitchen, Chant d'Oisel defends him, saying that "he loves to hear the Negroes tell their stories" (p. 109). Vieumaite carries this defense further, saying, "He likes the Negroes' tales? That's natural. Who of us at his age did not listen to them with pleasure? And let's not fool ourselves — there is sometimes a very subtle irony in these stories, and not just the interest of the plot" (p. 109). Vieumaite rightly sees in the LFC *contes* something more than empty entertainment; he appreciates their subtlety and irony. But even for him, they are something for children; and in any case, they are *contes* and not treatises.

This hierarchy is predictable; what white Louisiana intellectual at this time — what white intellectual anywhere, at this time — would take a Whorfian position on the relation between Parisian French and Louisiana Creole? What is less predictable is that the Saint-Ybars plantation is a place not only of strict linguistic hierarchy, but also of free linguistic circulation. Most of the characters, black and white, are bilingual; they choose to speak LSF or LFC for reasons of temperament or decorum or situation, but they understand both languages and often speak both languages, and language is almost never a barrier to communication.

Pélasge alone understands no LFC, and that only at the beginning of the novel. In two scenes his ignorance is dramatized, but in both cases interpreters are ready to hand, and in neither case does his ignorance keep him from getting to the heart of the matter. The chief effect of his initial ignorance of LFC is to emphasize the universal bilingualism of his new world. Consider the scene in which LFC makes its first appearance.

The young stranger slowed his pace, to see more clearly; but at first he did not understand what he was seeing. He turned, therefore, towards a Negro woman coming his way, and said,

"Tell me, Madame, I beg you: what is going on?"

On hearing herself called "Madame," the woman gave vent to one of those expansive, joyful laughs that are peculiar to the African race, and which no European can imagine before actually hearing them; then, partially regaining her decorum, she answered,

"Vou pa oua don, Michié? Cé nég pou vende."[7]

She saw that she was not understood; so, presuming that she was dealing with a foreigner, she continued in good French,

"They are Negroes for sale, Monsieur."

"Ah," said the stranger, and asked nothing further. (pp. 79–80)

A black woman sees a white man in the streets of New Orleans. He asks her a question in standard French. The question suggests that he might be a stranger; he does not understand the locally familiar institution of the slave auction, and he addresses the woman as Madame. The woman laughs at the unfamiliar form of address, but then answers the question in LFC; that, presumably, would be the language normally used by a person of color to speak with a white. And the white would normally understand. Or perhaps, with sly irony, she chooses to answer in a language he would not understand.

After enjoying the situation for a moment, the woman addresses him in his own language. She plays the polyglot cosmopolitan to Pélasge's ignorant visitor, and dramatizes the claim Mercier makes, that "Whoever speaks the creole here can also speak good French; any ordinary [*petit*] black man or woman, in the most remote streets of the city, will make it a point of honor, if you pose a question in French, to answer you in the language that you speak."[8]

The free circulation of language is accompanied by an equally free circulation of culture. Mamrie composes a *complainte* in LFC to the tune of the French song "Malbrouck s'en va-t-en guerre" (p. 143).[9] Chant d'Oisel sings opera arias to the old slave Ima, who later plays them, "with motifs and variations of his own" (p. 127), on the banjo. Mamrie's LFC letters to Démon, who is waiting out the Civil War in France, are published in a French philological journal, with commentary by Pélasge; and for a while, writes Mercier, "Mamrie was a subject of discussion among certain men of letters"(p. 201). And lest we think that LFC is always the raw material, and speakers of standard French always its consumers, Mercier suggests early in the novel that Mamrie has made use of French literature in developing her unservile ideas about freedom and slavery, and that the scheming black page, Duc de Lauzun, has made use of other works of that same literature in developing his ideas about intrigue and seduction.

For a complicated example of how languages circulate, consider this incident. In Chapter VII, "Man Sophie et ses deux petites filles," Pélasge and Démon encounter Man Sophie, a harmless, demented black woman who carries two dolls around with her and believes they are her children. She and Démon talk for a while, Démon translating for Pélasge; then she leaves, singing what Mercier calls "la vieille romance de Saint-Domingue"(p. 124):

> Lisett' to kité la plaine;
> Mo perdi bonhair à moué;
> Ziés à moué semblé fontaine;
> Depi mo pa miré toué.
> Jour là can mo coupé canne,
> Mo chongé zamour à moué;
> Lanouitt' can mo dan cabane,
> Dan droumi mo tchombo toué.
>
> [Lisette, you left the plain;
> I lost my happiness.
> My eyes are like fountains
> since I stopped seeing you.
> Daytimes, when I cut cane,
> I think of my love;
> at night, in my cabin,
> in my sleep I dream of you.]

This is in fact the famous Haitian Creole song, "Lisette quitté la plaine," composed by the white planter Duvivier de la Mahautière. It was reprinted by Moreau de Saint-Méry in 1797, in an effort to prove that Creole was capable of nuance. How Mercier got hold of it is not clear; nor is it clear how the original Haitian Creole text was rewritten in LFC. Perhaps Mercier himself did the work; perhaps a version of the Haitian song made its way to Louisiana and into the local language. In any case, the result is a sort of merry-go-round: a song artfully composed by a white planter becomes a black folk song, the expressive utterance of a black woman. The black folk song is then perceived by Pélasge as a document of the black culture that he is coming to know, and is translated for his benefit into his language, which is also the language of the planter who wrote the song in the first place! — a remarkable summary of the easy circulation of culture that marks this novel everywhere.[10]

These large, abstract notions — the hierarchy of languages and modes of knowing on the one hand, the space of free linguistic and cultural circulation on the other — need to be supplemented by linguistic portraits of particular characters. Démon's has been sketched already; to it I should add that of Mamrie, the faithful black nurse, and that of the Duc de Lauzun, the scheming black page. These two sharply opposed portraits suggest the range of possibilities lying between them.

Mamrie is a cosmopolitan. She is bilingual and literate. She may in fact be trilingual; during the war she goes to New Orleans to make money for Démon in Europe by selling sweets to Union officers. Presumably she would speak English to them, but Mercier doesn't say so explicitly. She composes poetry and has musical gifts. Her taste in French literature is excellent; like Saint-Ybars himself, she admires Rousseau and Voltaire, Lamartine and Hugo.

Mamrie's own speech, however, is exclusively in her native language, in LFC, regardless of what her interlocutor speaks. This is in sharp contrast to, say, Man Miramis, a freed black woman who rules like a tyrant over the Saint-Ybars servants; Man Miramis adapts her speech to that of her interlocutor. Mamrie has the authenticity of people who always speak their own language; she will not change her language to gain an advantage in any specific situation, as others do.

If to speak LSF is to be ambitious, she has no ambition. But she does not judge other speakers' behavior by the standard of her own; in the passage quoted previously, her comment on Démon's French, she in fact articulates better than anyone else the rules of the bilingual system she functions in. Those rules are a consequence of slavery, and she is no partisan of it (p. 117), but she lives by the rules that slavery has produced.

Her opposite, and antagonist, is Saint-Ybars' quadroon page and illegitimate grandson, M. le duc de Lauzun, sarcastically named by Vieumaite after a seventeenth-century courtier. He is the novel's chief villain, and his scheming brings about three suicides. Presumably his linguistic usage is to be condemned as well; it is in any case quite distinctive, and marks him as a figure of linguistic dissimulation.

We know from what he says in his last scene that he speaks LFC, but until that scene we never observe him speaking it. Inverting Mamrie's linguistic code, he speaks LSF all the time. Notably, he speaks it with the slave Titia, whom he is attempting to seduce; still more notably, he speaks it to himself.[11] Moreover, unlike all the other black speakers of LSF, he has a particular (and particularly bad) LSF literary style, what Mercier calls "the bombastic language of M. le vicomte d'Arlincourt" (p. 202). D'Arlincourt was an early nineteenth-century pamphleteer of no literary distinction; that Lauzun admires him makes his taste as bad as Mamrie's is good. Lauzun is also a diarist, and no doubt his diary would be written in D'Arlincourt's language as well. He is thus the most literary and the most literarily productive of all the black speakers of LSF, and the most linguistically ambitious. Moreover, he is arguably the novel's most skilled polyglot; after the war, he goes about "haranguing the freed slaves and exciting them against their former masters, whom he made a point of calling *Bourbons*. He spoke only English now; he swore he had forgotten French"(pp. 261–62).

The duc de Lauzun embodies everything that Mercier dislikes in the use of language and languages: excessive verbal facility and self-conscious wit; forgetting or denying one's linguistic roots and history; pomposity of style; linguistic opportunism.[12] His grotesque death makes perfect sense in this context. Toward the end of the novel, after the double suicide of Démon and Blanchette for which Lauzun's scheming is ultimately responsible, Mamrie resolves to unmask and punish him. As she says to him, "tan pou réglé to conte vini" (p. 298; "time come to settle your account"). And at this point, he finally speaks LFC; Mamrie has unmasked not only his crimes but also, it seems, his true language. His last words are in LFC: "Mamrie, pa tranglé moin comme ça . . . ou sinon ma cognin vou" (p. 298; "Mamrie, don't choke me like that, or I'll hit you.") No more scheming, no more fine manners or sentences, and no more French or English; and after this revelation of self and language, Mamrie stabs the villain to death.

In some respects, the opposition between these two characters appears condescending. Mercier admires the slave who is loyal to her masters and her native language, modest in her ambitions, private in the sphere of her activity. He condemns the slave who plausibly calls his former masters

Bourbons, who learns and uses the language first of his francophone masters and then of his anglophone ones, who has large political ambitions and considerable oratorical gifts and public influence. M. le duc de Lauzun looks a little like a southern slaveholder's image of Frederick Douglass.

But the opposition has other meanings as well. This is, after all, a novel of 1881, and Mercier is devoting himself to the doomed struggle of Louisiana francophone culture in a world dominated by the anglophone north. In the context of that struggle, what Mamrie stands for is linguistic fidelity. She is loyal to those among her masters whom she loves, yes, but she is more loyal to her native language. She has no use for slavery and no qualms about throwing an axe at Saint-Ybars, but every word that she speaks is spoken in LFC. The opposition between Mamrie and Lauzun means to reveal not only two ways of being a black servant but also two ways of living in a multilingual world; not only the difference between subordination to one's masters and rebellion against them but also that between nurturing one's culture and betraying it.

If Mercier's novel became more widely known, it would inevitably be translated; and the task of translating it would raise some questions that translation theory has neglected.

Surprisingly, these questions do not concern the question of how to translate bilingual texts. It is true that translation theory has little to say about such texts; most theorists presume that the original text is unilingual. And generally they are right. And even when a book like Thomas Mann's *The Magic Mountain* comes along, with its long conversations in French amidst the vast German flow, the translator's options are clear: leave the passages in French or translate them into the target language in much the same way as the German.

Mercier's novel presents a more interesting problem. LSF and LFC are different languages, in that they are reciprocally unintelligible (and their reciprocal unintelligibility is dramatized in the novel), but they are also related. And the translator must determine what the relation is between them, and how to render it. In this sense, translating Mercier's novel would be less like translating *The Magic Mountain* and more like translating a richly multidialectal text, such as Mark Twain's *Huck Finn* or Alfred Döblin's *Berlin: Alexanderplatz*. *L'Habitation Saint-Ybars* is an extreme case in this category, in that its two "dialects" are reciprocally unintelligible. Nevertheless this is the category in which it belongs.

Unfortunately, translation theory has little to say about this sort of problem either. Moreover, few translations of multidialectal novels are very satisfying. Dialects are associated with places — the Pike County dialects of *Huck Finn*, the Berlin dialects of *Berlin: Alexanderplatz*, the French regional dialects recorded in Rabelais. Translating such novels usually means displacing their dialects, by one of two strategies. We might call them "re-situation" and "de-situation." Re-situation is what happens when, say, translator Eugene Jolas makes Döblin's characters speak in a dialect of New York, or a translator of Aristophanes renders Doric Greek with southern English.[13] We rebel at this, precisely because dialects are associated with places whereas standard languages are associated with transcendence of place; we can accept the fiction that Döblin's Berlin characters are speaking English, but not that they are speaking New York English.

De-situation is what happens when a translator, recognizing this problem, renders a placed dialect with an unplaced one: say, for a Berlin dialect of German substitutes an English dialect invented for the purpose — a dialect that never has been spoken by anyone but that has some *formal* relation to the dialect of the original text. We do not rebel at this strategy in the same way, since it does not produce the contradictions of location that re-situating does; but only rarely does it produce anyone's living speech.

In Mercier's case, and in the case of any author who treats multiple dialects as equally adequate varieties of speech, this last point matters a lot. Historically, the status of LFC was indeed contested, and the learned debates over the Creole language parallel the dangerous debates over the status of the race associated with it. Consider these remarks of Alcée Fortier's, made three or four years after Mercier's novel was published:

To the Negroes of Louisiana may be attributed the same characteristics that Prof. James A. Harrison recognizes in the American blacks of the South, that is to say, humor and a naïveté bordering on childishness, together with a great facility for imitating the sounds of nature and a wonderful aptitude for music. Their language partakes necessarily of their character, and is sometimes quaint, and always simple. Their plantation songs are quite poetical, and I may say, charming in their oddity.[14]

We know from Mercier's novel that he held a different view of these matters, if only from Vieumaite's astute comments on the subtlety of the LFC *contes,* and from the author's own narrative reference to "the precision of the Creole language" (p. 102); he is more explicit in his "Etude sur la langue créole": "It is a curious thing to follow the intellectual operations by which the savage of the African coast, transported to another continent, makes for himself [*se compose*] a grammar with the foreign words that strike his ear. We use the word 'grammar' deliberately; indeed, the Negro makes for himself a grammar; the words heard from the mouths of the whites are combined in his brain in such a way as to create all the parts of speech necessary for the expression of his thought" (p. 378). So no translation of the LFC passages in Mercier's novel should make them sound like a deficient version of some other language.

In successful translation, then, the dialect passages of a significantly multidialectal novel should be alive, self-sufficient, and as proximate geographically to the original location as possible. A successful translation should also maintain the original distance between one speech variety and another.

But there is a problem with this idea. Here is what happened in at least one test case. Writing in 1886, five years after the appearance of Mercier's novel, George Washington Cable translated an LFC broadside into an extreme African-American vernacular English. His rationale was precisely the one we have been discussing: "Should the Louisiana Creole Negro undertake to render his song to us in English, it would not be exactly the African-English of any other state in the Union. Much less would it resemble the gross dialects of the English-torturing Negroes of Jamaica, or Barbados, or the Sea Islands of Carolina."[15] But the results should give us pause.

> C'est Miché Cayetane,
> Qui sorti la Havane,
> Avec so chouals et so macacs.
> Li gagnein ein nhomme qui dancé dans sac;
> Li gagnein qui dancé si yé la main;
> Li gagnein zaut', à choual, qui boir' di vin;
> Li gagnein oussi ein zein, zoli mom'selle,

Qui monté choual sans bride et sans selle!
Pou' di' tou' ça mo pas capab';
Mé mo souvien ein qui 'valé sab'!
Yé n'en oussi tou' sort' bétail.
Yé pas montré pou' la négrail';
Gniapas là dotchians dos-brilé,
Pou'fé tapaze et pou' hirlé;
Cé gros madame et gros miché,
Qui ménein là tous pitits yé,
  'Oir Miché Cayétane,
   Qui 'rivé la Havane
Avec so chouals et so macacs.

Dass Cap'm Cayetano,
W'at comin' fum Hvano,
Wid 'is monkey' an' 'is nag'!
An' one man w'at dance in bag,
An' mans dance on dey hand' — cut shine'
An' gallop hoss sem time drink wine!
An' b'u'ful young missy dah beside,
Ridin' 'dout air sadd' aw brid'e;
To tell h'all dat — he cann' be tole.
Man teck a sword an' swall' im whole!
Beas'es? ev'y sawt o' figgah!
Dat show ain't fo' no common niggah!
Dey don't got deh no po' white cuss' -
Sunbu'nt back! — to holla an' fuss.
Dass ladies fine, and gennymuns gran',
Fetchin' dey chilluns dah — all han'!
  Fo' se Cayetano,
   W'at come fum Havano
Wid 'is monkey' an' 'is nag'! (pp. 411–13)

This example tells us that abstract considerations cannot solve the problems presented by multidialect novels; we need also to think about the local details of history. In Mercier's case, we have to remember that translating any black dialect from one American language to another means confronting the history of American slavery and Jim Crow. The particular trick in translating him is to find a living, self-sufficient, and geographically proximate language that will not end up sounding like a minstrel show. The dilemma that Mercier's novel poses to translation theory is how to do justice to the linguistic facts and preserve the human dignity of multiple varieties of speech.

How would our literary history change if we took account of Mercier? One way to look at literary history is hinted at in a remark made to Irving Howe by the great Yiddish poet Jacob Glatshteyn: "What does it mean to be a poet of an abandoned culture? It means that I have to be aware of Auden but Auden need never have heard of me."[16] Literary history of this sort might and should speak of the influence of Eliot and Auden on Glatshteyn and other Yiddish poets, but not, unless specific lines of connection could be traced, on Glatshteyn's influence on anglophone poets of his time or later. Such a history would be able to describe the reciprocal effects of American Yiddish poetry and American English poetry on one another only as of the moment when the writers of these two repertories of poetry begin to read each other — say, with the publication of the *Penguin Book of Modern Yiddish Verse* in 1987.

But a literary history might trace other patterns too, and for those patterns such details of reading and influence do not matter as much. A historian of American poetry might, for example, want to talk about how American poets reacted to the Sacco and Vanzetti case; and for that, Moyshe-Leyb Halpern's poem about Sacco and Vanzetti is relevant, if only to refine the historian's generalizations. A hypothetical critic who claimed that poems about this case were all political propaganda, with vulgar rhymes and simple diction, would have to refine those claims to deal with Halpern's subtle, indirect meditation.

In Mercier's case, the first sort of history is hard to do, absent more detailed information than we have about who outside the Creole community read Mercier and other Creole writings, and what works in English were read by Mercier and other Creole writers. The one story that surely needs to be told in this connection has to do with Lafcadio Hearn, who reviewed Mercier's book and drew richly on both francophone and anglophone Louisiana writing. Hearn and his novel *Chita* would surely gain new prominence in the context of multiple American (and international) literary traditions.

A little more can be said about how taking acount of Mercier's work would qualify literary historians' orienting generalizations. Let us consider in particular how it might affect two chapters, by Thomas Richardson and Lucinda Mackethan, in Louis Rubin's excellent *History of Southern Literature.*[17]

Mercier's novel surely belongs in Richardson's chapter on "Local Color in Louisiana." If it were there, then Mercier would presumably be set beside George Washington Cable; like Cable, "he saw the connections between the decline of the Creoles and their self-destructive racial pride, and his best work makes it clear that such racial arrogance has direct application to broader problems of Southern history, especially the black-white conflict after 1865" (p. 201). So Cable, who is often seen as standing alone, would have some company.

Accounts of Cable, though, tend to stress his status as an outsider; they link to that status both his ability to offer a balanced portrait of Creole society, and the outraged Creole reaction that the portrait evoked. And in so doing, they set up too simple a model of the relations between insiders and outsiders. Mercier's novel would complicate that model; he was an insider by birth and by language, and, at the time of his writing the novel, an insider by social position also.

Though Mercier should appear in any account of "Local Color in Louisiana," he was not a conventional local colorist, and *L'Habitation Saint-Ybars* is not distinguished chiefly for color. "Color" in this context normally means vividly observed and seductively presented local details of setting, of cuisine, of dress and appearance. Mercier observes details, but not details like these. From him we learn something about the architecture of the Saint-Ybars house, and about the books in the library, but not much about, say, the smell of the room or the taste of the cooking. We learn about the racial status of everyone in his book, but not that anyone's "soft, smooth skin was the color of *café-au-lait.*"[18] And few details go without analysis, whereas local colorists present details as decorations and leave them unexamined. Incorporating Mercier into an account of "local color in Louisiana" would mean shifting our sense of what that category means.

Local-color fiction is one of the principal literary stages for dramatizing language and dialect difference, and here, of course, taking account of Mercier would change the approach of literary history considerably. Take Richardson's claim that "the dialect writing of the local-color era, more quaint than realistic, quickly became dated" (p. 207). Richardson is right to suggest that "quaintness" is a problem in dialect writing, and right to say that a lot of dialect writing suffers from it. But he lumps diverse things together. "Dialect" means for him all speech varieties other than standard English. He quotes Beongcheon Yu praising Lafcadio Hearn's mastery of "the exotic rhythm of outlandish dialects, especially Creole and Spanish" (p. 207) and himself describes Cable as using "various dialects — Creole, German, Negro, Acadian" (p. 207). This is in fact a large and diverse group: it includes the dialects of native speakers of English, the English of non-native speakers marked by their native language, and three languages that are not English at all. Taking account of a book like Mercier's, with its vivid interest in distinctions of language and its indifference to distinctions of dialect, would help compel us to use more precise terms; and that in turn would let us see diverse works of literature more clearly.

Mercier would also seem to belong in any history of the plantation novel. Placed there, his work would call into question the idea of, to quote Lucinda Mackethan's excellent chapter on the subject, "a 'plantation school' of white Southern local-color writers, coming into being to vindicate a lost cause" (p. 212). Mercier had no interest in vindicating that cause.

Now, calling that idea into question does not require knowing Mercier; Mackethan herself only sets up the idea in order to refute it. But the gist of her refutation is equally at odds with what Mercier represents:

> To bring together [Thomas Nelson] Page's *In Ole Virginia*, [Joel Chandler] Harris' *Uncle Remus: His Songs and His Sayings*, and Charles Chesnutt's *The Conjure Woman* is to take the full measure of the potential for complexity that inheres in the exploitation of the plantation scene. The ground shared by these three works indicates common features that their authors saw as requirements for fiction treating the Old South. All placed the slave narrator at the center of the plantation scheme, not only because he fulfilled local-color standards but also because he provided an air of veracity and more subtly a persuasive doctrine of master-slave rela-

tions. These black narrators are the most valuable creations of the fictions for which they provided voice, for they embody the tensions that, with varying degrees of awareness, their authors brought to bear on the plantation they envisioned. (p. 218)

Mercier's narrator and central consciousness is of course not black but white, not slave but free. He is an outsider to both black and white plantation experience. Including Mercier in this analysis would mean interrogating rather than accepting the central position of the slave narrator.

Emerson wrote, "a new fact makes a new system." The goal of this chapter has been to show how taking account of the fact of Mercier's novel might change some aspects of literary history and criticism: our particular ideas about Louisiana local color and the plantation novel as well as our more general ideas about translation and the representation of language difference. Mercier was not a great artist, but his serious and thoughtful novel is refractory to our analysis, and needs to be taken account of.

Notes

1. Alfred Mercier, *L'Habitation Saint-Ybars, ou, Maîtres et esclaves en Louisiane, récit social* (Nouvelle-Orleans: Imprimerie franco-américaine [E. Antoine], 1881; repr. Montréal: Guérin, 1989, ed. Réginald Hamel).

   Louisiana Standard French is the plantation aristocracy version of Parisian Standard French; it is associated with whites, though blacks speak it also. Louisiana French Creole is, as its name implies, the Louisiana version of the language produced by contact between francophone slave traders and slave holders, and nonfrancophone slaves; it is associated with blacks, though whites speak it also. I shall use LSF for the former, and LFC for the latter.

2. I base the following account chiefly on Réginald Hamel's copious notes for his edition of Mercier's novel, but also on George Reinecke, "Alfred Mercier, French Novelist of New Orleans," *Southern Quarterly* 20-2 (Winter 1982):145–76; Edward Laroque Tinker, *Les Ecrits de langue française en Louisiane* (Paris: Honoré Champion, 1932), pp. 351–64; and Auguste Viatte, *Histoire littéraire de*

l'Amérique française des origines à 1950 (Quebec: Presses universitaires Laval, 1954), pp. 286–91.

3. "Vieumaite" is the LFC version of "vieux maître," "old master"; its effect would be something like "ole' massa'," though Saint-Ybars' father is called by this name by everyone, not just by the Saint-Ybars slaves and freed blacks, and the novel does not have any other name for him.

    There is a striking reciprocity here. Vieumaite creates most of the epithet-names in the book, for example, Chant d'Oisel and Démon; but his own name is created by the slaves and freed blacks in LFC.

4. I use this phrase because it is so hard to say with confidence whether Mercier's judgments in this matter are sound. It is almost impossible to get outside his novel; we cannot see independently what the novel is seeing. Consider, as an ironic demonstration of that impossibility, an article by the noted Creolist Albert Valdman, "La diglossie français-créole dans l'univers plantocratique," in Gabriel Manessy and Paul Wald, eds., *Plurilinguisme: normes, situations, stratégies* (Paris: Harmattan, 1979), pp. 173–85. Valdman takes Mercier's novel as raw sociolinguistic data, and uses it as the chief source for his account. To justify this strategy, he claims, as he must, that "stereotyping and caricature seem totally absent from the Creole dialogues" (p. 177). But how, except in relation to other trustworthy sources, can he know this?

    The answer, probably, is that there *are* no other trustworthy sources. This is true even for purely linguistic matters; the big Creolist website at the University of Stockholm (http://www.ling.su.se/Creole/Text_Collection.html) has a comprehensive collection of Creole texts, but the Creole passages from Mercier's novel make up ninety-nine percent of the Louisiana French Creole passages. And as for sociolinguistic matters — who would have spoken what to whom, and in what circumstances — there the evidence is scantier still. My own judgment differs from Valdman's; I find it hard to believe that communication in a bilingual community could be so unimpeded, so free of bewilderment and misunderstanding. But how can we know?

5. Mercier, "Etude sur la langue créole en Louisiane," *Comptes-rendus de l'Athénée Louisianais* 4 (1880):378.

6. Mercier, *L'Habitation Saint-Ybars*, p. 246; page numbers for subsequent quotations will be given in the text.

7. "So you don't see, Sir? They're Negroes for sale."

8. Mercier, "Etude," p. 378. Mercier is of course talking about the situation in 1880, not that in 1851.

    It's impossible not to assume that this scene suggests a connection between an unfamiliar language and an unfamiliar institution, between the Creole and slavery. What a novel Mercier might have made had he developed this connection! In fact, though, no other scenes develop it.

9. A *complainte* is a recognized literary genre; Littré's dictionary defines it as "a popular song dealing with a tragic event or a devotional legend."

10. I owe this account to extraordinarily helpful and generous personal communications from George Lang and Mikael Parkvall. For further information see Lang, "Islands, Enclaves, Continua: Toward a Comparative History of Caribbean Creole Literatures," in A. James Arnold, ed., *A History of Literature in the Caribbean* (Amsterdam: John Benjamins, 1997), vol. 3, pp. 29–56, and Perry Arthur Williams' 1982 Fordham University thesis, "La Fontaine in Haitian Creole."

   Several features of the chapter on Man Sophie anticipate Kate Chopin's 1893 story, "La Belle Zoraïde." Like the chapter, the story tells of a delusional black woman who treats a doll as her "piti," and quotes lines from "Lisette." It seems likely that Chopin read Mercier's novel and borrowed from it.

11. He is not the only black character to do this; the aged slave Lagniape does also (p. 219).

12. Mercier seems to dislike people who make a cult of playing with words. Certainly the three characters who do are all fools or knaves: the fatuous M. Héhé, Démon's previous and unsuccessful tutor; his bigoted and cowardly consort, Mlle Pulchérie; and the murderous duelist, M. des Assins.

13. See on this David Dollenmayer's excellent "'Wessen Amerikanisch?' — Zu Eugene Jolas' Übersetzung von Döblins 'Berlin Alexanderplatz'," in *Internationale Alfred-Döblin-Kolloquien* (Bern: Peter Lang, 1993), pp. 192–205.

14. Alcée Fortier, "The French Language in Louisiana and the Negro-French Dialect," *Transactions of the Modern Language Association of America* 1 (1884–85):102.

15. George Washington Cable, *Creoles and Cajuns* (Garden City: Doubleday, 1959), ed. Arlin Turner, p. 412; page numbers for subsequent quotations will be given in the text.

16. Irving Howe, *World of Our Fathers* (New York: Simon and Schuster, 1976), p. 452.

17. Louis D. Rubin, Jr. et al., *The History of Southern Literature* (Baton Rouge: Louisiana State University Press, 1985). Page numbers for subsequent quotations will be given in the text.

18. A phrase from Kate Chopin's "La Belle Zoraïde," in her *The Awakening and Selected Stories* (New York: Random House, 1981), p. 34.

CHAPTER TWELVE

Written in Sound: Translating the Multiple Voices of the Zuni Storyteller

■ **DENNIS TEDLOCK**

Among the Zuni of west-central New Mexico, as in many other Amerindian communities, storytelling is a fine art. There may be times when stories fit the larger purposes of a ritual or serve didactic ends, but they need no justification for being told other than the coming together of a willing performer and a willing audience. Their tellers claim to be neither eyewitnesses nor messengers for the gods, but only to be passing along what they heard from prior storytellers. Folklorists call such stories "tales," but Zunis call them *telapnaawe,* which means something like "words about the passage of time."[1]

Zuni storytellers, like many others in North America, spend about half their time making their characters speak to one another. These characters may sound authoritative or silly, articulate or confused, calm or anxious, kind or mean, and they may depart from ordinary talk to enter into more densely poetic modes of discourse, praying, making speeches, or breaking into song.[2] Even in the intervening narrative passages, constructed in the third person, the performer may echo the speaking style of one character or another, thus doubling the narrative voice with a voice from inside the world of the story. The result is a multivocal discourse of a kind that never existed — or so we have been solemnly told — until European novelists invented it.[3] It is true that multivocality becomes blurred or even obliterated when oral performances are routinely transcribed and translated as if they consisted of nothing but linear sequences of phonemes, segmented into words and sentences. Such reductions may have been a practical necessity during the era when performances were recorded by means of handwritten dictation, but sound recordings demand a better hearing.

Many of the received notions about oral literature — that it is repetitious and lacks characterization, for example — are little more than artifacts of textualization. The graphic conventions most commonly employed are not those of poetry or drama, which still show their relationship to speaking, but those of the kind of literature that packs the most words into the smallest space. And here is the crux of the matter: what the prose writer condenses in space the storyteller distributes broadly and unevenly across time, waiting long enough to let a proper name or a key phrase sink in, running quickly through ordinary routines, creating suspense by pausing in mid-clause, or evoking the orderliness of ritual by neatly pausing between clauses.

Effects such as these led me to recast my own transcriptions and translations of oral performances as scripts, scored for pauses, changes of amplitude, intonation, voice qualities, and gestures. Since I first began publishing such scripts in 1970–1972, others who work from sound recordings in various parts of the world have followed my methods.[4] Much of this work has been devoted to transcriptions and translations of Amerindian languages, among them the Inupiak and Yup'ik Eskimo of the Alaskan Arctic; the Tanacross and Koyukon of the Alaskan Subarctic; the Tlingit and Lushootseed of the Northwest Coast; the Assiniboin of the Plains; and the Hopi and Navajo of the Southwest.[5]

Throughout North America tales are properly told at night, during the colder months of the year. Except in the northernmost regions, the storytelling season is defined by the period when snakes are in hibernation. At Zuni, where snakes stay underground from October to March, it is said that telling a tale out of season would put the teller in danger of snakebite. As for telling one during the day, that might hasten the setting of the sun. The scenes of telling are intimate family gatherings (where television now competes for attention) and the nightly winter meetings of medicine societies (which provide media-free zones).

From November of 1964 through January of 1966, I did ethnographic field research at Zuni, tape-recording tales on many an evening during the snake-free months. The performers who traded stories back and forth for several hours at such gatherings were Andrew Peynetsa and Walter Sanchez, in their early sixties at the time. They were members of the same matrilineal clan and shared an interest in farming. Peynetsa told the tale I will quote from here on January 22, 1965.[6] It is just over half an hour long, which puts it in the middle of a range that runs from five minutes to an hour and a quarter.

The storyteller opens the way from the conversation of a particular winter's evening into the distant time of a tale by means of a pair of formulaic phrases. To utter them is to cast a spell over the audience, whose members will hopefully remain entranced until the spell is broken with another pair of formulas that marks the return from the world of the tale. The words of these spells are composed of the same sounds as ordinary language, but their meaning, beyond the fact that they mark the boundaries of a story, is somewhat elusive.[7] It is as if they themselves were relics of another time. The present performer gives a full rendition of the opening spell, pronouncing all the phonemes and speaking in a loud voice (here indicated by capitals). He follows each of the two phrases with a gaping pause that lasts two or three seconds (indicated by a strophe break with a raised dot).[8] He also stretches out the second syllable of *inoote* (indicated by a long dash), producing a gliding effect which not only emphasizes that the time of the story was long ago, but also indicates that the events in the story are not connected to the present by the rhythm of any countable number of moons or years:

> *SO'NAHCHI.*
> •
> *SONTI INOO —— TE*
> •
>
> [NOW THE ROAD STARTS LO —— NG AGO.
> •
> NOW WE TAKE IT UP.]
> •

During each of the long pauses the audience responds by saying *ee — so,* "ye — s indeed." Like the opening and closing spells, this affirmation is specific to tale-telling.[9] It may be used from time to time during the course of the story proper, but otherwise the listeners remain silent.

The performer then lists the places where his story's characters live, naming five different villages in five lines separated by brief pauses (ranging from a half to a full second). In the first line he continues to speak loudly, but by the time he reaches the fourth line he speaks entirely at the conversational level he will use for most of the story. He delivers the first four lines in the manner of operatic recitative, separating the rising and falling curves of normal intonation into two relatively stable pitches about three half-tones apart (indicated by running the text on two levels). The sound is similar to that of a Zuni priest announcing a ceremonial event from a housetop, but without the long, drawn-out syllables that carry an announcer's voice into the distance. All five lines follow the same syntactic pattern (but with different place-names), and they are formulaic in the sense that this same pattern is used to name places in the openings of countless other stories told by any number of narrators. The first four lines are formulaic in the additional sense of repeating the recitative mode of delivery, which is also familiar from the openings of other stories. But the performer breaks the pattern in the fifth line, signaling the completion of his list by switching to ordinary speech:

> *PINNAAW'ANLHUWALAP*
> *KWA'K'IN'AN lhuwalap*
> *ITIwan'an lhuwalap*
> *Kyakiima lhuwalap*
> *He'shoktan lhuwalap*

> [AT WINDS' PLACE THERE WERE VILLAGERS
> AT KWAKINA there were villagers
> AT THE MIDdle place there were villagers
> at Kyakima there were villagers
> at Resin Point there were villagers]

Each of these lines lacks a terminal drop in intonation (indicated by the lack of a punctuation mark), thus leaving the story's first sentence (or first oratorical period) unfinished. In the next line (which also leaves the sentence unfinished) the performer moves further away from the opening formalities by offering a comment on the list of places:

> *lesn holh lhuwalaa uulapnap*

> [it seems the villages were scattered around like this]

Most stories open with the names of one or two locations rather than a scattering. The present list of five villages tells the experienced listener that there will be four episodes in which the protagonist, either male or female and living at the first place on the list, will probably receive suitors from each of the other four and reject all but the last one. Except for the Middle Place (the present-day town otherwise known as Zuni), all these places are the ruins of villages inhabited by Zunis centuries ago. That the first village on the list is *Pinnaaw'an* or Winds' Place, a name which can also be taken to mean Spirits' Place, suggests that the protagonist may meet with a tragic end. This ruin, a short distance west of the present-day town of Zuni, is haunted by the ghosts of people who died before their time, especially suicides.

Despite the length of his unfinished sentence, the performer now slows his pace by shortening his lines. This has the effect of focusing audience attention on the introduction of the protagonist:

> *taachi*
> *PINNAAW'AN*
> *Pekwin an tsawak'*

> [and
> AT WINDS' PLACE
> the Word Priest had a son]

Now we know that if this does indeed turn out to be a courtship story, it will be one in which the normal course of real-life action is reversed, with girls coming to a boy's home to propose marriage instead of the other way around. The son of a priest would be a desirable mate in any case, and this boy is the son of the Word Priest, first in rank among a village's religious leaders. But it is pure fantasy to imagine that girls who desired such a husband would go after him in a public manner, walking all the way from their own villages and going directly to his house.

Now at last comes the line that completes the opening sentence: the performer brings his intonation down to the lowest pitch that has yet been heard (marked by a period) and follows with a brief pause. Then he creates a sort of reverberation, adding a one-line sentence that turns the last line of his previous sentence into the first line of a parallel couplet:

taap an tachchu, tewanaa holh an tachchu samma teyachchi'kowa iikwaanik'e'a.
Kwa' kyaak'i yam tachchu ansatto iikwaniky'ana'ma.

[and his father, every day it seems his father was alone as he worked
   in the field.
There was never a time when he helped his father do the work.]

Here, by means of a false start ("and his father") and a twist of syntax that shifts the father from the position of subject in the first line to that of object in the second, the speaker momentarily puts the father rather than the protagonist in the foreground, and then quickly reverses their positions. This turbulence has its origin in the personal (and ultimately social) voice that lies behind the narrative voice. The performer himself spends a good deal of time working in his fields, and he has trouble getting help. He is not alone: Zuni men and women who work in agriculture are shorthanded because their sons and daughters spend a great deal of time at workbenches in their homes, making silver and turquoise jewelry. His handling of this passage has the rhetorical effect of reminding us that his story might be interpreted, in part, as a parable. Sometimes he goes so far as to name characters after members of his own family when a story parallels their lives in some way.

The "long ago" time frame of the story does not allow the boy to be depicted as a silversmith. He does turn out to be an artisan, but for now the performer keeps us in the position of his first suitor, not knowing what he does until she finds out for herself. She takes a basket of cornmeal to the boy's house (the gift she would have given him if he had come to her house), and his family invites her to share their evening meal. Afterwards the boy's father asks her why she has come, and she states her interest in his son. The boy then invites her into his room, which would normally indicate his acceptance of her, but instead he informs her that she must pass a test. He is a weaver (traditionally a male occupation at Zuni), and the next day, while he goes to help his father in the field, she must work at his loom. If she does well, he will marry her.

Each of the first three girls fails the boy's test and goes home. The performer varies these episodes by selecting different details for description, or by changing his choices of words, points of emphasis, and line breaks. When he reaches the episode that brings the fourth suitor, he returns (for one line) to the recitative mode he used when he first listed the story's villages; it is almost as if the real story were just beginning. This girl will be different from the others, and the result of her effort will be different. He introduces her very slowly, using short lines and, at first, long pauses:

> *TAACHI ITIWAN'AN*
>
> •
>
> *lhuwal ona*
>
> •
>
> *e'lashtok'i*
> *kwa' tikwahna ho''i te'amme.*
> *Halhikwi*
> *e'lashtok'i.*
>
> [AND AT THE MIDDLE PLACE
>
> •
>
> one of the villagers
>
> •
>
> a girl
> was not living a just life.
> A witch
> girl.]

From the moment this girl gets ready to go to Winds' Place and propose to the boy, she lacks the proper reserve displayed by her predecessors. The performer tells us she "could hardly wait," and he portrays her as not bothering to grind the cornmeal she should take with her. Instead, he has her making do with some corn that has been soaking in preparation for grinding. In the first line of the passage below he notes this detail twice, producing an echo effect by using a soft voice (indicated by small type) the second time. He speaks rapidly, which is to say in long lines, running through eight different clauses before he brings a sentence-ending intonation into correspondence with a line break. In terms of syntax he stays in his role as a third-person narrator, but in his mode of delivery he speaks as if he were in the same frame of mind as the girl he is portraying:

> *S uhsona holh imati ants'ummehanna sunnaky'akkya, s yam chu k'ina olhashk'ya.*
> *Yam chu k'ina s olhashnan,*
> *sunnahap holh s aakya, Pinnaakwin,*
> *aa —————— elle holh te'chip, telikotip holhi te'chip,*
> *taa s elle itonaa, itonaky'ap s lholh*
> *taa lholh tunu''ati.*

[And that one could hardly wait until evening came, and she filled
  a basket with soaked corn. With her basketful of soaked corn,
she went there toward evening, to Winds' Place,
o —————— n until she was almost there, right around sunset she arrived,
and sure enough they were eating again, they were just about to eat
and again there came a thump.]

In the last two lines the performer shifts the point of view from the girl to the people in the boy's house. The "thump" is the sound of the girl setting foot on the roof, which tells them a visitor will be wanting to descend the ladder that enters their house through a trap door (an archaic arrangement preserved in stories and in today's kivas). But he artfully switches again: in quoting what the householders say to one another when they hear the thump, he drops to a soft voice, which fits what the girl would hear through the trap door. This alternation of positions is similar to the quick, back-and-forth cuts a filmmaker might use to show an arrival from both sides. Once the girl and the householders begin speaking to one another (partway through the second line below), the performer delivers both sides of their exchange in a normal voice:

> *"Iya''ati, chuwa ko'n iya," le' kwap, "E e," le'.*
> *Lholh taa pena kwatok'akkya. "Ukkwayi," le'. "Hayi," le'.*

"Hana'te, lalh hom anahnaawe," le'.
"Hana'te," le'.

["Someone's about to come, they're coming," so they said, "Yes yes," they said.
Then again came a voice. "Coming in," she said. "Very well," they said.
"Hurry, help me in," she said.
"Hurry," they said.]

The girl wants help with her basket. So far nothing unusual has happened, but that is about to change. During the next part of this scene the performer begins using the present tense, as if he were describing events going on right in front of him. First he focuses on the girl's basket, whose contents are unlike those of all the previous baskets. At his initial mention of the basket he suddenly drops to a soft voice, as if he were sharing a secret with us — a secret the householders have yet to discover. Next, after saying "her basket," he pauses for a moment and then changes it to "her seeming basketful," an ironic comment meant to remind us that the basket does not contain what the boy would expect. This line is suspended between the points of view of the performer and audience, as outside observers, and that of the boy who perceives the basket from inside the story. The next line continues the irony but shifts the balance toward the boy and his realization of what the audience already knows about the basket:

Tsawak'i elemaknan
an olha
an olhahna holh s, "Si, kwato," *le' anikwa s*
O'LE YUKTI.

[The boy takes care of
her basket
her seeming basketful and, "Now, come in," so she is told and
THE CORNMEAL IS HEAVY.]

The last line doubles the performer's third-person narrative voice with the inner voice of the boy's thoughts about the basket, which should have contained cornmeal but seems too heavy for that.[10] In fact, if the boy had commented aloud (which would have been impolite), he could have used these very same words.

Now the performer rushes through a standard exchange of greetings, but he slows down for the seating of the girl and goes on to speak slowly in lines that call attention to what makes the present episode different. In the third line below he again doubles his narrative voice with that of the boy's unspoken thoughts. That line stands out not only for its loudness, but for the long pause and soft voice that follow it:

S e'lashtok'i kwatonan. "Hom aatacchu, hom aatsitta, ko' to'n tewanan aateyaye?"
"K'ettsanisshe, ho'naawan cha'le, tosh iya." le'.
"Iimu," le' anik holh s iimu.
HISH HO''I K'OKSHI.

•

Tsawak'i lesn holh s
ampachchi iimu s
wolaatikya s itona'kya . . . .

[And the girl comes in. "My fathers, my mothers, how have you been
   passing the days?" "Happily, our child, so you've come," they say.
"Sit down," so she is told and she sits down.
SUCH A GOOD-LOOKING PERSON.

•

So then the boy
sits down next to her and
their meal was ready and they ate . . . .]

In none of the earlier episodes did the boy sit next to his suitor at dinner. Calling attention to this event with a soft voice, which adds a sly note to the observation, the performer quickly reverts to a normal voice for the routine event (in the last line) in which the characters eat a meal. At the same time he goes back to the past tense, which he last used when the girl was still at the doorway.

At first, the events that unfold after the meal are much like those in the earlier episodes. The boy's father asks the girl why she has come, and she says, with the proper degree of indirectness,

"Luk tom cha'le hom aan tse'mak telhakwiky'a, akkya ho' iya."

["My thoughts are fixed on your child here, that's why I've come."]

The father, replying on behalf of himself and the boy's mother, is equally delicate in his wording, but the performer gives him a solemn tone:

"Kwa' ho' aach, ma' ho' ikwena'ma, holh imat chish lukkya."

["But it's not for the two of us, I cannot say, it would seem
to be up to him."]

Now the son speaks. His words, which are proper for such an occasion, are noncommittal in themselves, but the performer gives him a friendly tone he did not display in any of the previous episodes:

"Hayi, kop ma' ho' ikenNA."

["Indeed, but what would I SAY?"]

Next the boy invites the girl to go to his room with him, but once inside she gets the same surprise as her predecessors: he makes separate beds and informs her that tomorrow he will test her by putting her to work at his loom.

In the passage that follows the performer uses the past tense in the first line, but as the story once more departs from the pattern of the previous episodes, he treats the events as ongoing ones. He heightens the drama by dangling the phrase "then the girl" over a long pause, before he begins to unfold her actions. The first line after that pause brings a moment of syntactic turbulence as he reveals that despite his previous statements, the girl hasn't actually been sleeping. He uses mock self-correction ("or rather she hadn't slept") to abandon the position of an observer, who would see the outer appearance of sleeping, and align the narrative voice with the girl, who has purposely stayed awake:

S aachi iisamma iichuunan s aachi alhkya.
Ala
a ——— telanaa ko' holh, taap e'lashtok'i
•
okwiky'aye, hayi kwa' alhna'ma, pilakna s tsawak'i ona
tuk'u''ak'e'a.

Ala tsawak'i.

•

Tsawak'i s alappa.

[And each of them lay down alone and the two of them went to sleep.
They sleep
o ———— n for some time, then the girl

•

wakes up, or rather she hasn't slept, she gets up and as for the boy
she pokes at him.
Sleeping boy.

•

The boy is asleep.]

During the second long pause in this passage, the performer turns to fix his gaze on a man in the audience who has slumped forward in a doze before he says, "The boy is asleep." Fortuitously, he is able to make this line doubly ironic. Whatever the girl in the story does next, the dozing man will be as much in the dark as the boy, and in that sense he has been transferred to a position inside the world of the story.

What happens next is that the girl calls out to the spiders in the houses all around, and when they come to her she utters a spell. This comes closer to being a fixed formula, both in its words and in its division into lines, than anything that has been heard since the opening lines of the story:

"*Luk tehlhinan, to'naawan asin ehkwi'kowa'*
ho' asi yalu
ho' iikwaaniky'anaawe," *le' holh ikwe*

["This very night, put your hands out front
I will put my hands behind
finish my work for me," she speaks like this]

In the last line the performer uses the evidential particle *holh* (rendered as "like" in this instance), which qualifies his quotation as approximate or probabilistic. After all, he would not want his audience to think he had precise knowledge of the methods used by real witches, and — whatever the nature of this spell — he would not want to succeed in getting a response from any real spiders that might be around. When the girl uses the spell again in a later scene he keeps her pauses in the same places, but he omits *Luk tehlhinan*, "This very night," from the first line. In the third line he drops the suffix *-na-* from the verb, which has the effect of changing "Finish my work for me," to "Do my work for me." Whatever the importance of the exact repetition of spells, the spiders dutifully weave for the girl on both occasions.

The first summoning of the spiders is a trial run, carried out while the boy sleeps. In describing the result, the performer adopts a percussive mode of delivery, sharply exaggerating the prominence of stressed syllables and keeping them at even intervals. The effect is similar to that of quantitative meter, but it is achieved by speeding up or slowing down the rate of articulation as needed, rather than by adhering to a mathematical scheme. The performer uses this mode to emphasize that a series of organized actions, in this case weaving procedures, yields a definitive result:

> *aawashe lesna holh s an ashnapkya s YAAk'anaawap UNappap, LESna'tep.*

> [they did as he had done and when they FINished and LOOKed,
> it was JUST right.]

With the boy still asleep, the spiders undo the weaving and leave. The next morning, after breakfast, the real test begins:

> *Tsawak'i les kwekkya, "SI — I*
> *lukkya to' iikwaaniky'anna. Ko'na ho' iikwan ill ona lesna'te to'*
> *ullha'up*
> *tom aan ho' tse'mak telhakwik'anna," le' holh anikwekkya.*

> [The boy said this, "NO — W
> this time you will do the work. If you can do my kind of work
> exactly right
> tamping the weft
> my thoughts will be fixed on you," he spoke like this to her.]

Note the sharp contrast between the recitative mode (beginning part way through the second line), in which the boy formally states what the test is, and the soft voice in which he states the reward for passing the test. In the

formal statement he speaks like a priest announcing a forthcoming ceremony to the general public (as his father might do), but in the quieter line
he sounds more like a boy having a conversation with his future bride.

This is the fourth time the boy has announced his terms to a girl. The
exact words have varied, but by now the sound of a recitative with three or
more alternations of high and low pitches has become his leitmotif.[11] Only
in the present episode is it heard twice. When the boy goes off to the field
to help his father and leaves the girl behind to weave a blanket, she calls
the spiders back. By the time he comes home for lunch,

> *itiw'ani sish ullhaye s itiwanahnap, an unap —*
> *KO'N IIKWAN ILL ONA LESNA'TE*

> [it's already half tamped and half left to go, and when he looks at it —
> SHE'S DOING HIS KIND OF WORK EXACTLY RIGHT]

In this last line the performer doubles the narrative voice with that of the
boy, using the boy's leitmotif and paraphrasing his earlier words. At the
same time he speaks loudly, maximizing the dramatic contrast between
this line and the next one, in which he lets the boy speak directly. He gives
him a high and excited voice that is heard nowhere else in the entire story:

> *Tsawak'i s k'ettsati, "Ma' ko'n ho' iikwan ill ona, ma' to' lesna't asha," le' anikwa.*

> [The boy is happy, "Well it's my kind of work, well you're making it just
> right," he tells her.]

This very long line expresses the boy's breathlessness, though it consists
only partly of his own words.

After lunch the boy helps his father in the field again, while the spiders
complete the weaving for the girl. When evening comes she does not wait
indoors for the boy's return (which would preserve their privacy), but instead goes outside to meet him. They have the following exchange, in
which the performer renders the girl's voice in a somewhat sing-song manner, with glides between the pitches. This voice will become her leitmotif,
coupled as it is here with an effusive choice of words. Even before he has
accepted her as his wife she calls him "father," as though they had already
been married long enough to have children and had settled into the intimate habit of calling one another "mother" and "father." And she uses two

different intensifiers — *ten* and *hish*, rendered here by "really" and "so very much" — with a verb, *ichem'a* (love), that is normally used only sparingly and therefore needs no added emphasis. The boy's reply is tensely reserved:

> *"Tacchu ten hish tom ho' ichem'a," le' anikwa.*
> *"Hayi, imat ten iiwichemanak'ekkya chi iiwillik'anna," le' holh tsawak'i ikwa.*

> ["Father I really do love you so very much," she tells him.
> "Indeed, when people marry they should certainly have love for
>   one another," the boy speaks like this.]

After dinner the boy invites her into his room. Once inside she uses her sing-song voice again, but this time his reply sounds relaxed and even placid:

> *S topinnte aach pewunan, chim s aach iiwill ichuun, lesn holh asse'a,*
> *"Hish*
> *hom tacchu*
> *hish ten tom ho' ichem'a," le' anikwa.*
> *"Ma' ten iiwillin iiwichemanaknan," tsawak'i holh le'.*
> •

> [And the two of them make one bed, lying together now, it seems she's
>   fondling him,
> "Really
> father of mine
> really I love you so very much," she tells him.
> "Well people who marry should have love for one another," the boy
>   speaks like this.]
> •

As time goes by (signaled by the long pause at the end of the above passage), the boy grows weary of hearing the girl's leitmotif and makes up his mind to do something about it. The performer neither quotes the boy's thoughts nor describes them, but rather doubles the narrative voice with the boy's inner voice through a percussive mode of delivery. A few lines later he will let the boy speak his thoughts out loud, but here the rhythmic use of strong stresses, last heard when the girl's weaving experiment turned out well, telegraphs that the boy has devised a solution to his problem:

> *Lesn holh s*
> *aateya, lesna s hish TOpinnte PEnanaky'a ASshu'wen AAN on AKkya*
> *tsawak'i ipisatikkya....*

> [So this is the way
> they lived, and beCAUSE of this ONE single LINE she KEPT on
>   GIVing him
> the boy got annoyed....]

Now the boy begins to explain his intentions to his father:

> "*Hish topinnte penan ho' ipisana.*
> '*Tac*CHUU —— *hish ten tom ho' ichem'a,' le' kwap.*"

> ["There is one line that really annoys me.
> 'FA —— ther I really do love you so very much,' she says."]

Here the performer represents the boy as not only quoting the girl's words, but as doing an exaggerated version of her leitmotif as well. The boy goes on to tell his father that he has decided to ask the Apaches to set up an ambush at the family field. On the appointed day, he will take his wife to that field. When he explains the purpose of these drastic actions to his father, he utters his own leitmotif (but using very different words) for the first time since he tested his wife's weaving ability:

> "*Honkw'at elleya hom ill ona ichemanan*
> *ho'na' aniwolohnaky'ap*
> *kwa' an aana'map*
> *ho'n iteh ho' aynanaky'anna.*"

> ["If it's true that my spouse really loves me
> then when we are ambushed
> she won't run away
> we'll both be killed."]

At this point, recall that the story is taking place at the village named Winds' (or Spirits') Place, now in ruins and said to be haunted by the ghosts of suicides.

On his way to Apache country the boy sees a crow, a bird whose feathers are worn by warriors. The crow has been circling but suddenly heads downward, flipping over and then turning right side up before it lands near the boy. The flipover is a bad omen, but from the boy's point of view it is good, in that it is consistent with his plan to arrange an attack. The crow questions him, whereupon he explains what drove him to go to the Apaches and quotes his wife's leitmotif:

"Ho' eet ooyelupte, sish topinnte penan ho' ipisana, 'Tacchu ten hish tom ho' ichem'a,' le'."

["I may be married, but there's one statement that really annoys me, 'Father I really do love you so very much,' she says."]

When the boy goes on to explain the purpose of the ambush, he plays a variation on his own leitmotif:

"Honk'wat elle hom ichemanan ho'n aniwolohap
kwa' an aana'map
ho'n ite ashenna."

["If it's true that she loves me when we're ambushed
she won't run away
we'll both die."]

The crow volunteers to take the boy's message to the Apaches, saving him a long journey. When the crow arrives, the Apaches see him flipping over in mid-flight again. In the course of explaining the boy's plan to them, he gives his own version of its purpose:

"Honkw'at elle an ooye ichemanan
to'n aachi aniwolohap,
kwa' aachi
kwa' an ooye an aana'map,
ma' elle ichem'an
achi iteh ashenna."

["If it's true that his wife really loves him
when you ambush the two of them

it will neither be both of them
nor his wife who runs away,
since if she really loves him
the two of them will die together."]

In the first line of this passage the sound of the boy's leitmotif has been doubled with a third-person narrative voice, but this time it is not the voice of the narrator of the story proper, but the voice of a narrator speaking within the story. As the crow continues to convey the boy's message, he recasts its content to fit his own voice. As befits a crow's astuteness in dark matters, the exposition proceeds logically, line by line, to the ending in a double death, which itself is rendered in a suddenly soft voice. As for the boy's leitmotif, it will never be heard again.

The Apaches agree to the plan, and the crow returns to the boy to give him the news. On the eve of the ambush, the boy tells his father what to do if his wife runs away and leaves him to be killed. He then takes his wife to the field to spend the night. When the Apaches come out of hiding the next morning he resists at first, hitting some of them with arrows. His wife, as might be expected from the way she has been portrayed, runs away, leaving him to die alone. His parents find his body in the field and, following his instructions, bury him in the middle of it.

Now the father, in his capacity as Word Priest, announces to the villagers that in eight days there will be a Yaaya dance. This, too, is part of the boy's plan. Like many other Zuni dances, the Yaaya involves the impersonation of the dead by men who wear masks, but with this important difference: unmasked performers, including women, may dance along with the dead. Ordinarily, women keep to the role of observers at masked dances and try to resist any attraction they may feel for any particular dancer, lest their thoughts turn to a lost loved one and they conceive a wish to join the dead. In the case of the Yaaya, the unmasked dancers protect themselves by joining hands with one another and moving around the maskers in closed, concentric rings.

Four days after the boy's death the rehearsals for the Yaaya begin. His widow joins in, although her formal eight-day mourning period will not be over until the day of the dance itself. When that day comes, an enormous crowd of spectators gathers in the plaza. With the sun a little past the meridian the boy rises from his grave, dressed in white clothing, and walks into the village. He reaches the entrance to the plaza and stands there in plain view. When his wife sees him, she tries to break out of her ring of dancers, but at first they manage to hold onto her. He walks around the perimeter of the plaza, and when he reaches the foot of the ladder that leads to the roof of his father's house, she gets loose and goes to him. For one last time she gives voice to her leitmotif:

> *"Tacchu ten hish tom ho' ichem'a," le'.* ToKWAN
> *ky'aky'ali yokkya.*
>
> ["Father I really do love you so very much," she said. At ONCE
> he turned into an eagle.]

That the boy's transformation is instantaneous is conveyed not only by the emphatic rendition of *tokwan,* but also by the fact that there is no pause between the end of the previous sentence and the beginning of the new one. The pause after *tokwan* corresponds to the moment a dumbfounded observer would need to grasp that in the same place where the boy had been standing a moment before there was now a *ky'aky'ali,* an eagle.

The eagle flies up and perches at the top of the ladder. There he (or the boy within him) delivers a brief soliloquy in a beneficent tone of voice. He blames his wife for his final transformation, but tells the people that henceforth they will have eagle feathers to use when they need to make valuable offerings. With that, he flies away to the top of the sky. The story's audience knows that the eagle, among the six powerful animals that guard the six directions, is in charge of the zenith. It is the direction of the region of the cosmos for which the boy's father, who belongs to a group of six priests, has responsibility.

Now the boy's father explains to the people that his son had been conducting an experiment. If not for his wife's rush to resume her intimacy with him, people might have been able to come back from the dead in the same way he did. For the final lines of the story, the performer adopts the percussive mode of delivery that signals a definitive outcome. In addition to using the formulas that end stories of the *telapnanne* genre, he makes an etiological statement, which is optional:

LE'n holh LEyati'kya
INoo — te TEyati'kya ko' akkya
le'na
ashenan kwa' INa' TE'amme, LEE —— semkonikya.

[THIS it seems is what HAPpened
LO — ng ago it was LIVED and so
because of this
the dead CANnot come BACK, eNOU ——gh the word was short.]

In a standard rendition, the etiological statement would have been worded as follows: *Le'n holh leyati'kya ko' akkya, ashenan kwa' ina' te'amme,* "It seems that because this happened, the dead cannot come back." Next would have come the first of a pair of spell-breaking phrases, *Le'n inoote teyatikya,* "This was lived long ago." The present performer often conforms to the usual order, but here he has allowed the etiological element to break through into the inner layer of the standard ending, producing a composite statement. For the second and final spell-breaker, *Lee semkonikya,* he returns to strictly canonical wording and delivery, which puts him back where he started.[12]

Between the first and last lines of a tale, a Zuni narrator has ample room for the practice of verbal arts that involve far more than producing a series of sentences or formulas. The present performer begins with the full formality prescribed by his chosen genre, but then overlaps this voice with a more conversational one as he moves into his chosen story, and concludes by merging a statement about this particular story with a generic ending. In the middle he comes closest to using formulas when he renders the spider spell and the leitmotifs of the boy and girl, and even in these cases there are variations. When the boy becomes irritated at the girl for the "one single line she kept on giving him," we hear a direct protest against repetition from *within* the story. Inside or outside the relatively formulaic passages, we can scarcely find any two lines — two strings of sounds punctuated by pauses — that are exactly alike, the most notable exception being *ho' asi yalu,* "I will put my hands behind," from the spider spell. It would seem that a speaker of tales, no less than a writer, is able to avoid exact repetition.

When the events in tales like this one are paraphrased or abstracted by literate interpreters, the dialogues among the characters disappear — as if speaking were something other than a form of action. With them disappears the richest part of the storyteller's art. When characters are made to talk, the features of a whole variety of speech modes or genres are interwoven with the idiosyncrasies that distinguish these characters. Between dialogues, the performer shifts the position of the narrative voice or doubles it with the voice of one character or another. And when one character quotes another or tells someone else's narrative, as in the case of the crow, the performer may pointedly double the voice of the speaker with that of the other character. All the while, running through all of these voices, is the sound of the artist's voice, neither submerged in sustained canonicity nor completely possessed by the characters whose presence the story summons.

Notes

1. Zuni vowels are approximately like those of Spanish; double vowels are held a bit longer than single ones, like the long vowels in Greek. Most consonants are pronounced approximately as in English, but *p* and *t* are unaspirated, and *lh* is like *ll* in the Welsh "Lloyd." The glottal stop (') is like *tt* in the Scottish pronunciation of "bottle," and when it follows other consonants, it is pronounced simultaneously with them. Double consonants are held a bit longer than single ones, like the double consonants in Italian; *cch* is double *ch*, *llh* is double *lh*, and *ssh* is double *sh*. Stress is nearly always on the first syllable of a word.

2. For a broad survey of narrative traditions in which the modes of discourse traditionally categorized as "verse" (including recitative and song) and "prose" are mixed, see the introduction in Karl Reichl and Joseph Harris, eds., *Prosimetrum: Crosscultural Perspectives on Narrative in Prose and Verse* (Woodbridge, Eng.: D. S. Brewer, 1997), pp. 1–16.

3. Mikhail Bakhtin, in setting up the multivocal novel as an advance over the univocal epic, ignores the folktale; see the essays on "Epic and the Novel" and "Discourse in the Novel" in M. M. Bakhtin, *The Dialogic Imagination,* tr. Caryl Emerson and Michael Holquist (Austin: University of Texas Press, 1981). Narratives of personal history, like tales, can be spoken with a rich multivocality, as in the case of the Nahuatl performance analyzed by Jane H. Hill in "The

Voices of Don Gabriel: Responsibility and Self in a Modern Mexicano Narrative," in *The Dialogic Emergence of Culture,* ed. Dennis Tedlock and Bruce Mannheim (Urbana: University of Illinois Press, 1995), pp. 97–147.

4. Dennis Tedlock, "Finding the Middle of the Earth," *Alcheringa* o.s. 1 (1970):67–80; "On the Translation of Style in Oral Narrative," *Journal of American Folklore* 84 (1971):114–33; *Finding the Center: Narrative Poetry of the Zuni Indians* (New York: Dial, 1972; rev. ed., Lincoln: University of Nebraska Press, 1999).

5. For Inupiak and Yup'ik narratives, see, respectively, Lawrence D. Kaplan, comp., *Ugiuvangmiut Quliapyuit: King Island Tales,* tr. Margaret Seegana and Gertrude Analoak (Fairbanks: Alaska Native Language Center and University of Alaska Press, 1988); and Anthony C. Woodbury, *Cev'armiut Qanemciit Qulirait-Llu: Eskimo Narratives and Tales from Chevak, Alaska* (Fairbanks: Alaska Native Language Center, 1984). Tanacross and Koyukon sources include Gaither Paul, *Stories for My Grandchildren,* ed. Ron Scollon (Fairbanks: Alaska Native Language Center, 1980); and Chief Henry of Huslia, *The Stories That Chief Henry Told,* tr. Eliza Jones (Fairbanks: Alaska Native Language Center, 1979). For the Northwest Coast, see Nora Marks Dauenhauer and Richard Dauenhauer, *Haa Shuká, Our Ancestors: Tlingit Oral Narratives* (Seattle: University of Washington Press, 1987); and Crisca Bierwert, *Lushootseed Texts: An Introduction to Puget Salish Narrative Aesthetics* (Seattle: University of Washington Press, 1996). On the Assiniboin see Brenda M. Farnell, *Do You See What I Mean? Plains Indian Sign Talk and the Embodiment of Action* (Austin: University of Texas Press, 1995). Two Southwestern sources are Andrew Wiget, "Telling the Tale: A Performance Analysis of a Hopi Coyote Story," in *Recovering the Word: Essays on Native American Literature,* ed. Brian Swann and Arnold Krupat (Berkeley: University of California Press, 1987), pp. 297–336; and Tódíchi'íi'nii Binalí Biye' (Timothy Benally Sr.), "Ma'ii Jooldloshí Hane': Stories about Coyote: The One Who Trots," in *Coming to Light: Contemporary Translations of the Native Literatures of North America,* ed. Brian Swann (New York: Random House, 1994), pp. 601–605.

6. My translation of the story Walter Sanchez told just before the one presented here appears in Dennis Tedlock, *The Spoken Word and the Work of Interpretation* (Philadelphia: University of Pennsylvania Press, 1983), chap. 2.

7. The translations offered here are based on the possibility that the formulas are contractions of longer phrases, *si ho'na ahhachi* in the case of the first one and *si onati inoote* in the case of the second. But the only plainly recognizable word in either formula is *inoote,* "long ago."

8. Some storytellers run the two opening formulas together and even omit the second one, but the present performer prefers the classical rendition.

9. *Ee — so* can occur as a response to a story told in the course of an everyday conversation, but in that context it is sarcastic, implying that the teller is passing off fiction as reality.

10. Similar effects are called "double voicedness" by Bakhtin (pp. 324–30), who finds them in the novels of Dostoevsky.

11. In some Paiute narratives, each character has an identifying melodic line to which the narrator may fit as many lines of the dialogue as he pleases (Edward Sapir, "Song Recitative in Paiute Mythology," *Journal of American Folklore* 23 [1910]:455–72). Among the Ammassalik Eskimo, an entire story may be built around a recitative monologue or dialogue and little else except a few lines of introduction (William Thalbitzer, *The Ammassalik Eskimo: Language and Folklore* [Copenhagen: Bianco Luno, 1923], pp. 207–35).

12. The translation given here is based on the possibility that this formula has been shortened, through long use, from *Lessi semme konikya*, in which *se-* is an archaic noun stem for "word" that survives in *selhasshi*, a compound term for traditional verbal art in which *lhasshi* means "old."

Part IV

LOSS AND GAIN

CHAPTER THIRTEEN

Contrapuntal Languages:
The Games They Play in Spanish

■ **DORIS SOMMER**

"No bueno," said the doctor grimly, as he walked in with Barbarita's X-rays. He told Mima, "Ask her if she had TB."

Mima turned to Barbarita. "He says if you have a television?"

"Tell him yes, but in Havana. Not in Miami. But my daughter has a television here."

Mima told the doctor, "She says she had a TV in Cuba, not in Miami. But her daughter has TV here."

"In that case we need to test her daughter for TB too."

Mima translated, "He says he needs to test your daughter's television to make sure it works, otherwise you cannot get your green card."

"Why the television?" asked a puzzled Barbarita.

"How many times did I tell you needed to buy one? Don't you know, Barbarita? This is America."

— Roberto Fernández, "Wrong Channel," 1996

"Ask the defendant if he stole a horse."

"The judge wants to know if you stole a horse."

"I stole a horse?"

"He says he stole a horse."

"Ask him why he stole the horse."

"The judge wants to know why you needed a horse."

"I needed a horse?"

"He says he needed the horse."

— Jewish-American joke

Immigrants who hold on to home languages after coming to the United States are not necessarily ungrateful; they are complicated.[1] Offended

263

neighbors may bristle, feeling excluded when they don't understand home languages spoken on the street (in bars, hospitals, businesses).[2] But displaced people will defend their freedom of speech and continue to live in double (or multiple) codes, sometimes for generations. If pressed to embrace the host culture after moving across the border — or having the border cross them, politically or economically, in increasingly transnational circuits — creative migrants are likely to double their response. They defer and demur, in counterpoint. Their language games can thrive under pressure, as the charm of diverse cultures survives in "posthumous" displays of originality. Purposeful mistranslation, a postponed punchline, a dialogue of the deaf (as we say in Spanish), relieve the law of one language by switching to another:

> sonriéndose se empina el bato la botella
> and wagging chapulín legs in-and-out
> le dice algo a su camarada
> y los dos avientan una buena carcajada
> y luego siguen platicando
> mientras la amiga, unaffected
> masca y truena su chicle
> viéndose por un espejo
> componiéndose el hairdo.[3]

These are some of the games that prosper in the tight spots where one language rubs against another.

Newcomers and their apparently assimilated children may not be quite modern when they hold something back from the universalist embrace.[4] Modernity, and the evidently attractive host culture that promotes it, would take for granted the appeal of universal codes, in which the difficulties of communication would be diminished. Maybe these slightly intractable subjects are postmodern, because they know that difficulty in language is not merely a nuisance. They know it even more intensely than do theorists who, after Paul de Man, call language allegorical because words are of a different order from their elusive referents.[5] Beyond elusive, everyday language can be downright opaque when it confronts another, intentionally opaque sometimes, as a reminder of surviving cultural differences. "We have a right to our opacity," begins Edouard Glissant's manifesto for Caribbean cultural self-determination.[6] Political and economic demands may founder if "cultural rights" are not included in the collective agenda. Consider that cultural survival became the center of Rigoberta Menchu's international mission, after she won the 1992 Nobel Prize. Her local Maya Quiché destiny turned out to depend on indigenous cultural rights worldwide, so that the local became global in perhaps an unanticipated way.

Does this kind of global reach stretch defenses too thin to shore up ancestral cultures? Probably. Yet how does one pull back from a world view, as the palpable movements of people, goods, and information continue to accelerate? At the origin of North and South American cultures, as well as of Europe's modernity, those movements are hardly new. The chronicles of conquest record dramatic impositions of culture and economy in narratives that sometimes linger on the ironies of mistranslation: Peru is the sound Spaniards mistook for an empire's name after forcing it from an Indian they had almost scared to death; "Yucatán," that is, "I don't understand you," is what the Mayas responded to Spaniards who asked where they were; Algonquin turned out to mean settled community, after the English routed the tribe on the grounds they were nomads. And subsequent histories record the intricate patterns of imposed or invited contact. Immigrant jokes on mistranslation are a staple of American literatures, from the time of the Inca Garcilaso's sixteenth-century stories through the multilingual publications that are again claiming our attention.[7] Were they destined to disappear in the pressure toward assimilation? Did immigrants and Indians prefer to fit in, rather than to stand out? Not everyone, and not always, as we are now acknowledging after *mestizaje* and melting pots have shown their persistent remainders. Perhaps it is the apparently unprecedented pace of demographic and economic movement today that brings our multinational origins into focus, as we coin new words like "translationalism" and "globalization" for foundational processes.[8] The only defense against getting homogenized may be helpless denial. Almost everywhere, local economies, along with political and cultural lives, are apparently pressed into versions of the international style. Markets cannot resist the universalizing demands of capital; even Asian-style corporatism has foundered and failed to put people first, over the cold rationality of profits.[9] Equally dire for guardians of traditional diversity are the reports about particular languages and cultures that are losing ground to the sprawl of uniformity. Hinterlands become slum. The American Anthropological Association, for instance, has become so concerned about cultural erosion that it has commissioned a task force to study the losses and to speculate on defensive remedies.[10]

Here, though, I want to consider some of the vanguard practices that I mentioned above, as relief from the conspicuous leveling of culture. They are the bi- (or multi-) lingual games that take advantage of live residues, after particular languages are forced into universal codes.[11] Interruptions, delays, code-switching, syncopated communication are rhetorical features of bicultural language games; they are also symptoms of democratic engagement that should not presume mutual understanding among citizens.[12] However much we may grieve over the real losses of cultural difference in the wake of modernity, it would be even sadder, and counterproductive, to let lamentation drown out the sounds of cultural counterpoint and creative survival.

EROSION AND ITS MISCHIEVOUS RESIDUES

The importance of local origins fades for readers of late-modern, or postmodern literature. By now, most of us have given up defending the uniqueness of literary sources, even though until recently, and throughout a long "populist" moment of modernization, local authenticity had been for many readers a practically indispensable literary value. Students of Latin American literature, for example, can sense the difference between Juan Rulfo's translation-resistant regionalism of the 1950s, and the international style of the Boom publishing house only a decade later. Rulfo's Mexican style, so sparse and arid in the original, sounds unexceptional in English translation, in which the staccato rhythm of tired Faulknerian phrases seems quite normal compared to this writer's style when it is set against the lush cadences of everyday Spanish. But regional flavor got ever more diluted after the deterritorialized Boom promoted García Márquez's moveable magical realism and Vargas Llosa's worldly urban melodramas from a publishing house in Barcelona that brokered almost seamless translations into English, French, German.[13] Transnational Latin Americans had caught up with their 1940s precursor Jorge Luis Borges, who used to joke that his essays and some idea-driven stories sounded better in English than in Argentine Spanish. This was Borges the ironist, not the poet who would sing local *milongas* for inspiration, nor the narrator of romantically violent fantasies of tango bars and knife fights on the vast pampas or in moonlit slums of Buenos Aires.

Catching up in order to leave behind. Between Borges's antipopulist irony and postmodern marketability there is a qualitative difference. Today there are good writers who apparently devalue their own native languages by pitching their style toward facile translation, since the books are destined to sell on the homogenized world market. According to Stephen Owen, some writers appear more interested in selling film rights than in reaching readers.[14] Perhaps there's no help for it. Everyone is producing goods for the international export market. Global markets for standardized tastes make digestible food for thought irresistible as an industry for authors. And the pattern of migrations that — as host countries complain — overwhelms national cultures, might prompt a skeptic to ask if there are enough educated consumers left in the home market to read more "authentic" stuff? The grounds for complaint are more than possible.

"Possible, but not interesting," as Borges's independent detective said to the reasonable police inspector. With that dismissal, detective Eric Lonnrot of "Death and the Compass" (1945) overrides the inspector's truth claim and his instant solution of the homicide case, in favor of a more interesting, literally erroneous, sidetrack. (Lonnrot resembles the proverbial rabbi, who responds to an obviously correct biblical exegesis with a disdainful "That's only one answer to the question," because right answers overlook the inexhaustible mystery of sacred texts.) Plausible solutions to a murder mystery, or justified complaints against globalization, are hardly the most creative responses to the challenges at hand. If detective Lonnrot were at today's scene of violence against cultures, he would probably delay any conclusions about guilt or damage in order to develop more interesting questions: Does everyone suffer losses? When victims incur damage, is it a net loss, or are there mitigating factors? Lonnrot might have observed, mischievously, that in Argentina and other Latin American countries where European and North American books have long been staples of reading, a strong national tradition continues to thrive. Educated Argentines, who sometimes learn their first lessons in English or French or German, may be amused at an almost provincial anxiety over eroding linguistic specificity. Perhaps they feel the satisfaction of watching the whole literate world finally advance toward Argentina, southward, where Argentines have always found their frontier. There, and in Mexico, or Cuba, or anywhere in Latin America (especially in Brazil) patriots have long known that economics and education oblige them to cross national lines and languages. And the most "authentic" literature can be hilariously hybrid. Think of Guillermo Cabrera Infante's novel written in "Cuban," *Three Trapped Tigers*, where Sam Clemens follows San Anselmo in the list of Enlightened Philosophers (p. 269). The book opens with a very funny, imperfectly bilingual, nightclub routine that could certainly have added a few ironic lines about a First World worried that creativity is lost in translation.

> "*Showtime!* Señoras y señores. *Ladies and gentlemen. Muy* buenas noches, damas y caballeros, tengan todos ustedes. . . . *In the marvelous production of our Rodney the Great* . . . En la gran, maravillosa producción de nuestro GRANDE, ¡Roderico Neyra! . . . "*Going to Brazil*" . . . Intitulada, "*Me voy pal Brasil*" . . . Taratará tarará, taratará tarará taratareo . . . *Brazuil terra dye nostra felichidade* . . . *That was Brezill for you, ladies and gentlemen. That is, my very very particular version of it.!* . . . en el idioma de *Chakespeare,* en *English.*[15]

In order to measure the alleged damage globalization does to local languages, one would have to question what native language means today, whether it is a single code or whether "native" language is an archaic signifier too narrow to name the bi- or trilingual cultural homes that so many writers inhabit. Does globalization drown out competitors (as some celebratory and other guilt-ridden compatriots assume, as if it meant "Americanization"), or does it tune in to internal differences that play in counterpoint against the dominant theme? Is everything sped up by globalization, or does the process retard some rhythms and create some engaging syncopations? Definitely mixed effects, is the response at the Social

Science Research Council: "It has become commonplace to observe that globalization accentuates heterogeneity even as it exposes ever increasing portions of the globe to common influences," though little is yet known about specific trade-offs by social actors.[16] Should we, as readers of literature (and viewers of film) simply lament the decline of linguistic specificity as we have known it? Or would it be more responsible (in the sense of responsive to the mystery of unanticipated meanings) to listen to the heterogeneous new language games? Wittgenstein himself might have predicted them, as results of the new circumstances for readers and writers.

Borges's detective Lonnrot certainly preferred playing games over winning them. Even after he finally loses, Lonnrot's last words manage to adjust the rules of the game for a rematch in another life. He could have closed the first homicide case with unimaginative answers; instead he opened it up with arcane questions that send us on a delightfully brain-teasing chase. Had the case been merely solved, it could not have been Borges's vehicle for one of his favorite themes, that of codependence between law and crime, detectives and delinquents, signs and things. Detective Lonnrot was notorious in the underworld for his clever skirmishes with crime; this time, he is lured to engage through a hermeneutical sidetrack that the murderer apparently left as a personal trap. Lonnrot, in fact, (mis)construes a certain circumstance into an inviting sign. He takes up the invitation, confident that he is at least equal to his prey. Their deadly game begins by spelling out God's unspeakably holy Hebrew name.

Among the reasons for quoting at length from this story is the segue it offers from the law's arid monolingualism to the seamy adventures in mistranslation. Lonnrot's refusal to be simple leads him directly to the sort of complicity that "foreign" language games establish in the face of an indifferent or hostile "home" language.

"No need to look for a three-legged cat here," Treviranus was saying as he brandished an imperious cigar. "We all know that the Tetrarch of Galilee owns the finest sapphires in the world. Someone, intending to steal them, must have broken in here by mistake. [Rabbi] Yarmolinsky got up; the robber had to kill him. How does it sound to you?"

"Possible, but not interesting," Lonnrot answered. . . . "I would prefer a purely rabbinical explanation, not the imaginary mischances of an imaginary robber."

Treviranus reprised ill-humoredly:

"I'm not interested in rabbinical explanations. I am interested in capturing the man who stabbed this unknown person."

"Not so unknown," corrected Lonnrot. "Here are his complete works." He indicated in the wall-cupboard a row of tall books: a *Vindication of the Cabala;* an *Examination of the Philosophy of Robert Fludd;* a literal translation of the *Sepher Yezirah;* a *Biography of the Baal Shem;* a *History of the Hasidic Sect;* . . .

One of the agents had found in the small typewriter a piece of paper on which was written the following unfinished sentence:

The first letter of the Name has been uttered

Lonnrot . . . ordered a package made of the dead man's books and carried them off to his apartment. Indifferent to the police investigation, he dedicated himself to studying them.[17]

CODED CONNECTIONS

Law (in Spanish, or in English translation) is a system that includes everyone; it is clear, uniformly available, and therefore indifferent to foreign distractions. But some speakers, bored by the uniformity, prefer the distractions. Why repeat the tedious game of being right, when the game of being clever is more fun? So Lonnrot takes up the particularist language of sacred lore and communes with his counterpart, the killer. Their game may have little to do with the texts that make it possible, unless Cabbalism offers clues to codependence and complicity that lead to the killer. In that case, the motif is an avatar of deconstruction and offers one answer to the question of what the *Sefer Yezirah* is doing among the dead man's legacy. Or perhaps the Hebrew language itself is vehicle enough for the special connection between the players. The special vehicle leads to no conflict with the public language. Nothing here happens outside the law, nor despite it, and certainly not against it. Lonnrot, after all, has defended the law so effectively that criminals target him personally as enemy number one. But the inclusive code is thin in places; it is tedious when compared to the option of a particular language that the law finds irrelevant. Thanks to the law's (in this case, the chief inspector's) indifference or dismissal of foreign signs, players can sometimes revel unpoliced while staying inside a generally powerful system. Their games are collective, but restricted, hermeneutic adventures. And though their virtuosity seems pointless to the other characters, to the protagonists it is the medium of creative communication.

How strange that the shared language should be the mechanism of exclusion, and that minor characters are distinguished by their ignorance of a minor language. Yet the paradox can surprise only monolinguals. Those who hear nothing but the universal language in Borges's story (and in many others) actually. miss the available fun. Specifically, his language game depends on the option to spar in a difficult, privileged language. More generally, it depends on the simultaneous availability of universal and particularist languages. To stay inside only one is already to forfeit the possible games, or to be their target.

I might have noticed the literary charms of code switching as long ago as my first reading of "Death and the Compass," or far earlier, in the multilingual games we immigrant children would play at the expense of competent English-only speakers, including our teachers. But theory can lag embarrassingly behind practice; and catching up now that the practice is so general, varied, and culturally significant is hardly an intellectual achievement. It is more of a pedagogical obligation. We live inside dominant languages that often sparkle with the survivals of resistant speech, yet teachers either decline to notice or they feel beleaguered by the range of references that somehow, they feel, should be mastered. Otherwise, what could they add to a reading? Sometimes educators conclude, prematurely, that multicultural games are meant to enrich the dominant experience, so they complain if the material is hard to digest. Enrichment is what Bill Buford hastily celebrated when he praised contemporary Indian authors for refreshing the English language. They responded, however, that English enrichment was neither the goal nor the most significant effect of their writing.[18] In fact, the appetite for enlarged and improved master codes misses the point of some particularist games. They are played at the center's expense. Readers are sometimes the targets of a minority text, not its co-conspirators. Lonnrot confronted the difference at the end of the story, when the Jewish crook who had scoffed at the *goyim* dabbling in Cabala took aim and shot the detective.

The book that first made me suspect of being an author's target rather than the object of her desire was Rigoberta Menchú's peculiar 1983 testimony about a genocidal war in Guatemala. The young Indian woman, who would win a Nobel prize in 1992, insisted repeatedly that she was keeping secrets. Why proclaim silence instead of keeping quiet, I wondered, as if announcing that secrets mattered more than guarding them? Another feature that keeps Rigoberta distant is her peculiar Spanish, which she studied for only three years before she testified. The sometimes discordant language is a reminder of difficult negotiations that make up her life and story, and a measure of the editor's respect for the informant's voice.[19] Paradoxically, in this rhetorical tug-of-war, pulling backwards from the "modernizing" Western codes to the indigenous ones may be going forward. Rigoberta sometimes brings back the forgotten egalitarian assumptions of the community's Law. The combined results of so many secrets and her foreign constructions was that no amount of information she shared could establish a mood of intimacy or conspiracy with me as a reader. Maybe that was the point of her performance, I began to think: to engage me without surrendering herself.

A formidable lesson.[20] It taught me to recognize moves that I had ignored elsewhere and that proudly keep a distance from the center. There was El Inca Garcilaso's superior Quechua that Spaniards would have to envy; Toni Morrison's mention of the African language that set Sethe's mother apart from her tormentors; Roberto Fernández's literal renderings of Cuban clichés that make bilinguals laugh ("Thanks!" for the bonito, says Mrs. Olsen as she rushes Barbarita out. "For nothing," answers Barbarita.[21]); and even the cold shoulder that Richard Rodriguez turns to his Anglo allies who will never understand his grandmother's message, because it did not reside *in* the words but *through* their intimate Spanish language.[22] The list of examples that drew me back and brought me up short is almost arbitrary; I happened to have read those. Anyone can think of different or overlapping lists.[23]

The point is that foreign disturbances can be flagrant and on purpose.

They can be signatures of particular languages through a universal medium. In the asymmetry of reception that they impose, in the deferred stress or delayed apprehension of meaning, in the skipped beat of a conversation that achieves the rhythm of a joke, spaces open up to esthetic and political experiment. Skewed rhythms and dissonant notes are more than noise; they are the very conditions of possibility for liberal improvisation. We share a polity, after all, and differences coexist in time as well as through time. Blockage comes, instead, from rushing to fill the gaps, from understanding too quickly or empathizing. Those hasty games mistake globalization as neutralization.

THE WHOLE TRUTH

Let me illustrate with a dramatic contrapuntal text, *The Ballad of Gregorio Cortez* (1983). The film, based on a popular ballad, stars Edward James Olmos, who promoted the commercial distribution of this updated historical *corrido* about border violence in turn-of-the-century Texas. Unlike the written versions of the Cortez legend, the movie targets the presumption of competence among English speakers; in the first instance it implicates the law enforcers, and by the end, the monolingual audience. Histories tell the same story, complete with misfired translations and better aimed bullets. And the oral variants have been singing the story for years. But only the film performs a particular effect on the audience, a guilt-provoking effect of delayed information, when viewers realize that the whole truth in English was only partial, and that it excluded justice. For all the deadpan humor that Américo Paredes brought to his book about the *corrido,* and that Renato Rosaldo applauds, his written version plays no joke on the reader.[24] Paredes does not withhold correct translations. He shares information openly, and welcomes English-language readers as intimates of the misunderstood Mexicans.

But the movie holds back reliable translation by playing the bilingual scene of conflict and sheriff-shooting without subtitles. It thereby withholds intimacy and guards its distance, the way Cortez himself did when he refused to speak English to the law. The film includes us all, but border people (now all of us, by extension, in this increasingly Hispanized country and de-colonized world) who live on the English-speaking side only will see the movie very differently from the bilingual straddlers.

Put a bit provocatively, *The Ballad* sets a trap for its Anglo viewers and eludes their efforts to grasp its meaning until the end, when reasons for the initial violence and for the hour-long chase scenes are finally cleared up in court. Meaning escapes monolinguals for as long as Cortez manages to escape his pursuers. The film repeats the Mexican's regional mastery, so embarrassingly superior to that of 600 Texas Rangers, at the expense of a similarly embarrassed Anglo audience. The movie, in other words, makes us worry about more than what we watch; it corners us into considering who watches and from what position on the language divide. And for all the incongruities of interpretation possible on either side, this film — like other resistant texts — performs the necessary gesture of highlighting a fatal incongruity between the sides.[25]

The force of the movie's black humor falls mostly on Deputy Choate, the subject who presumes to know and to translate, and also on those of us who don't bother to question his competence. To Gregorio's dignified courtesy *(a sus órdenes, ¿en qué les puedo ayudar?)*, Choate offers innuendo about reluctance to cooperate. Then the sheriff's suggestion of contradictory reports about a horse sale escalates to a charge of lying. And Cortez's informative banter about the mare who isn't quite a horse, along with more information about the precise timing of the admitted trade, is traduced into a report of intransigence. ("Ask him if he stole a horse." "The sheriff wants to know if you stole a horse." "I didn't steal a horse. It was a mare, two days ago.") Finally, *nada* is confused with *nadie* to twist Gregorio's legal logic about grounds for arrest into resistance against the law.

It would be impractical to object to the inevitable linguistic damage done in translation from one language to another, literally from one side to the other. To hear quotes misplaced or misused is hardly surprising, given what deconstructionists have been telling us about slippage in a single language, through iterability, decontextualized life, and the attendant problem of shifty signifiers.[26] My point here is merely to notice the moments in which the sides of translation are inscribed or circumscribed, to discover when moving across requires paying tolls or stopping. Instead of bringing us to the other side, Choate's translations block understanding. Patient re-construction of the linguistic detours that lost our way finally does rescue comprehension. The Texas court eventually authorized a competent trans-lation by Carolot Muñoz, who had been active in the general effort to free Cortez.[27] But by then the man had spent twelve years in prison. His health was broken, and he died soon afterwards.

In legal terms the fight was worth the effort. White Anglos have had to acknowledge the potential universality of their own law, and they will have to assume the burden of halting, tentative translation. From this promising perspective, the desire of the filmmaker is to produce compe-tent viewers and interlocutors from an English-speaking audience that is, by definition, not ideal. But this happy legal ending faces its unhappy and defiant parallel ending: Cortez suffered unjustly and died. In other words, alongside the film's desire to bridge differences through universally bind-ing law, there is a defensive desire to preserve the distance. Otherwise, Cortez would not have refused to speak English. That uncooperativeness suggests a "Mexican" stance that hesitates before it welcomes Anglo un-derstanding and interference. "Badly formed" and misunderstood phrases have meaning. This is a Wittgensteinian point that helps Lyotard to ac-count for speech that refuses exact translation. The meaning is precisely the refusal to move from one language regime to another, the insistence on untranslatability that situates the speaker at a distance from the ad-dressee.[28] Truer to the heroic spirit of the *corridos* than to the extended and exonerating history of legalities, this more prickly perspective prefers to keep resistance alive. Instead of encouraging correct translations from the local language into imperious universals, the film's alternative desire is to interfere with collaboration, to paint a fresh coat of local color on the stop signs in translation's way. Its ideal subjects are double; they remain Mexi-can *and* demand their rights as Americans.

CONTRAPUNTAL CONSCIOUSNESS

Ever since W. E. B. Du Bois published *Souls of Black Folk* (1903), double con-sciousness has been the bane of American minorities, an obstacle to accul-turation.[29] Doubleness has meant the unproductive tension between contradictory cultural identities, one particular, the other universal. This is an unhappy consciousness by definition, in its structural duplicity. In fact, double consciousness makes a mockery of the word "identity" as a single thing by splitting it into contending signs held apart by hyphens (African-American; Jewish-American; Hispanic-American; Irish-American). Or the signs are braced together by that hyphen as an unstable, transitional prop, while the citizen develops towards a more perfect alignment with a universal language. Braces are a nice figure, I think, for the voluntary growing pains of becoming American; they are a necessary nuisance that is scheduled to disappear once citizens achieve an unencumbered and attractive maturity. The young country was absorbing citizens from many different backgrounds. And their lingering ties to a culture based elsewhere interrupted a sense of belonging here. The unhappy if understandable and transitory result was a fissured "double consciousness" that could be straightened out through training and through time. Orthopedic imagery would have seemed unnecessary to Emerson, for its implication of meddling, since the Anglo-Saxon race would naturally align itself to history. For him, double consciousness had meant a kind of juvenile inability to adjust fate to freedom. Adults would normally make the adjustment (as cultivators of the soil or as guano for it).[30] If they could not adjust they would, evidently, become problems for the country.

But doubleness has not always been a predicament. A long history of premodern options is instructive for postmodern society. Consider medieval England, where Normans were wise enough to know that they ruled a nation of foreigners. Jews, Germans, Danes, and others could not "speak the same language" in any literal way, but they were enjoined to deal fairly with one another. Prudent listening for the "differend" was a medieval practice, long before it became Lyotard's postmodern hope.[31]

Now that our postmodern nations are adjusting to culturally mixed populations, to unstoppable waves of immigration and the continuing sounds of different languages in public places, we might take a lead from the Normans, and from the Moors in Spain, to cite one more example. They used to tax thriving infidels rather than to eliminate them as so much guano for conquest. Medieval Spanish lyric is typically bi- and trilingual; and its "frontier romances" celebrate the passion of border-crossing lovers.

More rational than Christian tradition has portrayed them, Moslem empires have traditionally been hosts to the cultural differences that Christendom did not abide. Spanish modernity came with cultural and political coherence: the consolidation of reluctant and even embattled kingdoms, the expulsion of miscreants, and the continued surveillance of private devotions by public authority.[32] Modernity drove England to overcome internal differences too; a uniform Common Law replaced the ad hoc mixed jury, and Jews were expelled (as elsewhere) because they preferred double consciousness over the coherence of one intolerant culture. Then the English language congealed, nourished and satisfied after absorbing foreign sounds, as Walter Scott reminded his defensive Saxon readers. The code and the language then resisted regular interruption.

Interruption is another name for creativity, both linguistic, and political. It opens congealed forms to specific circumstances. It is a sign of debate, and of wit. Were it not for the possibility of interruption and interception, democratic processes could congeal into predictable formulae, and citizens might forget how opaque countrymen can be. Literary readings might narrow down to tracing predictable patterns and pointing to inevitable loss as words miss meanings and tradition fades in the rush of change. Dire expectations might distract us from the charms and lessons of mistranslation. Language games of hide and seek, both purposeful and unintended, can, for example, interrupt an economic demand with an invitation to talk. Let a light-hearted example suggest a range of promising shifts from one, apparently intolerant, phrase-regime to a more dialogic engagement (Lonnrot would have appreciated the move): when a Dominican immigrant sees the flashing sign "Dime" on the cigarette vending machine, he leans over and answers, "Marlboro."

Notes

1. Suzanne Oboler calls them strategically ambivalent; that is ironic, subtle. See her *Ethnic Labels: Latino Lives* (Minneapolis: University of Minnessota Press, 1994). See, for examples, pp. 11–12; 93–98; 145–50; 161–62.

2. Consider the complicated California case of telemarketing employees, hired for their bilingualism and repeatedly censured for gossiping about Anglo co-workers in Spanish. Management finally forbade casual conversation in Spanish. The workers brought suit and the boss relocated. NPR report of Feb. 19, 1998. This is certainly a more interesting illustration than the story about the judge who fined a mother for speaking to her daughter in Spanish, alleging that she was dooming the child to the life of a maid.

3. Evangelina Vigil, *Thirty an' Seen a Lot* (Houston: Arte Publico Press, 1982), last section of "Por la Calle Zarzamora."

4. Nevertheless, "subtractive bilingualism" — Wallace Lambert's term to describe French-Canadian immigrant children — prevails for recent immigrant children generally. They are apparently losing their native languages more quickly than did earlier groups. "The only difference is that the process appears to be taking place much more rapidly today. Few among us realize what is really happening. Quite the contrary. Over the past several years, there has been an increasing concern among educators, policymakers, and members of the public that the new immigrants are not assimilating fast enough." Quoted in Lily Wong Fillmore, "When Learning a Second Language Means Losing the First," *Early Childhood Research Quarterly* 6 (1991):324.

5. "One particular advantage that bilingual children have is in the area of metalinguistic awareness — the ability to analyze the form as well as the content of language, knowledge of how to talk about language, and control over non-literal uses of language, like puns, irony, and figures of speech. Certain kinds of metalinguistic skills — such as recognizing that words have no intrinsic connection to the objects they refer to — typically emerge several years earlier in bilingual than in monolingual children. Nor is it surprising that the process of learning a second language or of switching back and forth between two languages would heighten one's likelihood of becoming aware of the formal aspects of the linguistic system and one's understanding of the arbitrariness of the linguistic code." Catherine Snow, "Rationales for Native Language Instruction: Evidence from Research," in *Bilingual Education: Issues and Strategies,* ed. Amado M. Padilla, Halford H. Fairchild, and Concepción M. Valadez (Newbury Park, Calif.: Sage Publications, 1990), p. 65.

6. Edouard Glissant, *Le Discours Antillais* (Paris: Editions du Seuil, 1981), p. 11. "Nous réclamons le droit à l'opacité."

   And Henry Giroux argues that the "politics of clarity . . . becomes a code word for an approach to writing that is profoundly Eurocentric in both context and content." See his "Language, Power and Clarity or 'Does Plain Prose Cheat?'" *Living Dangerously: Multiculturalism and the Politics of Difference* (New York: Peter Lang, 1993), p. 166. Della Pollock glosses his argument against flattening the relationship between language and audience, dismissing subaltern claims on language use. "Claims for such writing assume a correspondence theory of language that effaces questions of voice, style and difference." See Pollock, "Performing Writing," in *The Ends of Performance*, ed. Peggy Phelan and Jill Lane (New York: NYU Press, 1998), p. 77.

7. The Longfellow Institute, directed by Marc Shell and Werner Sollors at Harvard University, is dedicated to studying literature written in languages other than English in the United States.

8. See Carola and Marcelo Suárez-Orozco, *Trans-formations: Migration, Family Life and Achievement Motivation Among Latino Adolescents* (Stanford: Stanford University Press, 1995). The turning point was 1965, when the quantity of immigration (now more Latino and Asian than European and Canadian) began amounting to a qualitative change in American demography. By 1997, seven million Mexican citizens resided in the United States; more than 25% of them having arrived in the previous 5 years. Latin American immigration is a long-term phenomenon; after a billion-dollar expenditure to insure the border against illegal crossings, no measurable change in flows is recorded.

9. See, among many related articles, "Learning to Go Against Japan's Corporate Grain," by Sheryl WuDunn. Entrepreneurship, she writes, is now imported as a concept and a word in Japanese: "antorepurenah." "As the Asian economic crisis continues, it has become painfully obvious here that traditional Japanese values are interfering with the country's attempt to build the kind of entrepreneurial spirit that could lead it out of its seven-year slump." *New York Times*, Sunday, March 8, 1998, WK 3.

10. For this reference I thank Marcelo Suárez-Orozco, who is a member of the Commission.

11. Néstor García Canclini develops similar observations regarding everyday artisanal productions among working-class and rural populations in Mexico. See *Hybrid Cultures* (Durham: Duke University Press, 1994).

12. This is a commonplace of political philosophy. See John Rawls, "Justice as Fairness: Political Not Metaphysical," in *Philosophy and Public Affairs* 14 (1985):223–51. "[L]iberalism as a political doctrine supposes that there are

many conflicting and incommensurable conceptions of the good, each compatible with the full rationality of human persons," p. 248; and Robert Dahl, *Dilemmas of Pluralist Democracy: Autonomy Versus Control* (New Haven: Yale University Press, 1982); Milton Fisk, "Introduction: The Problem of Justice," in Fisk, *Key Concepts in Critical Theory: Justice* (Atlantic Highlands, N.J.: Humanities Press, 1993), pp. 1–8. "There has to be at least a conflict based on an actual lack of homogeneity for what is distinctive about justice to become relevant," p. 1.

13. I am indebted to Professor Maider Dravasa's work in progress about the Boom in Barcelona.

14. See Stephen Owen's essay in *Fieldwork,* ed. Marge Garber (New York: Routledge, 1995).

15. Guillermo Cabrera Infante, *Tres tristes tigres* (Barcelona: Seix Barral, 1967), p. 15.

16. Social Science Research Council, "Globalization, Local Institutions and Development," August 1997, p. 1.

17. Jorge Luis Borges, "Death and the Compass," *Labyrinths: Selected Stories and Other Writings,* ed. Donald A. Yates and James E. Irby (New York: New Directions Books, 1962), pp. 77–78.

18. Bill Buford, "Declarations of Independence: Why Are There Suddenly so Many Indian Novelists?" *The New Yorker* 73-17 (June 23 & 30, 1997), pp. 6–11. See responses in same issue by Salman Rushdie, G. V. Desani, Abraham Verghese, Amit Chaudhuri. I thank Greta Slobin for this reference.

19. Recent experiments in coauthored ethnography with bicultural informants develop this feature. (See, for example, Bernard and Salinas, and Diskin's review). Minor language errors distract us in our reading of Rigoberta, while the flavor of translation consistently suggests a foreign code. Just to give one stunning feature, the figural assumptions embedded in Spanish seem to be lost on her. This allows her own Quiché associations to disturb what would otherwise be a rather closed and less promising code. In Spanish as in many Western languages, the word "earth" is regularly metaphorized as woman; that is, woman is substituted by the Land which is the prize of struggle among men as well as their material for (re)production. On the other hand, man is metonymized as earth's husband; his agency and power are extended through the figure. From this follows a scheme of associations, including the passive and irrational female contrasted by the active, reasoning male. This opposition has generated a populist rhetoric in Spanish America that functions left, right, and center of the political spectrum. The most bitter enemies will agree that the People's goal is to preserve or re-possess the beloved Land from a Usurper (Doris Sommer, *One Master for Another: Populism as Patriarchal*

Rhetoric in Dominican Novels [Lanham: University Press of America, 1983]). Rigoberta would surely sympathize, but first she would have to know who the people are and how they relate to the land; her gender lines are quite different. "The earth gives food and the woman gives life. Because of this closeness the woman must keep this respect for the earth as a secret of her own. The relationship between the mother and the earth is like the relationship between husband and wife. There is a constant dialogue between the earth and the woman. This feeling is born in women because of the responsibilities they have, which men do not have" (pp. 220, 342).

20. For an excellent discussion of these anthropological traps, see Frederick Cooper and Ann Laura Stoler, "Introduction" to *Tensions of Empire: Colonial Cultures in a Bourgeois World* (Berkeley: University of California Press, 1996).

21. Roberto G. Fernández, *Raining Backwards* (Houston: Arte Público Press, 1997), p. 86.

22. Richard Rodriguez, *Hunger of Memory: The Education of Richard Rodriguez* (New York: Bantam, 1983), p. 37.

23. They might include urban musical innovations intended to leave the mainstream behind. "A style nobody can deal with" is the goal, says Fab Five Freddy, an early rapper and graffiti writer. See Tricia Rose, "A Style Nobody Can Deal With," in *Microphone Fiends: Youth Music and Youth Culture,* ed. Andrew Ross and Tricia Rose (New York: Routledge, 1994), pp. 71–88. Excerpted from Tricia Rose, *Black Noise: Rap Music and Black Culture in Contemporary America* (Middletown, Conn.: Wesleyan Press, 1994). I thank Arnaldo Cruz Malavé for this suggestion.

24. Renato Rosaldo, "Politics, Patriarchs, and Laughter," in *The Nature and Context of Minority Discourse,* ed. Abdul R. JanMohamed and David Lloyd (New York: Oxford University Press, 1990), pp. 124–45. I am grateful to Lora Romero for pointing out this essay.

25. Stuart Hall, "Notes on Deconstructing 'the Popular,'" in *People's History and Socialist Theory,* ed. R. Samuel (London: Rutledge & Kegan Paul, 1981), pp. 227–40.

26. Jacques Derrida, "Signature, Event, Context," in *A Derrida Reader Between the Blinds,* ed. Peggy Kamuf (New York: Columbia University Press, 1991), pp. 80–111.

27. Frank Javier García Berumen, *The Chicano/Hispanic Image in American Film* (New York: Vantage Press, 1995), p. 200.

28. Jean-François Lyotard, *The Differend* (Minneapolis: University of Minnesota Press, 1988), pp. 77–79.

29. I thank Werner Sollors for pointing out recent explorations of the philosophi-

cal origins of the term "double-consciousness" and of its meaning in contemporary America. See Shamoon Zamir, *Dark Voices: W. E. B. Du Bois and American Thought, 1888–1903* (Chicago: University of Chicago Press, 1995); and Gerald Early, ed., *Lure and Loathing: Essays on Race, Identity, and the Ambivalence of Assimilation* (New York: Allen Lane/Penguin, 1993).

30. Ralph Waldo Emerson, "Fate," published in *The Conduct of Life*, (Boston: Ticknor and Fields, 1860), pp. 1–42. A version existed in 1851, delivered as a lecture (*The Norton Anthology of American Literature*, 1979, p. 815). "The German and Irish millions, like the Negro, have a great deal of guano in their destiny. They are ferried over the Atlantic, and carted over America, to ditch and to drudge, to make corn cheap, and then to lie down prematurely to make a spot of green grass on the prairie" (p. 801).

31. Jean-François Lyotard, "The Other's Rights," in *On Human Rights: The Oxford Amnesty Lectures 1993*, ed. Stephen Shute and Susan Hurley (New York: Harper Collins, 1993), p. 139.

    A medieval mixed jury, which combined local subjects and foreigners as members of the same tribunal, would hear cases between culturally different litigants who could not be subject to one existing rule. The mixed jury predates the contradiction between nation and republic that Lyotard locates at the inconsistent core of modern polities. Perhaps American law would do well to retrieve and adapt medieval respect for cultural specificity as a vehicle and safeguard for justice. See Marianne Constable, *The Law of the Other: The Mixed Jury and Changing Conceptions of Citizenship, Law, and Knowledge* (Chicago: University of Chicago Press, 1994).

32. See Marc Shell, *Children of the Earth* (New York: Oxford University Press, 1993) for a critique of Spanish and other versions of universality.

CHAPTER FOURTEEN

America: Everybody's Other World

▉ ALICIA BORINSKY

WHERE AM I? NEW YORK?

What does the United States mean to newcomers, or to the not-so-recent arrivals who see themselves as belonging to an already established culture? Some of the observers and participants in American society criticize the mainstream, often through humor or denunciation; others desire to transform it by inflecting it with other dictions, inundating it with hitherto unheard rhythms, new foods and customs. The country may be a spectacle to be described with the amazement of one who believes that whatever happens in the States may be a clue to the future. Tourists have their own way of reporting their finds. Their testimony tends to justify the cost and distance of the trip, for it permits them to enjoy the spectacle always in the context of the sheltering conditions of home, having no doubt that they will be returning to their point of departure. But while a tourist's time may be encapsulated in photos, souvenirs, and other forms of the collector's detached curiosity, those who arrive with a one-way ticket have a much different set of concerns. Senses are heightened, and differences from the known to the new can feel threatening and acquire an apocalyptic hold on the viewer.

The trip with no return for those who have been persecuted and have been saved by chance presents very few possibilities for nostalgia. Nostalgia is the province of those who believe that their homeland is a welcoming place which is theirs by right. They hold a key that will eventually bring them back to a lost childhood and the safety of unspoken bonds. Such a feeling is shared even by descendants of groups who nourish a floating identity that connects them to an imaginary place of unproblematic be-

283

longing. *I am Italian, I am Greek, I am Cuban, Dominican,* we are told by people who may have never set foot in their alleged homelands. The peculiarities of life in the States allow and even encourage these feelings of virtual membership in foreign societies that are, nevertheless, essential to the construction of identities within the United States.

Polish Jews have a distinct place in this gallery of one-way ticket holders because they do not have the cushion of nostalgia for a place where the vast majority of their people were massacred. What could they long for, and from what vantage point? Writing about the United States from the United States by nostalgic foreigners, outcasts, survivors, and former aristocrats reveals to us, the readers, the instability of the country as reference, the ungraspable quality it has as a grounding for individual experiences. Isaac Bashevis Singer's survivor characters, for example, attempt to reach some kind of congruence in their lives with the idea they have of their own destinies. Brought to the city by sheer happenstance, they speak to each other in Yiddish, English, Polish, Russian.

Shadows on the Hudson, serialized in the Jewish newspaper *The Forward* in the 1950s, provides a gallery of familiar Bashevis Singer characters seeking the meaning of their lives and struggling with personal betrayals.[1] Stanislaw Luria, abandoned by his wife, decides to take his life. In an attempt to discuss the measure, he visits Professor Shrage, a man he had met in Warsaw, with whom he shared, among other things, the fact they had both belonged to a moneyed and learned circle. In New York this bond appears to persist. Luria apologizes for not having announced his visit and says that he telephoned but nobody answered. When he suggests that the professor avoids using the phone, he is told: "Avoid? I can't cope with it. The callers speak English, and it's difficult for me to make out what they're saying. I learned English from Shakespeare, but here they speak English so fast and it's all slang" (p. 13). The professor cannot bring himself to acknowledge a shortcoming of his own; it is New Yorkers who speak the wrong kind of English. And it is the world of New York that seems elusive and pointless to these immigrants, despite their efforts to grasp it by means of religious and philosophical readings. Disregarding the professor's arguments against suicide, his visitor persists in his decision: "Here, Professor, I find it tedious. I have nothing more to do. I have, so to speak, wrapped up all my business. As Shakespeare says, 'He that dies pays all debts'" (p. 136). Luria is a desperate man. His first wife and children were murdered by the Nazis, and Anna, the wife he took in the States, has left him. The other-worldly Professor Shrage has no power of persuasion over him, but Shakespeare constitutes a sure bond between them. They may not speak English well enough, but they can quote Shakespeare to each other and know what they mean. As for life in the States, the understanding of what drives it varies according to one's mood. To an angry Stanislaw Luria, the reason for his wife's betrayal is money: "She's going to a man who deals in stocks on Wall Street . . . She's become an American. There's only one love here — love for the dollar" (p. 252). Anna totters between love affairs but refuses to join in the pessimism of those around her; her failures open the door to bittersweet success: "This is America, not Europe! Anna told herself. Here one has to shake a leg and do things, not wander about with one's head in the clouds. Since the whole of America was predicated on achieving success, one had to be a success oneself" (p. 342). And a success she becomes: business woman, thin, elegant, capable of saving her father's fortune but nevertheless incapable of settling down with a man. The certainty about life in the States is the dollar and, for Anna, the key to understanding the world that it creates lies in Freud. As she drives along Fifth Avenue, she glances at store windows. "There was no end to the costly goods on display — clothes, jewelry, lingerie, furniture, silver — all the latest styles. Even the dust jackets of the new books seemed to be more colourful this year than ever before. There were thousands of talented people in New York who kept devising new charms, new variations, new attractions to entice customers, in exactly the same way as flowers decked themselves out in every imaginable color to attract the bees that pollinated them. Yes, Freud was right — everything was sex" (p. 343).

What is New York? How to gauge it as a place for conducting one's life? Singer's characters wander in the city. Stockbrokers, professors, theosophists, actors, swindlers, holy men and women, pretenders and pathological truth sayers navigate in a space that is in fact shaped by their faithfulness — often unwitting — to what may loosely be termed their original culture. The New York that serves as a backdrop to their discussions and travails varies with their mood as though it were a kaleidoscope. Each time they try to define it, they find a version of their own circumstances. New York is a mirage, and when the illusion of newness wears out, they find a familiar underside. As Stanislaw Luria takes a ride in the El, he considers the pawn shops, scrap-metal dealers selling their wares, and the mediocre eateries along the way. People share the bleakness of their surroundings: "How shabby they all looked! Raw faces, rough-hewn as though with an ax, wild-eyed, outsized hands and feet. One woman heaved herself in, so fat that she could barely squeeze through the doorway. Her angry glance seemed to say: I'm not fat for fun! When she sat down she occupied two seats. And look at the clothes. Where did these people find such garments? Their outlandish blouses and jackets the color of sulphur, with clashing stripes and checks, reminded Luria of Polish peasants and their *ciuchy*, the second-hand clothes they used to sell in Targówek. Here in this poverty, ugliness, tastelessness seemed to have crowded together. These people had no scruples either: give them power and they would do exactly what had been done in Russia. Each of them gave Luria a single glance, then averted his eyes. Where did they live? Where were they going? He would not have been surprised if this El was headed for Kowicz or Nizhni-Novgorod" (p. 292). Feeling that New York is Poland or Russia is not at all sheltering. On the contrary, for Luria it is a proof that his torment continues. Inextricably tied to the grotesque, America becomes part of a bad joke played against his hope of taking distance from his past.

Isaac Bashevis Singer's characters either are or wish to become travelers. Sometimes, as in the early *The Certificate,* their lives are dominated by the administrative maneuvers needed to ensure the departure from Europe that may save their lives. Once in America, they still want to leave: some consider suicide; others find hope in another trip. In *Shadows on the Hudson,* the ultimate geographical escape place is Florida. Two characters, living a love affair that is taking them back to their young passion for each other while in Poland, leave their mates to enjoy an adulterous affair among palm trees by the ocean. The thrill of foreignness greets them in Florida. The temperature, the air, the sky; for a brief moment we believe they are experiencing a sense of renewal. America may be emerging here. Are we to revisit the familiar idea that links the optimism of a new life to an exuberant New World landscape? Not so. Real-estate speculators, gossipy New

Yorkers, and fellow Polish and Russian survivors emerge to prove to the couple that here they are again; they have missed their chance to make a change. For them, the Old World masquerades as the New. Florida's distance from New York (and from Eastern Europe) is an illusion, a trivial, weather-related perception.

To Singer the United States is a place where Jews become grotesque because they are disconcerted, scattered, and hopeless. Scholars grapple with thoughts that do not help them organize their lives; ordinary people fall into exchanges that frequently lead them to betray their friends and spouses, and holy men and women, although admired and respected, represent an almost impossible ideal. Even without nostalgia, some look for their roots in the familiar surroundings, such as the hopeless character who goes back to Poland from Argentina in *Scum*, or the man who, in Poland, falls in love with dim-witted Shosha (in the novel by the same name), hoping thereby to regain his lost religiosity. Singer's American fictions pose the characters' need to escape because of embarrassment and lack of purpose. The lost European communities of the survivors had provided a unity, a background against which the talk about Freud, para-psychology, philosophy, art, and the practice of religion had a fundamentally cohesive function. In America, the unknown terrain takes aspects of the old but lacks its glue. The characters, exposed as if on stage, act with an uncanny sense of repetition that causes them shame and a desire to flee.

Where do they go? Some choose religion, like Grein in *Shadows on the Hudson*. He practiced so rigorously that, in a successful bid out of history, his features change to resemble his own father's looks. Others decide to go to Israel. Such is the plan of the characters in *Meshuge*, after becoming entangled in love affairs and pitiful rivalries. In Fellini-like fashion, they assemble for a trip that will, no doubt, return them to their aimlessness.

The ghost of an elusive America permeates Singer's work. Ungraspable and yet all-enveloping, this perception is fed by a rage and dissatisfaction with Europe. We sense that the problem with America is that it cannot detach itself completely from the Old World. Yet where are these characters to look for America? They find it in the streets, the trains and restaurants, the clothes that people wear, and in a certain use of English. America is consumerism. It is not outside; its contagious nature shapes the newcomers and turns them into grotesque and disheveled versions of what they should have been. "No, Grein did not really understand America. He complained at every opportunity that American minds functioned according to categories different from those that operated in Europe, that people here were the biological antitheses of Europeans. Nonetheless Americanness had entered his bones" (*Shadows on the Hudson*, pp. 73–74). New York, Miami, are names for the scattering of Jewish culture, places in which the nakedness of secular Jewish life is exposed, condemned, and celebrated. The streets of New York are alternatively seen as the dreaded stage for the destruction of European Jewry or the clue for an enveloping but unexplainable newness. Everything is New York in Singer's United States, because New York is the web in which the individual destinies of the characters are entangled, and their possibility of becoming a community is dispersed.

LIFE AND THE TUBE

Polish and Russian accents, Hebrew prayers, conversations in Yiddish and broken English that take place in the coffee shops, apartments, and cars of New York are replaced by different elements to name the same city in the work of Oscar Hijuelos.[2] We are still in New York, but to be certain we must turn on the television and watch. His novel *The Mambo Kings Play Songs of Love* opens with an evocation of *I Love Lucy* and the energy that the character of Desi Arnaz infuses in a group of New York Cubans. The dark-haired entertainer with a heavy Spanish accent married to Lucille Ball embodies — in ways that make some cringe — a certain ideal of success. The television show grants him visibility as a stereotype, and though it makes him into a joke at times, it invariably tells his story through a diction that encapsulates travel and distance. He is at home in the States, smiling, aggressively foreign, and unfailingly intense. The television screen has been redefined as a kind of passport, and, grounded in everyday comical situations, it generates the sort of charge that in a very different way used to be produced by Hollywood movies for generations of Latin Americans. No doubt about it: Desi is a clown, his lines include canned laughter as a punctuation mark, but the same is true for his wife. And together, Lucille — the

cream-puff of an all-American dim-witted housewife — and her Cuban mu-
sician husband stand for the inclusion of a certain kind of good-natured
situational humor that owes much to Desi's recent arrival in the United
States. The emergence of a Hispanic literature written in English within the
United States produces in some the same kind of unease as the presence of
Desi. What to do, how to react to an English so textured with Spanish
phrases and rhythms? And, no less important, what to say about the fading
of Spanish into English prose? These are questions about authenticity, cohesion of literary traditions, and the nature of new communities created by
art and literature. Here nobody misses the language of Shakespeare. Characters understand one another, and when they do not find the right English word, Spanish comes to the rescue. Oscar Hijuelos is part of a new generation of writers working in a highly textured language. Born in New
York, he is the son of a Cuban family that emigrated in 1951. Hijuelos
writes in his native English in an oblique relationship to the vibrant cultural and literary tradition of the island. *Mambo Kings* beckons us to find
Cuba again in the world of American popular culture.

Gone is the tinge of caricature featured in the frighteningly wide-eyed,
hyper energetic Carmen Miranda, with her outrageous hats and gestures,
and also in Desi's accented speech. For one of the characters in *The Mambo
Kings*, it was an honor to have been in the *I Love Lucy* show. It was the kind
of collective passport that granted the most heightened form of reality: being watched, being broadcasted: "When I heard the opening strains of the *I
Love Lucy* show I got excited because I knew she was referring to an item
of eternity, that episode in which my dead father and my uncle Cesar had
appeared playing Ricky Ricardo's singing cousins fresh off the farm in
Oriente Province, Cuba, and north in New York for an engagement at
Ricky's night club, the Tropicana" (p. 3). The story of the two brothers,
their love travails and involvement with music, is told in an easy-flowing
language that highlights the sensual aspects of their lives. Food, love-making, betrayals, and everyday chatter take place in a musical background.
The golden era of the past, represented by the wholeness of the immigrant
family in New York and the excellence of the Cuban musical tradition they
had left behind and that was brought back in the suitcases of the new arriv-

als, are encapsulated by the episode of *I Love Lucy*. Ricky Ricardo is a key to the naturalization of Hispanic vocabulary and diction within the English language. Having been part of that, having appeared in the show, is for these characters an achievement that justifies their lives.

Spanish words appear in the English text without any sense of foreignness: "*Nene* his uncle called out to him, and Eugenio charged down the hall. When Cesar lifted him up, Eugenio's feelings of emptiness went away" (p. 221). And later: "*Oyeme, hombre,* he said, straightening Nestor's bow tie. 'Be strong. It'll be great. Don't be nervous, just do as we did during the rehearsals with Mr. Arnaz.'" (p. 312). These are characters who live out their lives without being hampered by language differences; they say what they mean in whatever way seems to best serve their needs. The apparent absence of a preoccupation about style in language develops into a style of its own. Hijuelos has captured a speech. Despite the inclusion of non-English words into English, it is not fractured because the Spanish does not feel imported. It is a crucial medium for rendering a particular kind of experience. What is the quality of this experience? Music, sex, and food become the main connectors among characters satisfied with the eloquence they can attain with their language.

Books, even words, have nearly disappeared as subjects of the narrative, except for song lyrics and comments and television shows. Life is identified with popular culture. *The Mambo Kings* locates itself in a terrain of sheer intuition and pleasure. The readers forget whether they are reading Spanish or English and enjoy the unproblematic show.

Neither Shakespeare nor Cervantes are evoked as means of communication. A representative group of modern writers working in the United States is creating a language that wants to undo the differences between English and Spanish. Cristina García makes the point in this vignette: "I met Max at a downtown basement club a few months ago. He came over and started speaking to me in Spanish (his mother is Mexican) as if he'd known me for years. I liked him right away. When I brought him around to meet my parents, Mom took one look at his beaded headband and the braid down his back and said, *Sácalo de aquí*. When I told her that Max spoke Spanish, she simply repeated what she said in English: "Take him away."[3] This kind of writing at its best is removed from the merely pictur-esque, and addresses itself to a community of readers that does not see be-ing Hispanic as a pretext for situational humor or public introspection. Television and popular music played and continue to play an important role in the naturalization of Hispanic intellectuals as a cultural group that is both separate and integrated to the mainstream of the United States, rede-fining the terms in which we think of writing in English and Spanish. Phrases in Spanish referring to food, parts of the body, nicknames, and in-sults become part of the new sound of English in a writing style that is openly colloquial and rooted in everyday reality. It is understood that this writing, these television shows and musical sounds are here because art and literature reflect the reality of the country. Desi, the newcomer of the past, has now defined a norm and may be despised as a demeaned incar-nation of the terminally simpático Latin American. For Lourdes, a Cuban character in *Dreaming in Cuban,* her Brooklyn neighborhood gives her an opportunity to ponder relationships with people from different places, converging in the spectacle of the city. She wonders: "What happens to their languages? The warm burials they leave behind? What to their pas-sions lying stiff and untranslated in their breasts?"(p. 73). Far from experi-encing an optimistic cosmopolitanism or a nostalgic Cuban patriotism, Lourdes feels herself to be wholly in the United States. But the United States evoked here is made up of the patchwork of languages and unfin-ished business brought by people she sees on the street. The very meaning of being there, in New York, is sustained by the uncertainty about the lay-ers making up the city.

What does happen to their languages? Works such as García's and Hijuelos's suggest a solution. No longer concerned about the picturesque representations of Latin Americans, Spanish becomes part of the normal, everyday diction of English. Isaac Bashevis Singer's Professor Shrage walks these same streets, and although he has Shakespeare on his side, he posits the radical foreignness of English to itself. The problem with Americans is that they speak slang. Let's keep languages distinct, he would say. Paradox-ically, these Yiddish-speaking characters embody a certain purist relation-ship to their group. It is an allegiance to the quality of the connections among certain individuals, inextricably linked together by history yet hesitant to define their bond as a clear-cut culture when it strays from religious practice.

BEYOND THE NATIONAL: LET'S WATCH TOGETHER

If the United States is defined by these groups as New York, Hollywood provides characterizations not only for the Americas, but for the world.

Guillermo Cabrera Infante, a Cuban émigré widely acclaimed as one of the great innovators of Latin American fiction, has taken up residence in London. His work, characterized by relentless parody and punning, is wedded to the musical rhythms of Latin America and the images produced by Hollywood. Cabrera Infante and Manuel Puig, the Argentine novelist who lived in Europe, New York, and Brazil, and is best known for his novel *The Kiss of the Spider Woman,* are the two most salient representatives of a certain vision of the United States as provider of the ultimate machine of cultural interpretation: film.[4] In a series of lectures devoted to film gathered in *Arcadia todas las noches,* Cabrera Infante maintains that film fulfills the function once accorded to myth.[5] It is through films that the tasks of great literature and classical myth are fulfilled. He admires the great directors and actors of the American screen, above all Orson Welles, John Huston, Howard Hawks, and Alfred Hitchcock, and shows how they offer interpretations of reality through the lens of the camera, making powerful cultural interventions and providing perspectives on story telling. Cabrera Infante carries this admiration into his fictions, framing characters and structuring scenes in writing that seeks to invoke sights and sounds. American film has given Cabrera Infante a language and a vision. Or has it? How well did he actually understand these movies? It was amusing for me to learn that, speaking of Orson Welles's famous radio broadcast that sent people into a panic over an invasion from Mars, Cabrera Infante said he would not have been frightened had he been living in New Jersey then. The reason? He did not know English at the time. This of course, did not diminish in any way his feelings about the relationship of film to literature. Film is a language beyond all, the great matrix of contemporary culture. But what kind of language does it provide?

Sitting in a prison cell in the 1970s, Molina, a gay man convicted of corrupting minors, and Arregui, a left-wing revolutionary, two characters in Manuel Puig's *The Kiss of the Spider Woman,* suggest the writer's response. The police have planted Molina in the cell to induce Arregui to give away the names and plans of the members of his group so they can catch and destroy them. Meanwhile, Molina spends most of his time recounting movies to Arregui in cinematic detail. The novel describes, through dialogue, how the film stories create a relationship between the two men that goes beyond the police plans and the men's original personalities and expectations. Entangled in the plots that Molina has been telling, his political will obscured by the conflict in a film in which a suffering diva is bound by her passion to a Nazi, Arregui appears to return the love that Molina feels for him, and entrusts him with a message to his comrades once his cellmate is released. The novel closes with Molina being shot in the street while Arregui is tortured by the police.

Flirting with the representation of life in films, Puig presents the emotions of melodrama as a phenomenon of contagion. Life imitates film, and Molina dies for the man he loves. Movie-like intensity; the artificial translated into everyday life; clothes, jewelry, and special light effects; moonlight; shiny dance floors and meaningful glances are simultaneously offered and denied to the characters in Puig's novels. Friends and lovers live in a world of heightened feelings based on films, and when life comes to a tragic ending, readers understand it as a triumph of art over the meaninglessness of everyday events. If the characters in Hijuelos's novel stay in the density of aromas, rhythms, and dictions that spell the reality of home, those of Puig suspect that daily life is just a mirage that hides the elusive but essential truth of the screen. Arguably the writer who has best understood that the art of storytelling has taken up residence in film, Puig suggests that the stories are not there for mere consumption. They inspire, shape, and make our lives real because they give sense to our interactions with others. For the same reason boleros and tangos appear in his novels as lyrics without music. Unlike the world of Hijuelos, in which the presence of music implies a certain way of moving through life, with the cadences of a dance that shows itself in love-making, drinking, and eating, Puig uses popular music for its stories. Tangos and boleros that speak of unfailing love and death or of failed love and betrayals are there to bring popular culture into the personal and the intimate. Introspection is a matter of focusing on the *outside,* on films and songs. Against the police and sometimes through them, the search for meaning takes the form of trusting the collective sensibility and mainstream entertainment of the 1940s. His homelands are the screen and the record-player, perceived in retro fashion, and contemporary political brutality.

Puig offers us the eloquence of a Latin American-North American language rooted in ubiquitous cultural forms. Little old ladies who mind their neighbors' business inhabit *Cae la noche tropical;* boys who describe movies to their friends in small provincial towns show up in *Betrayed by Rita Hayworth;* and women who listen to boleros and tangos in *Heartbreak Tango* strive to speak the language of mass-produced passion. If women's hearts are broken by the death of the undeserving don Juan of *Heartbreak Tango,* it is not simply because this semi-literate, charming, good-looking young man is so irresistible. It is because the women themselves gave him this power by putting him in the context of the music and the films that shaped their lives. Only in this way do their experiences acquire the prestige and importance of belonging to a tradition. It is this capacity to shape life that Cabrera Infante wants to convey when he says that film is the great myth of our time.

In this view, Hollywood, more than a producer of illusions, is the creator of a matrix that inflects experience and grants meaning to daily chatter. The field of influence of film is so strong that even local literary tradition is redefined by the magnetism of film stars. In a moving and humorous eulogy for Manuel Puig, Guillermo Cabrera Infante described how Puig had given him a much cherished gift. It was a list of leading Latin American writers renamed as female movie stars: "Borges, blind, was cross-eyed Norma Shearer. Commentary: 'Oh, how dignified.' Carpentier was Joan Crawford, 'Oh, how fierce.' Asturias was Greta Garbo: 'only for that favor of the Nobel.' Juan Rulfo was Greer Garson; Cortázar was Hedy Lamarr, 'so cold and remote'; Lezama was, surprise! Lana Turner. Vivien Leigh, 'so sick and temperamental,' was Sábato. Vargas Llosa was Esther Williams, 'so disciplined'; and Carlos Fuentes was Ava Gardner, who had an aura of glamour but Puig wondered, 'Can she act?' García Márquez was Elizabeth Taylor: 'Beautiful face, awful body.'"[6]

The language of Shakespeare? Cervantes? The great innovators of the Spanish language, whose linguistic creativity prompted many a writer and scholar to say that there are truly only two great periods of writing in Spanish — the Golden Age, meaning the Renaissance, and the contemporary era — ought to be translated so that they may be properly understood. And the appropriate translation is not into English, or French, or any other written language, but into film. Movie stars provide instant recognition, eloquence, and immediacy so that movies, the new makers of myth, can give life to the silence of the written word.

The lives of Puig's characters and the references in Cabrera Infante rest on the assumption of a virtual homeland, a community of imaginary lives and heightened passions that are beyond nationality and hence profoundly intimate. United States culture is perceived as though it came from nowhere, that is, as though it could come from everywhere. Singer's characters, barely able to escape introspection, grapple with the repetition of experiences that make them see flashes of Europe in U.S. streets, and because of that, they are unable to forge cohesive destinies for themselves. Some reviewers deplore the shapelessness of *Shadows on the Hudson,* not realizing that it is a necessary correlative of the lives the book portrays. Shot through with pangs of nostalgia and humor and bits of Spanish, novels such as *Dreaming in Cuban* and *The Mambo Kings* suggest that the resolution of nostalgia does not lie in the past but in the forging of a literature that is neither here nor there. Considering the United States from within and from without, these contemporaries agree: the place is a mirage constructed by those willing to invest their destinies in its exploration. Its hook for the imagination may very well lie in the lack of urgency with which it poses questions about its own cultural identity.

Notes

1. Isaac Bashevis Singer, *Shadows on the Hudson* (New York: Farrar, Straus and Giroux, 1998). Page numbers refer to this edition.

2. Oscar Hijuelos, *The Mambo Kings Play Songs of Love* (New York: Harper and Row, 1996). Page numbers refer to this edition.

3. Cristina García, *Dreaming in Cuban* (New York: Ballantine Books, 1992). Page numbers refer to this edition.

4. See Manuel Puig, *The Kiss of the Spider Woman* (New York: Random House, 1978).

5. Guillermo Cabrera Infante, *Arcadia todas las noches* (Madrid: Alfaguara, 1995).

6. Guillermo Cabrera Infante, "La última traición de Manuel Puig," *El País* (Madrid), July 24, 1990, pp. 22–23. My translation.

CHAPTER FIFTEEN

The Gothic and the American-Exotic: Baron Ludwig von Reizenstein's *Die Geheimnisse von New-Orleans*

■ **STEVEN ROWAN**

While themes and material are known to circulate freely among diverse literary fields and cultures, the influence of scientific and technical writing on literary works is less frequent. It is not unknown, however: Edgar Allan Poe, for instance, rendered the scientific philosophy of Alexander von Humboldt's *Cosmos* in verse under the title *Eureka*. Accounts of exploration of the American West would be expected to appear principally in frontier tales, such as the German-American adventure tales of Charles Sealsfield or Karl May. It may come as a surprise, then, that the reports on one major Western expedition in 1852 served as a direct inspiration for an urban Gothic horror story, *Die Geheimnisse von New-Orleans* [The Mysteries of New Orleans], by Baron Ludwig von Reizenstein.

Ludwig von Reizenstein was born in Marktsteft am Main on 14 July 1826, the eldest son of Baron Alexander von Reitzenstein-Hartungs (1797–1890) and his first wife, Baroness Philippine von Branca (1800–1864). Baroness von Branca, the mother of eleven children, eventually suffered mental illness and was accused of unspecified immorality. The parents were divorced in 1843, and the Baroness was taken to a convent.[1] As early as 1843, Ludwig began giving signs of being a problematic child. By the start of 1848, Baron Alexander had decided his son had to leave Bavaria. King Ludwig I was asked to release Ludwig from his Bavarian military obligation so he could go abroad.[2] Manifest in this petition was the father's obvious fear that his son might repeat his mother's downward spiral into insanity, and there was soon a suggestion that young Ludwig was gay.[3]

When a Herr Steinberger from Bayreuth recruited Ludwig to run his farm in America, Baron Alexander agreed to ship his son there. During the passage to America, however, Steinberger died of cholera. Jobless, Ludwig soon ran out of cash and had to go to work with no marketable skills.

On 12 May 1851 Ludwig von Reizenstein entered the public arena in America by launching a weekly German newspaper, *Alligator,* published by a group called Saurians for New Orleans and its suburb of Lafayette.[4] He was not long at it; by the next year he was living in Pekin, Illinois, near Peoria, and on 23 March 1852 he circulated the prospectus for a paper called *Der Pekin Demokrat,* in which he promised he would soon publish a novel entitled *Die Geheimnisse von New-Orleans.*[5] He is mentioned as secretary for an assembly hastily called in Pekin in late April 1852 to hear an address by the German revolutionaries Armand Goegg and Ernst Violand.[6] The New Orleans city directory, published in late 1852, first records his name for 1853, and he continued to be listed as a New Orleans resident until his death.[7] After his efforts to launch a journal of his own failed, Ludwig von Reizenstein wrote for the *Louisiana Staats-Zeitung* (1850–1866), the more radical of the two major German dailies there, and later for its rival, the *Deutsche Zeitung* (1848–1915).[8]

Despite his episodic involvement with journalism, Reizenstein usually stated his profession as "draughtsman," "architect," "engineer," "surveyor," or "civil engineer."[9] Much of his income, however, appears to have derived from surveying or preparing illustrations of property posted at auctions (an occupation for marginal artists which he describes in detail in Book II of *The Mysteries*).

The novel he completed in December 1853, *Die Geheimnisse von New-Orleans,* had clearly been on Reizenstein's mind ever since he announced it in *Der Pekin Demokrat* early in 1852, but later commentators argued he was moved to publish it by the horrors of the New Orleans yellow fever epidemic of summer 1853, as well as by his disgust at the reception social New Orleans accorded Duke Paul of Württemberg in autumn 1853.[10]

Publication of *The Mysteries of New Orleans* began on 1 January 1854. The first three books were published in continuous daily installments, but at the end of Book III, Reizenstein announced that there would be a delay of a week, for reasons which were already known to German readers, particularly the ladies — namely, the objections raised by the story's libidinous extremes. He promised that Books IV and V would confound these critics. The devotees of morality would lose their sleeping-caps and be put to flight.[11] It was not until 20 July, 1854, however, after an interval of almost three months, that Book IV was begun.[12] Even then, the excerpts were shorter than before, and the book was not completed until the end of September.[13] After another interval of well over two months, a notice appeared in mid-December, in time for readers to renew their subscriptions, declaring that the fifth book of *Die Geheimnisse* would begin the next day and be serialized without a break until finished.[14]

There are reasons to believe that Book IV was expanded during the interval prior to its publication in 1854, because material about recent events was incorporated into the narrative. The preface to Book V, which speaks of the Kansas-Nebraska Bill of 1854, was clearly added to the text after the novel's putative date of completion. The conclusion of the book was finally reached on 4 March 1855.[15] The book edition, issued book by book from 1854 to 1855, was soon withdrawn from publication by the author's decision, and the text all but vanished and has remained an extreme rarity until now.

In later years, although Reizenstein would attempt one further long novel and some short comic sketches, his main publications in local New Orleans newspapers were the observations of a naturalist. It was in this capacity that he became a friend of the New Orleans novelist George Washington Cable, and after Reizenstein's death Cable would exploit his persona in a novella entitled *The Entomologist*.[16] Ludwig von Reizenstein died on 19 August 1885, barely 59 years of age.[17]

Despite its title, Baron Ludwig von Reizenstein's *Mysteries of New Orleans* is not the sort of "urban mystery novel" adapted from the genre established by Eugène Sue. Rather, it is a particularly dramatic example of a Gothic horror novel in the tradition of E. T. A. Hoffmann and the Romantics, extending German Gothic horror into American space and adumbrating in German language the Southern Gothic novel and drama. Its central theme is the appearance of a black messiah, a predestined leader who will punish the South for its sins by means of an apocalyptic race war. For that reason, it is the very antithesis of the urban mystery, which relied on conspiracy and crime to explain the malign motion of events. Reizenstein's novel relies instead on magic and fate. Compared to the supernatural motive forces, the only other agents of evil are mere criminals and psychopaths, not conspirators. Fate intervenes in the ordinary course of events throughout the novel in the form of the bizarre figure of Hiram, a magician hundreds of years old who is compelled at this time to carry out a commission to bring about terrible events.

Usually, however, Hiram is a visitor from an alien world. On only two occasions is Hiram allowed to appear in his own mythical setting, the Mesa, the source of the Red River. Although the Mesa is only portrayed in the prefaces of the fourth and fifth books, it is already mentioned in the earliest portions of the novel as the place whence Hiram comes.

The Mesa is not the only setting for purple passages in the novel. Mundane dealings in New Orleans are also punctuated by mythic episodes, such as a prophetic night vision of a slave rebellion seen by one of the female characters in the straits near Haiti, a vision of racial warfare seen in the clouds over the Masonic Hall in New Orleans, and several *Doppelgänger* episodes pointing to the portentous nature of the characters' actions. Still, the Mesa remains the sole fully developed mythic setting.

What is interesting about the Mesa is that we can actually locate it in space and time and trace the route by which it entered the dark mind of Baron Ludwig in New Orleans and in Pekin, Illinois, between 1852 and 1854. Its genesis is to be found in reports on the exploration up the Red River by Randolph B. Marcy and his son-in-law, the future General George B. McClellan, in 1852. Marcy, who would author a famous guide to crossing the "Great American Desert," led an adventurous exploration of the Red River and other rivers of Texas, Oklahoma, and New Mexico in 1852.[18] His earliest impressions were published shortly after the expedition in a report to the Geographical Society in New York in March 1853.[19]

In 1854 Marcy published a full narrative as part of a lavish official report that included splendid lithographs of the landscape of the course of the Red River, the flora and fauna of the region, and a large if sketchy map. Reizenstein, a very serious student of botany, biology, and entomology, certainly followed this exploration closely and incorporated the reports of this exploration into his story. Marcy himself, along with the equally historical figure of the explorer and collector Duke Paul of Württemberg, would appear as a character in the novel's climax in New Orleans in Book V.

In the preliminary reports as well as in the final narrative, Marcy located the source of the Red River in the Palo Duro Canyon bordering the Llano Estacado, and it is described as a place of great solemnity and beauty, haunted by panthers but strangely devoid of Native American population. Marcy and his soldiers approached this spot after a sequence of ordeals, nauseated by the bitter waters until they attained the pure water of the river's source in a place of grandeur and silence.

> The gigantic escarpments of sandstone, rising to the giddy height of eight hundred feet upon each side, gradually closed in until they were only a few yards apart, and finally uniting over head, leaving a long, narrow corridor beneath, at the base of which the head spring of the principal or main branch of Red River takes its rise. This spring bursts out from its cavernous reservoir, and, leaping down over the huge masses of rock below, here commences its long journey to unite with the other tributaries in making the Mississippi the noblest river in the universe.[20]

The lithographs of the 1854 report reinforce the awesome impression the vast, monumental, and empty landscape made on the explorers. This is one of the earliest attempts to depict the visible form of the desert Southwest, unfamiliar as yet to both viewers and readers. It is an utterly alien landscape for which a vocabulary does not yet exist. The progression of images in the report moves from a view of the expedition in camp (image 1) to repeated efforts to show the *sanctum sanctorum* of the source (image 2) as well as the general character of mesa landscape. We stand at the beginning of a tradition of Southwestern imagery that will eventually include Ansel Adams and Georgia O'Keeffe.

To Reizenstein, the awesome spot reached by Marcy cannot be the true source of the Red River. The true source, in his vision, is a sacred place similar to the mythic source of the Nile, imagined by ancient geographers to be located in a numinous place called The Mountains of the Moon. But

15.1. "Encampment on 6th June" (1852). Lithograph by H. Lawrence, illustrating explorations of the Red River of Louisiana.

more than water issues forth from the spring creating the Red River of Louisiana. Reizenstein makes it the native habitat of a plant called the *Mantis religiosa,* whose pods spread the deadly yellow fever which periodically decimated the population of New Orleans. The central event of the final part of the novel is the great yellow fever visitation of the summer of 1853, spreading from the Mesa by a decree of fate. The black messiah is also conceived there, the offspring of a black prostitute and an effete German aristocrat, and the messiah's nursemaid, the Haitian Diana Robert, resides there awaiting her moment.

The Mesa is a utopia where nature thrives in harmony and peace, but where every act is fated and significant. The Marcy expedition approached but did not violate this sanctuary. Instead, the denizens of the Mesa came out and paid Marcy a visit at the confluence of the Red River and Cache Creek. This meeting, described at the start of Book IV, marks an encounter between the prosaic real world of Marcy and the dream world of the Mesa. The scene then shifts to the mythic realm for the proclamation of the coming epidemic.

The final book of the novel opens with an allegorical condemnation of

15.2. "Head of Ke-Che-Ah-Que-Ho-Ho, or the Main Branch of the Red River [in Louisiana]" (1852). Lithograph by H. Lawrence.

the moral bankruptcy of America in the early months of 1854, marked by the passage of the Kansas-Nebraska Act. Hiram denounces the three allegorical birds of America: the palsied Bald Eagle of the United States, the mournful mother Pelican of Louisiana, and the opportunistic and ephemeral Nebraska Owl. In the midst of this downfall, the black messiah is conceived in a ritualized act of intercourse between the German nobleman and his black paramour. His name is to be Toussaint l'Ouverture, after the Haitian hero.

After the completion of the political allegory, the protagonist, Emil, is permitted a vision of the catastrophe of his own family, punished for his own moral failings. This precipitates the disastrous events of the final book and the death of most of the characters of the novel. At the conclusion, the future messiah of the black race is taken from New Orleans by a Haitian warship, to return in 1871 when the time will be ready for his revolution.

A close reading of the Mesa passages of the *Mysteries* shows us Reizenstein's mythic evocation of a location both Ur-American and exotic, combining the narrative of Captain Marcy with a virulent condemnation of what America has become. When the time comes, the black messiah will purify a society much in need of purging.

Notes

1. Munich, Hauptstaatsarchiv, MF 33832, petition of Alexander Freiherr von Reizenstein to King Ludwig I, 28 September 1845, 1v. The name "Reizenstein" came to be spelled "Reitzenstein" in the mid-nineteenth century due to a new spelling convention.

2. Munich, Hauptstaatsarchiv, MA 27239, petition of Alexander Freiherr von Reizenstein to King Ludwig I, dated Munich, 22 January 1848, approved by the king on 31 January 1848. A royal order carrying out the petition, directed to the Government of Oberbayern, was issued on 14 March 1848.

3. Helene Freifrau von Reitzenstein, ed., *Ein Mann und seine Zeit 1797–1890. Erinnerungen von Alexander Freiherr von Reitzenstein-Hartungs* (Eggstätt: for the author, 1990), p. 118.

4. Karl J. R. Arndt and May E. Olson, eds., *The German Language Press of the Americas*, vol. 1: *U.S.A.*, 3rd ed. (Munich: Verlag Dokumentation, 1976), p. 176, with nothing to add to the New Orleans German historian J. Hanno Deiler.

5. Arndt and Olson, *German Language Press*, vol. 1, p. 183, also from Deiler. Both appeared to believe this ephemeral paper was to be published in New Orleans, despite the title reference to Pekin, Illinois.

6. St. Louis, *Anzeiger des Westens*, weekly edition, 1 May 1852, p. 2, entry for 27 April, article "Aus Pekin." Ludwig Reizenstein was the secretary (second presiding officer) of the meeting, and he was named first secretary of the organizing committee of the Revolution Society in Pekin, which was to seek affiliation with the American Revolutionary League for Europe headquartered in Philadelphia.

7. The New Orleans city directories which mention Ludwig von Reizenstein begin with *Cohen's New Orleans Directory* (New Orleans, 1852), p. 220, and end with *Soard's New Orleans City Directory for 1885* (New Orleans, 1885), p. 767.

8. Arndt and Olson, *German Language Press*, vol. 1, pp. 181–82, entry on the *Louisiana Staats-Zeitung*, differs from Robert T. Clark, who believed the paper folded in 1864.

9. Reizenstein appears as a "draughtsman" in 1852, as an "architect" in 1858, 1859, 1867, 1871, 1872, 1876, 1877, and 1885, as an "engineer" in 1866, 1867, 1882, and 1883, as a "surveyor" in 1873, 1874, 1880, and 1881, and as a "civil engineer" in 1878 and 1884.

10. Glenn R. Conrad, ed., *A Dictionary of Louisiana Biography* (New Orleans: Louisiana Historical Association; Center for Louisiana Studies of the University of Southwestern Louisiana, 1988), vol. 2, p. 678.

11. *Louisiana Staats-Zeitung*, 27 April 1854, p. 1.

12. Ibid., 20 July 1854, p. 1.

13. Ibid., 24 Sept. 1854, p. 1.

14. Ibid., 10 Dec. 1854, p. 1.

15. Ibid., 4 March 1855, p. 1.

16. Published as one of three novellas in George Washington Cable, *Strong Hearts* (New York: Scribner's, 1899). Cable's daughter Lucy Leffingwell Cable Bikle, describing the study at the Cable house at 229 8th Street in New Orleans, mentions "a large glass case of moths and butterflies, given him by the old Baron von Reizenstein, the Entomologist of his later story," in *George W. Cable: His Life and Letters* (New York: Scribner's, 1928), p. 77. The original working title for the novella was "The Old Baron Rodenberg"; see Arlin Turner, *George W. Cable: A Biography* (Baton Rouge: Louisiana State University Press, 1966), p. 315. Also on Reizenstein and Cable, see Mattie Russell, "George

Washington Cable's Letters in Duke University Library," *Library Notes: A Bulletin Issued for the Friends of Duke University Library* 25 (Jan. 1951):1–13. On the moth named after Cable, see L. von Reizenstein, "A New Moth," *Scribner's Monthly, An Illustrated Magazine for the People* 22 (May–Oct. 1881):864–65.

17. J. Hanno Deiler and all who rely on him give the fall of 1888 as the date of Reizenstein's death, with only Turner, *George W. Cable,* p. 114, dating it in 1885. The obituary register at Tulane University Library does not have a listing for Ludwig von Reizenstein, but there is one for Augusta von Reizenstein (née Schröder) in 1886, which describes her as the widow of Ludwig von Reizenstein. In *Soard's 1885 Directory* for New Orleans, Ludwig von Reizenstein is listed as an architect resident at 309 Gasquet in the First District (p. 767), but in *Soard's 1886 Directory* there is no entry. Reizenstein, *Ein Mann,* p. 146, gives 1885 as the year of Ludwig von Reizenstein's death. Schloss Reitzenstein, *Stammbuch* of Lt. Gen. Wilhelm von Reitzenstein, p. 57, gives the complete date.

18. Randolph B. Marcy, *The Prairie Traveler* (1859; reprint, Old Saybrook, Conn.: The Globe Pequot Press, n.d.).

19. *Louisiana Staats-Zeitung,* 20 July 1854, p. 1, with Reizenstein's own reference to Marcy's report to the Geographic Society of New York, 22 March 1853.

20. Randolph B. Marcy and George B. McClellan, *Exploration of the Red River of Louisiana in the Year 1852,* United States House of Representatives, 33rd Congress, 1st Session (Washington, D.C., 1854), p. 55, 1 July 1852.

CHAPTER SIXTEEN

Grave Matters: Poetry and the Preservation of the Welsh Language in the United States

■ **MELINDA GRAY**

In 1891, at the beginning of a decade of especially strong nativist sentiment, *The Nation* published an editorial which suggested that immigration
to the United States be restricted to those who spoke English. The editorial
depicted the English language as an agent of social, moral, and ideological
conformity: "It is through the community of language that men are able to
feel and think the same way about public affairs, and cherish the same political ideals. Every immigrant who comes to this country speaking or understanding the English language becomes, from the day he lands, exposed to all the moral and social influences and agencies on which we rely
for the maintenance and preservation of the American nationality."[1] The
same decade saw the publication, in Welsh-American journals such as *Y
Drych* [*The Mirror;* est. 1851], *Y Cenhadwr Americanaidd* [*The American Messenger;* 1840–1901], and *The Cambrian* (1880–1908), of scores of poems and essays that vigorously exhorted the preservation of the Welsh language.[2]
There can be no doubt, however, that Welsh preservationists shared many
of *The Nation*'s beliefs about the unifying power of the English language in
the United States. At the end of the nineteenth century, Welsh-Americans
were struggling to envision an American life for a language that was believed to be dying in Britain and to do their part in the newly opened campaign for Welsh national identity, but they were also interested in contributing to "the maintenance and preservation of the American nationality."[3]
They wrote poetry in a spirit of linguistic renewal, securing the value
and the vitality of the Welsh language; yet their project was also fraught
with ambiguities and contradictions, and preservationist writing some-

times seemed to wish for the very event it appeared to be arguing against: the death of the Welsh language as a practice in the United States. This chapter will explore the project of linguistic preservation as a strategy of generating a sense of American belonging for the Welsh immigrant to the United States.

From the 1850s through the early twentieth century, Welsh-American writers worked to formulate an appropriate place for the Welsh language in the United States. To the refrain of "Keep to your mother tongue," they urged their readers to learn English and other languages: "Take every opportunity to learn every other language, yet keep to your mother tongue after all."[4] They confirmed the notion of English as the language of American citizenship and proposed Welsh as a private language, for use in the church, the home, and at specified cultural activities. In thus imagining language as a static, protective barrier around traditional practices and modes of knowledge, those who argued for the preservation of the Welsh language joined and took strength from a dominant ideological trend codifying the domestic as a sanctified space separate from the spheres of market production and public discourse:[5]

> To be attached to English as the language of government and the courts, commerce and the market, art and science: to be thoroughly proficient in it in these contexts is not a hindrance to embracing Welsh in its own proper circles. Observe the merchant on the exchange or the dealer in his market; there is some special affinity and agreement among them; but in their private lives, and particularly in their families, they have their own sacred characteristics that do not belong to the court or the marketplace. Thus should the Welsh language be to the Welsh amidst the boiling speech of the English language.[6]

Some writers, however, expressed skepticism and even disapproval of preservationist schemes; they feared that continued practice of the Welsh language among American immigrants from Wales would compromise patriotic commitment to the United States. The argument that the two languages — Welsh and English — might coexist in separate domestic and public spheres fostered anxiety that one language would threaten the integrity of the other. Such linguistic miscegenation was thought to damage the individual's successful entrance into American life. As one observer put it,

> many of the children of the Welsh thus become *confused* between the two languages, and this is a great disadvantage to their growth and their success. Thus many of the Welsh settlements in this country are very similar to those on the borders between England and Wales where the two nations are mixed and both languages are being spoken unclearly and at times in a mixed fashion. Perhaps there is some necessity for that, but it is truly painful to the heart and ear and feelings of every *monoglot* Welshman who has come here from Wales, and especially from Anglesey and Caenarvonshire.[7]

Such fear of mixture also frequently surfaced in opinions about the use of the English language in the United States. Thus one Welsh reviewer of Joseph E. Worcester's *Dictionary of the English Language* (Boston, 1860) joined many of his contemporary contributors to American journals in arguing against the Americanization of the English language, which, he felt, would amount to a degenerate version of standard British English:[8]

> It would not be desirable to try to shape an American language. One of this respectable writer's most praiseworthy characteristics is that he looks to the authority of the Old Country's writers for his standard. The English language is spreading so rapidly through the world that the only plan for maintaining uniformity is to have some standard to which all can conform; without this, we will very likely and soon have American, Australian, Indian, and Polynesian English, in unceasing mixture.[9]

The irony of such an argument lies in its failure to recognize the varieties of imperial offspring as the success story of the English language. The widely shared feeling against mixed languages in the United States mirrored and took its strength from the taboo of interracial couplings; both provoked fear of reproductive failure and impeded success.[10]

One magnet for such anxiety was the poetry that Welsh-American journals published in quantity in the second half of the nineteenth century. Not only did poets make occasional light-hearted experiments with the two languages, but their compositions also expressed fervent patriotism for Wales. Alarmed at the nostalgia for Wales that much of this poetry articulated, one correspondent to *Y Drych* in 1896 proposed to ship the poets back to Wales, where their nationalist yearnings would be better appreciated. The following poem, composed by Rowland Walter (Ionoron Glan Dwyryd), is one of many published in the Welsh-American journals that were occasioned by patriotic longing for the Old Country:

LLINELLAU A ANFONWYD MEWN LLYTHR I'R "HEN WLAD"
(I'r "Cylchgrawn")

Rhyw ofid a byd rhyfedd — yw aros
    Mewn hiraeth am Wynedd;
  Uthr yw bod yn nhrothwy'r bedd,
  A'r fonwent ger fy anedd.

Ymroi 'i aros, er dwyn mawr hiraeth,
Yma yr ydwyf, am Gymru odiaeth;
A byw yn adyn o dan boenydiaeth,
Ag ysig olwg yn gwisgo alaeth; —
Wrth rodio'n cwyno fel caeth, — bron syrthio,
A 'mhrôi i wylo hyd fy marwolaeth.

Os marw yn ngwres Amerig — a fyddaf,
    Caf fedd yn y goedwig;
  A daw gwâr adar y wig
  A chanant i'm llwch unig.

Ar ymweliad daw'r milyn — ar fy medd
    Er fy mwyn bob blwyddyn;
  A thyf gwellt, glaswellt y glyn
  I lochi 'm dystaw lwchyn.

Yn yr Ywen yr awel — a gwyna
    Ganwaith uwch fy argel:
  Y gwys a'm ceidw dan gel,
  A mynwesa 'mhen isel.

Aneirif flodau'n arwydd — a nodant
   Fy nedwydd ddystawrwydd;
   A deigryn caredigrwydd
   A rêd tros eu gruddiau'n rhwydd.

Yn y rhan hon yr hunaf; — yn nhŷ'r bedd
   Unrhyw boen ni theimlaf;
   Ni wna tês trwm wrês yr hâf
   Un niwed, na blin auaf.

[LINES SENT IN A LETTER TO THE "OLD COUNTRY"
(For the "Magazine")

Some sorrowful and strange world it is, still
   To be longing for Gwynedd;
   Dreadful to be on the grave's threshold,
   And the graveyard by my birthplace.

Here am I, committed to staying,
In spite of great longing for exquisite Wales;
A wretch living in torment,
Wearing grief's bruised aspect,
Lamenting like a captive, close to sinking,
To giving up in tears 'til my death.

If I am to die in America's heat,
   I will get a grave in the woods;
   Tame birds of the trees will visit
   And sing to my solitary dust.

The animals will visit my grave
   Year in and year out for my sake;
   And grass will grow, a glen's green grass,
   For sheltering my quiet bones.

The wind cries out a hundred times
   In the Yew above my secret place:
   The furrow keeps me hidden
   And embraces my head below.

> Countless flowers a disclosure, attesting
>> To my blessed silence;
> A sympathetic teardrop
> Makes haste across their faces.
>
> Here shall I sleep; in the house of the grave
>> No pain shall I suffer;
> Nor will the heavy heat of summer's sun
> Harm such a one, nor weary winter.]

The title and subtitle of this poem indicate its double destination: it addresses itself to the reader in the Old Country, to whom apparently the verses were posted in a letter; and to the American subscriber to the magazine *Y Cylchgrawn Cenedlaethol*, where the poem first appeared.[11] The poem's speaker is of two minds as well; he mourns his lost birthplace in Gwynedd, North Wales, and yet he specifically refrains from returning to it; he is committed, he claims, to staying in the United States despite his great longing for home; he is captive (or slave, *caeth*) to his own nostalgic desire. Furthermore, the speaker imagines an American grave as a solution to his homesick striving. According to his description, the grave resembles a home: it is a house (*tŷ*) that shelters and protects. Does the poet aim to create a sense of American belonging through this figure? Does the woodland grave promise to naturalize the Welsh-speaking poet, to authenticate his claim to a place in his new world? Or is it the shelter of Welsh patriotism that the poet chooses, a stubborn languishing for the old country?

Only in depicting the birthplace as an abandoned graveyard, and in maintaining a distance between America and Gwynedd, is there a reason for the poem itself. In a single stanza (*englyn*) from one of Rowland Walter's longer poems, "Gwlad fy Nhadau" [Land of My Fathers], the poet elucidates the close connection between the genesis of his poetry and the unyielding absence of his birthplace and forbears:

> Rhaid gadael Gwlad fy Nhadau — i eraill,
>> A morio trwy'r tonau;
> Er hyn mae hon yn parhau,
> Yn nôd fy nymuniadau.[12]

[I must leave to others the Land of my Fathers
  And sail across the sea;
  And yet it is unceasing
  As the object of my dreams.]

The poet's desiring or dreaming (*dymuniadau*) functions as a kind of endless return voyage, enlivening the fatherland and poetry itself.

As Walter's poem opens with the imaginative invocation of the birthplace, so distant from America, it also keeps the Welsh language in play. In "Letter to 'The Old Country,'" the Welsh language survives as the medium of the poet's longing; we might say that the speaker's failure to return to the lost birthplace makes the poem's preservationist contribution. While it refrains from naming either the Welsh language or the project of preserving it, the poem does illustrate the possibility that the value of the Welsh language was most secure in poetry itself (and poetry the safest place for the Welsh language).

The proposal to send the poets back to Wales elicited a number of replies that were printed in *Y Drych;* one defended the poet's sentiments on the grounds that nostalgic poetry sustained and authenticated an American belonging, precisely because it embodied traditional histories and modes of knowledge:

> Loving America does not mean hating Wales. When a lad weds his heart's desire, he does not take an oath to despise his mother and his old home. He continues to love his parents, but he loves his wife more. When love is professed for the old, it extends to the new. It is in this sense that we should view our poets' patriotic compositions. It would be unkind to understand their songs of praise, "Fair Wales" [Cymru Lan] or "The Little Thatched Cottage" [Bwthyn Bach Tô Gwellt], as treasons and to send them back across the pond. They are poets, persons moved by exceptional inspiration to say common things in a sublime and heart-stirring style. Sometimes they speak gloriously of this land's characteristics or places or circumstances... We should remember as well that a poet's language is figurative. It is not the humble cottage that is dear to him but the old connections and relationships. If he were to pass over these sacred things, he would not be a worthy citizen of any country but the country

of eternal poverty. It is not more treasonous to sing a song of the old home in Wales than it would be a transgression against the State of California for one who had moved there to sing a song of his old home in Utica, New York. And in the same vein, if it were a physical possibility, who among us would not like to be able to return to the days of his youth once more? We are conscious that we cannot, and so we make the blessed time in the company of mother and father that much dearer to us. Thanks to the poet for sometimes giving voice to our turmoil. If he can manage a head clear enough and a heart warm enough to cherish Wales under the yoke of the English oppressor, he can manage the head and the heart to be a patriotic citizen of "freedom's land." Fair play to the poets. Do not send them back overseas. There is need of them here.[13]

This rejoinder justifies the patriotism of Welsh-American poetry with an appeal to the value of an inviolate private sphere of domestic and childhood virtues. The sense of self necessary for American citizenship is accomplished only by recognizing, rather than suppressing, the authority of ethnic origin, constructed through and as the Welsh language. By reminding the reader that these origins are necessarily lost to the present place and time, subverted to and thereby enriching a new, mature allegiance to the United States, he reinforces the importance of the effort to retrieve them, to give them voice, to keep them alive.

Preservationist writings imagined a number of fates (or futures) for the language. One was the renewal or continuity of linguistic practices in the community, whether imagined as home and church, or more broadly as Welsh race or nation. However, the call to preserve the Welsh language also often depicted the language as a marker of ethnic identity, outside of practice. The following poem, for example, epitomizes the pervasive ambiguity in the message of preservation; it celebrates the life of the Welsh language and at the same time projects the death of the language as practice in order to open the door on its symbolic afterlife:[14]

Y GYMRAEG

Chwi Gymry iaith-garol ymunwch yn llu,
I gadw'r hen iaith fendigedig,

Rhag cwympo yn farw i fedd angof du,
Yn mynwent hen ieithoedd methedig.

Hon ydoedd iaith Adda yn Eden, pwy wad?
Iaith gyntaf barablodd ei dafod;
Drwy hon y cyfiawnai ein parchus hen dad
Gyfrinion ei fynwes i'w briod. [. . .]

Ymbrancio'n Gymraeg wna'r wyn ar y bryn,
A'r meirch ar y ddol a'i gweryant;
Cymraeg yw brefiadau y fuwch ger y llyn,
A'r cwn yn Gymraeg a gyfarthant.

Hi ydyw iaith aelwyd pob Cymro gwir, glan,
Ac enwog iaith ber ein pwlpudau;
Iaith beirdd a cherddorion, iaith awen a chan,
Iaith gweddi a mawl ac amenau.

Os trenga'n hen iaith a newidio ei gwedd,
O cladder hi'n barchus, mae'n haeddu;
Argraffer yn eglur ar garreg ei bedd:
"Fan yma mae hen iaith y Cymry."

Wrth ochr fy mam iaith, O torwch i'm fedd,
Neu doder ni'n ddau mewn un beddrod;
O boed i'm gael marw, a huno mewn hedd,
Tra Cymraeg floesg sibrwd fy nhafod.

[THE WELSH LANGUAGE

Welsh people, lovers of language, join forces this day,
And prevent our blessed old tongue
From dropping dead into black oblivion
In the graveyard of failed old languages.

Doubtless the language of Eden's Adam,
This one he spoke from the start;
In it our honest father confided
To his wife the secrets of his heart. [. . .]

The lambs on the hillside frolic in Welsh;
This the horses in the meadow neigh;
In Welsh the lakeside cattle low,
And in Welsh the dogs bay.

Sweet, famed tongue of our pulpits
Tongue of each good Welshman's hearth;
Language of poets and minstrels, poesy and song,
Language of prayer, praise, and amens.

If the old language will wither and die,
Then bury it with honor and care;
Favor its gravestone with reverent inscription:
"Here lies the old language of the Welsh."

Oh dig me a grave at my mother-tongue's side
Or set us in one grave together;
Oh let me die and sleep in peace,
And it's Welsh to the shadows I'll whisper.]

The poet's opening plea to prevent the language from "falling dead into the grave of black oblivion" is specifically a demand that the language not be forgotten; while it might "wither and die" in practice, it might yet be maintained in memory. The poem itself acts as a "living" memorial, enumerating the contexts to which the language gives access; these include the natural world, the worlds of marriage and home, the sacred world of the church, and the aesthetic and communal worlds of poetry, song, and prayer. Preserved "in memoriam," the language might continue to vouch for genealogical, religious, and aesthetic inheritances.

The figure of the grave embodies the ambiguity of this poem's message. Thus the poet proposes to protect a version of the language by honoring it with a gravestone; acceptance of the death of the language might, he suggests, be the most effective way to keep it intact and to shield it from "withering" and "changing its aspect." The last lines of the poem, however, designate the grave as a site of regeneration. The poet's willingness to lie down beside his mother tongue in the grave might be read as a subversive pledge to practice the Welsh language in the face of adversity: "Oh let me die and sleep in peace / And it's Welsh to the shadows I'll whisper." At the very least, the image of poet and mother tongue together in the grave suggests the power of the dead to "speak" across a radical divide. Perhaps a Welsh poem could never wish for the death of the Welsh language, however much it might toy with the idea. To see the Welsh language fall out of practice would be to relinquish the poem itself as unreadable.

Other writings (other modes of writing) from the end of the nineteenth century more freely explore the idea that the death of the Welsh language in the United States could generate a sense of American belonging beyond the confines of Welsh language practice in the United States. In an essay from 1891 on "The Welsh in the United States," one journalist suggested that the best way to accomplish such an American belonging was to let all sign of Welsh origin or allegiance lapse, even in memory. Only in forgetfulness could the immigrant hope to attain the liberties and opportunities of American life: "The Welshman [who] loves the free air of the United States, its educational and industrial advantages, . . . so often desires to forget he is a Welshman only that he may remember that he is an American citizen."[15] The essay itself, however, functions as a deliberate remembering, and the journalist moves on to list the names of people with Welsh ancestry who had, in his opinion, made important contributions to American society. This curious contradiction suggests the need for a particular kind of remembering and an equally powerful need to create a rupture between a (Welsh) past and an (American) present. According to this view, the Welsh language functioned only when it was attached to a past that was discontinuous with the present.

Other writers elaborated the idea that the memory of the Welsh language served an important purpose in the United States. Associated with a remote and cultured past and bearing a freight of "ideality, emotion, and poetic purpose," the language was imagined to be fundamentally necessary to the idea of America. The qualities of the language might be translated and preserved as "spirit":

> It is surmised, and certainly cannot be disproved, that far back in Eden, it was the Welsh tongue that was first loosened to the accents of love, and that Adam told the first sweet story to Eve in rippling and pellucid Cam-

brian; and that this language alone percolated through the wild diversion of Babel, to carry to the latest generations the lovely scent of Paradise. I cannot say this is absolutely true, but I mean no flattery, when I say, there is a peculiar fitness of the historic trend to the actual situation. . . . It is this kindred sentiment, unfolded down through the ages, growing stronger and sweeter in the light of knowledge, always loyal to God, to truth, to country, to home, that finds its best expression in American citizenship, which it adorns and ennobles. The Welsh spirit illustrates that form of virtue upon which this republic rests. It embodies more than knowledge, more than power, more than loyalty, even. It touches the emotions, and sweeps the strings of love, religion, courage, sacrifice, and attunes itself with the duties of life. It seeks the diviner graces of truth. These are not glittering generalities. There is a positive force in ideality, in emotion, in poetic purpose; and under the menace of materialism, one of the needs of the time.[16]

The excess and abstraction inherent in "the Welsh spirit" have the same effect as a language barrier; they seem to pose a threat until they are translated (from "language" to "kindred sentiment"). When trained to a purpose, however — when they are understood as the founding "virtues" of "this republic" — the "force of ideality, emotion, and poetic purpose" inherent in the idea of the Welsh language serves as a powerful counterforce to the "menace of materialism" facing American society.

Imagined as a sign, as a relic of a mythologized, Edenic past that, dead or translated, would generate a narrative of values useful in defense against American materialism, the Welsh language resembles the sort of souvenir that Susan Stewart has described:

The double function of the souvenir is to authenticate a past or otherwise remote experience and, at the same time, to discredit the present. The present is either too impersonal or too alienating compared to the intimate and direct experience of contact which the souvenir has as its referent. This referent is authenticity. What lies between here and there is oblivion, a void marking a radical separation between past and present. The nostalgia of the souvenir plays in the distance between the present and an imagined, prelapsarian experience, experience as it might be "directly lived."[17]

The souvenir is an object, a material sign, the purpose of which is to conjure meaning through narrative; Stewart's prototype is the antique. The dead or abandoned language, the language which has been translated into modern virtues, can also be seen to have a materiality: for example, in the unreadable book (a family Bible; a diary or journal) or in a commemorative poem, perhaps enclosed in a letter or inscribed on a headstone. The narrative such an item elicits is an account of ethnic origin, of values and spirit, of a authentic past that confers authenticity. As the abandoned language has once been a practice — a mode of human communication and exchange — it also suggests something of the potent anti-souvenir, in which the transformation of meaning into materiality accomplishes a profound discontinuity, a refusal of history:

> The antique as souvenir always bears the burden of nostalgia for experience impossibly distant in time: the experience of the family, the village, the firsthand community. One can better understand the antique's stake in the creation of an intimate distance if the antique is contrasted to the physical relic, the souvenir of the dead which is the mere material remains of what had possessed human significance. Because they are souvenirs of death, the relic, the hunting trophy, and the scalp are at the same time the most intensely *potential* souvenirs and the most potent antisouvenirs. They mark the horrible transformation of meaning into materiality more than they mark, as other souvenirs do, the transformation of materiality into meaning. If the function of the souvenir proper is to create a continuous and personal narrative of the past, the function of such souvenirs of death is to disrupt and disclaim that continuity. Souvenirs of the mortal body are not so much a nostalgic celebration of the past as they are an erasure of the significance of history.[18]

In the proposal to preserve the Welsh language as an idea, as an antique, is embedded a particular conception of what it means to be American: American identity depends both on creating a narrative of authentic and personal origin and on a fundamental and irreparable rupture with the past.

Notes

1. "The Proper Sieve for Immigrants," *The Nation,* 16 April 1891, p. 312.

2. Several other important sources for nineteenth-century Welsh-American writing are as follows: *Y Cyfaill o'r Hen Wlad yn America* [*Old Country's Companion in America;* 1838–69]; *Y Cylchgrawn Cenedlaethol* [*The National Magazine;* 1853–56]; *Y Traethodydd yn America* [*The Essayist in America;* 1857–60]; *Y Cyfaill: sef, Cylchgrawn Misol y Methodistiaid Calfinaidd yn America* [*The Companion, or, The Monthly Magazine of the Calvinist Methodists in America;* 1870–1933].

3. For more on the subject of the status of the Welsh language in nineteenth-century Wales, see John Davies, *A History of Wales* (London: Penguin, 1993); Prys Morgan, "From Long Knives to Blue Books," in *Welsh Society and Nationhood,* R. R. Davies et al., eds. (Cardiff: University of Wales Press, 1984); and Gwyn Williams, *When Was Wales? A History of the Welsh* (New York: Viking Penguin, 1985).

4. W. H. Owen, "Y Cymry a'r Gymraeg" [The Welsh and the Welsh Language], *Y Drych,* 18 Jan. 1851. The translation of this passage and all subsequent translations are my own.

5. Drawing on the work of social historians Leonore Davidoff and Catherine Hall (1987), Rod Edmond has described the "cult of domesticity" along with the compartmentalization of private and public spheres and the stratification of gender roles in middle-class Victorian England. See Edmond, *Affairs of the Hearth: Victorian Poetry and Domestic Narrative* (London: Routledge, 1988).

6. Syllog, "Yr Iaith Gymraeg. Pa un ai Mantais ai Anfantais i'r Cymry yn y Wlad Hon yw Cadw eu Hiaith yn Fyw" [Whether It Is a Disadvantage or an Advantage to the Welsh in This Country to Preserve the Welsh Language], *Y Drych,* 24 May 1906.

7. R. D. Thomas, *Hanes Cymry America* (Utica, N.Y., 1872); *A History of the Welsh in America,* trans. Phillips G. Davies (Lanham, Md.: University Press of America, 1983), p. 337.

8. For a thorough account of the lively conversations about language in the journals and criticism of late nineteenth-century United States, see Elsa Nettels, *Language, Race, and Social Class in Howells's America* (Lexington, Ky.: The University of Kentucky Press, 1988).

9. "Nodiadau Lenyddol" (Literary Notes), *Y Traethodydd yn America* (Mehefin/ June 1860):290.

10. See Werner Sollors, *Neither Black Nor White Yet Both: Thematic Explorations of Interracial Literature* (Oxford: Oxford University Press, 1997), p. 10: "Is there

such a thing as 'amalgophobia' or 'mixophobia'? As Diana Williams observed, it is still hard for Americans to recognize 'racial mixing, both between and within persons.'"

11. The poem first appeared in *Y Cylchgrawn Cenedlaethol*, Sept. 1853, together with a reply composed by a friend in Wales — a single *englyn* in praise of Walter's talent — and a last *englyn* by Walter in praise of the American journal's cultural endeavor. The poem was later included in Walter's American collection, *Caniadau Ionoron* (Utica, N.Y.: T. J. Griffiths, 1872).

12. From "Awdl — Gwlad fy Nhadau," included in Rowland Walter, *Caniadau Ionoron* (1872), p. 101.

13. Llew o'r Lliain. "Gwladgarwch" [Patriotism], *Y Drych*, 30 Jan. 1896.

14. Gwyngyll, *Y Drych*, 24 Dec. 1891.

15. Thomas L. James, "The Welsh in the United States," *Cosmopolitan*, Feb. 1891, p. 476.

16. E. S. Wilson, "The Welsh People as American Citizens," *The Cambrian*, May 1897, p. 223.

17. Susan Stewart, *On Longing: Narratives of the Miniature, the Gigantic, the Souvenir, the Collection* (Durham, N.C.: Duke University Press, 1993), p. 139.

18. Ibid., p. 140.

CHAPTER SEVENTEEN

Beyond the National Tradition: Thuong Vuong-Riddick's *Two Shores / Deux Rives*

■ **DAN DUFFY**

In the Boston Public Library, main branch, readers' annex, the mezzanine is devoted to books in languages other than English. The shelves are open. The collection is not catalogued, but shelved by language. The books are purchased blind on the recommendations of specialist dealers, and re-placed on a regular basis as they wear out. When I visited the collection in March 1997 after a meeting of the Longfellow Seminar, there were one hundred linear feet of Vietnamese books: four cases of five shelves apiece, filed by author.[1]

I sampled the collection by looking for standards of literature from Viet Nam, then examining the books on either side. For instance, I found just one copy of Nguyen Du's *Truyen Kieu,* known as the Vietnamese national poem.[2] It was filed under "Nguyen," the common family name. Of the five books to each side, one was a California edition of a contemporary Ha Noi author, Nguyen Huy Thiep.[3] The rest were novels, written in the United States. Browsing freely the length of the collection, I did find some fiction from Saigon before 1975, and many translations of U.S. popular fiction and self-help books. But nearly every volume there was printed in Vietnamese in the United States, and a great many of them are imaginative literature.

Vietnamese-language literature in the United States is a great untold story, if you can call a story untold that is spelled out in the Boston Public Library. Criticism in English is mostly limited to work on a few authors by dedicated scholars.[4] Translations have appeared in English-language com-pilations by literary editors with other goals.[5] Stray stories have been pub-lished in collections that address the topic of reconciliation between the

United States and Viet Nam; travel to Viet Nam; contemporary Vietnamese fiction; and Vietnamese American identity.[6] None have directly addressed the topic of Vietnamese authors at work in their native language in the New World.

To be sure, it is a difficult topic to address. Since my serendipitous discovery of the Boston collection, deliberate research has led me to similar stacks of Vietnamese books in the public libraries of Raleigh and Fayetteville, North Carolina. Other researchers at Longfellow seminars have told me of their personal discoveries of substantial non-English literatures in American libraries. The stories we trade are of what students of ethnography call the "arrival scene" of the field researcher among the people he or she will study.[7] Malinowski stands among his gear on a beach; Geertz flees a vice raid with his informants; Longfellow researchers follow a tip into the stacks.[8]

We find something unexpected that we feel specially prepared to explain to those who have not yet noticed that a great deal of the literature produced in the United States can't be read by most Americans. We face problems of national literature, posed by fitting these shelves of books into a tradition. My immediate concern was not so much with the tradition of American as with that of Vietnamese literature. When I stumbled into the Boston stacks I was just back from a working visit at a publishing house in Ha Noi, where I gathered contemporary short stories for publication in the United States.[9] Deeply involved in bringing fiction from one country to another, I looked at those shelves and asked, "What is the nationality of these books?"

This question falls squarely within academic discussions of nationalism, post-colonialism, and Asian American literature now taking place in the humanities and social sciences.[10] I would like to start instead from the observation that imaginative literature itself is interpretive and explanatory. For example, the power of Benedict Anderson's work on nationalism flows from his close attendance to the novels of Rizal and Pramoedya, rather than from the many works in political science on this subject.[11] If we are to regard literature as a social activity, why not look to a work of literature to frame questions about this area of life?[12] This will be my purpose here: in explicating a book of poetry by a woman born in Ha Noi, living in Canada, writing in French and English, I will seek to explore the nationality of her book. In conclusion I will draw upon the poet's views to propose an approach to Vietnamese writing in the United States.[13]

TWO SHORES / DEUX RIVES

The book was published in Vancouver in 1995 by an independent literary press.[14] The poems are short, seldom more than a page in length. They are presented in French on the right and English on the left. Whichever language has priority, the practical effect is that one opens the book and sees both versions together. The publisher's blurb says that the poet wrote her work in English, and "recreated/*recréé*" them in French. Whatever the process, the two versions are always close in meaning but usually expand or contract this meaning from one language to the other.

For instance, the first poem of the book is "Searching/*Errance.*" "Errance" doesn't mean "Searching," but to search can mean to wander. A knight errant, for example, was a man on a quest.[15] Another title with an expansive, nuanced discrepancy is "Blues/Spleen." Epigraphs are translated, but snatches of song or poem in the body of verse are not. When this happens in "Searching/*Errance,*" the epigraph and quotation are the same line of verse, translated on the top of the English page but not below, pointing to the different literal and evocative meanings of words. Sometimes the language of the page seems to indicate a place from which the poet speaks: for instance, in "Youth/*Jeunesse*" the stanza

> Maintenant
> J'ai atterri
> sur votre territoire, France

simply disappears from the English page. But the stanza may have dropped out by accident, since the first line of that particular poem announces itself in Nice, whose summer's heat recalls Saigon.

Throughout the book, it is not always clear when a discrepancy between right- and left-hand pages asserts an unambiguous distinction. This is to the point. "Searching/*Errance*" makes a statement with all the persuasive ambiguity of a modernist lyric. The statement is about the nationality of the poet. It is worth citing in English:

SEARCHING

I belong to a country that I have left.
— Colette

> I belong to a country that I have left.
> A country of small streets and villages
> where people know their neighbours
> from birth to old age.
>
> I belong to a country where
> the seasons bring few changes.
> Between winter and summer no difference
> except for the rains, when it rains.
>
> I belong to a country
> you cannot look for
> on maps, in books, movies.
> Even I hardly recognize it from the pictures
> I saw the other day in a calendar.
>
> I belong to a country of the mind
> with friends and relatives
> scattered in Canada, America, France, Australia,
> Vietnam.

[The ending lines of the English version are word-for-word those of the French version:]

> J'appartiens
> à un pays
> que j'ai quittée.
>
> Thuong thuoc ve, Thuong thuoc ve . . .

What is her country? That described in the first stanza is Viet Nam, in terms that are nostalgic even for those who have never left Ha Noi. Sentimentalists speak of the "small streets" of Ha Noi.[16] The "villages" are more than small towns, they are the heartland of the rice-growing Red River delta, where the ancestors settled, any of which may be remembered as the "home town" of families who have been in Ha Noi for generations.[17] Indeed, one may know one's neighbors from birth to old age, in the course of normal life in a Vietnamese village, but in what we laughingly call modern times, "normal" is always a nostalgic category.[18]

The second stanza locates the poet in the natural world, over and beyond the streets and village. She fiddles with the facts of weather in that part of the world to convey a sense of brooding timelessness, an eternal space subject to lasting storms.[19] In the third stanza she denies the ability of the reader to find her country in the representations of Viet Nam in maps, books, and movies. One can presume a gainsaying spirit here, which is fair enough about maps that do not show the streets of Ha Noi, and books and movies which narrate one or another fantasy about Viet Nam. But Riddick is more thorough; she resists as well the representation of the country in photographs on the calendars distributed by overseas Vietnamese businesses, though their staff can figure their homeland as well as anyone can.

Scholars often write of Anderson's "imagined communities" as if nations were intentional communities like Twin Oaks, versus imaginary communities like Shangri-La. That is weak understanding. His work describes our present world, where it can be meaningful to say that distant events proceed simultaneously, as is figured in the conventions of the novel and the newspaper. Riddick's poem embraces this idea of "meanwhile," while rejecting all possible manifestations of her country of origin in maps, books, movies, and calendars made for sale. "I belong to a country of the mind," she writes, meaning a country of nationalism without any particular nation.

The poem ends with a nugget of cryptic, untranslatable Vietnamese that (fails to) articulate this difficult point of view. The final refrain, "Thuong thuoc ve" sounds, or looks, poetic to those who don't read the language. It *is* poetry, finally, and here's how it works. The vocabulary is administrative, from that Vietnamese vocabulary which has roots in the Chinese of scholarly bureaucrats. *Thuong* means the poet; *thuoc ve* means to belong to a unit, in the sense of reporting to it, being counted by it, being under its administration. The very last word, taken as a Vietnamese monosyllable out of the Sino-Vietnamese compound, is also a pun: *ve* means to return to, especially to return to the city where you were born, or to travel to the city of Ha Noi — even if you were born in Saigon, you can't properly "go" — *di* — to Ha Noi, you have to "return" — *ve* — there.[20] She is saying, I belong by local authority, I am going back, I am going back to Ha Noi where I was born. The force of these meanings is intensified by a pun on the poet's name, the adverb *thuong*, which means to do something repeatedly, with seriousness.

But the object of this strong phrase "thuong thuoc ve" — "I continually return with seriousness to Ha Noi my place of birth where I belong" — is just an ellipsis. She doesn't belong to anything. "I belong to a country that I have left . . . Thuong thuoc ve, Thuong thuoc ve . . ." What follows this introductory poem is (not) the poet's nation.

The argument of "Searching/*Errance*" is borne out by the poems of the collection. The book is not about two countries. The *Two Shores / Deux Rives* of the title, going by the references in the poem, could as easily be the West and East coasts of Canada as Canada and Viet Nam, or Viet Nam and France.[21] The two shores are indeterminate. They refer to belonging to a place that lies between boundaries, that doesn't exist anywhere in particular. The first section of the book, "Viet Nam," is a travesty of the idea of the nation of Viet Nam. The second and third sections, "Canada" and "France," chase the poet around a world constituted by her interior subjectivity and domestic life existing inside a rickety structure of public events that no one would take seriously, given a choice.

THE VIET NAM SECTION

The first section begins with a folk song. "When you come back, will you remember me?" asks the couplet that makes up half of "Black Teeth/ *Dents Noires.*" The other half is an editorial aside, explaining that country women used to lacquer their teeth, and that one's beloved was moved by the sight.

The poem is about nostalgia. For some time, in a gesture of modernity, scholars in Viet Nam have made a subject of the songs and customs of rural people, blocking off the "traditional" and locating it in the living past.[22] The poet takes this tradition of modernizing scholarship and uses it to objectify

Viet Nam itself in fascination. The archaic custom she refers to in the title serves as an image of the beautiful that has become strange and distant.[23] The response line of the couplet, "I will remember your teeth when you smile," a passionate image from a love song, which would be quaint in the hands of an antiquary, in this poem is a representation of ambivalent attraction.

Love of country is palpable in "Itinerant Merchants / *Marchandes Ambulantes*," three stanzas about the women who walk into every Vietnamese town in the morning, carrying fruit to sell from two baskets slung from a pole over the shoulder.[24]

> I remember
> itinerant merchants
> passing the house front
> with their yokes and baskets
> full of guavas,
> sweet and fragrant,
> cinnamon-apples, rose-apples . . .

The country, one often hears, is like two baskets on a pole, Ha Noi and Saigon connected by a thin coastline. Just so, the poet moves on from her sense-memories of the ladies who sell fruit in Ha Noi, to give equal time to the different dress and fruit of the southern women who work the same trade in Saigon. Happy memories from childhood combine with images of regional costume and local delicacies, in the concoction of national feeling familiar to us all.

So why is she ambivalent? After patriotic feeling comes history, in the grand manner. In "Games/*Jeux*," planes bomb Ha Noi and Hai Phong. These might be Japanese or American bombers fighting the Japanese, but "We didn't know who they were." In a trench, the poet and her birth family play with Chinese cards. The poem is terse, elevating sense memory to survey the nation, as "Itinerant Merchants/*Marchandes Ambulantes*" does, but without the warm feeling. "Big Hunger: 1945/*Grande Famine: 1945*" uses the same technique to show the consequences of the Japanese seizure of the Vietnamese food supply:[25]

Millions of peasants
walking in towns:

ghost-like,
fleshless
hollow eyes,
carrying ghost-babies in baskets,
on ghost-hips . . .

Considered in historical terms, the famine of 1945 was a foundational moment in modern Viet Nam, from which many learned that the nation must at all costs become free and independent.[26] The poet doesn't tell that story, though. In her memory, children play cards in a trench, then watch history staggering down the streets of her country asking for food.

Young people all over Tonkin were moved by such cues to join the Viet Minh revolutionary movement. In "Remembering My Brother/*En Souvenir de Mon Frère*" the poet speaks of the compassion of her brother, who went without to feed a hungry man. But she writes of it as family myth, a gesture whose meaning was to illustrate the character of one of those with whom she shared a domestic world while the public one became problematic. This domestic world is remembered as several subjectivities at close quarters, "Unreachable/*Inaccessible*" as one poem puts it, not domestic bliss. But it has context and depth as the scenes from the streets do not. After the (unannounced) poems of the Japanese occupation in Ha Noi, "Civil War/*Guerre Civile*" moves (without announcement) to a scene of mayhem in Saigon, when soldiers climb the walls, plunder the house, and break the family's gate. It could be the early 1950s, or maybe 1968, but who's counting? History intrudes on the poet's world, but it speaks only in the voice of "The Mad Uncle/*L'Oncle Fou*":

He would sing with all his heart
the national anthem of Red China.

In all my memories of Hanoi
he sings loud and clear.
Throughout the wasted land

> I will hear this song
> 'til the end of time . . .

These poems of Viet Nam from the first section of the book articulate a position that is distinct from the turns away from public life into individualism, domesticity, or aestheticism that are familiar to readers in any modern tradition. The poet loves her country, but she thinks it is a heartbreak. She surveys its history attentively, but she denies it status as a story with which she must engage. She holds to the idea of a nation, but she does not want the particular one whose memory she clings to. The point is made with devastating power in a strong poem that is hardly a poem at all, like the Vietnamese refrain that ends "Searching/*Errance.*"

"My beloved is dead in Viet Nam/*Celui que j'aime est mort au Vietnam*" is dedicated to Trinh Cong Son, whom the *New York Times* aptly described in the 1960s as the Bob Dylan of Viet Nam. Son is about Dylan's age, and like him is a popular artist with a gift for singing what is going on right now. "My beloved is dead in Viet Nam/*Celui que j'aime est mort au Viet Nam*" is a revision of Son's great "Tinh ca cua nguoi mat tri (Love Song of a Madwoman)."[27] Banned in Viet Nam since 1975 because it narrates the war as a disaster among Vietnamese people, rather than the glorious fight against the Americans which Ha Noi remembers, the song goes like this in one English version:

> I love someone killed in the Battle of Pleime
> I love someone killed in Battle Zone D.
> Killed at Dong Xoai, killed in Hanoi,
> Killed along the border, suddenly.
>
> I love someone killed at Chu Prong,
> I love someone who floats down a river,
> Killed in the jungle, killed in the field,
> Killed in cold blood, burned like coal.
>
> I want to love you as I love Viet Nam,
> I whisper your name as I wander in the storm,
> Your Vietnamese name,
> Bound to you by our yellow-skin tongue.

I want to love you as I love Viet Nam,
Both of us raised to the sound of guns.
Our hands and lips are full,
Let us forget all foreign tongues.

Here is how Vuong-Riddick sings it:

My beloved is
Dead in Dien Bien Phu
Dead in Lao Kay, dead in Cao Bang
Dead in Langson, dead in Mong Cai
Dead in Thai Nguyen, dead in Hanoi,
Dead in Haiphong, dead in Phat Diem
Dead in Ninh-Binh, dead in Thanh Hoa
Dead in Vinh, dead in Hatinh
Dead in Hue, dead in Danang, dead in Quang Tri
Dead in Quang Ngai, dead in Qui Nhon
Dead in Kontum, dead in Pleiku
Dead in Dalat, dead in Nha-Tranh
Dead in My Tho, Dead in Tuy Hoa
Dead in Bien-Hoa, dead in Ban Me Thuot
Dead in Tayninh, dead in Anloc
Dead in Saigon, dead in Bien Hoa
Dead in Can Tho, dead in Soc Trang[28]

Vuong-Riddick takes a lovely song and makes it as ugly as the situation it describes. No war is mentioned. The lover isn't killed, he's just dead. Human agency isn't important, only the fact of wasted lives. Rhyme disappears. Where Son mentions a few disastrous battles, Vuong-Riddick gives a systematic North to South gazetteer of the country, which is indeed a list of battles. Her list evokes — just barely — the southward expansion of Vietnamese over the Champa, with their strange place names, over the Khmer. For someone who knows Vietnamese geography and the popular understanding of the national history, who knows Son's previous song, Vuong-Riddick's poem is a recital of the flat face of the past. There is no story, just the same result again and again: all these lovers are dead.

For other readers, the ideal readers of the poem, her list is impenetrable.

On both French and English sides of the page, it might as well be Vietnamese — the only Western words are the repetition, "Dead in . . . dead in . . ." One is not supposed to understand the list, to take part in the story of Vietnamese people. The reader stands with the poet outside her history. She ends it with a sentence in italics:

> Vietnam, how many times
> I have wanted to call your name
> I have forgotten
> the human sound.

Here she elides Trinh Cong Son's sentiment, "I whisper your name as I wander in the storm, your Vietnamese name, . . . Let us forget all foreign tongues." Where Trinh Cong Son's is after all a love song, as well as a plea for national unity and self-determination, Vuong-Riddick's is something bleaker, a dry elegy for a past she wants no part of.[29]

THE FRANCE AND CANADA SECTIONS

France and Canada are the settings, not the subjects of these sections. France is an account of the poet's student years, developing a sense of self in isolation from family, paddling in the world. The first poem, "Blues/ *Spleen*," complains of the short days of Paris winter, boredom at the Sorbonne, but then flits on to the bookstores and coffee shops and movies like a student settling into a life of her own. The poems of the France section explore Europe — many conjure jaunts in Germany, Greece, Belgium — and make tentative, truncated essays at romantic love.

Two kinds of threatening images interrupt these poems of student days. Together they first appear at the end of "Blues/*Spleen*":

> Use an x-ray
> to photograph our souls —
> you will glimpse
> a landscape
> incomprehensible
> even to ourselves.

Coming after an account of the poet beginning to read recent history of Indochina, speaking of Vietnamese expatriates, this is the same predicament posed in the Viet Nam section — a national problem. But it is also a statement about not yet knowing one's self, a public-health assessment about students.

That is a problem that can solve itself. As the poems come by, scenes of travel and romance build a sense of instrumentality and interiority. Night terrors appear in "Night/*Nuit*" for what they are at this time, namely grief and loneliness, not the end of the world. The poet grows up, and by the section's end, when "The Whirlwind of History/*Le Tourbillon de L'Histoire*" makes its dizzying entrance, politics, narrated with coherence and context, provides an occasion of adult competence. It is May 1968 in Paris, it has been Tet 1968 in Viet Nam. The poet's sister arrives from Saigon in time for the barricades, feels right at home, and sets out to stockpile rice among the demonstration supplies. In search of a nation that will take her entire family out of their mad homeland, the poet finds a job in Montreal. She gets all of them out by January 1975, all but one. The last poem says:

> Saigon fell in April,
> my father died in December.

Canada, the longest section of the collection, is a deeply moving fiction of adult integration into the human community. "*Poudrerie,*" the first poem, has no English title because the direct translation is incorrect. It is not a gunpowder factory but a blizzard, a random event of harsh power which the people of Quebec turn into a party. The poet meets her husband, and over the two dozen poems to come she gets used to him, adopts a child, and gives birth. A single round of the seasons unrolls as many years pass. They move west to Victoria, and she begins to speak English.

Life is arduous, and history has not become more agreeable. "Stress/*Stress*" recounts marriage and community duties in stanzas that alternate tenure review and the fall of Saigon. "Nightmare II/*Cauchemare II*" is more frightening than its first version, in the Viet Nam section. Then she was dreaming that her mother might die, and now her father has. The woman we see maturing so marvelously in "Canada" remains the damaged creature who will write "Viet Nam." In "Hospital/*Hôpital,*" visiting the sick, she panics and runs until restrained by three or four orderlies. The longest poem in the collection, "Pacific/*Pacifique*," follows Uncle Hoai, who set sail from Quang Ngai in 1978 to beat around the South China Sea with three hundred passengers for seventy days, turned away by nation after nation:[30]

> They called you the Pacific
> and rightly so, since
> you calm
>   the anguish, terror and despair
> of people
> who drown in your waves.

Integration is not necessarily a cheerful outlook. The Canada section and *Two Shores/Deux Rives* itself end with a textile metaphor in "He Covered Me With a Blanket/*Il M'a Recouverte*." Her husband's care is like a blanket, one that she felt in the presence of her father, one that the nuns at school knitted with their prayers. The image includes the network of Quebec women who have supported the poet, and even the people she greets daily on the streets of Victoria:

> It is this human warmth
> of the country
> I belong to.

These lines cut me to the quick. The blanket metaphor is quite ungrounded: there is no actual fabric in the poem. We already know that she belongs to no country. This is affirmation in the willed and human sense, the instrumental belief of a subject who knows that she is in the hands of persons like herself. The poet stands within a web of life which she understands and supports, which she invites us to understand. Let history rage.

CONCLUSION

Shall I spell it out? Thuong Vuong-Riddick, in her *Two Shores/Deux Rives*, articulates a particular transnational position from which I would like to consider Vietnamese writing in the New World. She emphasizes subjectivity: adult instrumentality and interiority. What do people actually do with books, I can ask, and for what purpose? She associates mere identity with sorrow and emptiness, and Vietnamese national identity with grief. I can hypothesize that these sentiments are not the basis of the vibrant industry that I observe on the shelves in Boston Public Library.

Those books remain mute here, except as social facts. It is also a fact that there are a great many people in the United States writing, publishing, and reading Vietnamese-language books.[31] I am not yet ready to interpret them as literature. Not that those volumes will rest mute until I do. Right now they wear themselves out, speaking to Boston readers. There is no call for salvage ethnography of this literature, no mission to explain these books, to give Viet Nam a voice in America.[32] A number of American authors already move between these special markets and the general English-language markets, and soon there will be more.[33] I stand instead with Vuong-Riddick, skeptical of Viet Nam, in love with my memories, convinced that we are all in this together and that there is a global space in which my subjectivity can speak of its interests to my fellows.[34]

Notes

1. The second seminar of the Longfellow Institute on Literature of the United States in Languages Other Than English, conducted by Marc Shell and Werner Sollors at Harvard, Spring 1997.

2. It is available in English as *The Tale of Kieu: A Bilingual Edition of Truyen Kieu,* by Nguyen Du, translated and annotated by Huynh Sanh Thong, with a historical essay by Alexander B. Woodside (New Haven: Yale Southeast Asia Studies and Yale University Press, 1983).

3. A different selection of his short stories is available in English: Nguyen Huy Thiep, *The General Retires and Other Stories,* trans. Greg Lockhart (Singapore: Oxford University Press, 1992).

4. English-language criticism is reviewed in John C. Schafer, "Vietnamese Exile Narratives," in his *Vietnamese Perspectives on the War in Vietnam: An Annotated Bibliography of Works in English* (New Haven: Yale Southeast Asia Studies, 1997), pp. 97–108.

5. Schafer is an invaluable guide to translations.

6. On reconciliation, see *The Other Side of Heaven: Post-War Fiction by Vietnamese and American Writers*, ed. Wayne Karlin, Le Minh Khue, and Truong Vu (Willimantic, Conn.: Curbstone Press, 1995). On travel, see *Vietnam: A Traveler's Literary Companion*, ed. John Balaban and Nguyen Qui Duc (San Francisco: Whereabouts Press, 1996). On fiction, see *Night, Again: Contemporary Fiction from Vietnam*, ed. Linh Dinh (New York: Seven Stories Press, 1996). On identity: for a constructive view, see *Watermark: Vietnamese American Poetry and Prose*, ed. Barbara Tran, Monique T. D. Truong, and Luu Truong Khoi (New York: Asian American Writers Workshop, 1998). For a skeptical view, see *Not a War: American Vietnamese Fiction, Poetry and Essays*, ed. Dan Duffy (New Haven: Yale Southeast Asia Studies, 1997).

7. Mary Louise Pratt, "Fieldwork in Common Places," in *Writing Culture: The Poetics and Politics of Ethnography*, ed. James Clifford and George E. Marcus (Berkeley: University of California Press, 1986), pp. 27–50. Pratt discusses the arrival scene as a literary trope. I suggest that researchers do bodily arrive in locations, and that what Pratt views as repetition and revision in ethnographic narrative is also news of the social situation of research.

8. Bronislaw Malinowski, *Argonauts of the Western Pacific* (New York: E. P. Dutton, 1961); Clifford Geertz, *The Interpretation of Cultures* (New York: Basic Books, 1973).

9. N.x.b. The Gioi (World Publishers) are publishers of such works as the monumental *Vietnamese Literature*, ed. Nguyen Khac Vien and Huu Ngoc (Ha Noi, 1976) and *Ho so van hoa My* (A File on American Culture), ed. Huu Ngoc and Lady Borton (Ha Noi, 1996). The stories were published in *North Viet Nam Now: Fiction and Essays from Ha Noi*, ed. Dan Duffy (New Haven: Yale Southeast Asia Studies, 1996) and in *Literature News: Nine Stories from the Viet Nam Writers Union Newspaper, Bao Van Nghe*, selected and trans. with intro. and ills. by Rosemary Nguyen (New Haven: Yale Southeast Asia Studies, 1997).

10. The critical essays of Tran Qui Phiet, a professor of English, review the applicable authorities. See, for instance, "Contemporary Vietnamese American Feminine Writing: Exile and Home," *Amerasia Journal* 19-3 (1993):71–83.

11. Benedict Anderson, *Imagined Communities: Reflections on the Origin and Spread of Nationalism*, rev. ed. (London: Verso, 1991). The novels are: Pramoedya Ananta Toer, *This Earth of Mankind*, trans. and with an afterword by Max Lane (New York: Penguin Books, 1996), and Jose Rizal, *Noli Me Tangere*, trans. Soledad Lacson-Locsin (Honolulu: University of Hawaii, 1997).

12. Three British geographers have collected essays on several topics in migration, investigated through imaginative literature. See *Writing Across Worlds:*

Literature and Migration, ed. Russell King, John Connell, and Paul White (Routledge, New York: 1995).

13. A critic in Australia, Nguyen Hung Quoc, in an article available in English, proposes a periodization of modern literature of Viet Nam that incorporates the overseas tradition into a national narrative. See his "Vietnamese Literature in Exile (1975–1990)," trans. Hoai An, in *Vietnamese Studies in a Multicultural World,* ed. Nguyen Xuan Thu (Melbourne: Vietnamese Language & Culture Publications, 1994), pp. 144–57.

14. Thuong Vuong-Riddick, *Two Shores / Deux Rives: Poems/Poèmes* (Vancouver: Ronsdale Press, 1995).

15. While learning Vietnamese, it has often seemed to me in retrospect that English (my native tongue) and French (what I learned in secondary school) are the same language.

16. *Pho nho* evokes a sense of street as market, as in the thirty-six streets *pho* of Ha Noi's old quarter, where the poet grew up.

17. *Que huong.* It is polite in conversation to inquire where someone was born, and where their home town is. The poet's nostalgia for Viet Nam is more notional and achieved than that of many other Ha Noi natives, in that her father was born to a Fukien merchant family sojourning in Viet Nam. She has no Vietnamese home town.

18. It is a convention here in the metropolis to think of life in the periphery proceeding at a more leisurely pace, in terms of the acceleration of dislocation associated with modernity. That is a mistake. Peripheries whirl around the core at breakneck speed. Life in Viet Nam, peripheral to China as well as to Europe and the United States, has seldom been normal. In the last words of the title character in Nguyen Huy Thiep's "Sa," "With these final years, living an ordinary life like everyone else in Hua Ta, I have now truly achieved extraordinary accomplishments." See Nguyen Huy Thiep, "The Winds of Hua Tat," trans. Peter Saidel, in Duffy, *North Viet Nam Now: Fiction and Essays from Ha Noi,* pp. 10–46.

19. Ha Noi citizens discern four seasons. Sentimentalists sing of fall in Ha Noi as others sing of Paris in spring. Riddick elides this for the dry and wet "seasons" of tropical Saigon.

20. At least, that is what they taught me in Hoan Kiem district, downtown Ha Noi. This is not an opinion uniformly held among Vietnamese speakers.

21. Marc Shell has pointed out to me the direct significance of this poem, and the whole collection, in its bilingual Canadian context. The poet is in plain fact a Canadian national addressing the problematics of that national identity. While in Montreal, she taught both at anglophone McGill University and at francophone Université de Montréal. But I met the poet in New York, where

she was reading at the Asian American Writers Workshop as I was seeking Vietnamese writers. This essay interprets her work in this global setting.

22. In English, see the essential work of Huu Ngoc, for instance *Sketches for a Portrait of Vietnamese Culture* (Ha Noi: The Gioi Publishers, 1995).

23. By my observation, the practice is still common and contemporary.

24. Shouldn't all writing be in English/French?

25. A black hole in the human record. Nobody knows how many hundreds of thousands simply wound down like clockwork and stopped breathing, on the roads, in the villages. See the poem "They starved, they starved . . ." by Ba Van Lan, trans. Huynh Sanh Thong, in *Viet Nam Forum* 5 (New Haven: Yale Southeast Asia Studies, 1985).

26. The English-language historian of anticolonialism in Viet Nam is David Marr. See his *Viet Nam 1945: The Quest for Power* (Berkeley: University of California Press, 1996).

27. The original Vietnamese and the following English version of the song are available in: "Love Songs of a Madman: Trinh Cong Son," trans. and intro. by Joseph Do Vinh and Eric Scigliano, with a portrait by Ho Thanh Duc, in Duffy, ed., *Not a War: American Vietnamese Fiction, Poetry and Essays*. Vuong-Riddick's revision is also reprinted in that volume.

28. The spelling of place names in this poem is not standard. The poet holds a French doctorate. She has not worked as an author in Vietnamese language.

29. Compare her poem as well to a precursor which she might expect her bilingual readers to recall. See "Le Conscrit des cent villages," in Louis Aragon, *La Diane française, suivi de En Etrange Pays dans mon pays lui même* (Paris: Seghers, 1946), pp. 41–43. Aragon's speaker, even more than Trinh Cong Son's madwoman, is a historical actor. The composite son of all those villages that gave to the last man for war, he speaks beautifully of his country, chanting the names of those small places, as a national anthem complete with incense. Vuong-Riddick is party to this discourse, in playing her revisionary game, in nostalgia for Viet Nam. But she stands to the side. Karl Britto pointed out to me Vuong-Riddick's allusion to this poem, moments before several francophones in our panel audience leaped to do the same. Indeed, she quotes from Aragon and Eluard, and names French, English, and American modernist poems and plays, at points throughout the collection.

30. Quang Ngai is the province of the My Lai villages.

31. This essay and its notes are for anglophones.

32. I spent years doing that sort of thing. See *Viet Nam Forum* and the *Lac Viet* monograph series (New Haven: Yale Southeast Asia Studies, 1994–97), and "Not a War: Suggestions from a College Reading Course in Fiction and Poetry

from Viet Nam and Vietnamese America," *Education About Asia*, 2-2 (Ann Arbor: Association for Asia Studies), pp. 9–13.

33. To pick two, Andrew Lam and Nguyen Qui Duc are English-language U.S. authors who are literate as adults in their native Vietnamese.

34. Several who responded in two Association for Asia Studies panels: Eric Henry, Patrick Laude, and Margaret Wiener; Karl Britto, Renny Christopher, Nancy Florida, Laurie Sears, and Tran Qui Phiet.

Part V

NATIONALISM AND INTERNATIONALISM

CHAPTER EIGHTEEN

The Welsh Atlantic: Mapping the Contexts of Welsh-American Literature

■ DANIEL WILLIAMS

"Beyond the parochial boundaries of British political life," states Paul Gilroy in discussing the implicit nationalism informing much of the British Left's cultural criticism, "the idea that identity and culture are exclusively *national* phenomena, and the related notion that unchanging essences of ethnic or national distinctiveness are automatically, though mysteriously produced from their own guts, have come to constitute a major political problem. These ideas can be effectively counterposed to the forms of identity and struggle developed — of necessity — by dispersed peoples for whom nationality, ethnicity and the nation state are perhaps not so tightly associated."[1] While the "dispersed peoples" of whom Gilroy speaks are the African and Asian communities of Western Europe and North America, his observations are equally relevant to the peripheral, stateless peoples within the established nation-states of Europe. In Wales, for instance, the problem of weighing the claims of a precarious national identity against other contrasting varieties of subjectivity and identification has been a key preoccupation of much recent creative and historical writing.[2] Welsh cultural studies is now entering a crucial phase. During the past decade, the 1980s revisionism of Dai Smith and Tim Williams — that linguistic decline was inevitable and any attempts at reinforcing the status of the Welsh language were delusional dreams of nationalist mythologizers — has given way to a crucial reconsideration of questions of national and cultural identity.[3] In the process, cultural theory, having seemingly sounded the death-knell of the nationalist cause, at least in academia, has struck a chord with critical nationalists. A key figure in this shift is Raymond Williams, who, in

343

his late writings on "Welshness," sought a place for the nation and the myths and dreams that informed that "imagined community" between the local and the global collectivities — which were themselves being transformed in an age characterized by the transnational character of modes of production, social movements, and informational exchanges.[4] In a discussion of the multiple relationships between Wales and England, he usefully noted: "If there is one thing to insist on in analysing Welsh culture it is the complex of forced and acquired discontinuities: a broken series of radical shifts, within which we have to mark not only certain social and linguistic continuities but many acts of self-definition by negation, by alternation and by contrast."[5] The story of the Welsh in nineteenth-century America may be considered as representing a "radical shift" in the cultural history of the people. The Welsh attempts at constructing a functional ethnic identity in the new American context emphasize the processes of "self-definition by negation, by alteration and by contrast" that Williams identifies as being characteristic of Welsh history. It is this process of "self-definition" that I seek to explore in what follows.

The first official recognition of a Welsh people by the modern British state was the Welsh Sunday Closing Act of 1881; a major victory for the temperance movement led by the Nonconformist church. Britain, however, was not the first modern state to acknowledge the existence of a Welsh nation, for this was granted by the United States Immigration Service in 1875.[6] There may therefore be some basis for claiming that Wales is an American invention. In any such general statements, of course, all the real complications of history are temporarily overridden. This fact is significant, however, in that it suggests that any account of the rise of Welsh national consciousness in the nineteenth century should not ignore the role of the United States in that process. "Welshness" was being invented simultaneously on both sides of the Atlantic. The literature of Welsh America needs to be contextualized within two distinct sociohistorical formations : that of Wales and that of the United States. We may theorize this process by invoking Raymond Williams's notion of "residual, dominant and emergent" social values and forces. In his *Marxism and Literature* Williams refers to ideas and traditions which link the present to the past as "residual forces": "What I mean by the residual is very different [from the archaic].

The residual, by definition, has been effectively formed in the past, but it is still active in the cultural process, not only and often not at all as an element of the past, but as an effective element of the present."[7] Linking the present with the future are the "emergent" social forces, signifying the emergence of new modes of thought and action. These are useful concepts for discussing the construction of ethnic identity in the United States, particularly in comparing those acts of construction with the emergence of nationalist identities in Europe. While the Welsh in Wales could draw on Celtic mythology, the Druids, and a residual rural tradition of oral poetry and song in the forging of a national identity, the Welsh in America were also part of an American context where other residual forces were active within the cultural process: the myths of Puritan origins, divine Providence, and upward social mobility.[8] A comparative account of the invention of nationalisms and ethnicities must account for the different residual forces in operation within each cultural context. Thus, while the Welsh in America could utilize traditions of nationalist invention developed in Wales, they were actively participating in constructing identities within a different cultural matrix. It is somewhat appropriate that one of the most widely read Welsh-American periodicals, boasting twelve thousand subscribers in its prime, was called *Y Drych / The Mirror*.[9] For as Welsh-Americans looked across the Atlantic they saw a slightly distorted and sometimes troubling reflection of their idealized homeland; conversely, the Welsh who turned their gaze toward their relatives in America saw there a reflection of their own problems of constructing a Welsh identity within a dominant English context. My central claim here is that the Welsh in nineteenth-century America cannot be disconnected from their kindred in nineteenth-century Wales.

CONSTRUCTING WELSH ETHNICITY

First impressions would suggest that the nineteenth century was a successful century for Wales. The population quadrupled, the stranglehold of the gentry class was broken, wealth increased tenfold, chapels and churches attracted vast and devoted followings, educational institutions multiplied, and Welsh-language culture flourished as never before. The number of

Welsh speakers increased decade by decade, publications in Welsh proliferated, and the recently re-invented cultural festival — the Eisteddfod —
proved to be an unmitigated success. Circumstances seemed right for a
confident assertion of national awareness, for the creation of firm political
foundations for the nation, and for the emergence of a Welsh literature of
maturity and innovation.[10]

But this did not happen. One of the key events of the century, as many
historians have argued, was the 1847 Royal Commission into the state of
education in Wales. The proposal which led to the establishment of the
commission responsible for the report was put forward by William Williams, a native of Llampumsaint, Carmarthenshire, and MP for Coventry.
In light of the concern for the growing hold of Dissent or Nonconformity
over the common people, the lack of provision for education in Wales and
the growth of political unrest over the previous decades, culminating in the
working class Merthyr Rising of 1831, the Chartist risings of 1839, and the
agrarian anti-tollgate riots of the movement known as Rebecca's Daughters
from 1839–1843, Williams urged the government to inquire into the state
of education in Wales, and "especially into the means afforded to the la-
bouring classes of acquiring a knowledge of the English language."[11] The
three English commissioners reported on much besides education in their
official blue books, attributing the backwardness and immorality of the
people (especially the women) to the influences of Dissent and the Welsh
language. Within a day's journey of the center of the world's most powerful empire, the Welsh lived a life of moral laxity, dishonesty, perjury, and
drunkenness that marked them out for bitter condemnation. Hywel Teifi
Edwards has traced the Welsh uproar that attended the publication of the
Report and, as a mythological tradition was still part of the heritage of
the Welsh at that time, it came to be known as Brad y Llyfrau Gleision,
The Treachery of the Blue Books — an epithet which referred back to the
Treachery of the Long Knives, a plot which had furthered the interests of
the English in the age of Vortigern.[12] This storm of protest led to paradoxi-
cal and contradictory results. On the one hand, it made the Welsh more na-
tionalistic than they had been; on the other, it implanted in the leaders of
the official Welsh way of life a terror of further *exposés*. This led them to engage in a committed effort to answer the criticisms of the commissioners

by encouraging the people to become more like the dominant model of Englishness, thus re-inventing themselves as practical, hardheaded, businesslike, English-speaking Britons.

In the realm of literature this process took the form of emphasizing "yr hyn sydd dda" / "that which is good" in Welsh national life.[13] The commission that was stimulated by the industrial riots of Merthyr and the Chartists thus led to the kind of literature represented by the following *englyn*, which is a traditional form of Welsh verse:

> Cymru lân, Cymru lonydd — Cymru wen,
> Cymru annwyl beunydd.
> Cymru dêg, cymer y dydd
> Gwlad y Gân, gwêl dy gynnydd.

> [Clean Wales, still Wales, white Wales,
> Daily dear Wales.
> Fine Wales steals the day
> Witness the progress of the land of song.]

The adjectives "clean" and "still" were the keywords of Welsh Victorian nationalism. Welsh literature of the late nineteenth century was a literature of "purity"; a literature that, in its celebration of the Welsh language as "the language of heaven" and of a "clean and pure Wales," was the vehicle for proving to the world — or more specifically, to the English — that the Welsh were the most respectable people on earth.

This nineteenth-century context has considerable relevance to the history of the Welsh in America, for it demonstrates that for them, as for many other immigrant groups, the invention of ethnicity was not a new phenomenon but had been a tool of resistance, solidarity, and acceptance within the British state.[14] The steady stream of Welsh who emigrated to the United States throughout the nineteenth century brought with them an idea of Welshness formed in nineteenth-century Britain; an identity which stressed peacefulness, thrift, and religious devotion.[15] This model of Welshness was continually recreated and reinvented in response to changing realities both within the boundaries of the Welsh ethnic group and within the wider context of American society. A significant example of this process may be found in the following speech on "Wales: The Native Land of Fancy," given by the leading American novelist and man of letters, William Dean Howells. It is worth quoting this little known piece at length:

> The Welsh chief Owen Glendower, who held the English at bay for many years, no earlier than the fifteenth century, was regarded as little better than a myth by the Sasenachs of his own time, in spite of all the hard knocks he gave them . . . Such is the force of fancy among our race that the English succession of the native princes of Wales was established by the lovely Welsh supposition that the son of an English king if born in Wales, was a native prince: and the effect of this has since gone so far that it is no longer necessary for any prince of Wales to be born in his own country. Wales is the only land which can impart this virtue of nativity to an alien and it is purely by the power of her most potent fancy that she does it. She was indeed never conquered by the English, as is known to all but Welshmen. She was captivated by them through her fancy. But her sovereign became Welsh, instead of her becoming English . . . As for some other Welsh fancies, I confess that I like to indulge them, and I feel free to do so because they flatter my pride ethnically and not personally. I like to think of myself the son of a people whose courage is as questionless as their history is blameless: of a race wedded from the first to the love of letters whose saints were scholars and whose princes were poets; whose peaceful rivalries in love and music at the Eisteddfods are immortal memorials of a golden age, in our iron times; and whose national name is a synonym for honesty, industry, sobriety, piety and all the other virtues and, so far as I know, none of the vices . . . Our fancy has kept us first pure and then peaceable in all high ideals: and by force of the rarest imagination in history a certain Welshman whose name I mentioned at the beginning of these maunderings, was inspired in an age of bigotry and cruelty, simply to fancy himself in another man's place and to wish for his neighbor the same freedom he desired for himself. No one but a man of inspired fancy could have done this, and it remained for Roger Williams, so late as the seventeenth century, to imagine that principle of perfect spiritual charity, which none aforetime, holiest saint or wisest sage, had conceived of. With him, with that greatest of all possible Welshmen, a new light came into the world, and men at last perceived

that freedom to worship God meant the freedom of men to worship God, each in his own way, or even not at all.[16]

The passage is primarily light-hearted in tone and intent, but in stating that the Welsh national name is a synonym for "honesty, industry, sobriety, piety and all the other virtues" Howells is explicitly reinforcing the dominant view of Welsh ethnicity which the ruling Welsh bourgeoisie brought with it from Victorian Britain. Howells's speech is also clearly designed to appeal to the ideological values of the Welsh-American elite; not only do the Welsh have a proud nationalist tradition that goes back to the revolts of Owain Glyndŵr against the Sasenach, but, in the figure of the democratic Puritan leader, Roger Williams, they are also amongst the most prophetic and democratic of America's founding fathers. By invoking the name of Roger Williams, Howells testifies to the prevalence of the ideology of Puritan origins in nineteenth-century America (as traced by Sacvan Bercovitch among others), while simultaneously suggesting that it is possible to be American and also "the greatest of all Welshmen."[17] Howells thus seeks to transcend the boundaries defining a distinctive Welsh ethnicity by forging a contributionist narrative in which the historical narrative of Welsh-Americans is fused with the dominant narrative of American expansion.

Howells's fusion of Welsh and American national histories suggests that the construction of a Welsh ethnicity in the United Sates was not wholly a matter of adopting formulas developed in nineteenth-century Wales. The "St. David's Day Address" suggests that ethnic identities in America developed in a complex dialogue with the invention of an American nationalist tradition. The nineteenth century saw considerable energy expended in the invention of a unitary American national identity, with an attendant nationalist history and literary canon. Thanksgiving Day, celebrating the Protestant Anglo-Saxon tradition, and the festivities of the Fourth of July, celebrating the Revolution and the Founding Fathers, were invented traditions designed to imbue the populace with a sense of being part of an identifiable "American" nation.[18] George Bancroft's spirited defense of Jacksonian America in his *History of the United States* (1834) tracked the country's origins back to the Puritan origins famously interrogated in the works of Nathaniel Hawthorne. Ralph Waldo Emerson pronounced Bancroft's book "a noble work," and his call upon artists to take on the challenge of representing America's "ample geography" which "dazzles the imagination" finds its correlative in the Hudson River School of painters, led by Thomas Cole, who found a pantheistic majesty in American landscapes that differentiated them from the historically saturated landscapes of European painting.[19] Marcus Klein argues in *Foreigners* that the creation of an American nationalist ideology, particularly the strategy of elevating the Puritans in the history of national origins, was part of an essentially reactionary defense of Anglo-Saxon, English-speaking norms, against the increasing influx of immigrants into industrializing America.[20] Dale Knobel has traced how Americans began viewing the Irish in ethnic terms in the 1850s, a category which depended on an idea of "Americanness against which the Irish could be defined," and Kathleen Conzen has usefully noted that a significant influence in the shaping of ethnicities was the changing perceptions of the various ethnic groups by the dominant society, and the stereotyping and labeling which ensued.[21] Before proceeding to a discussion of literature written in Welsh, it may therefore be useful to gain a sense of the ways in which the Welsh were perceived by the dominant culture by turning to some of the texts of the Anglo-American tradition.

In Hamlin Garland's "God's Ravens," from his collection of stories *Main Travelled Roads*, described as "a robust and terribly serious" book by Garland's mentor, William Dean Howells, the tensions between the country and a rapidly industrializing city are dramatized when the main protagonist attempts to return to his rural Wisconsin from the dehumanizing landscape of Chicago.[22] He explains his failure to reintegrate with the rural community as follows: "'Life in these coulees goes on rather slower than in Chicago. Then there are a great many Welsh and Germans and Norwegians living way up the coulees, and they're the ones you notice. They're not all so.' He could be generous toward them in general; it was in special cases where he failed to know them."[23] The Welsh, Germans, and Norwegians are singled out as those "you notice," as ethnic others, which is perhaps primarily due to a linguistic difference which Garland's English text is unable to represent and thus ignores. Kathleen Conzen notes that only some immigrants were perceived and judged as what would come to be called ethnic groups: "English immigrants, for example, often exhibited distinctive behaviours, yet generally were not placed within this category. Their foreignness was not problematic in the same way as that of immigrants of other European origins, hence it was not 'seen'; the English had no ethnicity in American eyes."[24] Conzen usefully points out the relation between the observer and the observed in her emphasis on the act of "seeing," an insight which is reinforced by Garland's observation.

The reiterated "look" is inseparable from the documentary strategy of much late nineteenth-century realist and naturalist fiction. Mark Seltzer notes that "the naturalist investment in seeing entails a policing of the real," an insight which is amply demonstrated in Rebecca Harding Davis's early realist novel, *Life in the Iron Mills* (1861).[25] The novel opens with the narrative voice asking the reader: "A cloudy day: do you know what that is in a town of iron-works? . . . I open the window, and, looking out, can scarcely see through the rain the grocer's shop opposite, where a crowd of drunken Irishmen are puffing Lynchburg tobacco in their pipes."[26] The narrator's gaze soon settles on the Wolfe family, whose primary defining feature is their ethnicity:

> The old man, like many of the puddlers and feeders of the mills, was Welsh — had spent half of his life in the Cornish tin-mines. You may pick the Welsh emigrants, Cornish miners, out of the throng passing the windows any day. They are a trifle more filthy; their muscles are not so brawny; they stoop more. When they are drunk, they neither yell, nor shout, nor stagger, but skulk along like beaten hounds. A pure, unmixed blood, I fancy, shows itself in the slight angular bodies and sharply cut facial lines. It is nearly thirty years since the Wolfes lived here. Their lives are like those of their class; incessant labor, sleeping in kennel-like rooms, eating rank pork and molasses, drinking — God and the distillers only know what; with an occasional night in jail to atone for some drunken excess. Is that all of their lives? — of the portion given to them and their duplicates swarming the streets today? — nothing beneath? — all? So many a political reformer has gone among them with a heart tender with Christ's charity, and come out outraged, hardened.[27]

There is a narrative development here from ethnic identity to class, from physical characteristics to the quality of life, with both constituents of

Wolfe's social identity rendered as identifiably "other." In a different context, Raymond Williams noted that Elizabeth Gaskell's pity for her working class subjects could not alone sustain the structure of feeling that informed her novel *Mary Barton,* and was thus joined by a "fear of violence" which led "finally, to a kind of writing off, when the misery of the actual situation can no longer be endured."[28] His observations are equally applicable to Davis's novel, which was greatly influenced by Gaskell's work; the progression from pity to rejection that Williams identifies is inscribed within the passage above. Class and ethnicity are complexly intertwined in the passage, with the Welshmen's drinking and general filthiness seeming as much an ethnic characteristic as their "sharply-cut facial lines." Both class and ethnicity contribute to the political reformer's ultimate "outrage."

Ethnicization — in the sense of evoking a symbolically constitutive sense of "us" in relation to "them" — had already provided a valuable strategy for the Welsh in Britain. The above examples of ethnic stereotyping suggest that the American context imposed its own pressures on the processes of ethnic formulation. The invention of ethnicity, which was not a new strategy for many immigrants, took on new forms under new conditions. William Dean Howells's "St David's Day Address" may thus be regarded as a powerful example of the way in which the Welsh-American bourgeoisie sought to construct an ethnic identity in which Welsh characteristics formed the basis for the model American citizen. The contributionist argument of Howells' address is reinforced by the fact that it is expressed in English, but similar notions were also expressed in Welsh. The following poem, written in 1885 by a poet going by the bardic name of Glanmabddwr, offers an untempered celebration of American glories.

F'EWYRTH SAM

Amerig yw'r wlad wyf yn garu
Mae'r wybren yn glir ac yn iach
Ei dyfroedd grisialaidd estynant
Drugaredd i'r mawr ac i'r bach
Y pleidiau fu gynt yn ymryson,
Gefnogant lywyddiaeth heb gam:

Un doeth yn ei ffyrdd a'i gynlluniau
Bob amser y ce's F'ewyrth Sam.

Nid unwaith cyhoeddodd fy Ewyrth
I'w ddeiliaid y cant gartref rhad;
Mae digon trwy'r De a thrwy'r Gogledd
O diroedd rhagorol y wlad;
Un cant chwe' deg mae yn rhoddi
O erwau i'r tad ac i'r fam;
Mae digon o dir amaethyddol
Ar gyfer holl blant F'ewyrth Sam.

Nid ydyw ein Hewyrth yn gofyn
Ond un dreth y flwyddyn am hyn; .
Mae'n rhanu ei dir yn gyfartal
Yn gartref i'r du ac i'r gwyn.
Dewch fechgyn a merched Amerig,
Cydsyniwch am gartref dinam;
Cewch dyddyn o dir yn gynysgaeth
Ond gofyn yn swyddfa'r hen Sam.

[MY UNCLE SAM

America is the land that I love
The air is clear and healthy;
Its crystalline waters will lend
Mercy to both poor and wealthy.
The parties that once were in conflict
Of its government are united in praise;
Uncle Sam, I've always discovered,
Is wise in his plans and his ways.

Not only once has my Uncle announced
Cheap homes for his tenants aplenty;
Through North and South there's abundant
Fruitful land to be had in this country.
He gives a hundred and sixty acres
To each woman and to each man;

There's enough farmland here to all
The children of my Uncle Sam

Our Uncle asks us no more
Than one yearly payment of tax.
He shares out his land equally
A home for both whites and for blacks.
Come lads and lasses of America
Let's sing to a home clean and prim
He'll endow you a farm at his office;
If you approach old Sam and ask him.][29]

This celebration of American virtues significantly contains no mention of Wales. Welsh ethnic identity is thus not constructed in opposition to an American identity but is actually subsumed by it. "F'ewyrth" means "my uncle," thus the title itself establishes a connection between the Welsh-American poet and the symbolic representative of his adopted country. This connection is reinforced in the final reference to "hen Sam" / "old Sam," for "hen" is often used as a term of endearment in Welsh. The emphasis on "my uncle" is significant for, to use Werner Sollors's terms, a narrative of consent — the adoption of the United States as one's nation — is inscribed within a narrative of descent, where the kinship between poet and Uncle Sam forms the basis of national identity.[30] This tension between strategies of consent and descent in the poem is mirrored, and reinforced, by the tension created between the poem's assimilationist rhetoric and the fact that it is written in Welsh. While the language creates an inevitable boundary between the poet and the dominant Anglo-American culture, the poem's narrative seeks to dissolve that boundary in its celebration of America as the nation where divisions between political parties, the poor and wealthy, north and south, black and white, will cease to exist.

The fact that this espousal of an inclusive American national identity is expressed through the medium of Welsh suggests that the poet, Glanmabddwr, believed in the concept of a multilingual America. He sees no contradiction in celebrating American unity through the medium of Welsh. Writing six years later, another poet, Gwyngyll, cannot share this optimism:

Y GYMRAEG

Chwi Gymry iaith-garol ymunwch yn llu,
I gadw'r hen iaith fendigedig,
Rhag cwympo yn farw I fedd angof du,
Ym mynwent hen ieithoedd methedig.

Hon ydoedd iaith Adda yn Eden, pwy wad?
Iaith gyntaf barablodd ei dafod;
Drwy hon y cyflwynai ein parchus hen dad
Gyfrinion ei fynwes i'w briod.

Hon ydoedd iaith anwyl fy nhaid a fy nain,
Fy nhad a fy mam a'i parablent;
Mewn mawl cysegredig, mor swynol ei sain,
Duw eu cyndadiau addolent.

Mae adar bach Cymru yn canu Cymraeg,
Yn sibrwd Cymraeg hefo'u gilydd;
Y ffrydiau grisialog sisialent yr aeg,
A sibrwd Cymraeg wna y coedydd.

. . . . .

Os trenga'n hen iaith a newidio ei gwedd,
O cladder hi'n barchus, mae'n haeddu;
Argraffer yn eglur ar garreg ei bedd:
"Fan yma mae hen iaith y Cymry."

Wrth ochr fy mam iaith, O torwch i'm fedd,
Neu doder ni'n dau mewn un beddrod;
O boed i'm gael marw, a huno mewn hedd,
Tra Cymraeg floesg sibrwd fy nhafod.

[THE WELSH LANGUAGE

You language-loving Welshmen, come to save
Your beautiful language so old
From falling into a dark forgotten grave
Of tongues whose words are never told.

Adam's words were Welsh — to deny who'd dare
The first language of the first life;
And in Eden his innermost secrets he'd share
Whispered in Welsh with his wife.

This dear language my Grandpa and Grandma would utter
And my parents Welsh words would they cast;
In a heavenly worship how melodious her sound
In worshipping the God of the past.

The small birds of Wales do their singing in Welsh
All whispering Welsh with each other;
The crystalline waters mutter her sounds,
And the trees in Welsh do they whisper.

. . . . .

If our language ever changes and dies
It deserves a respectful marker — To attest
To its greatness written clearly on the place it lies
"Here the old language of the Welsh does rest."

Next to my mother-tongue dig me a grave when I cease
Or put us in one tomb together;
Oh, let me die, and then rest in peace
While Welsh words my tongue can still whisper.][31]

Here, ethnic identity is inextricably linked to linguistic identity; the poet even equates the language's demise with his own death. The poem may be read as the antithesis to "F'ewyrth Sam." The latter contained no reference to Wales; "Y Gymraeg" contains no reference to the United States; "F'ewyrth Sam" sought to transcend ethnic, gender, and racial boundaries; "Y Gymraeg" calls on Welshmen who love their language to preserve their linguistic difference. "Y Gymraeg" develops narratively from the Garden of Eden to Welsh pastoral scenes where the animals converse in Welsh to scenes of Welsh domesticity where the emphasis is on the cleanliness, religiosity, and purity that were the invented characteristics of Victorian Welshness. The poet's celebration of "the ancient language" ends, however, on a profoundly fatalistic note in the final two stanzas; the image of the language's tombstone and the poet's own death suggests that there is no hope for the preservation of Welsh identity in America.

The poem is one of many written in the 1890s lamenting language decline and raising key questions with regards to the politics of identity.[32] "Y Gymraeg" suggests that once the Welsh-speakers stop speaking Welsh, then their identity will be lost, the people will not have survived. The poet asks that the words "Here the ancient language of the Welsh does rest" be put on the gravestone, thus equating "the Welsh people" with "the Welsh language." But what exactly was lost when Welsh-Americans stopped transmitting the language? Why would people whose parents spoke Welsh, but who speak English themselves, think they have lost their identity? This is a question of equal relevance to contemporary Wales, where, according to the 1991 census, the number of Welsh speakers is now at an all-time low of 18.6 percent of the population.[33] The point is that without some way of explaining how what people used to do but no longer do constitutes their real identity, while what they now do does not, it cannot be said that what the English-speaking generation has lost is "identity." This is not to say that nothing of value is lost, but that identity is never lost; it is transformed.

Indeed, there were already significant transformations taking place on the ground in Wales and Welsh America that challenged the image of all-embracing Welsh respectability that community leaders on both sides of the Atlantic strove to emphasize in their actions and words. The industrialization of Wales is a complex story. Suffice here to note that between 1851 and 1914 the population of Wales increased from 1,163,139 to 2,523,500; an increase of 117 percent.[34] Between 1861 and 1911, because of the explosive growth of the coal industry, the population of the county of Glamorgan in south Wales grew by 253 percent. The Rhondda Valley in 1851 housed under 1,000 people, by 1911 it had over 150,000 and was still growing. Most important, between 1801 and 1901 the population of the counties of Glamorgan and Monmouthshire in relation to all other Welsh counties changed from a ratio of 1 to 4, to 3 to 1.[35] Into industrial Wales poured anything from two-thirds to three-quarters of the existing Welsh population. This phenomenon, as Brinley Thomas noted, explains the relatively small number of Welshmen who emigrated to the United States in comparison with the other British nations.[36] This phenomenon also carries a wider international significance, for during the decade just before the First World War, Wales was the only country outside the United States to register a plus in the immigration tables. In that decade something in the region of 130,000 people flooded into the coal fields of south Wales; from Scotland, England, and also Ireland, Spain, and Italy. With an immigration rate of 45 per 10,000, Wales ranked second to the United States itself as a world center for immigration.[37]

From the late nineteenth century, then, a new culture emerged in south Wales. European in intellectual content, American in its supplementary reading (primarily in English), it led many to conclude that Wales had become two nations: a rural, Welsh-speaking north, and an industrial, anglicized south.[38] While such simplifications are as distorting as they are illuminating, neglecting as they do the complex interrelation between residual and emergent forces within the dominant social formation, it is significant that the sociologist Alfred Zimmern, visiting Wales in the early 1920s, suggested that "The Wales of today is not a unity. There is not one Wales; there are three . . . There is Welsh Wales; there is industrial or, as I sometimes think of it, American Wales; and there is upper class or English Wales. These three represent different types and different traditions. They are moving in different directions and, if they all three survive, they are not likely to re-unite."[39] While a residual Welsh-speaking working-class culture remained active within the dominant society, the communities of south Wales were increasingly perceived as, in the words of the novelist Gwyn Thomas, "the parts of America that never managed to get the boat."[40] South Wales, to quote Thomas again, was the place "where the Mississippi and Taff kiss with dark lubricity under an ashen hood of years," a place of considerable ethnic, linguistic, and cultural diversity, and much to the consternation of the Welsh bourgeois elite, an alternative concept of Welshness was being constructed there, aligned to radical politics, civil disobedience, and a vibrant popular culture.[41] The predicament of working people in Wales during the late nineteenth and early twentieth centuries reflected that of working people in industrializing America.

If the Welsh immigrants brought their chapels, religion, and cultural festivals — the Eisteddfodau — to America, they also brought with them aspects of the culture of an industrial society which equally gave meaning and identity to their lives. As early as July 1870 one "Huw o'r Ddol" asked in the *Drych*, with regards to a Welsh area in Scranton, Pennsylvania; "Ond beth am foesau Hyde Park? Ar lawer cyfrif y mae yn ail i Sodom, ac yn gyffelyb i Gomorah." ("But what of the morals of Hyde Park? In many respects they are second to those of Sodom, and the equal of Gomorrah.") He was in no doubt as to whom was to blame for this state of affairs: "Pwy sy'n euog am hyn? Cymru a Chymraesau Tredegar, Rhymni, Dowlais, Merthyr, Aberdar etc., y rhai nad ydynt newydd ddyfod oddi yno, neu o fewn y ddwy flynedd ddiwethaf. Mae *scum* gweithfeydd Cymru wedi eu shipio i Hyde Park yn y blynyddoedd diwethaf." ("Who's to blame for this? Welshmen and Welshwomen from Tredegar, Rhymney, Dowlais, Merthyr, Aberdare etc., those that have recently arrived, or who have come within the last two years. The scum of the works of Wales has been shipped to Hyde Park in recent years.") With characteristic religious rhetoric he noted that "Mae y saloons Cymraeg yma cyn amled a llyffaint yr Aipht . . . Cewch weled meibion a merched, gwyr a gwragedd, blith draphlith, a'u haner yn haner meddw, yn ffwlio a potio, ac yn canu Cymraeg." ("Welsh saloons here are as numerous as the frogs of Egypt. You can see sons and daughters, husbands and wives, lying around, forever half drunk, fooling and singing in Welsh.")[42] The product of an increasingly "American" Wales was upsetting "Welsh" America.

Along with the popular culture of industrial Wales, the immigrants also brought a fairly advanced notion of class consciousness which could form the basis for an alternative definition of Welsh ethnicity.[43] The following poem represents a powerful call for Welsh unionization.

P'LE MAE'R UNION, CHWARLEWYR

P'le mae'r Union, bobol anwyl
Ym mhle gebyst mae y drwg?
P'le mae dewrder meib y creigiau,
A raid i ni ofni gwg?
Byddin arfog gref gormesiaeth,
Byddin golud, trais a ffawd,

A'u mangelau poethion saethant
Drwy galonau gweithwyr tlawd!

. . . . .

Oes mae'i eisiau, meddai llyfrau
Duon shopwyr Talaeth York;
Anhawdd dal i weithio'n galed
Tra yn bwyta sych a phorc;
Mêr yr esgyrn lifa allan
O dan wres yr haul drwy'r cnawl;
Pwy a ddylai gael danteithion
Cryfion, ond y gweithiwr tlawd?

Oes mae'i eisiau, dewch chwarelwyr
Dewr Americ o un fryd,
Pa'm y rhaid i ni fod isaf
O bob dosbarth yn y byd?
P'le mae'r annibyniaeth hwnnw
Gawsom gan ein Hewyrth Sam.
Fudodd hwnnw o'n calonau
Nôl i Gymru, rhag cael cam?

Son am lwfdra pobl Bethesda,
'N cario cynffon Lord y Plas,
Blinodd rheiny ar ffieidd-dra
Yr hen oruchwyliaeth gas;
Ond chwarelwyr gwlad Jonathon,
Gwlad y rhyddid mwyaf gaed!
Ynt yn ofni cysgod boses
Bychain — llyfant wadnau'i traed.

. . . . .

Holl chwarelwyr y Gorllewin,
O Virginia boeth i Maine,
Ymfyddinwn o dan faner
Wen yr Undeb, a chawn wên

Duw y nefoedd — nes gorchfygu
Byddin gormes — er ein ffawd-
Llid y nefoedd sy'n enynu
'N fflam ar elyn dyn tylawd.

[WHERE'S THE UNION, QUARRYMEN?

Where's the Union, dear people,
Where is evil's threat?
Where's the bravery of the rockface's sons,
Does retribution make us fret?
Powerful armed forces of exploitation
The force of progress, harm and fate,
With heated weapons they aim and fire,
Through workers hearts so desolate.

Yes, we need one, say the Black Books
Of workers from the state of York,
It's difficult to keep working hard
On only dried bread and pork
The worker's marrow turns to liquid
The sun's heat beating through skull bone;
Who should have the tastiest dishes
Shouldn't the worker take them home?

Yes we need one, come Quarrymen
The brave of America should unite,
Of all the classes in the world
Why should we be the lowest, quite?
Where's that famous independence
That we got from Uncle Sam,
Has that migrated from our hearts
Back to Wales, afraid of harm?

Talk of the cowards of Bethesda,
Always at his Lordship's side,
They got tired of the evil

Overlordship, found their pride.
But quarrymen of the land of Jonathon
Where the greatest freedom men did meet!
They're afraid of their bosses shadows
Licking soles of small Master's feet.

Western Quarrymen, listen to me,
From hot Virginia up to Maine,
Let's unite under Union's white banner
And put an end to our needless shame.
The God of heaven will smile upon us
As we fight the force of greed,
The anger of heaven, despite our fate,
Will burn the enemy of men in need.][44]

Here ethnicity is fundamentally linked with class. As was the case in "F'ewyrth Sam," it is American ethnic identity that is emphasized, with America in this case being compared unfavorably to the activism of the workers of Bethesda, north Wales. The dream of American freedom is contrasted with the reality of human exploitation, and the poet wonders if the ideals of the American Constitution have fled from the American workers' hearts back to their homeland. The final stanza calls on American quarrymen to unite in the struggle against "gormesiaeth" / "exploitation." Rather than espouse a narrowly defined concept of Welshness based on language or religion, this poem advocates a common working class identity in America. It is surely significant that the Welsh language was believed to be a suitable vehicle for such a message. A school of revisionist historians in Wales have used America as a model in arguing that the demise of the Welsh language in south Wales was inevitable, the result of individual choices in a culture which was turning more democratic as it severed the "ties of custom, traditions, religion, language and deference."[45] Such a view clearly pays no attention to the interplay of residual and emergent forces within the dominant culture. To be sure, there is little doubt that large numbers of the Welsh in Wales and America were eager to trade their seemingly outmoded language for that of modernity and progress.

Yet it should be noted that this democratic choice, on both sides of the ocean, took place within a context in which public and commercial aspects of life were firmly reinforcing the increasing dominance of English. "P'le Mae'r Union Chwarlewyr" is significant in that it suggests that the Welsh language could indeed be the vehicle for democratic aspirations, for communicating constructions of Welshness other than those invented by the dominant cultural elite.

CONCLUSION

The three Welsh language poems discussed above offer quite different bases for the construction of a Welsh-American identity; assimilation, language, and class, respectively. They suggest that Welsh-American identity developed from many roots and was a plural experience. The words of the Trinidadian Marxist, C. L. R. James, may be of particular relevance here: "Now one of the chief errors of thought is to continue to think in one set of forms, categories, ideas, etc., when the object, the content, has moved on, has created or laid premises for an extension, a development of thought."[46] Welsh-American literature of the nineteenth century needs to be read beyond the "forms, categories, ideas" of familiar national histories. Although the Welsh brought with them an idea of Welshness based on the Victorian notion of the peacefulness, thrift, and purity found in Wales, the American setting exerted its own set of pressures resulting in the continual recreation and re-invention of the dominant model of Welsh identity. The story of the Welsh in America represents a crucial chapter in the history of discontinuities and radical shifts that Raymond Williams believed characterized Welsh culture.[47] An analysis of their literature yields an insight into the essential instability and mutability of ethnic identities, for the Victorian ideal of Welshness coexisted with other emergent conceptions of identity produced by the forces of industrialization and immigration. If, as Paul Gilroy suggests, an "Atlantic" perspective may allow us to transcend the "moribund categories of merely national history," then it is surely significant that this reconstruction of identity was taking place on both sides of the "Welsh Atlantic."[48]

Notes

Hoffwn gyflwyno'r erthygl yma i'r Dr. Eirug Davies, am ei gyfeillgarwch yn ystod fy mlynyddoedd yn yr Unol Daleithiau, ac am ei ymchwil a'i ddiddordeb ym myd y Cymry yn America. Daw'r cerddi yr wyf yn eu trafod yma o'i gasgliad yntau. Diolch i Sioned Jones hefyd am ei chymorth gyda'r cyfieithu.

1. Paul Gilroy, "Nationalism, History and Ethnic Absolutism," *History Workshop Journal* 30 (1990):116.

    Reprinted in Gilroy, *Small Acts* (London: Serpent's Tail, 1993), pp. 63–73. My title is a variation on the theme of Gilroy's *Black Atlantic; Modernity and Double Consciousness* (Cambridge, Mass.: Harvard University Press, 1993).

2. Most notable in historical studies have been the late Gwyn A. Williams's *When Was Wales?* (London: Penguin, 1985) and *The Welsh in Their History* (Beckenham: Croom Helm, 1985). The latter volume contains the article "Imperial South Wales" which has direct relevance to my subject here, and has been central to the development of my ideas on Welsh America. In literary criticism, M. Wynn Thomas studies questions of national identity in his *Internal Difference; Literature in Twentieth-Century Wales* (Cardiff: University of Wales Press, 1992); see also the theoretically less sophisticated but equally illuminating Tony Conran, *Frontiers in Anglo-Welsh Poetry* (Cardiff: University of Wales Press, 1997).

3. Dai Smith, *Wales! Wales?* (London: Allen and Unwin, 1984) and *Aneurin Bevan and the World of South Wales* (Cardiff: University of Wales Press, 1993). Dai Smith's controversial works are amongst the most important and influential productions of recent Welsh historiography. Tim Williams, "The Anglicisation of South Wales," in *Patriotism; The Making and Unmaking of British National Identity.* Vol. 2: *Minorities and Outsiders,* ed. Raphael Samuel (London: Routledge, 1989), pp. 193–203.

4. The term "imagined community" comes for Benedict Anderson's seminal *Imagined Communities; Reflections on the Origin and Spread of Nationalism* (London: Verso, 1983). For revisions of Anderson's thesis see the articles by Gopal Balakrishnan and Partha Chatterjee in *Mapping the Nation*, Balakrishnan, ed. (London: Verso, 1996).

5. Raymond Williams, "Wales and England," in *What I Came to Say* (London: Hutchinson, 1989), p. 68

6. Noted by Gwyn A. Williams, *The Welsh in Their History*, p. 171.

7. Raymond Williams, *Marxism and Literature* (1977; Oxford: Oxford University Press, 1989), p. 122.

8. For an account of the symbolic construction of "Welshness" see Prys Margan's chapter "From Death to a View: The Hunt for the Welsh Past in the Romantic Period," in *The Invention of Tradition,* ed. Hobsbawm and Ranger (Cambridge: Cambridge University Press, 1983), pp. 43–100. On constructions of America see Sacvan Bercovitch, *The Rites of Assent: Transformations in the Symbolic Construction of America* (New York: Routledge, 1993).

9. *Y Drych* first made its appearance on January 2, 1851, and is still going today. Throughout the nineteenth century it was wholly in the Welsh language. It became bilingual in the 1920s and wholly English from the 1940s onwards. See E. G. Hartmann, *Americans from Wales* (Boston: Christopher Publishing House, 1967), pp. 127–38, and (since the completion of this essay) Aled Jones and Bill Jones, *Welsh Reflections; 'Y Drych' and America 1851–2001* (Llandysul: Gomer Press, 2001).

10. The following section on the nineteenth-century history of Wales is largely a synthesis of many sources. Of particular relevance in English are Smith's *Wales! Wales?,* Gwyn Williams's *The Welsh in Their History,* particularly chaps. 6–8, and Ieuan Gwynedd Jones's *Communities; Essays in the Social History of Victorian Wales* (Llandysul: Gomer, 1987). Also John Davies's magisterial *A History of Wales* (London: Penguin, 1993), chap. 8. In Welsh, I am greatly indebted to the work of Hywel Teifi Edwards, particularly *Gwyl Gwalia: yr Eisteddfod Genedlaethol yn Oes Aur Victoria* (Llandysul: Gomer, 1980), *Codi'r Hen Wlad yn ei Hol 1850–1914* (Llandysul: Gomer, 1989), and *Eisteddfod Ffair y Byd, Chicago 1893* (Llandusul: Gomer, 1990). Hywel Teifi Edwards, Ieuan Gwynedd Jones, and Prys Morgan have emphasized the central importance of the Royal Commission into the State of Education in Wales in the history of the nineteenth century.

11. Quoted in Prys Morgan, ed., *Brad y Llyfrau Gleision* (Llandysul: Gomer, 1991), p. 26. For an account of the emergence of working-class activism in Wales, see Gwyn A. Williams, *The Merthyr Rising* (1978; Cardiff: University of Wales Press, 1988).

12. John Davies recounts this story in his *History of Wales,* p. 391.

13. Hywel Teifi Edwards offers reams of examples of this process in *Gwyl Gwalia* and *Codi'r Hen Wlad yn ei Hol.*

14. For a comparative account of the invention of ethnicity in the United States, see *The Invention of Ethnicity,* ed. Werner Sollors (Oxford: Oxford University Press, 1989).

15. Among the published surveys on the history of the Welsh in America, the most recent and penetrating account is William D. Jones, *Wales in America: Scranton and the Welsh 1860–1920* (Cardiff: University of Wales Press, 1993). See also earlier analyses by Rowland T. Berthoff, "The Welsh," in *Harvard*

Encyclopaedia of American Ethnic Groups, ed. Stephan Thernstrom (Cambridge, Mass.: Harvard University Press, 1980), pp. 1011–17; Alan Conway, ed., *The Welsh in America* (Cardiff: University of Wales Press, 1961), a selection of letters written by Welsh Americans, all translated by Conway, but without the Welsh originals; Hartmann, *Americans from Wales;* Maldwyn A. Jones, "From the Old Country to the New: The Welsh in Nineteenth-Century America," in *Flintshire Historical Society Publications* 27 (1975–76):85–100; David Williams, *Cymru ac America: Wales and America* (Cardiff: University of Wales Press, 1946); Glanmor Williams, "A Prospect of Paradise?" in his *Religion, Language and Nationality in Wales* (Cardiff: University of Wales Press, 1979), pp. 217–36.

16. William Dean Howells, "Wales: The Native Land of Fancy," an address delivered at the St. David's Banquet, New York, March 1, 1895, and published in *The Cambrian* (April 1895):106–108. *The Cambrian* was a Welsh-American journal published in English, and made its first appearance in January 1880. It lasted until 1919, and, as E. G. Hartmann notes, "is one of the most important sources of information concerning the activities of the Welsh in America during the period 1880–1919."

 Howells speaks of his Welsh ancestry in his autobiographical *Years of my Youth* (1916), and *A Boy's Town* (1890).

17. Sacvan Bercovitch, *The Puritan Origins of the American Self* (New Haven: Yale University Press, 1975).

 Roger Williams (1603–83), excommunicated and exiled to Rhode Island for his heretical beliefs, was among the first to show a degree of sympathy toward the Native Americans. He made an effort to live "with them in their smoky holes . . . to gain their tongue," efforts which resulted in *A Key into the Language of America* (1643). Several Welsh poems of the nineteenth century are dedicated to Roger Williams and, like Howells's "St David's Day Address," they seek to merge the narrative history of the Welsh nation with that of the United States. See especially A. Jones, "Roger Williams, Y Puritan," *Y Drych,* 10 April 1891, and Jonathan Lewis, "Roger Williams," *Y Drych,* 13 March 1891.

18. Eric Hobsbawm, "Mass-Producing Traditions: Europe, 1870–1914," in *The Invention of Tradition,* pp. 279–80.

19. On Bancroft see Sacvan Bercovitch's "Continuing Revolution: George Bancroft and the Myth of Process" in his *The Rites of Assent.* For the role of artists and painters in the creation of a national aesthetic, see Albert Gelpi, "White Light in the Wilderness," in *American Light: The Luminist Movement 1850–1875,* ed. John Wilmerding (Princeton: Princeton University Press, 1989).

20. Marcus Klein, *Foreigners: The Making of American Literature* (Chicago: University of Chicago Press, 1981).

21. Dale T. Knobel, *Paddy and the Republic: Ethnicity and Nationality in Antebellum America* (Middleton, Conn.: Wesleyan University Press, 1986). Kathleen Neils

Conzen, David A. Gerber, Ewa Morawska, George E. Pozzetta, and Rudolph J. Vecoli, "The Invention of Ethnicity: A Perspective from the USA," in *Journal of American Ethnic History* (Fall 1992):12.

22. Hamlin Garland, *Main Travelled Roads* (1891; New York: Signet, 1961), p. 104. Howells wrote of Garland in his "The Editor's Study," *Harper's Monthly*, Sept. 1891. Reprinted in Edward H. Cady, ed., *W. D. Howells as Critic* (London: Rotledge, 1973), p. 202.

23. Garland, *Main Travelled Roads*, p. 104.

24. Conzen et al., "Invention of Ethnicity," p. 7.

25. Mark Seltzer, *Bodies and Machines* (London: Routledge, 1991), p. 96.

26. Rebecca Harding Davis, *Life in the Iron Mills*, in *The Heath Anthology of American Literature*, vol. 2, ed. Paul Lauter (Lexington: D. C. Heath, 1994), p. 43.

27. Ibid., pp. 45–46.

28. Raymond Williams, *Culture and Society* (1958; reprint London; Hogarth Press, 1992), p. 91.

29. Glanmabddwr, "F'ewyrth Sam" in *Y Drych*, 31 Dec. 1885, p. 3. The poet lived in Sir Park, Colorado.

30. Werner Sollors, *Beyond Ethnicity: Consent and Descent in American Culture* (New York: Oxford University Press, 1986).

31. Gwyngyll, "Y Gymraeg," *Y Drych*, 24 Dec. 1891. p. 3. Gwyngyll lived in Lake Crystal, Minnesota.

32. Other notable examples are "A Yw'r Gymraeg yn Marw" / "Is the Welsh Language Dying?," *Y Drych*, 16 Jan. 1896, p. 3 and "O Rhowch I Mi Bregeth Gymraeg" / "Oh, Give Me a Sermon in Welsh," *Y Drych*, 28 May 1896, p. 1. In these poems ethnicity is based on language, while the language itself relies on religion for its existence.

33. John Aitchison and Harold Carter, *A Geography of the Welsh Language 1961–1991* (Cardiff: University of Wales Press, 1994), p. 88. For an account of the Welsh language's decline in the twentieth century see Mari C. Jones, *Language Obsolescence and Revitalization* (Oxford: Oxford University Press, 1998), and *"Let's Do Our Best for the Ancient Tongue": The Welsh Language in the Twentieth Century*, ed. Geraint Jenkins and Mari A. Williams (Cardiff: University of Wales Press, 2000).

34. John Davies, *A History of Wales*, p. 398.

35. Quoted in T. Williams, "The Anglicisation," p. 195. See also Gwyn A. Williams, "Mother Wales, Get Off Me Back," in *Marxism Today*, Dec. 1981, pp. 14–20.

36. Brinley Thomas, "Wales and the Atlantic Economy," in *The Welsh Economy; Studies in Expansion*, ed. B. Thomas (Cardiff: University of Wales Press, 1962).

The implications of Thomas's work are explored by Gwyn A. Williams in "Imperial South Wales," in *The Welsh in Their History*.

37. Gwyn A. Williams, *When Was Wales?* and *The Welsh in Their History*, p. 177. For complementary accounts of Welsh industrialization see Dai Smith, "Transforming Wales" in *Wales! Wales?* and John Williams, *Was Wales Industrialised? Essays in Modern Welsh History* (Llandysul: Gomer Press, 1995).

38. The historian of this "split" has been Dai Smith. Gwyn A. Williams's work represents a committed attempt to create unity and celebrate diversity at the same time. His warning to the revisionists remains relevant, and problematic, today: "If you reject the concept of Wales as a valid historical concept, then you free yourself from Wales to become the slave of some other, equally non-rational concept." "Are Welsh Historians Putting on the Style," *Planet; The Welsh Internationalist* 68 (April–May 1988):30.

39. Alfred E. Zimmern, *My Impressions of Wales* (London, 1921), quoted by Dai Smith in *Aneurin Bevan and the World of South Wales*, p. i.

40. Quoted in Smith, *Wales! Wales?*, p. 152.

41. Gwyn Thomas, *A Few Selected Exits* (reprint Bridgend: Seren, 1987), p. 103.

42. Huw o'r Ddol, "Scranton — Y Ddinas Fawr, a Hyde Park" / "Scranton — the Big City, and Hyde Park," *Y Drych*, 28 July 1870, p. 235. This passage was drawn to my attention by William D. Jones in his *Wales in America*, p. 204.

43. The most historically fascinating expression of this class consciousness was the Scranton miners' strike of 1871. See William D. Jones in chap. 2 of his *Wales in America*.

44. Ifor Wyn, "P'le Mae'r Union Chwarelwyr?", *Y Drych*, 1 July 1875, p. 211. Another notable poem of proletarian protest is J. S. Jones's "Paid Gorthrymu'r Gweithiwr" / "Don't Exploit the Workers" in *Y Drych*, 11 March 1875.

45. Dai Smith, *Wales! Wales?*, p. 27. This is most especially the case in the writings of Tim Williams.

46. C. L. R. James, *Notes on Dialectics* (London: Alison and Busby, 1980), p. 15.

47. Raymond Williams's most important writings on Wales are "Wales and England" and "Commmunity" in *What I Came To Say*, and "Welsh Culture," "The Importance of Community," and "Decentralism and the Politics of Place" in *Resources of Hope* (London: Verso, 1989). I am currently completing an edition of Williams's writings on Wales to be published by the University of Wales Press.

48. Paul Gilroy, *The Black Atlantic*, and "Nationalism, History and Ethnic Absolutism," *History Workshop Journal* 30 (Autumn 1990):119.

CHAPTER NINETEEN

Carved on the Walls: The Archaeology and Canonization of the Angel Island Chinese Poems

■ TE-HSING SHAN

Island: Poetry and History of Chinese Immigrants on Angel Island, 1910–1940 can be rightly called a work of reclamation.[1] Compiled by three descendants of the Angel Island Chinese immigrants, Him Mark Lai, Genny Lim, and Judy Yung, this is the most comprehensive collection of the poems carved on the walls of the detention camp on Angel Island by the Chinese immigrants on their way to San Francisco or to be deported back to China. Falling into oblivion after this camp closed in 1940, these poems first came to the notice of park ranger Alexander Weiss in 1970 but received no attention from his superiors. It was through the concerted effort of the Asian-American community that this building was preserved in 1976 as a living monument in the history of these immigrants. Angel Island has thus become a "site of memory" where meanings can be constantly invested and contested, especially from the subject position of Chinese-Americans.[2] The publication of the poems in an English-Chinese bilingual format in 1980 at last reveals to a wider audience the inner world of the suffering Chinese detainees: "the canonical Chinese American experience of the period."[3]

In the context of U.S. history, Werner Sollors pinpoints Plymouth Rock, Jamestown, and Ellis Island as three such sites of memory, citing the latter two as "in different fashions, symbolic alternatives to the narrow interpretation of America as *Mayflower*-descended, yet alternatives that — even though they were both 'thresholds' — could also exclude each other."[4] Sollors mentions in passing, among others, Angel Island and Chinese-

369

American literature. Focusing on *Island* poetry, this essay has as one of its main purposes to bring Angel Island into this wider context of American immigrant history and to conceive these poetic inscriptions "relationally . . . in terms of [their] competitive, reinforcing, and determining relations with other objects and cultural forces."[5]

Taken as a whole, the *Island* collection is significant on several levels. First, these sad, angry, and bitter poems by Chinese immigrants who had some training in classical Chinese literature seek to express their deep feelings of anticipation, frustration, discrimination, and maltreatment at the very threshold of *chiu-chin-shan* (San Francisco or, literally, "Old Gold Mountain"). Second, the very anonymity of these poems, while creating a sense of collectivity among the detainees, reflects their authors' fear that this vent of anger, the feeling of uncertainty about their own fate, and the strong sense of injustice might put them in an unfavorable and even perilous situation, as they await the decision of the immigrant officials. Third, the fact that these poems are all written by men is evidence of the traditional Chinese patriarchy and its educational practice.[6] Fourth, though without identifiable authorship, these poems are dialogical in nature not only because these anonymous writers deal with similar themes — some even echo each other, following the convention of classical Chinese poetry — but also because these poets, through the literary and historical allusions in the poems, identify with ancient Chinese heroes who persevered in hard times and were finally able to gain fame and fortune for themselves and their posterity, and sometimes even to revenge themselves against their enemies. Fifth, these poems collectively speak about the Chinese diaspora at a particular historical moment in Chinese, Asian, and American histories, and, in serving as important founding texts of Chinese-American history/literature, they offer an alternative to American (literary) history.[7] Finally, publication of these memories of bygone days is oriented not only toward the past, even though the collection is "Dedicated to the Pioneers / Who Passed Through Angel Island" — *ching-yang ch'ien-hsien* (literally, "Paying homage to former sages"). It is not even restricted to the present, but also looks toward the future, "making this collection available to posterity."[8]

Rather than simply gather the poems in a collection, the editors/transla-tors aim at something more profound by presenting a bilingual, polyvocal, and photo-verbal text. By putting the "Chinese 'original'" (which is already the result of an assiduous textual study of the inscriptions on the wall and other earlier transcriptions) alongside of the English translation, and fur-nishing the historical and literary contexts whenever necessary, the editors endeavor to render these poems as faithfully as possible and, by so doing, implicitly claim their fidelity to the Chinese original and the authenticity of their work. This collection of poems not only appeals to the monolingual Chinese or English readers, but also provides to its bilingual readers a chance to judge the translatability or untranslatability of the poems by means of its typographical arrangement.

Further contributing to the multiple voices of this bilingual text are the editors' introduction, annotations on the poetic texts, and various inter-views with detainees, interpreters, immigrant inspectors, social workers, and other relevant persons at that time. The interviews, as recovered mem-ories, serve to situate these poetic expressions in their proper historical moment by advancing different perspectives from various persons in-volved; they are categorized under five headings and appear at the end of each group of poems. This grounding or embedding of the poems provides different voices and rounds out the situation of these detainees and their relationship to others.[9]

In addition, the book contains twenty-two photographs that help to authenticate the editors' arguments and arrangements in a graphic way. Generally speaking, these photographs flesh out the texts — the editors' in-troduction, the English and Chinese literary texts, annotations, and inter-views. The cover design of the book, emphasizing the photographic pre-sentation of the original Chinese poetic texts, testifies to this intention. The photographic evidence, like the various texts, is also subject to various analyses. Although "a picture is worth a thousand words," it can sometimes undermine the text it is intended to substantiate.[10]

When thirteen out of the 135 pieces in this collection (excluding the paired prose entitled "Imprisonment in the Wooden Building") were in-cluded in *The Heath Anthology of American Literature* ten years later with an introduction by the same three editors, this adoption enacted the problematics of trans-linguistic, cross-cultural representation.[11]

In "On Linguistic Aspects of Translation," Roman Jakobson stresses the untranslatability of poetry. To him, the English translation (or failure to translate adequately) of the famous Italian aphorism *traduttore, traditore* (translator, traitor) exemplifies the untranslatability of poetry.[12] Given that a total translation of the phonetic, semantic, and cultural aspects of one language into another is unattainable, the translator has to choose among a number of alternatives and to be held accountable for the choice. What complicates the situation is that while translation is bound to lose something of the source language (such as phonetic similarities, semantic exactness, poetic forms, and cultural associations in the original context), it also generates something new and perhaps wholly unexpected in the context of the target language. In other words, the performative effect of translation in another linguistic and cultural context should not be easily dismissed.[13]

So far as the *Island* poems are concerned, the translators were very clearsighted about the great difficulties they faced. The three-paragraph "Translators' Note" addresses the issues of linguistic difference, poetic translation, and transliteration. A scrutiny of these poems shows that besides English, they contain Cantonese vernacular, Chinese-American colloquialisms, standard Chinese, and classical Chinese.

The translators also had to make choices in dealing with poetic forms. They are unequivocal about the concessions they made when faced with the choice between the fidelity to the form and that to the content:

> The act of interpretation itself implies creation and the reader should bear in mind that the process of poetic translation must involve a certain compromise. While these poems express the thoughts of the individuals who wrote them, they are not reiterations of their original literal forms. The form is oftentimes compromised in order to retain the content, which we for historic reasons feel is our first priority. We do not claim adherence to the poets' original meters or rhyme-schemes. By imitating the poetic structure, we feel an injustice to the meaning of the poem would have been committed.[14]

In other words, fidelity to content is gained at the expense of the rhythm and rhyme scheme. Even the easiest part of the poetic form — the line division — is not always maintained (for instance, A4, A14, A55, and A65). Consequently, although classical Chinese poetry has had, for more than a thousand years, a very refined and strict set of regulations which these detainee poets try to follow, the translators chose to put their emphasis on the content. As a matter of fact, this is the general practice of translating classical Chinese poetry into English.

In addition to the reasons or rationales which the editors-cum-translators stated, the choice not to adhere strictly to the original poetic forms can also be justified by the assumption that some of these anonymous writers probably had only rudimentary training in Chinese poetry and literature and composed these poems with no rhyme-books in hand.[15] In view of sometimes loose construction, empty words, forced imagery, violation of the rhythm, cadence, and rhyme scheme, or even incompleteness, these poems cannot claim to meet the formal requirements of classical Chinese poetry and the literary standard of the language. Nor can the free-verse rendition of these poems, with their "exotic" allusions, boast high aesthetic value according to the criteria of English poetry. Similar to the immigrant authors of *Songs of Gold Mountain,* these writers on the walls are "unrecognized by the literary establishments in either China or the United States."[16] However, it is exactly this in-between linguistic and cultural status that characterizes their historical specificity and lays claim to the so-called Asian-American sensibility or, to be more precise, Chinese-American sensibility, whose influence is far and wide.[17]

Chinese immigration to the United States has been going on for more than two centuries. Sucheng Chan breaks this immigrant history into four periods: "years of free immigration from 1849 to 1882; an age of exclusion from 1882 to 1943; a period of limited entry under special legislation from 1943 to 1965; and an era of renewed immigration from 1965 to the present."[18] In this periodization the *Island* poems written from 1910 to 1940 fall exactly into the second period of exclusion.[19] Indeed, the discriminatory acts against the Chinese immigrants in American history in general and in this second period in particular — institutional acts such as the Chinese Ex-

clusion Law in 1882, the antimiscegenation laws, and the modeling of Angel Island after Ellis Island as a "filtering center" primarily for the Chinese
immigrants — were the government's formulations of the pervasive anti-
Chinese sentiments in the United States at that time. Some of the immigrants' testimonies showed that they were aware that this unequal treatment was due to the weakness of their motherland. For Japanese immigrants were allowed to enter San Francisco very soon, while their Chinese
counterparts had to stay on Angel Island from several days to even up to
three years.[20] And the discriminatory treatment left an indelible mark on
the psyches of the Chinese immigrants passing through Angel Island.[21]

Despite the editors' effort to classify these poems into five groups, the
richness and diversity of these poems defy so easy a categorization. One of
the themes pervading the individual accounts is the motivation for this
massive diaspora: the weakness of the nation and the poverty of the family.
Here the national, the communal, the familial, and the personal intertwine.
Other themes include the economic pressure which forces the breadwin-
ner to separate from his beloved ones and leave his home country for the
Gold Mountain; the risks on the high seas; the suffering and maltreatment
caused by discrimination; the high anticipation and heartbreaking frustration; the anxiety of having no idea of one's fate; the sorrow for the weakness of the nation. All these are set in a history- and geography-specific
juncture.

The historical figures these poems refer to are many, some recalled from
hundreds and even thousands of years.[22] All these figures — among them
only one female (B28) and one Westerner (Napoleon, A60) — bear resemblance to the detainees. One of them, Taozhugong (5th century B.C., A11,
A43), probably *the* first famous man of fortune in Chinese history, serves as
a symbol of achievement and thus encouragement for the immigration. In
these poems, he appears as the only person with untainted success. All the
other historical figures are remarkable for a special kind of heroism: although suffering confinement, exile, homesickness, discrimination, and
frustration, they are able to persevere and wait for a time to fulfill their
wishes and even to revenge themselves. As these poems are composed
anonymously and often echo one another, these references to historical
figures promote a certain degree of collectivity.

China's history had produced a long-standing sense of cultural and economic superiority, with different names for the surrounding "barbarian" tribes in four directions: *tung-yi* (Eastern barbarians), *hsi-jung* (Western barbarians), *nan-man* (Southern barbarians), and *pei-ti* (Northern barbarians). Its inhabitants referred to China as *t'ien-ch'ao* (Celestial Regime). Even today, the Chinese name for China is, unequivocally, "Middle Kingdom," or "the Center of the Earth," suggesting that other countries are geographically and therefore culturally marginal and peripheral. There were some historical moments, however, when China suffered weakness and foreign invasions. Hence it is not unusual that this sense of cultural pride is sometimes mingled with an awareness of military and economic weakness. One of the most acute instances occurred when China encountered the West. When the Chinese immigrated to the United States and were detained on Angel Island, the same mixture of contempt and humiliation was manifest.

In this collection, the epithets applied to the Westerners (Americans) are numerous: *fan-nu* ("barbarian," A7, A48, B55), *man-yi* ("barbarian," A52), *hu* ("barbarian," A57, B34, B44), *kuei* ("devils," B49, B50), *wu-ch'ing pei-kuei* ("heartless white devils," B4), *lang-yi* ("savage doctors" [literally "wolf-like" doctors], B51). Some of these poets, especially those destined to be deported back to China, did not hesitate to pour their hatred against *barbarians* (B39, B40, B41, B44, B46). Since Japan invaded China, dealt another blow to the already dismal state of the rural economy, and hurt the national pride, these *wo-nu* ("dwarves") were also to be "annihilated" (B43). This peculiar combination of a strong sense of cultural superiority and an acute awareness of military and economic inferiority can be clearly seen from the way these poets refer to the "other." Given the poets' situation, these poems are more in the nature of verbal vent than real threat. However, the suffering is genuinely felt and conveyed.

The views conveyed in these poems are substantiated by the editors' introduction and extensive interviews with the people concerned. Although the interviews with the immigrant inspectors and Chinese interpreters show that the treatment of these immigrants on Angel Island was not totally inhuman, the legislation of Chinese Exclusion Laws (1882) and the establishment of Angel Island primarily for the Chinese immigrants were certainly unequal. And the photographic images attached usually lend strength and credibility to the editors' points.[23]

When one-tenth of the *Island* poems were included in the groundbreaking, canon-broadening *Heath Anthology of American Literature,* that step marked a milestone not only for Chinese-American literature, but also for the American literary canon.[24] A closer look at this development may gain us some glimpses into the politics of anthologizing and the problematics of representation and re-contextualization.

The Heath Anthology places this group of poems under the heading of "The Modern Period: 1910–1945." So far as the dates are concerned, it seems reasonable. However, note that Arnold Krupat, one of the editors of the fourth edition of *The Norton Anthology of American Literature,* points out that the periodization of American literature according to the mainstream American history does not stand to reason in the case of Native American literature.[25] This comment similarly applies to the *Island* poems in *The Heath Anthology.* The fact that 1910 marks both the establishment of Angel Island as an immigrant station and the beginning of the modern period is purely coincidental. What is more significant to the Chinese mentality or national spirit is the Chinese revolution in 1911, which established the first republic in Asia. Moreover, for Chinese immigrants to the United States, 1943 was the year when the Congress repealed the Chinese Exclusion Laws, while 1945 marks the end of the Second World War, when China finally obtained an equal status in the international community after decades of unequal treaties with many foreign countries, including the United States. Understandably, in compiling an anthology works must be placed somewhere; yet it is necessary to consider the complexity of such an act of dating, especially when dealing with literatures outside the mainstream, with their alternative cultural and historical contexts.

This is exactly what the introducers of these poems try to do. And it is indeed a wise choice to invite the editors and translators of the *Island* poems to write the introduction to this selection. In their succinct two-page introduction, the three editors of the Chinese immigrant poems put in a nutshell not only their historical context and cultural significance, but also the specific Chinese-American sensibility as it looks toward the past, present, and future. And it should be said that given this short space, the introducers have done a good job in representing this ethnic group's literature to the English readers.

Unlike most of the selections in the *Heath Anthology*, however, these Angel Island poems are English translations from a language which is famous for its rich allusions, historical complexity, and cultural associations. While this is not a proper place to discuss the question of translatability, the very fact that the poems are translated indicates that the multiethnic or comparative approach to American literature should be supplemented by a multilingual approach so as to render a better account of the rich and diverse literatures in the United States.[26]

This group of thirteen poems comes from Part A only: (I) 5, 8; (II) 20, 30, 31; (III) 35, 38, 42; (IV) 51, 55; and (V) 57, 64, 69. A look at the Chinese originals leaves no doubt that they are good, both in terms of content and in their strict adherence to the Chinese rhyme scheme. But the Chinese originals are not in this anthology — and the general readers lack the ability to read Chinese. Hence the failure to mention the translating strategy conceals much information from the readers of *The Heath Anthology*. And the brief introduction's failure to mention the format of Chinese classical poetic forms along with the translators' intention and choice impoverishes the cultural, transcultural, and translinguistic characteristics of this group of poems. Two examples will suffice. In the Chinese original, A20 is a poem in the form of the seven-character quatrain rhyming *aaba* (*Island* 57), one of the most popular poetic forms ever since the T'ang Dynasty (A.D. 618–907), the so-called golden age of Chinese poetry. The scheme is lost in the English version, which reads:

> Imprisonment at Youli, when will it end?
> Fur and linen garments have been exchanged; it is already another
>   autumn.
> My belly brims with discontent, too numerous to inscribe on bamboo
>   slips.
> Snow falls, flowers wilt, expressing sorrow through the ages. (*Island* 56)

Entitled "Crude Poem Inspired by the Landscape," A64 is another case in point. Written in the favorite form of five-character octave riming *aabacada* (*Island* 129), the poem is rendered into English as follows:

> The ocean encircles a lone peak.
> Rough terrain surrounds this prison.
> There are few birds flying over the cold hills.
> The wild goose messenger cannot find its way.
> I have been detained and obstacles have been put my way for
>   half a year.
> Melancholy and hate gather on my face.
> Now that I must return to my country,
> I have toiled like the *jingwei* bird in vain. (*Island* 128)

Even to those who do not know the Chinese language, a glimpse at the bilingual text immediately shows the typographical differences between the Chinese original and the English translation. In Chinese each line is of the same length, whereas the English lines are rather irregular. To bilingual readers, moreover, the failure of the English language to capture, even if slightly, the characteristic Chinese cadences and rhyme scheme is more than obvious. What can be best conveyed in this translingual communication are meaning and imagery. The remaining linguistic characteristics are almost totally missing, though the editors/translators did a fine job in identifying literary and historical allusions as well as expounding cultural connotations.[27]

Selected from the five sections of Part A, the poems do convey a strong sense of the suffering, worries, and sorrows of the Chinese immigrants, and the main themes of the whole collection are faithfully and forcefully represented by these selections. More than half (seven out of thirteen) use allusions in an apt way and show the writers' training; the ones that do not are still natural and moving. And the one dated the "13th Day of the 3rd Month in the 6th year of the Republic" (March 13, 1917) implicitly indicates the poet's allegiance to the newly emergent Republic of China in contrast to *mei-kuo* or *mei-li-chien ho-chung-kuo* (the United States of America or, literally, "the beautiful country" or "the beautiful-sharp-strong republic").

Moreover, the annotations, reproduced *almost* verbatim, help the English readers better to understand the historical, literary, and cultural intricacy of these texts.

However, negligence on the part of the anthology editors creates some confusion. For instance, ancient Chinese names and transliterations are different from the modern. Thus Su Wu is referred to in *Island* as "Ziqing" in A30 and "Su Wu" in A57.[28] That is why the annotation for A30 (the first annotation about this loyal envoy to a barbarian tribe) begins with "Another name for Su Wu." However, the repetition of the name Su Wu in the annotation for A57 leaves the readers wondering why "Su Wu" is "Another name for Su Wu."[29]

If this can be regarded as a sin of commission, a more serious sin of omission appears in the annotation for A69 about Chinese national hero Zu Di.[30] Thanks to his familiarity with classical Chinese literature and Chinese American immigrant history, editor Him Mark Lai admirably detects the allusion to Zu Di in this poem.[31] This allusion invokes the theme of nationalism which is closely connected with the dichotomy of barbarism/culture and the Other/China. General Zu Di and his comrades were obsessed with the idea of driving away the barbarian enemy who took possession of their territory, but this story and its rich associations are lost in the first edition of the anthology. This omission not only leaves the English readers puzzling over the meaning of "the whip of Zu Di" (what does "Zu Di" mean?!), but also does away with some major themes of the original, such as revenge, national recovery, and the sharp contrast between Chinese/non-Chinese (barbarian).[32]

The Heath Anthology marks the canonization of the *Island* poems in the literary and cultural scene of the United States. This act of inclusion is laudable in and of itself. Despite the effort to revise the literary canon from a comparative perspective, as advocated by Lauter, the *Heath Anthology*'s sampling and representation in this case — the English-only version — does not adequately address the bilingual, cross-cultural, transnational complexity, which is an important subject in American (ethnic) literature. Seen from another perspective, the "sins" mentioned above come from negligence which has much to do with the lack of understanding of cultural differences. It further testifies to the importance of the effort at mutual understanding through not only a comparative and multiethnic, but also a multilingual approach.

Now preserved as a state park, Angel Island becomes a site where memory and history intertwine. As Stan Yogi put it, "the island has come to symbolize the hardships endured by these early Chinese immigrants, who often underwent intense interrogations before being allowed into the U.S."[33] As a work of reclamation and verbal commemoration, *Island* re-inscribes and circulates the poems penned or carved by the Chinese immigrants on the walls of the detention camp. This very act, highlighting the peculiar materiality and textuality of the texts, characterizes a specific time and place in Chinese-American encounters and expresses a unique Chinese-American experience and sensibility. As one Chinese-American scholar avows: "without this book, I would have never come to know Angel Island as an immigration depot where thousands of our ancestors were bitterly incarcerated. I would have continued to view the island as the favorite picnic spot for seniors of Galileo High School."[34]

The ambivalence of hope and despair, longing and suffering expressed by the detainees — *Angel* Island, yet dominated by *pei-kuei* ("white devils"); *chin-shan* ("Gold Mountain") and *mei-kuo* ("the beautiful country"), and yet also the place of *fan, man, yi, hu* ("barbarians") — finds its pithy expression in Maxine Hong Kingston's bilingual title of her second novel, *China Men* (or *chin-shan yung-shih*, as the Chinese stamp shows).[35] The coexistence of these two titles, with the discriminatory ethnic connotations in the English and the recasting of the same people as "Gold Mountain Heroes" in Chinese, could serve as a metaphor for the Chinese immigrants who rushed to an island where angels feared to tread.

Notes

I would like to thank Stephen Greenblatt, Werner Sollors, and Doris Sommer for their comments on an earlier English version of this paper, as well as Him Mark Lai and two anonymous Chinese reviewers for comments on the Chinese version. Special thanks go to the Harvard-Yenching Institute, whose support was indispensable for the writing of this essay.

1. Him Mark Lai, Genny Lim, and Judy Yung, eds., *Island: Poetry and History of Chinese Immigrants on Angel Island, 1910–1940* (distributed by San Francisco Study Center, c. 1980; reprint Seattle: University of Washington Press, 1991).

2. Here I adopt Pierre Nora's term "sites of memory" *(lieux de mémoire)* and apply this concept to Angel Island. See Pierre Nora, "Between Memory and History: *Les Lieux de Mémoire,*" trans. Marc Roudebush, in *History and Memory in African-American Culture,* ed. Genevieve Fabre and Robert O'Meally (New York: Oxford University Press, 1994), pp. 284–300.

   Instead of embracing Nora's dichotomy between history and memory (past vs. present, relative vs. absolute, etc.), I view these two as being in constant interaction and interpenetration. The beautiful name "Angel Island" must contend with "Devil's Pass," the name the Chinese immigrants gave to the place. See also Te-hsing Shan, "Yi wo Ai-lun ju chuan-fu: T'ien-shih-tao pai-ke te ming-ke yu chai-hsien" ["Re-inscribing and Representing the Angel Island Poems"], in *Tsai-hsien cheng-chi yu hua-yi mei-kuo wen-hsueh* [Politics of Representation and Chinese-American Literature], ed. Ho Wen-ching and Shan Te-hsing (Taipei: Institute of European and American Studies, Academia Sinica, 1996), pp. 1–56.

3. Sau-ling C. Wong, "The Politics and Poetics of Folksong Reading: Literary Portrayals of Life under Exclusion," in *Entry Denied: Exclusion and the Chinese Community in America, 1882–1943,* ed. Sucheng Chan (Philadelphia: Temple University Press, 1991), p. 248.

4. Werner Sollors, "National Identity and Ethnic Diversity: 'Of Plymouth Rock and Jamestown and Ellis Island'; or, Ethnic Literature and Some Redefinitions of America," in *History and Memory in African-American Culture,* p. 113.

5. Cary Nelson, "Always Already Cultural Studies: Academic Conferences and a Manifesto." In *English Studies / Culture Studies: Institutionalizing Dissent,* ed. Isaiah Smithson and Nancy Ruff (Urbana: University of Illinois Press, 1994), p. 199.

6. Lai et al., *Island,* p. 25.

7. Sucheng Chan's *Asian Americans: An Interpretive History* (Boston: Twayne,

1991) offers a historical context for Asian-American immigrants; Elaine H. Kim's *Asian American Literature: An Introduction to the Writings and Their Social Context* (Philadelphia: Temple University Press, 1982) discusses this particular type of American literature from the perspective of its social context. Xiao-huang Yin's "Gold Mountain Dreams: Chinese American Literature and Its Socio-Historical Context, 1850–1963," Ph.D. diss., Harvard University, 1991, focuses on the sociohistorical context of Chinese-American literature for over a century. See also Sucheng Chan's chapter on "The Chinese Diaspora" in *This Bitter-Sweet Soil* (Berkeley: University of California Press, 1986), and Lynn Pan's *Sons of the Yellow Emperor: A History of the Chinese Diaspora* (New York: Kodansha International, 1994) for an understanding of the background and situation of the massive Chinese immigration over the centuries.

8. Lai et al., *Island*, "Acknowledgments." One anonymous reviewer of the Chinese version of this chapter supplements the following observations: (1) the explicit expression of the theme of revenge breaks the stereotype that the Chinese immigrants were passive, silent, and uncomplaining, and (2) the rich allusions in these poems also shatter the stereotype that earlier Chinese immigrants were illiterate.

9. The editors separate the collection into two major parts: the first part consists of 69 poems, subdivided into five groups ("The Voyage," "The Detainment," "The Weak Shall Conquer," "About Westerners," and "Deportees, Transients"); the second part consists of 66 poems. For the sake of convenience, poems will be referred to as belonging to Part A or B, followed by the poem number in each part. In a letter to me, Him Mark Lai remarks, "So far as I can remember, originally we chose only dozens of representative poems of higher literary quality and intended to publish a small anthology. Later on, we accepted friends' suggestions and added historical background and oral histories so as to enrich the content. Finally, we realized that since this kind of book did not attract publishers' interest and since we had already devoted so much energy, we might as well incorporate other poems as appendix for the readers' reference. But I also agree [with you] that since we have published all poems, it seems to stand to reason if we merge these two parts." Him Mark Lai, May 5, 1995, personal correspondence to the author.

10. For instance, A69 is the only one illustrated by a photograph. The editors' intention is to authenticate their source. However, a detailed scrutiny of the photograph shows that thematically, structurally, and typographically, A69 should be read as two poems instead. For a detailed analysis of the relationship as well as the discrepancy between the English translation and the Chinese original as represented by the photographic text, see Shan, "Reinscribing and Representing the Angel Island Poems," pp. 31–38.

11. Paul Lauter et al., eds., *The Heath Anthology of American Literature*, 2 vols. (Lexington, Mass.: D. C. Heath, 1990), vol. 2, pp. 1755–62.

12. Roman Jakobson, "On Linguistic Aspects of Translation," in *Theories of Translation: An Anthology of Essays from Dryden to Derrida*, ed. Rainer Schulte and John Biguenet (Chicago: University of Chicago Press, 1992), pp. 144–51.

13. See J. Hillis Miller, "Border Crossings: Translating Theory," in *New Starts: Performative Topographies in Literature and Criticism* (Taipei: The Institute of European and American Studies, Academia Sinica, 1993).

   As for the performative effect of translation, the editors/translators admit that "Some works have obscure meanings because of the frequent inclusion of Cantonese vernacular expressions as well as Chinese American colloquialisms. Such flaws, if such they are, are not evident in the English translations, because *by the very act of translating* from the original Chinese into the English language, *new literary works have been created* which, while keeping the meaning of the original, hide some of the defects" (Lai et al., *Island*, p. 25, emphasis added). In an early review of this work, Marlon K. Hom also points out that while the translation on the whole is faithful and accurate, "[i]n some instances the poems are over-translated with many translations appearing more erudite than the original." See Marlon K. Hom, "Review of *Island*," *Amerasia* 8-1 (1981):135.

14. Lai et al., *Island*, p. 31.

15. Ibid., p. 25.

16. Wong, "The Politics and Poetics of Folksong Reading," p. 247.

17. Lai et al., *Island*, p. 28; Lauter et al., *The Heath Anthology*, p. 1756.

18. Chan, *Asian Americans*, p. viii.

19. For a discussion of the significance of the *Heath Anthology*'s periodization in the context of American literature, see below.

20. Lai et al., *Island*, pp. 73, 96, 97.

21. In an interview conducted more than half a century after his detainment at Angel Island in 1934, Koon T. Lau says: "Angel Island did not adversely affect my livelihood, but it did affect me psychologically. I felt I was not equal. We were judged guilty although we had committed no crime. As I said earlier, the food was bad. Second, the space we were confined to was small. Why wouldn't they give us more freedom since we couldn't escape from the island anyway? Besides, as newcomers, even if we could swim, we couldn't swim that far or know where to go. Why wouldn't they let us go beyond the exercise yard? But the worst was their not allowing our relatives to come see us. I heard others say on the ship and in the barracks that criminals in America

have the right to visits from relatives. If they allowed criminals that right, why not us who had not committed any crime such as rob or kill anyone? Maybe we were considered criminals for coming in as paper sons, but what about those who were real sons? Why not let their relatives see them? Since landing here until now, I still wonder about this. I am seventy now and still do not understand why they treated us like that." Judy Yung, "Detainment at Angel Island: An Interview with Koon T. Lau," in *Chinese America: History and Perspectives* (San Francisco: Chinese Historical Society of America, 1991), p. 166.

22. The succinct annotations given by the editors/translators concerning these historical figures are of tremendous help not only to English readers, but also to modern Chinese readers who are no longer so familiar with their literary and historical traditions. It should also be noted that poems with allusions generally are more compact, erudite, and of better quality according to the standard of classical Chinese poetry.

23. It would be interesting to discuss the relation between verbal texts and photographic texts and to investigate how the photographs usually authenticate, yet sometimes undermine, the verbal texts. Moreover, some of the discrepancies between the English and Chinese titles of each section (Lai et al., *Island*, pp. 99, 121) and their relation to the photographs used as backgrounds indicate that this collection actually addresses three different groups of readers: English, Chinese, and bilingual. And since the introduction and interviews were written in English only, this book's major intended readers are English-speaking.

24. *The Heath Anthology of American Literature* is a continuation and partial realization of Paul Lauter's long-term project, Reconstructing American Literature. For a behind-the-scenes story of this anthology, see Lauter, "*The Heath Anthology* and Cultural Boundaries," in Smithson et al., *English Studies/Culture Studies*, pp. 180–90.

    For an understanding of his revisionist theory and praxis of American literature, see Lauter's *Reconstructing American Literature: Courses, Syllabi, Issues* (New York: The Feminist Press, 1983); *Canons and Contexts* (New York: Oxford University Press, 1991); and "To the Reader," in *The Heath Anthology of American Literature* (1990). The fact that *Island* poems are allotted a space in *The Heath Anthology*, itself a literary establishment, indicates that in comparison with other establishments this anthology is relatively canon-broadening.

25. Arnold Krupat (1994), personal correspondence to the author.

26. This is precisely the motivation behind the LOWINUS Project (Languages Of What Is Now the United States) headed by Werner Sollors and Marc Shell.

27. For detailed annotations and discussions of the discrepancies between the

Chinese original and the English translation of A69 (*Island* 134–35), see Shan, "Angel Island Poetry," in *The Multilingual Anthology of American Literature: A Reader of Original Texts with English Translations,* ed. Marc Shell and Werner Sollors (New York: New York University Press, 2000), pp. 577–81, 729–31.

28. Su Wu (140–60 B.C.) was an envoy of the Western Han Dynasty to "a nomadic people north of the Chinese empire" (Lai et al., *Island*, p. 66). Detained by the barbarian tribe for nineteen years, Su remained loyal to his emperor and was finally able to return to his home country with honors. This theme of prolonged exile and unflagging loyalty reveals the detainees' feelings and suggests they see a similarity between the barbarian countries past and present. A hint of nationalism is to be detected in this allusion.

29. Lauter et al., *The Heath Anthology*, p. 1761. In fact, this anthology also includes A30 and exactly the same annotation (ibid., p. 1758).

30. I use the expressions "sin of commission" and "sin of omission," which are generally associated with the discussion of translation, to highlight this translingual, cross-cultural representation.

31. Another translator, Hsu Kai-yu, failed to grasp this allusion and translated "Zu" literally. See Ruthanne Lum McCunn, *An Illustrated History of the Chinese in America* (San Francisco: Design Enterprises of San Francisco, 1979), p. 94.

32. This sin of omission has been corrected in the second edition of *The Heath Anthology*, whereas the sin of commission remains the same. See Paul Lauter et al., eds., *The Heath Anthology of American Literature*, 2nd ed., 2 vols. (Lexington, Mass.: D. C. Heath, 1994), p. 1963.

33. Stan Yogi, "Review of *Island*," *MELUS* 17-2 (1991–92):77.

34. Hom, "Review of *Island*," p. 136.

35. Kingston is the only well-known Chinese-American writer who is also included in the 1990 edition of *The Heath Anthology*. And it is worth noting that the "ghosts" in the subtitle of *The Woman Warrior* also refer to Americans as "white devils" and "barbarians." See Maxine Hong Kingston, *The Woman Warrior: Memoirs of a Girlhood Among Ghosts* (reprint, New York: Vintage, 1989); and *China Men* (reprint, New York: Vintage, 1989).

CHAPTER TWENTY

Immigration Blues: The Portrayal of Chinatown Life in Contemporary Chinese-Language Literature in America

▇ XIAO-HUANG YIN

As a product of the Chinese experience in America, Chinese-language literature understandably has many things in common with English-language works written by Chinese-Americans.[1] For example, the understated confrontation between immigrant parents and their American-born children in Chen Ruoxi's story "To the Other Side of the Pacific Ocean" parallels mother-daughter conflicts in Amy Tan's *The Joy Luck Club*.[2] Nie Hualing's novel *Mulberry and Peach*, featuring a female protagonist restlessly traversing the American landscape to explore the meaning of freedom and identity, brings to mind Maxine Hong Kingston's critically acclaimed *Trip Master Monkey: His Fake Book*.[3] Yet Chinese-language literature, with its own sensibility and perspective, also differs poignantly from that in English.

The fact that their prospective readers are Chinese, coupled with an intense desire to explore their own literary paths, has prompted Chinese-language authors to remain closely identified with the immigrant experience in theme and subject matter. While American-born Chinese writers often delve into the broad issues of cultural identity, generation conflicts, and sentiments of the native-born, Chinese-language authors are always dedicated to exploring compelling issues grounded in an immigrant sensibility, such as the agony of displacement, the dilemma of assimilation and alienation, and the hardship and struggle of daily life in a strange land. In other words, a major characteristic which distinguishes Chinese-language literature is its persistent focus on issues unique to the fate of immigrants. Indeed, for those who strive to interpret concerns of Chinese immigrants in American society, the literature provides a wealth of information and descriptive detail and offers a valuable conceptual framework to understand the forces and thoughts that shape and influence the lives of Chinese immigrants. The way of life in America's urban Chinatowns, especially the impact of the struggle for survival on Chinatown residents — the "Downtown Chinese" — in Chinese-language literature is a case in point.[4]

That poverty coexists with growing prosperity in Chinese-American life is not surprising. While recent decades have witnessed the coming of a different sort of Chinese immigrants, affluent and well educated, immigration laws such as the "family reunion act" and the upheavals in Southeast Asia have also brought to the United States large numbers of non-English speaking working-class Chinese immigrants and refugees with few readily transferable skills. In the words of a Chinese woman in Los Angeles: "It is not true that all Asians come to the United States with suitcases . . . full of cash. I came here with very limited resources."[5] There are also immigrant professionals who, failing to acquire positions in their fields, are forced to take manual and service work and get stuck in menial positions in Chinatowns. As a result, the Chinese-American community developed into a bi-model socioeconomic structure with two distinct groups: the "Uptown" and the "Downtown."

Compared with the Uptown Chinese who live comfortably in racially integrated suburbs, the Downtown Chinese are trapped in poverty-stricken urban enclaves. Caught in a world of gangs, drugs, and poverty, they differ dramatically from their Uptown counterparts in the American experience.[6] While the Uptown Chinese feel embittered about the "glass ceiling" that stops their career advancement, the Downtown Chinese, locked in dead-end jobs with little chance to move up, are more concerned for their immediate survival.

The depressed mood of the people who live in the cramped and run-down houses in overcrowded Chinatowns and the constraints and hardships of daily life for the Downtown Chinese are captured vividly by Chinese-language writers. Their stories, dealing with economic difficulties and the effects of mass uprooting, render a credible, at times scathingly pathetic, portrayal of Chinatowns as stagnant ponds. The sketches of New York's Chinatown by two women writers, representative of Chinese-language literature centered on Chinatown life, show how the consequences of poverty and alienation have turned the place into a "wasteland" and excluded its residents from mainstream social, economic, political, and cultural life:

> Chinatown. Hot with the sound of cicadas, dirty streets, gilded gates dotted with red paint . . . Under the heat, Chinatown residents line up to buy lottery tickets in front of newsstands. If you look closely at their faces, your heart would be filled with sorrow and disappointment: their faces are so rigid and stiff as if they were just carved out of wood . . . Bearing the burning heat, people stand there quietly . . . Under the expressionless faces, they are day-dreaming of making a big fortune.
>
> Nighttime in Chinatown. A pedestrian clutches the stub of a cigarette with his tired and numb fingers. A man walks across the street as he spits at the sidewalk . . . Cluttered shop windows of a curio store. Behind the dimly-lit counters sits a man, indistinguishable as to his age, staring blankly at passers-by, yet seemingly not seeing anything. Perhaps he is lost in thinking why he failed to grab a double-dragon card at a mahjong game last night."[7]

Such satirical and gloomy visions drive home the message that while there are individuals who thrive in Chinatowns, immigrants without skills or resources can expect only to spend a lifetime scraping and scrimping for a living.

However, what really catches the attention of Chinese-language writers is the impact of the struggle for survival on the Downtown Chinese rather than the sheer presence of poverty in Chinatown life. In fact, a particular strength of their writing is their realization that the contextual forces which cause and determine the extent and nature of problems in Chinatown life are not merely racial in nature. By examining how poverty and the struggle for survival exacerbate sharp divisions, ignite conflicts, and widen the schism among Chinese immigrants, their writing demonstrates that the process of racialization is never based just on race but is determined by a number of factors, and most certainly among them, economic conditions.

China Town（中国城）。酷暑，蝉鸣，肮脏不堪的街道，红字烫金的牌楼，中国餐馆一家连一家，使人感到目不暇接。中国人也好，美国人也好；穷人也好，富人也好，在纽约绝不会不知道 China Town 的。我惊诧这里的肮脏，可是肮脏中却散发着生气。这里有一堆堆小山般堆起的新鲜瓜果以及各式各样的海鲜，书摊上都是些封面印有乱七八糟的港台裸体女人照的刊物。广东和上海的移民在这里叫卖葱油饼、菜肉包等各式各样的风味小吃，酷暑下人们排着一条条长龙等候着小报亭出售乐透彩票。如果你仔细研究一下这些中国人的脸，你会感到揪心的失望和切肤的痛心；每个人的脸都像是木雕般的呆板，人与人之间都不讲话。也许是美国社会的感情淡薄症传到了每一个角落，也包括中国城吧！他们忍受着酷暑，静静地、像美国人那样排着大队，死板的表情下面人人藏着发财的美梦。

20.1. Chinese text interspersed with English words, p. 322 from Zhou Li, *Manhadun de Zhongguo Nuren* (1992).

"Two Ways to Eat American Meals" (1984), a short story by Zhou Feili, deals with this aspect of Chinatown life.[8] Like the author, the protagonist is an immigrant from Taiwan and lives in the Los Angeles Chinatown. Being laid off four times within two years in the mainstream job market, he and his wife decide to open a small restaurant with their old friends from Taiwan. They hope that the rising popularity of Chinese food will give them a chance to earn an easier livelihood.

This is not purely wishful thinking. The spread of Chinese cuisine and a corresponding increase in customer sophistication in recent years has turned Chinese restaurants into a booming business and provided an opportunity for economic sufficiency to immigrant laborers. Unfortunately, for the characters in the story, the dream is shattered by the ruthless reality. The risk of conducting business in a crime-ridden urban ghetto and the cut-throat competition in the industry soon exhaust their resources and drive their business partnership into an ugly game of mutual deception. In order to survive on the knife-edge profits, they resort to cheating and playing tricks against one another. In the end, the protagonist outwits and out-maneuvers his friends in a dramatic gamble and seizes the ownership of the restaurant.

The narrator's voice, occasionally cursory, is rich and percussive. It shifts from the emotional to the matter-of-fact with an effect that is both comic and coolly illuminating, showing vividly the unpleasant reality of Chinatown life:

> "I have calculated," my wife insisted, "if we don't hire anyone but do everything ourselves, we can net about one thousand dollars more a month from the savings on the labor costs . . . If we make two hundred dollars more, we may even afford medical insurance. Then we won't fear being sick."
>
> "If we make another one hundred dollars, we can even afford life insurance. Then we won't fear death," I replied in a cynical tone. ". . . but where can we borrow the money [to buy the restaurant]?"
>
> "How about from your friends?"
>
> "I have only two sorts of friends in this country: those who have money but won't lend it to me and those who want to help me but don't have money."[9]

Beneath the self-mocking and seemingly light-hearted tone, there are notes of doubt, anxiety, and bitterness, and a sense of insecurity for these Downtown Chinese. By attributing their agony and moral deterioration to the constraints and hardships in Chinatown life, the author implies that what happens to the characters in the story is a predictable consequence of the struggle for survival. Uprooted from their native land and inserted into an alienated and impoverished environment, they have failed miserably and are unable to rise, on a moral or spiritual plane, above the deranging displacement.

The clashes and rivalries among the friends in Zhou's story make it explicit that despite sharing a common cultural background, Chinese immigrants do not always live in cooperative harmony. Competition for limited resources turns Chinatowns into places where tensions and mutual distrust flourish. Unable to find the real sources of their problems, Chinatown residents often blame members of their own community for a deteriorating living environment, slashed wages, and worsening working conditions. The irrational vehemence with which they lash out against each other reflects their frustration over failed expectations and shattered dreams. The sad phenomenon is frequently seen among immigrants who are struggling in poverty. "The people at the bottom tend to strike out at whoever is closest," explains an author of immigration studies. "It is not a rational decision."[10] At a large gathering of garment factory workers in New York's Chinatown several years ago, discussions of problems in sweatshops quickly turned into an ugly confrontation between legal and illegal immigrants. While the former angrily denounced the latter for their declining wages and demanded that all illegal immigrants be sent home, the latter cried bitterly that they were mistreated and exploited by everyone, including their fellow Chinese workers. The emotional dispute almost escalated into violence between the two groups.[11] The case reveals clearly how competition for scarce opportunities causes discord among Chinatown residents and fragments the community.

In addition to intensifying competition for limited resources, the struggle for survival has also isolated and thwarted the Downtown Chinese from actively participating in the fight for racial justice and political rights. All too often, immigrants act as alien and passive observers of their fate and are less sensitive than American-born Chinese toward racial prejudice. The controversy over the movie *Year of the Dragon* is a case in point. While most American-born Chinese felt outraged by the blatant racist tone and distortion of Chinatown life as depicted in the movie, there were immigrants who enjoyed the story and dismissed protests against the movie as being oversensitive.[12] It is also common to find immigrants shunning discussions of difficulty and racial prejudice in Chinese American life. "I feel uncomfortable with your coverage of problems and hardships in American life," complains a reader to a Chinese-language newspaper in California. "There are so many happy and pleasant things in this country. Why don't you write more about pretty scenes or stories of people who have made it?"[13] Some Asian-American scholars and activists believe that such a mentality is an outcome of an effort by mainstream society to "whitewash" immigrants and make them conform to dominant institutions. Others think that Chinese immigrants who arrived after the 1960s have no experiences or memories of living in a land that once openly discriminated against the Chinese and Asians. Therefore, they tend to feel content with the status quo and lack racial consciousness.[14] As Angela Oh, an articulate Korean-American leader, argues: "They [new Asian immigrants] don't understand what that concept [of minority] means in terms of historical treatment of non-English-speaking people and people who are racially different."[15]

Although it is difficult to find a single, satisfactory explanation for the phenomenon, the portrayal of Chinatown life by Chinese-language writers suggests that the passivity and apolitical tendency displayed by immigrants, especially by the Downtown Chinese, is a result of the survival mentality acquired from their experiences in American society. It is poverty and a sense of insecurity that distract them from fighting for racial equality. Spiritually and physically, they are confined to a narrow vision where the struggle for economic efficiency and the fight for political rights seem mutually exclusive. As Qian Ning, author of a critically acclaimed reportage on recent Chinese immigrants, points out, it is the anxiety and deprivation of being an immigrant class in "a strange land" that forces them to repress their political enthusiasm and emotional expressiveness in order to wrest a living.[16]

Qian's argument, resembling Oscar Handlin's use of estrangement as a centerpiece and an explanatory concept in immigration studies, is supported by his extensive surveys and interviews of Chinese immigrants. In one story, the interviewee used to have strong interests in political events when he first arrived in America. But economic necessity soon reduces his high aspirations to a mere desire for survival. Making a living cutting up chickens into breasts, legs, and wings in the basement of a Chinatown restaurant, he has lost all his enthusiasm for politics. Or as an Asian immigrant organizer in Los Angeles finds: "Most people in the community don't care about that [Asian American movement]. To them, the question is how to pay the bills."[17]

Ironically, a rash of purgatorial suffering notwithstanding, many Chinatown residents still see America as a "paradise." The feeling of being elevated in America while living in poverty is not contradictory. Much of it has to do with the newcomer's pre-immigration experience and expectations. For immigrant laborers from various parts of the Chinese world, coming to America means escape from starvation and destitution. They find America's promise of material abundance alluring, and they expect the rewards of the opportunities they see around them. Such a mentality — a "green-card mindset" — is well illustrated in subject matter, theme, and characters in "The Ship of Bananas" (1973), a short story by Zhang Xiguo.

The highly symbolic story centers on the meeting between a ship-jumping sailor and a student immigrant from Taiwan. Asked why he runs the risk of being caught entering America illegally, the sailor replies, "Don't laugh at me. There are many Chinese ship-jumping sailors [in New York]. Our salary is too low . . . [So] we all tried to find opportunities to jump ship once we got to New York . . . Working in a Chinese restaurant here for a year or two, I can save as much as several thousand dollars. It is much better than working on a ship."[18]

The story's title, alluding to Sebastian Brant's classic *The Ship of Fools*, evokes a sense of irony for the fate of Chinese immigrants in America. Obvious satirical overtones aside, its implication as an incarnation of the Chinese immigrant community is thought-provoking. In a broad sense, as a critic points out, Chinese immigrants such as the nameless sailor and other characters in the story are "bananas": they have lost their common sense and fail to understand the reality of American life.[19] This is confirmed by the tragic death of the sailor at the end of the story — he dies in an accident on a ship carrying bananas when he tries to re-enter America.

The sailor's dream, albeit ending as a nightmare, is widely shared by the Downtown Chinese. Compared to those in their homelands, salary levels for unskilled labor in the United States seem to be strikingly high, making America a "shining Gold Mountain" in the eyes of immigrant laborers. As a scholar explains: "Four dollars an hour means nothing to us Americans. [But] it means a lot to somebody for whom it once represented a month's rent [back home]. Even though they're not paying that rent here, they're still using that metric."[20] The mentality is shown poignantly in "A Hundred Thousand Dollars" (1987), a short story by Yi Li that takes place in the Chinatown of Los Angeles. In the story, a longtime resident of the Chinatown tells his newly arrived brother-in-law why he thinks America is a "promised land" for Chinese immigrants:

> In America, the most important thing is that you must be willing to work hard and endure more suffering than others. For example, if other people work eight hours a day, we Chinese do sixteen hours; if they can't stand the heat of the stoves in kitchen, we can . . . There is no paradise, we earned every penny with sweat and blood . . . This is a wealthy country, and there are too many Americans who just want to eat without having to work. It is under such circumstances that we Chinese have got a chance to make money.[21]

In other words, since most Downtown Chinese in their homelands lived in poverty and faced daily backbreaking physical labor, their expectations for what constitutes a happy life are quite moderate. Any improvement in living standards and working conditions, however small, is greeted by them as significant progress. It is such a mentality that makes Chinese immigrant laborers endure more than people of true pride should, turns them into visibly hardworking employees, and stifles their aspirations for political rights.

More significantly, ethnic Chinese immigrants' attitude toward America, especially that of refugees from Southeast Asia who currently make up a significant part of the Chinatown population, is influenced by another, even more powerful factor. In their eyes, American society is a sheltered realm that offers them a sense of protection unavailable in the overseas Chinese communities. Their view derives from the history of the Chinese diaspora, which, as defined by Andrew J. Nathan, "is in large part, a story of racist victimization."[22] The discrimination against and persecution of the ethnic Chinese in Indonesia help us understand this point. As a 1997 study reports: "Excluded from politics, the civil service and state companies, the ethnic Chinese [in Indonesia] must carry national identification cards with a special code. Places at state universities are restricted from the Chinese, forcing them to study at private institutions or abroad."[23] Compared with such blatant racial discrimination, prejudice in American society appears rather insignificant to these ethnic Chinese immigrants. As a writer pointed out in a Chinese-language newspaper: "We Chinese living in North America should be grateful that we don't have to fear such ugly anti-Chinese sentiments in our life."[24] Even in Hong Kong, which claimed to be more "democratic" under British rule than the rest of the Chinese world, Chinese were still treated only as second-class citizens throughout history. An immigrant from Hong Kong recalls:

> I can still remember vividly . . . my first job in Hong Kong as an engineer fresh out of school [in the 1950s] . . . A fellow white engineer, also freshly out of school from Britain, was paid a salary seven times mine. When I brought this gross discrepancy to the attention of my superior, I was told I can leave the colony if I don't like it there. Till this day I can not believe the gall of this foreigner to tell a local to leave. I was quite pleasantly surprised when I immigrated to Canada in 1972 to find out that whites in Canada and the U.S. do not behave the same way as the British do in Hong Kong.[25]

Such an impression inevitably affects the attitude of these immigrants in favor of American society. It also explains in part why Chinese and other Asian immigrants have the highest rate of naturalization: to them, U.S. citizenship symbolizes the right to live in American society, where stability and opportunity seem unquestioned.

The point is sharply illustrated in "Paradise" (1980), a short story by Yi Li on Chinese refugees from Vietnam. The title "Paradise" of course refers to the image of America in the eyes of the ethnic Chinese from Southeast Asia. The author's lively and artful unfolding of various details vividly reflects the mentality and feeling of great relief experienced by refugees after settling in America. The miserable life in their old homes and in refugee camps prompts them to embrace America as the "paradise." "Where can you find such a good government?" exclaims a character in the story when she is handed over a small settlement fee on arrival in America and finds that her family is eligible for welfare benefits.[26]

In other words, overwhelmed by their pre-immigration experience, many Downtown Chinese fail to understand the significance of the struggle for political rights. Their memories of the past, coupled with the relatively better treatment received in America, lead them to approach the issues of racial equality and social justice with rather modest expectations. A resident in San Francisco's Chinatown explains why he stayed away from the civil rights movement: "[One] does not eat butter unless one has had butter before. So if I never had butter it didn't mean a darn thing to me. Whether they allowed us in the Palace Hotel, it didn't matter because I never even tried to enter the place . . . . I accepted a lot of this as natural."[27] His problematic and limited vision of racial equality is highly representative of that of immigrants across racial and ethnic boundaries. Mario Puzo recalls that his mother, a peasant from Southern Italy, was always grateful to America even though she could barely survive in the new country. "Never mind about being happy," she liked to tell her children. "Be glad you're alive."[28]

It would be wrong, however, to assume that Chinese immigrants always remain passive toward the struggle for racial equality. On the contrary, most of them undergo dramatic changes once they secure economic sufficiency in American life. Joan Chen (Chen Chong), a recipient of the prestigious Golden Ring Award for her role in promoting Asian-American arts, is an outstanding example.

Under the pressure of economic necessity, Chen played parts in movies that debased the Chinese when she first arrived in America in 1981. But as she gradually established herself, she became outspoken in her criticism of racial bias against Asians in Hollywood. In her autobiographical writing, Chen meditates: "Most of my career up until now has been spent playing vulnerable Asian girls . . . As an Asian-American actress, I want to win acceptance and recognition based on racial equality. I may never succeed in this goal, but I'll keep fighting for it."[29]

Chen's story tacitly exposes the fraudulence in the argument that immigrants cannot appreciate the Chinese-American sensibility. It also indicates that although economic sufficiency does not automatically lead to the rise of ethnic consciousness, it grants immigrants a higher degree of freedom and power to define themselves and to challenge racism. In reality, there is not always a clear-cut line between the native-born and immigrants on the issue of racial assertiveness. While some American-born Chinese may compete to be "top bananas," a study of Chinese immigrant entrepreneurs in Los Angeles finds that despite having conservative views on many issues, "they do not shy away from asserting themselves, economically, culturally, or politically."[30] Opinion polls also indicate that Asian-American professionals, both native- and overseas-born, are more likely to challenge racial discrimination than their working-class counterparts.[31] In essence, as William Wei argues, the Asian-American movement is a middle-class movement.[32]

It is noteworthy that by exploring how the struggle for survival frustrates aspirations for political rights, Chinese-language writers have not only associated economic conditions with racial consciousness but also implied that the gap between the rich and the poor has played a significant role in dividing Chinese immigrants. Such an economic interpretation of problems in Chinatown life represents a perspective sharply different from theories of ethnic solidarity but close to the traditional Marxist ideology on the issues of race and ethnicity. As Eugene Genovese contends, "All good Marxist writing leads to an explication of class."[33] Judged by this standard, a large number of works in Chinese-language literature might be considered "good Marxist writing," because their authors seem to argue consciously or unconsciously that "class" is a critical factor that transcends Chinese identity and affects community unity. Or as Yu Lihua, one of the most prolific Chinese immigrant writers in America, says, "I agree that racial and ethnic conflicts in essence are an issue of class struggle."[34]

Indeed, conspicuous or half-hidden class struggle features in virtually every major Chinese-language work, serving as background for the dynamics of intra-ethnic confrontations in the Chinese community. For example, in the short story "Abortion," the author provides snapshots of another side of problems in Chinatown life.[35] The yawning chasm between the poor and the rich in the story constitutes a challenge to prospects of Chinese unity and the establishment of a single and unified Chinese-American agenda. The protagonist's husband, a chef in a Chinatown restaurant, complains bitterly that after working hard for nearly twenty years, he cannot even afford to pay medical insurance, while his boss has bought a mansion with the money exacted from the blood and sweat of restaurant workers.[36] In the story, the gap between the life of those who enjoy extravagances and those who extract mere sustenance from their work reveals that life in Chinatown is not always a tale of wealthy white Americans taking advantage of helpless immigrants, but of Chinese exploiting members of their own community — the bosses are just as Chinese as the peons.

The bestseller *American Moon* by Cao Youfang makes an even more powerful case for the claim that the real division in the Chinese community is often drawn along socioeconomic lines rather than the remote or recent immigrant past or degrees of acculturation.[37] Set in New York's Chinatown, the novel tells a moving story of the joys and sorrows of a student-turned-waiter in his American life. Amidst the seemingly agreeable and lively scene, the author inserts a deeper story about a labor dispute in a restaurant in which the protagonist works and organizes a trade union. Cao's message is clear: it is disparity in economic status in American society rather than difference in birthplaces that causes the rift among Chinese immigrants.

This argument, deeply held and strongly felt by most Chinese-language authors, is at odds with that of some American-born Chinese writers such as Amy Tan, who sees cultural differences and the generation gap as the major sources of conflicts in the Chinese community. Nevertheless, research conducted by Chinese-American scholars on Chinatown politics appear to confirm such an economic interpretation of problems in the Chinese community, and the Downtown Chinese are aware of class differences in their lives.[38] Indeed, economic status has been a widely used criterion to guide personal relations and measure individuals' positions on the social ladder in Chinatowns, and there is intense antagonism between the "have-nots" and the "haves." Although rarely reported by the mainstream media, strikes and labor disputes in Chinatown businesses occur frequently.[39]

The impact of the struggle for survival on immigrants reflected in Chinese-language literature demonstrates that although racism remains a barrier to Chinese-American progress, it is neither the sole nor an unbridled locus of problems in Chinese-American life, especially that of the Downtown Chinese. By examining how the issue of race is twisted and deformed by the struggle for economic sufficiency and by the gap in class identifications, Chinese-language writers seem to argue that "classism" and "racism" in American society have been compounded together in a "crucible" and it is difficult to separate one from the other.[40] In other words, challenging racial prejudice requires having confidence in one's own strength. But subjected to the pressure of earning a livelihood, most Downtown Chinese do not have that confidence: life in isolation and squalor forces them to remain single-minded in their pursuit of survival alone. Therefore, a key to the successful integration of the Chinese into American life involves not only a struggle against racism, but also efforts to help them, especially the Downtown Chinese, to improve living conditions and achieve economic equality. Only in this way can we succeed in organizing Chinatown residents into an effective, consolidated, and coherent political force in the struggle to ensure Asian-American progress.

Notes

1. This article is based on a portion of my book *Chinese American Literature since the 1850s* (Champaign: University of Illinois Press, 2000). Unless otherwise noted, I have used the term "Chinese-language literature" in this article to refer to works written in Chinese by Chinese immigrant writers in America.

2. Chen Ruoxi, "Xiangzhe Taipingyang Bi'an" ["To the Other Side of the Pacific"], in *Haiwai Huaren Zhuojia Xiaoshuoxuan* [*A Selection of Short Stories by Chinese Immigrant Writers*], ed. Li Li (Bao Lili) (Hong Kong: Joint Publishing, 1983). For the readers' convenience, I have cited English translations of Chinese titles in the text of my article and placed the romanization (*pinyin*) in the notes.

3. Nie Hualing, *Sangqing yu Taohong* [*Mulberry and Peach*] (Hong Kong: Joint, 1976).

4. Socioeconomically, Chinese-Americans today have been divided into two distinctive groups, the "Uptown" and "Downtown": the former are Chinese professionals who reside in suburban towns and are well integrated into mainstream society; the latter are predominantly Chinese immigrant laborers on the lowest rungs of the job ladder in the Chinese-American community. For more information on the background and socioeconomic status of the

Chinatown population in recent times, see Chalsa M. Loo, *Chinatown: Most Time, Hard Time* (New York: Praeger, 1992).

5. Quoted in Timothy P. Fong, *The First Suburban Chinatown: The Remaking of Monterey Park, California* (Philadelphia: Temple University Press, 1994), p. 70.

6. Peter Kwong, *The New Chinatown* (New York: Noonday Press, 1987), pp. 3–10.

7. Zhou Li (Julia Zhou Fochler), *Manhadun de Zhongguo Nuren* [*Manhattan's China Lady*] (Beijing: Beijing Chubanshe, 1992), p. 322; Yu Lihua, *Kaoyan* [*The Ordeal*, 1974] (reprint, Hong Kong: Cosmos Books, 1993), p. 373. Unless otherwise noted, translations in this article are all mine.

8. Zhou Feili (Philip Chou), "Yangfan Erchi" ["Two Ways to Eat American Meals"], in Zhou Feili, *Yangfan Erchi* (reprint, Taipei: Erya, 1987), pp. 1–24.

9. Ibid, p. 9.

10. Peter A. Quinn, quoted in "Connecting the Past and Present," March 11, 1995, *Los Angeles Times*, B3.

11. *Yamei Shibao* [*Asian American Times*], Boston, Sept. 24, 1993, p. 11. For more information on the issue of division in and fragmentation of the Chinese communities, see Victor G. and Brett de Bary Nee, *Longtime Californ': A Documentary Study of an American Chinatown* (reprint; Stanford: Stanford University Press, 1986), p. 255; Fong, *The First Suburban Chinatown*; pp. 138–56; and Kwong, *The New Chinatown*, pp. 81–106. The fact that Chinese and Asian-Americans are deeply divided on issues such as Proposition 187 in California, which requires schools and hospitals to turn in illegal immigrants, is also evidence of the fragmentation of their communities. See *New York Times*, Oct. 13, 1994, B2.

12. Chen Ruoxi, *Zhihun* [*Paper Marriage*] (Hong Kong: Joint, 1987), pp. 193–94. Also see Kwong, *The New Chinatown*, pp. 116–23.

13. Zhu Ying, "Bie Laoxiang Geiren Chi Yikufan" ["Don't Always Feed Us with Bitter Stories about American Life"], *Xin Dalu* [*New Continent*], Los Angeles, Aug. 1, 1994, p. 16. Also see Pangzi, "I Am a Happy Slave," *Chinese Community Forum*, #9808, March 11, 1998. *Chinese Community Forum* (CCF) is an electronic journal sponsored by Chinese students and scholars in America and published on China-Net. Founded in 1991, it has more than 40,000 subscribers. For more information on the journal, visit its web site: http://www.cnd.org.

14. Fong, *The First Suburban Chinatown*, pp. 157–77; K. Connie Kang, "Chinese in the Southland: a Changing Picture," *Los Angeles Times*, June 29, 1997, A1. Also see Carla Rivera, "Asians Say They Fare Better Than Other Minorities," *Los Angeles Times*, Aug. 20, 1993, A1; and *Zhong Bao* [*Central Daily*], New York, Nov. 19, 1987, A3.

15. Angela Oh, "Adding an Asian American Voice to the Race Debate," *Los Angeles Times,* July 13, 1997, M3.

16. Qian Ning, *Liuxue Meiguo* [*Studying in the USA*] (Nanjing: Jiangsu Wenyi, 1996), pp. 174–92.

17. Quoted in Susan Moffat, "Splintered Society," *Los Angeles Times,* July 13, 1992, A1.

18. Zhang Xiguo, "Xianjao Chuan" ["The Ship of Bananas"], reprinted in *Zhang Xiguo Ji* [*Selected Stories of Zhang Xiguo*], ed. Chen Wanyi (Taipei: Qianwei, 1993), pp. 112–13.

19. Yang Mu, "Zhang Xiguo de Guanxin yu Yishu" ["Zhang Xiguo's Concerns and Arts of Literature"], in Chen, *Selected Stories of Zhang Xiguo*, pp. 245–47. Also see Pan Yatun and Wang Yisheng, *Haiwai Huawen Wenxue Mingjia* [*Distinguished Chinese-Language Writers Abroad*] (Guangzhou: Jinan University Press, 1994), pp. 176–79.

20. Mary C. Waters, "Interview: The Counterpoint of Race and Ethnicity," *Harvard Gazette,* Nov. 12, 1993, p. 5. Also see Zhou, "Two Ways to Eat American Meals," p. 18.

21. Yi Li (Pan Xiumei), "Shiwan Meijin" ["A Hundred Thousand Dollars"], in Yi, *A Hundred Thousand Dollars* (Hong Kong: Joint, 1987), p. 138.

22. Andrew J. Nathan, "But How Chinese Are They?" *New York Times Book Review,* Dec. 9, 1990, p. 26. Also see Garth Alexander, *The Invisible China: The Overseas Chinese and the Politics of Southeast Asia* (New York: Macmillan, 1974), pp. 150–66.

23. *South China Morning Post,* Hong Kong, May 29, 1997, A1. The ethnic Chinese make up about three percent of Indonesia's population of 202 million. Although a few are among the richest people in Indonesia, most are small businessmen or peddlers. However, they are often attacked as scapegoats during economic crises in that country. For more information on this issue, see Mely G. Tan, "The Ethnic Chinese in Indonesia," in *Ethnic Chinese as Southeast Asians,* ed. Leo Suryadinata (Singapore: Institute of Southeast Asian Studies, 1997), pp. 33–65; and Stephen Fitzgerald, *China and the Overseas Chinese* (New York: Cambridge University Press, 1972), pp. 1–11, 74–101.

24. Kong Xiangjiong, "Huaren Shouxi Cheng Daizui Gaoyang" ["Ethnic Chinese Again Become Scapegoats in Indonesia"], *Haojiao* [*Herald Monthly*], New York, 11-4 (April 1998):2.

25. Zhifu Du, "6.5 Million Hong Kong People Returning to the Communist Motherland," *Chinese Community Forum* #9733, July 1, 1997.

26. Yi Li, "Tian Tang" ["Paradise"], in Yi, *A Hundred Thousand Dollars,* pp. 116–20.

27. Quoted in Nee, *Longtime Californ',* pp. 245–46. Of course, in participating in

political movements in American society, Chinese immigrants are also handicapped by their "alien" status because they may be deported for their allegedly radical views. A Chinese writer recalls in her autobiography that she was deported to China in 1954 for her left-wing ideology during the wave of anti-Communist hysteria that swept America. See Wang Ying, *Liangzhong Meiguoren [Two Kinds of Americans]* (Beijing: Zhongguo Qingnian, 1980). For more information on this aspect of the Chinese-American experience, see L. Ling-chi Wang, "Roots and the Changing Identity of the Chinese in the United States," in *The Living Tree: The Changing Meaning of Being Chinese Today,* ed. Tu Wei-ming (Stanford: Stanford University Press, 1994), pp. 185–212.

28. Mario Puzo, "Choosing a Dream: Italians in Hell's Kitchen," reprinted in *Visions of America: Personal Narratives from the Promised Land,* ed. Wesley Brown and Amy Ling (New York: Persea Books, 1993), p. 58.

29. Quoted in Yan Geling, *Chen Chong — Helihuo de Zhongguo Nuren [Joan Chen: A Chinese Woman in Hollywood]* (Hong Kong: Cosmos, 1995), pp. 200, 224. In this respect, Chen seems to have followed in the footsteps of Anna May Wong, a pioneer for Asian-Americans in Hollywood. Anna became critical of racial prejudice in Hollywood once she had made a name in the entertainment industry. See Thi Thanh Nga (Tiana), "The Long March: From Wong to Woo," *Cineaste,* 21-4 (1995):38–40; Philip Leibfred, "Anna May Wong," *Films in Review,* 38-2 (March 1987):146–52; and Edward Sakamoto, "Anna May Wong and the Dragon-lady Syndrome," *Los Angeles Times Sunday Magazine,* July 12, 1987, p. 40.

30. Fong, *The First Suburban Chinatown,* p. 154. Also see Angelina T. Wong, "The Contest to Become Top Banana: Chinese Students at Canadian Universities," *Canadian Ethnic Studies,* 11-2 (1979):63–69.

31. Cited in Kang, "Chinese in the Southland: A Changing Picture," and in Rivera, "Asians Say They Fare Better Than Other Minorities."

32. William Wei, *The Asian American Movement* (Philadelphia: Temple University Press, 1993), pp. 1–43. Also see Gary Y. Okihiro, *Margins and Mainstreams: Asians in American History and Culture* (Seattle: University of Washington Press, 1994), pp. 148–75.

33. Quoted in Arif Dirlik, "Asians on the Rim: Transnational Capital and Local Community in the Making of Contemporary Asian America," *Amerasia* 22-3 (1996):7. Many Chinese-American scholars also argue that conflicts in economic interests are a primary source of tensions within the Chinese-American community. See L. Ling-chi Wang, "The Politics of Ethnic Identity and Empowerment: The Asian American Community Since the 1960s," *Asian American Policy Review,* 2-1 (Spring 1991):43–56. Also see Fong, *The First Suburban Chinatown;* pp. 138–56, and Kwong, *The New Chinatown,* pp. 81–106. The

interest of Chinese immigrant writers in Marxist views is obviously also a result of the influence of American academicians. Despite its practical and theoretical flaws, Marxist thought is still widely used by scholars in the humanities and social science. For more discussion on this issue, see Dario Fernandez-Morera, *American Academia and the Survival of Marxist Ideas* (New York: Praeger, 1996).

34. My interview with Yu Lihua at her residence in Albany, New York, Oct. 13, 1994.

35. Yi Li, "Duo Tai" ["Abortion"], in Li, *A Selection of Short Stories by Chinese Immigrant Writers.*

36. Ibid., pp. 102–103.

37. Cao Youfang, *Meiguo Yueliang* [*The American Moon*] (Hong Kong: Joint, 1986).

38. Wang, "The Politics of Ethnic Identity and Empowerment," pp. 45–54; Fong, *The First Suburban Chinatown*, pp. 138–56; and Kwong, *The New Chinatown*, pp. 81–106.

39. "When Restaurants Fail, Who Pays the Workers?" *Sampan*, Boston, Feb. 20, 1998, p. 7; *Qiao Bao* [*Overseas Chinese Daily*], New York, Dec. 9, 1997, A12. Also see Wang, "The Politics of Ethnic Identity."

40. Many Asian-American activists and scholars have expressed similar views on this issue. See Yen Le Espiritu, *Asian American Women and Men: Labor, Laws, and Love* (Thousand Oaks, Calif.: Sage Publications, 1997), pp. 113–16; Oh, "Adding an Asian American Voice to the Race Debate."

CHAPTER TWENTY-ONE

"China" in the American Diaspora

■ QIAN SUOQIAO

Not for the first time, but in a new context, waves of new immigrants to the United States since the 1960s have significantly changed the demographic features of various ethnic communities. As Arjun Appadurai wrote: "If, indeed, a postnational order is in the making, and Americanness changes its meanings, the whole problem of diversity in American life will have to be rethought . . . and we can become a federation of diasporas: American-Italians, American-Haitians, American-Irish, American-Africans."[1] Perhaps the acuteness of the diaspora question lies in its potential challenge to the theoretical foundations of identity politics, insofar as it forces the rethinking of the very notions of nation, border, home, location, and so forth. Then what kind of connotations does a diasporic discourse evoke in relation to a host of relevant concepts like home and exile, place and displacement, location and ground, border and boundary? And what do we mean by "diaspora" after all? Is the Anglo-American tradition a diasporic formation?

I do not attempt to engage in an all-encompassing theoretical study of diaspora. Instead, I will focus on the issue of representation and interpretation of "China" as revealed through a critical examination of the controversial works of Frank Chin and *Manhattan's China Lady* by Zhou Li. Although the former is usually placed in Asian-American studies and the latter in modern Chinese studies, one of my objectives here is precisely to cross and break such disciplinary boundaries. I will show that, despite the obvious experiential differences their texts invoke, their discursive realms are indeed interrelated and overlapping, not the least so far as the interpretive representation of "China" in the diaspora is concerned.

RE-LINKING WITH CHINESE CULTURAL
HISTORY AS "REAL"

In Asian-American cultural criticism, the issue of diaspora has also become the focus of attention, arousing much controversy and "chaos," as shown in a 1995 special issue of *Amerasia* entitled "Thinking Theory in Asian American Studies." As Sau-ling Wong admits, transnational and diasporic concerns can no longer be ignored as new waves of Asian immigrants became a formidable factor in Asian America. But Wong's seemingly "inclusive" account of the diasporic phenomenon is in fact aimed at its dismissal, since a diasporic refocusing will question the very validity of Asian-American cultural criticism itself. According to Wong, the field of Asian-American studies was founded upon "the cultural nationalist project as articulated by the *Aiiieeeee!* group" (Frank Chin as its foremost advocate) and the notion of "claiming America" (as coined by Maxine Hong Kingston), in which "culture" and "nation" refer to and are defined within the nation-state boundary of the United States. In their premises, Asian-American studies "explicitly or implicitly discourage, if not preclude, critical attention on things Asian."[2]

Wong's attribution of "cultural nationalism" to Frank Chin is accountable and at the same time misleading. It ignores and suppresses the complexity of Frank Chin's works, and conflates his stance with that of Maxine Hong Kingston in this respect merely for the sake of disciplinary unity. Nor does Wong's interpretation suffice to recognize the challenge of cultural nationalism in terms of a feminist critique of it, because what lies under the polemics between Chin and Kingston is not the problematics of gender *per se*, but rather the more fundamental question of the attitude toward "China" or "things Chinese" in the locality called Chinese America. I will show that, even though in his early work Frank Chin was responsible for the canonization of Asian-American studies in terms of a cultural nationalist project, if there ever were such a project, he has proven to be its own most serious rebel and critic given his repositioning toward Chinese cultural history as "real."

Frank Chin's play *The Year of the Dragon*, first produced in 1974 by the American Place Theater in New York, features a character called "China

Mama." Fresh from China to accompany her dying husband in the United States, the character is a rather freakish caricature in contrast to her almost-40-year-old, unmarried son Fred, a Chinatown tour guide. As China Mama gets up from her couch and tries to fix some food for Fred and talk to him in Chinese, Fred responds in English: "You want me to be Chinese too, huh? Everybody does . . . You know how the tourists tell I'm Chinese? No first person pronouns. No 'I,' 'Me' or 'We.' I talk like that lovable sissy, Charlie Chan, no first person personal pronouns . . . English lesson, China Mama. How do you say 'English' in Chinese." China Mama then gets an English lesson of pronouncing "I" from Fred in a comical confusion. And Fred declares, by way of "getting China Mama off him": "'I. Me. We.' You are now a citizen, congratulations . . . I'm not Chinese. This ain't China. Your language is foreign and ugly to me, so how come you're my mother?"[3] Then China Mama is dismissed and ends up smoking opium in the play.

Just like the father in *The Year of the Dragon*, the nameless father in "Food for All His Dead" is also dying, in Chin's short story that appeared in the widely read first anthology of Asian-American literature. The story focuses on Johnny's (the son) alienation from his father and the Chinatown community, which is celebrating Double Ten with a parade. To Johnny, the parade that carries deep emotional meaning for the father was like an American Indian curio show, with "the dark crowd of people standing in puddles of each other, moving like oily things and bugs floating on a tide."[4] As a disinterested and frustrated observer whose only reason for staying in Chinatown was waiting for his father to die, Johnny reflects that "the man was no longer like his father or a man; perhaps it was the parade. But the waiting, the lies and waiting so long with a flesh going to death that the person was no longer real as a life but a parody of live things, grinning."[5] So Johnny flatly tells his father: "Most of the people I don't like are Chinese. They even *laugh* with accents, Christ!"[6] The story ends, not with the closing of the Double Ten parade, but, not surprisingly, with the funeral procession of the nameless father, with Johnny marching with "a large photograph of the dead man," in "a parade of black coats and hats."[7]

The narrative strategy in the above two representative texts of Frank Chin's early writings, which have been regarded as pioneering literary landmarks in Asian-American literature, has made it quite clear that "China," through a symbolic personification of "China Mama," newly arrived from China and "Father," who has been a "longtime Californ'," stands for things "foreign and ugly." Whatever frustrations and problems the protagonists are grappling with, their attitude toward "Mother" and "Father" is consistent: one which Joseph S. M. Lau has aptly called an exercise of exorcism.[8] The question is whether the author identifies with the attitudes of the fictional protagonists of his creation, and if so, to what degree. As I will show, Chin later on tries to distance himself from his protagonists, and his narrative strategy in his later works changes dramatically in its representation of "China." To account for these apparent incongruities, we need to examine the notion of "Chinese American sensibility" and especially its related project of "stereotype critique," the creation and advancement of which have been largely credited to Frank Chin.

In the widely influential *Aiiieeeee! An Anthology of Asian American Writers,* Chin and his fellow anthologists attempt to define Chinese-American literature (and Chinese-American culture) according to a certain unique Chinese-American sensibility. But it is important to note that, behind the emotional rhetoric, what exactly constitutes Chinese-American sensibility was merely crudely suggested and remained elusive. The primary criterion was nativity: American-born and raised. Yet that was immediately qualified, for good reason. For instance, Chin claims that Louis Chu, who came to America when he was nine, authentically conveyed the "Chinese American sensibility." Conversely, the "fathers" his literary protagonists vehemently exorcise could very well be American-born, and indeed "longtime Californ'," just like his own father.[9] A more fruitful angle to examine what Chin admits to be such a "delicate" notion of Chinese-American sensibility is to understand the reasoning behind "stereotype critique," which has consumed most of the energy of the *Aiiieeeee!* group.

Thanks to the efforts of the civil rights movement, few will not acknowledge that racial stereotyping is a serious and continuing problem of American society. One has to constantly face the irony of watching a movie or television program "about me." To Frank Chin and Jeffery Paul Chan, stereotypes are false images imposed upon racial minorities for the sake of sustaining white supremacy — an argument, though much more straightforwardly put forward here, anticipating Edward Said's elaborate critique of Orientalism. So far as the Chinese in America are concerned, modern stereotyping is no longer instigated by fear and hatred, as was the Yellow Peril myth and the literary creation of Fu Manchu; rather, it is imbued with sentimentality, which Chin and Chan call "racist love," as in the Hollywood creation of Charlie Chan. As Chin and Chan see it, the real vice of anti-Asian stereotypes lies in its pernicious depiction of the Chinese as forever unassimilable aliens, foreigners to their land of abode, hence excluded from participation in American culture.

At the early stage, Chin's opposition to such stereotypes offered only a doubly negative solution. It is the key to understanding Chin's ambiguous attitude toward "China" at this time, and also points to the danger of a mere stereotype critique deprived of a reliable agent. Chinese-American sensibility is first and foremost defined as the opposite of what stereotypes have portrayed it to be, and, largely because of that, not "Chinese." The logic behind this connection is rather puzzling. If stereotypes are false images imposed upon racial minorities, it seems self-evident that one would show the "real" in order to dispel the falsity of such stereotypes. Yet to Chin and other Aiiieeeee! critics at this time, "stereotype critique" had become an enterprise for its own sake, a critical project led by the paradigmatic assumptions seen from outside, which ironically results in and functions as a tactic for internal differentiation and exclusion. Furthermore, the criteria for what counts as stereotypical were rather idiosyncratic and even dictatorial. The more established American-born writers of Chinese descent such as Pardee Lowe, Jade Snow Wong, Virginia Lee, and Betty Lee Sung were condemned as "confirming the popular stereotypes of Chinese-Americans."[10] The better-known China-born writers in English such as Lin Yutang and C. Y. Lee were excluded on the basis of both their nativity and their alleged self-stereotyping, since "they were intimate with and secure in their Chinese cultural identity in an experiential sense, in a way we American-born can never be. Again, unlike us, they are American by choice. They consciously set out to become American, in the white sense of the word, and succeeded in becoming 'Chinese American' in the stereotypical sense of the good, loyal, obedient, passive, law-abiding, cultured sense of the word."[11]

However, precisely because of its critical preoccupation with the negation of stereotypes, Chin's attitude toward "China" is also rather vexed. On the one hand, Chin seems to be adamant in affirming that a Chinese-American sensibility is radically different and dissociated from "things Chinese." In his correspondence with Frank Ching, editor of *Bridge* magazine, for instance, Chin claims that: "There is no cultural, psychological, Bridge between me and the Chinese immigrants. There are social, racist pressures that connect us. These connections must be broken."[12] This loud pronouncement of Chin's has been subsequently generalized into an institutional assumption of Asian-American studies, so we need to put it in its historical context to understand Chin's rhetorical rationale. An important clue to understanding stereotype critique lies in what Chin believes to be a primary function of racial stereotyping, namely, that it breeds self-contempt within the targeted minority. Living under the perpetual shadow of racial stereotyping that keeps telling them who they are, Asians in America are said to develop a negative psyche of self-contempt because they are told they acquire a "dual personality," which divides "the Chinese American into two incompatible segments: (1) the *foreigner* whose status is dependent on his ability to be accepted by the white natives; and (2) the *handicapped native* who is taught that identification with his foreignness is the only way to 'justify' his difference in skin color."[13] It is no wonder that according to such characterization of stereotypes, the oppositional strategy is directed at negating the "foreignness" and affirming the "nativeness." The striking and disturbing thing is that the *Aiiieeeee!* critics, instead of affirming that the Chinese were by no means foreign to the land of the Gold Mountain, made an internal differentiation between "Chinese" (from China) and "Chinese-American," largely on the ground that the white racial stereotyping does not make such a distinction. The result is Fred Eng's violent rejection of China Mama. Indeed, the role of China Mama makes sense only when we see that "China" is cast as the Other in order for Fred to break off his genealogical ties with Mama: her alienness opposes his citizenship; her "foreign and ugly" Cantonese contrasts with his "beautiful" English. It is most strange that, in order to dispel the stereotypes, Fred has to "get himself off" his China Mama, a China Mama fabricated as the fictional other, a stereotypical image the same as, if not worse than, that of Charlie Chan.

It is important to note that Chin here does not offer an affirmative definition of what Chinese-American sensibility really is. In his two plays — *The Chickencoop Chinaman* and *The Year of the Dragon* — and the short story "Food for All His Dead," while the "China" characters are portrayed negatively, the Chinese-American protagonists (Tam Lum, Fred Eng, and Johnny) can hardly be called positive portrayals. In *Chickencoop Chinaman*, for instance, when Tam is accused of being "prejudiced against Chinese," he replies: "Foreigners do not bother me, but ornamental Orientals like you make me sick."[14] While Tam seems to be certain that he does not belong to the Chinese who are foreigners nor to the stereotypical "ornamental Orientals," this Chinese-American also calls himself a "loser" who gives up and is bewildered about what to fight for.[15] Different from other political activists of the Asian-American movement, whether internationally oriented Maoists or domestic Black Panthers-inspired militants, Frank Chin is after all an artist of critical consciousness from the beginning. His later affirmative transition may be attributed to the fact that even in his early career he allows him an aesthetic space that significantly distances him from his protagonists. Exorcism of "China," while disturbing, has to be understood in the context of his overwhelming concern with stereotype critique. Even Johnny explains that it is not that he does not like to be in Chinatown where everybody is Chinese, but that he has become frustrated and overtaken by the outside white community's image of Chinatown (like an Indian curio show) *after* he has gone to school outside of Chinatown. As Johnny explains: "I remember when I was a kid. Man, then I knew everything. I knew all my aunts were beautiful, and all my cousins were small, and all my uncles were heroes from the war and the strongest guys in the world that smoked cigars and swore, and my grandmother was a queen of women . . . I really had it made then, really, and I knew more then than I do now."[16] Perhaps what is most revealing about Chin's vexed attitude toward "China" can be found in his own account of his personal relationship with his father. Son of the president of Six Companies, Chin is a member of the fifth generation of his family in California. He admits that he feels guilty of "coming down hard on anyone in Chinatown," and is quite aware that while his fictional protagonist Johnny regards Chinatown as a curio show, Chin's own family regards him as "sort of weirdo charity case." Moreover, he still identifies with his father and vice versa: "My father tried, in his own way he tried as hard as I am to make it in his terms in this country. Yeah, I think he failed and I think he thinks he's failed. But in his eyes, I'm irresponsible. I'm fooling around and I'm an insult to him . . . So I feel bad about that."[17]

It is not until Frank Chin discovers Guan Gong, the Chinese legendary hero, that his notion of Chinese-American sensibility matures into an affirmative elaboration. Now, however, he rarely uses the term "Chinese-American," and when he does, it is a pejorative reference to the assimilated group. The new term is "Chinaman." With Guan Gong, Chin's cultural criticism gains a positive agent — a Chinaman subjectivity. The nature of his cultural criticism changes from a mere stereotype critique for its own sake to a cross-cultural critique. Likewise his attitude toward "China" changes from vexed distancing to reconnecting.

The switch seems to be a consequence of Chin's reaction to the critical fame of Maxine Hong Kingston's writings and their incorporation into the canon of American literature and culture. But his early writings already contain a preview of what Chin now calls the "real," which has been somehow suppressed but could be revived. Johnny's problem with the Chinese and Chinatown is largely attributable to his school education outside Chinatown, while his knowledge of and familiarity with "things Chinese" are assumed. It is interesting that Frank Chin also tells us of his own personal experience with a certain Mr. Ma, his Chinese schoolteacher, who apparently left a deep impression on him. Mr. Ma, "a Chinese graduate student who had recently come to the United States," "shook everybody up" with his resounding contempt of the term "Chinese-American":

Why do you want to be called Chinese-Americans? Because you don't want to be called Chinamen, because that's what they called your grandfathers and your great-grandfathers who were the miners . . . What did they do to be bad guys? They mined gold, they dug out the tunnels, they carved the way for the railroad, what's so bad about that? The only thing that was bad was that the white man looked on them with contempt and called them Chinamen. And all we can remember is that they looked on them with contempt, you know. And we think it's all our fault, but it isn't, it's the white man's fault that Chinaman is a bad word. And you should never forget that, you should call yourselves Chinamen, not Chinese-Americans.[18]

Although young Frank Chin sets out to legitimize a certain Chinese-American sensibility, those words seem to have never left him. In his most recent novel, *Gunga Din Highway*, we find a fictional Chinese schoolteacher also named Mr. Ma, or Horse, who tells the story of Guan Gong to the protagonists in the novel, Ulysses, Benedict, and Diego, who swear to be brothers like the Peach Garden brotherhood of Liu, Guan, and Zhang in *Three Kingdoms*. While never really good students at the Chinese school, indeed, constantly fighting with Mr. Ma, the protagonists nevertheless visited the teacher at his deathbed. Before his last breath, he handed Ulysses "a vaguely cone-shaped lump of clay with Kwan Kung [Guan Gong] painted on it. Green for his robe and hat. Red for his face and hands. Little stripes of blue and red painted along the hem of his skirt and across his boots."[19]

According to Dorothy Ritsuko McDonald, Frank Chin seemed to have expressed great admiration of Guan Gong as early as 1976, in a letter to Michael Kirby, editor of *The Drama Review*.[20] It was not until 1985, however, that we find Chin fully embracing Guan Gong at the core of a Chinaman sensibility in his essay "This Is Not an Autobiography." Chin's retrieval of the Chinese heroic tradition *à la* Guan Gong certainly stems from his dissatisfaction with the popular reception of Kingston's writings, but he must have also been aware of where his own negative advancement of a Chinese-American sensibility could (mis)lead to. No wonder that in an interview with Robert Murray Davis conducted in 1985, Chin makes a special point of distancing himself from his own character, Fred Eng: "[Fred Eng] does use a stereotype and he does play on it and he knows he is lying and he knows he is exploiting. Am I that tourist guide? I don't think so, but that's not for me to say. I know the difference, I *think* I know the difference, between the real and the fake . . . I think that Fred Eng confronted his history. He found the real. He knows what he is doing is fake, but he believes in the stereotype at the same time so he hasn't bothered to read or understand the Chinatown that he is faking and living at the same time."[21]

Chin probably puts Maxine Hong Kingston in the same category. The polemic between Chin and Kingston is generally understated in Asian-American cultural criticism and glossed merely in terms of gender conflict. But Chin's argument is that gender is simultaneously, and more significantly, a matter of cultural representation. Kingston's feminist avenger in *The Woman Warrior,* the most widely taught text in American colleges, attempts to misrepresent and assault Chinese culture as a whole. As Judith Melton tells us, *The Woman Warrior* is taught in Women's Studies classes as reflecting "the historical portrait of a misogynist culture." Students are led to "share Kingston's fear and anger at the victimization of women in feudal China," and "like her, they find the traditions alien and abhorrent, and most of all shocking," so in the end "students begin to realize how practices that are significant in one . . . culture lose their importance in another."[22] Furthermore, even though Kingston attempts to recover a heroic tradition of Chinese experience in America in *China Men* (to interpret it as a "tacit call for empathy between Chinese American men and women," as King-kok Cheung suggests), she still misses and misinforms the fundamental issue at stake concerning the polemics between herself and Chin.[23] In the project of "claiming America," as Kingston explains her narrative intention in *China Men,* it is assumed that the "making of more Americans" simultaneously entails the act of exorcising the Chinese "ghosts." To the narrator's father, a vacant lot in Stockton becomes the "ancestral ground" after the ghost of Say Goong has been "startled away" back to China; Kau Goong has found his home in California and refused to be united with his long-time-no-seen wife, whether in China or Hong Kong. When he dies he is buried properly "like any American dead," and thereby "absolved of all duties to ancestors." Uncle Bun (which means Uncle Stupid) is stupid and fanatical because he goes back to China, Red China, and in the end is simply forgotten by the narrator's family, who have been "made" into "Americans." Kingston's narrative strategy to cast "China" as an Other to be exorcised turns into a farcical show in the story of Mad Sao. Having "firmly established his American citizenship by serving in the U.S. Army in World War II," he lives a happy normal American life until the real "mad" one, his irrational and bewitching mother in China, begins to haunt him, urging him to sell his American daughters and send the profits to her. And Mad

Sao literally has to accompany the dead mother's ghost back to China, solely for the purpose of burying it. Without spending "any time sightseeing or visiting relatives and old friends . . . He hurried home to America, where he acted normal again, continuing his American life."[24]

To Frank Chin, the assertion of a Chinaman subjectivity is meant precisely to prevent the irrelevance and extinction of once significant cultural practices in the "making of more Americans." To achieve that, Chin realizes that it is essential to go beyond a mere negative definition of the "Chinese American sensibility." It takes a "Chinaman 'I'" and a "Chinaman act" to fight against wishful assimilation and really claim America on their own terms. Language and nativity no longer assume primary significance here, for "whatever language a Chinaman speaks, it is always Chinaman."[25] Tam, the Chinaman in Chin's early play *The Chickencoop Chinaman,* claimed that "Chinamen are made . . . out of junk-imports, lies, railroad scrap iron, dirty jokes, broken bottles, cigars smoke, Cosquilla Indian blood, wino spit, and lots of milk of amnesia" where "the Word is [his] heritage."[26] The later use of Chinaman is directly handed down from Mr. Ma, deriving from Chin's unique interpretation of the Chinese (popular) cultural history as "real." As Chin now announces that "the Christian Chinese Americans coined the term *Chinese American* to distinguish themselves from heathen Chinamen," the term "Chinaman" is recuperated not merely in opposition to the racist connotations it has been historically imbued with, but in celebration of a subjectivity connected to and deriving from the Chinese popular/heroic cultural tradition.[27] This fundamental difference in cultural attitudes toward "China" lies at the core of the polemics between Chin and Kingston. Inspired by the new waves of Chinese immigrants coming to America from around the world, Chin explains to his interviewer, sounding very much like Frank Ching in their earlier correspondence, that "we [English-speaking American-born] shouldn't see ourselves as superior. Here's a real connection with our history and with the civilization, with the works of literature, childhood literature, adventure stories. What they see is that the English speaking American born don't know shit and are faking it and so our work is tending to have a white racist effect of separating the English speaking American born from the new immigrant."[28]

Chin's new representation of "China" has exerted a striking effect on his literary creativity and maturity, as shown in his novel *Donald Duk*. Certainly his masterpiece to date, *Donald Duk* will be regarded in a truly multicultural America as the great "kid's story" of a new America, a *Huckleberry Finn* for a different age. The father-son interplay here is drastically different from the alienated and conflict-ridden relationships in his earlier works. Donald Duk and his father are engaged in a reasoned interaction that ultimately leads to Donald's cultural awakening and enlightenment in becoming a Chinaman. Like the Chinese-American protagonists in Chin's early works, Donald is also experiencing a peculiar negation of China in revolt against racial stereotyping. But unlike the narrator in his earlier works, who could be said to be in complicity with his protagonists, the narrator in *Donald Duk* is in full control of the character portrayal and narrative structure, thanks to the Chinaman identification. It is also interesting to note that nativity is quite irrelevant to being a Chinaman. Donald's father, King Duk, was born in America, but he has no identity crisis. Rather, he is self-assured, knows the popular Chinese stories and legends, and feels completely at ease with Chinese cultural practices, including the proper manner of bringing up and educating his son. When Donald does the wrong thing, such as stealing a model airplane the father has been making, the father does not just scold and punish him, but rather makes sure that Donald realizes his own mistake and corrects it. The father teaches not just by words but by actions in matters related to Chinese cultural practices, such as the correct way to treat friends and relatives during the Chinese New Year holidays. Although King Duk is most friendly and accommodating to Donald's best friend at school, Arnold and his family, he does not do it to ingratiate himself but purely for Donald's sake. He teaches Donald the strategy of treasuring an ally in the fight against racism, and also gives him to understand that anger and frustration over racial stereotypes are themselves a sign of weakness. In order to be able to stand against racial stereotyping and injustice, it is most important to know where you yourself stand, that is, to firmly maintain your self-awareness. When Donald is upset because his father seems to be nonchalant about his discovery that Chinamen's contribution to the building of the railroad was neglected, King answers:

"They don't want our names in their history books. So what? You're surprised. If we don't write our history, why should they, huh?"

"It's not fair."

"Fair? What's fair? History is war, not sports! . . . You believe in the goodness of others to cover your butt, you're good for nothing. So, don't expect me to get mad or be surprised the *bokgwai* never told our history in any of their books you happen to read in the library, looking for yourself. You gotta keep the history yourself or lose it forever, boy. That's the mandate of heaven."[29]

During the Chinese New Year parade Donald participates in the dragon dance, which represents an old Chinese-language school he is enrolled in but has never attended. The dragon dance clears away the uncertainties that have been haunting the boy, as he is now linked to and has become part of his cultural legacy.

Frank Chin has not given up stereotype critique. Dispelling racial stereotypes still constitutes his major critical endeavor. The nature of his critique has changed, however. As Chin and other editors of *Aiiieeeee!* explain recently: "Before we can talk about our literature, we have to explain our sensibility. Before we can explain our sensibility, we have to outline our histories. Before we can outline our history, we have to dispel the stereotypes. Before we dispel the stereotypes, we have to prove the falsity of the stereotypes and the ignorance of easily accessible, once well-known common history."[30] Stereotype critique has thus merged into a *cross-cultural* critique, as Chin's critical priority shifted to recuperating (popular) Chinese cultural history in order to resist the assimilating power of what Chin deems are the historical practices of Christian religion. One may certainly take issue with Chin's particular Chinaman appropriation of (popular) Confucianism and with his gender bias, but he does offer us a valuable insight: in a cross-cultural encounter, what determines the validity of a certain culture lies not so much in the quintessence of its high culture as in the acceptability and durability of its popular cultural practices. It is this insight that prompts Chin to retrieve and advance the heroic tradition of Guan Gong particularly for Chinamen in America. And of course, in such a cross-cultural (re)-linking, Chinese-American history, or Chinamen's history in America, can never be exclusively demarcated within the nation-state boundary of the United States.

LEGITIMIZING THE "RED" GENERATION

At first glance, Frank Chin and Zhou Li could not be further apart in terms of their sensibilities, even though both are of Chinese descent and more or less of the same generation. Born (in 1940) and raised in California, Chin writes in English and inevitably for the English-speaking readership, while Zhou, born (in 1950) and raised in Shanghai, writes in Chinese in New York and inevitably for the Chinese-speaking readership. While Chin's major concern is to critique and fight against racial discrimination in American culture, Zhou seems to fully embrace the culture and strives to find her place in it. While "China" is something Chin needs to rejoin, overt declarations of patriotism toward "China" permeate Zhou's narratives. However, such a contrast is oversimplified and deceptive. A clearer picture will emerge from explicating the layered meaning of the discursive formations in Zhou's narrative.

It is generally agreed that the cultural scene in 1990s China has taken on quite a different shape from that of the 1980s. In the earlier half of the decade, the top two most popular literary texts in visual media were the television series *Kewang* [Yearning] and *Beijing ren zai Niuyue* [Beijinger in New York], and the top two in print media were Jia Pingwa's *Feidu* [Abandoned Capitol] and Zhou Li's *Manhadun de zhongguo nuren* [Manhattan's China Lady]. Of the four, two are about the Chinese diaspora in America. Published in July 1992, Zhou's work became the first sensational Chinese-language national bestseller since 1989, the June Fourth Incident (which is totally absent in Zhou's book), and by 1996 it had its eighth printing. Thousands of readers are said to have shed tears of sympathy, compassion, excitement, and envy over reading Zhou's book. Such popularity is warranted because, as a close reading of Zhou's text will show, the authorial sensibility quite tellingly reveals and helps to shape a peculiar ethos of the times.

Manhattan's China Lady (*Manhattan* for short) is a lengthy straightforward journalistic tale in the genre of autobiographical fiction, of a first-person narrator who grew up in Red China, went through the Cultural Revolution, came to the United States as a student in 1985 with $40, and became a marvelously successful businesswoman within four years, "handling over ten-million-US dollar-worth of international trade" in her own apartment overlooking Central Park in Manhattan. The text is almost squarely divided into her American experience (Chapters I, V, and VI), of studying in SUNY Binghamton, making it in the business world, and happily marrying a white man named Michael Fochler (whose "skin is so elegant, delicate and tender, especially his round, luxurious and beautifully delineated butt"[31]); and her experience in China (Chapters II, III, and IV), of growing up, going to the countryside during the Cultural Revolution, and falling into first love with an awesome Red Guard named Pei Yang.

The popularity of Zhou's book was initially ignited by media hype, and in a way set a precedent for later cultural production in 1990s China. The publicity arose from a controversy over the authenticity of Zhou's tale. A group of Chinese-American businessmen called a press conference in New York's Chinatown, claiming that they were derogatorily portrayed in Zhou's account and hence that their images were damaged. They subsequently published an article in a New York Chinese-language newspaper revealing the truth about Zhou. In their account she was a mere swindler; far from being a millionaire, she had a mortgaged, tiny two-bedroom apartment in Manhattan, which also served as the office for her one-person company, and she even rented out one room.[32] A major newspaper in Beijing republished the article and other tabloid newspapers around the country picked it up. Zhou replied that she was *handling* a million-dollar business and that the book was an "autobiographical fiction," and then threatened to sue the Beijing newspaper for irresponsibly republishing an article written by some ill-intentioned businessmen in New York. This triggered a nation-wide debate over the value of the book.

Immediately a handful of critics condemned the book as a bad piece of literary writing that promotes a bad philosophy of life. Wu Liang, for instance, points out that the book is merely a lengthy, tiresome pop memoir devoid of stylistic creativity, full of exclamation marks, encumbered with a laundry list of books she reads for "self-cultivation"; it is a tour guide of America filled with sensational love affairs, not to mention its unabashedly vulgar philosophy of life. As Dan Dan puts it, the book "reveals the author's longing for a life of vanity and fame. Her success is based on the satisfaction of her vanity, and it is precisely such vanity — money, mansion, luxury, power, fame, beautiful lady, white man, through elaborate promotion, indulgence and showing off that constitutes her success."[33] And Yang Ping simply calls it "a sales pitch for 'American Dream.'" This critic compares Zhou's book with Arthur Miller's *Death of a Salesman,* and concludes with an appreciation of the validity of the "Marxist critique of the hypocrisy of bourgeois values."[34] The problem is that most critics and Zhou's enthusiastic readers do not care a bit about the book's literary quality and have no inclination to re-appreciate Marxism. While it is certainly the story of the narrator's miraculous American Dream success, spiced by the controversy over its authenticity, that appeals to the imagination of millions of her readers, it is interesting to note how they express their appreciation. In 1993, Tongji University Press published a book of materials compiled to set the record straight about Zhou's book. The first chapter consists of statements, speeches, and recollections by Zhou's schoolmates, friends, and colleagues testifying to her personal integrity; the second consists of critical appraisals, and the third includes letters by enthusiastic readers from around the world. A glimpse of the headings of these letters will give us some idea of the book's appeal: "A Reflection of the Spiritual Journey of a Generation," "I Value Your Idealism," "Spiritual Food for the Spirit of an Age," "I Finished Reading It With Tears." Perhaps the critic Zeng Zhennan best summarized these sentiments: "Zhou Li's book touched hundreds of thousands of readers and aroused in their heart the excitement and enthusiasm to change their own fate and to struggle for promoting the Reform of our motherland; it aroused their yearning for and pursuit of a spiritual life, an ideal horizon, and moral faith higher than the mere quest for food — How rare is such a literary work today."[35]

How could a China lady's American success story offer "spiritual" and "moral" enlightenment to so many? Obviously, Zhou's narrative, plain, lengthy, tiresome as it is, has nevertheless proved to be powerful in a way that is both characteristic of and helps to characterize a peculiar ethos of the new decade. What is the nature of this ethos? Why is Zhou's narrative discourse so congenial to it? And how is this discourse constructed?

The answers to the first two questions are quite clear: the pervading ethos of China in the 1990s is *commercialism,* and the attraction and power of Zhou's narrative lies in its ability to add *culture* ("spirit") to an otherwise bare and banal "mere quest for food."

It is the third question that needs close and extensive examination, because answering it will reveal unique features of the "culture of commercialism." It is a transnational construction, a fusion of East and West *à la* Zhou. It is a composite involving the cultural spheres of China and the United States, written from a Chinese-American diasporic vantage point.

During the hot debate over Zhou's book, one critic made the shrewd remark that Zhou's book was really written *for* her husband. Very likely true, but there is also no denying that the book was about the China Lady's journey into the embrace of the "blue-eyed European guy." In this sense, *Manhattan* is best understood as an affirmation and justification of the marriage of China Lady and the white American. To use Sollors's striking metaphor: "American identity is like marriage, ethnicity is like ancestry."[36] *Manhattan* is a classic example of a transnational ethnic American identity construction, and it is within this context that the representation of "China" in Zhou's text should be understood: her lived experience during the Cultural Revolution, her portrayal of the tragic hero Pei Yang, and her overt reassertion of patriotism.

What Michael Fochler represents for the I-narrator (simply referred to as "Zhou Li" or "Julia," her English name throughout the text, hence I will use them interchangeably) is quite simple and clear: his whiteness, both physical and socially construed. When she first meets Michael, he is in a relationship with a friend of hers and she feels she must not get involved. "But, how blue his eyes are!"[37] Zhou's appreciation of Michael's white body is unabashed and straightforward: "I see the two nipples on his body, like two delicate and charming roses blossoming in white snow, little round crystals transparently covered with bright pinkness, and his breasts and arms so delicate and pure and white like jade porcelain, blonde and curly hair popping out here and there."[38] She portrays his body as a living sculpture, Michelangelo's David come to life. And Zhou tells us that it is not until age 35, after she met Michael, that she experienced a real sexual climax. In her journey to success and the American Dream, her marriage with Michael does indeed constitute a climax, not merely because her sexuality is gratified by whiteness, but also because she has now become part of (married to) what whiteness stands for in American social hierarchy, as Michael is "intelligent, rich, the elite of Investment Bank and the pride of Wall Street."[39] And furthermore, his German ethnic background adds the cultural enhancements of German classical philosophy, German classical music, German classical literature, plus his very pleasing Euro-accented English.

If assimilation means the melting away or melting down of one's ethnicity, however, Zhou's discourse is definitely not assimilationist. In fact, our China Lady writes her lengthy "autobiographical fiction" precisely to prove that her ethnicity is worthy of and compatible with the whiteness she marries. Manhattan's China Lady demonstrates that she retains her integral subjectivity in the union.

Zhou's subjective ethnic identity is first revealed as gendered self-image, based on her observations of difference. Julia, the new immigrant, is very quick to discern the prevailing taste for Asian women in America, as she warns her reader: "Americans do not like overly old-fashioned girls. They will think you lack sense of humor, falling into the so-called undesirable 'Asian stereotypical image.'"[40] In a modern fashion, Julia meets Michael at the tennis court on the campus of SUNY Binghamton. But a girl shouldn't be too open and vivacious either, as that would disqualify you as an Oriental lady. Throughout the book, Zhou consistently states that she consciously presents herself before American businessmen as a "pure and glittering" (qingcun liangli) Oriental lady with "class" (qizhi). That entails wearing light make-up and silky skirts — no jewelry or name-brand clothing. This differentiates her from those otherwise beautiful blonde girls who wear heavy make-up and dressy clothing and are only good enough to be secretaries. Yet a girl cannot be too Oriental: Zhou recounts an incident when she and Michael were visiting China and a prostitute suddenly "approached Michael in not so fluent English: 'That woman [referring to me] is Americanized, we are authentic Chinese.'"[41]

Most important, Zhou's diasporic ethnic identity is asserted as a *China* lady. Zhou's "China" as ethnic ancestry is certainly not Frank Chin's recovered Chinese heroic tradition. She uses her experiential history to prove its (advantageous) compatibility with whiteness. Yet like Chin's Chinaman, Zhou is fully endowed with a subjectivity of her own. And I believe it is this manifest subjectivity that prompts Xiaomei Chen, in discussing *Manhattan*, to call it "an extraordinary work."[42] But unlike Chen, who reads *Manhattan* as a "precise, realist, and vivid representations of a Chinese past … [which reflects] a longing for a China free of the tyranny and abuse that has characterized its sad history," I find no counterdiscursive effect whatsoever to the current ruling ideology of the Chinese government in Zhou's version of post-1949 history.[43] Rather, it fits in nicely with the current state ideology and official popular ethos. And more strikingly, Zhou's representation of "China" is derived from her ethnic identity affirmation as member of the diaspora.

Once Julia Zhou finally reaches her climax on Michael's snow-white body, she immediately reminds herself that for love to flourish, for her to be worthy of the Euro-American marriage, she must be on an "equal spiritual position."[44] What the I-narrator meant by "spiritual" is immediately clarified in the following paragraph: she will strive for American success. And, of course, *Manhattan* is first and foremost an American success story. But that does not seem to explain the significance of the lengthy China chapters in the book. In fact, as the narrator tells us, the motive for writing the book came after she became well established in the New York business world, where "I am already taken as an integral member — a business associate one can completely trust yet can also be openly angry with, a friend one would miss in a few days."[45] It is at this time that she decides to write the book, because Manhattan still does not know where she comes from. Already a successful Manhattanite, Zhou certainly does not want to deny her ethnicity. On the contrary, she feels it is almost her mission to make her "China-ness" fully known and recognized, because to Zhou, it is precisely her "ancestral past," her lived China experience, that gives a spiritual dimension (as well as competitive edge) to the fulfillment of the American Dream.

Zhou calls her book "an epic of an entire generation."[46] In her remembrance of the past, she reflects on a moment in her intellectual experience: "When a person began at the age of six to receive an education that makes you believe that Rightists are anti-Party, bad eggs, and now, at 25, you are suddenly told Rightists are good people and furthermore elite, how can you not be bewildered?"[47] For anybody growing up in the People's Republic of China through the Cultural Revolution, the bewilderment of such a reversal does indeed define the intellectual formation of a whole generation. But what is unique and amazing about Zhou's writing of PRC history is that the bewilderment is successfully overcome and solved. Zhou's account of her generational history shows a remarkable coherence, reconfigured in a peculiarly reconciliatory fashion that miraculously transcends the characteristic dilemma of the generation, reaching a new level in Zhou's journey to conquer the Avenue of the Americas. That is only possible because Zhou's generational epic is a discursive act meant to advance her American identity. China Lady's "China" has to be understood as a bedtime story for Michael, for his understanding, recognition, and appreciation.

The remarkable coherence in Zhou's account does not mean that her narrative is devoid of the conflicts and contradictions so characteristic of the experience of the generation. On the contrary, Zhou's story intends to reveal these conflicts and contradictions. In the chapter entitled "Childhood," for instance, Zhou recalls how she and her classmates in the primary school rejoiced when they heard the news of the assassination of John Kennedy, signifying the "end of the dark, reactionary imperialism." But now that she is in America, she realizes what a sad day it was for millions of Americans who loved their youngest talented president so much. The narrator then exclaims: "Ah, History! Who writes history anyway?"[48] Actually, to Zhou, it doesn't matter. What matters is her dictum: "You can't deny your History."[49] This sentiment permeates Zhou's narrative; for instance, she explains to Michael her reason for still keeping the Red Guard armband she wore when she was so fortunate as to be chosen to participate in the parade at Tiananmen Square to see Chairman Mao: "That is History."[50] And her History has become her ethnicity. History as an ethnic identity tag can embrace conflicts and contradictions, but it is ultimately mere nostalgia, both subjective and objective, which is incapable of and antithetical to critical reflection and judgment. Only in this light can we understand the juxtaposition of so many contradictory sentiments in the course of the turbulent historical events in her lifetime. Once history is understood as mere nostalgia, Zhou can proudly re-experience through her narrative the excitement of shouting rhythmically the slogans "Long Live Chairman Mao! Long Live the Communist Party!" and at the same time lament her sense of loss when she finds out that her own father has been named the enemy of the people, although lamentation here never turns into indignation. But when the historical tide itself overthrows the images of nostalgia — when citizens of Eastern European countries were tearing down Lenin statues, for example — Zhou's response becomes almost hysterical, as if "a relative is being lost," even though she was at the scene as an American businesswoman.[51] To a diasporic ethnic, "history" here means she is both a victim and product of her ancestry. When Michael tells the narrator that all he remembers about his childhood is "study, study, study," the "spiritual significance" of her ethnic background could not be clearer: our China Lady is so *historical*.

The theme of victimization also gets an interesting strategic deployment in Zhou's creation of the character Pei Yang, who is the hero of the second longest chapter entitled "A Young Girl's First Love." In the light of the debate over the authenticity of Zhou's narrative, the portrayal of Pei Yang is perhaps the most fictional, yet central. A close examination of this character will shed much light on Zhou's representation of China. First, in contrast to Frank Chin's complaint that Asian-American women writers portray Asian men as devoid of masculinity and heroism, Zhou's creation of Pei Yang is decidedly free of such stereotypes. Even though the love affair failed, Pei Yang is portrayed as a hero. This positive depiction enhances the subjectivity in Zhou's ethnic identity affirmation; she feels no need to hide or denigrate her Chinaman before Michael. In a culture in which virginity and divorce are irrelevant issues, the story of a romantic relationship with a heroic Chinaman makes her ethnicity more desirable and her current marriage more compatible.

But what kind of a hero is Pei Yang? A Red Guard hero. Or, a Red Guard strategically transformed in Zhou's representation as Hero. A top Red Guard leader at Fudan University, Pei was chosen as a "successor" to Party leadership at the Central Committee level. To mention the name of Pei Yang at Fudan in 1966, as Zhou puts it, "is like mentioning the name of General Schwarzkopf during the Persian Gulf War in 1991."[52] The narrator's passion for Pei is also comparable to her sister's excitement at seeing Chairman Mao, and Pei's attention to Zhou must have made up for her envy when the sister asks Zhou: "Do you want to touch my hand? This is the hand that has been shaken by Chairman Mao!"[53] During the Cultural Revolution, the narrator is cast as a victim because of a black spot in her "personal archive" (dang'an) due to a politically incorrect letter she submitted to a newspaper. But throughout her years in Beidahuang (Great Northern Wasteland) when her dang'an follows her like a ghost, her unquestionable love of Pei Yang, the "reddest" Red Guard, remains the source of her strength and intellectual enlightenment, despite the incongruity of such a match under the circumstances. Zhou's discursive ingenuity in rewriting that period of history lies in her subtle reshaping of a Red Guard image into a cross-culturally agreeable hero identifiable only in the post-Mao intellectual environment. The narrator's first impression of Pei Yang is: "What a handsome Jiangnan caizi (talent from Jiangnan)," a term that was hardly popular during the Cultural Revolution. She goes to Pei's office at Fudan and finds herself in an ideal setting: a roomful of books, clear and bright windows, a huge desk, and a telephone which would become their communication tool. When she tells him about her political "black spot," Pei first lectures her about the wonders of idealism and the spirit of self-devotion, quoting from various Soviet novels and books. But then he also murmurs somewhat secretively a passage from Montesquieu's L'Esprit des lois about freedom of speech. Finally he ends their conversation by quoting Wang Guowei's Renjian cihua (Worldly Sayings). The "roomful of books" contains a curious trio of cultural sources: Soviet, Western, and traditional Chinese. The Soviet contingent represents the "spirit of idealism," which is still to be upheld, valued, and appreciated, but the actual Red Guard practices of such idealism are conspicuously absent in Zhou's narrative representation. In fact, Pei is portrayed almost as a dissident in the movement given his Western knowledge. He talks with her of Beethoven, Mozart, Bach, Nietzsche, Plato, Socrates — all that during the Cultural Revolution. Such a Red Guard is bound to fall, as did Pei, but it was not because of his Western knowledge. At the end of the Cultural Revolution, he is put "under investigation" for his "history" as a Red Guard leader after 1976. Perhaps, after all, the bedtime story of the Chinaman hero-lover does have a limit. Pei has to become a *tragic* hero for the current legitimacy of her marriage. Nevertheless, even after Pei's diminished status as a mere historical figure, a victim of history, he continues to be a source of inspiration for the narrator. In the end, it is the traditional Chinese cultural cultivation in Pei that elevates the character into a statuesque tragic hero. Pei Yang, at the time of both his glory and disgrace, embodies the quintessence of Chinese cultural tradition. Before Zhou has to leave for the Great Northern Wasteland, he gives her Liu Xie's *Wenxin diaolong* (Literary Mind and the Carving of the Dragon) and Wang Xizi's *Lanting ji xu* (Preface to the Lanting Collection). While still a standing member of the Fudan Revolutionary Committee, Pei is already planning to translate Confucius's *Analects* and Qu Yuan's *Li Sao* into English. As a victim of changing political times, Pei sings lines from Qu Yuan's *Li Sao* at the top of Huangshan Mountain. To cast a Red Guard "successor" as a tragic hero bearing the symbolic suffering of China in its long history, traditional and modern, ultimately neutralizes the political vicissitudes of the Cultural Revolution. Whichever side you are on, you are a victim one way or another, part of the plight of China in its long history. The historical experience of suffering for an entire generation during the Cultural Revolution is legitimized as *experience* and *history*, which take on a new positive and alluring meaning as part of *ethnicity* in the American immigrant context.

Zhou's affirmation of ethnicity also entails fervent patriotism toward her homeland. "My biggest wish," Zhou proclaims after recounting her miraculous American success story, "is to return to my own motherland — not as an American-Chinese businesswoman, but as a [Chinese] of the diaspora, as a daughter, as a soldier of the 1970s *Beidahuang* Army — to return to the homeland of my dream, to repay my fellow compatriots and the loving and tragic land that has fed and nurtured me."[54] Her participation in the Cultural Revolution as a *Beidahuang* soldier is now listed as a sign of patriotism; Zhou's brand of diaspora patriotism is also strategically deployed. Thus when she observes the wild enthusiasm of Americans in celebrating the Fourth of July, she reaches a sudden enlightenment: "people all around the world are the same."[55] She finds no conflict in her "Chinese soul" about joining the American patriotic fervor — and it is on July 4 that Michael proposes to her. Patriotism as a manifestation of her ethnicity matches and complements her American marriage. But since Zhou decidedly sees her marriage as a license to joining whiteness, it is no wonder blackness in America poses an antithesis. And it is thus appropriate to reject blackness on the grounds of patriotism. For instance, Zhou gets indignant when a black female cop chases away some Chinese street artists in New York and calls them "shameless": "[hearing] the curse by a black, whether a cop or not, my face suddenly flushes, a sense of humiliation out of national dignity makes me furious. I shouted back: 'Those of your blacks who do drugs, rob, murder and rape, are they not all criminals? Why don't you take care of them? Punish them? . . . These artists are only making a living, or [work] for their tuition. They are making a living with a pen, at least they are not hurting anybody else!"[56] The fact that those artists are Chinese makes them a sympathetic target of Zhou's patriotism; conversely, the fact that they make a living on the street is antithetical to it. After all, despite her claim that she does not want to return to her motherland as an American-Chinese businesswoman, her brand of patriotism is only realized (and perhaps is most useful) in her trade with China. To her enthusiastic readers, the transnational business endeavors of JMF (Julia Michael Fochler) Company that help bring China to the world market represent the quintessential form of patriotism in 1990s China.

In *Manhattan*, the narrator describes a "language rule" for parties held at home: when the majority of the guests are Americans, everybody speaks English; when the majority are Chinese, everybody speaks Chinese (Michael "can now carry on a conversation in Chinese for ten minutes").[57] The amount he has learned, however, is not enough for him to read Julia's book. Here lies another irony of Zhou's work: while strategically deployed as a bedtime story for Michael, it is most enthusiastically embraced by her Chinese readers in China. But this is true only when we take "China" and "America" as separate entities in a mutually exclusive dichotomous sense. Indeed, the immense popularity of *Manhattan* further attests that America is in China and China in America. Hence Ethnic Studies in America has to be reconfigured cross-culturally and beyond the confines of the United States. For millions of Zhou's enthusiastic readers, the "moral encouragement" of her book to "struggle and change their fate" means immigrating to America, real or imagined, and claiming it for oneself just like the narrator.

To claim America as a Chinaman ethnic is what affords a "spiritual eleva-tion" to the culture of commercialism so prevalent in China today. In this light, the Chinaman subjectivities of Frank Chin and Zhou Li can be seen as competing modes of claiming America and representing China. And in such a competition, the immigrant writer in Chinese and the American-born writer in English share, after all, the same space involving "China" and "America," crisscrossing the Pacific.

Notes

1. Arjun Appadurai, *Modernity at Large: Cultural Dimensions of Globalization* (Min-neapolis: University of Minnesota Press, 1996), pp. 170, 173.

2. Sau-ling C. Wong, "Denationalization Reconsidered: Asian American Cul-tural Criticism at a Theoretical Crossroads," *Amerasia Journal* 21-1/2 (1995):3.

3. Frank Chin, *The Chickencoop Chinaman* and *The Year of the Dragon* (Seattle: Uni-versity of Washington Press, 1981), pp. 114, 115.

4. Frank Chin, "Food for All His Dead," in *Asian-American Authors*, ed. Kai-yu Hsu and Helen Palubinskas (Boston: Houghton Mifflin, 1972), p. 50.

5. Ibid.

6. Ibid., p. 53.

7. Ibid., p. 61.

8. Joseph S. M. Lau, "The Albatross Exorcised: The Rime of Frank Chin" in *Tamkang Review* 12-1 (1981):93–105.

9. See Frank Chin's own profile in Victor G. and Brett de Bary Nee, *Longtime Californ': A Documentary Study of an American Chinatown* (New York: Pantheon, 1972), pp. 377–89.

10. Ibid., p. 68.

11. Frank Chin, Jeffery Paul Chan, Lawson Fusao Inada, and Shawn Hsu Wong, "Preface to the Mentor Edition," in *Aiiieeeee! An Anthology of Asian American Writers* (New York: Mentor/Penguin, 1991), p. xiv.

12. Frank Chin, "Who's Afraid of Frank Chin, or Is It Ching?" *Bridge* 2-2 (Dec. 1972):31.

13. Frank Chin and Jeffery Paul Chan, "Racist Love," in *Seeing Through Shuck*, ed. Richard Kostelanetz (New York: Ballantine Books, 1972), p. 72.

14. Chin, *The Chickencoop Chinaman* and *The Year of the Dragon*, p. 59.

15. Chin, *The Chickencoop Chinaman*, p. 25.

16. Chin, "Food for All His Dead," pp. 58–59.

17. Chin, *Longtime Californ'*, pp. 388–89.

18. Ibid., pp. 378–79.

19. Frank Chin, *Gunga Din Highway* (Minneapolis: Coffee House Press, 1994), p. 287.

20. Dorothy Ritsuko McDonald, "Introduction," in *The Chickencoop Chinaman* and *The Year of the Dragon*, pp. xxv–xxix. The letter seems to be unpublished.

21. Robert Murray Davis, "Frank Chin: An Interview with Robert Murray Davis" in *Amerasia* 14-2 (1988):87–88.

22. Judith Melton, "*The Woman Warrior* in the Women's Studies Classroom," in *Approaches to Teaching Kingston's The Woman Warrior*, ed. Shirley Geok-lin Lim (New York: Modern Languages Association, 1991), pp. 74, 79.

23. King-kok Cheung, "*The Woman Warrior* Versus the Chinaman Pacific," in *Conflicts in Feminism*, ed. Marianne Hirsch and Evelyn Fox Keller (New York: Routledge, 1990), p. 241.

24. Maxine Hong Kingston, *China Men* (New York: Vintage, 1989), pp. 165–201.

25. Frank Chin, "This Is Not Autobiography" in *Genre* 18-2 (Summer 1985):110–11.

26. Chin, *The Chickencoop Chinaman* and *The Year of the Dragon*, p. 6.

27. Frank Chin, "Come All Ye Asian American Writers," in *The Big Aiiieeeee!*, ed. Jeffery Paul Chan, Frank Chin, Lawson Fusao Inada, and Shawn Wong (New York: Meridian Book, 1991), p. 13.

28. Chin, "Frank Chin: An Interview with Robert Murray Davis," p. 91.

29. Frank Chin, *Donald Duk* (Minneapolis: Coffee House Press, 1991), p. 122.

30. Chin et al., "Preface to the Mentor Edition," in *Aiiieeeee!*, p. xxvi.

31. Zhou Li, *Manhadun de zhongguo nuren* [Manhattan's China Lady] (Beijing: Beijing chubanshe, 1996), 8th print., p. 18. The translations here are mine.

32. You Zunming et al., *Shu: yingqi hongdong, Ren: yingqi zhengyi — Zhou Li qishu qiren* [The Book: A Hit; The Person: A Controversy — On Zhou Li, the Person and Her Book] in *Zhou Li zai qisu? — Manhadun de zhongguo nuren zengme le?* [Zhou Li Sues? — What's going on with *Manhattan's China Lady?*] ed. Jiang He and Zhuo Guo (Changsha: Hubei renmin chubanshe, 1993).

33. Dan Dan, *Man shu shi yiben bu zhide chuipeng de shu* [*Manhattan* Is Not a Book Worth Applauding] in *Zhou Li zai qisu?* p. 204.

34. Yang Ping, '*Meiguo meng' de tuixiaoshang* [Salesperson for 'American Dream'] in *Zhou Li zai qisu?* p. 185.

35. Zeng Zhennan, *Liuxuesheng wenxue yipie ji qita* [A Glimpse Into Students Abroad: Literature and More] in *Cengjing canghai nanwei shui* [Once Been to the Sea, Couldn't Stand Water Any More], ed. Lin Feng (Shanghai: Tongji University Press, 1993), p. 152.

36. Werner Sollors, "Forward: Theories of American Ethnicity," in *Theories of Ethnicity: A Classical Reader*, ed. Werner Sollors (New York: New York University Press, 1996), p. xx.

37. Zhou Li, *Manhadun de zhongguo nuren* [Manhattan's China Lady], p. 343.

38. Ibid., p. 350.

39. Ibid., p. 345.

40. Ibid., p. 423.

41. Ibid., p. 495.

42. Xiaomei Chen, *Occidentalism* (New York: Oxford University Press, 1995), p. 161.

43. Ibid., p. 164.

44. Zhou Li, *Manhadun de zhongguo nuren*, p. 352.

45. Ibid., p. 509.

46. Ibid., p. 513.

47. Ibid., p. 234.

48. Ibid., p. 98.

49. Ibid., p. 99.

50. Ibid.

51. Ibid., p. 404.

52. Ibid., p. 120.

53. Ibid., p. 119.

54. Ibid., p. 80.

55. Ibid., p. 349.

56. Ibid., p. 265.

57. Ibid., p. 483.

CHAPTER TWENTY-TWO

Haitian Literature in the United States, 1948–1986

■ JEAN JONASSAINT

Any account of Haitian literary production in the United States obviously needs to refer not only to the history and sociology of Haitian immigration to America, which is itself linked to contemporary Haitian politics, but also to American political and literary history.

Indeed, from 1948, the year when Philippe Thoby-Marcelin established himself in Washington, which is my starting point, to 1986, the year the Duvalier dictatorship was overthrown, my end-point, American society has changed greatly and so has the nature of Haitian immigration to the United States, as much in the places where immigrants settle as in the types or conditions of settlement. Indeed, the Immigrant Act of 1965, which abolished the discriminatory policy of setting immigrant quotas by nationality, favored Haitian immigration to the United States, which rose from 2,082 immigrants in 1964 to 3,609 in 1965, and continued to rise annually, to a high point in 1971 of 7,444 new immigrants. In the 1940s and 1950s the immigrant Haitian population, mostly bilingual, was concentrated in the New York area and consisted mostly of businessmen, professionals, and students. Beginning in the 1970s it diversified greatly, notably with the massive arrival of boat people in Florida, who spoke only Creole.[1]

Such changes could not be without consequences for literary works. According to the periods and places (or conditions) of settlement, Haitian writers in the United States favor different genres (poetry, theater, novel, essay), work in different languages (French, Haitian Creole, or English), and concern themselves with different problematics. Of course, the American reception of their works differs as well. In other words, on a theoretical

431

level I am concerned with articulating an interpretation of a literary fact (that of being Haitian in North America) on the basis of a reading of the history (of this people) of/in the American space. Moreover, as Lionnet and Scharfman suggest in their introduction to *Post/Colonial Conditions: Exiles, Migrations, and Nomadism*, it is necessary to break with the monolinguistic approach to literature, in order to take into account the work of languages of (and in) migration.[2] This is all the more urgent for Haitian literature, which, after the exodus of the years 1960–1980, is radically postnational. Indeed, those works called Haitian (whether written in Haitian or in French) are more and more the products of transnational writers, who are thus inscribing themselves in more than one literary culture, and their texts are written in more than one language — French and Haitian, clearly, but more and more in English as well, especially in the United States. Michel-Rolph Trouillot, for example, now professor of anthropology at the University of Chicago, writes and publishes in English, French, and Haitian (both in Haiti and the United States); Dany Laferrière lives in Miami but publishes regularly in Quebec, where he lived for some time, and where he continues to travel in order to work on the cultural scene.

Faced with this explosion of places of belonging and of publication with respect to writers termed Haitian, it is important to provide a minimal definition of the notion of Haitian literary production in the United States. Traditionally, Haitian literature has been defined as literature produced by Haitian subjects in one or another of the languages of the Haitian space, French and Haitian Creole. But the American situation leads us to enlarge, at least provisionally, this defining framework and to propose a pragmatic definition inspired by, among other things, Dubois's Bourdieusian analysis of the institution of literature. Thus Haitian literary production is defined as any work produced in Haiti or by a Haitian or perceived as Haitian (at one level or another of instances of production/legitimation), and Haitian literary production in the United States is defined as any work by a Haitian living or having lived in the United States, or any Haitian work published in the United States.

Certainly, this definition leaves certain problems unaddressed, to which it will be necessary to return one day. For example: who is a Haitian subject? But this definition makes it at least possible to constitute a rather large inventory, thus a representative corpus, leading to a first classification and to a reading of this literary phenomenon that will not be *a priori* a simple projection but induced from a more or less nuanced analysis of what is available.

With these methodological principles established, let us proceed to our inventory, which can only be provisional, for the state of research in this area in no way permits definitive inventories. To measure the difficulty of the task of inventorying Haitian immigrant literary production, note that Laguerre's *The Complete Haitiana: A Bibliographic Guide to the Scholarly Literature, 1900–1980* does not even have a specific entry for "literary work," let alone for "fiction," and that national libraries, for reasons that remain unclear, do not provide any information on writers' birthplaces and places of residence. Yet this inventory, although partial, will also be a history, or at the least, notes for the history of the Haitian-American literary phenomenon (in a broad sense). I will thus analyze five decades (from 1940–1989), which are grouped into four historical periods:

The 1940s–1950s (the Thoby-Marcelin years, and the recourse to translation);

The 1960s (the empty years, or the takeover by politics);

The 1970s (marked by the emergence of Haitian as a literary language);

The 1980s (the decade of the essay: "The Rise of English," to borrow Terry Eagleton's expression).

THE 1940s–1950s

Despite the revolutions of 1946 and 1957, the 1940s and 1950s were relatively stable. Haiti even enjoyed a relative prosperity, and very few Haitians emigrated to the United States. To the best of my knowledge, Philippe Thoby-Marcelin (1904–1975) was the first Haitian writer to exile himself there, in 1948.[3] It is thus not astonishing that the 1940s and 1950s are above all marked by his novelistic output, which began in New York in 1944, with *Canapé-Vert*, published simultaneously in French and English by Editions de la Maison Française and by Farrar and Rinehart. This novel, which won an inter-American literary prize, had some success, and the same publishers, in 1946, brought out a second novel by the brothers Philippe Thoby-Marcelin and Pierre Marcelin, *La Bête de Musseau* [*The Beast of the Haitian Hills*], again published in French and English. They were not alone for long: Langston Hughes and Mercer Cook's translation of Jacques Roumain's *Gouverneurs de la Rosée* [*Masters of the Dew*] was published a year later, 1947, by a less important publisher, Reynal and Hitchcock, but it went through several American reprints, most recently in 1988, by Heinemann. It was perhaps the only real Haitian literary success in the United States since the 1940s.

The 1950s decade began with a very important work for Haitian studies: Max Bissainthe's *Dictionnaire de bibliographie haïtienne*, published in Washington in 1951 by Scarecrow Press. This book, the first of its magnitude on Haitian literary output, greatly marked Haitian bibliography due to its being taken up by Haitian bibliographers, notably Max Manigat in his *Haitiana 1971–1975* (1980) and *Haitiana 1991–1995* (1997). Also in 1951, Philippe Thoby-Marcelin published his third novel, *Le Crayon de Dieu*, but it came out only in the English translation, *The Pencil of God*, published in Boston by Houghton Mifflin and with a long preface by Edmund Wilson. The novel did not appear in its original version until the following year, 1952, at the Parisian firm of La Table Ronde.

The decade concluded in New York with W. Sloan Associates' publication of the English translation of Marie Chauvet's *La Danse sur le volcan* [*Dance on the Volcano*], which had appeared in French two years earlier, published by Plon. This was the only one of her works published in the United States. Cogdell-Travis translated *Amour* into English as part of her Ph.D. thesis at Brown University; unfortunately, it has not been published, despite the constant interest in the work in American universities.[4]

In fact, for this first period from 1940 to 1959, other than Stephen Alexis's 1949 *Black Liberator: The Life of Toussaint Louverture*, Bissainthe's 1951 bibliography, and Thoby-Marcelin's 1953 collection of poetry, *À fonds perdu*, Haitian publications in the United States comprise about a dozen titles, principally novels, and three authors: Thoby-Marcelin, Chauvet, and Roumain.

THE 1960s

Despite an important increase in the number of Haitian immigrants to the United States, the 1960s are not rich in literary output. Only about fifteen works can be counted, and with reason. Haiti underwent one of the gravest political and social crises in its history. The Duvalier dictatorship solidified its power. The decade opened, moreover, with the assassination of the writer Jacques Stephen Alexis and with the Haitian intelligentsia forced into exile, diverting its energy to the political struggle. This was the golden age of failed invasions, which led to more and more brutal repressions, leading to ever larger waves of departures of the political class and the intelligentsia.

This decade, although somber, is not without interest from a literary point of view. It even begins with the publication, in Port-au-Prince, of a capital work, *L'Histoire de la littérature haïtienne* by Ghislain Gouraige, an important figure in Haitian literary production in America. While teaching at SUNY-Albany in the 1970s, he published many important essays, among them *La Diaspora d'Haïti et l'Afrique* (1974), *Amour, révolution de la femme* (1976), and *Continuité noire* (1977). This decade also saw the arrival of Maurice A. Lubin (professor at Howard University, 1978–1985) on the American scene as literary critic, with an article on "Five Haitian Poets" (1965), which appeared in the journal *Américas* in 1965, and an *Anthologie de la jeune poésie d'Haïti* (1967), published in Honolulu. This same year, Philippe Thoby-Marcelin's *Contes et légendes d'Haïti* was published by the Paris firm of Nathan. It became available in English only in 1971 under the title *The Singing Turtle and Other Tales from Haiti*.

Toward the end of this decade, in 1968, Gallimard brought out Chauvet's great trilogy *Amour, colère et folie* [Love, Anger, and Madness], which provoked Papa Doc's ire and sent her into exile in New York, where she worked on her last novel, *Les Rapaces*, before dying there in 1973. This last work would only be published in 1986, under her maiden name, Marie Vieux. It was also at the end of this decade, specifically on September 20, 1969, that the Kuidor troupe presented its first show, "Les Puits Errants," at the Brooklyn Academy of Music. This was a troupe inspired by, among other things, Brecht and voodoo theatricality, and it had a great influence on Haitian literature in America. We must also note that 1969 was the year of publication of the translation of the great Milo Rigaud's *Tradition voodoo et le voodoo haïtien* [*Secrets of Voodoo*].

THE 1970s

This was quite an extraordinary decade as regards Haitian literary production in America: more than thirty titles by some twenty writers, and a public to read them. The decade began admirably. Thoby-Marcelin, who had not published anything since 1952, published the English translation (at Farrar, Straus & Giroux) of his first and only novel written entirely in the United States, *Tous les hommes sont fous* [*All Men Are Mad*].[5] This was also the last Haitian work to be published in English by a major American publisher, for various reasons. In general, developments on the Haitian political scene, coupled with the emergence of Black African literatures in French and English and an ever more marked interest in Africa on the part of African-American intellectuals, resulted in Haiti's losing the appeal of its status as the first independent black state. There was little interest in Haitian literature in American literary circles, and aside from the Marcelin brothers' novel, the only work translated during this decade is *Un arc-en-ciel pour l'Occident chrétien* by René Depestre, which appeared in two translations under the title *A Rainbow for the Christian West*. The first translation was by Jack Hirschman in 1972, and the second in 1977 by an American of Haitian origin, Joan Dayan.[6]

Countering this lack of English translations, the 1970s, which were also the golden age of patriotic action (the militant left), marked a resurgence of Haitian literary production in both French and Haitian Creole, notably in North America. Indeed, 1970 was the year in which Georges Castera published his first collections of poetry in Haitian, in New York, and the year in which Albert Valdman produced his *Basic Course in Haitian Creole*. Although this last is not a Haitian text, it seems important to note it here. For it was part of an already strong tendency, not without some connection to the political struggle against the Duvalier regime — notably by the journal *Sèl* (founded in 1972 by Haitian Catholic priests in New York) and the work of cultural groups such as the Kouidor troupe or Tanbou libèté — to inscribe the Haitian language in the American space. Some of the remarkable texts in the Haitian language were Castera's *Konbèlann* (1976) and Trouillot's *Ti difé boulé sou istoua Ayiti* (1977).[7]

The year 1971 marked the publication, in New York, of the weekly newspaper *Haïti-Observateur*, today probably the most widespread Haitian publication. It was also the year in which the first issue of the journal *Nouvelle Optique*, closely linked to the Kouidor troupe, was published in Montreal. Moreover, it was in this first issue of *Nouvelle Optique* that Hervé Denis, one of the troupe's co-founders, published his "Introduction to a Manifesto for Haitian Theatre," which defined the principal issues of the aesthetics and practice of Kouidor, traces of which can be found in the works of Castera, Charlier, and Large. These writers are among the best poets of their generation, those who have most contributed to a new Haitian aesthetics that maintains an awareness of both the popular Haitian forms and the formal requirements of contemporary poetics.

That said, let us keep in mind Ruben François (1945–1973?), who was probably the first Haitian-American to write and publish in Montreal two collections of poems in English, in 1972: *The Scavengers and Other New Collected Poems* and *My Soul in Tears and Other Collected Poems*. Another, more militant poet is Paul Laraque, who has continued to publish since his first collection, *Ce qui demeure* (1973).[8] He is without a doubt one of the most prolific Haitian writers in the United States, writing in both French and Haitian. He is also one of the best known writers, as his work has been translated into English (*Camourade: Selected Poems*, 1988; *Fistibal/Slingshot*, 1989) and Spanish (*Poesía cotidiana; Las armas cotidianas*, 1981).

Although poetry was by far the favorite genre of Haitian immigrant writers at this time, some writers were drawn to the novel and short story, and it is through prose that they have expressed their American experience. Indeed, by 1972 Pierre Carrié published the first Haitian novel on the immigrant experience in New York, *Bonjour New-York*. But it was in 1977, the same year that Frantz Bataille reported on *La Vie Haïtienne à New York*, that Jean-Claude Charles in *Sainte dérive des cochons* produced the most gripping and also the most disturbing portrait of the Haitian exile. It is a short, polytonal work in which English, Spanish, French, and Haitian come together. Charles's book, and Charles himself, would make an interesting subject, and their status in the American space remains ambiguous. For although he wrote several books in part in the United States — among them *Négociations* (1972), *De si jolies petites plages* (1982), *Manhattan Blues* (1985) — he was never truly an American resident.

The 1970s also saw the emergence of a number of Haitian-American places of publication, notably in 1975, which was quite exceptional in displaying a certain "taking charge" of Haitian writing in the American space. On this point, it is necessary to draw attention in particular to the creation of a bilingual (French-Haitian) literary journal in New York, *Lakansièl*, which allowed Michel-Rolph Trouillot to experiment with his work in Haitian and to define his aesthetics and his relation to the Haitian sociopolitical arena. And it was not by chance that he published his first book, in 1977, under the *Lakansièl* imprint. This was *Ti difé boulé sou istoua Ayiti*, a magnificent historical work written in Haitian from a Marxist perspective, but framed like a popular Haitian narrative. It was the first text of its length in Haitian (some 200 pages), and also, along with Castera's *Konbèlann* (published in Montreal a year earlier), the most significant work in Haitian written by a Haitian in the United States.

The end of this decade confirms the emergence of the Haitian language, and marks the next period as the decade of the essay and of the emergence of English as the language of choice for Haitians in the United States. For the first time, two Haitian-Americans published in English (in 1979): Régine Latortue did the English translation of Louisiana Creole poems from the nineteenth century, *Les Cenelles*, and Maurice A. Lubin co-edited an important academic work, *Caribbean Writers: A Bio-bibliographical Critical Encyclopedia.*

THE 1980s

This was the end of Communism, the debacle of the Duvalier regime, and without doubt the emergence of the first generation of Haitians educated in the United States and of American-born Haitians. A significant (in number, of course) first generation of the contemporary period, properly speaking, of Haitian-Americans.

In literature, the decade begins with Michel Laguerre's first book in English, *Voodoo Heritage*, followed by Jean-Claude Charles's *Le Corps noir*, strongly influenced by the work of the African-American writer Chester Himes, and probably also, at the level of writing, by Jerry Rubin's *Do It!* Jack Hirschman's English translation of Depestre's *Végétation de clarté* [Vegetations of Splendor] also came out at that time. Published in Chicago, it announced a certain renewal of interest in Haitian texts by American publishers, who also later published, among other things, Depestre's *The Festival of the Greasy Pole* [*Le Mât de cocagne*] in 1990, re-issued Milo Rigaud's *Secrets of Voodoo* (1985) and the Marcelin brothers' *The Beast of the Hills* (1986), and in 1988 published an English translation of selected poems of Paul Laraque, *Camourade*. That there was an interest in Haitian texts is clear from the number of essays published in English in the 1980s. Here the first name to remember is that of Michel S. Laguerre, who in addition to his bibliography *The Complete Haitiana*, published five essays during this period, all in English.

In the late 1980s Trouillot started to publish in English. His *Peasants and Capital: Dominica in the World Economy* was published in 1988 by Johns Hopkins University Press. It was also the decade in which a number of young academics came to the forefront, and the first books by some Haitian-American faculty members were published, most notably in 1984 Ginette Adamson's *Le Procédé de Raymond Roussel;* Pierre Saint-Amand's *Diderot, le labyrinthe de la relation;* a year later Patrick Bellegarde-Smith's *In the Shadow of Powers: Dante's Bellegarde in Haitian Social Thought;* and in 1989, Alex Dupuy's *Haiti in the World Economy.*

These are, in large part, the authors to keep in mind for this decade, but from a strictly literary viewpoint, there were fewer writers active in a variety of genres (poetry, novels, drama) than there had been in the 1970s.

CONCLUSION

At the end of this survey, what first comes to mind is the strong correlation between literary production and periods of political stability (the 1970s) as well as of political agitation (the 1960s). The greater the political turbulence, the less literary creation. In this sense, the 1980s are significant. The departure of Jean-Claude Duvalier, leading to a mounting obsession with politics within the intellectual class, created a considerable decline in creative production in Haiti and even more so in the United States, where nonfiction became dominant.

It is also interesting to note that until the end of the 1980s, Haitian-Americans did not write fiction in English, at least not to my knowledge. By contrast, Haitian-American academics, particularly in the humanities, have a clear tendency to publish directly in English. This was the case for Laguerre, Bellegarde-Smith, and Dupuy. Yet literary writers, with the exception of Maurice A. Lubin, publish their works in French, and have not produced any book in English on Haitian literature.

Thus Haitian academics in one group write about Haiti principally in English. In another group there are Haitians who publish literary works, sometimes about Haitian literature, but in French.

This language divide repeats itself on the level of literary creation. On the one hand there is an important poetic production in French and Haitian, and this seems to be the tendency in the United States. In fact, except for Denizé Lauture (Denize Lotu), author of *When the Denizen Weeps* (1988) and *Boula pou yon metamófoz zéklè nan peyi a* (1988) who seems to prefer to write and publish in Haitian and English, Haitian poets, be they Castera, Large, Laraque, or Morisseau-Leroy, publish in the two national Haitian languages. On the other hand, a fairly important novelistic output has been produced exclusively in French (with some English translations), at least until the beginning of the 1990s, for since then we must take into account Edwidge Danticat, who writes and publishes with great success directly in English. In contrast to Quebec and despite the important figures of Thoby-Marcelin, Chauvet, and Charles, the novel remains relatively poor in Haitian-American literary production in the United States, which is dominated by essay-writing and poetry.

But what of the status of these texts and of their authors in the American literary establishment?

These books, notably those published in Haitian and at the author's expense, do not reach a wide audience and have not had many critical readings, if one relies on databases such as the Dissertation Abstracts and the MLA Bibliography; and also, according to WorldCat, they are found only in a few American libraries. For example, only one of the two titles by Ruben François, *My Soul in Tears and Other Collected Poems,* is available at only four American university libraries: Brown, Michigan, Minnesota, and Northeastern. More surprisingly, *Les Exploits du Colonel Pipe suivi de l'Averse* (1974), by the novelist Roger Pradel (who lived in the 1970s in Ann Arbor, Michigan, where he worked at the library of the University of Michigan), cannot be found in the database of WorldCat, even though the book was published by a commercial publisher in Montreal, Les Presses Libres. The same is true for the collection of "creole poems" by J. T. M. (Ti Ton Ton), *Nan jadin lakay,* published in New York in 1976.

In short, it seems clear that the Haitian sociological or historical discourse, in English, has found its place in the American institutional space. Literary discourse, for its part, has for the moment little opportunity to emerge. Indeed, within the African-American body of work, Haitian-American production is limited to the framework of multiculturalism. What constitutes African-American production is the great production, in English, by black writers in the United States; many consider it is not part of American literature as such but a separate African-American literature, an ethnic literature. The African-American canon does not legitimate French as a literary language (in this sense it conforms to any other literary canon, which functions first of all in terms of forms, languages, and genres), and besides, the Haitians discuss problems which are not those of the African-American majority. Finally, we must not discount the tension that exists between the two (black American) communities, which is real, as the work of E. Magloire has shown.[9] Tension, doubtless, that has a basis in some very old political conflicts between Haiti and the United States, and which probably constitutes another brake on the desire of Haitian-Americans to affirm themselves, or at least to truly integrate themselves into the great American mosaic.

Consequently, only a radical redefinition of the American literary scene, which would take into account what Marc Shell rightly calls "The Politics of Language Diversity in the United States," could bring a greater awareness of Haitian-American literature (which, as I have shown, goes beyond monolingualism, and in this way creates problems for researchers who have not mastered the three languages at play.)[10]

But is it not a pipe dream to think of such a radical change? It is discouraging to realize that in the 468 pages of essays in *MultiAmerica: Essays on Cultural Wars and Cultural Peace* (1997), edited by Ishmael Reed (whom it is difficult to accuse of being insensitive or even indifferent to the Haitian problematic), there is not a single page devoted, even in part, to Haitian-Americans, and the word "Haitian" only appears, it seems to me, once (p. 192).[11] Yet efforts such as those of the Longfellow Institute may after all prove to be the harbingers of a positive change in the politics of language diversity.

Haitian Works in the United States (1944–1997): An Indicative Bibliography

Adamson, Ginette. *Le Procédé de Raymond Roussel.* Amsterdam: Rodopi, 1984.

Alexis, Stephen. *Black Liberator: The Life of Toussaint Louverture.* New York: Macmillan, 1949.

Bataille, Frantz. *La Vie haïtienne à New York.* Port-au-Prince: Éditions Fardin, 1977.

Bellegarde-Smith, Patrick. *In the Shadow of Powers: Dante's Bellegarde in Haitian Social Thought.* Atlantic Highlands, N.J.: Humanities Press International, 1985.

—— *Haiti: The Breached Citadel.* Boulder: Westview Press, 1990.

Bissainthe, Max. *Dictionnaire de bibliographie haïtienne.* Washington: Scarecrow Press, 1951.

—— *Dictionnaire de bibliographie haïtienne, premier supplément.* Metuchen, N.J.: Scarecrow Press, 1973.

Carrié, Pierre. *Bonjour New-York.* Ville Saint-Laurent [Imprimerie] Journal Offset, 1972.

Castera, Georges. *Bwa Mitan.* New York, 1970.

—— *Panzou.* New York, 1970.

—— *Le Retour à l'arbre.* Illustrations by Bernard Wah. n.p. [Montréal]: Calfou Nouvelle Orientation, 1974.

—— *Konbèlann.* Montréal: Éditions Nouvelle Optique, 1976.

—— *Bisuit léta.* n.p. [New York]: Éditions Idées nouvelles, idées prolétariennes, 1978.

Célestin, Julio B. *Sous les manguiers. Sept histoires du folklore haïtien.* Sherbrooke: Naaman, 1976.

Célestin, Roger. *From Cannibals to Radicals: Figures and Limits of Exoticism.* Minneapolis: University of Minnesota Press, 1996.

Chancy, Myriam J. A. *Framing Silence: Revolutionary Novels by Haitian Women.* New Brunswick: Rutgers University Press, 1997.

—— *Searching for Safe Spaces: Afro-Caribbean Women Writers in Exile.* Philadelphia: Temple University Press, 1997.

Charles, Jean-Claude. *Négociations.* Paris: P. J. Oswald, 1972.

—— *Sainte Dérive des cochons,* Montréal: Nouvelle Optique, 1977.

—— *Le Corps noir.* Paris: Hachette-P.O.L., 1980.

—— *De si jolies petites plages.* Paris: Stock, 1982

—— *Bamboola Bamboche.* Paris: Barrault, 1984.

—— *Manhattan Blues.* Paris: Barrault, 1985.

Charlier, Jacques. *Le Scapulaire des armuriers.* New York: n.p., 1976.

—— *La Part des pluies.* New York: n.p., 1977.

Chauvet, Marie. *La Danse sur le volcan.* Paris: Plon, 1957.

—— *Dance on the Volcano.* New York: W. Sloan Associates, 1959.

—— *Amour, colère et folie.* Paris: Gallimard, 1968.

[Chauvet] Vieux, Marie. *Les Rapaces.* Port-au-Prince: Deschamps, 1986.

Crosley, Bernadette Carré. *Haïtianité et mythe de la femme dans Hadriana dans tous mes rêves de René Depestre.* Montréal: CIDIHCA, 1993.

—— *René Depestre et la défense et l'illustration de la créolité/haïtianité dans Bonjour et adieu à la négritude (1980) et Hadriana dans tous mes rêves (1988).* Port-au-Prince: Deschamps, 1993.

Crosley, Reginald. *Immanences.* Montréal: CIDIHCA, 1988.

—— *The Second Coming of Christ May Be Postponed Again: Is the Church Mistaken in Its Messianic Expectations?* New York: Vantage Press, 1991.

Danticat, Edwidge. *Breath, Eyes, Memory.* New York: Soho, 1994.

—— *Krik? Krak!* New York: Soho Press, 1995.

—— *The Farming of Bones.* New York: Soho Press, 1998.

Danticat, Edwidge, ed. *The Beacon Best of 2000: Creative Writing by Women and Men of All Colors and Cultures.* Boston: Beacon Press, 2000.

—— *The Butterfly's Way: Voices from the Haitian Diaspora in the United States.* New York: Soho Press, 2001.

Dambreville, Claude. *Un goût de fiel.* Port-au-Prince: Deschamps, 1983.

Dambreville, Claude and Frankétienne. *L'Amérique saigne (Gun Blesse America).* Port-au-Prince: Imprimeur II, 1995.

Dejean, Yves. *Dilemme en Haïti: français en péril ou péril français?* New York: Éditions Connaissance d'Haïti, 1975.

—— *Comment écrire le créole d'Haïti.* Outremont, Québec: Collectif Paroles, 1980.

Delphin, Jacques M. *Une Robe au destin.* Québec: Éditions Garneau, 1972.

Depestre, René. *A Rainbow for the Christian West.* Trans. Jack Hirschman. Fairfax: Red Hill Press, 1972.

—— *A Rainbow for the Christian West.* Trans. Joan Dayan. Amherst: University of Massachussets Press, 1977.

—— *Vegetations of Splendor.* Trans. Jack Hirschman. Chicago: Vanguard Books, 1980.

—— *The Festival of the Greasy Pole.* Trans. Carrol Coates. Charlottesville: University Press of Virginia, 1990.

Dezire, Jajan. *Powèm pou youn Ayiti to nèf.* Miami: Kolesksyon Koukouy, 1994.

Dupuy, Alex. *Haiti in the World Economy: Class, Race and Underdevelopment since 1700.* Boulder: Westview Press, 1989.

Étienne, Assely. *Dolope, espace du non-sens et de l'absence.* Paris: La Pensée universelle, 1990.

François, Ruben. *My Soul in Tears and Other Collected Poems.* Montréal: Spare Change? Press, 1972.

—— *The Scavengers and Other New Collected Poems.* Montréal: Spare Change? and Canadian Poets Press, 1972.

Gouraige, Ghislain. *Histoire de la littérature haïtienne (de l'Indépendance à nos jours).* Port-au-Prince: Imprimerie Théodore, 1960.

—— *La Diaspora d'Haïti et l'Afrique.* Sherbrooke: Naaman, 1974.

—— *Amour, révolution de la femme: la femme et l'amour, de l'antiquité à nos jours.* Sherbrooke: Naaman, 1976.

—— *Continuité noire.* Dakar: Nouvelles éditions africaines, 1977.

—— *Les Semences de l'esprit: propos sur l'esclavage moderne.* Sherbrooke: Éditions Naaman, 1987.

Heurtelou, Maude. *Lafami Bonplezi.* Coconut Creek: Educa Vision, 1993. [*The Bonplezi Family: The Adventures of a Haitian Family in North America.* Trans. John Nickroz. Temple Terrace: Educa Vision, 1996.]

—— *Sezisman.* Coconut Creek: Educa Vision, 1995.

J. T. M. [Titonton]. *Nan jadin lakay: rékèy n° 1.* New York: n.p., 1976.

—— *Ansan-m Ansan-m Nèg Dayiti.* N.p., n.p., 1977.

Laferrière, Dany. *Comment faire l'amour avec un Nègre sans se fatiguer.* Montréal: VLB Éditeur, 1985. [*How to Make Love to a Negro: A Novel.* Trans. David Homel. Toronto: Coach House Press, 1987.]

—— *Éroshima.* Montréal: VLB Éditeur, 1987. [*Eroshima: A Novel.* Trans. David Homel. Toronto: Coach House Press, 1991.]

—— *L'Odeur du café.* Montréal: VLB Éditeur, 1991. [*An Aroma of Coffee.* Trans. David Homel. Toronto: Coach House Press, 1993.]

—— *Le Goût des jeunes filles.* Montréal, VLB Éditeur, 1992. [*Dining with the Dictator.* Trans. David Homel. Toronto: Coach House Press, 1994.]

—— *Cette grenade dans la main du jeune nègre est-elle une arme ou un fruit?* Montréal, VLB Éditeur, 1993. [*Why Must a Black Writer Write About Sex?* Trans. David Homel. Toronto: Coach House Press, 1994.]

—— *Chronique de la dérive douce.* Montréal, VLB éditeur, 1994. [*A Drifting Year.* Trans. David Homel. Vancouver: Douglas & McIntyre, 1997.]

—— *Pays sans chapeau.* Montréal: Lanctôt Éditeur, 1996. [*Down Among the Dead Men.* Trans. David Home. Vancouver: Douglas & McIntyre, 1997.]

—— *La Chair du maître.* Outremont: Lanctôt Éditeur, 1997.

—— *Le Charme des après-midi sans fin.* Outremont: Lanctôt Éditeur, 1997.

—— *Le Cri des oiseaux fous.* Outremont: Lanctôt Éditeur, 2000.

—— *J'écris comme je vis: entretien avec Bernard Magnier.* Outremont: Lanctôt Éditeur, 2000.

Laguerre, Michel S. *Voodoo Heritage.* Beverly Hills: Sage Publications, 1980.

—— *The Complete Haïtiana: A Bibliographic Guide to the Scholarly Literature, 1900–1980.* 2 vols. Millwood: Kraus International Publications, 1982.

—— *Urban Life in the Caribbean: A Study of a Haitian Urban Community.* Cambridge, Mass.: Schenkman [1983], 1982.

—— *American Odyssey: Haitians in New York City.* Ithaca: Cornell University Press, 1984.

—— *Afro-Caribbean Folk Medicine.* South Hadley: Bergin & Garvey, 1987.

—— *Voodoo and Politics in Haiti.* New York: St. Martin's Press, 1989.

—— *The Military and Society in Haiti.* Knoxville: University of Tennessee Press, 1993.

—— *The Informal City.* New York: St. Martin's Press, 1994.

—— *Diasporic Citizenship: Haitian Americans in Transnational America.* New York: St. Martin's Press, 1998.

Laraque, Franck. *La Révolte dans le théâtre de Sartre vu par un homme du Tiers Monde.* Paris: J.-P. Delarge, 1976.

—— *Défi à la pauvreté.* Montréal: CIDIHCA, 1987.

Laraque, Paul. *Ce qui demeure.* Montréal: Nouvelle Optique, 1973.

—— *Fistibal.* Montréal: Nouvelle Optique, 1974.

—— *Les Armes quotidiennes/Poésie quotidienne.* La Havana: Casa de las Américas, 1979.

—— *Poesía cotidiana; Las armas cotidianas.* Trans. Nancy Mojerón. La Havana: Casa de las Américas, 1981.

—— *Camourade: Selected Poems.* Trans. Rosemary Manno. Willimantic: Curbstone Press, 1988.

—— *Fistibal/Slingshot.* Trans. Jack Hirschman. Port-au-Prince: Éditions Samba; San Francisco: Seaworthy Press, 1989.

—— *Œuvres incomplètes: poésie.* Montréal: Éditions du CIDIHCA, 1998.

—— *Lespwa.* Port-au-Prince: Éditions Mémoire, 2001.

Laraque, Paul and Jack Hirschman, eds. *Open Gate: An Anthology of Haitian Creole Poetry.* Willimantic: Curbstone Press, 2001.

Large, Josaphat. *Nerfs du vent.* Paris: P. J. Oswald, 1975.

—— *Chute de mots.* Paris: Éditions Saint-Germain-des-Prés, 1989.

—— *Les Sentiers de l'enfer.* Paris: Éditions L'Harmattan, 1990.

—— *Pè sèt! Powèm.* Miami: Edisyon Mapou, 1994.

Latortue, Régine [co-trans.]. *Les Cenelles: A Collection of Poems by Creole Writers of the Early Nineteenth Century*. Boston: G. K. Hall, 1979.

Lauture, Denizé [Lotu, Denize]. *When the Denizen Weeps*. New York: Denizenism Editions, 1988.

Lotu, Denize [Lauture, Denizé]. *Boula pou yon metamòfoz zèklè nan peyi a*. [New York]: Edisyon Denizenis, 1988.

—— *Father and Son*. New York: Philomel Books, 1992.

—— *Running the Road to ABC*. New York: Simon & Schuster Books for Young Readers, 1996.

Léonidas, Jean-Robert. *Sérénade pour un pays ou la génération du silence*. Montréal: CIDIHCA, 1992.

—— *Prétendus créolismes: le couteau dans l'igname*. Montréal: CIDIHCA, n.d.

Lerebours, Philippe. *Le Roi suivi de Temps mort*. New York: Éditions Connaissance d'Haïti, 1975.

—— *Haïti et ses peintres de 1804 à 1980: souffrances et espoirs d'un peuple*. 2 vols. Port-au-Prince: Imprimeur II, 1989.

Lubin, Maurice A. *Anthologie de la jeune poésie d'Haïti*. Honolulu: Mele, 1967.

—— [Associate ed.]. *Caribbean Writers: A Bio-Bibliographical-Critical Encyclopedia* [ed. Donald E. Herdeck]. Washington: Three Continents Press, 1979.

—— *Panorama de la poésie haïtienne. Tome 1, 1790–1950*. 2nd ed. Coconut Creek: Educa Vision, 1995.

Magloire, Eddy. *Regards sur la minorité ethnique haïtienne aux États-Unis*. Sherbrooke: Naaman, 1984.

Manigat, Max. *Haïtiana 1971–1975: bibliographie haïtienne*. Montréal: Collectif Paroles, 1980.

—— *Haïtiana 1991–1995: bibliographie haïtienne*. Montréal: CIDIHCA, 1997.

Mapou, Jan. *Bajou kasi: sòt pa touyé — sòt fè soué*. N.p.: Koleksyon Koukouy, 1974.

—— *Pwezigram*. New York: Koleksyon Koukouy, 1981.

—— *D-P-M Kanntè: boat people ayisyen*. Miami: Edisyon Mapou, 1996.

Morisseau-Leroy, Felix. *La Ravine aux diables*. Paris: L'Harmattan, 1982.

—— *Vilbone: kont chante*. Miami: Jaden Kreyròl, 1982.

—— *Dyakout 1,2,3, ak twa lòt poèm; Sa m-di nan sa, Depestre; Yon veye Mòn Hèkil pou Jak Aleksi; Botpipèl*. Miami: Jaden Kreyròl, 1983.

—— *Les Djons d'Aïti Tonma*. Paris: L'Harmattan, 1996.

Numa, E. N. *Clercina Destiné*. New York: Cabella French Printing & Publishing, n.d.

Paquin, Lyone. *The Haitians, Class and Color Politics*. New York: n.p. 1983.

Paul, Cauvin L. *Nuit sans fond*. N.p., n.p., 1976.

—— *Le Vieux Samuel*. Port-au-Prince: Impr. Henri Deschamps, 1996.

—— *Les Sédentaires*. Brossard: Humanitas, 1998.

—— *La Belle Eurydice*. Brossard: Humanitas, 2001.

Philoctète, Raymond and Silvio F. Baridon. *Poésie vivante d'Haïti*. Paris: Lettres nouvelles, 1978.

Pradel, Roger. *Les Exploits du Colonel Pipe suivi de l'Averse.* Montréal: Les Presses libres, 1974.

Rigaud, Milo. *Vè-vè: diagrammes rituels du voudou.* New York: French and European Publications, 1974

—— *Secrets of Voodoo.* New York: Arco, 1969.

—— *Secrets of Voodoo.* San Francisco: City Lights Books [1969], 1985.

Roumain, Jacques. *Gouverneurs de la rosée.* Port-au-Prince: Imprimerie de l'État, 1944.

—— *Masters of the Dew.* Trans. Langston Hughes & Mercer Cook. New York: Reynal & Hitchcock, 1947.

—— *Masters of the Dew.* Trans. Langston Hughes & Mercer Cook. New York: Collier Books, African/American Library Series, 1971.

—— *Masters of the Dew.* Trans. Langston Hughes & Mercer Cook. Portsmouth, NH: Heinemann, Caribbean Writers Series, 1988.

Saint-Amand, Pierre. *Diderot, le labyrinthe de la relation.* Paris: Vrin, 1984.

—— *Séduire, ou la passion des lumières.* Paris: Seuil, 1987.

—— *Les Lois de l'hostilité: la politique à l'âge des lumières.* Paris: Seuil, 1992.

Thoby-Marcelin, Philippe and Pierre Marcelin. *Canapé-Vert.* New York: Éditions de la Maison française, 1944.

—— *Canapé-Vert.* Trans. Edward Larocque Tinker. New York: Farrar & Rinehart, 1944.

—— *La Bête de Musseau.* New York: Éditions de la Maison française, 1946.

—— *The Beast of the Haitian Hills.* Trans. Peter C. Rhodes. New York: Rinehart, 1946.

—— *The Beast of the Haitian Hills.* Trans. Peter C. Rhodes. New York: Time, 1946, 1964.

—— *The Pencil of God.* Trans. Leonard Thomas. Boston: Houghton Mifflin, 1951.

—— *Le Crayon de Dieu.* Paris: La Table Ronde, 1952.

—— *Contes et légendes d'Haïti.* Paris: Nathan, 1967.

—— *All Men Are Mad.* Trans. Eva Thoby-Marcelin. New York: Farrar, Straus and Giroux, 1970.

—— *The Singing Turtle, and Other Tales from Haiti.* Trans. Eva Thoby-Marcelin. New York: Farrar, Straus and Giroux, 1971.

—— *Tous les hommes sont fous.* Montréal: Nouvelle Optique, 1980.

Trouillot, Michel-Rolph. *Ti difé boulé sou istoua Ayiti.* New York: Koléksion Lakansièl, 1977.

—— *Les Racines historiques de l'État duvalierien.* Port-au-Prince: Éditions Deschamps, 1986.

—— *Peasants and Capital: Dominica in the World Economy.* Baltimore: Johns Hopkins University Press, 1988.

—— *Haiti, State against Nation: The Origins and Legacy of Duvalierism.* New York: Monthly Review Press, 1990.

—— *Silencing the Past: Power and the Production of History.* Boston: Beacon Press, 1995.

Vilsaint, Féquière and Maude Heurtelou. *Diksyonè Kreyól Vilsen.* Coconut Creek: Educa Vision, 1990.

Wainwright, Kiki. *Pikliz.* Miami: Kolesksyon Koukouy, 1988.

—— *Les Sentiers de l'aube.* N. p.: À Contre Courant, 1993.

—— *Bonifas ak Malefis: kont kreyòl.* [Miami]: Edisyon Mapou, 1999.

Notes

Stephanie O'Hara translated this chapter.

Special thanks to C. Coates, M. Manigat, N. Pireddu and M. Shell for their help and encouragement.

1. See Michel Laguerre, *American Odyssey: Haitians in New York City* (Ithaca: Cornell University Press, 1984), pp. 169–73; and Eddy Magloire, *Regards sur la minorité ethnique haïtienne aux États-Unis* (Sherbrooke: Naaman, 1984), pp. 17–18.

2. Françoise Lionnet and Ronnie Scharfman, "Editors' Preface," *Yale French Studies* 82 (1993):1–3.

3. Of course, one could also point out the Santo Domingo writer Moreau de Saint-Méry, who lived and published in the United States at the end of the eighteenth century (see Laguerre, *American Odyssey,* pp. 162–63), but as far as Haitian literary criticism is concerned he is not a Haitian writer, since there was no such thing as a Haitian writer until after independence in 1804.

4. See Joyce Marie Cogdell-Travis, "A Translation of *Amour,* the First Book of the Trilogy Novel *Amour, colère et folie* by Marie Vieux Chauvet with a Critical Introduction 'Haiti — From a Woman's Point of View,'" Ph.D diss., Brown University, 1980; Madeleine Cottenet-Hage, "Violence libératoire/violence mutilatoire dans *Amour* de Marie Chauvet," *Francofonia: Studie Ricerche Sulle Letterature di Lingua Francese* 4-6 (1984):17–28; Joan Dayan, "Reading Women in the Caribbean: Marie Chauvet's Love, Anger, and Madness," in *Displacements: Women, Tradition, Literatures in French,* ed. Joan DeJean & Nancy K. Miller (Baltimore: Johns Hopkins University Press, 1991), pp. 228–53; Adrienne Gouraige, "Littérature haïtienne: Le Rôle des femmes dans la société chez deux romancières," *Revue-Francophone-de-Louisiane,* 4-1 (1989):30–38; Janis-A. Mayes, "Mind-Body-Soul: Erzulie Embodied in Marie Chauvet's *Amour, colère, folie,*" *Journal of Caribbean Studies,* 7-1 (1989):81–89; Laurie K. Lavine, "The Feminizing of the Trojan Horse: Marie Chauvet's *Amour* as War Machine," *Women in French Studies* 2 (1994):9–18; Ronnie

Scharfman, "Theorizing Terror: The Discourse of Violence in Marie Chauvet's *Amour, colère, folie*," in *Postcolonial Subjects. Francophone Women Writers*, ed. Mary Jean Green et al. (Minneapolis: University of Minnesota Press, 1996), pp. 229–45.

5. The original French edition did not appear until six years later (Montréal: Nouvelle Optique, 1976).

6. This first translation does not seem to have had any real impact, since Joan Dayan was completely unaware of it in the preface to her translation of Depestre's book five years later. See René Depestre, *A Rainbow for the Christian West*, trans. Joan Dayan (Amherst: University of Massachussets Press, 1977), pp. vii–xi.

7. The emergence in the United States of a literature in Haitian echoes what is happening in Haiti, where, clearly, there is a renewal of literary production in Haitian. It is important to remember here the creation of the "Sosoyèté Koukouy" — an association of writers and scholars devoted to the study and the promotion of Haitian Creole — under Jan Mapou (who in the 1970s and 1980s published several texts in the United States), Pierre Bambou and others at the end of the 1960s, and especially the publication in 1975 in Port-au-Prince of Franketienne's *Dézafi*. This first novel published in Haitian had considerable success, opening a debate on the language of Haitian literature(s) and a discussion of possible Haitian aesthetics.

8. Ruben François left the United States for Canada to avoid the Vietnam War. He died, probably from an overdose, in Montreal in 1972 or 1973. As was true for many young poets of his generation, his life and work were marked by the Beat Generation.

9. See Magloire, *Regards*, pp. 75–77.

10. See Marc Shell, "Babel in America; or, The Politics of Language Diversity in the United States," *Critical Inquiry* 20-1 (1993):103–27.

11. Ishmael Reed, *MultiAmerica. Essays on Cultural Wars and Cultural Peace* (New York: Penguin, 1998).

CHAPTER TWENTY-THREE

Translingualism and the American Literary Imagination

■ **STEVEN G. KELLMAN**

Though he is the most illustrious of all basketball guards, Michael Jordan failed spectacularly when he attempted a career in professional baseball. Like a language, each sport entails a distinctive aptitude, history, protocol, and Weltanschauung. There is no reason to suppose that a star in one sport will necessarily excel in another, any more than that Demosthenes would have become a consummate orator in Malinke, Gujarati, or Ojibwa as well as Greek. William Blake and Michelangelo each produced important paintings and poems, but few other major creators have distinguished themselves in more than one art. The history of sculpture was not transformed by anyone who also transformed the history of music.

For an explanation, look no further than the law of the conservation of cultural energy. Each art makes sufficient demands of its own to monopolize the talents and energies of anyone. In the throes of composing *Moby Dick*, Melville had no compulsion to express himself symphonically, even if he had had the temperament, the talent, and the orchestra. In post-Renaissance capitalist culture, industrial specialization has reduced the *uomo universale* — and his female counterpart — to a mere dilettante.

The same might be said of the polyglot, in whatever language it is said. A majority of the world's population is at least *bi*lingual. Fortunately, few are writers. Fewer still write well. Even rarer are those who write well in a second language. It is arduous enough to put the right words in the right place in one's native tongue. "All you have to do," noted sportswriter Red Smith, "is sit down at a typewriter and open a vein." How vain, then, are those who presume to write imaginative literature in a foreign tongue.

450

"No instance exists of a person's writing two languages perfectly," wrote Thomas Jefferson, in English, from Paris.[1] But the author of the blotted Declaration of Independence would be hard put to cite the instance of a person's writing even *one* language perfectly. Perfection is not an attribute of postlapsarian, post-Babelian expression. Yet numerous instances exist of literary translingualism, of a person's writing compellingly in a second language — even in the United States.[2] The national motto, *E pluribus unum*, expresses a communal yearning for unity that often becomes a desire to be done with other tongues, as though "English only" were the only ingredient lacking for continental comity.

Benjamin Franklin, who studied more than a dozen languages and was agile enough in French to translate the American Constitution into it, began his career by publishing a newspaper in German. The United States, a plural noun for most of its first century, were a tumultuous linguistic mix, until World War I led to prohibition of instruction and even conversation in German and other languages, and restrictive immigration laws in 1924 radically reduced the fresh supply of xenophones. In contrast to the multilingualism of Franklin and other founders, few modern American presidents could speak anything but English. When John F. Kennedy attempted German, he was translating verbatim from English, and the superfluous indefinite article in the resultant calque, "Ich bin ein Berliner," had him proclaiming: "I am a jelly doughnut." Yet this is also a nation of pan dulce, dim sum, and mandelbrot, as well as literary bakers whose repertoire exceeds apple pie. The most celebrated of modern translinguals are Europeans Joseph Conrad (Polish to French to English), Samuel Beckett (English to French), and Isak Dinesen (Danish to English) but, despite the monolingual impulse of American culture, the phenomenon is common, too, in literatures of the United States.

Though born in Hempstead, New York, Stuart Merrill wrote exclusively in French, adeptly enough to become a notable Symbolist poet. Yet the four undistinguished poems that T. S. Eliot wrote in French in 1917 disillusioned him about the very possibility of translingualism. "I don't think that one can be a bilingual poet," he contended. "I don't know of any case in which a man wrote great poetry or even fine poems equally well in two languages. I think one language must be the one you express yourself in poetry, and you've got to give up the other for that purpose."[3] Eliot ought to have known the cases of Petrarch, who wrote great poetry in both Italian and Latin, and Rainer Maria Rilke and Fernando Pessoa, who wrote fine poems in both German and French, and Portuguese and English, respectively.

Though raised in Spanish, George Santayana wrote his poetry in English. Yet he declared that no poets can be great who do not use the language in which their mothers sang them lullabies. For that reason, he slighted his own verse:

> Of impassioned tenderness or Dionysiac frenzy I have nothing, nor even of that magic and pregnancy of phrase — really the creation of a fresh idiom — which marks the high lights of poetry. Even if my temperament had been naturally warmer, the fact that the English language (and I can write no other with assurance) was not my mother-tongue would of itself preclude any inspired use of it on my part; its roots do not quite reach to my center. I never drank in childhood the homely cadences and ditties which in pure spontaneous poetry set the essential key. I know no words redolent of the wonder-world, fairy-tale, or the cradle.[4]

Vladimir Nabokov described his own switch from brilliant Russian to bravura English (via exquisite French, in which he wrote short fiction in Paris, before moving to Massachusetts) as "exceedingly painful — like learning anew to handle things after losing seven or eight fingers in an explosion."[5] There seems something not only painful but unnatural, almost matricidal, about an author who abandons the *Muttersprache, langue maternelle, mama loshen, sfat em, lengua materna, modersml, lingua madre, matesk jazyk,* and it is instructive that the most universally venerated of all authors, William Shakespeare, never left England or English. Chinua Achebe left Nigeria for the United States and, because he wrote *Things Fall Apart* in English, not Ibo, has had to counter charges of cultural treason by, among others, Ngugi wa Thiong'o (who renounced his own Anglographic career to write in Gikuyu).

Just as languages are incessantly evolving within communities, so that John Barth and Thomas Pynchon had to acquire proficiency in what is virtually a foreign tongue in order to write *The Sot-Weed Factor* and *Mason and*

Dixon, respectively, in eighteenth-century American English, neither language nor the relationship between languages is ever static for an individual speaker. In a sense, every speaker is translingual, moving with if not through languages.

Eva Hoffman lived in Polish for her first thirteen years, but when she revisits Cracow in middle age, she describes herself, in her 1990 memoir *Lost in Translation: A Life in a New Language,* as struggling to find the right local words.[6] Gerda Lerner fled Vienna at the age of eighteen, and half a century later, when she returned from the United States to lecture, in labored German, on a book she had written in English, she warned her audience: "You may wonder at my peculiar accent, and often at my choice of words. Although I am a native German speaker, I have not really spoken German in fifty years, and I have never before lectured in German."[7] When, fifty years after quitting St. Petersburg, Nabokov, whose books were available to native speakers only in *samizdat,* translated *Lolita* into Russian, it was a quaint, archaic language foreign to them and the author.

What gives George Frideric Handel a credible claim to the title of greatest English composer is the fact that, despite his thick German accent, the music he composed in London eclipses that of Henry Purcell, Edward Elgar, and Benjamin Britten. Tardiness in acquiring American English did not prevent Albert Bierstadt, Willem De Kooning, Arshile Gorky, Hans Hofmann, Mark Rothko, Ben Shahn, Joseph Stella, and Max Weber from attaining prominent positions in American painting. However, poetry is not nearly as portable. Much more than music, painting, sculpture, or dance, language is anchored to a particular time and place. "He who wants to dedicate himself to painting should start by cutting out his tongue" is the sentence with which Henri Matisse starts his book *Jazz,* and by which he distinguishes his wordless, nomadic art from that of poets.[8] If Handel had been an author, he would have had to confront two options after choosing exile: either continue, like Elias Canetti and W. G. Sebald, to compose in German, in stubborn isolation from the environment in which he lived, or else switch to English, though it is difficult for an adult to attain the fluency and even mastery in a second language that is necessary for literary virtuosity. After escaping Nazi Europe in her adolescence, Lerner aspired to be a writer but found herself caught between the native German she sought to discard and the American English that tormented her: "Living in translation is like skating on wobbly skates over thin ice. There is no sure footing; there are no clear-cut markers; no obvious signposts. It helps to trust in one's balance, to swing free and make leaps of the imagination. I suppose what I am saying is that it is immensely strenuous. Quite apart from being alienating."[9] For those who live in and through words, living in translation is to be racked between life and death.

W. H. Auden continued to create important poetry after leaving his native land, but he merely traded one Anglophonic country, England, for another, the United States. "Due to the Curse of Babel," proclaimed Auden, "poetry is the most provincial of the arts." However, he saw grandeur in that affliction, the fact that an art that depends on language thwarts its own potential for relocation. To sabotage a sonnet by encouraging it to limp to other lands, either deprive it of its feet or compose it in Uzbek — or any other finite language. "Today, when civilization is becoming monotonously the same all the world over," declared Auden in 1962, "one feels inclined to regard this [poetry's provincialism] as a blessing rather than a curse; in poetry, at least, there cannot be an 'International Style.'"[10] For Vincent Van Gogh, living in Arles instead of Amsterdam would have been more of a handicap and less of an inspiration had he tried to use words rather than pigments to portray starry nights.

And yet modernism is largely a literature of exile, a project of psychic, if not geographical, dislocation, and many of its champions have clung to their native languages thousands of miles from where they are spoken. Consider Gertrude Stein parsing her perverse English in Paris, Czeslaw Milosz composing his Polish in Berkeley, Isaac Bashevis Singer persisting with Yiddish in New York, Marguerite Yourcenar spinning fine French on Mount Desert Island, Thomas Mann conjuring up *Doktor Faustus* in Santa Monica, Lars Gustaffson creating Swedish fiction in Austin, Alexander Solzhenitsyn pronouncing in Russian from the fastness of rural Vermont. O. E. Rölvaag did not abandon his native Norwegian when he settled in Minnesota and wrote *I de dage* (1924) and *Riket grundlæges* (1925), which, translated as *Giants in the Earth* in 1928, entered the canon of American literature. Nor did Federico García Lorca resort to the ambient English to compose *Poeta en Nueva York* when he was a poet in New York in 1929. Ernest Hemingway and F. Scott Fitzgerald in Paris, Paul Bowles in Tangier, Ezra Pound in Italy, Pearl Buck in China — all are heroic figures of the artist who maintains literary loyalty to a native language far from the native land.

However, the past century also offers abundant examples of the converse: authors who, sometimes even without relocating, excelled in a second, third, or even fourth language. George Steiner, himself equally fluent in English, French, and German, has pondered the "extraterritoriality" of much twentieth-century literature, how poets have become "unhoused and wanderers across languages."[11] Within the United States, Felipe Alfau, Louis Begley, Abraham Cahan, Louis Chu, Ariel Dorfman, Raymond Federman, Khalil Gibran, Jerzy Kosinski, Bharati Mukherjee, Gabriel Preil, Henry Roth, Phyllis Wheatley, and Louis Zukofsky, among many others, developed commanding voices in languages in which their mothers did not sing them lullabies. Elie Wiesel — who writes in French, his fifth language, after Yiddish, Hebrew, Hungarian, and German, while residing in the United States — combines the linguistic agility of a Nabokov with the geographical itinerancy of Marco Polo, who himself chose French, not Italian, to recount his travels to China. Colonialism, war, increased mobility, and the aesthetics of alienation have combined to create a canon of translingual literature.

Nor is translingualism a categorical contrivance, a classification concocted to serve the purposes of idle pedantry. It is a genuine and rich tradition, in which authors are acutely aware of shared conditions and aspirations. Achebe responds, explicitly and implicitly, to Conrad, Eva Hoffman to Mary Antin. Both J. M. Coetzee — who grew up in an Afrikaner household but writes in English — and Raymond Federman have written extensively about Beckett. Even when Nabokov is belittling "Conrad's souvenir-shop style, bottled ships and shell necklaces of romanticist clichés," he is acknowledging affinity with another Anglophonic author who left behind a Slavic land and language.[12]

The most ostentatious and willful case of translingualism is the small body of fiction and poetry created in Esperanto, the vernacular of no one, an artificial language barely a century old. And the oddest contribution of American Esperantists is *Incubus* (1965), a movie directed by Leslie Stevens and starring William Shatner and Milos Milos that is the only feature film ever made in that fabricated language. But the phenomenon of translingualism antedates the modern aspiration to purify the words of the tribe by substituting synthetic speech or the words of another tribe. Spanish-American literature commences with Garcilaso de la Vega, a native speaker of Quechua, who wrote his masterpiece, *Comentarios reales*, in Spanish. Latin literature, which is said to have begun with Livius Andronicus, a Greek slave who wrote a Latin version of the *Odyssey*, was largely the creation of men who adopted the language of Rome though they were, like Seneca, Quintilian, Martial, and Lucan, from Spain, like Ausonius, from Gaul, or like Apuleius, Terence, and Augustine, from Africa. Arabic, Mandarin, Persian, Russian, and Sanskrit have also served as linguae francae, the dominant second language of heterogeneous speech communities, as has English during the period of American hegemony, enlisting the accented talents of Walter Abish and Ved Mehta but also repelling Louis Wolfson. In *Le Schizo et les langues* (1971), Wolfson, a native New Yorker hospitalized for schizophrenia, records, in brilliant French and fragments of Russian, German, Hebrew, and other languages, his psychotic rejection of his mother's — and father's — tongue, the one that he was reared to speak: English.[13]

For all the pathos of his plight as a Russian writer forced to start over again in Germany, France, and the United States, Nabokov, who admits in his autobiography *Speak, Memory* that he read English before Russian, was from childhood (a privileged one) almost equally fluent in Russian, English, and French.[14] His translingual dexterity is only underscored by the elegance with which he berates — in English — his own command of English for lacking the resources of a mother tongue: "the baffling mirror, the black velvet backdrop, the implied associations and traditions — which the native illusionist, frac-tails flying, can magically use to transcend the heritage in his own way."[15] Nabokov's claims of linguistic inadequacy, like those of Apuleius in the Preface to *The Golden Ass*, are manifestly inaccurate.

Many translinguals are consummate technicians, all the more fastidious for the fact that they are conscious of working with unfamiliar materials. It is hard to take words for granted when writing in a foreign language. Translingual writers represent an exaggerated instance of what the Russian

Formalists maintained is the distinctive quality of *all* imaginative literature: *ostranenie,* making strange. "The technique of art is to make objects 'unfamiliar,'" writes Victor Shklovsky, "to make forms difficult, to increase the difficulty and length of perception because the process of perception is an aesthetic end in itself and must be prolonged. *Art is a way of experiencing the artfulness of an object; the object is not important.*"[16] Working with a strange language is an obvious way to defamiliarize verbal expression, and the work of translinguals, more so than that of most other writers, foregrounds and challenges its own medium, creates that impediment to fluency that is the hallmark of the aesthetic according to Shklovsky, Boris Eichenbaum, and Jan Mukařovský. Puerto Rican novelist Rosario Ferré attributes a similar impeding power to her use of a second language: "English makes me slow down. I have to think over what I'm going to say twice, maybe three times — which is often healthy because I can't put my foot, or rather my pen, in my mouth so easily. I can't be trigger-happy in English because words take too much effort."[17] Repeated use of a native language automatizes writing, reduces idioms to formulas depleted of expressive power.

But some translinguals are simply clumsy in the alien idiom. In recounting *How the García Girls Lost Their Accents* in meticulous English prose, Julia Alvarez, a Dominican immigrant to the United States, demonstrates, through her first novel, that she lost hers. Yet some translingual texts expose the accents that their authors never quite discard. It is easy to spot occasional calques in the writings of some of the most respected translinguals, instances in which the author is thinking in one language but employing the locutions of another.

Though Joseph Brodsky was a major figure in Russian poetry, who also managed to become Poet Laureate of the United States, his ability to create a volume of poetry in English did not in itself impress John Bayley. Reviewing *So Forth: Poems,* the British critic complained: "There is an inherent clumsiness about this, like a bear playing the flute, that is embarrassing."[18] Canine rather than ursine, the metaphor in Samuel Johnson's infamous quip about homiletic women is equally applicable to translingual efforts: "Sir," observed the lexicographer to James Boswell, "a woman's preaching is like a dog's walking on his hinder legs. It is not done well: but you are surprised to find it done at all."[19] Though the mere existence of translingual literature is a marvel, some of the writing has been done surprisingly well, and a few misplaced adverbs or inappropriate prepositions do not negate the odd fascination of the phenomenon.

All else being equal, translingualism is a more arduous process for a poet or a short story writer, whose primary unit is the individual, irreducible word, than it is for the novelist or playwright, who can divert us from solecisms with plots and characters and for whom language might be merely instrumental. It is difficult to imagine Stéphane Mallarmé writing in any language other than his inimitable, untranslatable French, though another poet, one less dependent on the evocative sonics and semiotics of particular syllables, might manage the transition. One can more easily picture Henry Wadsworth Longfellow — who was in fact an accomplished linguist and, as the first professor of comparative literature at Harvard, a champion of multilingualism — composing in German. When a storyteller stumbles over an idiom or two, you are still inclined to turn the page. The fact that Rafael Sabatini, who was born in Italy and schooled in Portugal and Switzerland, chose to write all his novels in his *sixth* language, English, did not diminish their popularity. Sabatini attributed his translingual choice to the fact that "all the best stories are written in English," and devoted readers of *Scaramouche, Captain Blood,* and *The Sea Hawk,* who do not pause for verbal nits, consider those among them. Ten years after immigrating to the United States from Russia in 1926, Ayn Rand wrote her first novel, *We the Living,* in English — like all her subsequent books — and devoted disciples of Objectivism do not cavil over language.

Beyond qualitative distinctions, some categorical ones are useful. A taxonomy of literary translingualism would begin by differentiating between ambilinguals — authors who have written important works in more than one language — and monolingual translinguals — those who have written in only one language, but a language other than their native one. Just as Petrarch is a significant figure in both Latin and Italian, Nabokov, a master of American prose, would still be counted a major author in Russian literature even if he had never left Europe and written stories and novels in English. A canonical figure in French literature, Julien Green, who was born in Paris to American parents, wrote most of his fiction in French, though he set much of it in the American South and wrote an autobiography in English. After Karl Anton Post escaped from a monastery in Prague, he resurfaced in North America as Charles Sealsfield, a prolific author in both English and German. Other ambilinguals active on American soil include Abraham Cahan (Yiddish and English), Raymond Federman (French and English), Rosario Ferré (Spanish and English), and Joseph Tusiani (Italian and English). Charles V proclaimed: "I speak German to my horses, Spanish to my God, French to my friends, and Italian to my mistresses." As Emperor of the Holy Roman Empire, he spoke with authority in each. As agile as Proteus, ambilinguals promise the comprehensive, stereoscopic wisdom of Tiresias.

If *le style c'est l'homme même,* translingualism reconfigures style and makes of a single author a multiple man — or woman. Studying how the peculiar ways in which Hopi organizes tense dictates its speakers' orientation toward time, Edward Sapir famously declared that: "Human beings are very much at the mercy of the particular language which has become the medium of expression for their society."[20] Refusing to be constrained by the structures of any single language, ambilinguals seem both to acknowledge and defy the claims of linguistic determinism. It is precisely because they recognize the power of particular languages that they attempt to transcend them. To think about language in general requires the ability to step outside the prism of a particular system, an exercise in translingualism. Ludwig Wittgenstein, the philosopher who did most in the twentieth century to focus attention on the constraints of language, inhabited the space between German and English, and it was the polyglot Roman Jakobson who did more than most to advance the modern science of linguistics. Translinguals also seem especially well equipped, and compelled, to pose enigmas of personal identity. "Then who will solve this riddle of my day?" asks Tusiani in his poem "Song of the Bicentennial." "Two languages, two lands, perhaps two souls . . . / Am I a man or two strange halves of one?"[21] Tusiani and other ambilinguals are able to raise pointed questions about choice in the adoption of a particular literary medium. Does the writer choose the language, or does the language choose the writer?

The case of monolingual translinguals suggests the limitations and illusions of linguistic freedom, that even those able to step outside their native tongues are restricted in the further steps they take. Though ambilingual Ferré makes her choice between Spanish and English each time she writes, Elie Wiesel has stuck with French, a language he learned in Paris after liberation from Auschwitz, as the medium of all his fiction, even after he moved to the United States. Other monolingual translinguals, who jumped a tongue and stuck with it, include Mary Antin (Yiddish to English), Andrei Codrescu (Romanian to English), Ha Jin (Chinese to English) and Carlos Bulosan (Tagalog to English). The prodigious Isaac Asimov was born in Russia and reared in Yiddish, but he wrote all of his 477 books in English. Though she sets her novels — *Ein Sommer in der Woche der itke K.* (1971), *Die Töchter* (1978), *Uberbleibsel* (1995) — in Atlanta, where she moved as a child from her native New York, Jeannette Lander, who emigrated to Berlin in the 1960s, has adopted German exclusively as her literary medium. Richard Rodriguez's memoir *Hunger of Memory* recounts his life as a trajectory from Spanish, the mother tongue he now barely remembers, to English, the language in which he has created a career as professional author.

Much translingual writing in the United States is the literature of immigration, and much immigration is reluctant, the product of historical forces over which the individual has little control. So translingualism is not always an expression of autonomy, of independence from a culture that forces us to think and speak along its particular lines. Though she managed to write important poetry in English rather than her native Fulani, Phyllis Wheatley did not choose to be transported from Africa to America, as a slave. Eva Hoffman recounts how she ceased being Ewa Wydra; how, at the age of thirteen, she was uprooted from her beloved Cracow and resettled in North America, where English inevitably supplanted her native Polish, though certain feelings, like *tęsknota,* a blend of nostalgia, sadness, and longing, she can articulate only in Polish. It is not uncommon for a young immigrant, like Mary Antin or Anzia Yezierska, to excel in the language of the adopted country. In the classic of modern immigration fiction, *Call It Sleep,* translingual Henry Roth fashioned an English style so supple it could represent the Yiddish, Polish, Hebrew, English, and Italian of his characters.

Texts by translinguals usually betray traces of other tongues, but most are written entirely in one language or another. Linguistic purity is of course a chimera; English, Korean, and Arabic are each already mongrel, and creolization among existing languages proceeds wherever cultures touch and collide, which is to say virtually everywhere. Franglais, Spanglish, Germerican, Fanagalo, Gullah, Bajan, Papiamentu, Tok Pisin, Manipravalam, and other composites testify to how porous are linguistic boundaries. Code-switching is common among bilinguals, and authors who would represent speech as actually spoken create internally translingual texts, often between colloquial and formal or regional and standard forms of the same language. Toni Morrison, Ishmael Reed, and other African-Americans often switch between standard and Ebonic English.

Code-switching is especially prominent among Mexican-American authors, who assert their hybrid identity by producing sentences that are neither entirely Spanish nor entirely English. Celebrating her own *mestizaje*, Gloria Anzaldúa, for one, announces: "I am a border woman," and justifies the mingling of different registers of Spanish and English in *Borderlands/La Frontera* by explaining: "The switching of codes in this book from English to Castillian Spanish to the Northern Mexican dialect to Tex-Mex to a sprinkling of Nahuatl to a mixture of all of these, reflects my language, a new language — the language of the Borderlands."[22]

In his *Klail City Death Trip* cycle, a novelistic project that attempts to represent Chicano experience in the Rio Grande Valley throughout the twentieth century, Rolando Hinojosa writes his narrative entirely in Spanish for the early decades and entirely in English for the more recent ones. To create plausible dialogue among his bilingual characters, however, Hinojosa often switches codes within the same sentence. For example, one of the letters that Jehú Malacara sends to Rafa Buenrostro in the epistolary novel *Mi querido Rafa* begins: "Lunch at the Camelot; Noddy me mandó (& *that's* the word, son) a que fuera a look over a deal; Noddy se quiere deshacer de la agencia de carros y el buyer wants (has) to use the bank's money for said purpose."[23] Though it might exasperate purists of Spanish and English, the Klail City cycle simulates the code-switching actually employed by speakers in the south Texas context that Hinojosa evokes.

John Sayles has no personal ethnic connections to Spanish, but when, in 1991, he published a novel about Cuban exiles in Miami, he appropriated *Los Gusanos* (the worms), the derogatory term that Fidel Castro applied to his opponents, as title.[24] And Sayles taught himself Spanish in order to represent the speech that the characters would in fact employ. He made *Hombres armados / Men with Guns*, his 1998 film about Central American guerrillas, largely in Spanish, with occasional dialogue in the indigenous Nahuatl, Tzotzil, Maya, and Kuna languages. The only English syllables are uttered by two North American tourists (Mandy Patinkin and Kathryn Grody), who are a crass caricature of gringo arrogance and obtuseness. Barely bilingual, they speak Spanish, when they do, haltingly, defectively, in an accent as thick as a New York salami. "What's the word for fajitas?" asks Andrew, the burlesque of a monolingual monoculturalist who serves — in a crude, self-congratulatory way — to highlight Sayles's own accomplishment in stepping outside the *norteamericano* prisonhouse of his native language.

Since 1927, when movies began to speak, starting with the Yiddish inflections of the assimilation fable *The Jazz Singer*, Hollywood has been the world's dominant purveyor of words. Though hundreds of films in Cantonese, Spanish, Yiddish, and other languages have been made — mostly by native speakers — in the United States, it is English that dominates the industry. One of the protocols of commercial movie production is that characters such as Oskar Schindler, Christopher Columbus, Eva Perón, and Jesus are really speaking something else when what we hear from the actor's mouth is the Queen's — or Queens — English. Tony Curtis's portrayal in *Spartacus* of a Roman slave with a Bronx inflection is legendary. The convention of cinematic monolingualism obviates the clumsy mechanisms of subtitles and dubbing, even as it reinforces a quaint belief that all the world speaks English, only and always. However, Hollywood owes much of its glory to what xenophonic émigrés such as Michael Curtiz, Fritz Lang, Ernst Lubitsch, Rouben Mamoulian, Douglas Sirk, Josef von Sternberg, Billy Wilder, and Fred Zinnemann were able to accomplish with screenplays in English. And recent American cinema has continued to recruit translingual directors, including Ang Lee, Constantin Costa-Gavras, Roland Emmerich, Milos Forman, Agnieszka Holland, Louis Malle, Wolfgang Petersen, Paul Verhoeven, and John Woo.

The linguistic amalgam that T. S. Eliot creates in *The Waste Land* and Ezra Pound in his *Cantos* is aimed at a synoptic vision that transcends the limitations of any particular language. Along with the ideal insomnia that it demands of readers, James Joyce's *Finnegans Wake* aspires to a consummate translingualism, a state beyond any of the many natural languages out of which the novel is compounded. Translinguals move beyond their native languages, but for many, particularly in the twentieth century, theirs is an aspiration to transcend language in general, to be pandictic, to utter everything. Impatient with the imperfections of finite verbal systems, they yearn to pass beyond words, to silence and truth.

Notes

1. Thomas Jefferson, Letter to John Bannister, Jr., October 15, 1785. In *Writings* (New York: The Library of America, 1984), p. 839.

2. Steven G. Kellman, *The Translingual Imagination* (Lincoln: University of Nebraska Press, 2000).

3. T. S. Eliot, Interview, conducted by Donald Hall. In *Writers at Work: The Paris Review Interviews*, ed. George Plimpton (second series. New York: Penguin, 1963), p. 99.

4. George Santayana, *Poems* (New York: Charles Scribner's Sons, 1923), pp. vii–viii.

5. Vladimir Nabokov, *Strong Opinions* (New York: McGraw-Hill, 1973), p. 54.

6. Eva Hoffman, *Lost in Translation: A Life in a New Language* (New York: Penguin, 1990).

7. Gerda Lerner, *Why History Matters: Life and Thought* (New York: Oxford University Press, 1997), p. 47.

8. Henri Matisse, *Jazz* (Paris, 1947).

9. Lerner, *Why History Matters*, p. 40.

10. W. H. Auden, *The Dyer's Hand* (New York: Random House, 1962), p. 23.

11. George Steiner, *After Babel* (New York: Oxford University Press, 1975), p. 11.

12. Nabokov, *Strong Opinions*, p. 42.

13. Louis Wolfson, *Le Schizo et les langues* (Paris: Gallimard, 1971).

14. Vladimir Nabokov, *Speak, Memory: An Autobiography Revisited* (New York: G. P. Putnam's Sons, 1966).

15. Vladimir Nabokov, "On a Book Entitled *Lolita,*" in *The Annotated Lolita,* ed. Alfred Appel, Jr. (New York: McGraw-Hill, 1970), p. 319.

16. Victor Shklovsky, "Art as Technique," trans. Lee T. Lemon and Marion J. Reis, in *Critical Theory Since Plato,* ed. Hazard Adams (rev. ed. Orlando, Fla.: Harcourt Brace Jovanovich, 1992), p. 754.

17. Rosario Ferré, "Writers and Artists Speaking on the Frontier," in *Review: Latin American Literature and Arts* 54 (spring 1997):62.

18. John Bayley, "English as a Second Language," *The New York Times Book Review,* Sept. 1, 1996, p. 6.

19. James Boswell, *Life of Johnson* (London: Oxford University Press, 1953), p. 287.

20. Edward Sapir, "The Status of Linguistics as a Science," *Language* 5 (1929):209.

21. Joseph Tusiani, *Gente Mia* (Stone Park, Ill.: Italian Cultural Center, 1978), p. 7.

22. Gloria Anzaldúa, preface to *Borderlands / La Frontera: The New Mestiza* (San Francisco: Aunt Lute, 1987).

23. Rolando Hinojosa, *Mi querido Rafa* (Houston: Arte Publico, 1981), p. 17.

24. John Sayles, *Los Gusanos* (New York: Harper Collins, 1991).

CHAPTER TWENTY-FOUR

What Is *Aufklärung* (in Pennsylvania)?

■ PETER FENVES

The parenthesis in my title "(in Pennsylvania)" runs against the grain of the question — not because Pennsylvania is not a possible place of *Aufklärung*, but because the general project of *Aufklärung*, as it is generally understood, does not define itself in relation to places. Rather, it defines itself in terms of time and, above all, the time of maturation, which in German — or, more accurately, in one of the officially sanctioned German *Mundarten* (dialects) — is expressed by the term *Mündigkeit. Mündigkeit*, "maturity," could be translated by "mouthyness": I come of age when I am able to use my mouth and thus to let my voice be heard as my own voice, not as the voice of another, especially not the voice of my ancestors or ancestral land.

"*Aufklärung* is the departure of the human being from its self-incurred immaturity *(aus seiner selbst verschuldeten Unmündigkeit).*"[1] This is the most famous answer (Kant's) to the question "what is *Aufklärung?*" and it defines the term by referring to a temporal process: releasing oneself from one's self-imposed debts by gaining control over one's mouth, which, in turn, allows one to make promises and announce treaties. The project of Enlightenment does not depend on the place from which it is launched but on the time it takes for the mouth to transcend the particularity of its place and join the discourse of a world community: a cosmo-polis in which each mouth serves only the mind to which it (somewhat mysteriously) is attached. To ask "what is *Aufklärung* in X?" (where X stands for a particular place), as though this question would not receive the same response no matter what X stood for, is not so much to question Kant's all-too-famous answer as to plead for a further inquiry into the motility of the mouth that makes up *Mündigkeit*. For it is upon this strange (and not easily translatable) term that the pithiness and power of Kant's answer depend. If one were to

465

accept the mere possibility of a *divided* mouth, a mouth that, because of its place, incurs a debt *by* speaking — by speaking a *particular* language — then the act of gaining *Mündigkeit* (gaining a voice, becoming articulate) runs counter to the supposed goal of this act, namely disencumbering oneself of one's debts. Every movement toward *Mündigkeit* is a movement away from the debt-free existence toward which the project of Enlightenment aims, according to this, its classical formulation.

In making a choice about the language in which to address the question of Enlightenment as a problem of *Mündigkeit*, Kant seems certain that he incurs no debts. He responds to a question posed by the *Berlinische Monatsschrift* in German — or in a certain *Mundart* of German — and he responds in kind, as if no choice were implied in this response. His almost somnambulist certainty that no choice of language has been or needs to be made rests less on the nature of the places of reading and writing, namely Königsberg and Berlin, than in his prior understanding of these Prussian (and sometimes Russian) places as ones in which the choice of language has already been made — by someone else. It is not *his* choice when he chooses to write in German, and it is not *his* choice that he chooses a German *Mundart* hardly anyone *speaks*. Each choice is, rather, a passive "having been chosen." And yet passivities of this kind are precisely the ones that bear witness to a failure of *Mündigkeit*: Kant does not own up to his decision to leave the choice of language to certain authorities in whose decisions he has had no say. More importantly, he does not own up to the *inevitability* of this choice of language, an inevitability rooted in the nature of *Mündigkeit* itself: the choice of languages in which one gains one's voice always precedes and is therefore ahead of the voice one gains.

At the end of his response Kant quotes the voice of the enlightened ruler who, "fearing no shadows," lays the ground for further progress toward Enlightenment and therefore opens the way to a perpetually sunny existence: "argue [*räsonnieren*] as much as you want and about whatever you want, only obey!"[2] Because the original command of the enlightened sovereign is silent about the medium in which to argue, the command can be heard to say: you are allowed to talk as much as you want, and you are allowed to talk about whatever you want, as long as you talk in the language of this allowance. But, of course, the sovereign whom Kant quotes,

Friedrich II, issued this command in French, and a trace of this language is preserved in the very word by which Kant speaks of mature speaking, namely the Latin-French-German word *räsonnieren*. Kant, as usual, is ahead of his commentators: from the very beginning of his response to the question "what is Enlightenment," he shows the extent to which he is aware that he cannot avoid choosing a language in which to obey the command to talk as much as you want, for he shows that he *could have* chosen another language and that his choice does not go without saying, and that by choosing to speak in a particular language, which is to say, by choosing to speak at all, he incurs a debt. Kant goes so far as to express the "motto of Enlightenment" in a language other than officially sanctioned German. But — and this is the decisive point — the other language he chooses is even further removed from a living *Mundart* than the first one. This other language is a language of undeniable *Mündigkeit* precisely because *it is never spoken:* it is a language for which there are no longer any mouths, a mouthless language, or one in which no mouth gains its voice — a dead language, namely Latin, and more exactly, the heroic Latin of Horace as opposed to the servile Latin of Church services. Thus Kant writes at the end of the first paragraph: "*Sapere aude!* 'Have the courage to use your own understanding!' — that is the motto of Enlightenment."[3]

As long as the choice is limited to one between a dead Latin and "high" German — and these are indeed the two languages in which Kant wrote — he can justify his choice in terms of the highest aesthetic and therefore the highest communicative principle, namely the principle of liveliness. With only the slightest change in inflection or tone, however, the imperative he issues in the language he chooses to avoid — "have the courage to use your own understanding" — can turn in on itself and turn into "have the courage to use your own language so that you can have an understanding of your own." But here, in the phrase "your own language," or "my own language," the principle of *Mündigkeit,* of gaining your voice by departing from the debts you owe but have not made for yourself, is not so much abandoned as made into a point of perplexity: the "ownness" of "my own language" is one for which I cannot be held responsible.[4]

In the concluding footnote to his essay Kant asks his readers to compare his response to the question "what is *Aufklärung?*" with one he has not yet been able to read — that of Moses Mendelssohn. But Mendelssohn does not in fact respond to *this* question; instead, he responds to another one: "Was *heißt* aufklären?" (What does the term "to enlighten" mean? Or, what calls for enlightenment?) Unlike Kant, Mendelssohn makes it clear from the beginning that the question of enlightenment cannot be divorced from a question of language, and so he takes his point of departure from the new word "to enlighten" (*aufklären*) rather than from the — for Mendelssohn — very old phenomenon of enlightenment: "The words *enlightenment, culture,* and *education* [Aufklärung, Kultur, Bildung] are newcomers to our language. They belong at this point merely to the language of books" — which is to say, to a language disengaged from the mouth, a language in which a certain articulateness is already presupposed.[5]

But this analysis of the word *aufklären* "in our language" does not exhaust Mendelssohn's attentiveness to the linguistic character of enlightenment. Indeed, he is less concerned with the enlightenment of ages or peoples than with the enlightenment of language: "A language achieves enlightenment through the sciences and achieves culture through social interaction, poetry, and rhetoric. Through the first it becomes more fitting for theoretical pursuits, through the latter for practical ones. Both together give a language *Bildung*."[6] Language indicates the level of enlightenment, and any contribution to linguistic clarification, including the clarification of the word *Aufklärung*, is itself a contribution to enlightenment. But such contributions *also* contribute to the death of this language: as a language begins to separate out concepts on the basis of scientific knowledge, it also begins to disintegrate into two distinct dialectics — a living language of speech, on the one hand, and a dead language of writing, on the other.[7] As a language achieves enlightenment, it begins to die. Or, to cite the closing words of Mendelssohn's essay: "A nation that has come through *Bildung* to the highest pinnacle of national prosperity is, precisely because of that, in danger of falling."[8] Nowhere is the law more apparent than in the one nation that, according to Mendelssohn, achieved the highest degree of *Bildung* — the Greeks: "The Greeks had both, culture and enlightenment. They were a *gebildete* nation, just as their language is a *gebildete* language."[9] They *were,* their language *is:* the language outlives the nation and is, for this reason, a dead language. Language is not only the index of enlightenment; it is also its archive. Every achievement of enlightenment, however small, secures a language against decay but for this very reason makes it a little less alive, a little more a book language — until it becomes a dead language in which knowledge and taste are petrified and preserved.[10]

Kant and Mendelssohn's responses to the question of enlightenment took place at a time in which the ideals of the Enlightenment began to appear more and more questionable to the very class of people who had hitherto been its principal champions: members of what Kant calls the "reading world" *(Leserwelt)*.[11] By concerning itself with universals, the project of Enlightenment seemed to lose track of particularity — and especially of particular languages. Without admitting so, a countermovement to the cause of Enlightenment took its point of departure from the law Mendelssohn comes close to formulating: the enlightenment of a language contributes to its death. Accordingly, a living language, a language in which the Word lets itself be spoken in human mouths, should keep itself free of enlightenment: "Not only does the whole ability to think rest on language . . . but language is also the *middle point of reason's misunderstanding of itself,*" Hamann declared, and armed with this clarification of the misunderstandings into which unaided reason inevitably falls, he launched an enigmatic and yet — or perhaps for this reason — enormously effective countermovement to the enlightenment ideals that Kant and Mendelssohn, each in his own way, espoused.[12] According to Hamann, proponents of Enlightenment never fail to miss the living language, which is to say, the particular language spoken in particular locations by particular peoples. Whereas responses to the question of enlightenment generally emphasize the dimension of time, especially the time of maturation, celebrations of vital languages tend to concern themselves with specific localities: this nation, that territory, these customs, "our" mode of speaking. A living language does not belong to a "reading world" but, rather, to a localized people whose expression it is. This idea of language can then function as a powerful objection to the universal and cosmopolitan claims of Enlightenment. By celebrating the wonder of language as such — and by doing so with an exuberant overabundance of obscure citations in dead languages — Hamann was able to revive certain tendencies of German pietism and make them attractive to members of the German "reading world" who still wished to keep their distance from pietistic doctrines, preachers, and communities.

During the same time — but in another place — members of the "reading world" saw no need to distance themselves from German pietism, for they were its preachers, expounded its doctrines, and established communities on the basis of its principles. This place was, of course, Pennsylvania during the eighteenth century. The leaders of the sectarian communities in Pennsylvania were far removed from the debates sponsored by the *Berlinische Monatsschrift*, but they, unlike the majority of the German-speaking immigrants to America, were members of an active "world of reading" and productive culture of writing.[13] The German poetry written in the eighteenth century was largely the work of educated (even if not in Mendelssohn's sense *gebildete*) scholars, and almost all of this poetry was dedicated to a single thematic complex — which also happens to be the one to which Hamann devoted himself: the sublimity of God, the vanity of earthly things, and the darkness in which we lead our lives.[14] Johann Adam Gruber, who functioned as something of a liaison between the sectarian communities in Pennsylvania and pietist groups in Europe, was more explicit than many of his contemporaries; but the stilted anaphora with which he begins an extensive poem on divine grace expresses the general disposition of much German poetry written in eighteenth-century Pennsylvania:

> Weg mit allerley Verstellung,
> Weg mit Falshheit, Gleissnerey!
> Weg mit Frechheit, Welt-Gleichstellung,
> Weg mit Fleisches Trügerey! [. . .]
> Weg Vernunfts-Philosophiren,
> Weg der Argheit Schlangen-Tück!
> Weg, was Selbstsucht thut einführen:
> Menschensucht weich nur zürück!

> [Away with dissimulation,
> Away with falsehood, hypocrisy!

Away with insolence, making everything worldly,
Away with the deceptions of the flesh! . . .
Away with rational philosophizing,
Away with the snake-trick of maliciousness!
Away with what selfishness introduces:
Humanism simply recede!]][15]

Gruber's poem represents the position of radical pietism: all human pursuits consist in selfishness. This position may not define the entire discursive space of eighteenth-century Pennsylvanian-German poetry, but it does mark out one of its central points, and it extends beyond the realm of poetry — and beyond the boundaries of the sectarian communities. The most prolific publishers of German writing in colonial Pennsylvania, the Sauer family, added a free Sunday supplement to their German-town newspaper, *Ein Geistliches Magazien* (A Spiritual Magazine), which was less inclined than contemporaneous poetry toward visions of mystical union with the divine "Ungrund."[16] Like much of the poetry of the period, however, it was dedicated to the glorification of God: "this work is a magazine in which all kinds of things are to be found: admonitions, punishments, edifying letters, life-histories of blessed human beings, edifying events, and whatever else can serve . . . the honor of God."[17]

Other works of prose in German, including the numerous newspapers, generally concerned themselves with daily affairs, and even as they ventured into primarily "secular" territory — travel reports, accounts of hardship, complaints about mistreatment, denunciations of rebellion, celebrations of the young republic — they refrained from giving voice to *Vernunfts-Philosophiren* or, in other words, to Enlightenment ideals.[18] This is true even of the *Wöchentliche Pennsylvanische Staatsbote*, perhaps the best-established and most widely circulated German newspaper of the eighteenth century and the first newspaper in the world to announce the signing of an influential Enlightenment document: the Declaration of Independence.[19] Unlike the "reading world" in Berlin or Königsberg, in short, the one in Pennsylvania had few, if any, places where it was possible to *interpret* the pursuit of earthly happiness as something other than "selfishness" (*Selbstsucht*) — unless, of course, members of this world ventured into another one and read texts published outside of America or written in languages other than German.

Yet it is for precisely these reasons that the discursive space of German in eighteenth-century Pennsylvania offers an auspicious site from which to pose once again the question: "was ist Aufklärung"? Responses to this question, even if they are only implicit, cannot fail to take into consideration the language in which they are formulated, for Enlightenment *in this place* is a mortal threat to this language. When Hamann presents Enlightenment as the death of language, "death" must be understood in a figural sense, for German will doubtless survive the Berlin Enlightenment: only its ability to communicate something of spiritual significance to someone in particular will — he supposes — be lost. Not so with German in Pennsylvania: here the language could very well die as its speakers become more *aufgeklärt*, which is to say, as they begin to distance themselves from communities founded on the doctrine that our earthly lives are shrouded in a darkness we ourselves are incapable of illuminating. For these communities not only seek to preserve the Word in its original purity; they keep the language alive. Departing from "self-incurred immaturity" — to invoke Kant's definition of *Aufklärung* once again — means leaving the particular sphere where it makes sense to speak one language (German, say) rather than another (say, English); it is a *rational* decision to speak the former rather than the latter language because it goes without saying that it is simply the language of the community. Departing from *Unmündigkeit* means, in other words, having to *justify* the choice of language — without being able to base this choice on immature attachments to mother tongues, fatherlands, fraternal feelings, or sisterly relations. In Berlin, growing up does not mean renouncing the language of childhood but simply making it into the medium of one's own voice. In Pennsylvania, by contrast, departing from immaturity means coming to terms with the debt of language: a debt that falls due with the prospect of its death. Because this debt cannot be discounted, answers to the question "was ist Aufklärung?" in eighteenth-century Pennsylvania may be strangely in advance of the ones found in the much more sophisticated philosophical culture of eighteenth-century Berlin or Königsberg: these answers must argue for the arbitrary choice of the language in which they are cast without glorifying the arbitrariness of this — or any other — decision.

This task may be an impossible one. The choice of language may always be too closely connected with the arbitrariness of place to allow anyone to give a reason — or a *good* reason — for it. And perhaps for this reason there are almost no responses to the question "was ist Aufklärung?" in eighteenth-century Pennsylvania — almost none, but not quite. There is at least one, even if it is only implicit, and it can be found in the *Philadelphisches Magazin*, the sole number of which came out in 1798.[20] Unlike the *Berlinische Monatsschrift*, the *Philadelphisches Magazin* (which its editors hoped to turn into the *Philadelphische Monatsschrift* after receiving an appropriate number of subscriptions) does not solicit responses to the question of enlightenment, and yet its very appearance is the sign of enlightenment: it is not another *Geistliches Magazien*. And if anyone is tempted to confuse the two, the subtitle of the new periodical clears things up: *Philadelphisches Magazin, oder Unterhaltender Gesellschafter, für die Deutschen in America* (The Philadelphia Magazine or an Entertaining Companion for the Germans in America). In Philadelphia — if not in all of Pennsylvania and America at large — the answer to the question "what is *Aufklärung?*" is *Unterhaltung:* "conversation" or, more to the point, "entertainment."

To be entertained means, above all, to be diverted from worries about what is to come, and the point of having an "entertaining companion" during a trip is to allow travelers to forget at least for a moment their destination — if there is one. To be more precise, the *Philadelphisches Magazin* is "enlightened" to the degree that it gives its readers time to think about something other than the topics on which the *Geistliches Magazien* concentrates: the next world, the finitude of our earthly life, the end of this world and the beginning of the *Himmelreich* ("heavenly kingdom"). Insofar as the *Philadelphisches Magazin* lightens the burden of life on this earth, it is a genuinely enlightening companion. Without explicitly referring to theological doctrines, pietistic practices, charismatic preachers, or sectarian communities — and this total silence about such matters is the truly daring aspect of the magazine — the editors offer "believable news about the most wonderful inventions, changes, and events that have taken place in nature and art, from the earliest times to the present incidents of this time"[21] — "believable" (*glaubwürdig*) means something other than "faith" (*Glauben*), and "wonderful" (*wunderbar*) means something other than divine "miracles" (*Wunder*). At the very inception of this periodical, the editors make a reasonable promise: nothing based on faith, no miracles, only the present and what conforms with it.

So careful are the editors of the *Philadelphisches Magazin* to emphasize that they want nothing to do with destinies and destinations that they promise in the preface not to print any article or story that might leave the reader anxious about its conclusion: each issue will avoid the unpleasant prospect of having to wait for the next issue for the continuation of an article or story. It is not hard to understand this promise as a pledge not to worry its readers about the world to come. Immediately after announcing, without further comment, that this magazine is "the first writing of its kind that, as far as we know, has ever appeared in America in the German language," the editors go on to claim that everyone must admit that "nothing can be more unpleasant" than reading an article or story, only to find out that it has been broken off in the middle and its conclusion is forthcoming.[22] "The reader," the editors remark, thus indicating the sense of their subtitle and the direction of their efforts, "is immediately disturbed in his entertainment."[23] In the *Philadelphisches Magazin,* by contrast, everything is already here, without waiting, on demand. That's entertainment.

Or it is entertainment for a certain readership: Germans in America. The editors of the *Philadelphisches Magazin* do not indicate anywhere in the magazine that they are making up for a lack — a dearth of entertainment, say, in a dour religious atmosphere. On the contrary, the preface to the magazine defines Germans in America according to a certain tendency: they are not presented in terms of their religious practices, sectarian communities, or spiritual discourses but, instead, as those who are "otherwise very much for culture [*sonsten sehr für Cultur*]."[24] The entertainment of the *Philadelphisches Magazin* has no "higher" goal, but it is nevertheless justified, for it is offered in the name of culture. Because of the unexploited cultural resources of its readership, moreover, the magazine can expect to find "readers of taste and talents [*Lesern von Geschmack und Talenten*]" who will be able to make their own "prosaic and poetic" contributions to it. As it entertains, the *Philadelphisches Magazin* allows those who are "for culture" to become active participants in a newly created "world of reading" — one that has nothing to do with spiritual doctrines or religious practices.

Entertainment undertaken in the name of culture is, moreover, a refuge from politics. Germany as a political space, for example, is entirely absent from the pages of the *Philadelphisches Magazin:* the predominantly German-speaking territories are subsumed under the category of Europe, which, in turn, is set off against America. Beyond reporting "believable" stories and "the most wonderful events," the editors promise to give accounts and descriptions of the "most important patriots and the most remarkable persons in Europe and America": in the one issue that appeared, this meant American patriots and European persons.[25] The opening and longest article is devoted to George Washington, whose portrait graces the first page, and the second article consists of a lengthy description of Mount Vernon. But Washington is celebrated as one who freed his homeland from an unspecified "yoke" and who therefore deserves a pleasant end to his long days. When the magazine does touch upon a point at which the term "patriot" might assume a considerable polemical edge, it shies away from politics: in the section of the "Political Journal" devoted to France in 1797–98, for example, the editors say nothing about the events but, instead, only give some statistics about the number of deaths, births, and marriages. The same is true of the section of the "Political Journal" devoted to the United States — and these are the only two countries covered. The editors of the magazine not only shun theological controversies; they want nothing to do with political conflicts, whether in America or Europe. Instead of discussing such conflicts, the *Philadelphisches Magazin* prefers to "report on the customs and manners of various peoples."[26] The magazine presents itself, in short, as a neutral space of description — or entertainment — in the name of an ever-widening culture.

The magazine is not entirely neutral, however. It takes sides on at least one question: which language is the most productive? The politics of language thus gives direction to its program of entertainment. According to the editors, the most productive language is, not surprisingly, German. Nowhere does the *Philadelphisches Magazin* show any interest in the political, economic, social, "national," or religious character of predominantly German-speaking lands; but it is deeply concerned with the productive capacity of the language. In an article entitled "Progress der Deutschen Litteratur" (Progress of German Literature), the editors do not try to establish that German literature has proceeded from an earlier to a more advanced stage; rather, they list the number of books published in German according to their content and afterwards conclude that *some* good books must be among them:

> There is truly no country [*Land*] in the world where more books are written and published than in Germany.
>
> The following list of books that came out during the six years from 1785 to 1790 is taken from the *Jena gelehrete Schrift*, which Professor Schütz edits:

1. General Literature [Allgemeine Litteratur]	63 works
2. Philology	1527
3. Theology [Gottesgelahrtheit]	4863
4. Law	2158
5. Medicine and Healing	1899
6. Metaphysics and Philosophical Morality[. . .]	965
7. History of Literature	762
8. Miscellaneous Content	689
	Total 27,372 works

One can easily imagine that many more have been published that escaped the notice of the editor of a scholarly journal; one will then be able to count thirty thousand with a fair degree of certainty, which makes five thousand a year. Certainly an enormous number. That some of these books are bad is certain, but it is just as certain that many fine ones are to be numbered among them. This is the reason why even in England, where they otherwise treat the German language with contempt, everyone who claims scholarship and taste learns this excellent and rich language [*diese vertreffliche und reiche Sprache*]; in addition, an extraordinary number of German works are translated into English.[27]

German literature is making progress because of the unparalleled richness of its language. The language is so rich that it almost seems to work — or produce works — entirely on its own. Indeed, German forces speakers of other languages to learn it — speakers who wish to consider themselves among the enlightened. The editors of the *Philadelphisches Magazin* do not use the word *Aufklärung,* but they use two words that in conjunction serve as its equivalent: *Gelehrsamkeit und Geschmack* ("scholarship and taste"). German produces the products of Enlightenment, and so English-speakers must either learn it or condemn themselves to ignorance and lack of taste. Those who participate in German literature, by contrast, can rest assured that their language will produce more and more works. The productivity of the language is, therefore, a reason to contribute to the progress of German literature, even in America.

But the article on the progress of German literature says nothing about America. Although it notes that a professor at Jena would obviously have overlooked a large number of publications, the article does not indicate that some of these works may have escaped his attention because they were published outside Europe.[28] The theologically inflected "reading world" of Pennsylvania German does not, it seems, contribute to the progress of German literature. Or it does not yet and perhaps cannot do so as long as it remains inflected by — or infected with — theology. The publication of "the first writing of its kind that has ever appeared in America in the German language" may therefore be a momentous event: the productive capacities of German take hold in America, unfettered by theological controversies and sectarian tendencies.[29] And, as it turns out, the American landscape is perfectly suited for the German language. Another article later in the magazine gives a list similar to the one in the article about the progress of German literature, but instead of showing the number of books produced, it displays the value of exports from the United States to various countries around the world along with a breakdown of foreign exports from each of the 13 states. The conclusion to the latter article reproduces the conclusion of the former one, with one difference: the United States, rather than predominantly German-speaking lands, is the place of production: "Perhaps no nation in the world has made such extraordinary progress [*Fortschritt*] in trade as the United States in the last twenty years. The fruits of the earth are in overflow. Taxes are low, and the farmer becomes richer and richer [*reicher und reicher*] every day, as long as he deserves it. Knowledge goes hand in hand with the other improvements. Merely the newspapers that are printed in the United States are more than 200 hundred at last count."[30]

With this last figure the article about the United States in the section of the "Political Journal" comes to a close. The editors of the *Philadelphisches Magazin* may not have intended to bring their account of the "progress in German literature" so closely into line with their description of the progress of the United States, but this is exactly what they do: the richness of the German language corresponds to the richness of the American nation, and this correspondence becomes an affinity at the precise site where the lines of publication and those of trade meet — with periodicals. Germany produces an enormous number of books; the United States an enormous number of newspapers. Linguistic and economic modes of productivity unite in a German "work" published on American soil — which is to say, in the very pages of the *Philadelphisches Magazin*.

The productivity of the United States makes it into a perfect place to produce literary works in the most productive literary language. The editors of the *Philadelphisches Magazin* chose to produce the magazine in German not because they had noticed a need for one; still less because they wished to offer a free dispensation of spiritual guidance; rather, they wished to make a commercial contribution to a doubly productive culture — the culture of the Germans developing in conjunction with U.S. agriculture and trade. And this choice of language also indicates why the promotion of enlightenment — culture, scholarship, and taste — takes the specific form of *Unterhaltung*: the magazine is entertainment for the sake of (more and more) conversation; or in eighteenth-century German, *Unterhaltung unterhaltungshalber*.

Far from fearing that *Philadelphisches Magazin*, as an exercise in enlightenment, will contribute to the death of the language in which it is written, the editors demonstrate an implicit faith in the capacity of this language to produce an ever-increasing number of works and force itself into the English "world of reading." But perhaps the implicitness of this faith is an expression of fear: fear that the magazine will not find "readers of taste and talents" who will make it into a commercial success and likewise contribute to the progress of German literature in America; fear that the language of culture will not in fact suit a country of trade, even though — or perhaps because — both the language and the country are so productive, each in its own distinct way; fear that this language will die in Pennsylvania after all. It is impossible to say if the editors, who are particularly fond of stories about heroic courage (*Heldenmut*), are confident about the longevity of the language of their magazine or are in fear of its disappearance, for their faith remains implicit: they may speak about German in England but not in America.[31] And they had only once chance to express themselves. The *Philadelphisches Magazin* disappeared after only one issue, presumably because its editors, the Krämmerer brothers, died of the yellow fever epidemic that devastated Philadelphia in the summer of 1798.[32] No one of "taste and talents" accepted their challenge and attempted anything similar ever again. Twenty-five years later another monthly periodical dedicated to "friends of German literature" was founded in Pennsylvania; but this longer-lasting journal, the *Readinger Magazin,* placed religion at the top of its list of preferred topics.[33] The daring nonchalance of the *Philadelphisches Magazin* — which neglects religion and theology entirely, treating them as though they were dead dogs — was gone.[34]

Near the beginning of "What Is Enlightenment?" Kant responds to an obvious question: why does enlightenment take so long? He does not hesitate to provide an answer — it is for lack of energy and courage, "Laziness and cowardice are the reasons why so great a proportion of human beings, long after nature has released them from alien guidance (*naturaliter maiorennes*), nevertheless gladly remain in lifelong immaturity, and why it is so easy for others to establish themselves as their guardians. It is so comfortable to be immature [*Es ist so bequem, unmündig zu sein*]."[35] Near the conclusion of the one and only number of the *Philadelphisches Magazin* the editors, who had in all likelihood never heard of Kant, much less read his essays in the *Berlinische Monatschrift,* print a satirical couplet that repeats almost word for word Kant's explanation for the failure of enlightenment:

> Warum es so wenig Weise gibt?
> Warum ist auf der Welt der Weisen Zahl so klein?
> Weil's so bequem ist, dumm zu seyn.

> [Why are there so few sages?
> Why is the number of sages so small a sum?
> Because it is so comfortable to be dumb.][36]

According to Kant, comfort lies in *Unmündigkeit:* it is easier and safer to allow others to speak in one's place than to speak up for oneself. According to the couplet in the *Philadelphisches Magazin,* comfort lies in being *dumm,* which is almost the exact same word as *unmündig* — but not quite. To be dumb is, of course, to be without a voice, mute, or inarticulate. But the inarticulateness of the dumb, unlike the inarticulateness of the *unmündig,* is not a matter of time: speaking up has nothing to do with growing up; dumbness is, rather, a permanent condition. There is an escape — such as wisdom — but this escape, as a "departure" from inarticulateness, does not correspond to any specifiable "ages of man." The *Philadelphisches Magazin* has nothing more to say in response to the question why so few can be counted among the enlightened or why the number of sages is so small, yet its own rarity in the midst of an ever-increasing amount of articulate, if not wise or enlightened, voices — thousands of books in German, hundreds of newspapers in the United States — indicates that the editors count on another answer: the greater the amount of speech, the greater the chances that something wise or enlightened will be said. It makes no sense and is therefore irrational to allow *any* language to remain unproductive — or, in other words, to play dumb. Of all the "peculiar events" (*sonderbare Begebenheiten*) the Krämmerer brothers promised to tell, none is quite as peculiar as the one-time appearance of the *Philadelphisches Magazin* itself.

Notes

1. Immanuel Kant, "Beantwortung der Frage: Was ist Aufklärung?" originally published in the *Berlinische Monatschrift* (1784), reprinted in *Gesammelte Schriften*, ed. Königlich Preußischen [later Deutschen] Akademie der Wissenschaften (Berlin: Reimer; later, De Gruyter, 1900–), vol. 8, p. 35 (hereafter, Aka); "An Answer to the Question: What Is Enlightenment?" in *Perpetual Peace and Other Essays*, trans. Ted Humphrey (Indianapolis: Hackett, 1983), p. 41. All translations are my own. (The best translation of *unmündig* is "nonage," but since this word is so rarely used I reluctantly avoid it.)

2. Aka, vol. 8, pp. 41, 37; *Perpetual Peace*, pp. 45, 42.

3. Ibid., p. 35; ibid., p. 41.

4. On the perplexing idea of "my own language," see Jacques Derrida, *Le Monolinguisme de l'autre* (Paris: Galilée, 1996).

5. Moses Mendelssohn, "Was heißt aufklären?" originally printed in the *Berlinische Monatschrift* (1784), reprinted in *Gesammelte Schriften: Jubiläumsausgabe*, ed. Ismar Elbogen, Julius Guttmann, Eugen Mittwoch, Alexander Altmann (Berlin, 1929–32, Breslau, 1938; repr. Stuttgart: Frommann-Holzboog, 1974–), vol. 6, p. 115 (hereafter, GS); "On the Question: What Does 'To Enlighten' Mean?" in Mendelssohn, *Philosophical Writings*, trans. Daniel Dahlstrom (Cambridge: Cambridge University Press, 1997), p. 313. Two anthologies, one in German and one in English, reprint many of the essays concerned with the eighteenth-century controversy over Enlightenment; see *Was ist Aufklärung?* ed. Erhard Bahr (Stuttgart: Reclam, 1978); *What Is Enlightenment?* ed. James Schmidt (Berkeley: University of California Press, 1996).

6. GS, vol. 6, p. 116; *Philosophical Writings*, p. 314.

7. The second section of Mendelssohn's *Jerusalem* is devoted in large part to this tendency of language to disintegrate in response to the force of writing. Indeed, Mendelssohn supposes that the origin of idolatry lies in the confusion of written image and the abstract quality it was meant to designate; see Mendelssohn, *Jerusalem: oder über religiöse Macht und Judentum* (Berlin: Maurer, 1783), reprinted in *GS*, vol. 8, pp. 169–87; *Jerusalem*, trans. Allan Arkush, intro. and commentary Alexander Altmann (Hanover, Vt.: Brandeis University Press, 1983), pp. 102–34.

8. GS, vol. 6, pp. 118–19; *Philosophical Writings*, p. 317.

9. Ibid., p. 116; ibid., p. 314.

10. In recent times and in certain places, Kant's answer to the question "Was ist

Aufklärung?" has been overshadowed by another answer — that of Foucault. See Michel Foucault, "What Is Enlightenment?" in *The Foucault Reader*, ed. Paul Rabinow (New York: Pantheon, 1984), pp. 32–50. Foucault begins his essay with a few cursory remarks about the *Berlinische Monatsschrift* and Moses Mendelssohn, but he quickly turns his attention to Kant. For all his insistence on the local and localizing character of power, Foucault nowhere pays attention to the locality of speech. Instead of local speech, Foucault speaks of discourse, more specifically, "a body of determined practices and discourses" — without regard for the languages in which these discourses are developed. Yet every discourse, regardless of how specific its function within a configuration of practice, knowledge, and power, presupposes a certain *Mündigkeit*, which Foucault rather routinely translates as "mature adulthood" (p. 34), and this presupposition makes it difficult, if not impossible, to pose the question implicit in Kant's definition of *Aufklärung* and his subsequent explanation of its failure — "It is so comfortable to be *unmündig*" (Aka, vol. 8, p. 35; *Perpetual Peace*, p. 41): why does enlightenment take so long, indeed why does it *take time* at all? Here it would be worthwhile to pursue the other side of *Mündigkeit:* the decision not to engage in discourse, not to make a choice of language; the decision, namely, which Foucault in an earlier work calls *madness.*

11.   Aka, vol. 8, p. 37; *Perpetual Peace*, p. 42.

12.   Johann Georg Hamann, "Metakritik über den Purismum der Vernunft," in Sämtliche Werke, ed. J. Nadler (Vienna: Herder, 1951), vol. 3, p. 286; "Metacritique of the Purism of Reason," in *J. G. Hamann: 1730–1788*, ed. and trans. R. G. Smith (New York: Harper & Brothers, 1960), p. 216. On Hamann's relation to Kant, see Josef Simon, "Vernunftkritik und Autorschaft," in *Johann Georg Hamann: Akte des Internationalen Hamann-Colloquium in Lüneberg, 1976*, ed. A. Henkel (Frankfurt am Main: Klostermann, 1979), pp. 135–64; see also Friedrich Beisner, *The Fate of Reason* (Cambridge, Mass.: Harvard University Press, 1987), pp. 16–43. For a broad discussion of Hamann's relation to the German Enlightenment, see Isaiah Berlin, *The Magus of the North: J. G. Hamann and the Origins of Modern Irrationalism* (New York: Farrar, Straus and Giroux, 1993).

13.   On the sense in which eighteenth-century America is comprehensible as a "reading world," see Michael Warner, *The Letters of the Republic: Publication and the Public Sphere in Eighteenth-Century America* (Cambridge, Mass.: Harvard University Press, 1990). Warner does not consider letters written in languages other than English, and this is particularly unfortunate since one of his principal points of analysis — the literary life of Benjamin Franklin — is deeply entangled in the politics of language. For a discussion of Franklin's literary life

that does not leave aside the question of language, see Marc Shell, "Babel in America: or, The Politics of Language Diversity in the United States," *Critical Inquiry* 20-1 (Autumn 1993):103–27; see also n18 below.

14. As Robert Bishoff succinctly explains, "the Pennsylvania German culture actively began to develop late in the seventeenth century, but this culture was directed and determined by a handful of scholars who had been educated in German universities" (R. Bishoff, "German-American Literature," in *Ethnic Perspectives in American Literature: Selected Essays on the European Contribution*, ed. Robert J. Di Pietro and Edward Ifkovic [New York: Modern Language Association, 1983], p. 48). Scholarship on German literature written in Pennsylvania during the eighteenth century is not vast, but it has grown significantly in the last twenty years. In addition to Bishoff's brief assessment, the following works offer valuable information on, and interpretations of, "the first century" of German American literature: Harold Jantz, "German-American Literature: Some Further Perspectives," in *America and the Germans: An Assessment of a Three-Hundred-Year History*, ed. Frank Trommler and Joseph McVeigh (Philadelphia: University of Pennsylvania Press, 1985), vol. 1, pp. 283–93; Christoph Schweitzer, "The Challenge of Early German-American Literature," in *America and the Germans: An Assessment of a Three-Hundred-Year History*, ed. Frank Trommler and Joseph McVeigh (Philadelphia: University of Pennsylvania Press, 1985), vol. 1, pp. 294–305; Robert Ward, "The Case for German-American Literature," *The German Contribution to the Building of the Americas*, ed. Gerhard Friesen and Walter Schatzberg (Worcester, Mass.: Clark University Press, 1977), pp. 373–89; *German-American Literature*, ed. Don Tolzmann (Metuchen, N.J.: Scarecrow Press, 1977); John Joseph Stoudt, "Introduction" to his anthology, *Pennsylvania German Poetry: 1685–1830* (Allentown, Pa.: Schlechter's, 1956), pp. xix–cvi; Earl Robacker, *Pennsylvania German Literature: Changing Trends from 1683–1942* (Philadelphia: University of Pennsylvania Press, 1943); Heinrich Rattermann, *Deutsch-Amerikanische Dichter und Dichtungen des 17ten und 18ten Jahrhunderts: eine Anthologie* (Chicago: Historische Gesellschaft von Illinois, 1915).

No research into German literature in early America can do without the pioneering efforts of Oswald Seidensticker, *The First Century of German Printing in America, 1728–1830* (Philadelphia: Schaefer & Koradi, 1893). Equally valuable are three more recent reference works: Robert Ward, "Dictionary of German-American Literature," *German-American Studies* 10 (Fall, 1975); Don Tolzmann, *German-Americana: A Bibliography* (Metuchen, N.J.: Scarecrow Press, 1975); Robert Ward, *Biobibliography of German-American Writers, 1670–1970* (New York: Kraus International, 1985).

15. This poem of Johann Adam Gruber (1694–1763) was first published in 1748

and is reprinted in *Pennsylvania German Poetry*, p. 31. On Gruber's role as a mediator, see Stoudt, *Pennsylvania German Poetry*, pp. lxii and 30; see also Ward, *Biobibliography*, p. 107.

16.　This term appears in Conrad Beissel's "Theosophische Gedichte," published in *Erster Theil der Theosophischen Lectionen, betreffende die Schulen des einsamen Lebens* (Ephrata, Pa.: Ephrata, 1752); partially reprinted in *Pennsylvania German Poetry: 1685–1830*, ed. J. Stoudt, p. 61. Unlike many of the Germans who founded sectarian communities in Pennsylvania, Beissel, leader of the Ephrata community, was self-taught; see Christopher Schweitzer, "The Challenge of German-American Literature," in *America and the Germans*, p. 299. On the mystical trends of these communities and their founders, see Fred Stoeffler, *Mysticism in the German Devotional Literature of Colonial Pennsylvania* (Allentown, Pa.: Pennsylvania German Folklore Society, 1949). *Ungrund*, a word that Friedrich Schelling would later incorporate into his theosophical reflections, can mean many things — or nothings: unground, monstrous ground, abyssal foundation, irrational basis, and so forth.

17.　Christoph Sauer II, *Ein geistliches Magazien, oder: aus den Schätzen der Schrifftgelehrten zum Himmelreich gelehrt, dargereichtes Altes und Neues*, ed. C. Sauer II, 1-1 (1764): penultimate and last page of unpaginated preface. Published in Germantown, the *Geistliches Magazien* lasted from 1764 to 1770. Seidensticker calls it the "first religious periodical in America" (*The First Century of German Printing in America, 1728–1830*, p. 66). For 40 years, the Sauer family (sometimes spelled "Sower") played a major role in the publication of German texts in Colonial Pennsylvania, and Christoph Sauer (1683–1758) was especially important. So widespread was his influence among the educated members of the German-speaking communities in Pennsylvania that a group of wealthy English-speakers, including Benjamin Franklin, established a newspaper, the *Philadelphische Zeitung*, with the primary purpose of opposing him; see Seidensticker, *The First Century of German Printing*, p. 45. Franklin's paper failed, whereas Sauer's *Der hoch-deutsch pennsylvanische Geschicht-Schreiber, oder, Sammlung wichtiger Nachrichten, aus dem Natur- und Kirchen-Reich* lasted almost 40 years. One of the possible reasons for the failure of Franklin's paper was his decision to print in roman letters. Sauer, who printed in blackletter, made the successful strategic decision in this, the politics not of language but of lettering. On Sauer and Franklin, see Christoph Schweitzer, "The Challenge of Early German-American Literature," in *America and the Germans*, vol. 1, p. 300. On Sauer and the publication of the *Geistliches Magazien*, see Robacker, *Pennsylvania German Literature*, pp. 30–31. The Sauer property was seized by anti-British and antipacifist forces in 1778 and sold at auction; see Karl J. R. Arndt and May E. Olsen, *German Language Press of the Americas* (Munich: Verlag Dokumentation Sauer, 1976), vol. 1, p. 569.

Christoph Sauer the elder contributed to the poetry of the period: a poem he included in the first issue of *Der hoch-deutsch pennsylvanische Geschicht-Schreiber* (August 20, 1739) is reprinted in *Pennsylvania German Poetry: 1685–1830*, ed. J. Stoudt, p. 30. (Stoudt uncharacteristically gives the wrong date of publication on p. 270.)

18. For an account of the principal themes of German writing during the years following the War of Independence, see Robert Ward, "The Case for German-American Literature," in *The German Contribution to the Building of the Americas*, p. 378. Notwithstanding the great efforts of Ward and others to recover and record German texts written during this time, it is still necessary to append a proviso to any general statement about their content and say: "as far as research has been able to ascertain." Not all manuscripts have come to light, as Christopher Schweitzer emphasizes ("The Challenge of Early German-American Literature," in *America and the Germans*, vol. 1, pp. 303–304); some documents may have been lost, and although it is unlikely, these texts may have contained critical remarks on contemporaneous theological doctrines — beyond partisan polemics.

19. See the July 5, 1776, issue of *Wöchentliche Pennsylvanische Staatsbote*, which has been reprinted at the beginning of the first volume of Arndt and Olsen's *German Language Press*. On the relation of German papers to the War of Independence, see Alexander Waldenrath, "The Pennsylvania-Germans," in *The German Contribution to the Building of the Americas*, pp. 57–71.

20. *Philadelphisches Magazin, oder Unterhaltender Gesellschafter, für die Deutschen in America:* Band 1, no. 1–2, May 1, Aug. 1798; edited and published by Heinrich and Joseph Kämmerer. Robacker notes the uniqueness of the *Philadelphisches Magazin:* "So far as the writer has been able to discover, this is the only authentic piece of literary work produced before 1800 not predominantly religious in tone" (Robacker, *Pennsylvania German Literature*, p. 34). There were, however, a few similar publications and publication projects around the turn of the century, including the poetry of Gustav Friedrich Goetz. His poems for the *Neue Philadelphische Correspondenz* during the last decade of the eighteenth century and first decade of the nineteenth are more akin to the verse published in the *Berlinische Monatsschrift* than to the poetry of the sectarian communities; but as is shown by the example Stoudt reprints, "Sehnsucht nach dem Unvergänglichen" (Longing for the Permanent), the idea of mystical union with "Gotteskraft" (divine power) remains a central theme; see Stoudt, *Pennsylvania German Poetry*, pp. 222–23. In Baltimore, the publisher G. Keating (with help from Samuel Sauer) launched a project to reprint nonreligious German publications in America, but only one volume appeared, and it contained nothing more than some poems by Salomon Gessner (1733–88); see the series entitled *Dem Andenken Deutscher Dichter und Philosopher [sic] gewidmet,*

von Deutschen in Amerika, erster Band (Baltimore: Keating, 1796); for a description of the enterprise, see Seidensticker, *The First Century of German Printing,* p. 142.

21. *Philadelphisches Magazin,* unpaginated preface.

22. Ibid.: "Wir legen hiemit unsern Lesern das erste Stück von unserem versprochenen 'Magazin' vor: Die erste Schrift dieser Art, die, so viel wir wissen, jemals in America in Deutscher Sprache herausgekommen."

23. Ibid.

24. Ibid.

25. *Philadelphisches Magazin,* frontispiece.

26. Ibid. The editors make good on this promise to broaden the horizons of their readership by including two articles in the opening issue on the custom and manners of peoples other than those of European descent. The first is entitled "Das Opfer: Eine Indianische Begebenheit" (Sacrifice: An Indian Event) and celebrates the "great heroic courage" of a man "who belonged to the Collapissa nation" and whose story of his self-sacrifice gives insight into "human nature from its noblest perspective" (p. 18). The second article, "Kurze Beschreibungen der Türkischen Art zu baden" (A Short Description of the Turkish Manner of Bathing), is a translation of a brief passage from James Capper's *Observations on the Passage to India through Egypt, and Across the Great Desert* (1783). Capper begins his description by noting that "the Turkish manner of bathing is much better that such baths in Europe" (p. 23).

27. Ibid., pp. 29–30.

28. Seidensticker lists approximately 80 works published between 1786 and 1790; see *The First Century of German Printing,* pp. 117–27. Almost all of these works, needless to say, would be classified under *Gottesgelahrtheit* ("theology").

29. *Philadelphisches Magazin,* unpaginated preface.

30. Ibid., pp. 47–48.

31. In addition to stories about George Washington's heroism and the story of self-sacrifice discussed in note 26 above, the editors include a report of "Weibliche Heldenmut" (Feminine Heroic Courage); see *Philadelphisches Magazin,* pp. 26–27.

32. A serious yellow fever epidemic broke out in Philadelphia in the late summer of 1798, and according to Arndt and Olsen, the journal failed to appear because the Kämmerer brothers succumbed to it; see Arndt and Olsen, *The German Language Press,* vol. 1, p. 563; see also James Knauss, *Social Conditions Among the Pennsylvania Germans in the Eighteenth Century, As Revealed in German*

Newspapers Published in America (Lancaster, Pa.: New Era Printing Company, 1922). Another periodical, *Die Pennsylvanische Correspondenz*, also suspended publication because of the plague; see Arndt and Olsen, *The German Language Press*, vol. 1, p. 567.

33. See *Readinger Magazin für Freunde der Deutschen Literatur in Amerika* (1824–25), 22 numbers in total, edited by Johann Carl Gossler and published in both Reading and Philadelphia. Tolzmann, strangely enough, lists it as the earliest "literary journal" published in German in the United States (forgetting the *Philadelphisches Magazin*); see *German-Americana*, p. 116. The subtitle of the *Readinger Magazin* reads: "eine Monatschrift, enthaltend: Aufsätze aus dem Gebiete der Religion, Natur, Kunst, Laune, and Phantasie" (a monthly journal containing essays from the domains of religion, nature, art, humor, and fantasy). Gossler explains in his foreword — as though it were a corrective to the long-deceased *Philadelphisches Magazin* — that "Belehrung und Unterhaltung" (instruction and entertainment) are the "principal laws" of the magazine. True to his word, the editor provides instructive discourses, including, for example, a pedantic essay by a certain G. Prömmel entitled "Virtue and Love Would Already Cease to Make Us Truly Happy Without the Prospect of a Beyond Where They Continue" (*Readinger Magazin* 1-1 [January, 1824]:5–11). As the title indicates, this article would be more appropriate for the *Geistliches* than the *Philadelphisches Magazin*; but in other respects, the *Readinger Magazin* more closely approximates the kind of Enlightenment periodicals that were published in Europe in the later half of the eighteenth century than does the *Philadelphisches Magazin*, for it, like they, addresses traditional questions of theology in nonsectarian, "universal" and strictly "rational" terms. A closer study of the *Readinger Magazin* would definitely make for a fuller answer to the question: what is *Aufklärung* in Pennsylvania? One article is of particular interest: it tells the story of an anonymous Doctor who, as a young student of theology in Frankfurt, travels to Königsberg in order to hear Kant; see "Eine Begebenheit aus meinem Leben" (An Event from My Life), *Readinger Magazin* 1-5 (May 1824):101–107.

34. The *Philadelphisches Magazin* appeared at a turning-point in the long history of German writing in North America: after the European-born scholars who wrote in "high" German had died and before a "lower" form of German, generally called Pennsylvania Dutch, became the vehicle for local literary activity — and before new immigrants from Europe arrived whose primary concerns no longer expressed themselves in theological terms. See Bishoff, "German-American Literature," in *Ethnic Perspectives in American Literature*, esp. pp. 44–48; Ward, "The Case for German-American Literature," *The German Contribution to the Building of the Americas*, esp. pp. 377–79. Along with a

study of Gossler's *Readinger Magazin* (see note 34 above), further research into the question of Enlightenment in Pennsylvania would have to concentrate on Johann Georg Wesselhöft's *Alte und neue Welt;* see Robert Cazden, "Wesselhöft and the German Book Trade," in *The German Contribution to the Building of the Americas,* pp. 217–34.

35.   Aka, vol. 8, p. 35; *Perpetual Peace,* p. 41.

36.   *Philadelphisches Magazin,* p. 44.

Part VI

AFTERWORD

"Prized His Mouth Open": Mark Twain's *The Jumping Frog of Calaveras County* In English, Then in French, Then Clawed Back into a Civilized Language Once More, by Patient, Unremunerated Toil

■ MARC SHELL

How is that gentilman who did speak by and by?

Is a German.

I did think him Englishman.

He is the Saxony side.

He speak the french very well.

Tough he is German, he speak so much well italyan, french, spanish, and english, that among the Italyans, they believe him Italyan, he speake the frenche as the Frenches himself. The Spanishesmen believe him Spanishing, and the Englishes, Englisman.

It is difficult to enjoy so well so much several languages.

— Mark Twain, "Introduction" to *The New Guide of the Conversation in Portuguese and English* (1883)

THE COMBAT ZONE; OR, A CANADIAN IN AMERICA

It's no accident that I, Marc Shell (born Meyer Selechonek), come to the problems of bilingualism with which the essay that follows — and much of the work of Mark Twain (born Samuel Clemens) — deals. I was born in Montreal in 1947, just after World War II, and raised in Quebec, where

491

questions of politics and language go hand in hand.[1] In that colonial setting, I did not consider myself a member of a people conquered within the boundaries of its own homeland, as did my Mohawk and French Canadian neighbors: both these groups made claims, often mutually exclusive, for special territorial and linguistic rights based on their peculiar understanding of their particular group's unique autochthony or indigenousness. Nor did I consider myself a member of a conquering people — as did my English Canadian neighbors. Neither *quebecois de souche* nor *britannique de souche*, I was, like so many immigrants, somehow neither conqueror nor conquered — or perhaps, like a person split in twain, both at once. No matter what language I spoke on the streets — French, English, Mohawk — it was not mine.

Scholars from around the world still use Quebec as something of a case study for the sociology of multilingualism.[2] It is not clear, though, just how typical or untypical an example of the politics of language Quebec is. My mother's generally Yiddish-speaking and Hebrew-praying Polish family often recalled for me, in Polish, the terms of a law enacted in Poland during "the liberal Polish revolution of the 1860s" which outlawed the use of Hebrew and Yiddish.[3] (It was, of course, a law typical for nineteenth-century liberal nation states, but even now unilingualism informs and, in some situations, defines our notions of nationhood and statehood.) For me the example of Quebec has been useful for understanding the politics of language, and its literary experience has been valuable for understanding polyglot literature elsewhere in the world. In fact, the generally peaceful language problems of Canada have been one subject of my writing, from an early series of essays on bilingual advertisement published in French-Canadian in Quebec City in 1973 to a large-scale comparative study published in English-Canadian in 1994. Quebec's language conflict originates in a war of conquest (1763) and erupts intermittently in bloodshed (1914), terrorism (1971), a separatist movement, and such consequential political countermeasures as the War Measures Act (1973), which suspended *habeas corpus* for many months.

Consider how language conflict pertains, on the level of urban development, to the bilingual city of Montreal. In Montreal the principal language border between the French-speaking east and the English-speaking west runs along an east-west line once known as "The Main" or "The Combat Zone." In 1973, urban architects and planners, by building a commercial tower at our local meeting place of English and French, sought to contribute a solution for the linguistic and imperialist problem of Babel.

A newspaper ad for their then new building built on this line, Complexe Desjardins, quotes Rudyard Kipling's colonial poem "The Ballad of East and West."

> Oh, East is East, and West is West, and never the twain shall meet,
> Till Earth and Sky stand presently at God's great Judgment Seat;
> But there is neither East nor West, Border, nor Breed, nor Birth,
> When two strong men stand face to face,
>   tho' they come from the ends of the earth!

But how, if at all, in that linguistically amphibious Combat Zone, does one jump the abyss, as it were, between eastern French and western English? Or, for that matter, how do shopkeepers and shoppers translate on the line?

As a student I found one kind of answer in Twain's *The Jumping Frog of Calaveras County*, apparently a children's story, written in a country where no two languages lord it over all others, but where one language dominates unofficially.

I read *The Jumping Frog* for the first time in 1967, while flying nonstop from Montreal, then celebrating Canada's constitutional centennial by hosting a World's Fair, to California, which was at the same time celebrating the hundredth anniversary of the publication of *The Jumping Frog* with a special international frog-jumping contest.[4] That day I read *The Jumping Frog* in its English-language version.[5] (The cover of my copy has decorative green cloth with a gilt jumping frog.) At the time it was clear to me that Twain likely had in mind not only the intralinguistic difference between the dialects of his western (California) and eastern (Yankee) English-speaking characters, but also the interlinguistic difference between Englishmen and Frenchmen. The very term *frog*, after all, means "francophone person." Thus the proudly binational quebecois singer Kevin Parent sings "about how proud he is 'to be a frog and a squarehead too.'" (English-speakers in Quebec are called *les têtes carrées*.)[6] Likewise, the refrain of the

1960s quebecois *superfrog* Robert Charlebois, in his well known Franglais "Frog Song," goes:[7]

> You're a frog I'm a frog. Kiss me,
> And I'll turn into a prince suddenly
> Donne moé des peanuts
> J'm'en va t'chanter Alouette sans fausse note.[8]

Moreover, many Canadian and American singers at the time knew the old African-American inspired Cajun song *Saut Crapaud* (or *Saute Crapeau*) as sung by Columbus "Boy" Fruge (probably pronounced like "frog").[9] (The work of Fruge, who hailed from Armaudville in Louisiana, is included in the *American Anthology of Folk Music*, which influenced Woody Guthrie and Bob Dylan.) The Cajun Fruge sometimes seems stuck on a line between — or cleft in twain by — two linguistic worlds. Unable to leave the jumping-off spot, Fruge exists somewhere between two lingoes.

Twain criticizes humorless Frenchmen generally for being unable to translate, or language-jump, from English to French; his *Jumping Frog*'s tall tale about how a shot-laden frog is rendered unable to jump — "like a Frenchman" — became the perfect vehicle. Two later versions of the story, which Twain published in 1875 together with his "original" English-language tale, suggest as much. One of these is a strangely introduced translation of *The Jumping Frog* into French. The other is Twain's "clawing" back of that French translation into English — or rather, into a literal English one might call Frenglish.

Such translinguistic concerns suffuse much of Twain's work. As for dialect, consider how, in *The Tragedy of Pudd'nhead Wilson* (1894), dialectal irregularity seems to match racial difference and even species variation. In *The Adventures of Huckleberry Finn* (1884), such difference drives the plot. The same dialectal theme suggests many of Twain's later essays on American interlingual difference.[10] For example, "The Awful German Language," "The German Chicago," and "The Horrors of the German Language" recall the melting-pot influence of the German-American language in St. Louis. Twain grew up there with German or Germerican as one of his lingoes.[11] Looking back in 1898 on his German literary experiences in Missouri, Twain wrote in a curious Germerican lingo: "Als ich ein Knabe war und

25.1. "A Complete Word." Original caption for illustration by W. Fr. Bowen in Mark Twain, *A Tramp Abroad*, 1879.

wohnte in einem Dorfe on the banks of the Mississippi, schon lange away back in the early Fifties our paper 'exchanged' with the St Louis [German-language newspaper] *Anzeiger des Westens.*"[12]

It is in this vein of ethnic cosmopolitanism that Twain's "Introduction" to *The New Guide of the Conversation in Portuguese and English* (1883) focuses on that *Guide's* lexical and syntactic "Portenglish" blunders.[13] One subject for relevant debate among Twain scholars has been whether Twain's own "exchanges" with the German language help to explain his "predilection" for humorous compound words.[14] Consider, in this context, Brown's illustration of a "grand mountain range": a word in Twain's superficially bilingual *A Tramp Abroad* (1885).[15]

In line with his fanciful meditation on interlingual difference, many of Twain's works present make-believe translations of nonexistent original texts. These works constitute almost a genre in their own right, at least in an American context of European models. They include *Adam's Diary: Translated from the Original Ms.* (1893); *Eve's Diary: Translated from the Original Ms.* (1906); *No. 44, The Mysterious Stranger: Being an Ancient Tale Found in a Jug and Freely Translated from the Jug* (1916 [posthumous]); and *Personal Recollections of Joan of Arc . . . by the sieur Louis de Conte [pseud.] (her page and secretary) Freely Translated out of the Ancient French* (1896).

In *The Jumping Frog* Twain presents a text that purports to be a rendering of an "original" text that he pretends exists, but does not. Twain also mocks interlinguistic translation, perhaps also intralinguistic translation, of actual texts.

A YANKEE IN CALIFORNIA ("MAYBE YOU UNDERSTANDS FROGS AND MAYBE YOU DONT UNDERSTAND EM")[16]

The jumping-off point for Mark Twain's career as a national figure in the American literary world was *The Jumping Frog*.[17] This was the "tall tale" that was called "quintessentially American literature" already in 1867.[18] It "catapulted" the nominally and thematically amphibian Twain to fame.[19]

Whence jumped to us this quintessentially American story?

The transmission of "the jumping frog legend" — from its "original source" to the story's narrator — is part of the puzzle of *The Jumping Frog* from the time of its first publication.[20] The narrator had the story from Simon Wheeler, whom the narrator sought out precisely in order that Wheeler convey the tale to him.

Did the events reported actually take place? In his "Private History of the 'Jumping Frog' Story" (1893), Twain says "the thing happened in Calaveras County in the spring of 1849."

Were the events already reported elsewhere? Twain says that the tale may have been transmitted from a California newspaper where it appeared as "A Toad Story" — as if it were not only about an amphibian frog but also about "a person regarded as loathsome, contemptible, etc."[21] (That is one of Webster's standard definitions for "toad.")

Are there earlier than nineteenth-century counterparts for the tale? In his "Note" written especially for the 1903 edition of *The Jumping Frog*, Twain seems seriously to wonder whether he may not have been an unwitting "literary thief" since he had discovered that there was a similar 1500-year-old ancient Greek counterpart.[22] "The Athenian and the Frog," supposedly written in Boetia, was published in Arthur Sidgwick's classical Greek-language textbook;[23] and Twain, following here "Professor Van Dyke of Princeton University," dryly compares that ancient Greek story with his own, almost as if he, Twain, were himself a professor of folklore and mythology.[24]

But are those ancient Greek originals anything other than imitations of earlier versions of the tale? Or are they instead merely counterfeit modern productions made to look ancient? Twain eventually lets on that Sidgwick's classical Greek Jumping Frog is really a paraphrase of Twain's own *Jumping Frog*. Sidgwick had translated it into Greek and then surreptitiously inserted it into his textbook as a Greek "original" that students should translate into English.[25]

Such problems of literary transmission are further refracted by typographical "errors" in the text — of the sort that Twain may wittingly have inserted into original documents when he was typographer for the German-language papers of Missouri. In any case, Twain, in an interview reported in 1895, said the following about the origin of the name of "Smiley": "He was a real character, and his name was Greeley. The way he got the name of Smiley was this — I wrote the story for the *New York Saturday Gazette*, a perishing weekly so-called literary newspaper — a home of poverty; it was the last number — the jumping frog killed it. They had not enough 'G's,' so they changed Greeley's name to 'Smiley.' That's a fact."[26]

The source games continued after Twain's death. For example, in 1929 William Robert Gillis — the son of Steven Gillis who had been Twain's "Jumping Frog" California companion — argued that many African-American tales inform nineteenth-century anglophone European-American tales, and claimed that Twain's "trickster story" was originally an African-language one.[27] In view of Twain's interest in dialect and interlinguistic differences, it is noteworthy that William Robert Gillis does not say from which African language-group the jumping frog story came. It is as if Gillis is carrying on a tradition that muzzles the captive frog or fails to deliver from silence its "native language."[28]

Twain asks us to read the English and French or Frenglish versions of his tale together: "I ask the reader to run his eye over the original English version of the *Jumping Frog*, and then read the French or my retranslation" (JF 4). If this is not a new kind of writing that Twain is presenting, it is, for most Americans, a new kind of reading that he is requesting. The reading is made more difficult because the page layout that Twain provides is the commonplace sequential linear sort (first English, then French, finally Frenglish) whereas what the reader requires is a triple-column set-up in facing-pages format. Just such a format one found in the newspapers of New Orleans that earlier in the century had published the "same" stories in facing (English, Spanish, and French) columns; one finds a similar format in some editions of the Talmud; Twain's own *Extracts from Adam's Diary* provides the reader with Adam's "hieroglyphics" printed to the left of Twain's English-language "translation." As it is, however, readers of the tri-lingual *Jumping Frog* must flip pages back and forth from English to French, from French to Frenglish, from English to Frenglish.

So Twain's publishing practice exacerbates his game of multilingual "telephone tag" — a linguistic leap-frog Americanized for the multilingual "gossip" of the New World.[29]

A PARISIAN IN AMERICA; OR, *LA GRENOUILLE SAUTEUSE DU COMTÉ DE CALAVERAS*

Eh bien! I no see not that that frog has nothing of better than another. (JF 49)

Eh bien! I no saw not that that frog had nothing of better than each frog. (Je ne vois pas que cette grenouille ait rien de mieux qu'aucune grenouille.) (JF 50)

"Possible that you not it saw not," said Smiley, "possible that you — you comprehend frogs; possible that you not you there comprehend nothing; possible that you had of the experience, and possible that you not be but an amateur. Of all manner (de toute manière) I bet forty dol-lars that she batter in jumping no matter which frog of the country of Calaveras." (JF 51)

Simon Wheeler's dialectal and oral interpretation of "The Jumping Frog" story is the starting point for the narrator's story in much the same way that Twain's *Jumping Frog* is the jumping-off place for the translator who Frenchified it as *La Grenouille Sauteuse du Comté de Calaveras.*

This translation was first published as part of a French-language essay, "American Humorists I: Mark Twain," in an 1872 issue of the *Revue des Deux Mondes,* an influential Continental journal in comparative literature and politics.[30] Twain translates the title literally, into Frenglish, as *Review of Some Two Worlds.*[31]

The "American Humorists" essay appeared under the name "Th. Bentzon." Who was this "Th. Bentzon"? Twain apparently first mistook Bentzon for "a gentleman": her real name was Marie-Thérèse [de Solms] Blanc (1840–1907).[32] Bentzon (as I will call her) was a scholar and writer in the comparatist tradition of Mme de Staël, but with a penchant for frequent visits to the New World. From 1870 to 1900 Bentzon was the chief spokesperson on American affairs for the *Revue.* Her output was prodigious, yet her work has been all but overlooked by literary historians both French and American. I thus take this opportunity to sketch briefly those aspects of Bentzon's work which touch on the dialectal humorists of the United States and on the changing American language. Her "American Humorists II," also published in 1872, concerns dialectal humorists such as Artemus Ward, Josh Billings, and the bi-dialectal "accent writer" Hans Breitman (Leland Charles Godfrey).[33]

In the same year Bentzon also published essays in the *Revue* on Harriet Beecher Stowe's *My Wife and I* and Bret Harte's *Mliss* as well as a more general study of Walt Whitman.[34] (Harte was a special interest. Bentzon wrote about him again in 1878.[35] Her translations of Hart's dialectal and humorous works include her popular *Récits californiens* [1873; 1884].)[36] Bentzon also wrote on William Dean Howells, Henry James, George W. Cable, Edgar Fawcett, W. H. Bishop, and Francis Marion Crawford, and provided studies of Arthur Sherburne Hardy's *But Yet a Woman,* Edgar Fawcett's *The Adventures of a Widow,* George Parson Lathrop's *Newport,* and Edward Bellamy's *Miss Ludington's Sister.*[37] Among Bentzon's books devoted to single writers would be *A Typical American: Thomas Wentworth Higginson* (1902).[38]

Bentzon's noteworthy predilection for reviewing books about women matches her disposition to focus on woman writers. She thus wrote on Sarah Orne Jewett's *A Country Doctor,* Harriet Beecher Stowe, Octave Thanet (Alice French), Amelie Rives, Frances Hodgson, Grace Elizabeth King, and

Mary E. Wilkins.[39] These essays constitute a basis for her *The Condition of Woman in the United States,* published in English in 1895.[40] The feminist sympathies of that book may help explain the eclipse of the author's reputation, although that, in itself, does not explain the century-long duration of that eclipse.

Bentzon's thinking about the biculturalism of the *deux mondes* clearly informs her own fiction-writing. Her novels, published in English, include *Aline's Widowhood* (1882), *Remorse* (1878), *Jacqueline* (1893), *Expiation* (1889), *Love's Atonement* (1892), and *Georgette* (1892).[41] For our purposes the most important would be her French-and-Creole novel, *Yette: Histoire d'une jeune Creole,* set in the French Antilles.[42] Writing about the language of the Antilles, Edouard Glissant, in his *Le Discours antillais* (1981), argues that "'lack does not reside in the ignorance [*méconnaissance*] of a language (the French language), but in the non-mastery (be it in Creole or in French) of an appropriated language)."[43] When American writers present shibboleth themes, Bentzon is quick to take them on. (Crawford, for example, discusses the shibboleth massacre on Easter Monday, 1282, when it is said that Frenchmen who could not pronounce properly the Italian word *ciceri* were killed.)[44] Bentzon studies other literary *francophonies*: Louisiana, including the English-language popularization of Creole culture by George Washington Cable; the Caribbean, as in *Yette;* and the northeastern part of North America, as in her comparative study, *Nouvelle-France et Nouvelle Angleterre* (1899).[45]

Bentzon often deals with pidgin and mixed-language literatures (see her writings about Ward and Billings), and she considers issues of malapropism, nonstandard orthography, and local dialect.[46] In her review of *The Jumping Frog,* Bentzon thus focuses on interculturally "incomprehensible" aspects of the American idiom. In particular, English-language American terms describing humor, such as "jolly," "bluffy," "funny," "telling," and "queer," are, for her, "épithètes intraduisibles" (untranslatable epithets).[47] Frenchmen, claims Bentzon, cannot understand the slang-filled American genre of the "eye-opener," the "screamer," and "tall tale."[48] Bentzon argues that humorous American narrators make fun of themselves in ways foreign to "witty" French culture.[49] "Humor," she says, is "the joking of an individual who keeps a serious expression while joking."[50] James Millington makes similar remarks in the 1880s about *The New Guide of the Conversation in Portuguese and English:* "A jest in sober earnest" is what he called this "incompetent" conversation-and-phrase *Guide.*[51]

Bentzon writes that "we French-speakers consider barbarous" all American work which toes the lines between standard English and slang and between one language and another.[52] (Among relevant slang terms in *The Jumping Frog* would be the American *j'int* [JF 13] which Bentzon weirdly translates into French as *articulation* [JF 29].) It is in the interstices between humor/wit and nontranslatability, says Bentzon, where the problem resides for the French translator of American "slang": "Mark Twain les conte avec un charme sauvage et une simplicité émue dont on ne peut donner qu'une idée imparfaite. *Ce qui est intraduisible* surtout, c'est ce qut [sic] fait le principal merite de ces bigarrures, le style original et mordant, le tour idiomatique, le mélange bizarre et souvent pittoresque de néologie, de patois et d'argot qu'on appelle le *slang*" (italics added).[53]

Bentzon expressed high hopes for the "American language" of the future. Noah Webster had argued that the American language would eventually become an amalgam of all the languages spoken — or once spoken — in the New World. He had claimed further that the United States "will produce, in a course of time, a language in North America, as different from the future language of England, as the modern Dutch, Danish and Swedish are from German, or from one another."[54] Bentzon saw in American linguistic humor something of this Babel-like quality. She argued that although "l'anglais reste la langue mère" (English remains its mother tongue), the American language was in the process of becoming a "mélange" of other languages from all over the world — a "confusion of tongues." And in a utopian vein, she predicted that, "bientôt nous serons accoutumés à une langue américaine" (soon we will be habituated to an American tongue) — a language that would be universally human.[55] Presumably American English would blend together English with French and myriad other languages in the same way that the English language centuries earlier blended together with French to form "the creolized language of Shakespeare."

AN AMERICAN IN PARIS; OR, *THE FROG JUMPING OF THE COUNTRY OF CALAVERAS*

The multilingual Kentish poet John Gower, who died in the fifteenth century, was the last of the great English poets to use Anglo-Norman. Whether or not Twain had Gower in mind when he translated *Sieur... de Conte's* recollections of Joan of Arc, Twain did know the French language, at least to write it. In the 1903 edition of *The Jumping Frog*, in fact, Twain wrote: "I cannot speak the French language, but I can translate very well, though not fast, being self-educated" (JF 4).[56] And "he speak the french very well," claimed Twain in his "Introduction" to *The New Guide of the Conversation in Portuguese and English*. Nevertheless, Twain disliked the French "race." In his 1899 essay about anti-Semitism, he wrote this about his antipathy towards Frenchmen: "I am quite sure that (bar one) I have no race prejudices."[57] That one race was the frog. He takes up a similar prejudice against the French in "How to Tell a Story," a work in keeping with Mme. Bentzon's assessment of him.[58] Twain was easily put out by the articulate inability of the witty French to translate, hence to understand, his dialectally complex work about a frog (Frenchman) whose mouth is filled with shot in such manner that he may as well have had "no hind legs" (JF 14).[59] That legless-ness, we recall, is also the condition of the dog who defeated — really *killed* — the canine Andrew Jackson figured in *The Jumping Frog*.

On the interlinguistic level, then, the frog-jumping contest is recapitulated by the contest between two writers with pen names: Twain and Bentzon. In 1875 Bentzon published in the *Revue* an unfavorable review of *The Gilded Age* by Mark Twain and C. Dudley Warner; that year was also the start of the *Revue's* publishing remarkable translations of Henry James's "Dernier des Valerus," "Premier Amour d'Eugène Pickering," "La Madone de l'Avenir," "Cousin et Cousine," and "Quatres Rencontres"[60] — but none of Twain's. Twain, stung by Bentzon's criticism of him as "barbarous" and likewise affected by the *Revue*, published in 1875 his "toothsome [mordant] reading" of Bentzon's translation.

Twain's linguistic exchange is suggested in Strothman's depiction of him translating or retranslating. Twain here works with a jumble of six-sided letter blocks that are presumably able, if appropriately arranged, to

25.2. "My Re-Translation from the French." Original caption for illustration by F. W. Strothman in Mark Twain, *The Jumping Frog of Calaveras County*, 1903.

represent the written form both of the language, French, out of which Twain has to claw the translation and that of the language, English, into which he supposedly wants to claw it. (These two languages — French and English — share pretty much the same alphabet, so Twain needs only uni-alphabet blocks. There are, however, multialphabet blocks for converting ancient Greek, say, or African languages into and out of English.[61]) Strothman's blocks recall the tumbled-down bricks of a Tower of Babel, the urban building which the God of Genesis destroyed. God destroyed that Tower when the city-dwellers made their assault, or *sault* (the Old English word for "assault"), on heaven. That word's homonym *saut* (the French term for "jump") yields the jumpy adjective *sauteuse* in Bentzon's title. *Assault* is also the partial homonym of *somersault* (*somerset* [JF 16] — which term Emerson uses in his celebrated essay on "the uses of great men" to name "merely" intellectual exercises.[62]

In *The Jumping Frog* the term *translation* partly means "a jumping from one language to another." Frog-jumping so understood is what the "Frenchman" does when, qua Bentzon, it bounds across the international *oceanic* divide from west to east, and what Twain does when, leapfrog style, he rebounds after Bentzon. This leapfrog is anthropomorphized when Smiley, a gambling addict, bounds after the wild swamp frog he must capture in order to make his wager.

There is another meaning of *saut*: "ransom for murder or manslaughter."[63] This meaning becomes especially salient when we consider, first, how the subject matter of Twain's tripartite book presents a distinct "economics of translation" where Twain's "clawing back" of Bentzon's French into English apparently goes "unremunerated"; and second, how Twain's various frog stories involve both "killing" and "payback."

Twain's tale is a killer. As Twain tells it in his "Private History of the 'Jumping Frog' Story," *The Jumping Frog* put the newspaper *Saturday Press* out of business.[64] Moreover, Wheeler's tale might be able to "bore [the narrator] to death" (JF 6). Humor, moreover, *must* kill. What Twain dislikes in the French translation is that it kills the killing quality of his humor. "In French the story is too confused, and chaotic, and unreposeful, and ungrammatical, and insane; consequently it could only cause grief and sickness — it could not kill" (PH 127–28). (More generally, all language may kill — as Maurice Blanchot suggests.[65])

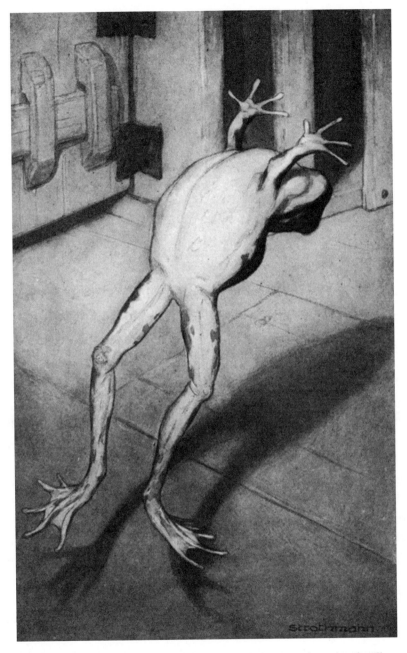

25.3. "Turn one summerset, or maybe a couple." Original caption for illustration by F. W. Strothman in Mark Twain, *The Jumping Frog*.

25.4. Detail from 25.2.

Twain claims, in his very title, that his work as translator goes "unre-munerated." Yet he does exact a payback (*saut*) for Bentzon's murder, that is, her translation into French, of his *Jumping Frog* (*grenouille sauteuse*). The murder victim jumps back to life, twain-like, both itself and not itself, thanks to a humorously metamorphic resurrection by translation that more closely resembles barter than monetary exchange. Even so a butterfly replaces the caterpillar — or a frog the tadpole. Just such identification also happens in Platonic and Euclidean geometry — the sort of intellectual exercise that Emerson associates with *somersaults*. That is one reason that Strothman includes geometric tools of comparison or monetary exchange tables in his *saut* illustration. Presumably such translational instruments help to "cipher" (JF 12) one group's dialectal or linguistic meaning in terms of another. *Saut*, after all, also means "to measure out."

In *The Jumping Frog* Twain presents himself as feeling that he has been *jumped* (suddenly attacked) by Bentzon. So he retaliates by *jumping* (suddenly attacking) the Bentzon text. *Jumping on* ("scolding") Bentzon, or maybe *jumping after* her (as Smiley does after the wild swamp frog), Twain shoots down frog Bentzon's critique. He fills the frog's mouth with leaden shot in much the same way that the Stranger in *The Jumping Frog* fills the mouth of the frog Daniel Webster and thus renders the other ineffective as a jumper. Daniel Webster can no longer jump; Bentzon can no longer kill American killing with her mordant froggy jumping.

Thanks to Twain's retranslation, his English-language original work is "restored to the English after martyrdom in the French."[66] "Martyrdom" here, as in Twain's biography of Joan of Arc, is the act of suffering "death as the penalty of . . . refusing to renounce . . . [a] religion or a . . . principle."[67] All Smiley has to do, in order to discover the wrong if not to right it, is to "turn . . . [the frog] upside down."

Some moralist readers of *The Jumping Frog* are bothered by the apparent injustice that "he who was so good at 'ketching' [frogs] never ketched him [the Yankee]" (JF 231). (In his 1950 opera *The Jumping Frog*, the Berlin-born German-American composer Lukas Foss has Smiley capture the stranger and retrieve his money.) But as it turns out, Twain himself, though he does not win remuneration from Bentzon, does get back the shot: "the amount due to be paid at a tavern or for entertainment" (the dictionary definition). In her book *Littérature et moeurs étrangères* (1882), Bentzon moderated her criticism of Twain as *barbarous*. And she generously acknowledged the "witty revenge" of Clemens's Frenglish translation of her French translation of his English "original."[68] Twain had the jump on her. Bentzon's French translation of Twain was now, glossophagically speaking, part of *his* killing "American tale."

Twain never reciprocated in complimentary kind. Whether this has to do with his generally strained relationships with women — or, for that matter, his becoming himself "the belle of New York" — I leave for another time.[69]

THE MORAL

In *The Jumping Frog*, frogs are not the only animals matched against each other in gambling contests. With only one or two exceptions, all the bets described in *The Jumping Frog* figure animals: horse-races, dog fights (including rat-terriers), cat fights (including tomcats; JF 9, 15), and cock fights (JF 9, 12–15).[70]

Smiley is always ready to bet on which bird will take flight first (JF 9), for example, or where "the straddle-bug" goes and how long it takes (JF 10, cf. 15).[71] The tale that Simon Wheeler hopes to tell when the narrator walks out on him would have told about "a yaller one-eyed cow" (JF 24). The story of the dog Andrew Jackson, who dies because his canine opponent has nowhere to plant his *prize* jaws, foreshows that of Daniel Webster — the captive frog if not also the American statesman.[72]

In the "talking-animal" tale of the sort that Aesop wrote in Asia Minor, the talking animals are thinly disguised human beings, and they talk, cartoon-like, just as if they were human. But unlike *Frog and Toad* — in the well-known children's series — the two amphibians in Twain's tale do *not* talk.[73] Their dumbness is especially noteworthy for a story about so "naturally" musical and famously noisome creatures. As captives, Twain's frogs have *no* voice of their own. There is no animal talking match, as there is in Aesop's anthropomorphic fable "The Fox and the Crow." (Twain's animal fable is no "animal-groom" tale such as *The Frog Prince*, in which the amphibian is happily re-translated, like Bottom the ass in *A Midsummer Night's Dream*, back into a human being.)

Neither is *The Jumping Frog* about animal "education" — *pace* the claims of the would-be animal trainer Smiley. True enough, we learn how to goad a captive animal into doing what it would do "naturally" — say to jump, which one spurs a frog to do by poking it with a sharp object — and how to compel that captive *not* to do what it otherwise would do "naturally" — say *not* to jump ship, which one compels it not to do by sticking it into a prison-box or filling it with shot. Hence the captive animals are never permitted to leave their "little lattice box" (JF 18) unless it be to entertain the master or earn money for him. Even so, Daniel Webster the frog can use his tongue to "snake a fly" (JF 17), as his namesake the human statesman could use his tongue to move the nation.

The Jumping Frog is also no traditional children's fable, because it has no simple moral. In a talk of 1895, Twain did append a moralistic ending to the piece. "Don't you put too much faith in the passing stranger. This life is full of uncertainties, and every episode in life, figuratively speaking, is just a frog. You want to watch every exigency as you would a frog, and don't you ever bet a cent on it until you know whether it is loaded or not."[74] But let's

25.5. "It might be a canary, maybe, but it ain't — it's only just a frog." Original caption for illustration by F. W. Strothman in Mark Twain, *The Jumping Frog*.

not *jump* at *this* moralistic conclusion — a concluding moral offered by a passing stranger, a money-making sophist by the name Twain. Every translator has to make a jump, a leap of faith that he will land on the other side. *Jumping* as such means "passing suddenly from one thing or topic to another"; often "with omission of intermediate points; an interval, gap, chasm involving such a transition."[75] In the lingo of late nineteenth-century electricity, a *jump spark* is one that is "produced by the jumping of an electric current across a space between permanently fixed poles, as in the ignition system of some engines." In most translation, in fact, we bank on the translation's being the *jump* equal of the original.

So we might say that two things — for example, a living person and a dead one ("the reports of my death are greatly exaggerated" said Clemens about Twain in 1910), or, as another example, some time today and some time yesterday — are in some ideal or geometrically measurable way, *jump* equals. The ghost in *Hamlet:* "Thus twice before, and *jump* at this dead hour, / With martial stalk hath he gone by our watch" (italics added).[76]

Our own *jumpiness* about translating, perhaps speaking in general, produces the disease called "the jump," which is but another word for *chorea*, or that insanity of "delirium tremens" (JF 55) which Twain says arises precisely from confronting French grammar and lexis in English context and, perhaps, English grammar and lexis in French context.

THE JUMP BID

"Well," says Yank, "I'll bet liquors on it." A chalk line was made and the toad put down. They struck the boards behind the toad and he leaped six feet, then the frog leaped seven. Yank paid the liquors. ("A Toad Story," in *Sonoma Herald,* 1849)

On the one hand, Twain's tripartite *Jumping Frog* seems to focus on how inadequate is Bentzon's translation.

I think the fault must be in the translation. I ought to have translated it myself. I think so because I examined into the matter and finally retranslated the sketch from the French back into the English, to see what the trouble was; that is, to see just what sort of focus the French people got upon it. Then the mystery was explained. In French the story is too confused, and chaotic, and unreposeful, and ungrammatical, and insane; consequently it could only cause grief and sickness — it could not kill. (PH 127–28)

On the other hand, Twain hints that good translation — an accurate "exchange" — is an impossibility. "It may be that there are people who can translate better than I can, but I am not acquainted with them."[77] And here, despite his not saying so, Twain is following Bentzon's lead in her comments about the difference between French and American joking. Honoring the differences and similarities between languages (instead of expressing one meaning in two languages) has long been recognized as a goal of translation, especially for the bilingual reader and the humorist. After all, Clemens's generically original study of intra- and interlinguistic jumping is set in the get-ever-richer contestant community of Angel's Camp in California. A *jump bid* is a bid that is higher than necessary to increase the previous bid.

I have heard many explanations for Samuel Clemens's *nom-de-plume*, which he first used in 1863. One of these has it that *mark twain* means "two fathoms" in riverboat talk. This explanation suggests to me the division into two, east and west, of North America, as by the Mississippi River, along which axis Twain grew up. At the time of the Civil War, the term *twain* hearkens also to the division of the body politic into North and South. Likewise, when it comes to the division of the individual human body, twain often informs tales about Siamese twins and Solomonic changelings. A second explanation for Clemens's *nom* involves that author's simply stealing his name from another writer. But let me place my bet on the proposition that when Twain wrote *The Celebrated Jumping Frog of Calaveras County* in 1865, the term *mark twain* also meant "allow two free drinks." Clemens's *nom* derives partly from the "on credit" drinking contests that he held with opponents in Virginia City's famous Old Corner Saloon.

Just such a contest is the overt subject matter of *The Jumping Frog*, with its drinker of shots (of liquor) and its gambler who fills his rival's dummy with shot (of lead). *That* frog dummy is named Daniel Webster, presumably after

25.6. Joseph Goodhue Chandler, *Daniel Webster at Bunker Hill.* Undated.

the rhetorician from Massachusetts, known as "expounder of the American constitution," famously depicted as bearing a text in his hand. A speaker who could jump his way around and through the rhetoric of a land divided between slave and free, Webster managed to postpone the Civil War by about ten years thanks to his enabling California, the gamblers' stage set for *The Jumping Frog,* to become slave-free.[78] "Liberty and Union!" was Web-

25.7. "Dan'l Webster." Original caption for illustration by F. W. Strothman in Mark Twain, *The Jumping Frog.*

ster's nearly oxymoronic cry. Daniel Webster the frog couldn't jump ship, despite Nat Turner's Rebellion. Whether Daniel Webster the rhetorician ever could deliver Twain's humanoid amphibian named Daniel Webster from the weighted silence of its prison-box is almost another question.

Notes

This essay was originally a lecture delivered in Samuel Clemens Hall, in Buffalo, New York, on March 24, 2000.

1. J. A. Laponce, "Relating Linguistic to Political Conflicts: The Problem of Language Shift in Multilingual Societies," in *Les États multilingues: Problèmes et solutions,* ed. J.-G. Savard and R. Vigneault (Québec: Les Presses de l'Université Laval, 1975), pp. 185–207.

2. R. Y. Bourhis, "Introduction: Language Policies in Multilingual Settings," in *Conflict and Language Planning in Quebec,* ed. Bourhis (Clevedon, Eng.: Multilingual Matters, 1984).

3. In a letter to the President of the United States, Louis Marshall, President of the American Jewish Committee, cites the law: "In consideration for the admission to the enjoyment of equal rights the Jews shall renounce the use of a language of their own in speech as well as in writing. After the promulgation of this act, no legal act, no will, no contract or guaranty, no obligation of any worth, no accounts or bills, no books or commercial correspondence shall be written or signed in Hebrew or Yiddish." MS "Marshall to Wilson," 7 Nov. 1918. Quoted in George J. Lerski, "Dmowski, Paderewski and American Jews: A Documentary Compilation," p. 101; in *POLIN: A Journal of Polish-Jewish Studies,* vol. 2 (Oxford: Basil Blackwell for the Institute for Polish-Jewish Studies, 1987):95–116.

4. Angels Camp, California (east of Stockton) still has an annual frog-jumping contest.

5. Mark Twain, *The Celebrated Jumping Frog Of Calaveras County. And Other Sketches* (New York: C. H. Webb, 1867). 1st ed., 2nd print. Subsequent references will appear in the text as JF.

6. Mike Zwerin, *International Herald Tribune,* April 26, 1996, p. 26.

7. "The Frog Song." Words and music by Jean Chevrier.

8. Transcriptions vary for the Franglais and/or Frenglish: for example, *pinottes*

instead of *peanuts,* and *fausses notes* instead of *fausse note.* This text is from So-lution SN-905. New edition, 1992: Gestion Son & Image SN-905 CD. This is the recording of Robert Charlesbois called *Longue Distance.*

9. Fruge's version is in *American Folk Music; Vol. 2, Social Music,* Folkways FA 2952/FP 292, LP (1952), cut# 37. Fruge sings with accordeon; recorded in Memphis, 18 Sept. 1929. Other recorded versions of the song include *Saute Crapeau* (Isom Fontenot AH 359c) and Wallace "Cheese" Reed (AH 415c), in the *Saut Crapaud* CD *Squeeze: A World Accordion Anthology.* Notes by Dick Spottswood.

10. David R. Sewell, *Mark Twain's Languages: Discourse, Dialogue, and Linguistic Variety* (Berkeley: University of California Press, 1987).

11. See John T. Krumpelmann, *Mark Twain and the German Language* (Baton Rouge: Louisiana State University Press, 1953).

12. "When I was a boy and lived in a village on the banks of the Mississippi, a long away back in the early Fifties, our paper 'exchanged' with the St. Louis *Anzeiger des Westens."* John J. Weishert, "Once Again: Mark Twain and German," *Mark Twain Journal* 12 (Summer 1965):16.

13. "Twain" quotes the English part of the Portuguese/English "Dialogue 17" in the epigraph to this chapter. Jose da Fonseca and Pedro Carolino, *The New Guide on the Conversation in Portuguese and English,* 1st American ed., rpr. verbatim et literatim, with an introduction by Mark Twain (Boston: J. R. Osgood and Company, 1883). First published as *O novo guia da conversação em Portuguez e Inglez; ou, Escolha de dialogos familiares sobre varios assumptos; precedido d'um copioso vocabulario de nomes proprios, com a pronuncia figurada das palavras inglezas, e o accento prosodico nas portuguezas, para se poder aprender com perfeicao e a inda sem mestre, qualquer dos dous idiomas. Offerecido a'estudiosa mocidade portugueza e brazileira* (Paris: Va. J. P. Aillaud, Monlon, 1855).

14. See Robert L. Ramsay and Frances G. Emerson, *A Mark Twain Lexicon* (Columbia, Mo.: 1938), p. lxxxix. Cited by Holger Kersten, "Mark Twain's First Joke on the German Language," *Mark Twain Journal* 31-1 (Spring 1993):18–21.

15. Mark Twain, *A Tramp Abroad,* illus. W. Fr. Brown, True Williams, B. Day, Mark Twain, and others (London, 1885), appendix D.

16. JF 19. Spoken by Smiley some time before the wager.

17. Writes Twain: "The 'Jumping Frog' was the first piece of writing of mine that spread itself through the newspapers and brought me into public notice," in "Private History of the 'Jumping Frog' Story," *North American Review* 158 (April 1894).

18. See Henry B. Wonham, *Mark Twain and the Art of the Tall Tale* (New York: Oxford University Press, 1993).

19. *The Jumping Frog* has been the focus of American cultural works ranging from operas and songs to films and videos. See Lukas Foss, *The Jumping Frog of Calaveras County*, libretto by Jean Karsavina, after a story by Mark Twain (New York: C. Fischer, c.1951).

20. First published in *The Saturday Press*, Nov. 18, 1865. For an early version of the origin of the tale, see Albert Bigelow Paine, *Mark Twain: A Biography* (New York: Harper & Brothers, 1912), pp. 270–273.

21. On "Toad Story" see *Sonora Herald,* June 11, 1853, and *San Andreas Independent,* Dec. 11, 1858. For the tale's appearance in early newspapers, see Oscar Lewis, *The Origin of the Celebrated Jumping Frog of Calaveras County* (San Francisco: The Book Club of California, 1931). .

22. Twain, "Note," Nov. 1903. In Mark Twain, *The Jumping Frog,* illus. F. W. Strothman (New York and London: 1903):64–66.

23. Arthur Sidgwick's *Introduction to Greek Prose Composition,* with exercises, was issued several times in the United States, including the widespread Ginn and Heath edition (Boston, 1877).

24. This is Henry Van Dyke (1852–1933).

25. "I could not help being suspicious of the Greek frog because he was willing to be fed with gravel" (JF 65).

26. "Interview: Mark Twain Put to the Question," *Adelaide South Australian Register,* Oct. 14, 1895. See Kersten, "Joke."

27. For the report about Gillis, see Lewis, *Origins,* p. 27. See also William Robert Gillis's *Memories of Mark Twain and Steve Gillis* (Sonora, Calif.: Printed by the Banner, c.1924) and *Gold Rush Days with Mark Twain* (New York: A. & C. Boni, 1930).

28. Twain begins his "Private History of the 'Jumping Frog' Story" with a reference to Hopkinson Smith's "negro stories."

29. The term *gossip* means "a humorous party pastime in which a sentence or anecdote is whispered from one person to the next around the group and the final version compared with the original statement" (*Webster's Third New International Dictionary, Unabridged,* s.v. "Gossip").

30. See Sidney Lamont McGee, *La Littérature américaine dans la "Revue des Deux Mondes" (1831–1900)* (Montpellier: Imprimerie de la Manufacture de la Charité, 1927) and Victor Du Bled, *Le Salon de la "Revue des Deux Mondes"* (Paris: Bloud and Gay, 1930).

31. *Revue des Deux Mondes* (henceforth *RDM*), July 15, 1872. Part II was published August 15, 1872.

32. Mark. K. Wilson, "Mr. Clemens and Madame Th. Bentzon: Mark Twain's First French Critic," *American Literature* 43 (Jan. 1974):537–56.

33. *RDM*, Aug. 15, 1872: "Les Humoristes américains II."

34. *RDM*, June 15, 1872: "Un Romancier californien" (on Harte); *RDM*, June 1, 1872: "Un Poète américain: Walt Whitman."

35. *RDM*, Aug. 15, 1878: "L'Histoire d'une mine."

36. *Récits* was first published in Paris (Michel Levy Frères, 1873); new ed. was published in 1884 by the same house.

37. *RDM*, Feb. 1, 1883 to April 15, 1884: "Les Nouveaux Romanciers américains"; *RDM*, Aug. 1, 1885: "Les Nouveaux Romans américains."

38. Published in English in London by H. W. Bell.

39. For Jewett and Beecher Stowe, *RDM*, Feb. 1, 1885: "Le Roman de la femme-médecin." See too *RDM*, Sept. 15, 1887: "Le Naturalisme aux Etats-Unis." For Thanet, *RDM*, Feb. 1, 1896: "Dans l'Arkansas." For Rives, *RDM*, Nov. 15, 1888: "Un Roman virginien." For Hodgson, *RDM*, March 15, 1890: "Un Romancier anglo-américain." For King, *RDM*, April 1, 1893: "Les Romanciers du Sud en Amérique." For Wilkins, *RDM*, Aug. 1, 1896: "Un Romancier de la Nouvelle-Angleterre."

40. Published in French as *Américaines chez elles*.

41. *Widowhood*, trans. Mary (Neal) Sherwood (New York, G. Munro, 1882); *Remorse* (New York: D. Appleton, 1878); *Jacqueline*, trans. Elizabeth Wormeley Latimer, ills. by Albert Lynch (New York. Boussod, Valadon, 1893); *Expiation* (New York: Welch, Fracker, 1889); *Love's Atonement* (New York: F. M. Lupton, 1892); *Georgette*, trans. E. P. Robbins (Chicago: Donohue, Henneberry, 1892).

42. Pref. by Gilbert Gratiant (Morne-Rouge, Martinque: Editions des Horizons Caraibes, 1977). This is vol. 2 in the series *Romans antillais du XIXe siècle*.

43. Edouard Glissant, *Le Discours antillais* (Paris, 1981). Quoted by Jacques Derrida, *Monolingualism of the Other; or, The Prosthesis of Origin*, trans. Patrick Mensah (Stanford: Stanford University Press, 1998), title page.

44. See Francis Marion Crawford, *The Rulers of the South: Sicily, Calabria, Malta*, drawings by Henry Brokman (New York: Macmillan, 1900–1901), p. 321.

45. Published in Paris: Lévy, 1899.

46. *RDM*, "Humoristes américains II," in Bentzon, *Littératures et moeurs étrangères* (Paris, 1882), esp. pp. 62–64. See Francis Shubael Smith, *Life and Adventures of Josh Billings: With a Characteristic Sketch of the Humorist* (New York: G. W. Carleton, 1883).

47. Bentzon, *Littératures et moeurs*, p. 323.

48. Twain, *Jumping Frog*; Bentzon, *Littératures et moeurs*, p. 321.

49. Cf. Hugh Reginald Haweis, *American humorists*, 2d. ed. (London: Chatto and

Windus, 1883). This work includes in its purview Artemus Ward with Mark Twain.

50. "L'*humour* . . . la plaisanterie d'un homme qui en plaisantant garde une mine grave" (Bentzon, *Littératures et moeurs,* p. 313).

51. Jose da Fonseca, *English As She Is Spoke; or, A Jest in Sober Earnest,* with an introduction by James Millington (New York: D. Appleton, 1884).

52. Bentzon, *Littératures et moeurs,* p. 313.

53. Ibid., p. 335.

54. Quoted in Bailey, *Images of English,* p. 104. Noah Webster also said that in the Federal Procession there was "a scroll, containing the principles of a [new] *Federal* language."

55. Bentzon, *Littératures et moeurs,* p. 335. Bentzon includes this statement: "*The Innocents at Home* et *Roughing It* fourmillent d'anecdotes du même genre, qui prouvent l'heureuse impossibilité où l'on est d'éteindre même sous la fièvre de l'or les sentiments tendres et les besoins naturels du coeur.. . . . L'anglais reste la langue mère, fondamentale, mais c'est une nourrice vieillie dont les mamelles se tarissent souvent; elle ne peut exprimer que la civilisation européenne, et se trouve à court devant la surabondance d'idées, d'inventions, de découvertes, dont s'énorgueillit la jeune Amérique. Pour désigner des choses nouvelles, il faut des mots nouveaux; à la souche antique on a donc greffé peu à peu de nombreux emprunts plus ou moins défigurés, plus ou moins corrompus, faits aux dialectes variés dont les emigrants venus de tous les points du globe avaient doté leur patrie adoptive; les Indiens à demi exterminés ont eux-mêmes laissé quelques traces de leur génie local, absorbé par le génie supérieur et envahissant de l'Anglo-Saxon, qui est devenu comme l'architecte d'une nouvelle Babel. De cette confusion des langues ont jailli, pareilles à autant de pousses vivaces, les expressions neuves, énergiques, ingénieuses et hardies. C'est en Californie, — et il est facile de comprendre pourquoi — que la révolution se produit avec le plus de vigueur. Les audaces d'un Bret Harte, les témérités les plus grossières d'un Mark Twain nous étonnent encore; mais bientôt nous serons accoutumés à une langue américaine dont la verdeur savoureuse n'est pas à dedaigner, en attendant les qualités plus délicates et plus relevées que le temps lui apportera sans doute" (Benzton, *Littératures et moeurs,* p. 335).

56. Twain had studied French since 1860. Albert Bigelow Paine, *Mark Twain: A Biography,* 3 vols. (New York, 1912), vol. 1, p. 151.

57. Mark Twain, "Concerning the Jews," in *Literary Essays: The Writings of Mark Twain.* Author's National Edition, 25 vols. (New York, 1907–1918), vol. 22, p. 264.

58. Twain writes in his "How to Tell a Story" that "the humorous story is Ameri-

can, . . . the witty story is French" (*Writings*, vol. 22, p. 7; cited in Wilson, "Mr. Clemens," p. 545).

59. "The Love Letters of Mark Twain," ed. Dixon Wecter, in *The Atlantic* 18 (Jan. 1948):86–87; cited in Wilson, "Mr. Clemens," p. 549.

60. *RDM*, March 15, 1875: "L'Age doré en Amérique"; *RDM*, Nov. 1, 1875; Jan. 1, 1876; April 1, 1876; Oct. 1, 1876; Dec. 15, 1878.

61. Boston Block & Toy currently have English, Cyrillic, Arabic, Hebrew, Sign Language, Braille, Greek, and Atomic blocks.

62. Ralph Waldo Emerson, "Use of Great Men," in *Representative Men* (London: H. G. Bohn, 1850), p. 260.

63. This term *saut* is probably originally Irish; see OED.

64. "I used to tell the story of the Jumping Frog in San Francisco, and presently Artemus Ward came along and wanted it to help fill out a little book which he was about to publish; so I wrote it out and sent it to his publisher Carleton; but Carleton thought the book had enough matter in it, so he gave the story to Henry Clapp as a present, and Clapp put it in his *Saturday Press*, and it killed that paper with a suddenness that was beyond praise. At least the paper died with that issue, and none but envious people have ever tried to rob me of the honor and credit of killing it." Twain, "Private History of the 'Jumping Frog' Story," p. 127, in Twain, *How to Tell a Story and Other Essays* (Hartford: American Publishing, 1901), pp. 120–30; hereafter abbreviated as PH. See also n.17.

65. See Maurice Blanchot, "Literature and the Right to Death," in *The Gaze of Orpheus*, trans. Lydia Davis (Barrytown, N.Y.: Station Hill Press, 1981). p. 42.

66. That is how the 1875 edition of the American publishing house has it.

67. *Webster's Third New International Dictionary*, Unabridged, 1993, s.v. "Martyr."

68. Bentzon, *Littérature et moeurs étrangerès*, p. 14; cf. Wilson, "Mr. Clemens," p. 554. Twain's PH includes relevant critical remarks about "Mme" Bentzon. Grace King complained to Twain about his treatment of "her." See Robert Bush, "Grace King and Mark Twain," *American Literature* 44 (March 1972):48. Cf. Wilson, "Mr. Clemens," pp. 554–55. Wrote Twain back: "The whole trouble lies in the French character. It hasn't a shred of humor in it."

69. "I have to live up to the name which Jamie Dodge has given me — the 'Belle of New York,'" he once said, "and it just keeps me rushing." See Peter Salwen, "Mark Twain, the New Yorker: They Called Him the 'Belle of New York,'" *New York Newsday*, Nov. 29, 1985, special feature.

70. See, for example, the bet on when Parson Walker's wife will die (JF 10).

71. See Hamlin Garland's "Land of the Straddle-Bug," 1894. The pioneering venture, which was to occupy the talents of many novelists, receives Garland's

attention in "Moccasin Ranch" (1909), based on his homesteading experiences; it was originally published in 1894–95 under the title "The Land of the Straddle-Bug."

72. Twain spent three months with prankster Steve Gillis at Jackass Hill and Angel's Camp. "Jackass" was one of President Andrew Jackson's nicknames.

73. See, for example, Arnold Lobel, *Frog and Toad Are Friends* (New York: Harper and Row, 1970).

74. The Clifton Waller Barrett Collection (University of Virginia) includes a transcript of Mark Twain's first performance on the "Round the World Tour," taken down by a reporter for the *Cleveland Plain Dealer*, which printed it 19 July 1895. In retelling his *Jumping Frog* tale, Mark Twain adds: "And Simon Wheeler said, 'That has been a lesson to me.' And I say to you, let that be a lesson to you. Don't you put too much faith in the passing stranger. This life is full of uncertainties, and every episode in life, figuratively speaking, is just a frog. You want to watch every exigency as you would a frog, and don't you ever bet a cent on it until you know whether it is loaded or not."

75. OED, s.v. 5.

76. Shakespeare, *Hamlet,* Act 1, Scene 1.

77. PH 130.

78. Daniel Webster endorsed Henry Clay's plan to assure sectional equilibrium in Congress. Passed after eight months of congressional wrangling, the legislation admitted California to the Union as a free state. The legislative package known as the *Compromise of 1850* postponed the Civil War by a decade. See, for example, his famous speech of 7 March 1850.

Contributors

ALA ALRYYES
Department of Comparative
  Literature
Yale University

YOTA BATSAKI
Department of Comparative
  Literature
Harvard University

ALICIA BORINSKY
Department of Modern Foreign
  Languages
Boston University

DAN DUFFY
Department of Anthropology
University of North Carolina at
  Chapel Hill

PETER FENVES
Department of German,
  Department of Philosophy
Northwestern University

**SUSANNAH YOUNG-AH
GOTTLIEB**
Department of English
Northwestern University

MELINDA GRAY
Literature Concentration
Harvard University

JEAN JONASSAINT
Department of Romance Studies
Duke University

STEVEN KELLMAN
Division of Foreign Languages,
  Comparative Studies in the
  Humanities
University of Texas at San Antonio

ELISABETH LENCKOS
Horace H. Rackham School of
  Graduate Studies
University of Michigan

JAMES LOEFFLER
Department of History
Columbia University

KENNETH NILSEN
Department of Celtic Studies
St. Francis Xavier University, Nova
  Scotia

QIAN SUOQUIAO
Department of Chinese,
  Translation and Linguistics
City University of Hong Kong

LAWRENCE ROSENWALD
Department of English
Wellesley College

STEVEN ROWAN
Department of History
University of Missouri — St. Louis

TE-HSING SHAN
Institute of European and American
  Studies
Academia Sinica, Taiwan

MARC SHELL
Department of English,
   Department of Comparative
   Literature
Harvard University

WERNER SOLLORS
Department of English
Harvard University

DORIS SOMMER
Department of Romance
   Languages
Harvard University

DENNIS TEDLOCK
Department of English
State University of New York at
   Buffalo

ESTHER WHITFIELD
Department of Romance
   Languages
Harvard University

DANIEL G. WILLIAMS
Department of English
University of Swansea, Wales

XIAO-HUANG YIN
Department of American Studies
Occidental College

DATE DUE

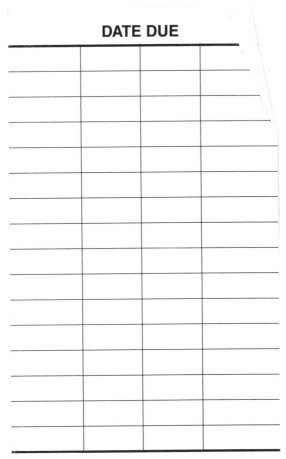

HIGHSMITH #45115